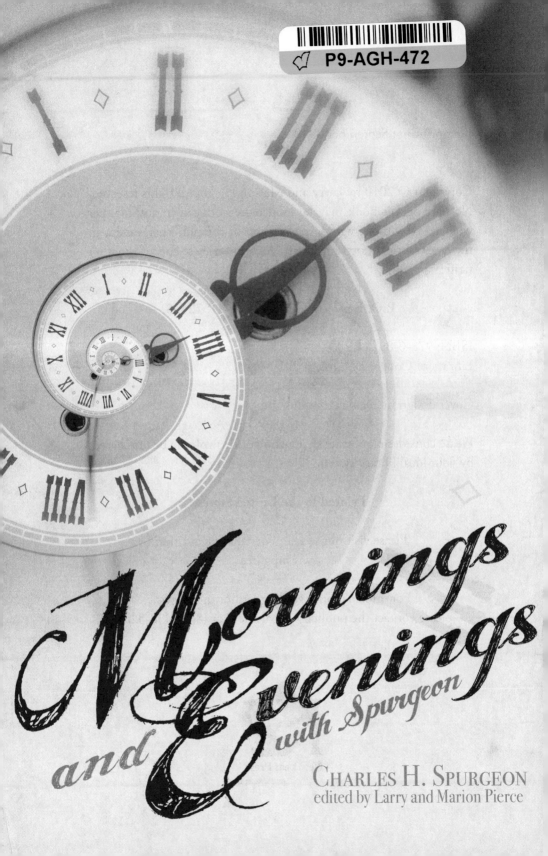

Mornings and Evenings with Spurgeon

CHARLES H. SPURGEON
edited by Larry and Marion Pierce

First printing: September 2010

New Leaf Publishing Group
P. O. Box 726, Green Forest, AR 72638

ISBN: 978-0-89221-700-7
Library of Congress Number: 2010934162

Cover design by Diana Bogardus

Please consider requesting that a copy of this volume be purchased
by your local library system.

Printed in the United States

Please visit our website for other great titles:
www.nlpg.net

For information regarding author interviews,
please contact the publicity department at (870) 438-5288.

New Leaf Press
A Division of New Leaf Publishing Group

Preface

Since 1978, we have been reading the Bible through each year using literature published by *Trans World Radio*. In 1993, we scanned in Spurgeon's *Morning and Evening* for the *Online Bible*. We started using his readings daily as part of our devotions. In 1999 when we added the audio to *Online Bible*, we added the daily readings so the computer could read the daily readings to us each day. You will find these Scripture readings on each page as well as the daily readings for the popular TV program *Quick Study*.

We have modernized the language of Spurgeon to make it more suitable for today's generation. We have not knowingly changed the intent of what he wrote. Likewise, using the King James translation of the Scriptures, we updated some of the language in the Bible verses Spurgeon used, so the entire devotion reads in a modern English style.

Each day we greet the morning with our daily Bible reading and these precious meditations from Spurgeon. The morning mediations from March 21 to April 24 contain very rich and moving mediations on the passion of Christ. Spurgeon was never better than when he preached on that subject. We have often sent the evening reading of March 22 to those who are bereaved. Likewise the morning reading of May 13 or the evening read of June 22 has comforted many going through deep waters.

May this little book be an introduction to Spurgeon Country and your taste for the deeper things of God be satiated as Spurgeon expounds the Scriptures for you each day. For an even richer treat, we encourage you to read Spurgeon's sermons each day as Answers In Genesis posts them on their website (AnswersInGenesis.Org). The English has been updated and footnotes added to aid your comprehension of what Spurgeon preached. Once you get a taste for Spurgeon, you will crave to read more by this man who was so greatly used by God in the nineteenth century. We pray you are as blessed by them as we are. "He being dead yet speaks." *(Hebrews 11:4)*

— Larry and Marion Pierce

"He awakens me morning by morning,
He awakens my ear
To hear as the learned."

(Isaiah 50:4)

"My soul shall be satisfied as with marrow and fatness;
And my mouth shall praise you with joyful lips;
When I remember you on my bed,
And meditate on you in the night watches."

(Psalms 63:5–6)

January 1 — Morning

{Daily Reading: Genesis 1:1–3:24} {Quick Study: Genesis 1:1–2:25}

**They ate the fruit of the land of Canaan
that year.** *{Joshua 5:12}*

Israel's weary wanderings were all over, and the promised rest was attained. No more moving tents, fiery serpents, fierce Amalekites, and howling wildernesses: they came to the land which flowed with milk and honey, and they ate the old grain of the land. Perhaps this year, beloved Christian reader, this may be your case or mine. Joyful is the prospect, and if faith is in active exercise, it will yield unalloyed delight. To be with Jesus in the rest which remains for the people of God is a cheering hope indeed, and to expect this glory so soon is a double bliss. Unbelief shudders at the Jordan which still rolls between us and the good land, but let us rest assured that we have already experienced more ills than death at its worst can cause us. Let us banish every fearful thought, and rejoice with exceedingly great joy in the prospect that this year we shall begin to be "for ever with the Lord."

A part of the host will tarry on earth this year, to do service for their Lord. If this should fall to our lot, there is no reason why the New Year's text should not still be true. "We who have believed do enter into rest." The Holy Spirit is the foretaste of our inheritance; he gives us "glory begun below." In heaven they are secure, and so we are preserved in Christ Jesus; there they triumph over their enemies, and we have victories, too. Celestial spirits enjoy communion with their Lord, and this is not denied to us; they rest in his love, and we have perfect peace in him: they hymn his praise, and it is our privilege to bless him too. We will this year gather celestial fruits on earthly ground, where faith and hope have made the desert like the garden of the Lord. Man ate angels' food of old, and why not now? Oh for grace to feed on Jesus, and so to eat the fruit of the land of Canaan this year!

January 1 — Evening

We will be glad and rejoice in you. *{Song of Solomon 1:4}*

We will be glad and rejoice in you. We will not open the gates of the year to the dolorous notes of the sackbut, but to the sweet strains of the harp of joy, and the high-sounding cymbals of gladness. "Oh come, let us sing to the Lord: let us make a joyful noise to the rock of our salvation." We, the called and faithful and chosen, we will drive away our griefs, and set up our banners of confidence in the name of God. Let others lament over their troubles, we who have the sweetening tree to cast into Marah's bitter pool, with joy will magnify the Lord. Eternal Spirit, our effectual Comforter, we who are the temples in which you dwell will never cease from adoring and blessing the name of Jesus. *We* WILL, we are resolved about it, Jesus must have the crown of our heart's delight; we will not dishonour our Bridegroom by mourning in his presence. We are ordained to be the minstrels of the skies, let us rehearse our everlasting anthem before we sing it in the halls of the New Jerusalem. We will BE GLAD AND REJOICE: two words with one sense, double joy, blessedness upon blessedness. Need there be any limit to our rejoicing in the Lord even now? Do not men of grace find their Lord to be camphire and spikenard, calamus and cinnamon even now, and what better fragrance have they in heaven itself? *We will be glad and rejoice* IN YOU. That last word is the meat in the dish, the kernel of the nut, the soul of the text. What heavens are laid up in Jesus! What rivers of infinite bliss have their source, indeed, and every drop of their fulness in him! Since, oh sweet Lord Jesus, you are the present portion of your people, favour us this year with such a sense of your preciousness, that from its first to its last day we may be glad and rejoice in you. Let January open with joy in the Lord, and December close with gladness in Jesus.

January 2 — Morning

{Daily Reading: Genesis 4:1–6:22} {Quick Study: Genesis 3:1–5:32}

Continue in prayer. *{Colossians 4:2}*

It is interesting to notice how large a portion of Sacred Writ is occupied with the subject of prayer, either in furnishing examples, enforcing precepts, or pronouncing promises. We scarcely open the Bible before we read, "Then men began to call upon the name of the Lord"; and just as we are about to close the volume, the "Amen" of an earnest supplication meets our ear. Instances are plentiful. Here we find a wrestling Jacob — there a Daniel who prayed three times a day — and a David who with all his heart called upon his God. On the mountain we see Elijah; in the dungeon Paul and Silas. We have multitudes of commands, and myriads of promises. What does this teach us but the sacred importance and necessity of prayer? We may be certain that whatever God has made prominent in his Word, he intended to be conspicuous in our lives. If he has said much about prayer, it is because he knows we have much need of it. So deep are our necessities that until we are in heaven we must not cease to pray. Do you not need anything? Then, I fear you do not know your poverty. Have you no mercy to ask from God? Then, may the Lord's mercy show you your misery! A prayerless soul is a Christless soul. Prayer is the lisping of the believing infant, the shout of the fighting believer, the requiem of the dying saint falling asleep in Jesus. It is the breath, the watchword, the comfort, the strength, and the honour of a Christian. If you are a child of God, you will seek your Father's face, and live in your Father's love. Pray that this year you may be holy, humble, zealous, and patient; have closer communion with Christ, and enter more often into the banqueting house of his love. Pray that you may be an example and a blessing to others, and that you may live more for the glory of your Master. The motto for this year must be, "Continue in prayer."

January 2 — Evening

Let the people renew their strength. *{Isaiah 41:1}*

All things on earth need to be renewed. No created thing continues by itself. "You renew the face of the year," was the psalmist's utterance. Even the trees, which are not burdened with care, nor shorten their lives with labour, must drink of the rain of heaven and suck from the hidden treasures of the soil. The cedars of Lebanon, which God has planted, only live because day by day they are full of sap fresh drawn from the earth. Neither can man's life be sustained without renewal from God. Just as it is necessary to repair the waste of the body by the frequent meal, so we must repair the waste of the soul by feeding upon the Book of God, or by listening to the preached Word, or by the soul-fattening table of the ordinances. How depressed are our graces when means are neglected! What poor starvelings some saints are who live without the diligent use of the Word of God and secret prayer! If our piety can live without God it is not of divine creating; it is only a dream; for if God had established it, it would wait upon him as the flowers wait upon the dew. Without constant restoration we are not ready for the perpetual assaults of hell, or the stern afflictions of heaven, or even for the strifes within. When the whirlwind shall be released, woe to the tree that has not sucked up fresh sap, and grasped the rock with many intertwisted roots. When tempests arise, woe to the mariners who have not strengthened their mast, nor cast their anchor, nor sought the haven. If we allow the good to grow weaker, the evil will surely gather strength and struggle desperately for the mastery over us; and so, perhaps, a painful desolation, and a lamentable disgrace may follow. Let us draw near to the footstool of divine mercy in humble entreaty, and we shall realise the fulfilment of the promise, "Those who wait upon the Lord shall renew their strength."

January 3 — Morning

{Daily Reading: Genesis 7:1–9:29} {Quick Study: Genesis 6:1–9:29}

I will give you for a covenant of the people. *{Isaiah 49:8}*

Jesus Christ is himself the sum and substance of the covenant, and as one of its gifts, he is the property of every believer. Believer, can you estimate what you have received in Christ? "In him dwells all the fulness of the Godhead bodily." Consider that word "God" and its infinity, and then meditate upon "perfect man" and all his beauty; for all that Christ, as God and man, ever had, or can have, is yours — out of pure free favour, passed over to you to be your entailed property forever. Our blessed Jesus, as God, is omniscient, omnipresent, omnipotent. Will it not console you to know that all these great and glorious attributes are altogether yours? Has he power? That power is yours to support and strengthen you, to over-come your enemies, and to preserve you even to the end. Has he love? Well, there is not a drop of love in his heart which is not yours; you may dive into the immense ocean of his love, and you may say of it all, "It is mine." Has he justice? It may seem a stern attribute, but even that is yours, for he will by his justice see to it that all which is promised to you in the covenant of grace shall be most cer-tainly secured to you. And all that he has as *perfect man* is yours. As a perfect man the Father's delight was upon him. He stood accepted by the Most High. Oh believer, God's acceptance of Christ is your acceptance; for do you not know that the love which the Father set on a perfect Christ, he sets on you *now*? For all that Christ did is yours. That perfect righteousness which Jesus worked out, when through his stainless life he kept the law and made it honourable, is yours, and is imputed to you. Christ is in the covenant.

> My God, I am yours — what a comfort divine!
> What a blessing to know that the Saviour is mine!
> In the heavenly Lamb thrice happy I am,
> And my heart it does dance at the sound of his name.

January 3 — Evening

The voice of one crying in the wilderness, "Prepare the way of the Lord, make his paths straight." *{Luke 3:4}*

The voice crying in the wilderness demanded *a way for the Lord, a way prepared, and a way prepared in the wilderness.* I wish to be attentive to the Master's proclamation, and give him a road into my heart, built up by gracious operations, through the desert of my nature. The four directions in the text must have my serious attention.

Every valley must be exalted. Low and grovelling thoughts of God must be given up; doubting and despairing must be removed; and self-seeking and carnal delights must be forsaken. Across these deep valleys a glorious causeway of grace must be raised.

Every mountain and hill shall be laid low. Proud creature sufficiency, and boastful self-righteousness, must be levelled, to make a highway for the King of kings. Divine fellowship is never given to haughty, highminded sinners. The Lord has respect towards the lowly, and visits the contrite in heart, but the lofty are an abomination to him. My soul, beseech the Holy Spirit to set you right in this respect.

The crooked shall be made straight. The wavering heart must have a straight path of decision for God and holiness marked out for it. Double-minded men are strangers to the God of truth. My soul, take heed that you are in all things honest and true, as in the sight of the heart-searching God.

The rough places shall be made smooth. Stumbling blocks of sin must be removed, and thorns and briers of rebellion must be uprooted. So great a visitor must not find miry ways and stony places when he comes to honour his favoured ones with his company. Oh that this evening the Lord may find in my heart a highway made ready by his grace, that he may make a triumphal procession through the utmost bounds of my soul, from the beginning of this year even to the end of it.

January 4 — Morning

{Daily Reading: Genesis 10:1–12:20} {Quick Study: Genesis 10:1–11:32}

Grow in grace, and in the knowledge of our Lord and Saviour Jesus Christ. *{2 Peter 3:18}*

Grow in grace" — not in one grace only, but in *all* grace. Grow in that root grace, *faith*. Believe the promises more firmly than you have done. Let faith increase in fulness, constancy, and simplicity. Grow also in *love*. Ask that your love may become extended, more intense, more practical, influencing every thought, word, and deed. Grow likewise in *humility*. Seek to lie very low, and know more of your own nothingness. As you grow *downward* in humility, seek also to grow *upward* — having nearer approaches to God in prayer and more intimate fellowship with Jesus. May God the Holy Spirit enable you to *"grow in the knowledge of our Lord and Saviour."* He who does not grow in the knowledge of Jesus, refuses to be blessed. To know him is "life eternal," and to advance in the knowledge of him is to increase in happiness. He who does not long to know more about Christ, knows nothing about him yet. Whoever has sipped this wine will thirst for more, for although Christ does satisfy, yet it is such a satisfaction that the appetite is not dulled, but whetted. If you know the love of Jesus — as the hart pants for the water brooks, so will you pant after deeper draughts of his love. If you do not desire to know him better, then you do not love him, for love always cries, "Nearer, nearer." Absence from Christ is hell; but the presence of Jesus is heaven. Do not rest then content without an increasing acquaintance with Jesus. Seek to know more about him in his divine nature, in his human relationship, in his finished work, in his death, in his resurrection, in his present glorious intercession, and in his future royal advent. Remain near the cross, and search the mystery of his wounds. An increase of love for Jesus, and a more perfect apprehension of his love for us is one of the best tests *of growth in grace.*

**And Joseph knew his brethren, but they did not
know him.** *{Genesis 42:8}*

This morning our desires went forth for growth in our acquaintance with the Lord Jesus; it may be well tonight to consider a related topic, namely, *our heavenly Joseph's knowledge of us.* This was most blessedly perfect long before we had the slightest knowledge of him. "His eyes beheld our substance, yet being imperfect, and in his book all our members were written, when as yet there was not one of them." Before we had a being in the world we had a being in his heart. When we were enemies to him, he knew us, our misery, our madness, and our wickedness. When we wept bitterly in despairing repentance, and viewed him only as a judge and a ruler, he viewed us as his well-beloved brethren, and his heart yearned towards us. He never mistook his chosen, but always beheld them as objects of his infinite affection. "The Lord knows those who are his," is as true of the prodigals who are feeding swine as of the children who sit at the table.

But, alas! *We did not know our royal Brother,* and out of this ignorance grew a host of sins. We withheld our hearts from him, and allowed him no entrance to our love. We mistrusted him, and gave no credit to his words. We rebelled against him, and paid him no loving homage. The Sun of Righteousness shone forth, and we could not see him. Heaven came down to earth, and earth did not perceive it. Let God be praised, those days are over with us; yet even now it is very little that we know of Jesus compared with what he knows of us. We have only begun to study him, but he knows us altogether. It is a blessed circumstance that the ignorance is not on his side, for then it would be a hopeless case for us. He will not say to us, "I never knew you," but he will confess our names in the day of his appearing, and meanwhile will reveal himself to us as he does not do to the world.

January 5 — Morning

{Daily Reading: Genesis 13:1–15:21} {Quick Study: Genesis 12:1–14:24}

**And God saw the light, that it was good: and God
divided the light from the darkness.** *{Genesis 1:4}*

Light might well be good since it sprang from that fiat of goodness, "Let there be light." We who enjoy it should be more grateful for it than we are, and see more of God in it and by it. *Physical*
light is said by Solomon to be sweet, but *gospel* light is infinitely more
precious, for it reveals eternal things and ministers to our immortal
natures. When the Holy Spirit gives us *spiritual* light, and opens our
eyes to behold the glory of God in the face of Jesus Christ, we behold
sin in its true colours, and ourselves in our real position; we see the
Most Holy God as he reveals himself, the plan of mercy as he pro-
pounds it, and the world to come as the Word describes it. Spiritual
light has many beams and prismatic colours, but whether they are
knowledge, joy, holiness, or life, all are divinely good. If the received
light is thus good, what must the *essential* light be, and how glorious
must be the place where he reveals himself. Oh Lord, since light is so
good, give us more of it, and more of yourself, the true light.

No sooner is there a good thing in the world, than *a division is
necessary*. Light and darkness have no communion; God has divided
them, let us not confound them. Sons of light must not have fellowship with deeds, doctrines, or deceits of darkness. The children of
the day must be sober, honest, and bold in their Lord's work, leaving the works of darkness to those who shall dwell in it for ever. Our
churches should by discipline divide the light from the darkness,
and we should by our distinct separation from the world do the
same. In judgment, in action, in hearing, in teaching, in association,
we must discern between the precious and the vile, and maintain
the great distinction which the Lord made upon the world's first
day. Oh Lord Jesus, be our light throughout all of today, for your
light is the light of men.

January 5 — Evening

And God saw the light. *{Genesis 1:4}*

This morning we noticed the goodness of the light, and the Lord's dividing it from the darkness, we now note the special eye which the Lord had for the light. "God saw the light" — he looked at it with complacency, gazed upon it with pleasure, and saw that it "was good." If the Lord has given you light, dear reader, he looks on that light with special interest; for not only is it dear to him as his own handiwork, but because it is like himself, for "He is light." It is pleasant for the believer to know that God's eye is thus tenderly observant of that work of grace which he has begun. He never loses sight of the treasure which he has placed in our earthen vessels. Sometimes we cannot see the light, but God always sees the light, and that is much better than our seeing it. Better for the judge to see my innocence than for me to think I see it. It is very comforting for me to know that I am one of God's people — but whether *I* know it or not, if the Lord knows it, I am still safe. This is the foundation, "The Lord knows those who are his." You may be sighing and groaning because of inbred sin, and mourning over your darkness, yet the Lord sees "light" in your heart, for he has put it there, and all the cloudiness and gloom of your soul cannot conceal your light from his gracious eye. You may have sunk low in despondency, and even despair; but if your soul has any longing towards Christ, and if you are seeking to rest in his finished work, God sees the "light." He not only *sees* it, but he also *preserves* it in you. "I, the Lord, do keep it." This is a precious thought to those who, after anxious watching and guarding of themselves, feel their own powerlessness to do so. The light thus preserved by his grace, he will one day develop into the splendour of noonday, and the fulness of glory. The light within is the dawn of the eternal day.

January 6 — Morning

{Daily Reading: Genesis 16:1–18:33} {Quick Study: Genesis 15:1–17:27}

Casting all your care upon him; for he cares for you. *{1 Peter 5:7}*

It is a happy way of soothing sorrow when we can feel — "HE cares for *me*." Christian! Do not dishonour religion by always wearing a brow of care; come, cast your burden upon your Lord. You are staggering beneath a weight which your Father would not feel. What seems to you a crushing burden would be to him only as the small dust of the balance. Nothing is so sweet as to

> Lie passive in God's hands,
> And know no will but his.

Oh, child of suffering, be patient; God has not passed you over in his providence. He who is the feeder of sparrows will also furnish *you* with what you need. Do not sit down in despair; hope on, hope always. Take up the arms of faith against a sea of trouble, and your opposition shall end your distresses. *There is* one who cares for you. His eye is fixed on you, his heart beats with pity for your woe, and his omnipotent hand shall yet bring you the needed help. The darkest cloud shall scatter itself in showers of mercy. The blackest gloom shall give place to the morning. If you are one of his family, he will bind up your wounds, and heal your broken heart. Do not doubt his grace because of your tribulation, but believe that he loves you as much in seasons of trouble as in times of happiness. What a serene and quiet life might you lead if you would leave providing to the God of providence! With a little oil in the cruse, and a handful of meal in the barrel, Elijah outlived the famine, and you will do the same. If God cares for you, why do you need to care, too? Can you trust him for your soul, and not for your body? He has never refused to bear your burdens; he has never fainted under their weight. Come, then, soul! Be done with fretful care, and leave all your concerns in the hand of a gracious God.

January 6 — Evening

Now the hand of the Lord was upon me in the evening. *{Ezekiel 33:22}*

In the way of *judgment* this may be the case, and, if so, it is mine to consider the reason for such a visitation, and bear the rod and him who has appointed it. I am not the only one who is chastened in the night season; let me cheerfully submit to the affliction, and carefully endeavour to profit by it. But the hand of the Lord may also be felt in another manner, *strengthening* the soul and lifting the spirit upward towards eternal things. Oh that I may in this sense feel the Lord dealing with me! A sense of the divine presence and indwelling bears the soul towards heaven as upon the wings of eagles. At such times we are full to the brim with spiritual joy, and forget the cares and sorrows of earth; the invisible is near, and the visible loses its power over us; the servant body waits at the foot of the hill, and the master spirit worships upon the summit in the presence of the Lord. Oh that a hallowed time of divine communion may be given to me this evening! The Lord knows that I need it very greatly. My graces languish, my corruptions rage, my faith is weak, my devotion is cold; all these are reasons why his healing hand should be laid upon me. His hand can cool the heat of my burning brow, and stop the tumult of my palpitating heart. That glorious right hand which moulded the world can renew my mind; the unwearied hand which bears up the earth's huge pillars can sustain my spirit; the loving hand which encloses all the saints can cherish me; and the mighty hand which breaks the enemy in pieces can subdue my sins. Why should I not feel that hand touching me this evening? Come, my soul, address your God with the potent plea, that Jesus' hands were pierced for your redemption, and you shall surely feel that same hand upon you which once touched Daniel and set him upon his knees so that he might see visions of God.

January 7 — Morning

{Daily Reading: Genesis 19:1–21:34} {Quick Study: Genesis 18:1–19:38}

For me to live is Christ. *{Philippians 1:21}*

The believer did not always live for Christ. He began to do so when God the Holy Spirit convicted him of sin, and when by grace he was brought to see the dying Saviour making a propitiation for his guilt. From the moment of the new and celestial birth the man begins to live for Christ. Jesus is to believers the one pearl of great price, for whom we are willing to part with all that we have. He has so completely won our love that it beats alone for him; to his glory we would live, and in defence of his gospel we would die; he is the pattern of our life, and the model after which we would sculpture our character. Paul's words mean more than most men think; they imply that the *aim and end of his life* was Christ — indeed, his life itself was Jesus. In the words of an ancient saint, he did eat, and drink, and sleep eternal life. Jesus was his very breath, the soul of his soul, the heart of his heart, the life of his life. Can you say, as a professing Christian, that you live up to this ideal? Can you honestly say that for you to live is Christ? Your business — are you doing it *for Christ*? Is it not done for self-aggrandizement and for family advantage? Do you ask, "Is that a poor reason?" For the *Christian* it is. He professes to live for Christ; how can he live for another object without committing spiritual adultery? There are many who carry out this principle in some measure; but who is there that dares to say that he has lived wholly for Christ as the apostle did? Yet, this alone is the true life of a Christian — its source, its sustenance, its fashion, its end, all gathered up in two words — *Christ Jesus*. Lord, accept me; I here present myself, praying to live only in you and for you. Let me be as the young bull which stands between the plough and the altar, to work or to be sacrificed; and let my motto be, "Ready for either."

January 7 — Evening

My sister, my spouse. *{Song of Solomon 4:12}*

Observe the sweet titles with which the heavenly Solomon with intense affection addresses his bride the church. *My sister,* one near to me by ties of nature, partaker of the same sympathies. *My spouse,* nearest and dearest, united to me by the most tender bands of love; my sweet companion, part of myself. *My sister,* by my incarnation, which makes me bone of your bone and flesh of your flesh; *my spouse,* by heavenly betrothal, in which I have espoused you to myself in righteousness. *My sister,* whom I knew of old, and over whom I watched from her earliest infancy; *my spouse,* taken from among the daughters, embraced by arms of love, and affianced to me for ever. See how true it is that our royal Kinsman is not ashamed of us, for he dwells with obvious delight upon this twofold relationship. We have the word "my" twice in our version; as if Christ dwelt with rapture on his possession of his church. "His delights were with the sons of men," because those sons of men were his own chosen ones. He, the Shepherd, sought the sheep, because they were his sheep; he has gone about "to seek and to save those who were lost," because those who were lost were *his* long before they were lost to themselves or lost to him. The church is the exclusive portion of her Lord; no one else may claim a partnership, or pretend to share her love. Jesus, your church delights to have it so! Let every believing soul drink solace out of these wells. Soul! Christ is near to you in ties of relationship; Christ is dear to you in bonds of marriage union, and you are dear to him; behold he grasps both of your hands with both of his own, saying, "*My* sister, *my* spouse." Notice the two sacred holdfasts by which your Lord gets such a double hold on you that he neither can nor will ever let you go. Oh beloved, do not be slow to return the hallowed flame of his love.

{Daily Reading: Genesis 22:1–24:67} {Quick Study: Genesis 20:1–22:24}

The iniquity of the holy things. *{Exodus 28:38}*

What a veil is lifted up by these words, and what a disclosure is made! It will be humbling and profitable for us to pause a while and see this sad sight. The iniquities of our public worship, its hypocrisy, formality, lukewarmness, irreverence, wandering of heart, and forgetfulness of God, what a full measure have we there! Our work for the Lord, its jealous rivalry, selfishness, carelessness, slackness, unbelief, what a mass of defilement is there! Our private devotions, their laxity, coldness, neglect, sleepiness, and vanity, what a mountain of dead earth is there! If we looked more carefully we should find this iniquity to be far greater than appears at first sight. Dr. Payson, writing to his brother, says, "My parish, as well as my heart, very much resembles the garden of the sluggard; and what is worse, I find that very many of my desires for the improvement of both proceed either from pride or vanity or indolence. I look at the weeds which cover my garden, and breathe out an earnest wish that they were eradicated. But why? What prompts the wish? It may be that I may walk out and say to myself, 'In what fine order is my garden kept!' This is *pride*. Or, it may be that my neighbours may look over the wall and say, 'How finely your garden flourishes!' This is *vanity*. Or I may wish for the destruction of the weeds, because I am weary of pulling them up. This is *indolence*." So even our desires for holiness may be polluted by bad motives. Under the greenest sods worms hide themselves; we do not need to look long to find them. How cheering is the thought, that when the high priest bore the iniquity of the holy things he wore upon his brow the words, "HOLINESS TO THE LORD": and even so while Jesus bears our sin, he presents before his Father's face not our unholiness, but his own holiness. Oh for grace to view our great High Priest by the eye of faith!

January 8 — Evening

Your love is better than wine. *{Song of Solomon 1:2}*

*N*othing gives the believer so much joy as fellowship with Christ. He has enjoyment as others have in the common mercies of life, he can be glad both in God's gifts and God's works; but in all these individually, yes, and in all of them added together, he does not find such substantial delight as in the matchless person of his Lord Jesus. He has wine which no vineyard on earth ever yielded; he has bread which all the grain fields of Egypt could never bring forth. Where can such sweetness be found as we have tasted in communion with our Beloved? In our esteem, the joys of earth are little better than husks for swine compared with Jesus, the heavenly manna. We would rather have one mouthful of Christ's love, and a sip of his fellowship, than a whole world full of carnal delights. What is the chaff to the wheat? What is the sparkling paste to the true diamond? What is a dream to the glorious reality? What is time's mirth, in its best form, compared to our Lord Jesus in his most despised estate? If you know anything about the inner life, you will confess that our highest, purest, and most enduring joys must be the fruit of the tree of life which is in the midst of the Paradise of God. No spring yields such sweet water as that well of God which was dug with the soldier's spear. All earthly bliss is of the earth, earthy, but the comforts of Christ's presence are like himself, heavenly. We can review our communion with Jesus and find no regrets of emptiness in it; there are no dregs in this wine, no dead flies in this ointment. The joy of the Lord is solid and enduring. Vanity has not looked upon it, but discretion and prudence testify that it abides the test of years, and is in time and in eternity worthy to be called "the only true delight." For nourishment, consolation, exhilaration, and refreshment, no wine can rival the love of Jesus. Let us drink to the full this evening.

January 9 — Morning

{Daily Reading: Genesis 25:1–27:46} {Quick Study: Genesis 23:1–24:67}

I will be their God. *{Jeremiah 31:33}*

Christian! Here is all you can require. To make you happy you need something that shall satisfy you; and is not this enough? If you can pour this promise into your cup, will you not say, with David, "My cup is running over; I have more than a heart can wish for?" When this is fulfilled, *"I am your God,"* are you not possessor of all things? Desire is as insatiable as death, but he who fills all in all can fill it. Who can measure the capacity of our wishes? But the immeasurable wealth of God can more than overflow it. Are you not complete when God is yours? Do you need anything except God? Is his all-sufficiency not enough to satisfy you if all else should fail? But you need more than quiet satisfaction; you desire *rapturous delight.* Come, soul, here is music fit for heaven in your portion, for God is the Maker of Heaven. Not all the music blown from sweet instruments or drawn from living strings can yield such melody as this sweet promise, "I will be their God." Here is a deep sea of bliss, a shoreless ocean of delight; come, bathe your spirit in it; swim for an age, and you shall find no shore; dive throughout eternity, and you shall find no bottom. "I will be their God." If this does not make your eyes sparkle, and your heart beat high with bliss, then assuredly your soul is not in a healthy state. But you need more than present delights — you crave something concerning which you may exercise *hope*; and what more can you hope for than the fulfilment of this great promise, "I will be their God?" This is the masterpiece of all the promises; its enjoyment makes a heaven below, and will make a heaven above. Dwell in the light of your Lord, and let your soul be always ravished with his love. Get the marrow and fatness from this portion for yourself. Live up to your privileges, and rejoice with unspeakable joy.

January 9 — Evening

Serve the Lord with gladness. *{Psalms 100:2}*

Delight in divine service is a token of acceptance. Those who serve God with a sad countenance, because they do what is unpleasant to them, are not serving him at all; they bring the form of homage, but the life is absent. Our God requires no slaves to grace his throne; he is the Lord of the empire of love and would have his servants dressed in the livery of joy. The angels of God serve him with songs, not with groans; a murmur or a sigh would be a mutiny in their ranks. That obedience which is not voluntary is disobedience, for the Lord looks at the heart, and if he sees that we serve him by compulsion, and not because we love him, he will reject our offering. Service coupled with cheerfulness is heart service, and therefore true. Take away joyful willingness from the Christian, and you have removed *the test of his sincerity*. If a man is driven to battle, he is no patriot; but he who marches into the fray with flashing eye and beaming face, singing, "It is sweet to die for one's country," proves himself to be sincere in his patriotism. Cheerfulness is *the support of our strength*; in the joy of the Lord we are strong. It acts as *the remover of difficulties*. It is to our service what oil is to the wheels of a railway car. Without oil, the axle soon grows hot, and accidents occur; and if there is not a holy cheerfulness to oil our wheels, our spirits will be clogged with weariness. The man who is cheerful in his service for God proves that obedience is his element; he can sing,

> Make me to walk in your commands,
> 'Tis a delightful road.

Reader, let us ask this question — do *you* serve the Lord *with gladness*? Let us show to the people of the world, who think our religion to be slavery, that it is to us a delight and a joy! Let our gladness proclaim that we serve a good Master.

January 10 — Morning

{Daily Reading: Genesis 28:1–30:43} {Quick Study: Genesis 25:1–26:35}

There is laid up for me a crown of righteousness. *{2 Timothy 4:8}*

Doubting one! You have often said, "I fear I shall never enter heaven." Do not fear! All the people of God shall enter there. I love the quaint saying of a dying man, who exclaimed, "I have no fear of going home; I have sent all before me; God's finger is on the latch of my door, and I am ready for him to enter." "But," one said, "are you not afraid lest you should miss your inheritance?" "No," he said, "no; there is one crown in heaven which the angel Gabriel could not wear, it will fit no head except mine. There is one throne in heaven which Paul the apostle could not fill; it was made for me, and I shall have it." Oh Christian, what a joyous thought! Your portion is secure; "there remains a rest." "But can I not forfeit it?" No, it is entailed. If I am a child of God I shall not lose it. It is mine as securely as if I were there. Come with me, believer, and let us sit upon the top of Nebo, and view the goodly land, even Canaan. Do you see that little river of death glistening in the sunlight, and across it do you see the pinnacles of the eternal city? Do you see the pleasant country, and all its joyous inhabitants? Know, then, that if you could fly across you would see written upon one of its many mansions, "This remains for such a one; reserved for him only. He shall be caught up to dwell for ever with God." Poor doubting one, see the fair inheritance; it is *yours*. If you believe in the Lord Jesus, if you have repented of sin, if you have been renewed in heart, you are one of the Lord's people, and there is a place reserved for you, a crown laid up for you, a harp specially provided for you. No one else shall have your portion, it is reserved in heaven for you, and you shall have it before long, for there shall be no vacant thrones in glory when all the chosen are gathered in.

January 10 — Evening

In my flesh I shall see God. *{Job 19:26}*

Notice the subject of Job's devout anticipation "I shall see *God*." He does not say, "I shall see the saints" — though doubtless that will be untold felicity — but, "I shall see God." It is not — "I shall see the pearly gates, I shall behold the walls of jasper, I shall gaze upon the crowns of gold," but "I shall see God." This is the sum and substance of heaven; this is the joyful hope of all believers. It is their delight to see him now in the ordinances by faith. They love to behold him in communion and in prayer; but there in heaven they shall have an open and unclouded vision, and thus seeing "him as he is," shall be made completely like him. *Likeness to God* — what more can we wish for? And *a sight of God* — what better can we desire? Some read the passage, "Yet, I shall see God in my flesh," and find here an allusion to Christ, as the "Word made flesh," and that glorious beholding of him which shall be the splendour of the latter days. Whether that is so or not it is certain that Christ shall be the object of our eternal vision; nor shall we ever need any joy beyond that of seeing him. Do not think that this will be a narrow sphere for the mind to dwell in. It is only one source of delight, but that source is infinite. All his attributes shall be subjects for contemplation, and since he is infinite under each aspect, there is no fear of exhaustion. His works, his gifts, his love for us, and his glory in all his purposes and in all his actions, these shall make a theme which will be for ever new. The patriarch looked forward to this sight of God as a *personal* enjoyment. "Whom my eye shall behold, and not another." Anticipate heaven's bliss; think what it will be *to you*. "*Your eyes* shall see the King in his beauty." All earthly brightness fades and darkens as we gaze upon it, but here is a brightness which can never dim, a glory which can never fade — *"I shall see God."*

January 11 — Morning

{Daily Reading: Genesis 31:1–33:20} {Quick Study: Genesis 27:1–28:22}

These have no root. *{Luke 8:13}*

My soul, examine yourself this morning by the light of this text. You have received the word with joy; your feelings have been stirred and a lively impression has been made; but remember, that to receive the word in the ear is one thing, and to receive Jesus into your very soul is quite another; superficial feeling is often joined to inward hardness of heart, and a lively impression of the word is not always a lasting one. In the parable, the seed in one case fell upon ground having a rocky bottom, covered over with a thin layer of earth; when the seed began to take root, its downward growth was hindered by the hard stone and therefore it spent its strength in pushing its green shoot aloft as high as it could, but having no inward moisture derived from root nourishment, it withered away. Is this my case? Have I been making a fair show in the flesh without having a corresponding inner life? Good growth takes place upward and downward at the same time. Am I rooted in sincere fidelity and love for Jesus? If my heart remains unsoftened and unfertilized by grace, the good seed may germinate and grow for a while, but it must ultimately wither, for it cannot flourish on a rocky, unbroken, unsanctified heart. Let me dread a godliness as rapid in growth and as lacking in endurance as Jonah's gourd; let me count the cost of being a follower of Jesus, above all let me feel the energy of his Holy Spirit, and then I shall possess an abiding and enduring seed in my soul. If my mind remains as obdurate as it was by nature, the sun of trial will scorch, and my hard heart will help to cast the heat the more terribly upon the poorly covered seed, and my religion will soon die, and my despair will be terrible; therefore, oh heavenly sower, plough me first, and then cast the truth into me, and let me yield for you a bounteous harvest.

January 11 — Evening

I have prayed for you. *{Luke 22:32}*

How encouraging is the thought of the Redeemer's never ceasing intercession for us. When we pray, he pleads for us; and when we are *not* praying, he is advocating our cause, and by his supplications shielding us from unseen dangers. Notice the word of comfort addressed to Peter — "Simon, Simon, Satan has desired to have you so that he may sift you as wheat; but" — what? "But go and pray for yourself." That would be good advice, but it is not so written. Neither does he say, "But I will keep you watchful, and so you shall be preserved." That would be a great blessing. No, it is, "*But I have prayed for you*, that your faith does not fail." We little know what we owe to our Saviour's prayers. When we reach the hill tops of heaven, and look back upon all the way by which the Lord our God has led us, how we shall praise him who, before the eternal throne, undid the mischief which Satan was doing upon earth. How shall we thank him because he never held his peace, but day and night pointed to the wounds upon his hands, and carried our names upon his breastplate! Even before Satan had begun to tempt, Jesus had forestalled him and entered a plea in heaven. Mercy outruns malice. Notice, he does not say, "Satan has sifted you, and therefore I will pray," but "Satan has *desired* to have you." He checks Satan even in his very desire, and nips it in the bud. He does not say, "But I have desired to pray for you." No, but "I *have* prayed for you: I have done it already; I have gone to court and entered a counterplea even before an accusation is made." Oh, Jesus, what a comfort it is that you have pleaded our cause against our unseen enemies; countermined their mines, and unmasked their ambushes. Here is a matter for joy, gratitude, hope, and confidence.

January 12 — Morning

{Daily Reading: Genesis 34:1–36:43} {Quick Study: Genesis 29:1–30:43}

You are Christ's. *{1 Corinthians 3:23}*

You *are* Christ's." You are his by donation, for the Father gave you to the Son; his by his bloody purchase, for he counted down the price for your redemption; his by dedication, for you have consecrated yourself to him; his by relation, for you are named by his name, and made one of his brethren and joint heirs. Labour practically to show the world that you are the servant, the friend, the bride of Jesus. When tempted to sin, reply, "I cannot do this great wickedness, for I am Christ's." Immortal principles forbid the friend of Christ to sin. When wealth is before you to be won by sin, say that you are Christ's, and do not touch it. Are you exposed to difficulties and dangers? Stand firm in the evil day, remembering that you are Christ's. Are you placed where others are sitting down idly, doing nothing? Rise to the work with all your powers; and when the sweat stands upon your brow, and you are tempted to loiter, cry, "No, I cannot stop, for I am Christ's. If I were not purchased by blood, I might be like Issachar, crouching between two burdens; but I am Christ's, and cannot loiter." When the siren song of pleasure would tempt you from the path of right, reply, "Your music cannot charm me; I am Christ's." When the cause of God invites you, give yourself to it; when the poor require you, give your goods and yourself away, for you are Christ's. Never betray your profession. Always be one of those whose manners are Christian, whose speech is like the Nazarene, whose conduct and conversation are so redolent of heaven, that all who see you may know that you are the Saviour's, recognising in you his features of love and his countenance of holiness. "I am a Roman!" was of old a reason for integrity; far more, then, let it be your argument for holiness, "I am Christ's!"

January 12 — Evening

I have yet to speak on God's behalf. *{Job 36:2}*

We ought not to court publicity for our virtue, or notoriety for our zeal; but, at the same time, it is a sin to be always seeking to hide what God has bestowed upon us for the good of others. A Christian is not to be a village in a valley, but "a city set upon a hill"; he is not to be a lamp under a bushel, but a lamp on a lampstand, giving light to all. Retirement may be lovely in its season, and to hide one's self is doubtless modest, but the hiding of *Christ* in us can never be justified, and the keeping back of truth which is precious to ourselves is a sin against others and an offence against God. If you are of a nervous temperament and of retiring disposition, take care that you do not indulge this trembling propensity too much, lest you should be useless to the church. Seek in the name of him who was not ashamed of you to ignore your feelings, and tell others what Christ has done for you. If you cannot speak with trumpet tongue, use the still small voice. If the pulpit must not be your tribune, if the press may not carry your words on its wings, say with Peter and John, "I do not have any silver and gold; but what I have I give to you." By Sychar's well, talk to the Samaritan woman, if you cannot preach a sermon on the mountain; utter the praises of Jesus in the house, if not in the temple; in the field, if not in the stock exchange; in the midst of your own household, if you cannot do it among your fellow men. From the hidden springs within let sweetly flowing rivulets of testimony flow forth, giving drink to every passerby. Do not hide your talent, trade with it, and you shall bring in good interest for your Lord and Master. To speak for God will be refreshing to ourselves, cheering to saints, useful to sinners, and honouring to the Saviour. Dumb children are an affliction to their parents. Lord, unloose all your children's tongues.

January 13 — Morning

{Daily Reading: Genesis 37:1–39:23} {Quick Study: Genesis 31:1–32:32}

Jehoshaphat made merchant ships to go to
Ophir for gold: but they did not go; for the ships were
wrecked at Eziongeber. *{1 Kings 22:48}*

Solomon's ships had returned in safety, but Jehoshaphat's vessels never reached the land of gold. Providence prospers one and frustrates the desires of another, in the same business and in the same place, yet the Great Ruler is as good and wise at one time as another. May we have grace today, in the remembrance of this text, to bless the Lord for ships wrecked at Eziongeber, as well as for vessels freighted with temporal blessings; let us not envy the more successful, nor murmur at our losses as though we were singularly and especially tried. Like Jehoshaphat, we may be precious in the Lord's sight, although our schemes end in disappointment.

The secret cause of Jehoshaphat's loss is well worthy of notice, for it is the root of very much of the suffering of the Lord's people; it was his alliance with a sinful family, his fellowship with sinners. We are told that the Lord sent a prophet to declare, "Because you have joined yourself with Ahaziah, the Lord has broken your works." *{2 Chronicles 20:37}* This was a fatherly chastisement, which appears to have been blest to him; for in the verse which succeeds our morning's text we find him refusing to allow his servants to sail in the same vessels with those of the wicked king. Oh, that Jehoshaphat's experience might be a warning to the rest of the Lord's people, to avoid being unequally yoked together with unbelievers! A life of misery is usually the lot of those who are united in marriage, or in any other way of their own choosing, with the men of the world. Oh, for such love for Jesus that, like him, we may be holy, harmless, undefiled, and separate from sinners; for if it is not so with us, we may expect to hear it often said, *"The Lord has broken your works."*

January 13 — Evening

The iron did float. *{2 Kings 6:6}*

The axe head seemed hopelessly lost, and since it was borrowed, the honour of the prophetic band was likely to be imperilled, and so the name of their God to be compromised. Contrary to all expectation, the iron was made to mount from the depth of the stream and to float; for things impossible with man are possible with God. I knew a man in Christ only a few years ago who was called to undertake a work far exceeding his strength. It appeared so difficult as to involve absurdity in the bare idea of attempting it. Yet he was called to it, and his faith rose to the occasion; God honoured his faith, unlooked for aid was sent, and the iron did float. Another of the Lord's family was in grievous financial straits, he was able to meet all claims, and much more if he could have realised a certain portion of his estate, but he was overtaken with a sudden pressure; he sought for friends in vain, but faith led him to the unfailing Helper, and lo, the trouble was averted, his footsteps were enlarged, and the iron did float. A third had a sorrowful case of depravity to deal with. He had taught, reproved, warned, invited, and interceded, but all in vain. Old Adam was too strong for young Melancthon, the stubborn spirit would not relent. Then came an agony of prayer, and before long a blessed answer was sent from heaven. The hard heart was broken, the iron did float.

Beloved reader, what is your desperate case? What heavy matter have you in hand this evening? Bring it here. The God of the prophets lives, and lives to help his saints. He will not allow you to lack any good thing. Believe in the Lord of hosts! Approach him pleading the name of Jesus, and the iron shall float; you too shall see the finger of God working marvels for his people. According to your faith be it to you, and yet again the iron shall float.

January 14 — Morning

{Daily Reading: Genesis 40:1–42:38} {Quick Study: Genesis 33:1–36:43}

Mighty to save. *{Isaiah 63:1}*

By the words "to save," we understand all the great work of salvation, from the first holy desire onward to complete sanctification. The words are *multum in parvo*: indeed, here is all mercy in one word. Christ is not only "mighty to save" those who repent, but he is able to make men repent. He will carry those to heaven who believe; but he is, moreover, mighty to give men new hearts and to work faith in them. He is mighty to make the man who hates holiness love it, and to constrain the despiser of his name to bend the knee before him. Indeed, this is not all the meaning, for the divine power is equally seen in the later work. The life of a believer is a series of miracles performed by "the Mighty God." The bush burns, but is not consumed. He is mighty to keep his people holy after he has made them so, and to preserve them in his fear and love until he consummates their spiritual existence in heaven. Christ's might does not lie in making a believer and then leaving him to shift for himself; but he who begins the good work carries it on; he who imparts the first germ of life in the dead soul prolongs the divine existence, and strengthens it until it bursts asunder every bond of sin, and the soul leaps from earth, perfected in glory. Believer, here is encouragement. Are you praying for some beloved one? Oh, do not give up your prayers, for Christ is "mighty to save." You are powerless to reclaim the rebel, but your Lord is Almighty. Lay hold on that mighty arm, and rouse it to put forth its strength. Does your own case trouble you? Do not fear, for his strength is sufficient for you. Whether to begin with others, or to carry on the work in you, Jesus is "mighty to save"; the best proof of which lies in the fact that he has saved *you*. What a thousand mercies that you have not found him mighty to destroy!

January 14 — Evening

Beginning to sink, he cried, saying,
"Lord, save me." *{Matthew 14:30}*

Sinking times are praying times with the Lord's servants. Peter neglected prayer when starting upon his venturous journey, but when he began to sink his danger made him a supplicant, and his cry though late was not too late. In our hours of bodily pain and mental anguish, we find ourselves as naturally driven to prayer as the wreck is driven upon the shore by the waves. The fox hies to its hole for protection; the bird flies to the forest for shelter; and even so the tried believer hastens to the mercy seat for safety. Heaven's great harbour of refuge is All Prayer; thousands of weather-beaten vessels have found a haven there, and the moment a storm comes on, it is wise for us to make for it with all sail.

Short prayers are long enough. There were only three words in the petition which Peter gasped out, but they were sufficient for his purpose. Not length but strength is desirable. A sense of need is a mighty teacher of brevity. If our prayers had less of the tail feathers of pride and more wing they would be all the better. Verbiage is to devotion as chaff is to the wheat. Precious things lie in small compass, and all that is real prayer in many a long address might have been uttered in a petition as short as that of Peter's.

Our extremities are the Lord's opportunities. Immediately a keen sense of danger forces an anxious cry from us and then the ear of Jesus hears, and with him ear and heart go together, and the hand does not linger long. At the last moment we appeal to our Master, but his swift hand makes up for our delays by instant and effectual action. Are we nearly engulfed by the boisterous waters of affliction? Let us then lift up our souls to our Saviour, and we may rest assured that he will not allow us to perish. When we can do nothing Jesus can do all things; let us enlist his powerful aid upon our side, and all will be well.

January 15 — Morning

{Daily Reading: Genesis 43:1–45:28} {Quick Study: Genesis 37:1–38:30}

Do as you have said. *{2 Samuel 7:25}*

God's promises were never meant to be thrown aside as waste paper; he intended that they should be used. God's gold is not miser's money, but is minted to be traded with. Nothing pleases our Lord better than to see his promises put into circulation; he loves to see his children bring them up to him, and say, "Lord, do as you have said." We glorify God when we plead his promises. Do you think that God will be any the poorer for giving you the riches he has promised? Do you dream that he will be any the less holy for giving holiness to you? Do you imagine he will be any the less pure for washing you from your sins? He has said, "Come now, and let us reason together, says the Lord: though your sins are as scarlet, they shall be as white as snow; though they are red like crimson, they shall be as wool." Faith lays hold upon the promise of pardon, and it does not delay, saying, "This is a precious promise, I wonder if it is true?" but it goes straight to the throne with it, and pleads, "Lord, here is the promise. Do as you have said." Our Lord replies, "Be it to you even as you wish." When a Christian grasps a promise, if he does not take it to God, he dishonours him; but when he hastens to the throne of grace, and cries, "Lord, I have nothing to recommend me but this, 'You have said it' "; then his desire shall be granted. Our heavenly Banker delights to cash his own notes. Never let the promise rust. Draw the word of promise out of its scabbard, and use it with holy violence. Do not think that God will be troubled by your importunately reminding him of his promises. He loves to hear the loud outcries of needy souls. It is his delight to bestow favours. He is more ready to hear than you are to ask. The sun is not weary of shining, nor the fountain of flowing. It is God's nature to keep his promises; therefore, go at once to the throne with, "Do as you have said."

January 15 — Evening

But I give myself to prayer. *{Psalms 109:4}*

Lying tongues were busy against the reputation of David, but he did not defend himself; he moved the case into a higher court, and pleaded before the great King himself. Prayer is the safest method of replying to words of hatred. The psalmist prayed in no cold-hearted manner, he *gave himself* to the exercise — threw his whole soul and heart into it — straining every sinew and muscle, as Jacob did when wrestling with the angel. Thus, and thus only, shall any of us prosper at the throne of grace. Just as a shadow has no power because there is no substance in it, even so that supplication, in which a man's proper self is not thoroughly present in agonizing earnestness and vehement desire, is utterly ineffectual, for it lacks what would give it force. "Fervent prayer," says an old divine, "like a cannon planted at the gates of heaven, makes them fly open." The common fault with the most of us is our readiness to yield to distractions. Our thoughts go roving here and there, and we make little progress towards our desired end. Like quicksilver our mind will not hold together, but rolls off this way and that. How great an evil this is! It injures us, and what is worse, it insults our God. What should we think of a petitioner, if, while having an audience with a prince, he should be playing with a feather or catching a fly?

Continuance and perseverance are intended in the expression of our text. David did not cry once, and then relapse into silence; his holy clamour was continued until it brought down the blessing. Prayer must not be our chance work, but our daily business, our habit and vocation. Just as artists give themselves to their models, and poets to their classical pursuits, so must we addict ourselves to prayer. We must be immersed in prayer as in our element, and so pray without ceasing. Lord, teach us so to pray that we may be more and more prevalent in supplication.

January 16 — Morning

{Daily Reading: Genesis 46:1–48:22} {Quick Study: Genesis 39:1–41:57}

"I will help you," says the Lord. *{Isaiah 41:14}*

This morning let us hear the Lord Jesus speak to each one of us: "I will *help* you." "It is only a small thing for me, your God, to help you. Consider what I have done already. What! Not help you? Why, I bought you with my blood. What! Not help you? I have died for you; and if I have done the greater, will I not do the less? *Help* you! It is the least thing I will ever do for you; I *have* done more, and *will* do more. Before the world began I chose you. I made the covenant for you. I laid aside my glory and became a man for you; I gave up my life for you; and if I did all this, I will surely help you now. In helping you, I am giving you what I have bought for you already. If you had need of a thousand times as much help, I would give it to you; you require little compared with what I am ready to give. It is much for you to need, but it is nothing for me to bestow. '*Help* you?' Do not fear! If there was an ant at the door of your granary asking for help, it would not ruin you to give him a handful of your wheat; and you are nothing but a tiny insect at the door of my all-sufficiency. 'I will help you.' "

Oh, my soul, is not this enough? Do you need more strength than the omnipotence of the united Trinity? Do you need more wisdom than exists in the Father, more love than displays itself in the Son, or more power than is revealed in the influences of the Spirit? Bring here your empty pitcher! Surely this well will fill it. Hurry, gather up your requests, and bring them here — your emptiness, your woes, your needs. Behold, this river of God is full for your supply; what can you desire beside? Go forth, my soul, in this your might. The eternal God is your helper!

> Fear not, I am with you,
> Oh, be not dismayed!
> I, I am your God,
> And will still give you aid.

January 16 — Evening

The Messiah shall be cut off, but not for himself. *{Daniel 9:26}*

Blessed is his name, there was no cause of death in him. Neither original nor actual sin had defiled him, and therefore death had no claim upon him. No man could have taken his life from him justly, for he had done no man wrong, and no man could even have killed him by force unless he had been pleased to yield himself to die. But lo, one sins and another suffers. Justice was offended by us, but found its satisfaction in him. Rivers of tears, mountains of offerings, seas of the blood of young bulls, and hills of frankincense, could not have availed for the removal of sin; but Jesus was cut off for us, and the cause of wrath was cut off at once, for sin was put away for ever. Herein is wisdom, by which substitution, the sure and speedy way of atonement, was devised! Herein is condescension, which brought the Messiah, the Prince, to wear a crown of thorns, and die upon the cross! Herein is love, which led the Redeemer to lay down his life for his enemies!

It is not enough, however, to admire the spectacle of the innocent bleeding for the guilty, we must make sure of our interest in it. The special object of the Messiah's death was the salvation of his church; have we a part and a lot among those for whom he gave his life for a ransom? Did the Lord Jesus stand as our representative? Are we healed by his stripes? It will be a terrible thing indeed if we should come short of a portion in his sacrifice; it would be better for us that we had never been born. Solemn as the question is, it is a joyful circumstance that it is one which may be answered clearly and without mistake. To all who believe on him the Lord Jesus is a present Saviour, and upon them all the blood of reconciliation has been sprinkled. Let all who trust in the merit of the Messiah's death be joyful at every remembrance of him, and let their holy gratitude lead them to the fullest consecration to his cause.

January 17 — Morning

{Daily Reading: Genesis 49:1–Exodus 1:22} {Quick Study: Genesis 42:1–44:34}

And I looked, and, lo, a Lamb stood on the mount Sion. *{Revelation 14:1}*

The apostle John was privileged to look within the gates of heaven, and in describing what he saw, he begins by saying, "I looked, and, lo, a Lamb!" This teaches us that the primary object of contemplation in the heavenly state is "the Lamb of God, who takes away the sins of the world." Nothing else attracted the apostle's attention so much as the person of that Divine Being, who has redeemed us by his blood. He is the theme of the songs of all glorified spirits and holy angels. Christian, here is joy for you; you have looked, and you have seen the Lamb. Through your tears your eyes have seen the Lamb of God taking away your sins. Rejoice, then. In a little while, when the tears in your eyes shall have been wiped away, you will see the same Lamb *exalted on his throne*. It is the joy of your heart to hold daily fellowship with Jesus; you shall have the same joy to a higher degree in heaven; you shall enjoy the constant vision of his presence; you shall dwell with him for ever. "I looked, and, lo, a Lamb!" Why, that Lamb is heaven itself; for as good Rutherford says, "Heaven and Christ are the same thing"; to be with Christ is to be in heaven, and to be in heaven is to be with Christ. That prisoner of the Lord very sweetly writes in one of his glowing letters — "Oh my Lord Jesus Christ, if I could be in heaven without you, it would be a hell; and if I could be in hell, and have you still, it would be a heaven to me, for you are all the heaven I want." It is true, is it not, Christian? Does not your soul say so?

> Not all the harps above can make a heavenly place,
> If God his residence remove, or but conceal his face.

All you need to make you blessed, supremely blessed, is "to be with Christ."

January 17 — Evening

And it came to pass in the evening, that David arose from off his bed, and walked upon the roof of the king's house. *{2 Samuel 11:2}*

At that hour David saw Bathsheba. We are never out of the reach of temptation. Both at home and abroad we are liable to meet with allurements to evil; the morning opens with peril, and the shades of evening find us still in jeopardy. They are well kept whom God keeps, but woe to those who go forth into the world, or even dare to walk their own house unarmed. Those who think themselves secure are more exposed to danger than any others. The armourbearer of Sin is Self-confidence.

David should have been engaged in fighting the Lord's battles, but instead he remained in Jerusalem, and gave himself up to luxurious repose, for he arose from his bed in the evening. Idleness and luxury are the devil's jackals, and find him abundant prey. In stagnant waters noxious creatures swarm, and neglected soil soon yields a dense tangle of weeds and briars. Oh, for the constraining love of Jesus to keep us active and useful! When I see the king of Israel sluggishly leaving his couch at the close of the day, and falling at once into temptation, let me take warning, and set holy watchfulness to guard the door.

Is it possible that the king had gone up to his housetop for retirement and devotion? If so, what a caution is given to us to consider no place, however secret, a sanctuary from sin! While our hearts are so like a tinderbox, and sparks so plentiful, we need to use all diligence everywhere to prevent a blaze. Satan can climb housetops, and enter closets, and even if we could shut out that foul fiend, our own corruptions are enough to work our ruin unless grace prevents it. Reader, beware of evening temptations. Do not be secure. The sun is down but sin is up. We need a watchman for the night as well as a guardian for the day. Oh blessed Spirit, keep us from all evil tonight. Amen.

January 18 — Morning

{Daily Reading: Exodus 2:1–4:31} {Quick Study: Genesis 45:1–47:31}

Therefore there remains a rest for
the people of God. *{Hebrews 4:9}*

How different will be the state of the believer in heaven from what it is here! Here he is born to toil and suffer weariness, but in the land of the immortal, fatigue is never known. Anxious to serve his Master, he finds his strength unequal to his zeal: his constant cry is, "Help me to serve you, oh my God." If he is thoroughly active, he will have much labour; not too much for his will, but more than enough for his power, so that he will cry out, "I am not wearied *of* the labour, but I am wearied *in it.*" Ah! Christian, the hot day of weariness does not last for ever; the sun is nearing the horizon; it shall rise again with a brighter day than you have ever seen upon a land where they serve God day and night, and yet rest from their labours. *Here*, rest is only partial, *there*, it is *perfect. Here*, the Christian is always unsettled; he feels that he has not yet attained. *There*, all are at rest; they have attained the summit of the mountain; they have ascended to the bosom of their God. Higher they cannot go. Ah, toil worn labourer, only think when you shall rest for ever! Can you conceive it? It is an *eternal* rest; a rest that "remains." *Here*, my best joys bear "mortal" on their brow; my fair flowers fade; my dainty cups are drained to dregs; my sweetest birds fall before death's arrows; my most pleasant days are shadowed into nights; and the flood tides of my bliss subside into ebbs of sorrow; but *there*, everything is immortal; the harp abides unrusted, the crown unwithered, the eye undimmed, the voice unfaltering, the heart unwavering, and the immortal being is wholly absorbed in infinite delight. Happy day! Happy! When mortality shall be swallowed up in life, and the Eternal Sabbath shall begin.

January 18 — Evening

He expounded to them in all the Scriptures the things concerning himself. *{Luke 24:27}*

The two disciples on the road to Emmaus had a most profitable journey. Their companion and teacher was *the best of tutors*; the interpreter one of a thousand, in whom are hid all the treasures of wisdom and knowledge. The Lord Jesus condescended to become a preacher of the gospel, and he was not ashamed to exercise his calling before an audience of two people, neither does he now refuse to become the teacher of even one. Let us court the company of so excellent an instructor, for until he is made to us wisdom we shall never be wise to salvation.

This unrivalled tutor used as his class book *the best of books*. Although able to reveal fresh truth, he preferred to expound the old. He knew by his omniscience what was the most instructive way of teaching, and by turning at once to Moses and the prophets, he showed us that the surest road to wisdom is not speculation, reasoning, or reading human books, but meditation upon the Word of God. The quickest way to be spiritually rich in heavenly knowledge is to dig in this mine of diamonds, to gather pearls from this heavenly sea. When Jesus himself sought to enrich others, he laboured in the quarry of Holy Scripture.

The favoured pair were led to consider *the best of subjects*, for Jesus spoke of Jesus, and expounded the things concerning himself. Here the diamond cut the diamond, and what could be more admirable? The Master of the House unlocked his own doors, conducted the guests to his table, and placed his own dainties upon it. He who hid the treasure in the field himself guided the searchers to it. Our Lord would naturally discourse upon the sweetest of topics, and he could find not one sweeter than his own person and work: with an eye to these we should always search the Word. Oh, for grace to study the Bible with Jesus as both our teacher and our lesson!

January 19 — Morning

{Daily Reading: Exodus 5:1–7:25} {Quick Study: Genesis 48:1–50:26}

I looked for him, but I did not find him. *{Song of Solomon 3:1}*

Tell me where you lost the company of Christ, and I will tell you the most likely place to find him. Have you lost Christ in the prayer closet by restraining prayer? Then it is there you must seek and find him. Did you lose Christ by sin? You will find Christ in no other way except by the giving up of the sin, and seeking by the Holy Spirit to mortify the member in which the lust dwells. Did you lose Christ by neglecting the Scriptures? You must find Christ in the Scriptures. It is a true proverb, "Look for a thing where you dropped it, it is there." So look for Christ where you lost him, for he has not gone away. But it is hard work to go back to Christ. Bunyan tells us, the pilgrim found the piece of the road back to the Arbour of Ease, where he lost his roll, the hardest he had ever travelled. Twenty miles onward is easier than to go one mile back for the lost evidence.

Take care, then, when you find your Master, to cling close to him. But why is it you have lost him? One would have thought you would never have parted with such a precious friend, whose presence is so sweet, whose words are so comforting, and whose company is so dear to you! Why is it that you did not watch him every moment for fear of losing sight of him? Yet, since you have let him go, what a mercy that you are seeking him, even though you mournfully groan, "Oh, that I knew where I might find him!" Go on seeking, for it is dangerous to be without your Lord. Without Christ you are like a sheep without its shepherd; like a tree without water at its roots; like a sere leaf in the tempest — not bound to the tree of life. With your whole heart seek him, and he will be found by you: only give yourself thoroughly up to the search, and truly, you shall yet discover him to your joy and gladness.

January 19 — Evening

Then he opened their understanding, so that they might understand the Scriptures. {Luke 24:45}

He whom we viewed last evening as opening Scripture, we see here opening the understanding. In the first work he has many fellow labourers, but in the second he stands alone; many can bring the Scriptures to the mind, but the Lord alone can prepare the mind to receive the Scriptures. Our Lord Jesus differs from all other teachers; they reach the ear, but he instructs the heart; they deal with the outward letter, but he imparts an inward taste for the truth, by which we perceive its savour and spirit. The most unlearned of men become mature scholars in the school of grace when the Lord Jesus by his Holy Spirit unfolds the mysteries of the kingdom to them, and grants the divine anointing by which they are enabled to see the invisible. We are happy if we have had our understandings cleared and strengthened by the Master! How many men of profound learning are ignorant of eternal things! They know the killing letter of revelation, but they cannot discern its living spirit; they have a veil upon their hearts which the eyes of carnal reason cannot penetrate. Such was our case a little while ago; we who now see were once utterly blind; truth was to us as beauty in the dark, a thing unnoticed and neglected. Had it not been for the love of Jesus we would have remained to this moment in utter ignorance, for without his gracious opening of our understanding, we could no more have attained spiritual knowledge than an infant can climb the pyramids, or an ostrich fly up to the stars. Jesus' college is the only one in which God's truth can be truly learned; other schools may teach us what is to be believed, but Christ's alone can show us how to believe it. Let us sit at the feet of Jesus, and by earnest prayer call in his blessed aid so that our dull wits may grow brighter, and our feeble understandings may receive heavenly things.

January 20 — Morning

{Daily Reading: Exodus 8:1–10:29} {Quick Study: Exodus 1:1–2:25}

Abel was a keeper of sheep. *{Genesis 4:2}*

As a shepherd, Abel *sanctified his work to the glory of God, and offered a sacrifice of blood upon his altar, and the Lord had respect for Abel and his offering.* This early type of our Lord is exceedingly clear and distinct. Like the first streak of light which tinges the east at sunrise, it does not reveal everything, but it clearly indicates the great fact that the sun is coming. As we see Abel, a shepherd and yet a priest, offering a sacrifice of sweet smell to God, we discern our Lord, who brings before his Father a sacrifice to which Jehovah always has respect. Abel was hated by his brother — hated without a cause; and even so was the Saviour: the natural and carnal man hated the accepted man in whom the Spirit of grace was found, and did not rest until his blood had been shed. Abel fell, and sprinkled his altar and sacrifice with his own blood, and in it sets forth the Lord Jesus slain by the enmity of man while serving as a priest before the Lord. "The good Shepherd lays down his life for the sheep." Let us weep over him as we view him slain by the hatred of mankind, staining the horns of his altar with his own blood. *Abel's blood speaks.* The Lord said to Cain, "The voice of your brother's blood cries to me from the ground." The blood of Jesus has a mighty tongue, and the intention of its prevailing cry is not vengeance but mercy. It is precious beyond all preciousness to stand at the altar of our good Shepherd! To see him bleeding there as the slaughtered priest, and then to hear his blood speaking peace to all his flock, peace in our conscience, peace between Jew and Gentile, peace between man and his offended Maker, peace all down the ages of eternity for blood-washed men. Abel is the first shepherd in order of time, but our hearts shall always place Jesus first in order of excellence. You great Keeper of the sheep, we the people of your pasture bless you with our whole hearts when we see you slain for us.

January 20 — Evening

*Turn away my eyes from beholding vanity; and
revive me in your way.* {Psalms 119:37}

There are various kinds of vanity. The cap and bells of the fool, the mirth of the world, the dance, the lyre, and the cup of the dissolute, all these men know to be vanities; they wear upon their forefront their proper name and title. Far more treacherous are those equally vain things, the cares of this world and the deceitfulness of riches. A man may follow vanity as truly in business as in the theatre. If he is spending his life in amassing wealth, he passes his days in a vain show. Unless we follow Christ, and make our God the great object of life, we only differ in appearance from the most frivolous. It is clear that there is much need of the first prayer of our text. "Revive me in your way." The psalmist confesses that he is dull, heavy, lethargic, all but dead. Perhaps, dear reader, you feel the same. We are so sluggish that the best motives cannot revive us, apart from the Lord himself. What! Will hell not motivate me? Shall I think of sinners perishing, and yet not be awakened? Will not heaven motivate me? Can I think of the reward that awaits the righteous, and yet be cold? Will not death motivate me? Can I think of dying, and standing before my God, and yet be lazy in my Master's service? Will not Christ's love constrain me? Can I think of his dear wounds, can I sit at the foot of his cross, and not be stirred with fervency and zeal? It seems so! No mere consideration can motivate us to zeal, but God himself must do it, hence the cry, "*You* revive me." The psalmist breathes out his whole soul in vehement pleadings: his body and his soul unite in prayer. "Turn away my eyes," says the body: "Revive me," cries the soul. This is a fitting prayer for every day. Oh, Lord, hear it in my case tonight.

January 21 — Morning

{Daily Reading: Exodus 11:1–13:22} {Quick Study: Exodus 3:1–4:31}

And so all Israel shall be saved. *{Romans 11:26}*

Then Moses sang at the Red Sea, it was his joy to know that *all* Israel was safe. Not a drop of spray fell from that solid wall until the last of God's Israel had safely planted their foot on the other side of the flood. That done, immediately the floods dissolved into their proper place again, but not until then. Part of that song was, "You in your mercy have led forth the people whom you have redeemed." In the last time, when the elect shall sing the song of Moses, the servant of God, and of the Lamb, it shall be the boast of Jesus, "Of all whom you have given to me, I have lost no one." In heaven there shall not be a vacant throne.

> For all the chosen race
> Shall meet around the throne,
> Shall bless the conduct of his grace,
> And make his glories known.

As many as God has chosen, as many as Christ has redeemed, as many as the Spirit has called, as many as believe in Jesus, shall safely cross the dividing sea. We are not all safely landed yet:

> Part of the host has crossed the flood,
> And part are crossing now.

The vanguard of the army has already reached the shore. We are marching through the depths; today we are following close after our Leader into the heart of the sea. Let us be of good cheer: the rearguard shall soon be where the vanguard already is; the last of the chosen ones shall soon have crossed the sea, and then shall be heard the song of triumph, when all are secure. But oh! if one were to be absent — oh! if one of his chosen family should be cast away — it would make an everlasting discord in the song of the redeemed, and cut the strings of the harps of paradise, so that music could never be extorted from them.

January 21 — Evening

He was very thirsty, and called on the LORD, and said,
"You have given this great deliverance into the hand of your
servant: and now shall I die of thirst?" {Judges 15:18}

Samson was thirsty and ready to die. The difficulty was totally different from any which the hero had met before. Merely to get thirst assuaged is nothing like so great a matter as to be delivered from a thousand Philistines! But when the thirst was upon him, Samson felt that little present difficulty was more weighty than the great past difficulty out of which he had so specially been delivered. It is very usual for God's people, when they have enjoyed a great deliverance, to find a little trouble too much for them. Samson kills a thousand Philistines, and piles them up in heaps, and then faints for a little water! Jacob wrestles with God at Peniel, and overcomes Omnipotence himself, and then goes "halting on his thigh!" Strange that there must be a shrinking of the sinew whenever we win the day. As if the Lord must teach us our littleness, our nothingness, in order to keep us within bounds. Samson boasted very loudly when he said, "I have killed a thousand men." His boastful throat soon grew hoarse with thirst, and he resorted to prayer. God has many ways of humbling his people. Dear child of God, if after great mercy you are laid very low, your case is not an unusual one. When David had mounted the throne of Israel, he said, "I am weak today, although anointed king." You must expect to feel weakest when you are enjoying your greatest triumph.

If God has performed for you great deliverances in the past, your present difficulty is only like Samson's thirst, and the Lord will not let you faint, nor allow the daughter of the uncircumcised to triumph over you. The road of sorrow is the road to heaven, but there are wells of refreshing water all along the route. So, tried brother, cheer your heart with Samson's words, and rest assured that God will deliver you before long.

January 22 — Morning

{Daily Reading: Exodus 14:1–16:36} {Quick Study: Exodus 5:1–7:25}

Son of man, how is the vine tree better than any tree, or than a vine branch which is among the trees of the forest? *{Ezekiel 15:2}*

These words are for the humbling of God's people; they are called God's vine, but what are they by nature more than others? They, by God's goodness, have become fruitful, having been planted in a good soil; the Lord has trained them upon the walls of the sanctuary, and they bring forth fruit to his glory; but what are they without their God? What are they without the continual influence of the Spirit, creating fruitfulness in them? Oh believer, learn to reject pride, seeing that you have no basis for it. Whatever you are, you have nothing to make you proud. The more you have, the more you are in debt to God; and you would not be proud of what renders you a debtor. Consider your origin; look back to what you were. Consider what you would have been if not for divine grace. Look upon yourself as you are now. Does your conscience not reproach you? Do your thousand wanderings not stand before you, and tell you that you are unworthy to be called his son? And if he has made you anything, are you not taught by it that it is grace which has made you to differ? Great believer, you would have been a great sinner if God had not made you to differ. Oh you who are valiant for truth, you would have been as valiant for error if grace had not laid hold upon you. Therefore, do not be proud, though you have a large estate — a wide domain of grace, you had not once a single thing to call your own except your sin and misery. Oh! strange infatuation, that you, who have borrowed everything, should think of exalting yourself; a poor dependent pensioner upon the bounty of your Saviour, one who has a life which dies without fresh streams of life from Jesus, and yet proud! Fie on you, oh silly heart!

January 22 — Evening

Does Job fear God for nothing? {Job 1:9}

This was the wicked question of Satan concerning that upright man of old, but there are many in the present day concerning whom it might be asked with justice, for they love God after a fashion because he prospers them; but if things went poorly with them, they would give up all their boasted faith in God. If they can clearly see that since the time of their supposed conversion the world has gone prosperously with them, then they will love God in their poor carnal way; but if they suffer adversity, they rebel against the Lord. Their love is the love of the table, not of the Host; a love for the cupboard, not to the Master of the house. As for the true Christian, he expects to have his reward in the next life, and to endure hardness in this. The promise of the old covenant was prosperity, but the promise of the new covenant is adversity. Remember Christ's words — "Every branch in me that does not bear fruit he takes away, and every branch that bears fruit." — What? *"He purges it, so that it may bring forth more fruit."* If you bring forth fruit, you will have to endure affliction. "Alas!" you say, "that is a terrible prospect." But this affliction works out such precious results that the Christian who is the subject of it must learn to rejoice in tribulations, because as his tribulations abound, so his consolations abound by Christ Jesus. Rest assured, if you are a child of God, you will be no stranger to the rod. Sooner or later, every bar of gold must pass through the fire. Do not fear, but rather rejoice that such fruitful times are in store for you, for in them you will be weaned from earth and made suitable for heaven; you will be delivered from clinging to the present, and made to long for those eternal things which are so soon to be revealed to you. When you feel that concerning the present you do serve God for nothing, you will then rejoice in the infinite reward of the future.

I have exalted one chosen out of the people. *{Psalms 89:19}*

Why was Christ chosen out of the people? Speak, my heart, for heart thoughts are best. Was it not so that he might be able to be *our brother*, in the blessed tie of kindred blood? Oh, what relationship there is between Christ and the believer! The believer can say, "I have a Brother in heaven; I may be poor, but I have a Brother who is rich, and is a King, and will he allow me to lack while he is on his throne? Oh, no! He loves me; he is my Brother." Believer, wear this blessed thought, like a necklace of diamonds, around the neck of your memory; put it, as a golden ring, on the finger of remembrance, and use it as the King's own seal, stamping the petitions of your faith with confidence of success. He is a Brother born for adversity, treat him as such.

Christ was also chosen out of the people that he might know our needs and sympathise with us. "He was tempted in all points like we are, yet without sin." In all our sorrows we have his sympathy. Temptation, pain, disappointment, weakness, weariness, poverty — he knows them all, for he has felt them all. Remember this, Christian, and let it comfort you. However difficult and painful your road, it is marked by the footsteps of your Saviour; and even when you reach the dark valley of the shadow of death, and the deep waters of the swelling Jordan, you will find his footprints there. In all places wherever we go, he has been our forerunner; each burden we have to carry has once been laid on the shoulders of Emmanuel.

> His way was much rougher
> And darker than mine;
> Did Christ, my Lord, suffer,
> And shall I repine?

Take courage! Royal feet have left a blood-red track upon the road, and consecrated the thorny path for ever.

January 23 — Evening

We will remember your love
more than wine. *{Song of Solomon 1:4}*

Jesus will not let his people forget his love. If all the love they have enjoyed would be forgotten, he will visit them with fresh love. "Do you forget my cross?" he says, "I will cause you to remember it; for at my table I will reveal myself anew to you. Do you forget what I did for you in the council chamber of eternity? I will remind you of it, for you shall need a counsellor, and shall find me ready at your call." Mothers do not let their children forget them. If the boy has gone to Australia, and does not write home, his mother writes — "Has John forgotten his mother?" Then there comes back a sweet epistle, which proves that the gentle reminder was not in vain. So it is with Jesus, he says to us, "Remember me," and our response is, "We will remember your love." We *will* remember your love and its matchless history. It is ancient as the glory which you had with the Father before the world was. We remember, oh Jesus, your eternal love when you became our Surety, and espoused us as your Betrothed. We remember the love which suggested the sacrifice of yourself, the love which, until the fulness of time, mused over that sacrifice, and longed for the hour of which in the volume of the book it was written about you, "Lo, I come." We remember your love, oh Jesus, as it was revealed to us in your holy life, from the manger of Bethlehem to the garden of Gethsemane. We track you from the cradle to the grave — for every word and deed of yours was love — and we rejoice in your love, which death did not exhaust; your love which shone resplendent in your resurrection. We remember that burning fire of love which will never let you hold your peace until your chosen ones are all safely housed, until Zion is glorified, and Jerusalem settled on her everlasting foundations of light and love in heaven.

January 24 — Morning

{Daily Reading: Exodus 20:1–22:31} {Quick Study: Exodus 11:1–13:22}

**Surely he shall deliver you from the snare
of the fowler.** *{Psalms 91:3}*

God delivers his people from the snare of the fowler in two senses. *From*, and *out of*. First, he delivers them from the snare — does not let them enter it; and secondly, if they should be caught in it, he delivers them *out of* it. The first promise is the most precious to some; the second is the best to others.

"He shall deliver you *from* the snare." How? Trouble is often the means by which God delivers us. God knows that our backsliding will soon end in our destruction, and he in mercy sends the rod. We say, "Lord, why is this?" not knowing that our trouble has been the means of delivering us from far greater evil. Many have been thus saved from ruin by their sorrows and their crosses; these have frightened the birds from the net. At other times, God keeps his people *from* the snare of the fowler by giving them great spiritual strength, so that when they are tempted to do evil they say, "How can I do this great wickedness, and sin against God?" But what a blessed thing it is that if the believer shall, in an evil hour, come into the net, yet God will bring him *out* of it! Oh backslider, be cast down, but do not despair. Wanderer though you have been, hear what your Redeemer says — "Return, oh backsliding children; I will have mercy upon you." But you say you cannot return, for you are a captive. Then listen to the promise — "Surely he shall deliver you out of the snare of the fowler." You shall yet be brought out of all evil into which you have fallen, and though you shall never cease to repent of your ways, yet he who has loved you will not cast you away; he will receive you, and give you joy and gladness, so that the bones which he has broken may rejoice. No bird of paradise shall die in the fowler's net.

January 24 — Evening

Martha was encumbered with much serving. *{Luke 10:40}*

Her fault was not that she *served*: the condition of a servant well becomes every Christian. "I serve," should be the motto of all the princes of the royal family of heaven. Nor was it her fault that she had "*much* serving." We cannot do too much. Let us do all that we possibly can; let head, and heart, and hands, be engaged in the Master's service. It was no fault of hers that she was busy preparing a feast for the Master. Happy Martha, to have an opportunity of entertaining so blessed a guest; and happy, too, to have the spirit to throw her whole soul so heartily into the engagement. Her fault was that she grew "*encumbered* with much serving," so that she forgot *him*, and only remembered the service. She allowed service to override communion, and so presented one duty stained with the blood of another. We ought to be Martha and Mary in one: we should do much service, and have much communion at the same time. For this we need great grace. It is easier to serve than to commune. Joshua never grew weary in fighting with the Amalekites; but Moses, on the top of the mountain in prayer, needed two helpers to sustain his hands. The more spiritual the exercise, the sooner we tire in it. The choicest fruits are the hardest to rear: the most heavenly graces are the most difficult to cultivate. Beloved, while we do not neglect external things, which are good enough in themselves, we ought also to see to it that we enjoy living, personal fellowship with Jesus. See to it that sitting at the Saviour's feet is not neglected, even though it is under the specious pretext of doing him service. The first thing for our soul's health, the first thing for his glory, and the first thing for our own usefulness, is to keep ourselves in perpetual communion with the Lord Jesus, and to see that the vital spirituality of our religion is maintained over and above everything else in the world.

January 25 — Morning

{Daily Reading: Exodus 23:1–25:40} {Quick Study: Exodus 14:1–15:27}

I will mention the lovingkindnesses of the Lord,
and the praises of the Lord, according to all
that the Lord has bestowed on us. *{Isaiah 63:7}*

And can *you* not do this? Are there no mercies which you *have experienced*? Even though you are gloomy now, can you forget that blessed hour when Jesus met you, and said, "Come to me?" Can you not remember that rapturous moment when he snapped your fetters, dashed your chains to the earth, and said, "I came to break your bonds and set you free?" Or if the love of your espousals is forgotten, there must surely be some precious milestone along the road of life not quite grown over with moss, upon which you can read a happy memorial of his mercy towards you? What, did you never have a sickness like what you are suffering now, and did he not restore you? Were you never poor before, and did he not supply your needs? Were you never in distress before, and did he not deliver you? Arise, go to the river of your experience, and pull up a few bulrushes, and weave them into an ark, into which your infant faith may float safely on the stream. Do not forget what your God has done for you; look over the book of your remembrance, and consider the days of old. Can you not remember the hill Mizar? Did the Lord never meet with you at Hermon? Have you never climbed the Delectable Mountains? Have you never been helped in time of need? Indeed, I know you have. Go back, then, a little way to the choice mercies of yesterday, and though all may be dark now, light up the lamps of the past, they shall glitter through the darkness, and you shall trust in the Lord until the day breaks and the shadows flee away. "Remember, oh Lord, your tender mercies and your lovingkindnesses, for they have been from of old." *{Psalms 25:6}*

January 25 — Evening

Do we then make the law void through faith? Certainly not! Indeed we establish the law. *{Romans 3:31}*

When the believer is adopted into the Lord's family, his relationship to old Adam and the law ceases at once; but then he is under a new rule, and a new covenant. Believer, you are God's child; it is your first duty to obey your Heavenly Father. You have nothing to do with a servile spirit: you are not a slave, but a child; and now, inasmuch as you are a beloved child, you are bound to obey your Father's faintest wish, the least intimation of his will. Does he bid you fulfil a sacred ordinance? It is at your peril that you neglect it, for you will be disobeying your Father. Does he command you to seek the person of Jesus? Is it not your joy to do so? Does Jesus tell you, "Be perfect, even as your Father who is in heaven is perfect?" Then not because the law commands, but because your Saviour desires it, you will labour to be perfect in holiness. Does he bid his saints to love one another? Do it, not because the law says, "Love your neighbour," but because Jesus says, "If you love me, keep my commandments"; and this is the commandment that he has given to you, "that you love one another." Are you told to distribute to the poor? Do it, not because charity is a burden which you dare not shirk, but because Jesus teaches, "Give to him who asks of you." Does the Word say, "Love God with all your heart?" Look at the commandment and reply, "Ah! commandment, Christ has fulfilled you already — I have no need, therefore, to fulfil you for my salvation, but I rejoice to yield obedience to you because God is my Father now and he has a claim upon me, which I would not dispute." May the Holy Spirit make your heart obedient to the constraining power of Christ's love, so that your prayer may be, "Make me to go in the path of your commandments; for I delight in it." Grace is the mother and nurse of holiness, and not the apologist of sin.

Your Heavenly Father. *{Matthew 6:26}*

God's people are doubly his children, they are his offspring by creation, and they are his sons by adoption in Christ. Hence they are privileged to call him, "Our Father who is in heaven." Father! Oh, what a precious word is that. Here is *authority*: "If I am a Father, where is my honour?" If you are sons, where is your obedience? Here is *affection* mingled with authority; an authority which does not provoke rebellion; an obedience demanded which is most cheerfully rendered — which would not be withheld even if it might. The obedience which God's children yield to him must be *loving* obedience. Do not go about the service of God as slaves to their taskmaster's toil, but run in the way of his commands because it is your *Father's* way. Yield your bodies as instruments of righteousness, because righteousness is your Father's will, and *his* will should be the will of his child. Father! — Here is a kingly attribute so sweetly veiled in love, that the King's crown is forgotten in the King's face, and his sceptre becomes not a rod of iron, but a silver sceptre of mercy — the sceptre indeed seems to be forgotten in the tender hand of him who wields it. *Father!* — Here is honour and love. How great is a Father's love for his children! What friendship cannot do, and mere benevolence will not attempt, a father's heart and hand must do for his sons. They are his offspring, he must bless them; they are his children, he must show himself strong in their defence. If an earthly father watches over his children with unceasing love and care, how much more does our Heavenly Father? Abba, Father! He who can say this has uttered better music than cherubim or seraphim can reach. There is heaven in the depth of that word — Father! There is all I can ask; all my necessities can demand; all my wishes can desire. I have all in all to all eternity when I can say, "Father."

All those who heard it wondered about those things. *{Luke 2:18}*

We must not cease to wonder about the great marvels of our God. It would be very difficult to draw a line between holy wonder and *real worship*; for when the soul is overwhelmed with the majesty of God's glory, although it may not express itself in song, or even utter its voice with bowed head in humble prayer, yet it silently adores. Our incarnate God is to be worshipped as "the Wonderful." That God should consider his fallen creature, man, and instead of sweeping him away with the besom of destruction, should himself undertake to be man's Redeemer, and to pay his ransom price, is, indeed marvellous! But to each believer redemption is most marvellous as he views it in relation to himself. It is a miracle of grace indeed, that Jesus should forsake the thrones and royalties above, to suffer ignominiously below *for you*. Let your soul lose itself in wonder, for wonder is in this way a very practical emotion. Holy wonder will lead you to *grateful worship* and *heartfelt thanksgiving*. It will cause within you *godly watchfulness*; you will be afraid to sin against such a love as this. Feeling the presence of the mighty God in the gift of his dear Son, you will take off your shoes from your feet, because the place where you are standing is holy ground. You will be moved at the same time to *glorious hope*. If Jesus has done such marvellous things on your behalf, you will feel that heaven itself is not too great for your expectation. Who can be astonished by anything, when he has once been astonished by the manger and the cross? What is left that is wonderful after one has seen the Saviour? Dear reader, it may be that from the quietness and solitariness of your life, you are scarcely able to imitate the shepherds of Bethlehem, who told what they had seen and heard, but you can, at least, fill up the circle of the worshippers before the throne, by wondering over what God has done.

And we have all received of his fulness. *{John 1:16}*

These words tell us that there is a fulness in Christ. There is a fulness of essential deity, for "in him dwells all the fulness of the Godhead." There is a fulness of perfect manhood, for in him, bodily, that Godhead was revealed. There is a fulness of atoning efficacy in his blood, for "the blood of Jesus Christ, his Son, cleanses us from all sin." There is a fulness of justifying righteousness in his life, for "there is therefore now no condemnation to those who are in Christ Jesus." There is a fulness of divine prevalence in his plea, for "He is able to save to the uttermost those who come to God by him; seeing he ever lives to make intercession for them." There is a fulness of victory in his death, for through death he destroyed him who had the power of death, that is the devil. There is a fulness of efficacy in his resurrection from the dead, for by it "we are begotten again to a lively hope." There is a fulness of triumph in his ascension, for "when he ascended up on high, he led captives captive, and received gifts for men." There is a fulness of blessings of every sort and shape; a fulness of grace to pardon, of grace to regenerate, of grace to sanctify, of grace to preserve, and of grace to perfect. There is a fulness at all times; a fulness of comfort in affliction; a fulness of guidance in prosperity. A fulness of every divine attribute, of wisdom, of power, of love; a fulness which it would be impossible to survey, much less to explore. "It pleased the Father that in him should *all* fulness dwell." Oh, what a fulness must this be of which *all* receive! Fulness, indeed, must there be when the stream is always flowing, and yet the well springs up as free, as rich, as full as ever. Come, believer, and get all your need supplied; ask largely, and you shall receive largely, for this "fulness" is inexhaustible, and is treasured up where all the needy may reach it, even in Jesus, Emmanuel — God with us.

January 27 — Evening

But Mary kept all these things, and pondered them in her heart. *{Luke 2:19}*

There was an exercise, on the part of this blessed woman, of three powers of her being: her *memory* — she kept all these things; her *affections* — she kept them in her heart; her *intellect* — she pondered them; so that memory, affection, and understanding were all exercised about the things which she had heard. Beloved, remember what you have heard of your Lord Jesus, and what he has done for you; make your heart the golden pot of manna to preserve the memorial of the heavenly bread on which you have fed in days gone by. Let your memory treasure up everything about Christ which you have either felt, or known, or believed, and then let your fond affections hold *him* firmly for evermore. Love the person of your Lord! Bring forth the alabaster box of your heart, even though it is broken, and let all the precious ointment of your affection come streaming onto his pierced feet. Let your intellect be exercised concerning the Lord Jesus. Meditate upon what you read: do not stop at the surface; dive into the depths. Do not be as the swallow which touches the brook with her wing, but as the fish which penetrates the lowest depth. Abide with your Lord: do not let him be to you as a wayfaring man, who tarries for a night, but constrain him, saying, "Abide with us, for the day is far spent." Hold him, and do not let him go. The word "ponder" means to weigh. Make ready the balances of judgment. Oh, but where are the scales that can weigh the Lord Christ? "He takes up the isles as a very little thing": — who shall take him up? "He weighs the mountains in scales" — in what scales shall we weigh *him*? Let it be that if your understanding cannot comprehend, then let your affections apprehend; and if your spirit cannot encompass the Lord Jesus in the grasp of understanding, let it embrace him in the arms of affection.

January 28 — Morning

{Daily Reading: Exodus 32:1–34:35} {Quick Study: Exodus 22:1–24:18}

Perfect in Christ Jesus. *{Colossians 1:28}*

Do you not feel in your own soul that perfection is not in you? Does not every day teach you that? Every tear which trickles from your eye, weeps "imperfection"; every sigh which bursts from your heart, cries "imperfection"; every harsh word which proceeds from your lip, mutters "imperfection." You have too frequently had a view of your own heart to dream for a moment of any perfection *in yourself.* But amid this sad consciousness of imperfection, here is comfort for you — you are "perfect *in Christ Jesus.*" In God's sight, you are "complete in him"; *even now* you are "accepted in the Beloved." But there is a second perfection, yet to be realised, which is sure to all the seed. Is it not delightful to look forward to the time when every stain of sin shall be removed from the believer, and he shall be presented faultless before the throne, without spot, or wrinkle, or any such thing? The church of Christ then will be so pure, that not even the eye of Omniscience will see a spot or blemish in her; so holy and so glorious, that Hart did not go beyond the truth when he said —

> With my Saviour's garments on,
> Holy as the Holy One.

Then shall we know, and taste, and feel the happiness of this vast but short sentence, "Complete in Christ." Not until then shall we fully comprehend the heights and depths of the salvation of Jesus. Does your heart not leap for joy at the thought of it? Black as you are, you shall be white one day; filthy as you are, you shall be clean. Oh, it is a marvellous salvation this! Christ takes a worm and transforms it into an angel; Christ takes a black and deformed thing and makes it clean and matchless in his glory, peerless in his beauty, and fit to be the companion of seraphs. Oh my soul, stand and admire this blessed truth of perfection in Christ.

January 28 — Evening

And the shepherds returned, glorifying and
praising God for all the things that they had heard
and seen, as it was told to them. *{Luke 2:20}*

What was the subject of their praise? They *praised God for what they had heard* — for the good tidings of great joy that a Saviour was born to them. Let us copy them; let us also raise a song of thanksgiving that we have heard of Jesus and his salvation. They also *praised God for what they had seen*. There is the sweetest music — what we have experienced, what we have felt within, what we have made our own — "the things which we have made touching the King." It is not enough to *hear* about Jesus: mere hearing may tune the harp, but the fingers of living faith must create the music. If you have seen Jesus with the God-given sight of faith, allow no cobwebs to linger among the harp strings, but awaken your psaltery and harp to the loud praise of sovereign grace. One point for which they praised God was *the agreement between what they had heard and what they had seen*. Observe the last sentence — "As it was told to them." Have you not found the gospel to be in yourselves just what the Bible said it would be? Jesus said he would give you rest — have you not enjoyed the sweetest peace in him? He said you should have joy, and comfort, and life through believing in him — have you not received all these? Are not his ways — ways of pleasantness, and his paths — paths of peace? Surely you can say with the queen of Sheba, "The half has not been told to me." I have found Christ more sweet than his servants ever said he was. I looked upon his likeness as they painted it, but it was a mere daub compared with himself; for the King in his beauty outshines all imaginable loveliness. Surely what we have "seen" keeps pace with, indeed, far exceeds, what we have *"heard."* Let us, then, glorify and praise God for a Saviour so precious, and so satisfying.

The things which are not seen. *{2 Corinthians 4:18}*

In our Christian pilgrimage it is well, for the most part, to be looking forward. Forward lies the crown, and onward is the goal. Whether it is for hope, for joy, for consolation, or for the inspiring of our love, the future must, after all, be the grand object of the eye of faith. Looking into the future we see sin cast out, the body of sin and death destroyed, the soul made perfect, and fit to be a partaker of the inheritance of the saints in light. Looking further yet, the believer's enlightened eye can see death's river passed, the gloomy stream forded, and the hills of light attained on which stands the Celestial City; he sees himself enter within the pearly gates, hailed as more than conqueror, crowned by the hand of Christ, embraced in the arms of Jesus, glorified with him, and made to sit together with him on his throne, even as he has overcome and has sat down with the Father on his throne. The thought of this future may well relieve the darkness of the past and the gloom of the present. The joys of heaven will surely compensate for the sorrows of earth. Hush, my fears! This world is only a narrow span, and you shall soon have passed it. Hush, hush, my doubts! Death is only a narrow stream, and you shall soon have forded it. Time, how short — eternity, how long! Death, how brief — immortality, how endless! I think I even now eat of Eshcol's clusters, and sip from the well which is within the gate. The road is so, so short! I shall soon be there.

> When the world my heart is rending
> With its heaviest storm of care,
> My glad thoughts to heaven ascending,
> Find a refuge from despair.
> Faith's bright vision shall sustain me
> Till life's pilgrimage is past;
> Fears may vex and troubles pain me,
> I shall reach my home at last.

January 29 — Evening

The dove came in to him in the evening. {Genesis 8:11}

Blessed be the Lord for another day of mercy, even though I am now weary with its toils. To the preserver of men I lift up my song of gratitude. The dove found no rest outside of the ark, and therefore returned to it; and my soul has learned yet more fully than ever, today, that there is no satisfaction to be found in earthly things — God alone can give rest to my spirit. As for my business, my possessions, my family, my attainments, these are all well enough in their way, but they cannot fulfil the desires of my immortal nature. "Return to your rest, oh my soul, for the Lord has dealt bountifully with you." It was at the still hour, when the gates of the day were closing, that with weary wing the dove came back to the master: oh Lord, enable me this evening thus to return to Jesus. She could not endure to spend a night hovering over the restless waste, nor can I bear to be even for another hour away from Jesus, the rest of my heart, the home of my spirit. She did not merely alight upon the roof of the ark, she "came in to him"; even so would my longing spirit look into the secret of the Lord, pierce to the interior of truth, enter into what is within the veil, and reach to my Beloved in very deed. I must come to Jesus: my panting spirit cannot remain short of the nearest and dearest communion with him. Blessed Lord Jesus, be with me, reveal yourself, and abide with me all night, so that when I awake up I may be still with you. I notice that the dove brought in her mouth an olive branch plucked off, the memorial of the past day, and a prophecy of the future. Have I no pleasing record to bring home? No pledge and earnest of lovingkindness yet to come? Yes, my Lord, I present to you my grateful acknowledgments for tender mercies which have been new every morning and fresh every evening; and now, I ask that you put forth your hand and take your dove into your bosom.

January 30 — Morning

{Daily Reading: Exodus 38:1–39:43} {Quick Study: Exodus 29:1–31:18}

When you hear the sound of marching in the tops of the mulberry trees, then you shall advance quickly. *{2 Samuel 5:24}*

The members of Christ's church should be very prayerful, always seeking the unction of the Holy One to rest upon their hearts, so that the kingdom of Christ may come, and that his "will be done on earth, even as it is in heaven"; but there are times when God seems especially to favour Zion, such times ought to be to them like "the sound of marching in the tops of the mulberry trees." We ought then to be doubly prayerful, doubly earnest, wrestling more at the throne than we have been accustomed to do. Action should then be prompt and vigorous. The tide is flowing — now let us pull manfully for the shore. Oh for Pentecostal outpourings and Pentecostal labours. Christian, in *yourself* there are times "when you hear the sound of marching in the tops of the mulberry trees." You have a particular power in prayer; the Spirit of God gives you joy and gladness; the Scripture is open to you; the promises are applied; you walk in the light of God's countenance; you have particular freedom and liberty in devotion, and more closeness of communion with Christ than was your habit. Now, at such joyous periods when you hear the "sound of marching in the tops of the mulberry trees," is the time to advance quickly; now is the time to get rid of any evil habit, while God the Spirit helps your infirmities. Spread your sail; but remember what you sometimes sing —

> I can only spread the sail;
> You! You! must breathe the auspicious gale.

Only be sure you have the sail up. Do not miss the gale for lack of preparation for it. Seek help from God, so that you may be more earnest in duty when made more strong in faith; so that you may be more constant in prayer when you have more liberty at the throne; so that you may be more holy in your conversation while you live more closely with Christ.

January 30 — Evening

In whom also we have obtained an inheritance. *{Ephesians 1:11}*

When Jesus gave himself for us, he gave us all the rights and privileges which went with himself; so that now, although as eternal God, he has essential rights to which no creature may venture to pretend, yet as Jesus, the Mediator, the Federal Head of the covenant of grace, he has no heritage apart from us. All the glorious consequences of his obedience to death are the joint riches of all who are in him, and on whose behalf he accomplished the divine will. See, he enters into glory, but not for himself alone, for it is written, "Where the Forerunner is *for us* entered." *{Hebrews 6:20}* Does he stand in the presence of God? — "He appears in the presence of God *for us*." *{Hebrews 9:24}* Consider this, believer. You have no right to heaven in yourself: your right lies in Christ. If you are pardoned, it is through *his* blood; if you are justified, it is through *his* righteousness; if you are sanctified, it is because *he* is made by God to you for sanctification; if you shall be kept from falling, it will be because you are preserved in Christ Jesus; and if you are perfected at the last, it will be because you are complete in *him*. Thus Jesus is magnified — for all is in him and by him; thus the inheritance is made certain to us — for it is obtained in him; thus each blessing is the sweeter, and even heaven itself the brighter, because it is Jesus our Beloved "in whom" we have obtained all. Where is the man who shall estimate our divine portion? Weigh the riches of Christ in scales, and his treasure in balances, and then think to count the treasures which belong to the saints. Reach the bottom of Christ's sea of joy, and then hope to understand the bliss which God has prepared for those who love him. Leap over the boundaries of Christ's possessions, and then dream of a limit to the fair inheritance of the elect. "All things are yours, for you are Christ's and Christ is God's."

January 31 — Morning

{Daily Reading: Exodus 40:1–40:38} {Quick Study: Exodus 32:1–34:35}

THE LORD OUR RIGHTEOUSNESS. *{Jeremiah 23:6}*

It will always give a Christian the greatest calm, quiet, ease, and peace, to think of the perfect righteousness of Christ. How often the saints of God are downcast and sad! I do not think they ought to be. I do not think they would if they could always see their perfection in Christ. There are some who are always talking about corruption, and the depravity of the heart, and the innate evil of the soul. This is quite true, but why not go a little further, and remember that we are "perfect in Christ Jesus." It is no wonder that those who are dwelling upon their own corruption should wear such downcast looks; but surely if we call to mind that "Christ is made to us righteousness," we shall be of good cheer. Though distresses afflict me, though Satan assault me, though there may be many things to be experienced before I get to heaven, those are done for me in the covenant of divine grace; there is nothing lacking in my Lord, Christ has done it all. On the cross he said, "It is finished!" and if it is finished, then I am complete in him, and can rejoice with joy unspeakable and full of glory, "Not having my own righteousness, which is of the law, but what is through the faith of Christ, the righteousness which is of God by faith." You will not find on this side of heaven a holier people than those who receive into their hearts the doctrine of Christ's righteousness. When the believer says, "I live on Christ alone; I rest on him solely for salvation; and I believe that, however unworthy, I am still saved in Jesus"; then there rises up as a motive of gratitude this thought — "Shall I not live for Christ? Shall I not love him and serve him, seeing that I am saved by his merits?" "The love of Christ constrains us," "that those who live should not henceforth live for themselves but for him who died for them." If saved by imputed righteousness, we shall greatly value imparted righteousness.

January 31 — Evening

Then Ahimaaz ran by the way of the plain, and outran Cushi. *{2 Samuel 18:23}*

Running is not everything, there is much in the way which we select: a swift foot over hill and down dale will not keep pace with a slower traveller upon level ground. How is it with my spiritual journey, am I labouring up the hill of my own works and down into the ravines of my own humiliations and resolutions, or do I run by the plain way of "Believe and live?" How blessed is it to wait upon the Lord by faith! The soul runs without weariness, and walks without fainting, in the way of believing. Christ Jesus is the way of life, and he is a plain way, a pleasant way, a way suitable for the tottering feet and feeble knees of trembling sinners: am I found in this way, or am I looking for another path such as priestcraft or metaphysics may promise me? I read of the way of holiness, that the wayfaring man, although a fool, shall not err in it: have I been delivered from proud reason and been brought as a little child to rest in Jesus' love and blood? If so, by God's grace I shall outrun the strongest runner who chooses any other path. This truth I may remember to my profit in my daily cares and needs. It will be my wisest course to go at once to my God, and not to wander in a roundabout manner to this friend and that. He knows my needs and can relieve them, to whom should I go except to himself by the direct appeal of prayer, and the plain argument of the promise. "Straight forward makes the best runner." I will not parlay with the servants, but hasten to their Master.

In reading this passage, it strikes me that if men compete with each other in common matters, and one outruns the other, I ought to be in solemn earnestness so to run that I may obtain. Lord, help me to gird up the loins of my mind, and may I press forward towards the mark for the prize of my high calling of God in Christ Jesus.

February 1 — Morning

{Daily Reading: Leviticus 1:1–3:17} {Quick Study: Exodus 35:1–37:29}

They shall sing in the ways of the Lord. *{Psalms 138:5}*

Christians first begin to sing in the ways of the Lord when they lose their burden at the foot of the cross. Not even the songs of the angels seem so sweet as the first song of rapture which gushes from the innermost soul of the forgiven child of God. You know how John Bunyan describes it. He says when poor Pilgrim lost his burden at the cross, he gave three great leaps, and went on his way singing —

> Blest cross! blest sepulchre! blest rather be
> The man that there was put to shame for me!

Believer, do you remember the day when *your* fetters fell off? Do you remember the place when Jesus met you, and said, "I have loved you with an everlasting love; I have blotted out as a cloud your transgressions, and as a thick cloud your sins; they shall not be mentioned against you any more for ever." Oh! what a sweet season is that when Jesus takes away the pain of sin. When the Lord first pardoned my sin, I was so joyful that I could scarcely refrain from dancing. I thought on my road home from the house where I had been set at liberty, that I must tell the stones in the street the story of my deliverance. My soul was so full of joy, that I wanted to tell every snow flake that was falling from heaven about the wondrous love of Jesus, who had blotted out the sins of one of the chief of rebels. But it is not only at the commencement of the Christian life that believers have reason for song; as long as they live they find reasons to sing in the ways of the Lord, and their experience of his constant lovingkindness leads them to say, "I will bless the Lord at all times: his praise shall continually be in my mouth." See to it, brother, that you magnify the Lord *today*.

> Long as we tread this desert land,
> New mercies shall new songs demand.

February 1 — Evening

Your love for me was wonderful. *{2 Samuel 1:26}*

Come, dear readers, let each one of us speak for himself about the wonderful love, not of Jonathan, but of Jesus. We will not relate what we have been told, but the things which we have tasted and handled concerning the love of Christ. Your love for me, oh Jesus, was wonderful when I was a stranger wandering far from you, fulfilling the desires of the flesh and of the mind. Your love restrained me from committing the sin which is to death, and withheld me from self-destruction. Your love held back the axe when Justice said, "Cut it down! Why does it encumber the ground?" Your love drew me into the wilderness, stripped me there, and made me feel the guilt of my sin, and the burden of my iniquity. Your love spoke thus comfortably to me when I was severely dismayed — "Come to me, and I will give you rest." Oh, how matchless was your love when, in a moment, you washed my sins away, and made my polluted soul, which was crimson with the blood of my nativity, and black with the grime of my transgressions, to be white as the driven snow, and pure as the finest wool. How you commended your love when you whispered in my ears, "I am yours and you are mine." Those accents were kind when you said, "The Father himself loves you." And sweet the moments, surpassingly sweet, when you declared to me "the love of the Spirit." Never shall my soul forget those places of fellowship where you have unveiled yourself to me. Had Moses his cleft in the rock, where he saw the train, the back parts of his God? We, too, have had our clefts in the rock, where we have seen the full splendours of the Godhead in the person of Christ. Did David remember the tracks of the wild goat, the land of Jordan and the Hermonites? We, too, can remember places dear to our memory, equal to these in blessedness. Precious Lord Jesus, give us a fresh draught of your wondrous love to begin the month with. Amen.

February 2 — Morning

{Daily Reading: Leviticus 4:1–6:30} {Quick Study: Exodus 38:1–40:38}

Without the shedding of blood is no remission. *{Hebrews 9:22}*

This is the voice of unalterable truth. In none of the Jewish ceremonies were sins, even typically, removed without blood shedding. In no case, by no means, can sin be pardoned without atonement. It is clear, then, that there is no hope for me apart from Christ; for there is no other blood shedding which is worth a thought as an atonement for sin. Am I, then, believing in him? Is the blood of his atonement truly applied to my soul? All men are on a level concerning their need of him. If we are ever so moral, generous, amiable, or patriotic, the rule will not be altered to make an exception for us. Sin will yield to nothing less potent than the blood of him whom God has set forth as a propitiation. What a blessing that there is the one way of pardon! Why should we seek another?

People of merely formal religion cannot understand how we can rejoice that all our sins are forgiven for Christ's sake. Their works, and prayers, and ceremonies, give them very poor comfort; and well may they be uneasy, for they are neglecting the one great salvation, and endeavouring to get remission without blood. My soul, sit down, and behold the justice of God as bound to punish sin; see that punishment all executed upon your Lord Jesus, and fall down in humble joy, and kiss the dear feet of him whose blood has made atonement for you. It is in vain when conscience is aroused to flee to feelings and evidences for comfort: this is a habit which we learned in the Egypt of our legal bondage. The only cure for a guilty conscience is a sight of Jesus suffering on the cross. "The blood is its life," says the levitical law, and let us rest assured that it is the life of faith and joy and every other holy grace.

> Oh! how sweet to view the flowing
> Of my Saviour's precious blood;
> With divine assurance knowing
> He has made my peace with God.

February 2 — Evening

And these are ancient things. *{1 Chronicles 4:22}*

Yet not as ancient as those precious things which are the delight of our souls. Let us for a moment recount them, tallying them over as misers count their gold. *The sovereign choice* of the Father, by which he elected us to eternal life before the earth was created, is a matter of vast antiquity, since no date can be conceived for it by the mind of man. We were chosen from before the foundations of the world. *Everlasting love* went with the choice, for it was not a bare act of divine will by which we were set apart, but the divine affections were concerned. The Father loved us in and from the beginning. Here is a theme for daily contemplation. *The eternal purpose* to redeem us from our foreseen ruin, to cleanse and sanctify us, and at last to glorify us, was of infinite antiquity, and runs side by side with immutable love and absolute sovereignty. *The covenant* is always described as being everlasting, and Jesus, the second party in it, had his goings forth of old; he struck hands in sacred suretyship long before the first of the stars began to shine, and it was in him that the elect were ordained to eternal life. Thus in the divine purpose a most blessed covenant union was established between the Son of God and his elect people, which will remain as the foundation of their safety when time shall be no more. Is it not well to be conversant with these ancient things? Is it not shameful that they should be so much neglected and even rejected by the majority of professors? If they knew more of their own sin, would they not be more ready to adore distinguishing grace? Let us both admire and adore tonight, as we sing —

> A monument of grace,
> A sinner saved by blood;
> The streams of love I trace
> Up to the Fountain, God;
> And in his sacred bosom see
> Eternal thoughts of Love for me.

February 3 — Morning

{Daily Reading: Leviticus 7:1–8:36} {Quick Study: Leviticus 1:1–3:17}

Therefore, brethren, we are debtors. *{Romans 8:12}*

As God's creatures, we are all debtors to him: to obey him with all our body, and soul, and strength. Having broken his commandments, as we all have, we are debtors to his justice, and we owe to him a vast amount which we are not able to pay. But of the *Christian* it can be said that he does not owe God's *justice* anything, for Christ has paid the debt his people owed; for this reason the believer owes all the more to *love*. I am a debtor to God's grace and forgiving mercy; but I am no debtor to his justice, for he will never accuse me of a debt already paid. Christ said, "It is finished!" and by that he meant that whatever his people owed was wiped away for ever from the book of remembrance. Christ, to the uttermost, has satisfied divine justice; the account is settled; the handwriting is nailed to the cross; the receipt is given, and we are debtors to God's justice no longer. But then, because we are not debtors to our Lord in that sense, we become ten times more debtors to God than we would have been otherwise. Christian, pause and ponder for a moment. What a debtor you are to divine *sovereignty*! How much you owe to his disinterested love, for he gave his own Son that he might die for you. Consider how much you owe to his forgiving *grace*, that after ten thousand affronts he loves you as infinitely as ever. Consider what you owe to his *power*; how he has raised you from your death in sin; how he has preserved your spiritual life; how he has kept you from falling; and how, though a thousand enemies have beset your path, you have been able to hold on your way. Consider what you owe to his *immutability*. Although you have changed a thousand times, he has not changed once. You are as deep in debt as you can be to every attribute of God. To God you owe yourself, and all you have — yield yourself as a living sacrifice, it is your only reasonable service.

February 3 — Evening

**Tell me . . . where you feed, where you make your flock
to rest at noon.** *{Song of Solomon 1:7}*

These words express the desire of the believer for Christ, and his longing for present communion with him. Where do you feed your flock? In *your house*? I will go, if I may find you there. In private *prayer*? Then I will pray without ceasing. In the *Word*? Then I will read it diligently. In your *ordinances*? Then I will walk in them with all my heart. Tell me where you feed, for wherever you stand as the Shepherd, there I will lie down as a sheep; for no one except you can supply my need. I cannot be satisfied to be apart from you. My soul hungers and thirsts for the refreshment of your presence. "Where do you make your flock to rest at noon?" for whether at dawn or at noon, my only rest must be where you are and your beloved flock. My soul's rest must be a grace-given rest, and can only be found in you. Where is the shadow of that rock? Why should I not repose beneath it? "Why should I be as one who turns aside by the flocks of your companions?" You have companions — why should I not be one? Satan tells me I am unworthy; but I always was unworthy, and yet you have loved me for a long time; and therefore my unworthiness cannot be a bar to my having fellowship with you now. It is true I am weak in faith, and prone to fall, but my very feebleness is the reason why I should always be where you feed your flock, so that I may be strengthened, and preserved in safety beside the still waters. Why should I turn aside? There is no reason why I should, but there are a thousand reasons why I should not, for Jesus beckons me to come. If he withdrew himself a little, it is only to make me prize his presence more. Now that I am grieved and distressed at being away from him, he will lead me yet again to that sheltered nook where the lambs of his fold are sheltered from the burning sun.

The love of the Lord. *{Hosea 3:1}*

Believer, *look back* through all your experience, and think of the way by which the Lord your God has led you in the wilderness, and how he has fed and clothed you every day — how he has borne with your bad manners — how he has put up with all your murmurings, and all your longings after the flesh pots of Egypt — how he has opened the rock to supply you, and fed you with manna that came down from heaven. Think of how his grace has been sufficient for you in all your troubles — how his blood has been a pardon to you in all your sins — how his rod and his staff have comforted you. When you have thus looked back upon the love of the Lord, then let faith survey his love *in the future*, for remember that Christ's covenant and blood have something more in them than the *past*. He who has loved you and pardoned you shall never cease to love and pardon. He is Alpha, and he shall be Omega also: he is first, and he shall be *last*. Therefore, do you think, when you shall pass through the valley of the shadow of death, you need fear any evil, for he is with you? When you shall stand in the cold floods of Jordan, you do not need to fear, for death cannot separate you from his love; and when you shall come into the mysteries of eternity you do not need to tremble, "For I am persuaded, that neither death; nor life, nor angels, nor principalities, nor powers, nor things present, nor things to come, nor height, nor depth, nor any other creature, shall be able to separate us from the love of God, which is in Christ Jesus our Lord." Now, soul, is not your love refreshed? Does not this make you love Jesus? Does not a flight through illimitable plains of the ether of love inflame your heart and compel you to delight yourself in the Lord your God? Surely as we meditate on "the love of the Lord," our hearts burn within us, and we long to love him more.

February 4 — Evening

Your refuge from the avenger of blood. *{Joshua 20:3}*

It is said that in the land of Canaan, cities of refuge were so arranged that any man might reach one of them within half a day at the utmost. Even so, the word of our salvation is near to us; Jesus is a present Saviour, and the way to him is short; it is only a simple renunciation of our own merit, and a laying hold of Jesus, to be our all in all. With regard to the roads to the city of refuge, we are told that they were strictly preserved; every river was bridged, and every obstruction removed, so that the man who fled might find an easy passage to the city. Once a year the elders went along the roads and saw to their order, so that nothing might impede the flight of anyone, and cause him, through delay, to be overtaken and slain. How graciously do the promises of the gospel remove stumbling blocks from the way! Wherever there were byroads and turnings, signs were posted with the inscription upon them — "To the city of refuge!" This is a picture of the road to Christ Jesus. It is no roundabout road of the law; it is no obeying this, that, and the other; it is a straight road: "Believe, and live." It is a road so hard that no self-righteous man can ever tread it, but so easy that every sinner who knows himself to be a sinner may by it find his way to heaven. No sooner did the manslayer reach the outskirts of the city than he was safe; it was not necessary for him to pass far within the walls, but the suburbs themselves were sufficient protection. Learn by this, that if you only touch the hem of Christ's garment, you shall be made whole; if you only lay hold upon him with "faith as a grain of mustard seed," you are safe.

> A little genuine grace ensures
> The death of all our sins.

Only waste no time, do not loiter by the way, for the avenger of blood is swift of foot; and it may be he is at your heels at this still evening hour.

February 5 — Morning

{Daily Reading: Leviticus 11:1–13:59} {Quick Study: Leviticus 7:1–9:24}

The Father sent the Son to be the
Saviour of the world. *{1 John 4:14}*

It is a sweet thought that Jesus Christ did not come forth without his Father's permission, authority, consent, and assistance. He was sent by the Father, so that he might be the Saviour of men. We are too apt to forget that while there are distinctions as to the *persons* in the Trinity, there are no distinctions of *honour*. We too frequently ascribe the honour of our salvation, or at least the depths of its benevolence, more to Jesus Christ than we do to the Father. This is a very great mistake. What if Jesus came? Did his Father not send him? If he spoke wondrously, did his Father not pour grace into his lips, so that he might be an able minister of the new covenant? He who knows the Father, and the Son, and the Holy Spirit as he should know them, never sets one before another in his love; he sees them at Bethlehem, at Gethsemane, and on Calvary, all equally engaged in the work of salvation. Oh, Christian, have you put your confidence in the man Christ Jesus? Have you placed your reliance solely on him? And are you united with him? Then believe that you are united to the God of heaven. Since to the man Christ Jesus you are brother, and hold closest fellowship, you are linked by it with God the Eternal, and "the Ancient of Days" is your Father and your friend. Did you ever consider the depth of love in the heart of Jehovah, when God the Father equipped his Son for the great enterprise of mercy? If not, make this your day's meditation. The *Father* sent him! Contemplate that subject. Think how Jesus works what the *Father* wills. In the wounds of the dying Saviour see the love of the great I AM. Let every thought of Jesus be also connected with the eternal, ever blessed God, for "It pleased the Lord to bruise him; he has put him to grief."

February 5 — Evening

At that time Jesus answered. *{Matthew 11:25}*

This is a singular way in which to commence a verse — "At that time Jesus answered." If you will look at the context you will not perceive that any person had asked him a question, or that he was in conversation with any human being. Yet it is written, "Jesus answered and said, 'I thank you, oh Father.' " When a man answers, he answers a person who has been speaking to him. Who, then, had spoken to Christ? His Father. Yet there is no record of it; and this should teach us that Jesus had constant fellowship with his Father, and that God spoke into his heart so often, so continually, that it was not a circumstance singular enough to be recorded. It was the habit and life of Jesus to talk with God. Even as Jesus was, in this world, so are we; let us therefore learn the lesson which this simple statement concerning him teaches us. May we likewise have silent fellowship with the Father, so that often we may answer him, and though the world does not know to whom we speak, may we be responding to that secret voice unheard by any other ear, which our own ear, opened by the Spirit of God, recognises with joy. God has spoken to us, let us speak to God — either to set our seal that God is true and faithful to his promise, or to confess the sin of which the Spirit of God has convicted us, or to acknowledge the mercy which God's providence has given, or to express assent to the great truths which God the Holy Spirit has opened to our understanding. What a privilege is intimate communion with the Father of our spirits! It is a secret hidden from the world, a joy with which even the nearest friend does not intermeddle. If we wish to hear the whispers of God's love, our ear must be purged and tuned to listen to his voice. This very evening may our hearts be in such a state that when God speaks to us, we, like Jesus, may be prepared at once to answer him.

February 6 — Morning

{Daily Reading: Leviticus 14:1–15:33} {Quick Study: Leviticus 10:1–12:8}

Praying always. *{Ephesians 6:18}*

What multitudes of prayers have we raised from the first moment when we learned to pray. Our first prayer was a prayer for ourselves; we asked that God would have mercy upon us, and blot out our sin. He heard us. But when he had blotted out our sins like a cloud, then we had more prayers for ourselves. We have had to pray for sanctifying grace, for constraining and restraining grace; we have been led to crave for a fresh assurance of faith, for the comforting application of the promise, for deliverance in the hour of temptation, for help in the time of duty, and for aid in the day of trial. We have been compelled to go to God for our souls, as constant beggars asking for everything. Bear witness, children of God, you have never been able to get anything for your souls elsewhere. All the bread your soul has eaten has come down from heaven, and all the water it has drunk has flowed from the living rock — Christ Jesus the Lord. Your soul has never grown rich in itself; it has always been a pensioner upon the daily bounty of God; and hence your prayers have ascended to heaven for a range of spiritual mercies all but infinite. Your needs were innumerable, and therefore the supplies have been infinitely great, and your prayers have been as varied as the mercies have been countless. Then have you not cause to say, "I love the Lord, because he has heard the voice of my supplication?" For just as your prayers have been many, so also have been God's answers to them. He has heard you in the day of trouble, has strengthened you, and helped you, even when you dishonoured him by trembling and doubting at the mercy seat. Remember this, and let it fill your heart with gratitude to God, who has thus graciously heard your poor weak prayers. "Bless the Lord, oh my soul, and do not forget all his benefits."

February 6 — Evening

Pray for one another. *{James 5:16}*

As an encouragement cheerfully to offer intercessory prayer, remember that *such prayer is the sweetest God ever hears*, for the prayer of Christ is of this character. In all the incense which our great High Priest now puts into the golden censer, there is not a single grain for himself. His intercession must be the most acceptable of all supplications — and the more our prayer is like Christ's, the sweeter it will be; thus while petitions for ourselves will be accepted, our pleadings for others, having in them more of the fruits of the Spirit, more love, more faith, more brotherly kindness, will be, through the precious merits of Jesus, the sweetest oblation that we can offer to God, the very fat of our sacrifice. Remember, again, that *intercessory prayer is exceedingly prevalent*. What wonders it has wrought! The Word of God teems with its marvellous deeds. Believer, you have a mighty engine in your hand, use it well, use it constantly, use it with faith, and you shall surely be a benefactor to your brethren. When you have the King's ear, speak to him for the suffering members of his body. When you are favoured to draw very near to his throne, and the King says to you, "Ask, and I will give you whatever you ask," let your petitions be not for yourself alone, but for the many who need his aid. If you have grace at all, and are not an intercessor, that grace must be small as a grain of mustard seed. You have just enough grace to float your soul clear from the quicksand, but you have no deep floods of grace, or else you would carry in your joyous bark a weighty cargo of the needs of others, and you would bring back from your Lord, for them, rich blessings which except for you they might not have obtained: —

> Oh, let my hands forget their skill,
> My tongue be silent, cold, and still,
> This bounding heart forget to beat,
> If I forget the mercy seat!

February 7 — Morning

{Daily Reading: Leviticus 16:1–18:30} {Quick Study: Leviticus 13:1–14:57}

Arise, and depart. *{Micah 2:10}*

The hour is approaching when the message will come to us, as it comes to all — "Arise, and go forth from the home in which you have lived, from the city in which you have done your business, from your family, from your friends. Arise, and take your last journey." And what do we know about the journey? And what do we know about the country to which we are bound? We have read a little about it, and some of it has been revealed to us by the Spirit; but how little do we know of the realms of the future! We know that there is a black and stormy river called "Death." God bids us to cross it, promising to be with us. And, after death, what comes? What wonderful world will open upon our astonished sight? What scene of glory will be unfolded to our view? No traveller has ever returned to tell. But we know enough of the heavenly land to make us welcome our summons there with joy and gladness. The journey of death may be dark, but we may go forth on it fearlessly, knowing that God is with us as we walk through the gloomy valley, and therefore we need not fear any evil. We shall be departing from all we have known and loved here, but we shall be going to our Father's house — to our Father's home, where Jesus is — to that royal "city which has foundations, whose Builder and Maker is God." This shall be our *last* move, to dwell for ever with him whom we love, in the midst of his people, in the presence of God. Christian, meditate much on heaven, it will help you to press on, and to forget the toil of the way. This vale of tears is only the pathway to the better country: this world of woe is only the stepping stone to a world of bliss.

Prepare us, Lord, by grace divine,
For your bright courts on high;
Then bid our spirits rise, and join
The chorus of the sky.

February 7 — Evening

And they heard a great voice from heaven saying to them,
"Come up here." {Revelation 11:12}

Without considering these words in their prophetic connection, let us regard them as the invitation of our great Forerunner to his sanctified people. In due time there shall be heard "a great voice from heaven" to every believer, saying, "Come up here." This should be to the saints *the subject of joyful anticipation*. Instead of dreading the time when we shall leave this world to go to the Father, we should be panting for the hour of our emancipation. Our song should be —

> My heart is with him on his throne, and ill can brook delay;
> Each moment listening for the voice, "Rise up and come away."

We are not called *down* to the grave, but *up* to the skies. Our heaven-born spirits should long for their native air. Yet should the celestial summons be *the object of patient waiting*, our God knows best when to bid us "Come up here." We must not wish to accelerate the period of our departure. I know that strong love will make us cry,

> Oh Lord of Hosts, the waves divide,
> And land us all in heaven;

but patience must have her perfect work. God ordains with accurate wisdom the most fitting time for the redeemed to abide below. Surely, if there could be regrets in heaven, the saints might mourn that they did not live longer here to do more good. Oh, for more sheaves for my Lord's garner! More jewels for his crown! But how, unless there is more work? True, there is the other side of it, that, living so briefly, our sins are the fewer; but oh! when we are fully serving God, and he is giving to us precious seed to scatter, and reap a hundredfold, we would even say it is better for us to abide where we are. Whether our Master shall say "go," or "stay," let us be equally well pleased as long as he indulges us with
his presence.

You shall call his name Jesus. *{Matthew 1:21}*

When a person is dear, everything connected with him becomes dear for his sake. Thus, so precious is the person of the Lord Jesus in the estimation of all true believers, that everything about him they consider to be inestimable beyond all price. "All your garments smell of myrrh, and aloes, and cassia," said David, as if the very vestments of the Saviour were so sweetened by his person that he could only love them. It is certain that there is not a spot where that hallowed foot has trodden — there is not a word which those blessed lips have uttered — nor a thought which his loving Word has revealed — which is not precious beyond all price to us. And this is true of the *names* of Christ — they are all sweet in the believer's ear. Whether he is called the Husband of the church, her Bridegroom, her Friend; whether he is called the Lamb slain from the foundation of the world — the King, the Prophet, or the Priest — every title of our Master — Shiloh, Emmanuel, Wonderful, the Mighty Counsellor — every name is like the honeycomb dropping with honey, and luscious are the drops that distil from it. But if there is one name sweeter than another in the believer's ear, it is the name of *Jesus*. Jesus! It is the name which moves the harps of heaven to melody. Jesus! The life of all our joys. If there is one name more charming, more precious than another, it is this name. It is woven into the very warp and woof of our psalmody. Many of our hymns begin with it, and scarcely any, that are good for anything, end without it. It is the sum total of all delights. It is the music with which the bells of heaven ring; a song in a word; an ocean for comprehension, although a drop for brevity; a matchless oratorio in two syllables; a gathering up of the hallelujahs of eternity in five letters.

> Jesus, I love your charming name,
> 'Tis music to my ear.

February 8 — Evening

He shall save his people from their sins. *{Matthew 1:21}*

Many people, if they are asked what they understand by salvation, will reply, "Being saved from hell and taken to heaven." This is one result of salvation, but it is not one tithe of what is contained in that boon. It is true our Lord Jesus Christ does redeem all his people from the wrath to come; he saves them from the fearful condemnation which their sins had brought upon them; but his triumph is far more complete than this. He saves his people "from their sins." Oh! sweet deliverance from our worst foes. Where Christ works a saving work, he casts Satan from his throne, and will not let him be master any longer. No man is a true Christian if sin reigns in his mortal body. Sin will be *in* us — it will never be utterly expelled until the spirit enters glory; but it will never have *dominion*. There will be a striving for dominion — a lusting against the new law and the new spirit which God has implanted — but sin will never get the upper hand so as to be absolute monarch of our nature. Christ will be master of the heart, and sin must be mortified. The Lion of the tribe of Judah shall prevail, and the dragon shall be cast out. Professor! Is sin subdued in you? If your *life* is unholy your *heart* is unchanged, and if your heart is unchanged you are an unsaved person. If the Saviour has not sanctified you, renewed you, given you a hatred of sin and a love of holiness, he has done nothing in you of a saving character. The grace which does not make a man better than others is a worthless counterfeit. Christ saves his people, not *in* their sins, but *from* them. "Without holiness no man shall see the Lord." "Let everyone who names the name of Christ depart from iniquity." If not saved from sin, how shall we hope to be counted among his people. Lord, save me now from all evil, and enable me to honour my Saviour.

February 9 — Morning

{Daily Reading: Leviticus 22:1–23:44} {Quick Study: Leviticus 19:1–21:24}

And David enquired of the Lord. *{2 Samuel 5:23}*

When David made this enquiry he had just fought the Philistines, and gained an outstanding victory. The Philistines came up in great hosts, but, by the help of God, David had easily put them to flight. Note, however, that when they came a second time, David did not go up to fight them without enquiring from the Lord. Once he had been victorious, and he might have said, as many have in other cases, "I shall be victorious again; I may rest quite sure that if I have conquered once I shall triumph yet again. Why should I wait to petition the Lord?" Not so, David. He had gained one battle by the strength of the Lord; he would not venture upon another until he had ensured the same. He enquired, "Shall I go up against them?" He waited until God's sign was given. Learn from David to take no step without God. Christian, if you wish to know the path of duty, take God for your compass; if you wish to steer your ship through the dark billows, put the tiller into the hand of the Almighty. Many a rock might be escaped, if we would let our Father take the helm; many a shoal or quicksand we might well avoid, if we would leave to his sovereign will to choose and to command. The Puritan said, "As sure as ever a Christian carves for himself, he will cut his own fingers"; this is a great truth. Another old divine said, "He who goes before the cloud of God's providence goes on a fool's errand"; and so he does. We must see God's providence leading us; and if providence tarries, wait until providence comes. He who goes before providence, will be very glad to run back again. "I will instruct you and teach you in the way which you shall go," is God's promise to his people. Let us, then, take all our perplexities to him, and say, "Lord, what will you have me to do?" Do not leave your room this morning without enquiring from the Lord.

February 9 — Evening

Do not lead us into temptation; but deliver us from evil [or, the evil one]. *{Luke 11:4}*

What we are taught to seek or shun in prayer, we should equally pursue or avoid in action. Very earnestly, therefore, we should avoid temptation, seeking to walk so guardedly in the path of obedience, that we may never tempt the devil to tempt us. We are not to enter the thicket in search of the lion. Dearly might we pay for such presumption. This lion may cross our path or leap upon us from the thicket, but we have nothing to do with hunting him. He who meets with him, even though he wins the day, will find it a stern struggle. Let the Christian pray that he may be spared the encounter. Our Saviour, who had experience of what temptation meant, thus earnestly admonished his disciples — "Pray that you do not enter into temptation."

But let us do as we wish, we shall be tempted; hence the prayer "deliver us from evil." God had one Son without sin; but he has no son without temptation. The natural man is born to trouble as the sparks fly upward, and the Christian man is born to temptation just as certainly. We must be always on our guard against Satan, because, like a thief, he gives no intimation of his approach. Believers who have had experience of the ways of Satan, know that there are certain seasons when he will most probably make an attack, just as at certain seasons bleak winds may be expected; thus the Christian is put on a double guard by fear of danger, and the danger is averted by preparing to meet it. Prevention is better than cure: it is better to be so well armed that the devil will not attack you, than to endure the perils of the fight, even though you come off a conqueror. Pray this evening first that you may not be tempted, and next that if temptation is permitted, you may be delivered from the evil one.

February 10 — Morning

{Daily Reading: Leviticus 24:1–25:55} {Quick Study: Leviticus 22:1–24:23}

I know how to abound. *{Philippians 4:12}*

There are many who know "how to be abased" who have not learned "how to abound." When they are set upon the top of a pinnacle their heads grow dizzy, and they are ready to fall. The Christian more often disgraces his profession in prosperity than in adversity. It is a dangerous thing to be prosperous. The crucible of adversity is a less severe trial to the Christian than the refining pot of prosperity. Oh, what leanness of soul and neglect of spiritual things have been brought on through the very mercies and bounties of God! Yet this is not a matter of necessity, for the apostle tells us that he knew how to abound. When he had much he knew how to use it. Abundant grace enabled him to bear abundant prosperity. When he had a full sail he was loaded with much ballast, and so floated safely. More than human skill is needed to carry the brimming cup of mortal joy with a steady hand, yet Paul had learned that skill, for he declares, "In all things I am instructed both to be full and to be hungry." It is a divine lesson to know how to be full, for the Israelites were full once, but while the flesh was yet in their mouth, the wrath of God came upon them. Many have asked for mercies so that they might satisfy their own hearts' lust. Fulness of bread has often made fulness of blood, and that has brought on wantonness of spirit. When we have much of God's providential mercies, it often happens that we have very little of God's grace, and little gratitude for the bounties we have received. We are full and we forget God: satisfied with earth, we are content to do without heaven. Rest assured it is harder to know how to be full than it is to know how to be hungry — so desperate is the tendency of human nature to pride and forgetfulness of God. Take care that you ask in your prayers that God would teach you "how to be full."

> Let not the gifts your love bestows
> Estrange our hearts from thee.

February 10 — Evening

*I have blotted out, as a thick cloud, your transgressions,
and, as a cloud, your sins: return to me;
for I have redeemed you. {Isaiah 44:22}*

Attentively observe THE INSTRUCTIVE SIMILITUDE: our sins are like *"a cloud."* Just as clouds are of many shapes and shades, so are our transgressions. Just as clouds obscure the light of the sun, and darken the landscape beneath, so do our sins hide from us the light of Jehovah's face, and cause us to sit in the shadow of death. They are earth born things, and rise from the miry places of our nature; and when so collected that their measure is full, they threaten us with storm and tempest. Alas! that, unlike clouds, our sins yield us no genial showers, but rather threaten to deluge us with a fiery flood of destruction. Oh you black clouds of sin, how can it be fair weather with our souls while you remain?

Let our joyful eye dwell upon THE NOTABLE ACT of divine mercy — *"blotting out."* God himself appears upon the scene, and in divine graciousness, instead of showing his anger, reveals his grace: he at once and for ever effectually removes the mischief, not by blowing away the cloud, but by blotting it out from existence once and for all. Against the justified man no sin remains, the great transaction of the cross has eternally removed his transgressions from him. On Calvary's summit the great deed, by which the sin of all the chosen was for ever put away, was completely and effectually performed.

Practically let us obey THE GRACIOUS COMMAND, *"return to me."* Why should pardoned sinners live at a distance from their God? If we have been forgiven all our sins, let no legal fear withhold us from the boldest access to our Lord. Let backslidings be bemoaned, but let us not persevere in them. To the greatest possible nearness of communion with the Lord, let us, in the power of the Holy Spirit, strive mightily to return. Oh Lord, restore us tonight!

February 11 — Morning

{Daily Reading: Leviticus 26:1–27:34} {Quick Study: Leviticus 25:1–27:34}

**And they took knowledge of them,
that they had been with Jesus.** *{Acts 4:13}*

A Christian should be a striking likeness of Jesus Christ. You have read lives of Christ, beautifully and eloquently written, but the best life of Christ is his living biography, written out in the words and actions of his people. If we were what we profess to be, and what we should be, we would be pictures of Christ; yes, such striking likenesses of him, that the world would not have to hold us up by the hour together, and say, "Well, it seems somewhat of a likeness"; but they would, when they once have seen us, exclaim, "He has been with Jesus; he has been taught by him; he is like him; he has caught the very idea of the holy Man of Nazareth, and he works it out in his life and every day actions." A Christian should be like Christ in his *boldness*. Never blush to own your religion; your profession will never disgrace you: take care you never disgrace *that*. Be like Jesus, very valiant for your God. Imitate him in your *loving* spirit; think kindly, speak kindly, and do kindly, so that men may say of you, "He has been with Jesus." Imitate Jesus in his *holiness*. Was he zealous for his Master? So should you be; always go around doing good. Do not waste time: it is too precious. Was he self-denying, never looking to his own interest? Be the same. Was he devout? Be fervent in your prayers. Had he deference to his Father's will? So submit yourselves to him. Was he patient? So learn to endure. And best of all, as the highest portrait of Jesus, try to forgive your enemies, as he did; and let those sublime words of your Master, "Father, forgive them; for they do not know what they are doing," always ring in your ears. Forgive, as you hope to be forgiven. Heap coals of fire on the head of your foe by your kindness to him. Good for evil, remember, is Godlike. Be Godlike, then; and in all ways and by all means, so live that all may say of you, "He has been with Jesus."

You have left your first love. *{Revelation 2:4}*

That best and brightest of hours is always to be remembered, when first we saw the Lord, lost our burden, received the roll of promise, rejoiced in full salvation, and went on our way in peace. It was spring time in the soul; the winter was past; the mutterings of Sinai's thunders were hushed; the flashings of its lightnings were no more perceived; God was seen as being reconciled; the law threatened no vengeance, justice demanded no punishment. Then the flowers appeared in our heart; hope, love, peace, and patience sprung from the sod; the hyacinth of repentance, the snowdrop of pure holiness, the crocus of golden faith, the daffodil of early love, all decked the garden of the soul. The time of the singing of birds was come, and we rejoiced with thanksgiving; we magnified the holy name of our forgiving God, and our resolve was, "Lord, I am yours, wholly yours; all I am, and all I have, I would devote to you. You have bought me with your blood — let me spend myself and be spent in your service. In life and in death let me be consecrated to you." *How have we kept this resolve?* Our espousal love burned with a holy flame of devotedness to Jesus — is it the same *now?* Might not Jesus well say to us, "I have something against you, because you have left your first love?" Alas! it is very little we have done for our Master's glory. Our winter has lasted all too long. We are as cold as ice when we should feel a summer's glow and bloom with sacred flowers. We give to God pence when he deserves pounds, indeed, he deserves our heart's blood to be coined in the service of his church and of his truth. But shall we continue like this? Oh Lord, after you have so richly blessed us, shall we be ungrateful and become indifferent to your good cause and work? Oh quicken us so that we may return to our first love, and do our first works! Send us a genial spring, oh Sun of Righteousness.

February 12 — Morning

{Daily Reading: Numbers 1:1–2:34} {Quick Study: Numbers 1:1–2:34}

For just as the sufferings of Christ abound in us, so our consolation also abounds by Christ. *{2 Corinthians 1:5}*

There is a blessed proportion. The Ruler of Providence bears a pair of scales — in this side he puts his people's trials, and in that he puts their consolations. When the scale of trial is nearly empty, you will always find the scale of consolation in nearly the same condition; and when the scale of trials is full, you will find the scale of consolation just as heavy. When the black clouds gather most, the light is more brightly revealed to us. When the night lowers and the tempest is coming on, the Heavenly Captain is always closest to his crew. It is a blessed thing, that when we are most cast down, then it is that we are most lifted up by the consolations of the Spirit. One reason is, because *trials make more room for consolation.* Great hearts can only be made by great troubles. The spade of trouble digs the reservoir of comfort deeper, and makes more room for consolation. God comes into our heart — he finds it full — he begins to break our comforts and to make it empty; then there is more room for grace. The humbler a man lies, the more comfort he will always have, because he will be more fitted to receive it. Another reason why we are often most happy in our troubles, is this — *then we have the closest dealings with God.* When the barn is full, man can live without God: when the purse is bursting with gold, we try to do without so much prayer. But once take our *gourds* away, and we want our God; once cleanse the idols out of the house, then we are compelled to honour Jehovah. "Out of the depths have I cried to you, oh Lord." There is no cry so good as what comes from the bottom of the mountains; no prayer half so hearty as what comes up from the depths of the soul, through deep trials and afflictions. Hence they bring us to God, and we are happier; for nearness to God is happiness. Come, troubled believer, do not fret over your heavy troubles, for they are the heralds of weighty mercies.

February 12 — Evening

He shall give you another Comforter, so that he may abide with you for ever. {John 14:16}

The Great Father revealed himself to believers of old before the coming of his Son, and was known to Abraham, Isaac, and Jacob as the God Almighty. Then Jesus came, and the ever blessed Son in his own proper person, was the delight of his people's eyes. At the time of the Redeemer's ascension, the Holy Spirit became the head of the present dispensation, and his power was gloriously revealed in and after Pentecost. He remains at this hour the present Emmanuel — God with us, dwelling in and with his people, quickening, guiding, and ruling in their midst. Is his presence recognised as it ought to be? We cannot control his working; he is most sovereign in all his operations, but are we sufficiently anxious to obtain his help, or sufficiently watchful lest we provoke him to withdraw his aid? Without him we can do nothing, but by his almighty energy the most extraordinary results can be produced: everything depends upon his revealing or concealing his power. Do we always look up to him both for our inner life and our outward service with the respectful dependence which is fitting? Do we not too often run before his call and act independently of his aid? Let us humble ourselves this evening for past neglects, and now entreat the heavenly dew to rest upon us, the sacred oil to anoint us, the celestial flame to burn within us. The Holy Spirit is no temporary gift, he abides with the saints. We have only to seek him properly, and he will be found by us. He is jealous, but he is full of pity; if he leaves in anger, he returns in mercy. Condescending and tender, he does not weary of us, but awaits to be gracious still.

> Sin has been hammering my heart
> To a hardness, void of love,
> Let supplying grace to cross his art
> Drop from above.

February 13 — Morning

{Daily Reading: Numbers 3:1–4:49} {Quick Study: Numbers 3:1–4:49}

Behold, what manner of love the Father has bestowed
upon us, that we should be called the sons of God: therefore
the world does not know us, because it did not know him.
Beloved, now we are the sons of God. *{1 John 3:1–2}*

"Behold, what manner of love the Father has bestowed upon us." Consider who we were, and what we feel ourselves to be even now when corruption is powerful in us, and you will wonder at our adoption. Yet we are called *"the sons of God."* What a high relationship is that of a son, and what privileges it brings! What care and tenderness the son expects from his father, and what love the father feels towards the son! But all *that*, and more than *that*, we now have through Christ. As for the temporary suffering we have in common with the older brother, this we accept as an honour: "Therefore the world does not know us, because it did not know him." We are content to be unknown with him in his humiliation, for we are to be exalted with him. *"Beloved, now we are the sons of God."* That is easy to read, but it is not so easy to feel. How is it with your heart this morning? Are you in the lowest depths of sorrow? Does corruption rise within your spirit, and grace seem like a poor spark trampled under foot? Does your faith almost fail you? Do not fear, it is neither your graces nor feelings on which you are to live: you must live simply by faith in Christ. With all these things against us, now — in the very depths of our sorrow, wherever we may be — *now*, as much in the valley as on the mountain, "Beloved, *now* we are the sons of God." "Ah, but," you say, "see how I am arrayed! my graces are not bright; my righteousness does not shine with apparent glory." But read the next verse: *"It does not yet appear what we shall be: but we know that, when he shall appear, we shall be like him."* The Holy Spirit shall purify our minds, and divine power shall refine our bodies, then *we shall see him as he is.*

February 13 — Evening

There is therefore now no condemnation. *{Romans 8:1}*

Come, my soul, think of this. Believing in Jesus, you are actually and effectually cleared from guilt; you are led out of your prison. You are no more in fetters as a bondslave; you are delivered *now* from the bondage of the law; you are freed from sin, and can walk at large as a freeman, your Saviour's blood has procured your full discharge. You have a right now to approach your Father's throne. No flames of vengeance are there to scare you now; no fiery sword; justice cannot strike the innocent. Your disabilities are taken away: you were once unable to see your Father's face: you can see it now. You could not speak with him: but now you have access with boldness. Once there was a fear of hell upon you; but you have no fear of it now, for how can there be punishment for the guiltless? He who believes is not condemned, and cannot be punished. And more than all, the privileges you might have enjoyed, if you have never sinned, are yours now that you are justified. All the blessings which you would have had if you had kept the law, and more, are yours, because Christ has kept it for you. All the love and the acceptance which perfect obedience could have obtained from God, belong to you, because Christ was perfectly obedient on your behalf, and has imputed all his merits to your account, so that you might be exceedingly rich through him, who for your sake became exceedingly poor. Oh! how great the debt of love and gratitude you owe to your Saviour!

> A debtor to mercy alone,
> Of covenant mercy I sing;
> Nor fear with your righteousness on,
> My person and offerings to bring:
>
> The terrors of law and of God,
> With me can have nothing to do;
> My Saviour's obedience and blood
> Hide all my transgressions from view.

February 14 — Morning

{Daily Reading: Numbers 5:1–6:27} {Quick Study: Numbers 5:1–6:27}

**And his allowance was a continual allowance given
to him by the king, a daily rate for every day,
all the days of his life. *{2 Kings 25:30}***

Jehoiachin was not sent away from the king's palace with a store to last him for months, but his provision was given to him as a daily pension. In this he is a good picture of the happy position of all the Lord's people. A daily portion is *all that a man really needs*. We do not need tomorrow's supplies; that day has not yet dawned, and its needs are as yet unborn. The thirst which we may suffer in the month of June does not need to be quenched in February, for we do not feel it yet; if we have enough for each day as the days arrive we shall never know need. Sufficient for the day is *all that we can enjoy*. We cannot eat or drink or wear more than the day's supply of food and clothes; the surplus gives us the care of storing it, and the anxiety of watching against a thief. One staff aids a traveller, but a bundle of staves is a heavy burden. Enough is not only as good as a feast, but is all that the greatest glutton can truly enjoy. This is *all that we should expect*; a craving for more than this is ungrateful. When our Father does not give us more, we should be content with his daily allowance. Jehoiachin's case is ours, we have a sure portion, a portion *given to us by the King, a gracious* portion, and a *perpetual portion*. Here is surely ground for thankfulness.

Beloved Christian reader, in matters of grace *you need a daily supply*. You have no store of strength. Day by day you must seek help from above. It is a very sweet assurance that *a daily portion is provided for you*. In the word, through the ministry, by meditation, in prayer, and waiting upon God you shall receive renewed strength. In Jesus all needful things are laid up for you. Then *enjoy your continual allowance*. Never go hungry while the daily bread of grace is on the table of mercy.

February 14 — Evening

She was healed immediately. *{Luke 8:47}*

One of the most touching and instructive of the Saviour's miracles is before us tonight. The woman was very ignorant. She imagined that virtue came out of Christ by a law of necessity, without his knowledge or direct will. Moreover, she was a stranger to the generosity of Jesus' character, or she would not have gone behind to steal the cure which he was so ready to bestow. Misery should always place itself right in the face of mercy. Had she known the love of Jesus' heart, she would have said, "I have only to put myself where he can see me — his omniscience will teach him my case, and his love at once will work my cure." We admire her faith, but we marvel at her ignorance. After she had obtained the cure, she rejoiced with trembling; she was glad that the divine virtue had performed a marvel in her; but she feared lest Christ would retract the blessing, and put a negative upon the grant of his grace; little did she comprehend the fulness of his love! We have not as clear a view of him as we could wish; we do not know the heights and depths of his love; but we know of a surety that he is too good to withdraw from a trembling soul the gift which it has been able to obtain. But here is the marvel of it; little as was her knowledge, her faith, because it was real faith, saved her, and saved her at once. There was no tedious delay — faith's miracle was instantaneous. If we have faith as a grain of mustard seed, salvation is our present and eternal possession. If in the list of the Lord's children we are written as the feeblest of the family, yet, being heirs through faith, no power, human or devilish, can eject us from salvation. If we dare not lean our heads upon his bosom with John, yet if we can venture into the crowd behind him, and touch the hem of his garment, we are made whole. Courage, timid one! Your faith has saved you; go in peace. "*Being* justified by faith, we *have* peace with God."

To him be glory both now and for ever. *{2 Peter 3:18}*

Heaven will be full of the ceaseless praises of Jesus. Eternity! your unnumbered years shall speed their everlasting course, but for ever and for ever, "to him be glory." Is he not a "priest for ever after the order of Melchizedek?" "To him be glory." Is he not king for ever? — King of kings and Lord of lords, the everlasting Father? "To him be glory *for ever*." Never shall his praises cease. What was bought with blood deserves to last while immortality endures. The glory of the cross must never be eclipsed; the lustre of the grave and of the resurrection must never be dimmed. Oh Jesus! You shall be praised for ever. Long as immortal spirits live — long as the Father's throne endures — for ever, for ever, to you shall be glory. Believer, you are anticipating the time when you shall join the saints above in ascribing all glory to Jesus; but are you glorifying him *now*? The apostle's words are, "To him be glory both now and for ever." Will you not today make it your prayer? "Lord, help me to glorify you; I am poor, help me to glorify you by contentment; I am sick, help me to give you honour by patience; I have talents, help me to extol you by spending them for you; I have time, Lord, help me to redeem it, so that I may serve you; I have a heart to feel, Lord, let that heart feel no love except yours, and glow with no flame except affection for you; I have a head to think, Lord, help me to think *of* you and *for* you; you have put me in this world for something, Lord, show me what that is, and help me to work out my life purpose: I cannot do much, but just as the widow put in her two mites, which were all her living, so, Lord, I cast my time and eternity too into your treasury; I am all yours; take me, and enable me to glorify you *now*, in all that I say, in all that I do, and with all that I have."

February 15 — Evening

By which they have made you glad. *{Psalms 45:8}*

And who are thus privileged to make the Saviour glad? His church — his people. But is it possible? He makes us glad, but how can *we make him glad*? By our love. Ah! we think it is so cold, so faint; and so, indeed, we must sorrowfully confess it to be, but it is very sweet to Christ. Hear his own eulogy of that love in the golden Canticle: "How fair is your love, my sister, my spouse! how much better is your love than wine!" See, loving heart, how he delights in you. When you lean your head on his bosom, you not only receive, but you give him joy; when you gaze with love upon his all glorious face, you not only obtain comfort, but impart delight. Our *praise*, too, gives him joy — not the song of the lips alone, but the melody of the heart's deep gratitude. Our *gifts*, too, are very pleasant to him; he loves to see us lay our time, our talents, our substance upon the altar, not for the value of what we give, but for the sake of the motive from which the gift springs. To him the lowly offerings of his saints are more acceptable than the thousands of gold and silver. *Holiness* is like frankincense and myrrh to him. Forgive your enemy, and you make Christ glad; distribute of your substance to the poor, and he rejoices; be the means of saving souls, and you reward him to see the travail of his soul; proclaim his gospel, and you are a sweet savour to him; go among the ignorant and lift up the cross, and you have given him honour. It is in your power even now to break the alabaster box, and pour the precious oil of joy upon his head, as did the woman of old, whose memorial is to this day set forth wherever the gospel is preached. Will you be backward then? Will you not perfume your beloved Lord with the myrrh and aloes, and cassia, of your heart's praise? Yes, oh ivory palaces, you shall hear the songs of the saints!

February 16 — Morning

{Daily Reading: Numbers 8:1–9:23} {Quick Study: Numbers 9:1–10:36}

I have learned, in whatever state I am, to be content. *{Philippians 4:11}*

These words show us that contentment is not a natural propensity of man. "Ill weeds grow apace." Covetousness, discontent, and murmuring are as natural to man as thorns are to the soil. We do not need to sow thistles and brambles; they come up naturally enough, because they are indigenous to earth: and so, we do not need to teach men to complain; they complain soon enough without any education. But the precious things of the earth must be cultivated. If we wish to have wheat, we must plough and sow; if we want flowers, there must be the garden, and all the gardener's care. Now, contentment is one of the flowers of heaven, and if we wish to have it, it must be cultivated; it will not grow in us by nature; it is the new nature alone that can produce it, and even then we must be especially careful and watchful that we maintain and cultivate the grace which God has sown in us. Paul says, "I have *learned* . . . to be content"; as much as to say, he did not know how at one time. It cost him some pains to attain to the mystery of that great truth. No doubt he sometimes thought he had learned, and then broke down. And when at last he had attained to it, and could say, "I have learned in whatever state I am, to be content," he was an old, grey-headed man, upon the borders of the grave — a poor prisoner shut up in Nero's dungeon at Rome. We might well be willing to endure Paul's infirmities, and share the cold dungeon with him, if we too might by any means attain to his good degree. Do not indulge the notion that you can be contented with *learning*, or learn without discipline. It is not a power that may be exercised naturally, but a science to be acquired gradually. We know this from experience. Brother, hush that murmur, natural though it is, and continue to be a diligent pupil in the College of Content.

February 16 — Evening

Your good Spirit. *{Nehemiah 9:20}*

Common, too common, is the sin of forgetting the Holy Spirit. This is folly and ingratitude. He deserves well at our hands, for he is good, supremely good. As God, he is good essentially. He shares in the threefold ascription of *Holy, holy, holy*, which ascends to the triune Jehovah. He is unmixed purity and truth, and grace. He is *good benevolently*, tenderly bearing with our waywardness, striving with our rebellious wills; quickening us from our death in sin, and then training us for the skies as a loving nurse fosters her child. How generous, forgiving, and tender is this patient Spirit of God. He is *good operatively*. All his works are good in the most eminent degree: he suggests good thoughts, prompts good actions, reveals good truths, applies good promises, assists in good attainments, and leads to good results. There is no spiritual good in all the world of which he is not the Author and Sustainer, and heaven itself will owe the perfect character of its redeemed inhabitants to his work. He is *good officially*; whether as Comforter, Instructor, Guide, Sanctifier, Quickener, or Intercessor, he fulfils his office well, and each work is fraught with the highest good for the church of God. Those who yield to his influences become good, those who obey his impulses do good, those who live under his power receive good. Let us then act towards so good a person according to the dictates of gratitude. Let us revere his person, and adore him as God over all, blessed for ever; let us acknowledge his power, and our need of him by waiting upon him in all our holy enterprises; let us hourly seek his aid, and never grieve him; and let us speak his praise whenever occasion occurs. The church will never prosper until it believes more reverently in the Holy Spirit. He is so good and kind that it is sad indeed that he should be grieved by slights and negligences.

February 17 — Morning

{Daily Reading: Numbers 10:1–11:35} {Quick Study: Numbers 11:1–13:33}

Isaac lived by the well Lahairoi. *{Genesis 25:11}*

Hagar had once found deliverance there and Ishmael had drank from the water so graciously revealed by the God who lives and sees the sons of men; but this was a merely casual visit, such as worldlings pay to the Lord in times of need, when it serves their purpose. They cry to him in trouble, but forsake him in prosperity. Isaac *lived* there, and made the well of the living and all-seeing God his constant source of supply. The usual tenor of a man's life, the *dwelling* of his soul, is the true test of his state. Perhaps the providential visitation experienced by Hagar struck Isaac's mind, and led him to revere the place; its mystical name endeared it to him; his frequent musings by its brim in the evening made him familiar with the well; his meeting Rebecca there had made his spirit feel at home near the place; but best of all, the fact that he enjoyed fellowship with the living God there, had made him select that hallowed ground for his dwelling. Let us learn to live in the presence of the living God; let us pray the Holy Spirit that today, and every other day, we may feel, "Oh God, you see me." May the Lord Jehovah be as a well to us, delightful, comforting, unfailing, springing up to eternal life. The bottle of the creature cracks and dries up, but the well of the Creator never fails; happy is he who dwells at the well, and so has abundant and constant supplies near at hand. The Lord has been a sure helper to others: his name is Shaddai, All-Sufficient God; our hearts have often had most delightful communion with him; through him our soul has found her glorious Husband, the Lord Jesus; and in him today we live, and move, and have our being; let us, then, dwell in closest fellowship with him. Glorious Lord, constrain us that we may never leave you, but dwell by the well of the living God.

February 17 — Evening

Whereas the Lord was there. *{Ezekiel 35:10}*

Edom's princes saw the whole country left desolate, and counted upon its easy conquest; but there was one great difficulty in their way — quite unknown to them — *"The Lord was there"*; and in his presence lay the special security of the chosen land. Whatever may be the machinations and devices of the enemies of God's people, there is still the same effectual barrier to thwart their design. *The saints* are God's heritage, and he is in the midst of them, and will protect his own. What comfort this assurance yields us in our troubles and spiritual conflicts! We are constantly opposed, and yet perpetually preserved! How often Satan shoots his arrows against our faith, but our faith defies the power of hell's fiery darts; they are not only turned aside, but they are quenched upon its shield, for "the Lord is there." *Our good works* are the subjects of Satan's attacks. A saint never yet had a virtue or a grace which was not the target for hellish bullets: whether it was hope bright and sparkling, or love warm and fervent, or patience all enduring, or zeal flaming like coals of fire, the old enemy of everything that is good has tried to destroy it. The only reason why anything virtuous or lovely survives in us is this, *"The Lord is there."*

If the Lord is with us through life, we do not need to fear for our dying confidence; for *when we come to die*, we shall find that "the Lord *is there"*; where the billows are most tempestuous, and the water is most chill, we shall feel the bottom, and know that it is good: our feet shall stand upon the Rock of Ages when time is passing away. Beloved, from the first of a Christian's life to the last, the only reason why he does not perish is because *"the Lord is there."* When the God of everlasting love shall change and leave his elect to perish, then may the church of God be destroyed; but not until then, because it is written, JEHOVAH SHAMMAH, *"The Lord is there."*

February 18 — Morning

{Daily Reading: Numbers 12:1–13:33} {Quick Study: Numbers 14:1–15:41}

Therefore show me why you contend with me. *{Job 10:2}*

Perhaps, oh tried soul, the Lord is doing this to develop your graces. There are some of your graces which would never be *revealed* if it were not for your trials. Do you not know that your faith never looks so grand in summer weather as it does in winter? Love is too often like a glow worm, showing very little light except when it is in the midst of surrounding darkness. Hope itself is like a star — not to be seen in the sunshine of prosperity, and only to be discovered in the night of adversity. Afflictions are often the black foils in which God sets the jewels of his children's graces, to make them shine the better. It was only a little while ago that on your knees you were saying, "Lord, I fear I have no faith: let me know that I have faith." Was not this really, though perhaps unconsciously, praying for trials? — for how can you know that you have faith until your faith is exercised? Depend upon it, God often sends us trials so that our graces may be revealed, and that we may be assured of their existence. Besides, it is not merely their existence, *real growth* in grace is the result of sanctified trials. God often takes away our comforts and our privileges in order to make us better Christians. He trains his soldiers, not in tents of ease and luxury, but by turning them out and using them in forced marches and hard service. He makes them ford through streams, and swim through rivers, and climb mountains, and walk many a long mile with heavy knapsacks of sorrow on their backs. Well, Christian, may this not account for the troubles through which you are passing? Is the Lord not bringing out your graces, and making them grow? Is this not the reason why he is contending with you?

> Trials make the promise sweet;
> Trials give new life to prayer;
> Trials bring me to his feet,
> Lay me low, and keep me there.

February 18 — Evening

Father, I have sinned. *{Luke 15:18}*

It is quite certain that those whom Christ has washed in his precious blood need not make a confession of sin, as culprits or criminals, before God the Judge, for Christ has for ever taken away all their sins in a legal sense, so that they no longer stand where they can be condemned, but are once and for all accepted in the Beloved; but having become children, and offending as children, ought they not every day to go before their Heavenly Father and confess their sin, and acknowledge their iniquity in that character? Nature teaches that it is the duty of erring children to make a confession to their earthly father, and the grace of God in the heart teaches us that we, as Christians, owe the same duty to our Heavenly Father. We daily offend, and ought not to rest without daily pardon. For, supposing that my trespasses against my Father are not at once taken to him to be washed away by the cleansing power of the Lord Jesus, what will be the consequence? If I have not sought forgiveness and been washed from these offences against my Father, I shall feel at a distance from him; I shall doubt his love for me; I shall tremble before him; I shall be afraid to pray to him: I shall grow like the prodigal, who, although still a child, was yet far off from his father. But if, with a child's sorrow at offending so gracious and loving a parent, I go to him and tell him all, and do not rest until I realise that I am forgiven, then I shall feel a holy love for my Father, and shall go through my Christian career, not only as saved, but as one enjoying present peace in God through Jesus Christ my Lord. There is a wide distinction between confessing sin *as a culprit*, and confessing sin *as a child*. The Father's bosom is the place for penitent confessions. We have been cleansed once and for all, but our feet still need to be washed from the defilement of our daily walk as children of God.

February 19 — Morning

{Daily Reading: Numbers 14:1–15:41} {Quick Study: Numbers 16:1–18:32}

Thus says the Lord God; "I will yet be enquired of for this by the house of Israel, to do it for them." *{Ezekiel 36:37}*

Prayer is the forerunner of mercy. Turn to sacred history, and you will find that scarcely ever did a great mercy come to this world unheralded by supplication. You have found this true in your own personal experience. God has given you many an unsolicited favour, but still great prayer has always been the prelude of great mercy with you. When you first found peace through the blood of the cross, you had been praying much, and earnestly interceding with God that he would remove your doubts, and deliver you from your distresses. Your assurance was the result of prayer. When at any time you have had high and rapturous joys, you have been obliged to look upon them as answers to your prayers. When you have had great deliverances out of severe troubles, and mighty helps in great dangers, you have been able to say, "I sought the Lord, and he heard me, and delivered me from all my fears." Prayer is always the preface to blessing. It goes before the blessing *as the blessing's shadow.* When the sunlight of God's mercies rises upon our necessities, it casts the shadow of prayer far down upon the plain. Or, to use another illustration, when God piles up a hill of mercies, he himself shines behind them, and he casts on our spirits the shadow of prayer, so that we may rest certain, if we are much in prayer, our pleadings are the shadows of mercy. Prayer is thus connected with the blessing *to show us the value of it.* If we had the blessings without asking for them, we would think them to be common things; but prayer makes our mercies more precious than diamonds. The things we ask for are precious, but we do not realise their preciousness until we have sought for them earnestly.

> Prayer makes the darken'd cloud withdraw;
> Prayer climbs the ladder Jacob saw;
> Gives exercise to faith and love;
> Brings every blessing from above.

February 19 — Evening

He first found his own brother Simon. *{John 1:41}*

This case is an excellent pattern of all cases where spiritual life is vigorous. *As soon as a man has found Christ, he begins to find others.* I will not believe that you have tasted of the honey of the gospel if you can eat it all yourself. True grace puts an end to all spiritual monopoly. Andrew first found his own brother Simon, and then others. *Relationship has a very strong demand upon our first individual efforts.* Andrew, you did well to begin with Simon. I doubt whether there are not some Christians giving away tracts at other people's houses who would do well to give away a tract at their own — whether there are not some engaged in works of usefulness abroad who are neglecting their special sphere of usefulness at home. You may or you may not be called to evangelise the people in any particular locality, but certainly you are called to see after your own employees, your own relatives and acquaintances. Let your religion begin at home. Many tradesmen export their best commodities — the Christian should not. All his conduct everywhere should be of the best kind; but let him be careful to put forth the sweetest fruit of spiritual life and testimony in his own family. When Andrew went to find his brother, he little imagined how eminent Simon would become. *Simon Peter was worth ten Andrews* as far as we can gather from sacred history, and yet Andrew was instrumental in bringing him to Jesus. You may be very deficient in talent yourself, and yet you may be the means of drawing to Christ one who shall become eminent in grace and service. Ah! dear friend, you little know the possibilities which are in you. You may only speak a word to a child, and in that child there may be slumbering a noble heart which shall stir the Christian church in years to come. Andrew had only two talents, but he found Peter. Go and do likewise.

February 20 — Morning

{Daily Reading: Numbers 16:1–18:32} {Quick Study: Numbers 19:1–21:35}

God, who comforts those who are cast down. *{2 Corinthians 7:6}*

And who comforts like him? Go to some poor, melancholy, distressed child of God; tell him sweet promises, and whisper in his ear choice words of comfort; he is like the deaf adder, he does not listen to the voice of the charmer, even though he charms ever so wisely. He is drinking gall and wormwood, and comfort him as you may, it will be only a note or two of mournful resignation that you will get from him; you will bring forth no psalms of praise, no hallelujahs, no joyful sonnets. But let *God* come to his child, let him lift up his countenance, and the mourner's eyes glisten with hope. Do you not hear him sing —

> 'Tis paradise, if you are here;
> If you depart, 'tis hell.

You could not have cheered him: but the Lord has done it; "He is the God of all comfort." There is no balm in Gilead, but there is balm in God. There is no physician among the creatures, but the Creator is Jehovah-Rophi. It is marvellous how one sweet word of God will make whole songs for Christians. One word of God is like a piece of gold, and the Christian is the gold beater, and can hammer that promise out for whole weeks. So, then, poor Christian, you do not need to sit down in despair. Go to the Comforter, and ask him to give you consolation. You are a poor dry well. You have heard it said, that when a pump is dry, you must pour water down it first of all, and then you will get water, and so, Christian, when you are dry, go to God, ask him to shed abroad his joy in your heart, and then your joy shall be full. Do not go to earthly acquaintances, for you will find them Job's comforters after all; but go first and foremost to your "God, who comforts those who are cast down," and you will soon say, "In the multitude of my thoughts within me your comforts delight my soul."

February 20 — Evening

Then Jesus was led up by the Spirit into the wilderness to be tempted by the devil. *{Matthew 4:1}*

A holy character does not avert temptation — Jesus was tempted. When Satan tempts us, his sparks fall upon tinder; but in Christ's case, it was like striking sparks on water; yet the enemy continued his evil work. Now, if the devil goes on striking when there is no result, how much more will he do it when he knows what inflammable stuff our hearts are made of. Though you become greatly sanctified by the Holy Spirit, expect that the great dog of hell will still bark at you. In the haunts of men we expect to be tempted, but even seclusion will not guard us from the same trial. Jesus Christ was led away from human society into the wilderness, and was tempted by the devil. Solitude has its charms and its benefits, and may be useful in checking the lust of the eye and the pride of life; but the devil will follow us into the most lovely retreats. Do not suppose that it is only the worldly minded who have dreadful thoughts and blasphemous temptations, for even spiritually minded people endure the same; and in the holiest position we may suffer the darkest temptation. The utmost consecration of spirit will not insure you against Satanic temptation. Christ was consecrated through and through. It was his food and drink to do the will of him who sent him: and yet he was tempted! Your hearts may glow with a seraphic flame of love for Jesus, and yet the devil will try to bring you down to Laodicean lukewarmness. If you will tell me when God permits a Christian to lay aside his armour, I will tell you when Satan has stopped his temptations. Like the old knights in wartime, we must sleep with helmet and breastplate buckled on, for the arch-deceiver will seize our first unguarded hour to make us his prey. The Lord keep us watchful in all seasons, and give us a final escape from the jaw of the lion and the paw of the bear.

He has said. *{Hebrews 13:5}*

If we can only grasp these words by faith, we have an all conquering weapon in our hand. What doubt will not be killed by this two-edged sword? What fear is there which shall not fall stricken with a deadly wound before this arrow from the bow of God's covenant? Will not the distresses of life and the pangs of death; will not the corruptions within, and the snares without; will not the trials from above, and the temptations from beneath, all seem to be very light afflictions, when we can hide ourselves beneath the bulwark of "He has said"? Yes; whether for delight in our tranquillity, or for strength in our conflict, "He has said" must be our daily resort. And this may teach us the extreme value of *searching* the Scriptures. There may be a promise in the Word which would exactly fit your case, but you may not know of it, and therefore you miss its comfort. You are like prisoners in a dungeon, and there may be one key in the bunch which would unlock the door, and you might be free; but if you will not look for it, you may still remain a prisoner, although liberty is so near at hand. There may be a potent medicine in the great pharmacopoeia of Scripture, and you may still remain sick unless you will examine and search the Scriptures to discover what "He has said." Should you not, besides reading the Bible, store your memories richly with the promises of God? You can remember the sayings of great men; you treasure up the verses of renowned poets; ought you not to be profound in your knowledge of the words of God, so that you may be able to quote them readily when you have to solve a difficulty, or overthrow a doubt? Since "He has said" is the source of all wisdom, and the fountain of all comfort, let it dwell in you richly, as "A well of water, springing up to everlasting life." So you shall grow healthy, strong, and happy in the divine life.

February 21 — Evening

Do you understand what you read? {Acts 8:30}

We would be more able teachers of others, and less liable to be carried about by every wind of doctrine, if we tried to have a more intelligent understanding of the Word of God. Just as the Holy Spirit, the Author of the Scriptures is the only one who can properly enlighten us to understand them, so we should constantly ask for his teaching, and his guidance into all truth. When the prophet Daniel had to interpret Nebuchadnezzar's dream, what did he do? He set himself to earnest prayer that God would open up the vision. The apostle John, in his vision at Patmos, saw a book sealed with seven seals which no one was found worthy to open, or so much as to look upon. The book was afterwards opened by the Lion of the tribe of Judah, who had prevailed to open it; but it is written first — "I wept much." The tears of John, which were his liquid prayers, were, so far as he was concerned, the sacred keys by which the folded book was opened. Therefore, if, for your own and others' profiting, you desire to be "filled with the knowledge of God's will in all wisdom and spiritual understanding," remember that prayer is your best means of study. Like Daniel, you shall understand the dream, and its interpretation, when you have looked for God; and like John you shall see the seven seals of precious truth unloosed, after you have wept much. Stones are not broken, except by an earnest use of the hammer; and the stone breaker must go down on his knees. Use the hammer of diligence, and let the knee of prayer be exercised, and there is not a stony doctrine in revelation which is useful for you to understand, which will not fly into shivers under the exercise of prayer and faith. You may force your way through anything with the leverage of prayer. Thoughts and reasonings are like the steel wedges which give a hold upon truth; but prayer is the lever, the prise which forces open the iron chest of sacred mystery, so that we may get the treasure hidden within.

February 22 — Morning

{Daily Reading: Numbers 21:1–22:41} {Quick Study: Numbers 24:1–25:18}

His bow abode in strength, and the arms of
his hands were made strong by the hands of
the Mighty God of Jacob. *{Genesis 49:24}*

That strength which God gives to his Josephs is real strength; it is not a boasted valour, a fiction, a thing of which men talk, but which ends in smoke; it is true — *divine strength*. Why does Joseph stand against temptation? Because God gives him aid. There is nothing that we can do without the power of God. All true strength comes from "the Mighty God of Jacob." Notice in what a *blessedly familiar way* God gives this strength to Joseph — "The arms of his hands were made strong by the hands of the Mighty God of Jacob." Thus God is represented as putting his hands on Joseph's hands, placing his arms on Joseph's arms. Just as a father teaches his children, so the Lord teaches those who fear him. He puts his arms upon them. Marvellous condescension! God Almighty, Eternal, Omnipotent, stoops from his throne and lays his hand upon the child's hand, stretching his arm upon the arm of Joseph, so that he may be made strong! This strength was also covenant strength, for it is ascribed to "the Mighty *God of Jacob*." Now, wherever you read about the God of Jacob in the Bible, you should remember the covenant with Jacob. Christians love to think about God's covenant. All the power, all the grace, all the blessings, all the mercies, all the comforts, all the things we have, flow to us from the wellhead, through the covenant. If there should be no covenant, then we would fail indeed; for all grace proceeds from it, as light and heat from the sun. No angels ascend or descend, except upon that ladder which Jacob saw, at its top stood a covenant God. Christian, it may be that the archers have severely injured you, and shot at you, and wounded you, but still your bow abides in strength; be sure, then, to ascribe all the glory to Jacob's God.

February 22 — Evening

**The Lord is slow to anger,
and great in power.** *{Nahum 1:3}*

Jehovah *"is slow to anger."* When mercy comes into the world she drives winged steeds; the axles of her chariot wheels are red hot with speed; but when wrath goes forth, it toils on with tardy footsteps, for God takes no pleasure in the sinner's death. God's rod of mercy is always in his outstretched hands; his sword of justice is in its scabbard, held down by that pierced hand of love which bled for the sins of men. "The Lord is slow to anger," because he is GREAT IN POWER. He is truly great in power who has power over himself. When God's power restrains himself, then it is power indeed: the power that binds omnipotence is omnipotence surpassed. A man who has a strong mind can bear to be insulted for a long time, and only resents the wrong when a sense of right demands his action. The weak mind is irritated by a little: the strong mind bears it like a rock which does not move, although a thousand breakers dash upon it, and cast their pitiful malice in spray upon its summit. God marks his enemies, and yet he does not bestir himself, but holds in his anger. If he were less divine than he is, he would long before this have sent forth all of his thunders, and emptied the magazines of heaven; he would long before this have blasted the earth with the wondrous fires of its lower regions, and man would have been utterly destroyed; but the greatness of his power brings us mercy. Dear reader, what is your state this evening? Can you by humble faith look to Jesus, and say, "My Substitute, you are my Rock, my trust?" Then, beloved, do not be afraid of God's power; for by faith you have fled to Christ for refuge, the power of God need no more terrify you, than the shield and sword of the warrior need terrify those whom he loves. Rather rejoice that he who is "great in power" is your Father and Friend.

February 23 — Morning

{Daily Reading: Numbers 23:1–25:18} {Quick Study: Numbers 26:1–27:23}

I will never leave you. *{Hebrews 13:5}*

No promise is of private interpretation. Whatever God has said to any one saint, he has said to all. When he opens a well for one, it is so that all may drink. When he opens a granary door to give out food, there may be one starving man who is the occasion of its being opened, but all hungry saints may come and feed, too. Whether he gave the word to Abraham or to Moses, does not matter, oh believer; he has given it to you as one of the covenanted seed. There is not a high blessing too lofty for you, nor a wide mercy too extensive for you. Lift up your eyes now to the north and to the south, to the east and to the west, for all this is yours. Climb to Pisgah's top, and view the utmost limit of the divine promise, for the land is all your own. There is not a brook of living water from which you may not drink. If the land flows with milk and honey, eat the honey and drink the milk, for both are yours. Be bold to believe, for he has said, "I will never leave *you*, nor forsake *you*." In this promise, God gives to his people everything. "*I* will never leave you." Then no attribute of God can cease to be engaged for us. Is he mighty? He will show himself strong on the behalf of those who trust him. Is he love? Then with lovingkindness he will have mercy upon us. Whatever attributes may compose the character of Deity, everyone of them to its fullest extent shall be engaged on our side. To put everything in one, there is nothing you can want, there is nothing you can ask for, there is nothing you can need in time or in eternity, there is nothing living, nothing dying, there is nothing in this world, nothing in the next world, there is nothing now, nothing at the resurrection morning, nothing in heaven which is not contained in this text — "I will never leave you, nor forsake you."

February 23 — Evening

Take up the cross, and follow me. *{Mark 10:21}*

You do not have to make your own cross, although unbelief is a master carpenter at cross making; neither are you permitted to choose your own cross, although self-will would attempt to be lord and master; but your cross is prepared and appointed for you by divine love, and you are cheerfully to accept it; you are to *take up* the cross as your chosen badge and burden, and not to stand complaining about it. Tonight Jesus bids you to submit your shoulder to his easy yoke. Do not kick at it in petulance, or trample on it in vain glory, or fall under it in despair, or run away from it in fear, but take it up like a true follower of Jesus. Jesus was a cross bearer; he leads the way in the path of sorrow. Surely you could not desire a better guide! And if he carried a cross, what nobler burden would you desire? The *Via Crucis* is the way of safety; do not fear to tread its thorny paths.

Beloved, the cross is not made of feathers, or lined with velvet, it is heavy and galling to disobedient shoulders; but it is not an iron cross, although your fears have painted it with iron colours, it is a wooden cross, and a man can carry it, for the Man of Sorrows tried the load. Take up your cross, and by the power of the Spirit of God you will soon be so in love with it, that like Moses, you would not exchange the reproach of Christ for all the treasures of Egypt. Remember that Jesus carried it, and it will smell sweetly; remember that it will soon be followed by the crown, and the thought of the coming weight of glory will greatly lighten the present heaviness of trouble. The Lord help you to bow your spirit in submission to the divine will before you fall asleep tonight, so that waking with tomorrow's sun, you may go forth to the day's cross with the holy and submissive spirit which becomes a follower of the Crucified.

February 24 — Morning

{Daily Reading: Numbers 26:1–27:23} {Quick Study: Numbers 28:1–30:16}

I will cause the shower to come down in its season;
there shall be showers of blessing. *{Ezekiel 34:26}*

Here is *sovereign mercy* — "I will give them the shower in its season." Is it not sovereign, *divine* mercy? — for who can say, "I will give them showers," except God? There is only one voice which can speak to the clouds, and bid them give the rain. Who sends down the rain upon the earth? Who scatters the showers upon the green herb? Do not I, the Lord? So grace is the gift of God, and is not to be created by man. It is also *needed* grace. What would the ground do without showers? You may break the clods, you may sow your seeds, but what can you do without the rain? The divine blessing is absolutely needful. In vain you labour, until God bestows the plenteous shower, and sends salvation down. Then, it is *plenteous* grace. "I will send them showers." It does not say, "I will send them drops," but "showers." So it is with grace. If God gives a blessing, he usually gives it in such a measure that there is not room enough to receive it. Plenteous grace! Ah! We need plenteous grace to keep us humble, to make us prayerful, to make us holy; plenteous grace to make us zealous, to preserve us through this life, and at last to land us in heaven. We cannot do without saturating showers of grace. Again, it is *seasonable* grace. "I will cause the shower to come down *in its season*." What is your season this morning? Is it the season of drought? Then that is the season for showers. Is it a season of great heaviness and black clouds? Then that is the season for showers. "As your days so shall your strength be." And here is a *varied* blessing. "I will give you *showers* of blessing." The word is in the plural. All kinds of blessings God will send. All God's blessings go together, like links in a golden chain. If he gives converting grace, he will also give comforting grace. He will send "showers of blessing." Look up today, oh parched plant, and open your leaves and flowers for a heavenly watering.

February 24 — Evening

Oh Lord of hosts, how long will you not have mercy upon Jerusalem? . . . And the Lord answered the angel . . . with good and comforting words. {Zechariah 1:12–13}

What a sweet answer to an anxious enquiry! Tonight let us rejoice in it. Oh Zion, there are good things in store for you; your time of travail shall soon be over; your children shall be brought forth; your captivity shall end. Bear patiently the rod for a while, and under the darkness still trust in God, for his love burns towards you. God loves the church with a love too deep for human imagination; he loves her with all his infinite heart. Therefore let her sons be of good courage; she cannot be far from prosperity to whom God speaks "good and comforting words." What these comforting words are the prophet goes on to tell us: "I am jealous for Jerusalem and for Zion with a great jealousy." The Lord loves his church so much that he cannot bear that she should go astray to others; and when she has done so, he cannot endure that she should suffer too much or too heavily. He will not have his enemies afflict her: he is displeased with them because they increase her misery. When God seems most to leave his church, his heart is warm towards her. History shows that whenever God uses a rod to chasten his servants, he always breaks it afterwards, as if he loathed the rod which gave his children pain. "Just as a father pities his children, so the Lord pities those who fear him." God has not forgotten us because he strikes — his blows are not an evidence of lack of love. If this is true of his church *collectively*, it is necessarily also true of *each individual member*. You may fear that the Lord has passed you by, but it is not so: he who counts the stars, and calls them by their names, is in no danger of forgetting his own children. He knows your case as thoroughly as if you were the only creature he ever made, or the only saint he ever loved. Approach him and be at peace.

February 25 — Morning

{Daily Reading: Numbers 28:1–29:40} {Quick Study: Numbers 31:1–32:42}

The wrath to come. *{Matthew 3:7}*

It is pleasant to pass through the country after a storm has spent itself; to smell the freshness of the herbs after the rain has passed away, and to note the drops while they glisten like purest diamonds in the sunlight. That is the position of a Christian. He is going through a land where the storm has spent itself upon his Saviour's head, and if there are a few drops of sorrow falling, they distil from clouds of mercy, and Jesus cheers him by the assurance that they are not for his destruction. But how terrible it is to witness the approach of a tempest: to note the forewarnings of the storm; to see the birds of heaven as they droop their wings; to see the cattle as they lay their heads low in terror; to discern the face of the sky as it grows black, and look to the sun which does not shine, and the heavens which are angry and frowning! How terrible to await the dread advance of a hurricane — such as occurs, sometimes, in the tropics — to wait in terrible apprehension until the wind shall rush forth in fury, tearing up trees from their roots, forcing rocks from their pedestals, and hurling down all the houses of man! And yet, sinner, this is your present position. No hot drops have as yet fallen, but a shower of fire is coming. No terrible winds howl around you, but God's tempest is gathering its dread artillery. As yet the flood waters are dammed up by mercy, but the flood gates shall soon be opened: the thunderbolts of God are yet in his storehouse, but lo! the tempest hastens, and how awful shall that moment be when God, robed in vengeance, shall march forth in fury! Where, where, where, oh sinner, will you hide your head, or where will you flee? Oh that the hand of mercy may now lead you to Christ! He is freely set before you in the gospel: his riven side is the rock of shelter. You know your need of him; believe in him, cast yourself upon him, and then the fury shall be past over for ever.

February 25 — Evening

But Jonah rose up to flee to Tarshish from the presence of the Lord, and went down to Joppa. *{Jonah 1:3}*

Instead of going to Nineveh to preach the Word, as God commanded him, Jonah disliked the work, and went down to Joppa to escape from it. There are occasions when God's servants shrink from duty. But what is the consequence? What did Jonah lose by his conduct? *He lost the presence and comforting enjoyment of God's love.* When we serve our Lord Jesus as believers should do, our God is with us; and although we have the whole world against us, if we have God with us, what does it matter? But the moment we start back, and seek our own inventions, we are at sea without a pilot. Then may we bitterly lament and groan out, "Oh my God, where have you gone? How could I have been so foolish as to shun your service, and in this way to lose all the bright shinings of your face? This is a price too high. Let me return to my allegiance, so that I may rejoice in your presence." In the next place, Jonah *lost all peace of mind.* Sin soon destroys a believer's comfort. It is the poisonous upas[1] tree, from whose leaves distil deadly drops which destroy the life of joy and peace. Jonah *lost everything upon which he might have drawn for comfort in any other case.* He could not plead the promise of divine protection, for he was not in God's ways; he could not say, "Lord, I meet with these difficulties in the discharge of my duty, therefore help me through them." He was reaping his own deeds; he was filled with his own ways. Christian, do not play the Jonah, unless you wish to have all the waves and the billows rolling over your head. You will find in the long run that it is far harder to shun the work and will of God than to at once yield yourself to it. Jonah *lost his time,* for he had to go to Nineveh after all. It is hard to contend with God; let us yield ourselves at once.

1. Upas tree: Javanese tree yielding milky sap used as poison for arrows. (*Oxford English Dictionary*)

Salvation is of the Lord. *{Jonah 2:9}*

Salvation is the work of God. It is he alone who quickens the soul "dead in trespasses and sins," and it is he who also maintains the soul in its spiritual life. He is both "Alpha and Omega." "Salvation is of the Lord." If I am prayerful, God makes me prayerful; if I have graces, they are God's gifts to me; if I hold on in a consistent life, it is because he upholds me with his hand. I do nothing whatever towards my own preservation, except what God himself first does in me. Whatever I have, all my goodness is of the Lord alone. When I sin, that is my own; but when I act rightly, that is of God, wholly and completely. If I have repulsed a spiritual enemy, the Lord's strength nerved my arm. Do I live before men a consecrated life? It is not I, but Christ who lives in me. Am I sanctified? I did not cleanse myself: God's Holy Spirit sanctifies me. Am I weaned from the world? I am weaned by *God's* chastisements sanctified for my good. Do I grow in knowledge? The great Instructor teaches me. All my jewels were fashioned by heavenly art. I find in God all that I want; but I find in myself nothing but sin and misery. "He only is my rock and my salvation." Do I feed on the Word? That Word would be no food for me unless the Lord made it food for my soul, and helped me to feed upon it. Do I live on the manna which comes down from heaven? What is that manna except Jesus Christ himself incarnate, whose body and whose blood I eat and drink? Am I continually receiving fresh increase of strength? Where do I gather my might? My help comes from heaven's hills: without Jesus I can do nothing. As a branch cannot bring forth fruit unless it abides in the vine, no more can I, unless I abide in him. What Jonah learned in the great deep, let me learn this morning in my prayer closet: "Salvation is of the Lord."

February 26 — Evening

Behold, if the leprosy has covered all his flesh, he shall pronounce him clean who has the plague. {Leviticus 13:13}

This regulation appears quite strange, yet there was wisdom in it, for the throwing out of the disease proved that the constitution was sound. This evening it would be good for us to see the typical teaching of so singular a rule. We, too, are lepers, and may read the law of the leper as applicable to ourselves. When a man sees himself to be altogether lost and ruined, covered all over with the defilement of sin, and in no part free from pollution; when he disclaims all righteousness of his own, and pleads guilty before the Lord, then he is clean through the blood of Jesus, and the grace of God. Hidden, unfelt, unconfessed iniquity is the true leprosy; but when sin is seen and felt, it has received its deathblow, and the Lord looks with eyes of mercy upon the soul afflicted with it. Nothing is more deadly than self-righteousness, or more hopeful than contrition. We must confess that we are "nothing else except sin," for no confession short of this will be the whole truth; and if the Holy Spirit is at work with us, convicting us of sin, there will be no difficulty about making such an acknowledgment — it will spring spontaneously from our lips. What comfort does the text afford to truly awakened sinners: the very circumstance which so grievously discouraged them is here turned into a sign and symptom of a hopeful state! Stripping comes before clothing; digging out the foundation is the first thing in building — and a thorough sense of sin is one of the earliest works of grace in the heart. Oh you poor leprous sinner, utterly destitute of a sound spot, take heart from the text, and come as you are to Jesus —

For let our debts be what they may, however great or small,
As soon as we have nothing to pay, our Lord forgives us all.
'Tis perfect poverty alone that sets the soul at large:
While we can call one mite our own, we have no full discharge.

February 27 — Morning

{Daily Reading: Numbers 32:1–33:56} {Quick Study: Deuteronomy 1:1–2:37}

**You have made the Lord, who is my refuge,
even the most High, your habitation.** *{Psalms 91:9}*

The Israelites in the wilderness *were continually exposed to change*. Whenever the pillar stopped its motion, the tents were pitched; but tomorrow, before the morning sun had risen, the trumpet sounded, the ark was in motion, and the fiery, cloudy pillar was leading the way through the narrow defiles of the mountain, up the hillside, or along the arid waste of the wilderness. They had scarcely time to rest a little before they heard the sound of "Away! This is not your rest; you must still be onward journeying towards Canaan!" They were never long in one place. Even wells and palm trees could not detain them. Yet they had an abiding home in their God, his cloudy pillar was their canopy, and its flame by night their household fire. They must go onward from place to place, continually changing, never having time to settle, and to say, "Now we are secure; in this place we shall dwell." "Yet," says Moses, "though we are always changing, Lord, you have been our dwelling place throughout all generations." The Christian knows no change with regard to God. He may be rich today and poor tomorrow; he may be sickly today and well tomorrow; he may be in happiness today; tomorrow he may be distressed — but there is no change with regard to his relationship to God. If he loved me yesterday, he loves me today. My unmoving mansion of rest is my blessed Lord. Let prospects be blighted; let hopes be blasted; let joy be withered; let mildews destroy everything; I have lost nothing of what I have in God. He is "my strong habitation whereto I can continually resort." I am a pilgrim in the world, but at home in my God. In the earth I wander, but in God I dwell in a quiet habitation.

February 27 — Evening

Whose goings forth have been from of old,
from everlasting. {Micah 5:2}

The Lord Jesus had goings forth for his people *as their representative before the throne, long before they appeared upon the stage of time.* It was "from everlasting" that he signed the compact with his Father, that he would pay blood for blood, suffering for suffering, agony for agony, and death for death, on behalf of his people; it was "from everlasting" that he gave himself up without a murmuring word. That from the crown of his head to the sole of his foot he might sweat great drops of blood, that he might be spit upon, pierced, mocked, torn asunder, and crushed beneath the pains of death. His goings forth as our Surety were from everlasting. Pause, my soul, and wonder! You have goings forth in the person of Jesus "from everlasting." Not only when you were born into the world did Christ love you, but his delights were with the sons of men before there were any sons of men. Often he thought of them; from everlasting to everlasting he had set his affection upon them. What! My soul, has he been so long about your salvation, and will he not accomplish it? Has he from everlasting been going forth to save me, and will he lose me now? What! Has he carried me in his hand, as his precious jewel, and will he now let me slip from between his fingers? Did he choose me before the mountains were brought forth, or the channels of the deep were dug, and will he reject me now? Impossible! I am sure he would not have loved me so long if he had not been a changeless lover. If he could grow weary of me, he would have been tired of me long before now. If he had not loved me with a love as deep as hell, and as strong as death, he would have turned from me long ago. Oh, joy above all joys, to know that I am his everlasting and inalienable inheritance, given to him by his Father before the earth ever was! Everlasting love shall be the pillow for my head tonight.

{Daily Reading: Numbers 34:1–35:34} {Quick Study: Deuteronomy 3:1–4:49}

My expectation is from him. *{Psalms 62:5}*

It is the believer's privilege to use this language. If he is looking for anything from the world, it is a poor "expectation" indeed. But if he looks to God for the supply of his needs, whether in temporal or spiritual blessings, his "expectation" will not be a vain one. Constantly he may draw from the bank of faith, and get his need supplied out of the riches of God's lovingkindness. This I know, I had rather have God for my banker than all the Rothschilds. My Lord never fails to honour his promises; and when we bring them to his throne, he never sends them back unanswered. Therefore I will only wait at his door, for he always opens it with the hand of munificent grace. At this hour I will try him anew. But we have "expectations" beyond this life. We shall die soon; and then our "expectation is from him." Do we not expect that when we lie upon the bed of sickness he will send angels to carry us to his bosom? We believe that when the pulse is faint, and the heart heaves heavily, some angelic messenger shall stand and look with loving eyes upon us, and whisper, "Sister spirit, come away!" As we approach the heavenly gate, we expect to hear the welcome invitation, "Come, you blessed of my Father, inherit the kingdom prepared for you from the foundation of the world." We are expecting harps of gold and crowns of glory; we are hoping soon to be among the multitude of shining ones before the throne; we are looking forward and longing for the time when we shall be like our glorious Lord — for "We shall see him as he is." Then if these are your "expectations," oh my soul, live for God; live with the desire and resolve to glorify him from whom comes all your supplies, and of whose grace in your election, redemption, and calling it is, that you have any "expectation" of coming glory.

February 28 — Evening

*The barrel of flour was not exhausted, neither did
the cruse of oil fail, according to the word of the Lord,
which he spoke by Elijah. {1 Kings 17:16}*

See the faithfulness of divine love. You observe that this woman had *daily needs*. She had herself and her son to feed in a time of famine; and now, in addition, the prophet Elijah was to be fed, too. But although the need was threefold, yet the supply of flour was not exhausted, for she had a *constant supply*. Each day she made calls upon the barrel, but yet each day it remained the same. You, dear reader, have daily needs, and because they come so frequently, you are apt to fear that the barrel of flour will one day be empty, and the cruse of oil will fail you. Rest assured that, according to the Word of God, this shall not be the case. Each day, though it brings its trouble, shall bring its help; and though you should live to outnumber the years of Methuselah, and though your needs should be as many as the sands of the seashore, yet God's grace and mercy shall last through all your necessities, and you shall never know a real lack. For three long years, in this widow's days, the heavens never saw a cloud, and the stars never wept a holy tear of dew upon the wicked earth; famine, and desolation, and death, made the land a howling wilderness, but this woman was never hungry, but always joyful in abundance. So shall it be with you. You shall see the sinner's hope perish, for he trusts his native strength; you shall see the proud Pharisee's confidence totter, for he builds his hope upon the sand; you shall see even your own schemes blasted and withered, but you yourself shall find that your place of defence shall be the munition of rocks: "Your bread shall be given to you, and your water shall be sure." Better to have God for your guardian, than the Bank of England for your possession. You might spend the wealth of the Indies, but the infinite riches of God you can never exhaust.

February 29 — Morning

{Daily Reading: Numbers 36:1–36:13}

With lovingkindness I have drawn you. *{Jeremiah 31:3}*

The thunders of the law and the terrors of judgment are all used to bring us to Christ; but the final victory is effected by lovingkindness. The prodigal set out to his father's house from a sense of need; but his father saw him a great way off, and ran to meet him; so that the last steps he took towards his father's house were with the kiss still warm upon his cheek, and the welcome still musical in his ears.

> Law and terrors do but harden
> All the while they work alone;
> But a sense of blood bought pardon
> Will dissolve a heart of stone.

The Master came one night to the door, and knocked with the iron hand of the law; the door shook and trembled upon its hinges; but the man piled every piece of furniture which he could find against the door, for he said, "I will not admit the man." The Master turned away, but by and by he came back, and with his own soft hand, using mostly that part where the nail had penetrated, he knocked again — oh, so softly and tenderly. This time the door did not shake, but, strange to say, it opened, and there upon his knees the once unwilling host was found rejoicing to receive his guest. "Come in, come in; you have so knocked that my heart is moved for you. I could not think of your pierced hand leaving its blood mark on my door, and of your going away homeless, Your head filled with dew, and your locks with the drops of the night. I yield, I yield, your love has won my heart." So in every case: lovingkindness wins the day. What Moses with the tablets of stone could never do, Christ does with his pierced hand. Such is the doctrine of effectual calling. Do I understand it from experience? Can I say, "He drew me, and I followed on, glad to confess the divine voice?" If so, may he continue to draw me, until at last I shall sit down at the marriage supper of the Lamb.

February 29 — Evening

Now we have received . . . the Spirit who is from God; so that we might know the things that are freely given to us by God. {1 Corinthians 2:12}

Dear reader, have you received the spirit which is by God, wrought by the Holy Spirit in your soul? The necessity of the work of the Holy Spirit in the heart may be clearly seen from this fact, that *all which has been done by God the Father, and by God the Son, must be ineffectual to us, unless the Spirit shall reveal these things to our souls.* What effect does the doctrine of election have upon any man until the Spirit of God enters into him? Election is a dead letter in my consciousness until the Spirit of God calls me out of darkness into marvellous light. Then through my calling, I see my election, and knowing myself to be called by God, I know myself to have been chosen in the eternal purpose. A covenant was made with the Lord Jesus Christ, by his Father; but what avails that covenant to us until the Holy Spirit brings us its blessings, and opens our hearts to receive them? There hang the blessings on the nail — Christ Jesus; however being short of stature, we cannot reach them; the Spirit of God takes them down and hands them to us, and thus they become actually ours. Covenant blessings in themselves are like the manna in the skies, far out of mortal reach, but the Spirit of God opens the windows of heaven and scatters the living bread around the camp of the spiritual Israel. Christ's finished work is like wine stored in the wine vat; through unbelief we can neither draw nor drink. The Holy Spirit dips our vessel into this precious wine, and then we drink; but without the Spirit we are as truly dead in sin as though the Father never had elected, and though the Son had never bought us with his blood. The Holy Spirit is absolutely necessary for our well-being. Let us walk lovingly towards him and tremble at the thought of grieving him.

March 1 — Morning

{Daily Reading: Deuteronomy 1:1–2:37} {Quick Study: Deuteronomy 5:1–7:26}

Awake, oh north wind; and come, oh south; blow upon my garden, that the spices of it may flow out. *{Song of Solomon 4:16}*

Anything is better than the dead calm of indifference. Our souls may wisely desire the north wind of trouble if that alone can be sanctified to the drawing forth of the perfume of our graces. So long as it cannot be said, "The Lord was not in the wind," we will not shrink from the most wintry blast that ever blew upon plants of grace. Did not the spouse in this verse humbly submit herself to the reproofs of her Beloved; only entreating him to send forth his grace in some form, and making no stipulation concerning the particular manner in which it should come? Did she not, like ourselves, become so utterly weary of deadness and unholy calm that she sighed for any visitation which would brace her to action? Yet she desires the warm south wind of comfort, too, the smiles of divine love, the joy of the Redeemer's presence; these are often mightily effectual to arouse our sluggish life. She desires either one or the other, or both; so that she may only be able to delight her Beloved with the spices of her garden. She cannot endure to be unprofitable, nor can we. How cheering a thought that Jesus can find comfort in our poor feeble graces. Can it be? It seems far too good to be true. Well may we court trial or even death itself if by it we shall be aided to make Emmanuel's heart glad. Oh that our heart would be crushed to atoms if only by such bruising our sweet Lord Jesus could be glorified. Graces unexercised are as sweet perfumes slumbering in the cups of the flowers: the wisdom of the great Husbandman overrules diverse and opposite causes to produce the one desired result, and makes both affliction and consolation draw forth the grateful odours of faith, love, patience, hope, resignation, joy, and the other fair flowers of the garden. May we know by sweet experience, what this means.

March 1 — Evening

He is precious. *{1 Peter 2:7}*

Just as all the rivers run into the sea, so all delights centre in our Beloved. The glances of his eyes outshine the sun: the beauties of his face are fairer than the choicest flowers: no fragrance is like the breath of his mouth. Gems of the mine, and pearls from the sea, are worthless things when measured by his preciousness. Peter tells us that Jesus is precious, but he did not and could not tell us *how* precious, nor could any of us compute the value of God's unspeakable gift. Words cannot set forth the preciousness of the Lord Jesus to his people, nor fully tell how essential he is to their satisfaction and happiness. Believer, have you not found in the midst of plenty a severe famine if your Lord has been absent? The sun was shining, but Christ had hidden himself, and all the world was black to you; or it was night, and since the bright and morning star was gone, no other star could yield you so much as a ray of light. What a howling wilderness is this world without our Lord! If once he hides himself from us, withered are the flowers of our garden; our pleasant fruits decay; the birds suspend their songs, and a tempest overturns our hopes. All earth's candles cannot make daylight if the Sun of Righteousness is eclipsed. He is the soul of our soul, the light of our light, the life of our life. Dear reader, what would you do in the world without him, when you wake up and look forward to the day's battle? What would you do at night, when you come home jaded and weary, if there would be no door of fellowship between you and Christ? Blessed is his name, he will not allow us to try our lot without him, for Jesus never forsakes his own. Yet, let the thought of *what life would be without him* enhance his preciousness.

March 2 — Morning

{Daily Reading: Deuteronomy 3:1–4:49} {Quick Study: Deuteronomy 8:1–11:32}

But all the Israelites went down to the Philistines,
each to sharpen his plowshare, and his pick,
and his axe, and his sickle. *{1 Samuel 13:20}*

We are engaged in a great war with the Philistines of evil. *Every weapon within our reach must be used.* Preaching, teaching, praying, giving, all must be brought into action, and talents which have been thought too lowly for service, must now be employed. Pick, and axe, and sickle, may all be useful in killing Philistines; rough tools may deal hard blows, and killing need not be elegantly done, as long as it is done effectually. Each moment of time, in season or out of season; each fragment of ability, educated or untutored; each opportunity, favourable or unfavourable, must be used, for our foes are many and our force is only slender.

Most of our tools need sharpening; we need quickness of perception, tact, energy, promptness, in a word, complete adaptation for the Lord's work. Practical common sense is a very scarce thing among the conductors of Christian enterprises. We might learn from our enemies if we would, and so *make the Philistines sharpen our weapons.* This morning let us be sure to sharpen our zeal during this day by the aid of the Holy Spirit. See the energy of the Papists, how they encompass sea and land to make one proselyte, are they to monopolise all the earnestness? See the heathen devotees, what tortures they endure in the service of their idols! Are they alone to exhibit patience and self-sacrifice? Observe the prince of darkness, how persevering in his endeavours, how unabashed in his attempts, how daring in his plans, how thoughtful in his plots, how energetic in all! The demons are united as one man in their infamous rebellion, while we believers in Jesus are divided in our service for God, and scarcely ever work with unanimity. Oh that from Satan's infernal industry we may learn to go about like good Samaritans, seeking whom we may bless!

**To me, who am less than the least of all saints,
this grace is given, that I should preach among the Gentiles
the unsearchable riches of Christ.** *{Ephesians 3:8}*

The apostle Paul felt it a great privilege to be allowed to preach the gospel. He did not look upon his calling as a drudgery, but he entered upon it with intense delight. Yet while Paul was thus thankful for his office, his success in it greatly humbled him. The fuller a vessel becomes, the deeper it sinks in the water. Idlers may indulge a fond conceit of their abilities, because they are untried; but the earnest worker soon learns his own weakness. If you seek humility, *try hard work*; if you wish to know your nothingness, attempt some great thing for Jesus. If you wish to feel how utterly powerless you are apart from the living God, attempt especially the great work of proclaiming the unsearchable riches of Christ, and you will know, as you never knew before, what a weak unworthy thing you are. Although the apostle thus knew and confessed his weakness, he was never perplexed concerning the *subject* of his ministry. From his first sermon to his last, Paul preached Christ, and nothing but Christ. He lifted up the cross, and extolled the Son of God who bled on it. Follow his example in all your personal efforts to spread the glad tidings of salvation, and let "Christ and him crucified" be your ever recurring theme. The Christian should be like those lovely spring flowers which, when the sun is shining, open their golden cups, as if saying, "Fill us with your beams!" But when the sun is hidden behind a cloud, they close their cups and droop their heads. So should the Christian feel the sweet influence of Jesus; Jesus must be his sun, and he must be the flower which yields itself to the Sun of Righteousness. Oh! to speak of Christ alone, this is the subject which is both "seed for the sower, and bread for the eater." This is the live coal for the lip of the speaker, and the master key to the heart of the hearer.

March 3 — Morning

{Daily Reading: Deuteronomy 5:1–7:26} {Quick Study: Deuteronomy 12:1–16:22}

I have chosen you in the furnace of affliction. *{Isaiah 48:10}*

Comfort yourself, tried believer, with this thought: God says, "I have chosen you in the furnace of affliction." Does not the word come like a soft shower, assuaging the fury of the flame? Yes, is it not an asbestos armour, against which the heat has no power? Let affliction come — God has chosen me. Poverty, you may stride in at my door, but God is in the house already, and he has chosen me. Sickness, you may intrude, but I have a balsam ready — God has chosen me. Whatever befalls me in this vale of tears, I know that he has "chosen" me. If, believer, you require still greater comfort, remember *that you have the Son of Man with you in the furnace.* In that silent bedroom of yours, there sits by your side One whom you have not seen, but whom you love; and often when you do not know it, he makes your bed in all your affliction, and smooths your pillow for you. You are in poverty but in that lovely house of yours the Lord of life and glory is a frequent visitor. He loves to come into these desolate places, so that he may visit you. Your friend sticks closely to you. You cannot see him, but you may feel the pressure of his hands. Do you not hear his voice? Even in the valley of the shadow of death he says, "Do not fear, I am with you; do not be dismayed, for I am your God." Remember that noble speech of Caesar: "Do not fear, you carry Caesar and all his fortune." Do not fear, Christian; Jesus is with you. In all your fiery trials, his presence is both your comfort and safety. He will never leave one whom he has chosen for his own. "Do not fear, for I am with you," is his sure word of promise to his chosen ones in the "furnace of affliction." Will you not, then, take firm hold of Christ, and say —

> Through floods and flames, if Jesus lead,
> I'll follow where he goes.

March 3 — Evening

He saw the Spirit of God
descending like a dove. *{Matthew 3:16}*

As the Spirit of God descended upon the Lord Jesus, the head, so he also, in measure, descends upon the members of the mystical body. His descent is to us in the same manner in which it fell upon our Lord. There is often a singular *rapidity* about it; before we are aware of it, we are impelled onward and heavenward beyond all expectation. Yet there is none of the hurry of earthly haste, for the wings of the dove are as soft as they are swift. *Quietness* seems essential for many spiritual operations; the Lord is in the still small voice, and like the dew, his grace is distilled in silence. The dove has always been the chosen type of *purity*, and the Holy Spirit is holiness itself. Where he comes, everything that is pure and lovely, and of good report, is made to abound, and sin and uncleanness depart. *Peace* reigns also where the Holy Dove comes with power; he bears the olive branch which shows that the waters of divine wrath are assuaged. *Gentleness* is a sure result of the Sacred Dove's transforming power: hearts touched by his benign influence are meek and lowly henceforth and for ever. *Harmlessness* follows, as a matter of course; eagles and ravens may hunt their prey — the turtledove can endure wrong, but cannot inflict it. We must be harmless as doves. The dove is an apt picture of *love*, the voice of the turtledove is full of affection; and so, the soul visited by the blessed Spirit, abounds in love for God, in love for the brethren, and in love for sinners; and above all, in love for Jesus. The brooding of the Spirit of God upon the face of the deep, first produced *order and life*, and in our hearts, he causes and fosters new life and light. Blessed Spirit, as you rested upon our dear Redeemer, even so rest upon us from this time forward and for ever.

My grace is sufficient for you. *{2 Corinthians 12:9}*

If none of God's saints were poor and tried, we would not know half so well the consolations of divine grace. When we find the wanderer who has nowhere to lay his head, who yet can say, "Still I will trust in the Lord"; when we see the pauper starving on bread and water, who still glories in Jesus; when we see the bereaved widow overwhelmed in affliction, and yet having faith in Christ, oh! what honour it reflects on the gospel. God's grace is illustrated and magnified in the poverty and trials of believers. Saints bear up under every discouragement, believing that all things work together for their good, and that out of apparent evils a real blessing shall ultimately spring — that their God will either work a deliverance for them speedily, or most assuredly support them in the trouble, as long as he is pleased to keep them in it. This patience of the saints proves the power of divine grace. There is a lighthouse out at sea: it is a calm night — I cannot tell whether the edifice is firm; the tempest must rage around it, and then I shall know whether it will stand. So with the Spirit's work: if it were not on many occasions surrounded with tempestuous waters, we would not know that it was true and strong; if the winds did not blow upon it, we would not know how firm and secure it was. The master works of God are those men who stand in the midst of difficulties, steadfast, unmoveable —

> Calm mid the bewildering cry,
> Confident of victory.

He who wishes to glorify his God must be prepared to encounter many trials. No man can be illustrious before the Lord unless his conflicts are many. If then, yours is a much tried path, rejoice in it, because you will the better demonstrate the all-sufficient grace of God. As for his failing you, never dream of it — hate the thought. The God who has been sufficient until now, should be trusted to the end.

March 4 — Evening

They shall be abundantly satisfied with the fulness of your house. *{Psalms 36:8}*

Sheba's queen was amazed at the sumptuousness of Solomon's table. She lost all heart when she saw the provision of a single day; and she marvelled equally at the company of servants who were feasted at the royal table. But what is this to the hospitalities of the God of grace? Ten thousand thousand of his people are daily fed; hungry and thirsty, they bring large appetites with them to the banquet, but not one of them returns unsatisfied; there is enough for each, enough for all, enough for evermore. Although the host that feed at Jehovah's table is countless as the stars of heaven, yet each one has his portion of food. Think how much grace one saint requires, so much that nothing but the Infinite could supply him for one day; and yet the Lord spreads his table, not for one, but many saints, not for one day, but for many years; not for many years only, but for generation after generation. Observe the full feasting spoken of in the text, the guests at mercy's banquet are satisfied, indeed, more "abundantly satisfied"; and that not with ordinary fare, but with fulness, the particular fulness of God's own house; and such feasting is guaranteed by a faithful promise to all those children of men who put their trust under the shadow of Jehovah's wings. I once thought if I might only get the broken food at God's back door of grace I would be satisfied; like the woman who said, "The dogs eat the crumbs that fall from the master's table"; but no child of God is ever served with scraps and leftovers; like Mephibosheth, they all eat from the King's own table. In matters of grace, we all have Benjamin's mess — we all have ten times more than we could have expected, and although our needs are great, yet we are often amazed at the marvellous plenty of grace which God gives us by experience to enjoy.

March 5 — Morning

{Daily Reading: Deuteronomy 11:1–13:18} {Quick Study: Deuteronomy 21:1–23:25}

Let us not sleep, as others do. *{1 Thessalonians 5:6}*

There are many ways of promoting Christian wakefulness. Among the rest, let me strongly advise Christians to converse together concerning the ways of the Lord. Christian and Hopeful, as they journeyed towards the Celestial City, said to themselves, "To prevent drowsiness in this place, let us fall into good discourse." Christian enquired, "Brother, where shall we begin?" And Hopeful answered, "Where God began with us." Then Christian sang this song —

> When saints do sleepy grow, let them come hither,
> And hear how these two pilgrims talk together;
> Yes, let them learn from them, in any wise,
> Thus to keep open their drowsy slumbering eyes.
> Saints' fellowship, if it is managed well,
> Keeps them awake, and that in spite of hell.

Christians who isolate themselves and walk alone are very liable to grow drowsy. Hold Christian company and you will be kept wakeful and refreshed and encouraged to make quicker progress on the road to heaven. But as you take "sweet counsel" with others in the ways of God, take care that the theme of your conversation is the Lord Jesus. Let the eye of faith be constantly looking to him; let your heart be full of him; let your lips speak of his worth. Friend, live near to the cross, and you will not sleep. *Labour to impress yourself with a deep sense of the value of the place to which you are going.* If you remember that you are going to heaven, you will not sleep on the road. If you think that hell is behind you, and the devil pursuing you, you will not loiter. Would the manslayer sleep with the avenger of blood behind him, and the city of refuge before him? Christian, will you sleep while the pearly gates are open — the songs of angels waiting for you to join them — a crown of gold ready for your brow? Ah! no; in holy fellowship continue to watch and pray so that you do not enter into temptation.

March 5 — Evening

Say to my soul, "I am your salvation." *{Psalms 35:3}*

What does this sweet prayer teach me? It shall be my evening's petition; but first let it yield to me an instructive meditation. The text informs me first of all that *David had his doubts*; for why should he pray, "Say to my soul, 'I am your salvation,' " if he was not sometimes exercised with doubts and fears? Let me, then, be of good cheer, for I am not the only saint who has to complain about weakness of faith. If David doubted, I need not conclude that I am not a Christian because I have doubts. The text reminds me that *David was not content while he had doubts and fears*, but he went at once to the mercy seat to pray for assurance; for he valued it as much fine gold. I too must labour after an abiding sense of my acceptance in the Beloved, and must have no joy when his love is not shed abroad in my soul. When my Bridegroom is gone from me, my soul must and will fast. I learn also that *David knew where to obtain full assurance*. He went to his God in prayer, crying, "Say to my soul 'I am your salvation.' " I must be much alone with God if I wish to have a clear sense of Jesus' love. Let my prayers cease, and my eye of faith will grow dim. Much in prayer, much in heaven; slow in prayer, slow in progress. I notice that *David would not be satisfied unless his assurance had a divine source*. "*Say* to my soul, 'Lord, do *you* say it!' " Nothing short of a divine testimony in the soul will ever satisfy the true Christian. Moreover, David could not rest unless his assurance had a *vivid personality* about it. "Say to *my* soul, 'I am *your* salvation.' " Lord, if you should say this to all the saints, it would be nothing, unless you would say it to me. Lord, I have sinned; I do not deserve your smile; I scarcely dare to ask for it; but oh! say to *my* soul, even to *my* soul, "I am *your* salvation." Let me have a present, personal, infallible, indisputable sense that I am yours, and that you are mine.

March 6 — Morning

{Daily Reading: Deuteronomy 14:1–16:22} {Quick Study: Deuteronomy 24:1–26:19}

You must be born again. *{John 3:7}*

Regeneration is a subject which lies at the very basis of salvation, and we should be very diligent to take heed that we really are "born again," for there are many who imagine they are, who are not. Be assured that the name of a Christian is not the nature of a Christian; and that being born in a Christian land, and being recognised as professing the Christian religion is of no avail whatever, unless there is something more added to it — the being "born again," is a matter so *mysterious*, that human words cannot describe it. "The wind blows where it wishes, and you hear its sound, but cannot tell where it comes from, and where it is going: so is everyone who is born by the Spirit." Nevertheless, it is a change which is *known and felt*: known by works of holiness, and felt by gracious experience. This great work is *supernatural*. It is not an operation which a man performs for himself: a new principle is infused, which works in the heart, renews the soul, and affects the entire man. It is not a change of my name, but a renewal of my nature, so that I am not the man I used to be, but a new man in Christ Jesus. To wash and dress a corpse is a far different thing from making it alive: man can do the one, God alone can do the other. If you have then, been "born again," your acknowledgment will be, "Oh Lord Jesus, the everlasting Father, you are my spiritual Parent; unless your Spirit had breathed into me the breath of a new, holy, and spiritual life, I would have been to this day 'dead in trespasses and sins.' My heavenly life is wholly derived from you, to you I ascribe it. 'My life is hidden with Christ in God.' It is no longer I who live, but Christ who lives in me." May the Lord enable us to be well assured on this vital point, for to be unregenerate is to be unsaved, unpardoned, without God, and without hope.

March 6 — Evening

Before destruction the heart of man is haughty. *{Proverbs 18:12}*

It is an old and common saying, that "coming events cast their shadows before them"; the wise man teaches us that a haughty heart is the prophetic prelude of evil. Pride is as safely the sign of destruction as the change of mercury in the barometer is the sign of rain; and far more infallibly so than that. When men have ridden the high horse, destruction has always overtaken them. Let David's aching heart show that there is an eclipse of a man's glory when he dotes upon his own greatness. *{2 Samuel 24:10}* See Nebuchadnezzar, the mighty builder of Babylon, creeping on the earth, devouring grass like oxen, until his nails had grown like bird's claws, and his hair like eagle's feathers. *{Daniel 4:33}* Pride made the boaster a beast, as once before it made an angel a devil. God hates high looks, and never fails to bring them down. All the arrows of God are aimed at proud hearts. Oh, Christian, is your heart haughty this evening? For pride can get into the Christian's heart as well as into the sinner's; it can delude him into dreaming that he is "rich and increased in goods, and has need of nothing." Are you glorying in your graces or your talents? Are you proud of yourself, that you have had holy frames and sweet experiences? Take note, reader, there is a destruction coming to you also. Your flaunting poppies of self-conceit will be pulled up by the roots, your mushroom graces will wither in the burning heat, and your self-sufficiency shall become as straw for the dunghill. If we forget to live at the foot of the cross in deepest lowliness of spirit, God will not forget to make us smart under his rod. A destruction will come to you, oh unduly exalted believer, the destruction of your joys and of your comforts, though there can be no destruction of your soul. Therefore, "He who glories, let him glory *in the Lord.*"

March 7 — Morning

{Daily Reading: Deuteronomy 17:1–20:20} {Quick Study: Deuteronomy 27:1–28:68}

Have faith in God. *{Mark 11:22}*

Faith is the foot of the soul by which it can march along the road of the commandments. Love can make the feet move more swiftly; but faith is the foot which carries the soul. Faith is the oil enabling the wheels of holy devotion and of earnest piety to move well; and without faith the wheels are taken from the chariot, and we drag heavily. With faith I can do all things; without faith I shall neither have the inclination nor the power to do anything in the service of God. If you want to find the men who serve God the best, you must look for the men with the most faith. Little faith will save a man, but little faith cannot do great things for God. Poor Little Faith could not have fought Apollyon[1]; it needed Christian to do that. Poor Little Faith could not have slain Giant Despair; it required Great Heart's arm to knock that monster down. Little Faith will go to heaven most certainly, but it often has to hide itself in a nut shell, and it frequently loses everything except its jewels. Little Faith says, "It is a rough road, beset with sharp thorns, and full of dangers; I am afraid to go"; but Great Faith remembers the promise, "Your shoes shall be iron and brass; as your days, so shall your strength be": and so she boldly ventures. Little Faith stands desponding, mingling her tears with the flood; but Great Faith sings, "When you pass through the waters, I will be with you; and through the rivers, they shall not overflow you": and she fords the stream at once. Would you be comfortable and happy? Would you enjoy religion? Would you have the religion of cheerfulness and not that of gloom? Then "have faith in God." If you love darkness, and are satisfied to dwell in gloom and misery, then be content with little faith; but if you love the sunshine, and would sing songs of rejoicing, covet earnestly this best gift, "great faith."

1. Apollyon, Giant Despair, Great Heart, and Little Faith are characters in John Bunyan's *Pilgrim's Progress*.

March 7 — Evening

It is better to trust in the Lord, than to put confidence in man. *{Psalms 118:8}*

Doubtless the reader has been tried with the temptation to rely upon the things which are seen, instead of resting alone upon the invisible God. Christians often look to man for help and counsel, and mar the noble simplicity of their reliance upon their God. Does this evening's portion meet the eye of a child of God anxious about temporals, then we would reason with him a while. You trust in Jesus, and only in Jesus, for your salvation, then why are you troubled? *"Because of my great care."* Is it not written, "Cast your burden upon the Lord?" "Be careful for nothing, but in everything by your prayer and supplication make known requests to God." Can you not trust God for temporals? *"Ah! I wish I could."* If you cannot trust God for temporals, how dare you trust him for spirituals? Can you trust him for your soul's redemption, and not rely upon him for a few lesser mercies? Is God not enough for your need, or is his all-sufficiency too narrow for your needs? Do you need another eye besides that of him who sees every secret thing? Is his heart faint? Is his arm weary? If so, seek another God; but if he is infinite, omnipotent, faithful, true, and all wise, why do you gad about so much to seek another confidence? Why do you rake the earth to find another foundation, when this is strong enough to bear all the weight which you can ever build on it? Christian, do not mix your wine with water, do not alloy your gold of faith with the dross of human confidence. Wait only upon God, and let your expectation be from him. Do not covet Jonah's gourd, but rest in Jonah's God. Let the sandy foundations of terrestrial trust be the choice of fools, but like one who foresees the storm, build for yourself an abiding place upon the Rock of Ages.

March 8 — Morning

{Daily Reading: Deuteronomy 21:1–23:25} {Quick Study: Deuteronomy 29:1–30:20}

**We must through much tribulation enter into
the kingdom of God.** *{Acts 14:22}*

God's people have their trials. When God chose his people, he never intended that they should be an untried people. They were chosen in the furnace of affliction; they were never chosen to worldly peace and earthly joy. Freedom from sickness and the pains of mortality was never promised to them; but when their Lord drew up the charter of privileges, he included chastisements among the things to which they should inevitably be heirs. Trials are a part of our lot; they were predestined for us in Christ's last legacy. So surely as the stars are fashioned by his hands, and their orbits fixed by him, so surely are our trials allotted to us; he has ordained their time and their place, their intensity and the effect they shall have upon us. Good men must never expect to escape troubles; if they do, they will be disappointed, for not one of their predecessors has been without them. See the patience of Job; remember Abraham, for he had his trials, and by his faith under them, he became the "Father of the faithful." Note well the biographies of all the patriarchs, prophets, apostles and martyrs, and you shall discover all those whom God made vessels of mercy, who were made to pass through the fire of affliction. It is ordained of old that the cross of trouble should be engraved on every vessel of mercy, as the royal mark by which the King's vessels of honour are distinguished. But although tribulation is thus the path of God's children, they have the comfort of knowing that their Master has traversed it before them; they have his presence and sympathy to cheer them, his grace to support them, and his example to teach them how to endure; and when they reach "the kingdom," it will more than make amends for the "much tribulation" through which they passed to enter it.

March 8 — Evening

She called his name Benoni (son of sorrow), but his father called him Benjamin (son of my right hand). {Genesis 35:18}

To every matter there is a bright as well as a dark side. Rachel was overwhelmed with the sorrow of her own travail and death; Jacob, although weeping for the mother's loss, could see the mercy of the child's birth. It is well for us if, while the flesh mourns over trials, our faith triumphs in divine faithfulness. Samson's lion yielded honey, and so will our adversities, if properly considered. The stormy sea feeds multitudes with its fishes; the wild wood blooms with beautiful flowers; the stormy wind sweeps away the pestilence, and the biting frost loosens the soil. Dark clouds distil bright drops, and black earth grows colourful flowers. A vein of good is to be found in every mine of evil. Sad hearts have particular skill in discovering the most disadvantageous point of view from which to gaze upon a trial; if there were only one slough in the world, they would soon be up to their necks in it, and if there were only one lion in the desert they would hear it roar. About us all there is a tinge of this wretched folly, and we are apt, at times, like Jacob, to cry, "All these things are against me." Faith's way of walking is to cast all care upon the Lord, and then to anticipate good results from the worst calamities. Like Gideon's men, she does not fret over the broken pitcher, but rejoices that the lamp blazes forth all the more. Out of the rough oyster shell of difficulty she extracts the rare pearl of honour, and from the deep ocean caves of distress she uplifts the priceless coral of experience. When her flood of prosperity ebbs, she finds treasures hidden in the sands; and when her sun of delight goes down, she turns her telescope of hope to the starry promises of heaven. When death itself appears, faith points to the light of resurrection beyond the grave, thus making our dying Benoni to be our living Benjamin.

Yes, he is altogether lovely. *{Song of Solomon 5:16}*

The superlative beauty of Jesus is all attracting; it is not so much to be admired as to be loved. He is more than pleasant and fair, he is *lovely*. Surely the people of God can fully justify the use of this golden word, for he is the object of their warmest love, a love founded on the intrinsic excellence of his person, the complete perfection of his charms. Look, oh disciples of Jesus, to your Master's lips, and say, "Are they not most sweet?" Do not his words cause your hearts to burn within you as he talks with you by the way? You worshippers of Emmanuel, look up to his head of much fine gold, and tell me, are not his thoughts precious to you? Is not your adoration sweetened with affection as you humbly bow before that countenance which is as Lebanon, excellent as the cedars? Is there not a charm in his every feature, and is not his whole person fragrant with such a savour of his good ointments, that therefore the virgins love him? Is there one member of his glorious body which is not attractive? — one portion of his person which is not a fresh lodestone to our souls? — one office which is not a strong cord to bind your heart? Our love is not as a seal set upon his heart of love alone; it is fastened upon his arm of power also; nor is there a single part of him upon which it does not fix itself. We anoint his whole person with the sweet spikenard of our fervent love. We wish to imitate his whole life; we wish to transcribe his whole character. In all other beings we see some defect, in him there is all perfection. The best even of his favoured saints have had blots upon their garments and wrinkles upon their brows; he is nothing but loveliness. All earthly suns have their spots: the fair world itself has its wilderness; we cannot love the all of most lovely things; but Christ Jesus is gold without alloy, light without darkness — glory without cloud — "Yes, he is *altogether* lovely."

March 9 — Evening

Abide in me. *{John 15:4}*

Communion with Christ is a certain cure for every ill. Whether it is the wormwood of woe, or the cloying excesses of earthly delight, close fellowship with the Lord Jesus will take bitterness from the one, and satiety from the other. Live near to Jesus, Christian, and it is a matter of secondary importance whether you live on the mountain of honour or in the valley of humiliation. Living near to Jesus, you are covered with the wings of God, and underneath you are the everlasting arms. Let nothing keep you from that hallowed communion, which is the choice privilege of a soul wedded to THE WELL BELOVED. Do not be content with an interview now and then, but always seek to retain his company, for only in his presence have you either comfort or safety. Jesus should not be to us a friend who calls upon us now and then, but one with whom we walk for evermore. You have a difficult road before you: see, oh traveller to heaven, that you do not go without your Guide. You have to pass through the fiery furnace; do not enter it unless, like Shadrach, Meshach, and Abednego, you have the Son of God to be your companion. You have to storm the Jericho of your own corruptions: do not attempt the warfare until, like Joshua, you have seen the Captain of the Lord's host, with his sword drawn in his hand. You are to meet the Esau of your many temptations: do not meet him until at Jabbok's brook you have laid hold upon the Angel and prevailed. In every case, in every condition, you will need Jesus; but most of all, when the iron gates of death shall open to you. Keep close to your soul's Husband, lean your head upon his bosom, ask to be refreshed with the spiced wine of his pomegranate, and you shall be found in him at last, without spot, or wrinkle, or any such thing. Seeing you have lived with him, and lived in him here, you shall abide with him for ever.

In my prosperity I said I shall never be moved. *{Psalms 30:6}*

Moab settled on his lees, he has not been emptied from vessel to vessel." Give a man wealth; let his ships bring home continually rich freights; let the winds and waves appear to be his servants to bear his vessels across the bosom of the mighty deep; let his lands yield abundantly; let the weather be propitious to his crops; let uninterrupted success attend him; let him stand among men as a successful merchant; let him enjoy continued health; allow him with braced nerve and brilliant eye to march through the world, and live happily; give him the buoyant spirit; let him have the song perpetually on his lips; let his eye be ever sparkling with joy — and the natural consequence of such an easy state to any man, let him be the best Christian who ever breathed, will be *presumption*; even David said, "I shall never be moved"; and we are not any better than David, nor half as good. Brother, beware of the smooth places in the way; if you are treading them, or if the way is rough, thank God for it. If God would always rock us in the cradle of prosperity; if we were always dandled on the knees of fortune; if we did not have some stain on the alabaster pillar; if there were not a few clouds in the sky; if we had not some bitter drops in the wine of this life, we would become intoxicated with pleasure, we would dream "we stand"; and stand we would, but it would be upon a pinnacle; like the man asleep upon the mast, each moment we would be in jeopardy.

We bless God, then, for our afflictions; we thank him for our changes; we extol his name for losses of property; for we feel that had he not chastened us thus, we might have become too secure. Continued worldly prosperity is a fiery trial.

> Afflictions, though they seem severe,
> In mercy oft are sent.

March 10 — Evening

**Man . . . is of few days,
and full of trouble.** *{Job 14:1}*

It may be of great service to us, before we fall asleep, to remember this mournful fact, for it may lead us to hold loosely earthly things. There is nothing very pleasant in our memory that we are not above the shafts of adversity, but it may humble us and prevent our boasting like the psalmist in our morning's portion. "My mountain stands firm: I shall never be moved." It may prevent us from taking too deep a root in this soil from which we are so soon to be transplanted into the heavenly garden. Let us remember the frail tenure upon which we hold our temporal mercies. If we would remember that all the trees of earth are marked for the woodman's axe, we would not be so ready to build our nests in them. We should love, but we should love with the love which expects death and separations. Our dear relations are only loaned to us, and the hour when we must return them to the lender's hand may be even at the door. The same is certainly true of our *worldly goods*. Do not riches take to themselves wings and fly away? Our *health* is equally precarious. Frail flowers of the field, we must not expect to bloom for ever. There is a time appointed for weakness and sickness, when we shall have to glorify God by suffering, and not by earnest activity. There is no single point in which we can hope to escape from the sharp arrows of affliction; out of our few days there is not one secure from sorrow. Man's life is a cask full of bitter wine; he who looks for joy in it had better seek for honey in an ocean of brine. Beloved reader, do not set your affections upon things of earth: but seek those things which are above, for *here* the moth devours, and the thief breaks through, but *there* all joys are perpetual and eternal. The path of trouble is the way home. Lord, make this thought a pillow for many a weary head!

March 11 — Morning

{Daily Reading: Deuteronomy 29:1–31:30} {Quick Study: Joshua 1:1–2:24}

Sin . . . exceedingly sinful. *{Romans 7:13}*

Beware of light thoughts of sin. At the time of conversion, the conscience is so tender, that we are afraid of the slightest sin. Young converts have a holy timidity, a godly fear lest they should offend against God. But alas! Very soon the fine bloom upon these first ripe fruits is removed by the rough handling of the surrounding world: the sensitive plant of young piety turns into a willow in later life, too pliant, too easily yielding. It is sadly true, that even a Christian may grow by degrees so callous, that the sin which once startled him does not alarm him in the least. By degrees men get familiar with sin. The ear in which the cannon has been booming will not notice slight sounds. At first a little sin startles us; but soon we say, "Is it not a little one?" Then there comes another, larger, and then another, until by degrees we begin to regard sin as only a little ill; and then follows an unholy presumption: "We have not fallen into open sin. True, we tripped a little, but we stood upright in the main. We may have uttered one unholy word, but as for the most of our conduct, it has been consistent." So we palliate sin; we throw a cloak over it; we call it by dainty names. Christian, beware how you think lightly of sin. Take heed lest you fall by little and little. Sin, a *little* thing? Is it not a poison? Who knows its deadliness? Sin, a little thing? Do not the little foxes spoil the grapes? Does not the tiny coral insect build a rock which wrecks a navy? Do not little strokes fell lofty oaks? Will not continual droppings wear away stones? Sin, a little thing? It girded the Redeemer's head with thorns, and pierced his heart! It made him suffer anguish, bitterness, and woe. Could you weigh the least sin in the scales of eternity, you would flee from it as from a serpent, and abhor the least appearance of evil. Look upon all sin as what crucified the Saviour, and you will see it to be "exceedingly sinful."

March 11 — Evening

You shall be called, "Sought out." *{Isaiah 62:12}*

The surpassing grace of God is seen very clearly in that we were not only sought, but sought *out*. Men *seek* for a thing which is lost upon the floor of the house, but in such a case there is only seeking, not seeking *out*. The loss is more perplexing and the search more persevering when a thing is sought *out*. We were mingled with the mire: we were as when some precious piece of gold falls into the sewer, and men gather out and carefully inspect a mass of abominable filth, and continue to stir and rake, and search among the heap until the treasure is found. Or, to use another illustration, we were lost in a labyrinth; we wandered here and there, and when mercy came after us with the gospel, it did not find us at the first coming, it had to search for us and seek us out; for we as lost sheep were so desperately lost, and had wandered into such a strange country, that it did not seem possible that even the Good Shepherd should track our devious roamings. Glory be to unconquerable grace, we were sought *out!* No gloom could hide us, no filthiness could conceal us, we were found and brought home. Glory be to infinite love, God the Holy Spirit restored us!

The lives of some of God's people, if they could be written would fill us with holy astonishment. Strange and marvellous are the ways which God used in their case to find his own. Blessed be his name, he never relinquishes the search until the chosen are sought out effectually. They are not a people sought today and cast away tomorrow. Almightiness and wisdom combined will make no failures, they shall be called, *"Sought out!"* That any should be sought out is matchless grace, but that we should be sought out is grace beyond degree! We can find no reason for it but God's own sovereign love, and can only lift up our heart in wonder, and praise the Lord that tonight we wear the name of *"Sought out."*

March 12 — Morning

{Daily Reading: Deuteronomy 32:1–34:12} {Quick Study: Joshua 3:1–5:15}

You shall love your neighbour. *{Matthew 5:43}*

Love your neighbour." Perhaps he rolls in riches, and you are poor, and living in your little cottage side by side with his lordly mansion; you see every day his estates, his fine linen, and his sumptuous banquets; God has given him these gifts, do not covet his wealth, and do not think harsh thoughts concerning him. Be content with your own lot, if you cannot better it, but do not look upon your neighbour, and wish that he were as yourself. Love him, and then you will not envy him.

Perhaps, on the other hand, you are rich, and near you reside the poor. Do not scorn to call them neighbour. Remember that you are bound to love them. The world calls them your inferiors. In what are they inferior? They are far more your equals than your inferiors, for "God has made of one blood all people who dwell upon the face of the earth." It is your coat which is better than theirs, but you are by no means better than they are. They are men, and what are you more than that? Take heed that you love your neighbour even though he is in rags, or sunken in the depths of poverty.

But, perhaps, you say, "I cannot love my neighbours, because for all I do they return ingratitude and contempt." So much the more room for the heroism of love. Would you be a featherbed warrior, instead of bearing the rough fight of love? He who dares the most, shall win the most; and if your path of love is rough, tread it boldly, still loving your neighbours through thick and thin. Heap coals of fire on their heads, and if they are hard to please, do not seek to please *them*, but to please *your Master*; and remember if *they* spurn your love, your Master has not spurned it, and your deed is as acceptable to him as if it had been acceptable to them. Love your neighbour, for in so doing you are following the footsteps of Christ.

March 12 — Evening

To whom do you belong? *{1 Samuel 30:13}*

No neutralities can exist in religion. We are either ranked under the banner of Prince Emmanuel, to serve and fight his battles, or we are vassals of the black prince, Satan. "To whom do you belong?"

Reader, let me assist you in your response. *Have you been "born again?"* If you have, you belong to Christ, but without the new birth you cannot be his. *In whom do you trust?* For those who believe in Jesus are the sons of God. *Whose work are you doing?* You are sure to serve your Master, for he whom you serve is by your very actions your lord. *What company do you keep?* If you belong to Jesus, you will fraternise with those who wear the livery of the cross. "Birds of a feather flock together." *What is your citizenship?* Is it heavenly or is it earthly? *What have you learned about your Master?* — for servants learn much from their masters to whom they are apprenticed. If you have served your time with Jesus, it will be said of you, as it was of Peter and John, "They took knowledge of them, that they had been with Jesus."

We press the question, "To whom do you belong?" Answer honestly before you give sleep to your eyes. If you are not Christ's you are in a hard service — *run away from your cruel master!* Enter into the service of the Lord of love, and you shall enjoy a life of blessedness. If you are Christ's, let me advise you to do four things. You belong to Jesus — *obey him*; let his word be your law; let his wish be your will. You belong to the Beloved, then *love him*; let your heart embrace him; let your whole soul be filled with him. You belong to the Son of God, then *trust him*; rest nowhere except on him. You belong to the King of kings, then *be decided for him*. Thus, without your being branded upon the brow, all will know to whom you belong.

March 13 — Morning

{Daily Reading: Joshua 1:1–3:17} {Quick Study: Joshua 6:1–8:35}

Why do we sit here until we die? *{2 Kings 7:3}*

Dear reader, this little book was mainly intended for the edification of believers, but if you are yet unsaved, our heart yearns over you: and we would attempt to say a word which may be blessed to you. Open your Bible, and read the story of the lepers, and notice their position, which was much the same as yours. If you remain where you are you must perish; if you go to Jesus you can only die. "Nothing ventured, nothing gained," is the old proverb, and in your case the venture is no great one. If you sit still in sullen despair, no one can pity you when your ruin comes; but if you die with mercy sought, if such a thing were possible, you would be the object of universal sympathy. No one escapes who refuses to look to Jesus; but you know that, at any rate, some are saved who believe in him, for some of your own acquaintances have received mercy: then why not you? The Ninevites said, "Who can tell?" Act upon the same hope, and try the Lord's mercy. To perish is so awful, that if there should be only a straw to grasp, the instinct of self-preservation would lead you to stretch out your hand. We have thus been talking to you on your own unbelieving ground, we would now assure you, as from the Lord, that if you seek him he will be found by you. Jesus casts out no one who comes to him. You shall not perish if you trust him; on the contrary, you shall find treasure far richer than the poor lepers gathered in Syria's deserted camp. May the Holy Spirit embolden you to go at once, and you shall not believe in vain. When you are saved yourself, publish the good news to others. Do not hold your peace; tell the King's household first, and unite with them in fellowship; let the porter of the city, the minister, be informed of your discovery, and then proclaim the good news in every place. May the Lord save you before the sun goes down today.

March 13 — Evening

Then he put forth his hand, and took her, and pulled her in to him into the ark. *{Genesis 8:9}*

Worn out with her wanderings, the dove returns at length to the ark as her only resting place. How heavily she flies — she will drop — she will never reach the ark! But she struggles on. Noah has been looking for his dove all day long, and is ready to receive her. She has just strength enough to reach the edge of the ark, she can hardly alight upon it, and is ready to drop, when Noah puts out his hand and pulls her in to him. Notice that: *"pulled her in to him."* She did not fly right in herself, but was too fearful, or too weary to do so. She flew as far as she could, and then he put out his hand and pulled her in to him. This act of mercy was shown to the wandering dove, and she was not chided for her wanderings. Just as she was she was pulled into the ark. So you, seeking sinner, with all your sin, will be received. "Only return" — those are God's two gracious words — "only return." What! Nothing else? No, "only return." She had no olive branch in her mouth this time, nothing at all but just herself and her wanderings; but it is "only return," and she does return, and Noah pulls her in. Fly, you wanderer; fly you fainting one, dove as you are, though you think yourself to be black as the raven with the mire of sin, back, back to the Saviour. Every moment you wait only increases your misery; your attempts to plume yourself and make yourself fit for Jesus are all vanity. Come to him just as you are. "Return, oh backsliding Israel." He does not say, "Return, oh *repenting* Israel" (there is such an invitation doubtless), but "you *backsliding* one," as a backslider with all your backslidings about you, "Return, return, return!" Jesus is waiting for you! He will stretch out his hand and "pull you in" — in to himself, your heart's true home.

March 14 — Morning

{Daily Reading: Joshua 4:1–6:27} {Quick Study: Joshua 9:1–10:43}

**Let him who thinks he stands take heed
lest he fall.** *{1 Corinthians 10:12}*

It is a curious fact, that there is such a thing as being proud of grace. A man says, "I have great faith, I shall not fall; poor little faith may, but I never shall." "I have fervent love," says another, "I can stand, there is no danger of my going astray." He who boasts about grace has little grace to boast about. Some who do this imagine that their graces can keep them, not knowing that the stream must flow constantly from the fountain head, or else the brook will soon be dry. If a continuous stream of oil does not come to the lamp, although it burns brightly today, it will smoke tomorrow, and its scent will be noxious. Take heed that you do not glory in your graces, but let all your glorying and confidence be in Christ and his strength, for only by this can you be kept from falling. Be much more in prayer. Spend a longer time in holy adoration. Read the Scriptures more earnestly and constantly. Watch your lives more carefully. Live nearer to God. Take the best examples for your pattern. Let your conduct be compatible with heaven. Let your hearts be perfumed with affection for men's souls. So live that men may take knowledge of you that you have been with Jesus, and have learned from him; and when that happy day shall come, when he whom you love shall say, "Come up higher," may it be your happiness to hear him say, "You have fought a good fight, you have finished your course, and henceforth there is laid up for you a crown of righteousness which does not fade away." On, Christian, with care and caution! On, with holy fear and trembling! On, with faith and confidence in Jesus alone, and let your constant petition be, "Uphold me according to your word." He is able, and he alone, "To keep you from falling, and to present you faultless before the presence of his glory with exceeding joy."

March 14 — Evening

I will take heed to my ways. *{Psalms 39:1}*

Fellow pilgrim, do not say in your heart, "I will go here and there, and I shall not sin"; for you are never so out of danger of sinning as to boast about your security. The road is very miry; it will be hard to pick your path so as not to soil your garments. This is a world of pitch; you will need to watch often, if in handling it you are to keep your hands clean. There is a robber at every turn of the road to rob you of your jewels; there is a temptation in every mercy; there is a snare in every joy; and if you ever reach heaven, it will be a miracle of divine grace to be ascribed entirely to your Father's power. Be on your guard. When a man carries a bombshell in his hand, he should mind that he does not go near a candle; and you too must take care that you do not enter into temptation. Even your common actions are edged tools; you must mind how you handle them. There is nothing in this world to foster a Christian's piety, but everything to destroy it. How anxious you should be to look up to God, that he may keep you! Your prayer should be, "Hold me up, and I shall be safe." Having prayed, you must also watch; guarding every thought, word, and action, with holy jealousy. Do not expose yourselves unnecessarily; but if called to exposure, if you are bidden to go where the darts are flying, never venture forth without your shield; for if once the devil finds you without your buckler, he will rejoice that his hour of triumph is come, and will soon make you fall down wounded by his arrows. Though you cannot be slain; you may be wounded. "Be sober; be vigilant, danger may be in an hour when all seems most secure to you." Therefore, take heed to your ways, and watch prayerfully. No man ever fell into error through being too watchful. May the Holy Spirit guide us in all our ways, so they shall always please the Lord.

Be strong in the grace that is in Christ Jesus. *{2 Timothy 2:1}*

Christ has grace without measure in himself, but he has not retained it for himself. As the reservoir empties itself into the pipes, so has Christ emptied out his grace for his people. "We have all received from his fulness, and grace for grace." He seems only to have in order to dispense to us. He stands like the fountain, always flowing, but only running in order to supply the empty pitchers and the thirsty lips which draw near to it. Like a tree, he bears sweet fruit, not to hang on boughs, but to be gathered by those who need. Grace, whether its work is to pardon, to cleanse, to preserve, to strengthen, to enlighten, to quicken, or to restore, is always to be had from him freely and without price; nor is there one form of the work of grace which he has not bestowed upon his people. Just as the blood of the body, though flowing from the heart, belongs equally to every member, so the influences of grace are the inheritance of every saint united to the Lamb; and herein there is a sweet communion between Christ and his church, inasmuch as they both receive the same grace. Christ is the head upon which the oil is first poured; but the same oil runs to the very skirts of the garments, so that the lowliest saint has an unction of the same costly moisture like what fell upon the head. This is true communion when the sap of grace flows from the stem to the branch, and when it is perceived that the stem itself is sustained by the very nourishment which feeds the branch. As we day by day receive grace from Jesus, and more constantly recognise it as coming from him, we shall behold him in communion with us, and enjoy the felicity of communion with him. Let us make daily use of our riches, and always go to him as to our own Lord in covenant, taking from him the supply of all we need with as much boldness as men take money from their own purse.

March 15 — Evening

**He did it with all his heart
and prospered.** *{2 Chronicles 31:21}*

This is no unusual occurrence; it is the general rule of the moral universe that those men prosper who do their work with all their hearts, while those are almost certain to fail who go to their labour leaving half their hearts behind them. God does not give harvests to idle men except harvests of thistles, nor is he pleased to send wealth to those who will not dig in the field to find its hidden treasure. It is universally confessed that if a man wishes to prosper, he must be diligent in business. It is the same in religion as it is in other things. If you wish to prosper in your work for Jesus, let it be *heart* work, and let it be done with *all* your heart. Put as much force, energy, heartiness, and earnestness into religion as you ever do into business, for it deserves far more. The Holy Spirit helps our infirmities, but he does not encourage our idleness; he loves active believers. Who are the most useful men in the Christian church? The men who do what they undertake for God *with all their hearts*. Who are the most successful Sunday School teachers? The most talented? No; the most zealous; the men whose hearts are on fire, those are the men who see their Lord riding forth prosperously in the majesty of his salvation. Whole heartedness shows itself in *perseverance*; there may be failure at first, but the earnest worker will say, "It is the Lord's work, and it must be done; my Lord has bidden me to do it, and in his strength I will accomplish it." Christian, are you thus "with all your heart" serving your Master? Remember the earnestness of Jesus! Think what heart work was his! He could say, *"The zeal of your house has eaten me up."* When he sweat great drops of blood, it was no light burden he had to carry upon those blessed shoulders; and when he poured out his heart, it was no weak effort he was making for the salvation of his people. Was Jesus in earnest, and are we lukewarm?

March 16 — Morning

{Daily Reading: Joshua 9:1–10:43} {Quick Study: Joshua 15:1–17:18}

I am a stranger with you. *{Psalms 39:12}*

Yes, oh Lord, *with* you, but not *to* you. All my natural alienation from you, your grace has effectually removed; and now, in fellowship with yourself, I walk through this sinful world as a pilgrim in a foreign country. *You* are a stranger in your own world. Man forgets you, dishonours you, sets up new laws and alien customs, and does not know you. When your dear Son came to his own, his own did not receive him. He was in the world, and the world was made by him, and the world did not know him. Never was a foreigner so speckled a bird among the denizens of any land as your beloved Son among his mother's brethren. It is no marvel, then, if I who live the life of Jesus, should be unknown and a stranger here below. Lord, I would not be a citizen where Jesus was an alien. His pierced hand has loosened the cords which once bound my soul to earth, and now I find myself a stranger in the land. My speech seems to these Babylonians among whom I dwell an outlandish tongue, my manners are singular, and my actions are strange. A Tartar would be more at home in Cheapside than I could ever be in the haunts of sinners. But here is the sweetness of my lot: I am a stranger *with you*. You are my fellow sufferer, my fellow pilgrim. Oh, what joy to wander in such blessed company! My heart burns within me by the way when you speak to me, and though I am a sojourner, I am far more blest than those who sit on thrones, and far more at home than those who dwell in their panelled houses.

> To me remains nor place, nor time: my country is in every clime;
> I can be calm and free from care, on any shore, since God is there.

> While place we seek, or place we shun,
>   the soul finds happiness in none:
> But with a God to guide our way, 'tis equal joy to go or stay.

Keep back your servant also from
presumptuous sins. *{Psalms 19:13}*

Such was the *prayer* of the *"man after God's own heart."* Did holy David need to pray thus? How needful, then, must such a prayer be for us babes in grace! It is as if he said, "Keep me back, or I shall rush headlong over the precipice of sin." Our evil nature, like an ill-tempered horse, is apt to run away. May the grace of God put the bridle upon it, and hold it in, so that it does not rush into mischief. What might not the best of us do if it were not for the restraints which the Lord places on us both in providence and in grace! The psalmist's prayer is directed against the worst form of sin — what is done with deliberation and wilfulness. Even the holiest need to be "kept back" from the vilest transgressions. It is a solemn thing to find the apostle Paul warning saints against the most loathsome sins. "Mortify therefore your members which are upon the earth; fornication, uncleanness, inordinate affection, evil concupiscence, and covetousness, which is idolatry." What! Do saints need warning against such sins as these? Yes, they do. The whitest robes, unless their purity is preserved by divine grace, will be defiled by the blackest spots. Experienced Christian, do not boast in your experience; you will still trip if you look away from him who is able to keep you from falling. You whose love is fervent, whose faith is constant, whose hopes are bright, do not say, "We shall never sin," but rather cry, "Do not lead us into temptation." There is enough tinder in the heart of the best of men to light a fire that shall burn to the lowest hell, unless God shall quench the sparks as they fall. Who would have dreamed that righteous Lot could be found drunken, and committing uncleanness? Hazael said, "Is your servant a dog, that he should do this thing?" and we are very apt to use the same self-righteous question. May infinite wisdom cure us of the madness of self-confidence.

March 17 — Morning

{Daily Reading: Joshua 11:1–13:33} {Quick Study: Joshua 18:1–21:45}

Remember the poor. *{Galatians 2:10}*

Why does God allow so many of his children to be poor? He could make them all rich if he pleased; he could lay bags of gold at their doors; he could send them a large annual income; or he could scatter abundance of provisions around their houses, as once he made the quails lie in heaps around the camp of Israel, and rained bread out of heaven to feed them. There is no necessity that they should be poor, except that he sees it to be best. "The cattle upon a thousand hills are his" — he could supply them; he could make the richest, the greatest, and the mightiest bring all their power and riches to the feet of his children, for the hearts of all men are in his control. But he does not choose to do so; he allows them to suffer want, he allows them to pine in penury and obscurity. Why is this? There are many reasons: one is, *to give us, who are favoured with enough, an opportunity of showing our love for Jesus.* We show our love for Christ when we sing of him and when we pray to him; but if there were no sons of need in the world we would lose the sweet privilege of evidencing our love, by ministering in alms giving to his poorer brethren; he has ordained that thus we should prove that our love does not stand in word only, but in deed and in truth. If we truly love Christ, we shall care for those who are loved by him. Those who are dear to him will be dear to us. Let us then look upon it not as a duty but as a privilege to relieve the poor of the Lord's flock — remembering the words of the Lord Jesus, "Inasmuch as you have done it to one of the least of these my brethren, you have done it to me." Surely this assurance is sweet enough, and this motive strong enough to lead us to help others with a willing hand and a loving heart — remembering that all we do for his people is graciously accepted by Christ as done for himself.

Blessed are the peacemakers: for they shall be called the children of God. *{Matthew 5:9}*

This is the seventh of the beatitudes: and seven was the number of perfection among the Hebrews. It may be that the Saviour placed the peacemaker the seventh in the list because he most nearly approaches the perfect man in Christ Jesus. He who would have perfect blessedness, as far as it can be enjoyed on earth, must attain to this seventh benediction, and become a peacemaker. There is a significance also in the position of the text. The verse which precedes it speaks of the blessedness of "the pure in heart: for they shall see God." It is well to understand that we are to be "first pure, then peaceable." Our peaceableness is never to be a compact with sin, or tolerance of evil. We must set our faces like flints against everything which is contrary to God and his holiness: purity being in our souls a settled matter, we can go on to peaceableness. No less does the verse that follows seem to have been put there on purpose. However peaceable we may be in this world, we shall still be misrepresented and misunderstood: and no marvel, for even the Prince of Peace, by his very peacefulness, brought fire upon the earth. He himself, though he loved mankind, and did no ill, was "despised and rejected by men, a man of sorrows and acquainted with grief." Lest, therefore, the peaceable in heart should be surprised when they meet with enemies, it is added in the following verse, "Blessed are those who are persecuted for righteousness' sake: for theirs is the kingdom of heaven." Thus, the peacemakers are not only pronounced to be blessed, but they are surrounded with blessings. Lord, give us grace to climb to this seventh beatitude! Purify our minds so that we may be "first pure, then peaceable," and fortify our souls, that our peaceableness may not lead us into cowardice and despair, when for your sake we are persecuted.

{Daily Reading: Joshua 14:1–16:10} {Quick Study: Joshua 22:1–24:33}

You are all the children of God by faith in Christ Jesus. *{Galatians 3:26}*

The *fatherhood of God is common to all his children.* Ah! Little Faith, you have often said, "Oh that I had the courage of Great Heart, that I could wield his sword and be as valiant as he! But, alas, I stumble at every straw, and a shadow makes me afraid." Listen, Little Faith. Great Heart is God's child, and you are God's child too; and Great Heart is not one whit more God's child than you are. Peter and Paul, the highly favoured apostles, were of the family of the Most High; and so are you also; the weak Christian is as much a child of God as the strong one.

> This cov'nant stands secure,
> Though earth's old pillars bow;
> The strong, the feeble, and the weak,
> Are one in Jesus now.

All the names are in the same family register. One may have more grace than another, but God our Heavenly Father has the same tender heart towards all. One may do more mighty works, and may bring more glory to his Father, but he whose name is the least in the kingdom of heaven is as much the child of God as he who stands among the King's mighty men. Let this cheer and comfort us, when we draw near to God and say, "Our Father."

Yet, while we are comforted by knowing this, let us not rest contented with weak faith, but ask, like the apostles, to have it increased. However feeble our faith may be, if it is real faith in Christ, we shall reach heaven at last, however we shall not honour our Master as much on our pilgrimage, neither shall we abound in joy and peace. If then you wish to live for Christ's glory, and be happy in his service, seek to be filled with the Spirit of adoption more and more completely, until perfect love shall cast out fear.

March 18 — Evening

Just as the Father has loved me,
so I have loved you. {John 15:9}

As the Father loves the Son, in the same manner Jesus loves his people. What is that divine method? He loved him *without beginning*, and thus Jesus loves his members. *"I have loved you with an everlasting love."* You can trace the beginning of human affection; you can easily find the beginning of your love for Christ, but his love for us is a stream whose source is hidden in eternity. God the Father loves Jesus *without any change*. Christian, take this for your comfort, that there is no change in Jesus Christ's love for those who rest in him. Yesterday you were on Tabor's top, and you said, "He loves me": today you are in the valley of humiliation, but he loves you still the same. On the hill Mizar, and among the Hermons, you heard his voice, which spoke so sweetly with the turtledove's notes of love; and now on the sea, or even in the sea, when all his waves and billows go over you, his heart is faithful to his ancient choice. The Father loves the Son *without any end*, and thus the Son loves his people. Saint, you do not need to fear the loosing of the silver cord, for his love for you will never cease. Rest confident that even down to the grave Christ will go with you, and that up again from it he will be your guide to the celestial hills. Moreover, the Father loves the Son *without any measure*, and the same immeasurable love the Son bestows upon his chosen ones. The whole heart of Christ is dedicated to his people. He "loved us and gave himself for us." His is a love which surpasses knowledge. Ah! We have indeed an immutable Saviour, a precious Saviour, one who loves without measure, without change, without beginning, and without end, even as the Father loves him! There is much food here for those who know how to digest it. May the Holy Spirit lead us into its marrow and fatness!

March 19 — Morning

{Daily Reading: Joshua 17:1–19:51} {Quick Study: Judges 1:1–2:23}

Strong in faith. *{Romans 4:20}*

Christian, take good care of your faith; for remember *faith is the only way by which you can obtain blessings*. If we want blessings from God, nothing can bring them down but faith. Prayer cannot draw down answers from God's throne except it is the earnest prayer of the man who believes. Faith is the angelic messenger between the soul and the Lord Jesus in glory. Let that angel be withdrawn, we can neither send up prayer, nor receive the answers. Faith is the telegraphic wire which links earth and heaven — on which God's messages of love fly so fast, that before we call he answers, and while we are yet speaking he hears us. But if that telegraphic wire of faith is snapped, how can we receive the promise? Am I in trouble? — I can obtain help for trouble by faith. Am I beaten about by the enemy? — My soul leans on her dear refuge by faith. But take faith away — in vain I call to God. There is no road between my soul and heaven. In the deepest wintertime faith is a road on which the horses of prayer may travel — indeed, and all the better for the biting frost; but blockade the road, and how can we communicate with the Great King? Faith links me with divinity. Faith clothes me with the power of God. Faith engages on my side the omnipotence of Jehovah. Faith ensures every attribute of God in my defence. It helps me to defy the hosts of hell. It makes me march triumphant over the necks of my enemies. But without faith how can I receive anything from the Lord? Do not let him who wavers — who is like a wave of the sea — expect that he will receive anything from God! Oh, then, Christian, watch well your faith; for with it you can win all things, however poor you are, but without it you can obtain nothing. "If you can believe, all things are possible for him who believes."

March 19 — Evening

And she ate, and was satisfied, and left. {Ruth 2:14}

Whenever we are privileged to eat the bread which Jesus gives, we are, like Ruth, satisfied with the full and sweet repast. When Jesus is the host no guest goes empty from the table. Our *head* is satisfied with the precious truth which Christ reveals; our *heart* is content with Jesus, as the altogether lovely object of affection; our *hope* is satisfied, for whom have we in heaven but Jesus? And our desire is satiated, for what can we wish for more than "to know Christ and to be found in him?" Jesus fills our *conscience* until it is at perfect peace; our *judgment* with persuasion of the certainty of his teachings; our *memory* with the remembrance of what he has done, and our *imagination* with the prospects of what he is yet to do. As Ruth was "satisfied, *and left*," so it is with us. We have had deep draughts; we have thought that we could take in all of Christ; but when we have done our best we have had to leave a vast remainder. We have sat at the table of the Lord's love, and said, "Nothing but the Infinite can ever satisfy me; I am such a great sinner that I must have infinite merit to wash my sin away"; but we have had our sin removed, and found that there was merit to spare; we have had our hunger relieved at the feast of sacred love, and found that there was an abundance of spiritual food remaining. There are certain sweet things in the Word of God which we have not enjoyed yet, and which we are obliged to leave for a while; for we are like the disciples to whom Jesus said, "I have yet many things to say to you, but you cannot bear them now." Yes, there are graces to which we have not attained; places of fellowship nearer to Christ which we have not reached; and heights of communion which our feet have not climbed. At every banquet of love there are many baskets of fragments left. Let us magnify the liberality of our glorious Boaz.

My beloved. *{Song of Solomon 2:8}*

This was a golden name which the ancient church in her most joyous moments was accustomed to give to the anointed of the Lord. When the time of the singing of birds was come, and the voice of the turtledove was heard in her land, *her* love note was sweeter than either, as she sang, "*My beloved* is mine and I am his: he feeds among the lilies." Always in her song of songs she calls him by that delightful name, "My beloved!" Even in the long winter, when idolatry had withered the garden of the Lord, her prophets found time to lay aside the burden of the Lord for a short time, and to say, as Isaiah did, "Now I will sing to my well beloved a song of my beloved touching his vineyard." Though the saints had never seen his face, though as yet he was not made flesh, nor had lived among us, nor had man beheld his glory, yet he was the consolation of Israel, the hope and joy of all the chosen, the "Beloved" of all those who were upright before the Most High. We, in the summer days of the church, are also accustomed to speak of Christ as the best beloved of our soul, and to feel that he is very precious, the "chiefest among ten thousand . . . he is altogether lovely." So true is it that the church loves Jesus, and claims him as her Beloved, that the apostle dares to defy the whole universe to separate her from the love of Christ, and declares that neither persecutions, distress, affliction, peril, or the sword have been able to do it; indeed, he joyously boasts, "In all these things we are more than conquerors through him who loved us." Oh that we knew more of you, oh ever precious one!

> My sole possession is your love;
> In earth beneath, or heaven above,
> I have no other store;
> And though with fervent suit I pray,
> And importune you day by day,
> I ask you nothing more.

Husbands, love your wives, even as Christ
also loved the church. *{Ephesians 5:25}*

What a golden example Christ gives to his disciples! Few masters could venture to say, "If you would practise my teaching, imitate my life"; but since the life of Jesus is the exact transcript of perfect virtue, he can point to himself as the paragon of holiness, as well as the teacher of it. The Christian should take nothing short of Christ for his model. Under no circumstances ought we to be content unless we reflect the grace which was in him. As a husband, the Christian is to look upon the portrait of Christ Jesus, and he is to paint according to that copy. The true Christian is to be such a husband as Christ was to his church. The love of a husband is *special.* The Lord Jesus cherishes for the church a particular affection, which is set upon her above the rest of mankind: "I pray for them, I do not pray for the world." The elect church is the favourite of heaven, the treasure of Christ, the crown of his head, the bracelet of his arm, the breastplate of his heart, the very centre and core of his love. A husband should love his wife with a *constant* love, for thus Jesus loves his church. He does not vary in his affection. He may change in his display of affection, but the affection itself is still the same. A husband should love his wife with an *enduring* love, for nothing "shall be able to separate us from the love of God, which is in Christ Jesus our Lord." A true husband loves his wife with a *hearty* love, fervent and intense. It is not mere lip service. Ah! Beloved, what more could Christ have done in proof of his love than he has done? Jesus has a *delighted* love towards his spouse: he prizes her affection, and delights in her with sweet complacence. Believer, you marvel at Jesus' love; you admire it — *are you imitating it?* In your domestic relationships is the rule and measure of your love — *"even as Christ loved the church?"*

March 21 — Morning

{Daily Reading: Joshua 22:1–24:33} {Quick Study: Judges 6:1–8:35}

**You shall be scattered, every man to his own,
and shall leave me alone.** *{John 16:32}*

Few had fellowship with the sorrows of Gethsemane. The majority of the disciples were not sufficiently advanced in grace to be admitted to behold the mysteries of "the agony." Occupied with the passover feast at their own houses, they represent the many who live upon the letter, but are mere babes concerning the spirit of the gospel. To twelve, indeed, to eleven only was the privilege given to enter Gethsemane and see "this great sight." Out of the eleven, eight were left at a distance; they had fellowship, but not of that intimate kind to which men greatly beloved are admitted. Only three highly favoured ones could approach the veil of our Lord's mysterious sorrow: within that veil even these must not intrude; a stone's throw distance must be left between. He must tread the winepress *alone*, and of the people there must be no one with him. Peter and the two sons of Zebedee represent the few eminent, experienced saints who may be written down as "Fathers"; these having done business on great waters, can in some degree measure the huge Atlantic waves of their Redeemer's passion. To some selected spirits it is given, for the good of others, and to strengthen them for future, special, and tremendous conflict, to enter the inner circle and hear the pleadings of the suffering High Priest; they have fellowship with him in his sufferings, and are made conformable to his death. Yet even these cannot penetrate the secret places of the Saviour's woe. "Your unknown sufferings" is the remarkable expression of the Greek liturgy: there was an inner chamber in our Master's grief, shut out from human knowledge and fellowship. There Jesus is *"left alone."* Here Jesus was more than ever an "Unspeakable gift!" Is not Watts right when he sings —

> And all the unknown joys he gives,
> Were bought with agonies unknown.

March 21 — Evening

Can you bind the sweet influences of Pleiades, or loose the bands of Orion? *{Job 38:31}*

If inclined to boast about our abilities, the grandeur of nature may soon show us how puny we are. We cannot move the least of all the twinkling stars, or quench so much as one of the beams of the morning. We speak about power, but the heavens laugh us to scorn. When the Pleiades shine forth in spring with vernal joy we cannot restrain their influences, and when Orion reigns aloft, and the year is bound in winter's fetters, we cannot relax the icy bands. The seasons revolve according to the divine appointment, neither can all of mankind change it. Lord, what is man?

In the spiritual, as in the natural world, man's power is limited on all hands. No one can disturb when the Holy Spirit sheds abroad his delights in the soul; all the cunning and malice of men are ineffectual to suspend the genial quickening power of the Comforter. When he deigns to visit a church and revive it, the most inveterate enemies cannot resist the good work; they may ridicule it, but they can no more restrain it than they can push back the spring when the Pleiades rule the hour. God wills it, and so it must be. On the other hand, if the Lord in sovereignty, or in justice, binds a man so that he is in soul bondage, who can give him liberty? He alone can remove the winter of spiritual death from an individual or a people. He looses the bands of Orion, and no one but him. What a blessing it is that he can do it. Oh that he would perform the wonder tonight. Lord, end my winter, and let my spring begin. I cannot with all my longings raise my soul out of her death and dulness, but all things are possible with you. I need celestial influences, the clear shinings of your love, the beams of your grace, the light of your countenance, these are the Pleiades to me. I suffer much from sin and temptation, these are my wintry signs, my terrible Orion. Lord, work wonders in me, and for me. Amen.

March 22 — Morning

{Daily Reading: Judges 1:1–2:23} {Quick Study: Judges 9:1–11:40}

And he went a little farther, and fell on his face, and prayed. *{Matthew 26:39}*

There are several instructive features in our Saviour's prayer in his hour of trial. It was *lonely prayer*. He withdrew even from his three favoured disciples. Believer, be much in solitary prayer, especially in times of trial. Family prayer, social prayer, prayer in the church, will not suffice. These are very precious, but the best beaten spice will smoke in your censer in your private devotions, where no ear hears but God's.

It was *humble prayer*. Luke says he knelt, but another evangelist says he "fell on his face." Where, then, must be your place, you humble servant of the great Master? What dust and ashes should cover *your* head! Humility gives us good foothold in prayer. There is no hope of prevalence with God unless we abase ourselves so that he may exalt us in due time.

It was *filial prayer*. "Abba, Father." You will find it a stronghold in the day of trial to plead your adoption. You have no rights as a subject, you have forfeited them by your treason; but nothing can forfeit a child's right to a father's protection. Do not be afraid to say, "My Father, hear my cry."

Observe that it was *persevering prayer*. He prayed three times. Do not cease until you prevail. Be as the importunate widow, whose continual coming earned what her first supplication could not win. Continue in prayer, and watch in the same with thanksgiving.

Lastly, *it was the prayer of resignation*. "Nevertheless, not as I will, but as you will." Yield, and God yields. Let it be as God wills, and God will determine for the best. Be content to leave your prayer in his hands, who knows when to give, and how to give, and what to give, and what to withhold. So pleading, earnestly, importunately, yet with humility and resignation, you shall surely prevail.

March 22 — Evening

Father, I will that they also, whom you have given to me,
be with me where I am. {John 17:24}

Oh, death! Why do you touch the tree beneath whose spreading branches weariness has rest? Why do you snatch away the excellent of the earth, in whom is all our delight? If you must use your axe, use it upon the trees which yield no fruit; you might be thanked then. But why will you fell the goodly cedars of Lebanon? Oh, withhold your axe, and spare the righteous. But no, it must not be; death strikes the best of our friends; the most generous, the most prayerful, the most holy, the most devoted must die. And why? It is through Jesus' prevailing prayer — "Father, I will that they also, whom you have given to me, be with me where I am." It is *that* which bears them on eagle's wings to heaven. Every time a believer mounts from this earth to paradise, it is an answer to Christ's prayer. A good old divine remarks, "Many times Jesus and his people pull against one another in prayer. You bend your knee in prayer and say 'Father, I will that your saints be with me where *I* am'; Christ says, 'Father, I will that they also, whom you have given me, be with me where *I* am.'" Thus the disciple is at cross purposes with his Lord. The soul cannot be in both places: the beloved one cannot be with Christ and with you, too. Now, which pleader shall win the day? If you had your choice; if the King should step from his throne, and say, "Here are two supplicants praying in opposition to one another, who shall be answered?" Oh! I am sure, although it should be agony, you would spring to your feet, and say, "Jesus, not my will, but yours be done." You would give up your prayer for your loved one's life, if you could realise the thoughts that Christ is praying in the opposite direction — "Father, I will that they also, whom you have given to me, be with me where I am." Lord, you shall have them. By faith we let them go.

His sweat was as it were great drops of blood falling down to the ground. *{Luke 22:44}*

The mental pressure arising from our Lord's struggle with temptation so forced his frame to an unnatural excitement, that his pores sent forth great drops of blood which fell down to the ground. This proves *how tremendous must have been the weight of sin* when it was able to crush the Saviour so that he distilled great drops of blood! This demonstrates *the mighty power of his love.* It is a very accurate observation of old Isaac Ambrose that the gum which exudes from the tree without cutting is always the best. This precious camphire tree yielded most sweet spices when it was wounded under the knotty whips, and when it was pierced by the nails on the cross; but see, it gives forth its best spice when there is no whip, no nail, no wound. This portrays the *voluntariness of Christ's sufferings*, since without a lance the blood flowed freely. No need to put on the leech, or apply the knife; it flows spontaneously. No need for the rulers to cry, "Spring up, oh well"; by itself it flows in crimson torrents. If men suffer great pain of mind apparently the blood rushes to the heart. The cheeks are pale; a fainting fit comes on; the blood has gone inward as if to nourish the inner man while passing through its trial. But see our Saviour in his agony; he is so utterly oblivious of self, that instead of his agony driving his blood to the heart to nourish himself, it drives it outward to bedew the earth. The agony of Christ, inasmuch as it pours him out upon the ground, pictures the fulness of the offering which he made for men.

Do we not perceive how intense must have been the wrestling through which he passed, and will we not hear its voice to *us*? "You have not yet resisted to blood, striving against sin." Behold the great Apostle and High Priest of our profession, and sweat even to blood rather than yield to the great tempter of your souls.

March 23 — Evening

I tell you that, if these should hold their peace,
the stones would immediately cry out. *{Luke 19:40}*

But could the stones cry out? Assuredly they could if he who opens the mouth of the dumb should bid them lift up their voice. Certainly if they were to speak, they would have much to testify in praise of him who created them by the word of his power; they could extol the wisdom and power of their *Maker* who called them into being. Shall not we speak well of him who made us anew, and out of stones raised up children to Abraham? The old rocks could tell of chaos and order, and the handiwork of God in successive stages of creation's drama; and cannot we talk about God's decrees, of God's great work in ancient times, in all that he did for his church in the days of old? If the stones were to speak, they could tell of their *breaker,* how he took them from the quarry, and made them fit for the temple, and can we not tell of our glorious Breaker, who broke our hearts with the hammer of his word, so that he might build us into his temple? If the stones should cry out they would magnify their *builder,* who polished them and fashioned them after the similitude of a palace; and shall not we talk of our Architect and Builder, who has put us in our place in the temple of the living God? If the stones could cry out, they might have a long, long story to tell by way of memorial, for many a time has a great stone been rolled as a memorial before the Lord; and we too can testify of Ebenezers, stones of help, pillars of remembrance. The broken stones of the law cry out against us, but Christ himself, who has rolled away the stone from the door of the sepulchre, speaks for us. Stones might well cry out, but we will not let them: we will hush their noise with ours; we will break forth into sacred song, and bless the majesty of the Most High, all our days glorifying him who is called by Jacob the Shepherd and Stone of Israel.

He was heard in that he feared. *{Hebrews 5:7}*

Did this fear arise from the infernal suggestion *that he was utterly forsaken?* There may be sterner trials than this, but surely it is *one* of the worst to be utterly forsaken. "See," said Satan, "you have a friend nowhere! Your Father has shut up the heart of his compassion against you. Not even an angel in his courts will stretch out his hand to help you. All heaven is alienated from you; you are left alone. See the companions with whom you have taken sweet counsel, what are they worth? Son of Mary, see there your brother James, see there your beloved disciple John, and your bold apostle Peter, how the cowards sleep when you are in your sufferings! Lo! You have no friend left in heaven or earth. All hell is against you. I have stirred up my infernal den. I have sent my missives throughout all regions summoning every prince of darkness to set upon you tonight, and we will spare no arrows, we will use all our infernal might to overwhelm you: and what will you do, you solitary one?" It may be, this was the temptation; we think it was, because the appearance of an angel to him strengthening him removed that fear. He was heard in that he feared; he was no more alone, but heaven was with him. It may be that this is the reason of his coming three times to his disciples — as Hart puts it —

> Backwards and forwards thrice he ran,
> As if he sought some help from man.

He would see for himself whether it was really true that all men had forsaken him; he found them all asleep; but perhaps he gained some faint comfort from the thought that they were sleeping, not from treachery, but from sorrow, the spirit indeed was willing, but the flesh was weak. At any rate, he was heard in that he feared. Jesus was heard in his deepest woe; my soul, you shall be heard also.

March 24 — Evening

In that hour Jesus rejoiced in spirit. *{Luke 10:21}*

The Saviour was "a man of sorrows," but every thoughtful mind has discovered the fact that down deep in his innermost soul he carried an inexhaustible treasury of refined and heavenly joy. Of all the human race, there was never a man who had a deeper, purer, or more abiding peace than our Lord Jesus Christ. "He was anointed with the oil of gladness more than his companions." His vast benevolence must, from the very nature of things, have afforded him the deepest possible delight, for benevolence is joy. There were a few remarkable occasions when this joy revealed itself. "At that hour Jesus rejoiced in spirit, and said, 'I thank you, oh Father, Lord of heaven and earth.' " Christ had his songs, though it was night with him; though his face was marred, and his countenance had lost the lustre of earthly happiness, yet sometimes it was lit up with a matchless splendour of unparalleled satisfaction, as he thought upon the recompence of the reward, and in the midst of the congregation sang his praise to God. In this, the Lord Jesus is a blessed picture of his church on earth. At this hour the church expects to walk in sympathy with her Lord along a thorny road; through much tribulation she is forcing her way to the crown. To bear the cross is her office, and to be scorned and counted an alien by her mother's children is her lot; and yet the church has a deep well of joy, of which no one can drink except her own children. There are stores of wine, and oil, and grain, hidden in the midst of our Jerusalem, upon which the saints of God are evermore sustained and nurtured; and sometimes, as in our Saviour's case, we have our times of intense delight, for, "There is a river, the streams of which shall make glad the city of our God." Exiles though we are, we rejoice in our King; yes, in him we exceedingly rejoice, while in his name we set up our banners.

March 25 — Morning

{Daily Reading: Judges 8:1–9:57} {Quick Study: Judges 19:1–21:25}

The kisses of an enemy are deceitful. *{Proverbs 27:6}*

Let me be on my guard when the world puts on a loving face, for it will, if possible, betray me as it did my Master, with a kiss. Whenever a man is about to stab religion, he usually professes very great reverence for it. Let me beware of the sleek-faced hypocrisy which is the armour bearer to heresy and infidelity. Knowing the deceitfulness of unrighteousness, let me be wise as a serpent to detect and avoid the designs of the enemy. The young man, void of understanding, was led astray by the kiss of the strange woman: may my soul be so graciously instructed all this day, that "the much fair speech" of the world may have no effect upon me. Holy Spirit, do not let me, a poor frail son of man, be betrayed with a kiss!

But what if I should be guilty of the same accursed sin as Judas, that son of perdition? I have been baptized into the name of the Lord Jesus; I am a member of his visible church; I sit at the communion table: all these are so many kisses of my lips. Am I sincere in them? If not, I am a base traitor. Do I live in the world as carelessly as others do, and yet make a profession of being a follower of Jesus? Then I must expose religion to ridicule, and lead men to speak evil of the holy name by which I am called. Surely if I act like this inconsistently I am a Judas, and it would be better for me that I had never been born. Dare I hope that I am clear in this matter? Then, oh Lord, keep me so. Oh Lord, make me sincere and true. Preserve me from every false way. Never let me betray my Saviour. I do love you, Jesus, and although I often grieve you, yet I would desire to abide faithful even to death. Oh God, forbid that I should be a high-soaring professor, and then fall at last into the lake of fire, because I betrayed my Master with a kiss.

March 25 — Evening

The Son of man. *{John 3:13}*

How constantly our Master used the title, the "Son of man!" If he had chosen, he might always have spoken of himself as the Son of God, the Everlasting Father, the Wonderful, the Counsellor, the Prince of Peace; but behold the lowliness of Jesus! He prefers to call himself the Son of man. Let us learn a lesson of humility from our Saviour; let us never court great titles nor proud degrees. There is here, however, a far sweeter thought. Jesus loved manhood so much that he delighted to honour it; and since it is a high honour, and indeed, the greatest dignity of manhood, that Jesus is the Son of man, he is accustomed to use this name, so that he may as it were hang royal stars upon the breast of manhood, and show forth the love of God to Abraham's seed. *Son of man* — whenever he said that word, he placed a halo around the head of Adam's children. Yet there is perhaps a more precious thought still. Jesus Christ called himself the Son of man to express his oneness and sympathy with his people. He thus reminds us that he is the one whom we may approach without fear. As a man, we may take to him all our griefs and troubles, for he knows them by experience; in that he himself has suffered as the "Son of man," he is able to help and comfort us. All hail, oh blessed Jesus! Inasmuch as you are for evermore using the sweet name which acknowledges that you are a brother and a near kinsman, it is to us a dear token of your grace, your humility, your love.

> Oh see how Jesus trusts himself
> To our childish love,
> As though by his free ways with us
> Our earnestness to prove!
>
> His sacred name a common word
> On earth he loves to hear;
> There is no majesty in him
> Which love may not come near.

March 26 — Morning

{Daily Reading: Judges 10:1–11:40} {Quick Study: Ruth 1:1–4:22}

Jesus said to them, "If you seek me, let these go their way." *{John 18:8}*

See, my soul, the care which Jesus showed even in his hour of trial, towards the sheep of his hand! The ruling passion is strong in death. He resigns himself to the enemy, but he interposes a word of power to set his disciples free. As for himself, like a sheep before her shearers he is dumb and did not open his mouth, but for his disciples' sake he speaks with almighty energy. Herein is love, constant, self-forgetting, faithful love. But is there not far more here than is to be found on the surface? Have we not the very soul and spirit of the atonement in these words? The Good Shepherd lays down his life for the sheep, and pleads that they must therefore go free. The Surety is bound, and justice demands that those for whom he stands as a substitute should go their way. In the midst of Egypt's bondage, that voice rings as a word of power, *"Let these go their way."* Out of slavery of sin and Satan the redeemed must come. In every cell of the dungeons of Despair, the sound is echoed, *"Let these go their way,"* and out comes Despondency and Much Afraid. Satan hears the well-known voice, and lifts his foot from the neck of the fallen; and Death hears it, and the grave opens her gates to let the dead arise. *Their way* is one of progress, holiness, triumph, glory, and no one shall dare to stop them in it. No lion shall be on their way, neither shall any ravenous beast go up on it. "The hind of the morning" has drawn the cruel hunters upon himself, and now the most timid roes and hinds of the field may graze at perfect peace among the lilies of his loves. The thunder cloud has burst over the cross of Calvary, and the pilgrims of Zion shall never be struck by the bolts of vengeance. Come, my heart, rejoice in the immunity which your Redeemer has secured for you, and bless his name all the day, and every day.

March 26 — Evening

When he comes in the glory of his Father
with the holy angels. *{Mark 8:38}*

If we have been partakers with Jesus in his shame, we shall be sharers with him in the lustre which shall surround him when he appears again in glory. Are you, beloved one, with Christ Jesus? Does a vital union knit you to him? Then you are today with him in his shame; you have taken up his cross, and gone with him outside the camp bearing his reproach; you shall doubtless be with him when the cross is exchanged for the crown. But judge yourself this evening; for if you are not with him in the regeneration, neither shall you be with him when he shall come in his glory. If you recoil back from the black side of communion, you shall not understand its bright, its happy period, when the king shall come, and *all his holy angels with him*. What! Are *angels with him*? And yet he did not take up angels — he took up the seed of Abraham. Are the holy angels *with him*? Come, my soul, if you are indeed his own beloved, you cannot be far from him. If his friends and his neighbours are called together to see his glory, what do you think if you are married to him? Shall you be distant? Although it is a day of judgment, yet you cannot be far from that heart which, having admitted angels into intimacy, has admitted you into union. Has he not said to you, oh my soul, "I will betroth you to me in righteousness, and in judgment, and in lovingkindness?" Have not his own lips said it, "I am married to you, and my delight is in you?" If the angels, who are only friends and neighbours, shall be with him, it is abundantly certain that his own beloved Hephzibah, in whom is all his delight, shall be near him, and sit at his right hand. Here is a morning star of hope for you, of such exceeding brilliance, that it may well light up the darkest and most desolate experience.

March 27 — Morning

{Daily Reading: Judges 12:1–14:20} {Quick Study: 1 Samuel 1:1–3:21}

Then all the disciples forsook him and fled. *{Matthew 26:56}*

He never deserted them, but they in cowardly fear for their lives, fled from him in the very beginning of his sufferings. This is only one instructive instance of the frailty of all believers if left to themselves; they are only sheep at the best, and they flee when the wolf comes. They had all been warned of the danger, and had promised to die rather than leave their Master; and yet they were seized with sudden panic, and took to their heels. It may be, that I, at the opening of this day, have braced up my mind to bear a trial for the Lord's sake, and I imagine myself to be certain to exhibit perfect fidelity; but let me be very jealous of myself, lest having the same evil heart of unbelief, I should depart from my Lord as the apostles did. It is one thing to promise, and quite another to perform. It would have been to their eternal honour to have stood at Jesus' side very manfully; they fled from honour; may I be kept from imitating them! Where else could they have been so safe as near their Master, who could presently call for twelve legions of angels? They fled from their true safety. Oh God, do not let me play the fool also. Divine grace can make the coward brave. The smoking flax can flame forth like fire on the altar when the Lord wills it. These very apostles who were timid as hares, grew to be bold as lions after the Spirit had descended upon them, and even so the Holy Spirit can make my cowardly spirit brave to confess my Lord and witness for his truth.

What anguish must have filled the Saviour as he saw his friends so faithless! This was one bitter ingredient in his cup; but that cup is drained dry; let me not put another drop in it. If I forsake my Lord, I shall crucify him afresh, and put him to an open shame. Keep me, oh blessed Spirit, from so shameful an end.

And she said, "Yes, Lord: yet the dogs even eat the crumbs
which fall from their master's table." *{Matthew 15:27}*

This woman gained comfort in her misery by thinking GREAT
THOUGHTS OF CHRIST. The Master had talked about the
children's bread: "Now," she argued, "since you are the Master of
the table of grace, I know that you are a generous housekeeper, and
there is sure to be abundance of bread on your table; there will be
such an abundance for the children that there will be crumbs to
throw on the floor for the dogs, and the children will fare none
the worse because the dogs are fed." She thought him to be one
who kept such a good table that all that she needed would only
be a crumb in comparison; yet remember, what she wanted was to
have the demon cast out of her daughter. It was a very great thing
to her, but she had such a high esteem of Christ that she said, "It
is nothing to him, it is only a crumb for Christ to give." This is the
royal road to comfort. Great thoughts of your sin alone will drive
you to despair; but great thoughts of Christ will pilot you into the
haven of peace. "My sins are many, but oh! it is nothing to Jesus to
take them all away. The weight of my guilt presses me down as a
giant's foot would crush a worm, but it is no more than a grain of
dust to him, because he has already borne its curse in his own body
on the tree. It will be only a small thing for him to give me full
remission, although it will be an infinite blessing for me to receive
it." The woman opens her soul's mouth very wide, expecting great
things from Jesus, and he fills it with his love. Dear reader, do the
same. She confessed what Christ laid at her door, but she laid firm
hold upon him, and drew arguments even out of his harsh words;
she believed great things of him, and she thus overcame him. SHE
WON THE VICTORY BY BELIEVING IN HIM. Her case is an
instance of prevailing faith; and if we wish to conquer like her, we
must imitate her tactics.

March 28 — Morning

{Daily Reading: Judges 15:1–17:13} {Quick Study: 1 Samuel 4:1–7:17}

The love of Christ which surpasses knowledge. *{Ephesians 3:19}*

The love of Christ in its sweetness, its fulness, its greatness, its faithfulness, surpasses all human comprehension. Where shall language be found which shall describe his matchless, his unparalleled love towards the children of men? It is so vast and boundless that, as the swallow only skims the water, and does not dive into its depths, so all descriptive words only touch the surface, while depths immeasurable lie beneath. Well might the poet say,

Oh love, you fathomless abyss!

for this love of Christ is indeed measureless and fathomless; no one can comprehend it. Before we can have any right idea of the love of Jesus, we must understand his previous glory in its height of majesty, and his incarnation upon the earth in all its depths of shame. But who can tell us about the majesty of Christ? When he was enthroned in the highest heavens he was very God of very God; by him were the heavens made, and all its hosts. His own almighty arm upheld the spheres; the praises of cherubim and seraphim perpetually surrounded him; the full chorus of the hallelujahs of the universe unceasingly flowed to the foot of his throne: he reigned supreme above all his creatures, God over all, blessed for ever. Who can describe his height of glory then? And who, on the other hand, can tell how low he descended? To be a man was something, to be a man of *sorrows* was far more; to bleed, and die, and suffer, these were much for him who was the Son of God; but to suffer such unparalleled agony — to endure a death of shame and desertion by his Father, this is a depth of condescending love which the most inspired mind must utterly fail to fathom. Herein is love! And truly it is love that "surpasses knowledge." Oh let this love fill our hearts with adoring gratitude, and lead us to practical displays of its power.

March 28 — Evening

I will accept you with your sweet savour. *{Ezekiel 20:41}*

The merits of our great Redeemer are as a sweet savour to the Most High. Whether we speak of the active or passive righteousness of Christ, there is an equal fragrance. There was a sweet savour in his active life by which he honoured the law of God, and made every precept to glitter like a precious jewel in the pure setting of his own person. Such, too, was his passive obedience, when he endured with unmurmuring submission, hunger and thirst, cold and nakedness, and at length sweat great drops of blood in Gethsemane, gave his back to the smiters, and his cheeks to those who plucked out his hair, and was fastened to the cruel wood, so that he might suffer the wrath of God on our behalf. These two things are sweet before the Most High; and for the sake of his doing and his dying, his substitutionary sufferings and his vicarious obedience, the Lord our God accepts us. What a preciousness must there be in him to overcome our lack of preciousness! What a sweet savour to put away our ill savour! What a cleansing power in his blood to take away sin such as ours! And what glory in his righteousness to make such unacceptable creatures to be accepted in the Beloved! Notice, believer, how sure and unchanging must be our acceptance, since it is *in him*! Take care that you never doubt your acceptance in Jesus. You cannot be accepted without Christ; but, when you have received his merit, you cannot be unaccepted. Notwithstanding all your doubts, and fears, and sins, Jehovah's gracious eye never looks upon you in anger; although he sees sin in you, in yourself, yet when he looks at you through Christ, he sees no sin. You are always accepted in Christ, are always blessed and dear to the Father's heart. Therefore lift up a song, and as you see the smoking incense of the merit of the Saviour coming up, this evening, before the sapphire throne, let the incense of your praise go up also.

March 29 — Morning

{Daily Reading: Judges 18:1–19:30} {Quick Study: 1 Samuel 8:1–10:27}

**Although he was a Son, yet he learned obedience
by the things which he suffered.** *{Hebrews 5:8}*

We are told that the Captain of our salvation was made perfect through suffering, therefore we who are sinful, and who are far from being perfect, must not wonder if we are called to pass through suffering too. Shall the head be crowned with thorns, and shall the other members of the body be rocked upon the dainty lap of ease? Must Christ pass through seas of his own blood to win the crown, and are we to walk to heaven dryshod in silver slippers? No, our Master's experience teaches us that suffering is necessary, and the true born child of God must not, would not, escape it if he might. But there is one very comforting thought in the fact of Christ's "being made perfect through suffering" — it is, that he can have complete sympathy with us. "He is not a high priest that cannot be touched with the feeling of our infirmities." In this sympathy of Christ we find a sustaining power. One of the early martyrs said, "I can bear it all, for Jesus suffered, and he suffers in me now; he sympathises with me, and this makes me strong." Believer, lay hold of this thought in all times of agony. Let the thought of Jesus strengthen you as you follow in his steps. Find a sweet support in his sympathy; and remember that to suffer is an honourable thing — to suffer for Christ is glory. The apostles rejoiced that they were counted worthy to do this. Just so far as the Lord shall give us grace to suffer *for* Christ, to suffer *with* Christ, just so far does he honour us. The jewels of a Christian are his afflictions. The regalia of the kings whom God has anointed are their troubles, their sorrows, and their griefs. Let us not, therefore, shun being honoured. Let us not turn aside from being exalted. Griefs exalt us, and troubles lift us up. "If we suffer, we shall also reign with him."

I called him, but he gave me no answer. *{Song of Solomon 5:6}*

Prayer sometimes tarries, like a petitioner at the gate, until the King comes forth to fill her bosom with the blessings which she seeks. The Lord, when he has given great faith, has been known to try it by long delayings. He has allowed his servants' voices to echo in their ears as from a brazen sky. They have knocked at the golden gate, but it has remained immovable, as though it were rusted upon its hinges. Like Jeremiah, they have cried, "You have covered yourself with a cloud, so that our prayer should not pass through." Thus have true saints continued long in patient waiting without reply, not because their prayers were not vehement, nor because they were unaccepted, but because it so pleased him who is a Sovereign, and who gives according to his own pleasure. If it pleases him to exercise our patience, shall he not do as he wishes with his own! Beggars must not be choosers either as to time, place, or form. But we must be careful not to take delays in prayer for denials: God's long dated bills will be punctually honoured; we must not permit Satan to shake our confidence in the God of truth by pointing to our unanswered prayers. Unanswered petitions are not unheard. God keeps a file for our prayers — they are not blown away by the wind, they are treasured in the King's archives. This is a registry in the court of heaven in which every prayer is recorded. Tried believer, your Lord has a tear bottle in which the costly drops of sacred grief are put away, and a book in which your holy groanings are numbered. By and by, your suit shall prevail. Can you not be content to wait a little? Will not your Lord's time be better than your time? By and by he will comfortingly appear, to your soul's joy, and make you put away the sackcloth and ashes of long waiting, and put on the scarlet and fine linen of full fruition.

March 30 — Morning

{Daily Reading: Judges 20:1–21:25} {Quick Study: 1 Samuel 11:1–13:23}

He was numbered with the transgressors. *{Isaiah 53:12}*

Why did Jesus allow himself to be enrolled among sinners? This wonderful condescension was justified by many powerful reasons. *In such a character he could the better become their advocate.* In some trials there is an identification of the counsellor with the client, nor can they be looked upon in the eye of the law as apart from one another. Now, when the sinner is brought to the bar, Jesus appears there himself. *He* stands to answer the accusation. He points to his side, his hands, his feet, and challenges Justice to bring anything against the sinners whom he represents; he pleads his blood, and pleads so triumphantly, being numbered with them and having a part with them, that the Judge proclaims, "Let them go their way; deliver them from going down into the pit, for he has found a ransom." Our Lord Jesus was numbered with the transgressors in order that they might *feel their hearts drawn towards him.* Who can be afraid of one who is written in the same list with us? Surely we may come boldly to him, and confess our guilt. He who is numbered with us cannot condemn us. Was he not written down in the transgressor's list *that we might be written in the red roll of the saints?* He was holy, and written among the holy; we were guilty, and numbered among the guilty; he transfers his name from that list to this black indictment, and our names are taken from the indictment and written in the roll of acceptance, for there is a complete transfer made between Jesus and his people. Jesus has taken all our estate of misery and sin; and all that Jesus has, comes to us. His righteousness, his blood, and everything that he has he gives to us as our dowry. Rejoice, believer, in your union to him who was numbered among the transgressors; and prove that you are truly saved by being publicly numbered with those who are new creatures in him.

March 30 — Evening

Let us search and try our ways, and turn again to the Lord. *{Lamentations 3:40}*

The spouse who fondly loves her absent husband longs for his return; a long protracted separation from her lord is a semi-death to her spirit: and so with souls who love the Saviour much, they must see his face, they cannot bear that he should be away upon the mountains of Bether, and hold communion with them no more. A reproaching glance, an uplifted finger will be grievous to loving children, who fear to offend their tender father, and are only happy in his smile. Beloved, it was once so with you. A text of Scripture, a threatening, a touch of the rod of affliction, and you went to your Father's feet, crying, "Show me why you contend with me?" Is it so now? Are you content to follow Jesus afar off? Can you contemplate suspended communion with Christ without alarm? Can you bear to have your Beloved walking contrary to you, because you walk contrary to him? Have your sins separated you from your God, and is your heart at rest? Oh let me affectionately warn you, for it is a grievous thing when we can live contentedly without the present enjoyment of the Saviour's face. *Let us labour to feel what an evil thing this is* — little love for our own dying Saviour, little joy in our precious Jesus, little fellowship with the Beloved! Hold a true Lent in your souls, while you sorrow over your hardness of heart. Do not stop at sorrow! Remember where you first received salvation. *Go at once to the cross.* There, and there only, can you get your spirit quickened. No matter how hard, how insensible, how dead we may have become, let us go again in all the rags and poverty, and defilement of our natural condition. Let us cling to that cross, let us look into those languid eyes, let us bathe in that fountain filled with blood — this will bring back to us our first love; this will restore the simplicity of our faith, and the tenderness of our heart.

March 31 — Morning

{Daily Reading: Ruth 1:1–4:22} {Quick Study: 1 Samuel 14:1–15:35}

With his stripes we are healed. *{Isaiah 53:5}*

Pilate delivered our Lord to the lictors to be scourged. The Roman scourge was a most dreadful instrument of torture. It was made of the sinews of oxen, and sharp bones were intertwisted every here and there among the sinews; so that every time the lash came down these pieces of bone inflicted fearful laceration, and tore off the flesh from the bone. The Saviour was, no doubt, bound to the column, and thus beaten. He had been beaten before, but this of the Roman lictors was probably the most severe of his flagellations. My soul, stand here and weep over his poor stricken body.

Believer in Jesus, can you gaze upon him without tears, as he stands before you the mirror of agonizing love? He is at once fair as the lily for innocence, and red as the rose with the crimson of his own blood. As we feel the sure and blessed healing which his stripes have worked in us, does not our heart melt at once with love and grief? If ever we have loved our Lord Jesus, surely we must feel that affection glowing now within our bosoms.

> See how the patient Jesus stands,
> Insulted in his lowest case!
> Sinners have bound the Almighty's hands,
> And spit in their Creator's face.
>
> With thorns his temples gor'd and gash'd
> Send streams of blood from every part;
> His back's with knotted scourges lash'd,
> But sharper scourges tear his heart.

We would desire to go to our bedrooms and weep; but since our business calls us away, we will first pray our Beloved to print the image of his bleeding self upon the tablets of our hearts all the day, and at nightfall we will return to commune with him, and sorrow that our sin should have cost him so dearly.

March 31 — Evening

*And Rizpah the daughter of Aiah took sackcloth,
and spread it for her upon the rock, from the beginning
of harvest until water dropped upon them out of heaven,
and allowed neither the birds of the air to rest on them by day,
nor the beasts of the field by night.* {2 Samuel 21:10}

If the love of a woman for her slain sons could make her prolong her mournful vigil for so long a period, shall we weary of considering the sufferings of our blessed Lord? She drove away the birds of prey, and shall not we chase from our meditations those worldly and sinful thoughts which defile both our minds and the sacred themes upon which we are occupied? Away, oh birds of evil wing! Leave the sacrifice alone! She bore the heats of summer, the night dews and the rains, unsheltered and alone. Sleep was chased from her weeping eyes; her heart was too full for slumber. Behold how she loved her children! Shall Rizpah thus endure, and shall we halt at the first little inconvenience or trial? Are we such cowards that we cannot bear to suffer with our Lord? She chased away even the wild beasts, with courage unusual in her sex, and will not we be ready to encounter every foe for Jesus' sake? These her children were slain by other hands than hers, and yet she wept and watched; what ought we to do who have by our sins crucified our Lord? Our obligations are boundless, our love should be fervent and our repentance thorough. To watch with Jesus should be our business, to protect his honour our occupation, to abide by his cross our solace. Those ghastly corpses might well have frightened Rizpah, especially at night, but in our Lord, where we are sitting at the foot of the cross, there is nothing revolting, but everything attractive. Never was living beauty so enchanting as a dying Saviour. Jesus, we will watch with you yet a while, and you graciously unveil yourself to us; then we shall not sit beneath sackcloth, but in a royal pavilion.

April 1 — Morning

{Daily Reading: 1 Samuel 1:1–3:21} {Quick Study: 1 Samuel 16:1–17:58}

Let him kiss me with the kisses of his mouth. *{Song of Solomon 1:2}*

For several days we have been dwelling upon the Saviour's passion, and for some little time to come we shall linger there. In beginning a new month, let us seek the same desires after our Lord as those which glowed in the heart of the elect spouse. See how she leaps at once to *him*; there are no prefatory words; she does not even mention his name; she is in the heart of her theme at once, for she speaks of *him* who was the only him in the world for her. How bold is her love! It was much condescension which permitted the weeping penitent to anoint his feet with spikenard — it was rich love which allowed the gentle Mary to sit at his feet and learn from him — but here, love, strong, fervent love, aspires to higher tokens of regard, and closer signs of fellowship. Esther trembled in the presence of Ahasuerus, but the spouse in joyful liberty of perfect love knows no fear. If we have received the same free spirit, we also may ask for the same. By kisses, we suppose to be intended those varied displays of affection by which the believer is made to enjoy the love of Jesus. We enjoyed the kiss of *reconciliation* at our conversion, and it was sweet as honey dropping from the honeycomb. The kiss of *acceptance* is still warm on our brow, as we know that he has accepted us and our works through rich grace. The kiss of daily, present *communion*, is what we pant after to be repeated day after day, until it is changed into the kiss of *reception*, which removes the soul from earth, and the kiss of *consummation* which fills it with the joy of heaven. Faith is our walk, but fellowship sensibly felt is our rest. Faith is the road, but communion with Jesus is the well from which the pilgrim drinks. Oh, lover of our souls, do not be strange to us; let the lips of your blessing meet the lips of our asking; let the lips of your fulness touch the lips of our need, and immediately the kiss will be consummated.

April 1 — Evening

It is time to seek the Lord. *{Hosea 10:12}*

This month of April is said to derive its name from the Latin verb *aperio* which means *to open*, because all the buds and blossoms are now opening, and we have arrived at the gates of the flowery year. Reader, if you are yet unsaved, may your heart, in accord with the universal awakening of nature, be opened to receive the Lord. Every blossoming flower warns you that *it is time to seek the Lord*; do not be out of tune with nature, but let your heart bud and bloom with holy desires. Do you tell me that the warm blood of youth leaps in your veins? Then, I entreat you, give your vigour to the Lord. It was my unspeakable happiness to be called in early youth, and I could gladly praise the Lord every day for it. Salvation is priceless, let it come when it may, but oh! an early salvation has a double value in it. Young men and maidens, since you may perish before you reach your prime, *"It is time to seek the Lord."* You who feel the first signs of decay, quicken your pace: that hollow cough, that hectic flush, are warnings which you must not trifle with; with you *it is indeed time to seek the Lord.* Did I observe a little grey mingled with your once luxurious tresses? Years are stealing on apace, and death is drawing nearer by hasty marches; let each return of spring arouse you to set your house in order. Dear reader, if you are now advanced in life, let me entreat and implore you to delay no longer. There is a day of grace for you now — be thankful for that, but it is a limited season and grows shorter every time that clock ticks. Here in this silent room, on this first night of another month, I speak to you as best I can by paper and ink, and from my innermost soul, as God's servant, I lay before you this warning, *"It is time to seek the Lord."* Do not slight that work, it may be your last call from destruction, the final syllable from the lip of grace.

April 2 — Morning

{Daily Reading: 1 Samuel 4:1–7:17} {Quick Study: 1 Samuel 18:1–19:24}

He answered him not a word. *{Matthew 27:14}*

He had never been slow of speech when he could bless the sons of men, but he would not say a single word for himself. "Never a man spoke like this man," and never was a man silent like him. Was this singular silence *the index of his perfect self-sacrifice*? Did it show that he would not utter a word to stop the slaughter of his sacred body, which he had dedicated as an offering for us? Had he so entirely surrendered himself that he would not interfere in his own behalf, even in the minutest degree, but be bound and slain a passive, uncomplaining victim? Was this silence *a type of the defencelessness of sin*? Nothing can be said in palliation or excuse for human guilt; and, therefore, he who bore its whole weight stood speechless before his judge. Is not patient silence *the best reply to a gainsaying world*? Calm endurance answers some questions infinitely more conclusively than the loftiest eloquence. The best apologists for Christianity in the early days were its martyrs. The anvil breaks a host of hammers by quietly bearing their blows. Did not the silent Lamb of God furnish us with *a grand example of wisdom*? Where every word was an occasion for new blasphemy, it was the line of duty to afford no fuel for the flame of sin. The ambiguous and the false, the unworthy and lowly, will before long overthrow and confute themselves, and therefore the truth can afford to be quiet, and finds silence to be its wisdom. Evidently our Lord, by his silence, furnished *a remarkable fulfilment of prophecy*. A long defence for himself would have been contrary to Isaiah's prediction. "He is led as a lamb to the slaughter, and as a sheep before her shearers is dumb, so he does not open his mouth." By his silence he conclusively proved himself to be the true Lamb of God. As such we greet him this morning. Be with us, Jesus, and in the silence of our heart, let us hear the voice of your love.

April 2 — Evening

He shall see his seed; he shall prolong his days, and the pleasure of the Lord shall prosper in his hand. *{Isaiah 53:10}*

Plead for the speedy fulfilment of this promise, all you who love the Lord. It is easy work to pray when we are grounded and established, concerning our desires, upon God's own promise. How can he who gave the word refuse to keep it? Immutable veracity cannot demean itself by a lie, and eternal faithfulness cannot degrade itself by neglect. God must bless his Son, his covenant binds him to it. What the Spirit prompts us to ask from Jesus, is what God decrees to give to him. Whenever you are praying for the kingdom of Christ, let your eyes behold the dawning of the blessed day which draws near, when the Crucified shall receive his coronation in the place where men rejected him. Courage, you who prayerfully work and toil for Christ with success of the very smallest kind, it shall not always be so; better times are coming. Your eyes cannot see the blissful future: borrow the telescope of faith; wipe the misty breath of your doubts from the glass; look through it and behold the coming glory. Reader, let us ask, *do you* make this your constant prayer? Remember that the same Christ who tells us to say, "Give us today our daily bread," had first given us this petition, "Hallowed be your name; your kingdom come; your will be done on earth as it is in heaven." Do not let your prayers be all concerning your own sins, your own needs, your own imperfections, your own trials, but let them climb the starry ladder, and get up to Christ himself, and then, as you draw near to the blood-sprinkled mercy seat, offer this prayer continually, "Lord, extend the kingdom of your dear Son." Such a petition, fervently presented, will elevate the spirit of all your devotions. Mind that you prove the sincerity of your prayer by labouring to promote the Lord's glory.

April 3 — Morning

{Daily Reading: 1 Samuel 8:1–11:15} {Quick Study: 1 Samuel 20:1–21:15}

They took Jesus, and led him away. *{John 19:16}*

He had been all night in agony, he had spent the early morning at the hall of Caiaphas, he had been hurried from Caiaphas to Pilate, from Pilate to Herod, and from Herod back again to Pilate; he had, therefore, very little strength left, and yet neither refreshment nor rest were permitted him. They were eager for his blood, and therefore led him out to die, loaded with the cross. Oh dolorous procession! Well may Salem's daughters weep. My soul, do you weep also?

What do we learn here as we see our blessed Lord led forth? Do we not perceive that truth which was set forth in shadow by *the scapegoat?* Did not the high priest bring the scapegoat, and put both his hands upon its head, confessing the sins of the people, so that those sins might be laid upon the goat, and cease from the people? Then the goat was led away by a fit man into the wilderness, and it carried away the sins of the people, so that if they were sought for they could not be found. Now we see Jesus brought before the priests and rulers, who pronounce him guilty; God himself imputes our sins to him, "The Lord has laid on him the iniquity of us all." "He was made sin for us," and, as the substitute for our guilt, bearing our sin upon his shoulders, represented by the cross, we see the great Scapegoat led away by the appointed officers of justice. Beloved, can you feel assured that he carried your sin? As you look at the cross upon his shoulders, does it represent your sin? There is one way by which you can tell whether he carried *your* sin or not. Have you laid your hand upon his head, confessed your sin, and trusted in him? Then your sin does not lie on you; it has all been transferred by blessed imputation to Christ, and he bears it on his shoulder as a load heavier than the cross.

Do not let the picture vanish until you have rejoiced in your own deliverance, and adored the loving Redeemer upon whom your iniquities were laid.

April 3 — Evening

*All we like sheep have gone astray; we have turned
every one to his own way; and the Lord has laid
on him the iniquity of us all.* {Isaiah 53:6}

Here is a confession of sin *common* to all the elect people of God. They have all fallen, and therefore, in common chorus, they all say, from the first who entered heaven to the last who shall enter there, "All we like sheep have gone astray." The confession, while thus unanimous, is also special and particular: "We have turned every one to his own way." There is a particular sinfulness about every one of the individuals; all are sinful, but each one with some *special* aggravation not found in his companion. It is the mark of genuine repentance that while it naturally associates itself with other penitents, it also takes up a position of loneliness. "We have turned every one to his own way," is a confession that each man had sinned against light particular to himself, or sinned with an aggravation which he could not perceive in others. This confession is *unreserved*; there is not a word to detract from its force, nor a syllable by way of excuse. The confession is *a giving up of all pleas of self-righteousness.* It is the declaration of men who are consciously guilty — guilty with aggravations, guilty without excuse: they stand with their weapons of rebellion broken in pieces, and cry, "All we like sheep have gone astray; we have turned every one to his own way." Yet we hear no dolorous wailings attending this confession of sin; for the next sentence makes it almost a song. "The Lord has laid on him the iniquity of us all." It is the most grievous sentence of the three, but it overflows with comfort. It is strange that where misery was concentrated, mercy reigned; where sorrow reached her climax, weary souls find rest. The Saviour bruised is the healing of bruised hearts. See how the lowliest penitence gives place to assured confidence through simply gazing at Christ on the cross!

**For he has made him to be sin for us,
who knew no sin; that we might be made the
righteousness of God in him.** *{2 Corinthians 5:21}*

Mourning Christian! Why do you weep? Are you mourning over your own corruptions? Look to your perfect Lord, and remember, you are complete in him; you are in God's sight as perfect as if you had never sinned; indeed, more than that, the Lord our Righteousness has put a divine garment upon you, so that you have more than the righteousness of man — you have the righteousness of God. Oh you who are mourning by reason of inbred sin and depravity, remember, not one of your sins can condemn you. You have learned to hate sin; but you have learned also to know that sin is not yours — it was laid upon Christ's head. Your standing is not in yourself — it is in Christ; your acceptance is not in yourself, but in your Lord; you are as much accepted by God today, with all your sinfulness, as you will be when you stand before his throne, free from all corruption. Oh, I beseech you, lay hold on this precious thought, *perfection in Christ!* For you are "complete in him." With your Saviour's garment on, you are holy as the Holy One. "Who is he who condemns? It is Christ who died, yes rather, who is risen again, who is even at the right hand of God, who also makes intercession for us." Christian, let your heart rejoice, for you are "accepted in the Beloved" — what have you to fear? Let your face always wear a smile; live near your Master; live in the suburbs of the Celestial City; for soon, when your time has come, you shall rise up where your Jesus sits, and reign at his right hand; and all this because the divine Lord "was made to be sin for us, who knew no sin; so that we might be made the righteousness of God in him."

April 4 — Evening

Come and let us go up to the mountain of the Lord. *{Isaiah 2:3}*

It is exceedingly beneficial to our souls to mount above this present evil world to something nobler and better. The cares of this world and the deceitfulness of riches are apt to choke everything good within us, and we grow fretful, desponding, perhaps proud and carnal. It is well for us to cut down these thorns and briers, for heavenly seed sown among them is not likely to yield a harvest; and where shall we find a better sickle with which to cut them down than communion with God and the things of the kingdom? In the valleys of Switzerland many of the inhabitants are deformed, and all have a sickly appearance, for the atmosphere is charged with miasma, and is close and stagnant; but up there, on the mountain, you find a hardy race, who breathe the clear fresh air as it blows from the virgin snows of the Alpine summits. It would be well if the dwellers in the valley could frequently leave their abodes among the marshes and the fever mists, and inhale the bracing element upon the hills. It is to such an exploit of climbing that I invite you this evening. May the Spirit of God assist us to leave the mists of fear and the fevers of anxiety, and all the ills which gather in this valley of earth, and to ascend the mountains of anticipated joy and blessedness. May God the Holy Spirit cut the cords that keep us here below, and assist us to mount! We sit too often like chained eagles fastened to the rock, only that, unlike the eagle, we begin to love our chain, and would, perhaps, if it really came to the test, be loath to have it snapped. May God now grant us grace, if we cannot escape from the chain of our flesh, yet to do so for our spirits; and leaving the body, like a servant, at the foot of the hill, may our soul, like Abraham, attain the top of the mountain, there to indulge in communion with the Most High.

They laid the cross on him, so that he might bear it after Jesus. *{Luke 23:26}*

In Simon's carrying the cross, we see a picture of the work of the church throughout all generations; she is the cross bearer after Jesus. Notice then, Christian, Jesus does not suffer to exclude your suffering. He bears a cross, not that you may escape it, but so that you may endure it. Christ exempts you from sin, but not from sorrow. Remember that, and expect to suffer.

But let us comfort ourselves with this thought, that in our case, as in Simon's, *it is not our cross, but Christ's cross which we carry.* When you are molested for your piety; when your religion brings the trial of cruel mockings upon you, then remember it is not *your* cross, it is *Christ's* cross; and how delightful it is to carry the cross of our Lord Jesus!

You carry the cross after him. You have blessed company; your path is marked with the footprints of your Lord. The mark of his blood red shoulder is upon that heavy burden. It is *his* cross, and he goes before you as a shepherd goes before his sheep. Take up your cross daily, and follow him.

Do not forget, also, *that you bear this cross in partnership.* It is the opinion of some that Simon only carried one end of the cross, and not the whole cross. That is very possible; Christ may have carried the heavier part, against the transverse beam, and Simon may have borne the lighter end. Certainly it is so with you; you only carry the light end of the cross, Christ bore the heavier end.

And remember, *though Simon had to bear the cross for a very little while, it gave him lasting honour.* Even so, the cross we carry is only for a little while at most, and then we shall receive the crown and the glory. Surely we should love the cross, and, instead of shrinking from it, *count it very dear,* when it works out for us "a far more exceeding and eternal weight of glory."

April 5 — Evening

Humility is before honour. *{Proverbs 15:33}*

Humiliation of soul always *brings a positive blessing with it.* If we empty our hearts of self, God will fill them with his love. He who desires close communion with Christ should remember the word of the Lord, "I will look to this man, even to him who is poor and of a contrite spirit, and trembles at my word." Stoop if you wish to climb to heaven. Do we not say of Jesus, "He descended that he might ascend?" So must you. You must grow downward, so that you may grow upward; for the sweetest fellowship with heaven is to be had by humble souls, and by them alone. God will deny no blessing to a thoroughly humbled spirit. "Blessed are the poor in spirit: for theirs is the kingdom of heaven," with all its riches and treasures. The whole treasury of God shall be transferred by deed of gift to the soul which is humble enough to be able to receive it without growing proud because of it. God blesses us all to the limit of the full measure and extremity of what it is safe for him to do. If you do not receive a blessing, it is because it is not safe for you to have one. If our Heavenly Father were to let your proud spirit win a victory in his holy war, you would pilfer the crown for yourself, and meeting with a fresh enemy you would fall a victim; so that you are kept low for your own safety. When a man is sincerely humble, and never ventures to touch so much as a grain of the praise, there is scarcely any limit to what God will do with him. Humility makes us ready to be blessed by the God of all grace, and makes us fit to deal efficiently with our fellow men. True humility is a flower which will adorn any garden. This is a sauce with which you may season every dish of life, and you will find an improvement in every case. Whether it is prayer or praise, whether it is work or suffering, the genuine salt of humility cannot be used in excess.

April 6 — Morning

{Daily Reading: 1 Samuel 17:1–18:30} {Quick Study: 1 Samuel 26:1–27:12}

Let us go forth therefore to him
outside the camp. *{Hebrews 13:13}*

J esus, bearing his cross, went forth to suffer outside the gate. The Christian's reason for leaving the camp of the world's sin and religion is not because he loves to be singular, but because *Jesus did so*; and the disciple must follow his Master. Christ was "not of the world." His life and his testimony were a constant protest against conformity with the world. Never was there such over-flowing affection for men as you find in him; but still he was separate from sinners. In like manner, Christ's people must "go forth to him." They must take their position "outside the camp," as witness-bearers for the truth. They must be prepared to tread the straight and narrow path. They must have bold, unflinching, lion-like hearts, loving Christ first, and his truth next, and Christ and his truth beyond all the world. Jesus would have his people "go forth without the camp" *for their own sanctification*. You cannot grow in grace to any high degree while you are conformed to the world. The life of separation may be a path of sorrow, but it is the highway of safety; and although the separated life may cost you many pangs, and make every day a battle, yet it is a happy life after all. No joy can excel that of the soldier of Christ: Jesus reveals himself so graciously, and gives such sweet refreshment, that the warrior feels more calm and peace in his daily strife than others in their hours of rest. The highway of holiness is the highway of communion. It is thus we shall hope *to win the crown* if we are enabled by divine grace to faithfully follow Christ "outside the camp." The crown of glory will follow the cross of separation. A moment's shame will be well rewarded by eternal honour; a little while of witness-bearing will seem like nothing when we are "for ever with the Lord."

April 6 — Evening

In the name of the Lord I will destroy them. *{Psalms 118:12}*

Our Lord Jesus, by his death, did not purchase a right to a *part* of us only, but to the *entire* man. He contemplated in his passion the sanctification of us wholly, spirit, soul, and body; so that in this triple kingdom he himself might reign supreme without a rival. It is the business of the newborn nature which God has given to the regenerate to assert the rights of the Lord Jesus Christ. My soul, so far as you are a child of God, you must conquer all the rest of yourself which yet remains unblest; you must subdue all your powers and passions to the silver sceptre of Jesus' gracious reign, and you must never be satisfied until he who is King by purchase also becomes King by gracious coronation, and reigns in you supreme. Seeing, then, that sin has no right to any part of us, we go about a good and lawful warfare when we seek, in the name of God, to drive it out. Oh, my body, you are a member of Christ: shall I tolerate your subjection to the prince of darkness? Oh, my soul, Christ has suffered for your sins, and redeemed you with his most precious blood: shall I allow your memory to become a storehouse of evil, or your passions to be firebrands of iniquity? Shall I surrender my judgment to be perverted by error, or my will to be led in fetters of iniquity? No, my soul, you are Christ's, and sin has no right to you.

Be courageous concerning this, oh, Christian! Do not be dispirited, as though your spiritual enemies could never be destroyed. You are able to overcome them — not in your own strength — the weakest of them would be too much for you in that; but you can and shall overcome them through the blood of the Lamb. Do not ask, "How shall I dispossess them, for they are greater and mightier than I?" But go to the strong for strength, wait humbly upon God, and the mighty God of Jacob will surely come to the rescue, and you shall sing of victory through his grace.

Oh you sons of men, how long will you turn my glory into shame? *{Psalms 4:2}*

An instructive writer has made a mournful list of the honours which the blinded people of Israel awarded to their long expected King.

1. They gave him *a procession of honour*, in which Roman legionaries, Jewish priests, men and women, took a part, he himself bearing his cross. This is the triumph which the world awards to him who comes to overthrow man's direst foes. Derisive shouts are his only acclamations, and cruel taunts his only paeans of praise.

2. They presented him with *the wine of honour*. Instead of a golden cup of generous wine they offered him the criminal's stupefying death draught, which he refused because he would preserve an uninjured taste by which to taste of death; and afterwards when he cried, "I thirst," they gave him vinegar mixed with gall, thrust to his mouth upon a sponge. Oh! wretched, detestable inhospitality to the King's Son.

3. He was provided with *a guard of honour*, who showed their esteem for him by gambling over his garments, which they had seized as their booty. Such was the bodyguard of the adored of heaven; a quaternion of brutal gamblers.

4. *A throne of honour* was found for him upon the bloody tree; no easier place of rest would rebel men yield to their liege Lord. The cross was, in fact, the full expression of the world's feeling towards him; "There," they seemed to say, "You Son of God, this is the manner in which God himself should be treated, if we could reach him."

5. *The title of honour* was nominally "King of the Jews," but that the blinded nation distinctly repudiated, and really called him "King of Thieves," by preferring Barabbas, and by placing Jesus in the place of highest shame between two thieves. His glory was thus in all things turned into shame by the sons of men, but it shall yet gladden the eyes of saints and angels, world without end.

April 7 — Evening

Deliver me from bloodguiltiness, oh God,
the God of my salvation; and my tongue shall
sing aloud of your righteousness. *{Psalms 51:14}*

In this SOLEMN CONFESSION, it is pleasing to observe that David plainly names his sin. He does not call it manslaughter, nor speak of it as an imprudence by which an unfortunate accident occurred to a worthy man, but he calls it by its true name, bloodguiltiness. He did not actually kill the husband of Bathsheba; but still it was planned in David's heart that Uriah should be killed, and he was still his murderer in the Lord's eyes. Learn in confession to be honest with God. Do not give fair names to foul sins; call them what you wish, they will smell no sweeter. Do strive to feel them to be as loathsome as God actually sees them to be; and with all honesty of heart acknowledge their real character. Observe that David was evidently oppressed with the heinousness of his sin. It is easy to use words, but it is difficult to feel their meaning. The fifty-first Psalm is the picture of a contrite spirit. Let us strive after the similar brokenness of heart; for however excellent our words may be, if our heart is not conscious of the hell deservingness of sin, we cannot expect to find forgiveness.

Our text has in it AN EARNEST PRAYER — it is addressed to the God of *salvation*. It is his prerogative to forgive; it is his very name and office to save those who seek his face. Better still, the text calls him the God of *my* salvation. Yes, blessed be his name, while I am yet going to him through Jesus' blood, I can rejoice in the God of *my* salvation.

The psalmist ends with A COMMENDABLE VOW: if God will deliver him he will sing — indeed, more, he will "sing *aloud*." Who can sing in any other manner of such a mercy as this! But note the subject of the song — "YOUR RIGHTEOUSNESS." We must sing of the finished work of a precious Saviour; and he who knows most of forgiving love will sing the loudest.

April 8 — Morning

{Daily Reading: 1 Samuel 22:1–24:22} {Quick Study: 1 Samuel 30:1–31:13}

If they do these things in a green tree,
what shall be done in the dry? *{Luke 23:31}*

Among other interpretations of this suggestive question, the following is full of teaching: "If the innocent substitute for sinners suffers thus, what will be done when the sinner himself — the dry tree — shall fall into the hands of an angry God?" When God saw Jesus in the sinner's place, he did not spare him; and when he finds the unregenerate without Christ, he will not spare them. Oh, sinner, Jesus was led away by his enemies: so you shall be dragged away by fiends to the place appointed for you. Jesus was deserted by God; and if he, who was only imputedly a sinner, was deserted, how much more shall you be? *"Eloi, Eloi, lama sabachthani?"* What an awful shriek! But what shall be your cry when you shall say, "Oh, God! Oh, God! Why have you forsaken me?" And the answer shall come back, "Because you have ignored all my counsel, and would have none of my reproof: I also will laugh at your calamity; I will mock when your fear comes." If God did not spare his own Son, how much less will he spare you! What whips of burning wire will be yours when conscience shall strike you with all its terrors. You rich, you most merry, you most self-righteous sinners — who would stand in your place when God shall say, "Awake, oh sword, against the man who rejected me; strike him, and let him feel the smart for ever?" Jesus was spit upon: sinner, what shame will be yours! We cannot sum up in one word all the mass of sorrows which met upon the head of Jesus who died for us, therefore it is impossible for us to tell you what streams, what oceans of grief must roll over your spirit if you die as you now are. You may die so, you may die now. By the agonies of Christ, by his wounds and by his blood, do not bring upon yourselves the wrath to come! Trust in the Son of God, and you shall never die.

April 8 — Evening

I will fear no evil: for you are with me. {Psalms 23:4}

Behold, how independent of outward circumstances the Holy Spirit can make the Christian! What a bright light may shine within us when it is all dark outside! How firm, how happy, how calm, how peaceful we may be, when the world shakes to and fro, and the pillars of the earth are removed! Even death itself, with all its terrible influences, has no power to suspend the music of a Christian's heart, but rather makes that music become more sweet, more clear, more heavenly, until the last kind act which death can do is to let the earthly strain melt into the heavenly chorus, the temporal joy into the eternal bliss! Let us have confidence, then, in the blessed Spirit's power to comfort us. Dear reader, are you looking forward to poverty? Do not fear; the divine Spirit can give you, in your poverty, a greater plenty than the rich have in their abundance. You do not know what joys may be stored up for you in the cottage around which grace will plant the roses of contentment. Are you conscious of a growing failure of your bodily powers? Do you expect to suffer long nights of languishing and days of pain? Oh, do not be sad! That bed may become a throne for you. How little you know that every pang that shoots through your body may be a refining fire to consume your dross — a beam of glory to light up the secret parts of your soul. Are the eyes growing dim? Jesus will be your light. Do the ears fail you? Jesus' name will be your soul's best music, and his person your dear delight. Socrates used to say, "Philosophers can be happy without music," and Christians can be happier than philosophers when all outward causes of rejoicing are withdrawn. In you, my God, my heart shall triumph, come what may of external ills! By your power, oh blessed Spirit, my heart shall be exceedingly glad, though all things should fail me here below.

April 9 — Morning

{Daily Reading: 1 Samuel 25:1–27:12} {Quick Study: 2 Samuel 1:1–2:32}

And there followed him a great company of people, and
of women, which also bewailed and lamented him. *{Luke 23:27}*

Amid the rabble rout which hounded the Redeemer to his
doom, there were some gracious souls whose bitter anguish
sought vent in wailing and lamentations — fit music to accompany that march of woe. When my soul can, in imagination, see the
Saviour bearing his cross to Calvary, it joins the godly women and
weeps with them; for, indeed, there is true cause for grief — cause
lying deeper than those mourning women thought. They bewailed
innocence maltreated, goodness persecuted, love bleeding, meekness about to die; but my heart has a deeper and more bitter cause
to mourn. My sins were the scourges which lacerated those blessed
shoulders, and crowned with thorns those bleeding brows: my sins
cried "Crucify him! Crucify him!" And laid the cross upon his gracious shoulders. His being led forth to die is sorrow enough for one
eternity: but my having been his murderer, is more, infinitely more
grief than one poor fountain of tears can express.

It would not be hard to guess why those women loved and wept
for him: but they could not have had greater reasons for love and
grief than my heart has. Nain's widow saw her son restored — but
I myself have been raised to newness of life. Peter's wife's mother
was cured of the fever — but I of the greater plague of sin. Out of
Magdalene seven demons were cast — but a whole legion out of me.
Mary and Martha were favoured with visits — but he dwells with
me. His mother bore his body — but he is formed in me the hope
of glory. Having a far greater debt than the women, I must show
even more gratitude or sorrow than they.

> Love and grief my heart dividing,
> With my tears his feet I'll lave —
> Constant still in heart abiding,
> Weep for him who died to save.

April 9 — Evening

Your gentleness has made me great. *{Psalms 18:35}*

The words are capable of being translated, "Your *goodness* has made me great." David gratefully ascribed all his greatness not to his own goodness, but the goodness of God. "Your *providence*," is another reading; and providence is nothing more than goodness in action. Goodness is the bud of which providence is the flower, or goodness is the seed of which providence is the harvest. Some render it, "Your *help*," which is only another word for providence; providence being the firm ally of the saints, aiding them in the service of their Lord. Or again, "Your *humility* has made me great." "Your *condescension*" may, perhaps, serve as a comprehensive reading, combining the ideas mentioned, including that of *humility*. It is God making himself little which is the cause of our being made great. We are so little that if God should reveal his greatness without condescension, we would be trampled under his feet; but God, who must stoop to view the skies, and bow to see what angels do, turns his eye yet lower, and looks to the lowly and contrite, and makes them great. There are yet other readings, as for instance, the Septuagint, which reads, "your discipline" — your fatherly correction — "has made me great"; while the Chaldee paraphrase reads, "Your Word has increased me." Still the idea is the same. David ascribes all his own greatness to the condescending goodness of his Father in heaven. May this sentiment be echoed in our hearts this evening while we cast our crowns at Jesus' feet, and cry, "Your gentleness has made me great." How marvellous has been our experience of God's gentleness! How gentle have been his corrections! How gentle his forbearance! How gentle his teachings! How gentle his drawings! Meditate upon this theme, oh believer. Let gratitude be awakened; let humility be deepened; let love be quickened before you fall asleep tonight.

April 10 — Morning

{Daily Reading: 1 Samuel 28:1–31:13} {Quick Study: 2 Samuel 3:1–5:25}

The place which is called Calvary. {Luke 23:33}

The hill of comfort is the hill of Calvary; the house of consolation is built with the wood of the cross; the temple of heavenly blessing is founded upon the riven rock — riven by the spear which pierced his side. No scene in sacred history ever gladdens the soul like Calvary's tragedy.

> Is it not strange, the darkest hour
> That ever dawned on sinful earth,
> Should touch the heart with softer power,
> For comfort, than an angel's mirth?
> That to the cross the mourner's eye should turn,
> Sooner than where the stars of Bethlehem burn?

Light springs from the midday midnight of Golgotha, and every herb of the field blooms sweetly beneath the shadow of the once accursed tree. In that place of thirst, grace has dug a fountain which always gushed with waters pure as crystal, each drop capable of alleviating the woes of mankind. You who have had your times of conflict will confess that it was not at Olivet that you ever found comfort, not on the hill of Sinai, nor on Tabor; but Gethsemane, Gabbatha, and Golgotha have been a means of comfort for you. The bitter herbs of Gethsemane have often taken away the bitters of your life; the scourge of Gabbatha has often scourged away your cares, and the groans of Calvary yields us comfort rare and rich. We would never have known Christ's love in all its heights and depths if he had not died; nor could we guess the Father's deep affection if he had not given his Son to die. The common mercies we enjoy all sing of love, just as the seashell, when we put it to our ears, whispers of the deep sea from where it came; but if we desire to hear the ocean itself, we must not look at everyday blessings, but at the transactions of the crucifixion. He who wishes to know love, let him retire to Calvary and see the man of sorrows die.

April 10 — Evening

For tonight there stood by me the angel of God. *{Acts 27:23}*

Tempest and long darkness, coupled with imminent risk of shipwreck, had brought the crew of the vessel into a sad state; one man alone among them remained perfectly calm, and by his word the rest were reassured. Paul was the only man who had heart enough to say, "Sirs, be of good cheer." There were veteran Roman legionaries on board, and brave old mariners, and yet their poor Jewish prisoner had more spirit than all of them. He had a secret friend who kept his courage up. The Lord Jesus dispatched a heavenly messenger to whisper words of consolation in the ear of his faithful servant, therefore he wore a shining countenance and spoke like a man at ease.

If we fear the Lord, we may look for timely interpositions when our case is at its worst. Angels are not kept from us by storms, or hindered by darkness. Seraphs think it is no humiliation to visit the poorest of the heavenly family. If angel's visits are few and far between at ordinary times, they shall be frequent in our nights of tempest and tossing. Friends may drop from us when we are under pressure, but our communion with the inhabitants of the angelic world shall be more abundant; and in the strength of love words, brought to us from the throne by the way of Jacob's ladder, we shall be strong to do exploits. Dear reader, is this an hour of distress with you? Then ask for special help. Jesus is the angel of the covenant, and if his presence is now earnestly sought, it will not be denied. What that presence brings in heart cheer remember those who, like Paul, have had the angel of God standing by them in a night of storm, when anchors would no longer hold, and rocks were near.

> Oh angel of my God, be near,
> Amid the darkness hush my fear;
> Loud roars the wild tempestuous sea,
> Your presence, Lord, shall comfort me.

April 11 — Morning

{Daily Reading: 2 Samuel 1:1–2:32} {Quick Study: 2 Samuel 6:1–8:18}

I am poured out like water,
and all my bones are out of joint. *{Psalms 22:14}*

Did earth or heaven ever behold a sadder spectacle of woe? In soul and body, our Lord felt himself to be weak as water poured upon the ground. The placing of the cross in its socket had shaken him with great violence, had strained all the ligaments, pained every nerve, and more or less dislocated all his bones. Burdened with his own weight, the august sufferer felt the strain increasing every moment of those six long hours. His sense of faintness and general weakness were overpowering; while to his own consciousness he became nothing but a mass of misery and swooning sickness. When Daniel saw the great vision, he thus describes his sensations, "There remained no strength in me, for my vigour was turned into corruption, and I retained no strength." How much more faint must have been our greater Prophet when he saw the dread vision of the wrath of God, and felt it in his own soul! To us, sensations such as our Lord endured would have been insupportable, and kind unconsciousness would have come to our rescue; but in his case, he was wounded, and felt the sword; he drained the cup and *tasted* every drop.

> Oh, King of Grief! (a title strange, yet true
> To you of all kings only due).
> Oh, King of Wounds! How shall I grieve for thee,
> Who in all grief preventest me!

As we kneel before our now-ascended Saviour's throne, let us remember well the way by which he prepared it as a throne of grace for us; let us in spirit drink from his cup, that we may be strengthened for our hour of heaviness whenever it may come. In his natural body every member suffered, and so it must be in the spiritual; but just as out of all his griefs and woes his body came forth uninjured to glory and power, even so shall his mystical body come through the furnace with not so much as the smell of fire upon it.

April 11 — Evening

Look upon my affliction and my pain;
and forgive all my sins. {Psalms 25:18}

It is well for us when prayers about our sorrows are linked with pleas concerning our sins — when, being under God's hand, we are not wholly taken up with our pain, but remember our offences against God. It is well, also, to take both sorrow and sin to the same place. It was to God that David carried his sorrow: it was to God that David confessed his sin. Observe, then, *we must take our sorrows to God.* You may even roll your little sorrows upon God, for he counts the hairs of your head; and your great sorrows you may commit to him, for he holds the ocean in the hollow of his hand. Go to him, whatever your present trouble may be, and you shall find him able and willing to relieve you. *But we must take our sins to God, too.* We must carry them to the cross, so that the blood may fall upon them, to purge away their guilt, and to destroy their defiling power.

The special lesson of the text is this — that *we are to go to the Lord with sorrows and with sins in the right spirit.* Note that all David asks concerning his sorrow is, "*Look upon* my affliction and my pain," but the next petition is vastly more expressive, definite, decided, plain — "*Forgive* all my sins." Many sufferers would have put it, "Remove my affliction and my pain, and look at my sins." But David does not say so; he cries, "Lord, as for my affliction and my pain, I will not dictate to your wisdom. Lord, look at them, I will leave them to you, I should be glad to have my pain removed, but do as you will; but as for my sins, Lord, I know what I want with them; I must have them forgiven; I cannot endure to lie under their curse for a moment." A Christian counts sorrow lighter in the scale than sin; he can bear that his troubles should continue, but he cannot support the burden of his transgressions.

April 12 — Morning

{Daily Reading: 2 Samuel 3:1–5:25} {Quick Study: 2 Samuel 9:1–12:31}

My heart is like wax; it is melted
in the midst of my body. *{Psalms 22:14}*

Our blessed Lord experienced a terrible sinking and melting of soul. "The spirit of a man will sustain his infirmity, but who can bear a wounded spirit?" Deep depression of spirit is the most grievous of all trials; all besides is as nothing. Well might the suffering Saviour cry to his God, "Be not far from me," for more than at any other time a man needs his God when his heart is melted within him because of heaviness. Believer, come near the cross this morning, and humbly adore the King of glory as having once been brought far lower, in mental distress and inward anguish, than anyone among us; and see his fitness to become a faithful High Priest, who can be touched with a feeling of our infirmities. Especially let those of us whose sadness springs directly from the withdrawal of a present sense of our Father's love, enter into near and intimate communion with Jesus. Let us not give way to despair, since through this dark room the Master has passed before us. Our souls may sometimes long and faint, and thirst even to anguish, to behold the light of the Lord's countenance: at such times let us console ourselves with the sweet fact of the sympathy of our great High Priest. Our drops of sorrow may well be forgotten in the ocean of his griefs; but how high ought our love to rise! Come in, oh strong and deep love of Jesus, like the sea at the flood in spring tides, cover all my powers, drown all my sins, wash out all my cares, lift up my earth bound soul, and float it right up to my Lord's feet, and there let me lie, a poor broken shell, washed up by his love, having no virtue or value; and only venturing to whisper to him that if he will put his ear to me, he will hear within my heart faint echoes of the vast waves of his own love which have brought me where it is my delight to lie, even at his feet for ever.

April 12 — Evening

The king's garden. *{Nehemiah 3:15}*

Mention of the king's garden by Nehemiah brings to mind the paradise which the King of kings prepared for Adam. Sin has utterly ruined that fair abode of all delights, and driven forth the children of men to till the ground, which yields thorns and briers to them. My soul, remember the fall, for it was your fall. Weep much because the Lord of love was so shamefully treated by the head of the human race, of which you are a member, as undeserving as any. Behold how dragons and demons dwell on this fair earth, which once was a garden of delights.

See over there another King's garden, which the King waters with his bloody sweat — *Gethsemane*, whose bitter herbs are sweeter by far to renewed souls than even Eden's luscious fruits. There the mischief of the serpent in the first garden was undone: there the curse was lifted from earth, and borne by the woman's promised seed. My soul, think much on the agony and the passion; resort to the garden of the olive press, and view your great Redeemer rescuing you from your lost estate. This is the garden of gardens indeed, in which the soul may see the guilt of sin and the power of love, two sights which surpass all others.

Is there no other King's garden? Yes, *my heart*, you are, or should be such. How do the flowers flourish? Do any choice fruits appear? Does the King walk within, and rest in the bowers of my spirit? Let me see that the plants are trimmed and watered, and the mischievous foxes hunted out. Come, Lord, and let the heavenly wind blow at your coming, so that the spices of your garden may flow abroad. Nor must I forget the King's garden of *the church*. Oh, Lord, send prosperity to it. Rebuild her walls, nourish her plants, ripen her fruits, and from the huge wilderness, reclaim the barren waste, and make of it "a King's garden."

April 13 — Morning

{Daily Reading: 2 Samuel 6:1–9:13} {Quick Study: 2 Samuel 13:1–14:33}

My well beloved is a bundle of myrrh to me. *{Song of Solomon 1:13}*

Myrrh may well be chosen as the type of Jesus on account of *its preciousness, its perfume, its pleasantness, its healing, preserving, disinfecting qualities, and its connection with sacrifice.* But why is he compared to "a *bundle* of myrrh?" First, for *plenty.* He is not just a drop of it, he is a casket full. He is not a sprig or flower of it, but a whole bundle. There is enough in Christ for all my necessities; let me not be slow to avail myself of him. Our well Beloved is compared to a "bundle" again, for *variety:* for there is in Christ not only the one thing needful, but in "him dwells all the fulness of the Godhead bodily," everything needful is in him. Take Jesus in his different characters and you will see a marvellous variety — Prophet, Priest, King, Husband, Friend, Shepherd. Consider him in his life, death, resurrection, ascension, second advent; view him in his virtue, gentleness, courage, self-denial, love, faithfulness, truth, righteousness — everywhere he is a bundle of preciousness. He is a "bundle of myrrh" for *preservation* — not loose myrrh to be dropped on the floor or trodden on, but myrrh tied up, myrrh to be stored in a casket. We must value him as our best treasure; we must prize his words and his ordinances; and we must keep our thoughts of him and knowledge of him as under lock and key, lest the devil should steal anything from us. Moreover, Jesus is a "bundle of myrrh" for *speciality.* The emblem suggests the idea of distinguishing, discriminating grace. From before the foundation of the world, he was set apart for his people; and he gives forth his perfume only to those who understand how to enter into communion with him, to have close dealings with him. Oh! Blessed people whom the Lord has admitted into his secrets, and for whom he sets himself apart. Oh! Choice and happy who are thus made to say, "my well beloved is a bundle of myrrh to me."

April 13 — Evening

And he shall put his hand upon the head of
the burnt offering; and it shall be accepted for him
to make atonement for him. *{Leviticus 1:4}*

Our Lord's being made "sin for us" is shown here by the very significant transfer of sin to the young bull, which was made by the elders of the people. The laying of the hand was not a mere touch of contact, for in some other places of Scripture the original word has the meaning of leaning heavily, as in the expression, "Your wrath lies hard upon me." *{Psalms 88:7}* Surely this is the very essence and nature of faith, which does not only bring us into contact with the great Substitute, but teaches us to lean upon him with all the burden of our guilt. Jehovah made to meet upon the head of the Substitute all the offences of his covenant people, but each one of the chosen is brought personally to ratify this solemn covenant act, when by grace he is enabled by faith to lay his hand upon the head of the "Lamb slain from before the foundation of the world." Believer, do you remember that rapturous day when you first realised pardon through Jesus the Sin Bearer? Can you not make a glad confession, and join with the writer in saying, "My soul recalls her day of deliverance with delight. Laden with guilt and full of fears, I saw my Saviour as my Substitute, and I laid my hand upon him; oh! how timidly at first, but courage grew and confidence was confirmed until I leaned my soul entirely upon him; and now it is my unceasing joy to know that my sins are no longer imputed to me, but laid on him, and like the debts of the wounded traveller, Jesus, like the good Samaritan, has said of all my future sinfulness, 'Add that to my account.' " Blessed discovery! Eternal solace of a grateful heart!

> My numerous sins transferred to him,
> Shall never more be found,
> Lost in his blood's atoning stream,
> Where every crime is drowned!

April 14 — Morning

{Daily Reading: 2 Samuel 10:1–12:31} {Quick Study: 2 Samuel 15:1–17:29}

**All those who see me ridicule me: they shoot
out the lip, they shake the head.** *{Psalms 22:7}*

Mockery was a great ingredient in our Lord's woe. Judas mocked him in the garden; the chief priests and scribes laughed him to scorn; Herod set him at naught; the servants and the soldiers jeered at him, and brutally insulted him; Pilate and his guards ridiculed his royalty; and on the tree all sorts of horrible jests and hideous taunts were hurled at him. Ridicule is always hard to bear, but when we are in intense pain it is so heartless, so cruel, that it cuts us to the quick. Imagine the Saviour crucified, racked with anguish far beyond all mortal guess, and then picture that motley multitude, all wagging their heads or thrusting out the lip in bitterest contempt for one poor suffering victim! Surely there must have been something more in the crucified one than they could see, or else such a great and mingled crowd would not unanimously have honoured him with such contempt. Was it not evil confessing, in the very moment of its greatest apparent triumph, that after all it could do no more than mock at that victorious goodness which was then reigning on the cross? Oh Jesus, "Despised and rejected of men," how could you die for men who treated you so poorly? Herein is love amazing, love divine, yes, love beyond degree. We, too, have despised you in the days of our unregeneracy, and even since our new birth we have set the world on high in our hearts, and yet you bleed to heal our wounds, and die to give us life. Oh, that we could set you on a glorious high throne in all men's hearts! We would ring out your praises over land and sea until men would as universally adore as once they did unanimously reject.

> Your creatures wrong you, oh you sovereign Good!
> *You are not loved, because not understood:*
> This grieves me most, that vain pursuits beguile
> Ungrateful men, regardless of your smile.

April 14 — Evening

**Say to the righteous, that it shall be
well with him.** *{Isaiah 3:10}*

It is well with the righteous ALWAYS. If it had said, "Say to the righteous, that it is well with him in his prosperity," we must have been thankful for so great a boon, for prosperity is an hour of peril, and it is a gift from heaven to be secured from its snares: or if it had been written, "It is well with him when under persecution," we must have been thankful for so sustaining an assurance, for persecution is hard to bear; but when no time is mentioned, all time is included. God's "shalls" must be understood always in their largest sense. From the beginning of the year to the end of the year, from the first gathering of evening shadows until the daystar shines, in all conditions and under all circumstances, it shall be well with the righteous. It is so well with him that we could not imagine it to be better, for he is *well fed*, he feeds upon the flesh and blood of Jesus; he is *well clothed*, he wears the imputed righteousness of Christ; he is *well housed*, he dwells in God; he is *well married*, his soul is knit in bonds of marriage union to Christ; he is *well provided for*, for the Lord is his Shepherd; he is *well endowed*, for heaven is his inheritance. It is well with the righteous — *well upon divine authority*; the mouth of God speaks the comforting assurance. Oh, beloved, if God declares that all is well, ten thousand demons may declare it to be ill, but we laugh them all to scorn. Blessed be God for a faith which enables us to believe God when the creatures contradict him. "It is," says the Word, "at all times well with you, you righteous one," then, beloved, if you cannot see it, let God's Word stand for you instead of sight; yes, believe it on divine authority more confidently than if your eyes and your feelings told it to you. Whom God blesses is blest indeed, and what his lip declares is truth most sure and steadfast.

April 15 — Morning

{Daily Reading: 2 Samuel 13:1–14:33} {Quick Study: 2 Samuel 18:1–20:26}

My God, my God, why have you forsaken me? *{Psalms 22:1}*

We here behold the Saviour in the depth of his sorrows. No other place shows the griefs of Christ so well as Calvary, and no other moment at Calvary is so full of agony as at the time when his cry rends the air — "My God, my God, why have you forsaken me?" At this moment physical weakness was united with acute mental torture from the shame and ignominy through which he had to pass; and to make his grief culminate with emphasis, he suffered spiritual agony surpassing all expression, resulting from the departure of his Father's presence. This was the black midnight of his horror; then it was that he descended the abyss of suffering. No man can enter into the full meaning of these words. Some of us think at times that we could cry, "My God, my God, why have you forsaken me?" There are times when the brightness of our Father's smile is eclipsed by clouds and darkness; but let us remember that God never does really forsakes us. It is only a seeming forsaking with us, but in Christ's case it was a real forsaking. We grieve at a little withdrawal of our Father's love; but the real turning away of God's face from his Son, who shall calculate how deep the agony which it caused him?

In our case, our cry is often dictated by unbelief: in his case, it was the utterance of a dreadful fact, for God had really turned away from him for a time. Oh you poor, distressed soul, who once lived in the sunshine of God's face, but are now in darkness, remember that he has not really forsaken you. God in the clouds is as much our God as when he shines forth in all the lustre of his grace; but since even the *thought* that he has forsaken us gives us agony, what must the woe of the Saviour have been when he exclaimed, "My God, my God, why have you forsaken me?"

April 15 — Evening

Lift them up for ever. *{Psalms 28:9}*

*G*od's people need lifting up. They are very heavy by nature. They have no wings, or, if they have, they are like the doves of old which lay among the pots; and they need divine grace to make them mount on wings covered with silver, and with feathers of yellow gold. By nature sparks fly upward, but the sinful souls of men fall downward. Oh Lord, "Lift them up for ever!" David himself said, "To you, oh God, do I lift up my soul," and here he feels the necessity that other men's souls should be lifted up as well as his own. When you ask this blessing for yourself, do not forget to seek it for others also. There are three ways in which God's people require to be lifted up. *They require to be elevated in character*. Lift them up, oh Lord; do not allow your people to be like the world's people! The world lies in the wicked one; lift them out of it! The world's people are pursuing after silver and gold, seeking their own pleasures, and the gratification of their lusts; but, Lord, lift your people up above all this; keep them from being "muckrakers," as John Bunyan calls the man who was always scraping after gold! Set their hearts upon their risen Lord and the heavenly heritage! Moreover, *believers need to be prospered in conflict*. In the battle, if they seem to fall, oh Lord, be pleased to give them the victory. If the foot of the foe is upon their necks for a moment, help them to grasp the sword of the Spirit, and eventually to win the battle. Lord, lift up your children's spirits in the day of conflict; do not let them sit in the dust, mourning for ever. Do not allow the adversary to vex them grievously, and make them fret; but if they have been, like Hannah, persecuted, let them sing about the mercy of a delivering God.

We may also ask our Lord to *lift them up at the last*! Lift them up by taking them home, lift their bodies from the tomb, and raise their souls to your eternal kingdom in glory.

April 16 — Morning

{Daily Reading: 2 Samuel 15:1–16:23} {Quick Study: 2 Samuel 21:1–22:51}

The precious blood of Christ. *{1 Peter 1:19}*

Standing at the foot of the cross, we see hands, and feet, and side, all distilling crimson streams of precious blood. It is "precious" because of its *redeeming and atoning efficacy*. By it the sins of Christ's people are atoned for; they are redeemed from under the law; they are reconciled to God, made one with him. Christ's blood is also "precious" in its *cleansing power*; it "cleanses from all sin." "Though your sins are as scarlet, they shall be as white as snow." Through Jesus' blood there is not a spot left upon any believer, no wrinkle nor any such thing remains. Oh precious blood, which makes us clean, removing the stains of abundant iniquity, and permitting us to stand accepted in the Beloved, notwithstanding the many ways in which we have rebelled against our God. The blood of Christ is likewise "precious" in its *preserving power*. We are safe from the destroying angel under the sprinkled blood. Remember it is *God's seeing* the blood which is the true reason for our being spared. Here is comfort for us when the eye of faith is dim, for God's eye is still the same. The blood of Christ is "precious" also in its *sanctifying influence*. The same blood which justifies by taking away sin, does, in its later action, quicken the new nature and lead it onward to subdue sin and to carry out the commands of God. There is no motive for holiness so great as what streams from the veins of Jesus. And "precious," unspeakably precious, is this blood, because it has an *overcoming power*. It is written, "They overcame through the blood of the Lamb." How could they do otherwise? He who fights with the precious blood of Jesus, fights with a weapon which cannot know defeat. The blood of Jesus! Sin dies at its presence, death ceases to be death: heaven's gates are opened. The blood of Jesus! We shall march on, conquering and to conquer, as long as we can trust its power!

April 16 — Evening

And his hands were steady until the going down of the sun. *{Exodus 17:12}*

So mighty was the prayer of Moses that all depended upon it. The petitions of Moses discomfited the enemy more than the fighting of Joshua. Yet both were needed. Indeed, in the soul's conflict, force and fervour, decision and devotion, valour and vehemence, must join their forces, and all will be well. You must wrestle with your sin, but the major part of the wrestling must be done alone in private with God. Prayer, like that of Moses, holds up the token of the covenant before the Lord. The rod was the emblem of God's working with Moses, the symbol of God's government in Israel. Learn, oh pleading saint, to hold up the promise and the oath of God before him. The Lord cannot deny his own declarations. Hold up the rod of promise, and have what you wish.

Moses grew weary, and then his friends assisted him. When at any time your prayer flags, let faith support one hand, and let holy hope uplift the other, and prayer seating itself upon the stone of Israel, the rock of our salvation, will persevere and prevail. Beware of faintness in devotion; if Moses felt it, who can escape? It is far easier to fight with sin in public, than to pray against it in private. It is remarked that Joshua never grew weary in the fighting, but Moses did grow weary in the praying; the more spiritual an exercise, the more difficult it is for flesh and blood to maintain it. Let us cry, then, for special strength, and may the Spirit of God, who helps our infirmities, as he allowed help for Moses, enable us like him to continue with our hands steady *"until the going down of the sun,"* until the evening of life is over; until we shall come to the rising of a better sun in the land where prayer is swallowed up in praise.

April 17 — Morning

{Daily Reading: 2 Samuel 17:1–18:33} {Quick Study: 2 Samuel 23:1–24:25}

We are come to the blood of sprinkling, that speaks better things than that of Abel. *{Hebrews 12:24}*

Reader, have *you* come to the blood of sprinkling? The question is not whether you have come to a knowledge of doctrine, or an observance of ceremonies, or to a certain form of experience, but *have you come to the blood of Jesus?* The blood of Jesus is the life of all vital godliness. If you have truly come to Jesus, we know how you came — the Holy Spirit sweetly brought you there. You came to the blood of sprinkling with no merits of your own. Guilty, lost, and helpless, you came to take that blood, and that blood alone, as your everlasting hope. You came to the cross of Christ, with a trembling and an aching heart; and oh! what a precious sound it was to you to hear the voice of the blood of Jesus! The dropping of his blood is as the music of heaven to the penitent sons of earth. We are full of sin, but the Saviour bids us lift our eyes to him, and as we gaze upon his streaming wounds, each drop of blood, as it falls, cries, "It is finished; I have made an end of sin; I have brought in everlasting righteousness." Oh! Sweet language of the precious blood of Jesus! If you have come to that blood once, you will come to it constantly. Your life will be "looking to Jesus." Your whole conduct will be epitomized in this — "to whom coming." Not to whom I *have* come, but to whom I am *always coming.* If you have ever come to the blood of sprinkling, you will feel your need of coming to it every day. He who does not desire to wash in it *every day*, has never washed in it at all. The believer always feels it to be his joy and privilege that there is still a fountain opened. Past experiences are doubtful food for Christians; a present coming to Christ alone can give us joy and comfort. This morning let us sprinkle our doorpost fresh with blood, and then feast upon the Lamb, assured that the destroying angel must pass us by.

April 17 — Evening

We would see Jesus. *{John 12:21}*

The worldling's cry is always, "Who will show us any good?" He seeks satisfaction in earthly comforts, enjoyments, and riches. But the quickened sinner knows of only one good. "Oh, that I knew where I might find HIM!" When he is truly awakened to feel his guilt, if you could pour the gold of India at his feet, he would say, "Take it away: I want to find HIM." It is a blessed thing for a man when he has brought his desires into a focus, so that they all centre in one object. When he has fifty different desires, his heart resembles a pool of stagnant water, spread out into a marsh, breeding miasma and pestilence; but when all his desires are brought into one channel, his heart becomes like a river of pure water, running swiftly to fertilize the fields. Happy is he who has one desire, if that one desire is set on Christ, though it may not yet have been realised. If Jesus is a soul's desire, it is a blessed sign of divine work within. Such a man will never be content with mere ordinances. He will say, "I want Christ; I *must* have him — mere ordinances are of no use to me; I want *him*; do not offer me these; you offer me the empty pitcher, while I am dying of thirst; give me water, or else I will die. Jesus is my soul's desire. I would see Jesus!"

Is this your condition, my reader, at this moment? Have you only one desire, and is that for Christ? Then you are not far from the kingdom of heaven. Have you only one wish in your heart, and that one wish that you may be washed from all your sins in Jesus' blood? Can you really say, "I would give all I have to be a Christian; I would give up everything I have and hope for, if I might only feel that I have an interest in Christ?" Then, despite all your fears, be of good cheer, the Lord loves you, and you shall come out into daylight soon, and rejoice in the liberty by which Christ makes men free.

April 18 — Morning

{Daily Reading: 2 Samuel 19:1–20:26} {Quick Study: 1 Kings 1:1–2:46}

She bound the scarlet line in the window. *{Joshua 2:21}*

Rahab depended for her preservation upon the promise of the spies, whom she looked upon as the representatives of the God of Israel. Her faith was simple and firm, but very obedient. To tie the scarlet line in the window was a very trivial act in itself, but she dared not run the risk of omitting it. Come, my soul, is there not here a lesson for you? Have you been attentive to all your Lord's will, even though some of his commands should seem non-essential? Have you observed in his own way the two ordinances of believers' baptism and the Lord's Supper? These neglected, argue much unloving disobedience in your heart. Be henceforth in all things blameless, even to the tying of a thread, if that is commanded.

This act of Rahab illustrates a yet more solemn lesson. Have I implicitly trusted in the precious blood of Jesus? Have I tied the scarlet cord, as with a Gordian knot in my window, so that my trust can never be removed? Or can I look out towards the Dead Sea of my sins, or the Jerusalem of my hopes, without seeing the blood, and seeing all things in connection with its blessed power? The passerby can see a cord of so conspicuous a colour, if it hangs from the window: it will be well for me if my life makes the efficacy of the atonement conspicuous to all onlookers. What is there to be ashamed of? Let men or demons gaze if they will, the blood is my boast and my song. My soul, there is one who will see that scarlet line, even when from weakness of faith you cannot see it yourself; Jehovah, the Avenger, will see it and pass over you. Jericho's walls fell flat: Rahab's house was on the wall, and yet it stood unmoved; my nature is built into the wall of humanity, and yet when destruction strikes the race, I shall be secure. My soul, tie the scarlet thread in the window afresh, and rest in peace.

And you said, "I will surely do you good." *{Genesis 32:12}*

When Jacob was on the other side of the brook Jabbok, and Esau was coming with armed men, he earnestly sought God's protection, and as a master reason he pleaded, "And you said, 'I will surely do you good.' " Oh, the force of that plea! He was holding God to his word — "You said." The attribute of God's faithfulness is a splendid horn of the altar to lay hold upon; but the promise, which has in it the attribute and something more, is an even more mighty holdfast — "You said, I will surely do you good." And has *he* said, and shall he not do it? "Let God be true, and every man a liar." Shall *he* not be true? Shall *he* not keep his word? Shall not every word that comes out of his lips stand true and be fulfilled? Solomon, at the opening of the temple, used this same mighty plea. He pleaded with God to remember the word which he had spoken to his father David, and to bless that place. When a man gives a promissory note, his honour is engaged; he signs his hand, and he must discharge it when the due date comes, or else he loses credit. It shall never be said that God dishonours his bills. The credit of the Most High never was impeached, and never shall be. He is punctual to the moment: he never is before his time, but he never is behind it. Search God's Word through, and compare it with the experience of God's people, and you shall find the two tally from the first to the last. Many a hoary patriarch has said with Joshua, "Not one thing has failed of all the good things which the Lord your God spoke concerning you; all are come to pass." If you have a divine promise, you need not plead it with an "if," you may urge it with certainty. The Lord meant to fulfil the promise, or he would not have given it. God does not give his words merely to quiet us, and to keep us hopeful for a while with the intention of putting us off at last; but when he speaks, it is because he means to do as he has said.

Behold, the veil of the temple was torn in two from the top to the bottom. *{Matthew 27:51}*

No mean miracle was performed in the tearing of so strong and thick a veil; but it was not intended merely as a display of power — this taught us many lessons. *The old law of ordinances was put away*, and like a worn out vesture, torn and laid aside. When Jesus died, the sacrifices were all finished, because all were fulfilled in him, and therefore the place of their presentation was marked with an evident token of decay. That tear also *revealed all the hidden things of the old dispensation*: the mercy seat could now be seen, and the glory of God gleamed forth above it. By the death of our Lord Jesus we have a clear revelation of God, for he was "not as Moses, who put a veil over his face." Life and immortality are now brought to light, and things which have been hidden since the foundation of the world are revealed in him. *The annual ceremony of atonement was thus abolished. The atoning blood* which was once every year sprinkled within the veil, was now offered once and for all by the great High Priest, and therefore the place of the symbolic rite was broken up. No blood of bulls or of lambs is needed now, for Jesus has entered within the veil with his own blood. Hence, *access to God is now permitted*, and is the privilege of every believer in Christ Jesus. There is no small space laid open through which we may peer at the mercy seat, but the tear reaches from the top to the bottom. We may come with boldness to the throne of the heavenly grace. Shall we err if we say that the opening of the Holy of Holies in this marvellous manner by our Lord's expiring cry was *the type of the opening of the gates of paradise* to all the saints by virtue of the Passion? Our bleeding Lord has the key of heaven; he opens and no man shuts; let us enter in with him into the heavenly places, and sit with him there until our common enemies shall be made his footstool.

April 19 — Evening

The Amen. *{Revelation 3:14}*

The word *amen* solemnly confirms what went before; and Jesus is the great Confirmer; immutable, for ever is "the Amen" in all *his promises. Sinner*, I would comfort you with this reflection. Jesus Christ said, "Come to me all you who labour and are heavy laden, and I will give you rest." If you come to him, he will say "amen" in your soul; his promise shall be true *to you*. He said in the days of his flesh, "I will not break the bruised reed." Oh, you poor, broken, bruised heart, if you come to him, he will say "Amen" to you, and that shall be true in *your* soul as in hundreds of cases in bygone years. *Christian*, is not this very comforting to you also, that there is not a word which has gone out of the Saviour's lips which he has ever retracted? The words of Jesus shall stand when heaven and earth shall pass away. If you get a hold of only half a promise, you shall find it true. Beware of him who is called "Clip promise," who will destroy much of the comfort of God's Word.

Jesus is "Yea and Amen" in all *his offices*. He was a Priest to pardon and cleanse once, he is Amen as Priest still. He was a King to rule and reign for his people, and to defend them with his mighty arm, he is an Amen King, the same still. He was a Prophet of old, to foretell good things to come, his lips are most sweet, and still drop with honey — he is an Amen Prophet. He is Amen concerning the merit of his blood; he is Amen concerning his righteousness. That sacred robe shall remain most fair and glorious when nature shall decay. He is Amen in every single title which he bears; your Husband, never seeking a divorce; your Friend, sticking closer than a brother; your Shepherd, with you in death's dark vale; your Help and your Deliverer; your Castle and your High Tower; the Horn of your strength, your confidence, your joy, your all in all, and your "Yea and Amen" in all.

April 20 — Morning

{Daily Reading: 2 Samuel 23:1–24:25} {Quick Study: 1 Kings 7:1–8:66}

**That through death he might destroy him
who had the power of death.** *{Hebrews 2:14}*

Oh, child of God, death has lost its sting, because the devil's power over it is destroyed. Then cease to fear dying. Ask grace from God the Holy Spirit, that by an intimate knowledge and a firm belief of your Redeemer's death, you may be strengthened for that dread hour. Living near the cross of Calvary you may think of death with pleasure, and welcome it when it comes with intense delight. It is sweet to die in the Lord; it is a covenant blessing to sleep in Jesus. Death is no longer banishment, it is a return from exile, a going home to the many mansions where the loved ones already dwell. The distance between glorified spirits in heaven and militant saints on earth seems great; but it is not so. We are not far from home — a moment will bring us there. The sail is spread; the soul is launched upon the deep. How long will be its voyage? How many wearying winds must beat upon the sail before it shall be reefed in the port of peace? How long shall that soul be tossed upon the waves before it comes to that sea which knows no storm? Listen to the answer, "Absent from the body, present with the Lord." That ship has just departed, but it is already at its haven. It had only spread its sail and it was there. Like that ship of old, upon the Lake of Galilee, a storm had tossed it, but Jesus said, "Peace, be still," and *immediately* it came to land. Do not think that a long period intervenes between the instant of death and the eternity of glory. When the eyes close on earth they open in heaven. The horses of fire are not an instant on the road. Then, oh child of God, what is there for you to fear in death, seeing that through the death of your Lord its curse and sting are destroyed? And now it is only a Jacob's ladder whose foot is in the dark grave, but its top reaches to glory everlasting.

April 20 — Evening

Fight the Lord's battles. *{1 Samuel 18:17}*

The sacramental host of God's elect is warring still on earth, Jesus Christ being the Captain of their salvation. He has said, "Lo! I am with you always, even to the end of the world." Listen to the shouts of war! Now let the people of God stand firm in their ranks, and let no man's heart fail him. It is true that just now in England the battle is turned against us, and unless the Lord Jesus shall lift his sword, we do not know what may become of the church of God in this land; but let us be of good courage, and play the man. There never was a day when Protestantism seemed to tremble more in the scales than now that a fierce effort is making to restore the Romish antichrist to his ancient seat. We greatly need a bold voice and a strong hand to preach and publish the old gospel for which martyrs bled and confessors died. The Saviour is, by his Spirit, still on earth; let this cheer us. He is always in the midst of the fight, and therefore the battle is not doubtful. And as the conflict rages, what a sweet satisfaction it is to know that the Lord Jesus, in his office as our great Intercessor, is prevalently pleading for his people! Oh anxious gazer, do not look so much at the battle below, for there you shall be enshrouded in smoke, and amazed with garments rolled in blood; but lift your eyes up there where the Saviour lives and pleads, for while he intercedes, the cause of God is safe. Let us fight as if it all depended upon us, but let us look up and know that all depends upon him.

Now, by the lilies of Christian purity, and by the roses of the Saviour's atonement, by the roes and by the hinds of the field, we charge you who are lovers of Jesus to do valiantly in the Holy War, for truth and righteousness, for the kingdom and crown jewels of your Master. Onward! "For the battle is not yours but God's."

April 21 — Morning

{Daily Reading: 1 Kings 1:1–2:25} {Quick Study: 1 Kings 9:1–11:43}

I know that my Redeemer lives. *{Job 19:25}*

The marrow of Job's comfort lies in that little word "my" — "my Redeemer," and in the fact that the Redeemer lives. Oh! to get hold of a living Christ. We must have a share in him before we can enjoy him. What is gold in the mine to me? Men are beggars in Peru, and beg their bread in California. It is gold in my purse which will satisfy my necessities, by purchasing the bread I need. So a Redeemer who does not redeem *me*, an Avenger who will never stand up for *my* blood, of what good is that? Do not rest content until by faith you can say, "Yes, I cast myself upon my living Lord; and he is mine." It may be you hold him with a feeble hand; you half think it is presumption to say, "He lives as *my* Redeemer," yet, remember if you only have faith as a grain of mustard seed, that little faith *entitles* you to say it. But there is also another word here, expressive of Job's strong confidence, *"I know."* To say, "I hope so, I trust so," is comforting; and there are thousands in the fold of Jesus who hardly ever get much further. But to reach the essence of consolation you *must* say, "I know." Ifs, buts, and perhapses, are sure murderers of peace and comfort. Doubts are dreary things in times of sorrow. Like wasps they sting the soul! If I have any suspicion that Christ is not mine, then there is vinegar mingled with the gall of death; but if I know that Jesus lives for me, then darkness is not dark: even the night is light around me. Surely if Job, in those ages before the coming and advent of Christ, could say, "I know," we should not speak less positively. God forbid that our positiveness should be presumption. Let us see that our evidences are right, lest we build upon an ungrounded hope; and then let us not be satisfied with the mere foundation, for it is from the upper rooms that we get the widest prospect. A living Redeemer, truly mine, is unspeakable joy.

April 21 — Evening

Who is even at the right hand of God. *{Romans 8:34}*

He who was once despised and rejected by men now occupies the honourable position of a beloved and honoured Son. The right hand of God is *the place of majesty and favour*. Our Lord Jesus is his people's representative. When he died for them they had rest; he rose again for them, they had liberty; when he sat down at his Father's right hand, they had favour, and honour, and dignity. The raising and elevation of Christ is the elevation, the acceptance, and enshrinement, the glorifying of all his people, for he is their Head and Representative. This sitting at the right hand of God, then, is to be viewed as the acceptance of the person of the Surety, the reception of the Representative, and therefore, the acceptance of our souls. Oh, saint, see in this your sure freedom from condemnation. "Who is he who condemns?" Who shall condemn the men who are in Jesus at the right hand of God?

The right hand is *the place of power*. Christ at the right hand of God has all power in heaven and in earth. Who shall fight against the people who have such power vested in their Captain? Oh, my soul, what can destroy you if Omnipotence is your helper? If the impregnable defence of the Almighty covers you, what sword can strike you? Rest secure. If Jesus is your all-prevailing King, and has trodden your enemies beneath his feet; if sin, death, and hell are all vanquished by him, and you are represented in him, by no possibility can you be destroyed.

> Jesus' tremendous name puts all our foes to flight:
> Jesus, the meek, the angry Lamb, a Lion is in fight.

> By all hell's host withstood; we all hell's host o'erthrow;
> And conquering them, through Jesus' blood
>   we still to conquer go.

April 22 — Morning

{Daily Reading: 1 Kings 2:26–4:34} {Quick Study: 1 Kings 12:1–13:34}

God has exalted him. *{Acts 5:31}*

Jesus, our Lord, once crucified, dead and buried, now sits upon the throne of glory. The highest place that heaven affords is his by undisputed right. It is sweet to remember that the exaltation of Christ in heaven is a *representative exaltation*. He is exalted at the Father's right hand, and though as Jehovah he had eminent glories, in which finite creatures cannot share, yet as the Mediator, the honours which Jesus wears in heaven are the heritage of all the saints. It is delightful to reflect how close Christ's union is with his people. We are actually one with him; we are members of his body; and his exaltation is *our* exaltation. He will give us the privilege of sitting upon his throne, even as he has overcome, and is seated with his Father on his throne; he has a crown, and he gives us crowns too; he has a throne, but he is not content with having a throne for himself, on his right hand there must be his queen, arrayed in "gold of Ophir." He cannot be glorified without his bride. Look up, believer, to Jesus now; let the eye of your faith see him with many crowns upon his head; and remember that you will one day be like him, when you shall see him as he is; you shall not be so great as he is, you shall not be so divine, but still you shall, in a measure, share the same honours, and enjoy the same happiness and the same dignity which he possesses. Be content to live unknown for a little while, and to walk your weary way through the fields of poverty, or up the hills of affliction; for by and by you shall reign with Christ, for he has "made us kings and priests to God, and we shall reign for ever and ever." Oh! wonderful thought for the children of God! We have Christ as our glorious representative in heaven's courts *now*, and soon he will come and receive us to himself, to be with him there, to behold his glory, and to share his joy.

April 22 — Evening

You shall not be afraid of the terror by night. {*Psalms 91:5*}

What is this terror? It may be the cry of fire, or the noise of thieves, or imagined appearances, or the shriek of sudden sickness or death. We live in the world of death and sorrow, we may therefore look for ills as well in the night watches as beneath the glare of the broiling sun. Nor should this alarm us, for whatever the terror may be, the promise is that the believer shall not be afraid. Why should he? Let us make it more personal, why should *we*? God our Father is here, and will be here all through the lonely hours; he is an almighty Watcher, a sleepless Guardian, a faithful Friend. Nothing can happen without his direction, for even hell itself is under his control. Darkness is not dark to him. He has promised to be a wall of fire around his people — and who can break through such a barrier? Worldlings may well be afraid, for they have an angry God above them, a guilty conscience within them, and a yawning hell beneath them; but we who rest in Jesus are saved from all these through rich mercy. If we give way to foolish fear we shall dishonour our profession, and lead others to doubt the reality of godliness. We ought to be afraid of being afraid, lest we should vex the Holy Spirit by foolish distrust. Down, then, oh dismal forebodings and groundless apprehensions, God has not forgotten to be gracious, nor shut up his tender mercies; it may be night in the soul, but there should be no terror, for the God of love does not change. Children of light may walk in darkness, but they are not therefore cast away, indeed, they are now enabled to prove their adoption by trusting in their Heavenly Father as hypocrites cannot do.

> Though the night be dark and dreary,
> Darkness cannot hide from thee;
> You are he, who, never weary,
> Watch where your people be.

April 23 — Morning

{Daily Reading: 1 Kings 5:1–7:51} {Quick Study: 1 Kings 14:1–15:34}

Yet, in all these things we are more than conquerors through the one who loved us. *{Romans 8:37}*

We go to Christ for forgiveness, and then too often look to the law for power to fight our sins. Paul thus rebukes us, "Oh foolish Galatians, who has bewitched you, that you should not obey the truth? This I would only learn from you, did you receive the Spirit by the works of the law, or by the hearing of faith? Are you so foolish? Having begun in the Spirit, are you now made perfect by the flesh?" Take your sins to Christ's cross, for the old man can only be crucified there: we are crucified *with him*. The only weapon to fight sin with is the spear which pierced the side of Jesus. To give an illustration — you want to overcome an angry temper, how do you go to work? It is very possible you have never tried the right way of going to Jesus with it. How did I get salvation? I came to Jesus just as I was, and I trusted him to save me. I must kill my angry temper in the same way. It is the only way in which I can ever kill it. I must go to the cross with it, and say to Jesus, "Lord, I trust you to deliver me from it." This is the only way to give it a death blow. Are you covetous? Do you feel the world entangle you? You may struggle against this evil as long as you please, but if it is your besetting sin, you will never be delivered from it in any way except by the blood of Jesus. Take it to Christ. Tell him, "Lord, I have trusted you, and your name is Jesus, for you do save your people from their sins; Lord, this is one of my sins; save me from it!" Ordinances are nothing without Christ as a means of mortification. Your prayers, and your repentances, and your tears — all of them put together — are worth nothing apart from him. "No one but Jesus can do helpless sinners good," or helpless saints either. You must be conquerors through him who has loved you, if conquerors at all. Our laurels must grow among his olives in Gethsemane.

**Lo, in the midst of the throne . . . stood a Lamb
as if had been slain.** *{Revelation 5:6}*

Why should our exalted Lord appear in his wounds in glory? The wounds of Jesus are his glories, his jewels, his sacred ornaments. To the eye of the believer, Jesus is surpassingly fair because he is "white and ruddy"; white with innocence, and ruddy with his own blood. We see him as the lily of matchless purity, and as the rose crimsoned with his own gore. Christ is lovely upon Olivet and Tabor, and by the sea, but oh! there never was such a matchless Christ as he who hung upon the cross. There we beheld all his beauties in perfection, all his attributes developed, all his love drawn out, all his character expressed. Beloved, the wounds of Jesus are far more fair in our eyes than all the splendour and pomp of kings. The thorny crown is more than an imperial diadem. It is true that he does not now bear the sceptre of reed, but there was a glory in it that never flashed from sceptre of gold. Jesus wears the appearance of a slain lamb as his court dress in which he wooed our souls, and redeemed them by his complete atonement. Nor are these only the ornaments of Christ: they are the *trophies* of his love and of his victory. He has divided the spoil with the strong. He has redeemed for himself a great multitude whom no man can number, and these scars are the memorials of the fight. Ah! If Christ thus loves to retain the thought of his sufferings for his people, *how precious should his wounds be to us!*

> Behold how every wound of his
> A precious balm distils,
> Which heals the scars that sin had made,
> And cures all mortal ills.
>
> Those wounds are mouths that preach his grace;
> The ensigns of his love;
> The seals of our expected bliss
> In paradise above.

April 24 — Morning

{Daily Reading: 1 Kings 8:1–8:66} {Quick Study: 1 Kings 16:1–18:46}

And because of all this we make
a sure covenant. *{Nehemiah 9:38}*

There are many occasions in our experience when we may very rightly, and with benefit, renew our covenant with God. After *recovery from sickness* when, like Hezekiah, we have had a new term of years added to our life, we may fitly do it. After any deliverance from trouble, when our joys bud forth anew, let us again visit the foot of the cross, and renew our consecration. Especially, let us do this after any *sin which has grieved the Holy Spirit*, or brought dishonour upon the cause of God; let us then look to that blood which can make us whiter than snow, and again offer ourselves to the Lord. We should not only let our troubles confirm our dedication to God, but *our prosperity* should do the same. If we ever meet with occasions which deserve to be called "crowning mercies," then, surely, if he has crowned us, we ought also to crown our God; let us bring forth anew all the jewels of the divine regalia which have been stored in the jewel chest of our heart, and let our God sit upon the throne of our love, arrayed in royal apparel. If we would learn to profit by our prosperity, we should not need so much adversity. If we would gather from a kiss all the good it might confer upon us, we would not so often smart under the rod. Have we recently received some blessing which we little expected? Has the Lord put our feet in a large room? Can we sing of mercies multiplied? Then this is the day to put our hand upon the horns of the altar, and say, "Bind me here, my God; bind me here with cords, even for ever." Inasmuch as we need the fulfilment of new promises from God, let us offer renewed prayers so that our old vows may not be dishonoured. Let us this morning make with him a sure covenant, because of the pains of Jesus which for the last month we have been considering with gratitude.

The flowers appear on the earth; the time of
the singing of birds is come, and the voice of the
turtledove is heard in our land. *{Song of Solomon 2:12}*

Sweet is the season of spring: the long and dreary winter helps us to appreciate its genial warmth, and its promise of summer enhances its present delights. After periods of depression of spirit, it is delightful to behold again the light of the Sun of Righteousness; then our slumbering graces rise from their lethargy, like the crocus and the daffodil from their beds of earth; then our heart is made merry with delightful notes of gratitude, far more melodious than the warbling of birds — and the comforting assurance of peace, infinitely more delightful than the turtledove's note, is heard within the soul. Now is the time for the soul to seek communion with her Beloved; now must she rise from her native sordidness, and come away from her old associations. If we do not hoist the sail when the breeze is favourable, we shall be blameworthy: times of refreshing ought not to pass over us unimproved. When Jesus himself visits us in tenderness, and entreats us to arise, can we be so base as to refuse his request? He has himself risen so that he may draw us after him: he now by his Holy Spirit has revived us, so that we may, in newness of life, ascend into the heavenlies, and hold communion with himself. Let our wintry state suffice us for coldness and indifference; when the Lord creates a spring within, let our sap flow with vigour, and our branch blossom with high resolve. Oh, Lord, if it is not springtime in my chilly heart, please make it so, for I am heartily weary of living at a distance from you. Oh! The long and dreary winter, when will you bring it to an end? Come, Holy Spirit, and renew my soul! Quicken me! Restore me, and have mercy on me! This very night I would earnestly implore the Lord to take pity upon his servant, and send me a happy revival of spiritual life!

April 25 — Morning

{*Daily Reading: 1 Kings 9:1–11:43*} {*Quick Study: 1 Kings 19:1–20:43*}

**Rise up my love, my fair one,
and come away.** {*Song of Solomon 2:10*}

Lo, I hear the voice of my Beloved! He speaks to *me!* Fair weather is smiling upon the face of the earth, and he would not have me spiritually asleep while nature is all around me awaking from her winter's rest. He bids me "rise up," and well he may, for I have been lying among the pots of worldliness long enough. He is risen, I am risen in him, why then should I cleave to the dust? From lower loves, desires, pursuits, and aspirations, I would rise towards him. He calls me by the sweet title of "my love," and considers me fair; this is a good argument for my rising. If he has thus exalted me, and thinks me thus comely, how can I linger in the tents of Kedar and find congenial associates among the sons of men? He bids me "come away." He calls me further and further away from everything selfish, grovelling, worldly, and sinful; indeed, he calls me from the outwardly religious world which does not know him, and has no sympathy with the mystery of the higher life. "Come away" has no harsh sound in it to my ear, for what is there to hold me in this wilderness of vanity and sin? Oh, my Lord, I wish that I could come away, but I am taken among the thorns, and cannot escape from them as I wish. I wish, if it were possible, to have neither eyes, nor ears, nor heart for sin. You call me to yourself by saying, "Come away," and this is a melodious call indeed. To come to you is to come home from exile, to come to land out of the raging storm, to come to rest after long labour, to come to the goal of my desires and the summit of my wishes. But Lord, how can a stone rise, how can a lump of clay come away from the horrible pit? Oh, raise me, draw me. Your grace can do it. Send forth your Holy Spirit to kindle sacred flames of love in my heart, and I will continue to rise until I leave life and time behind me, and indeed come away.

April 25 — Evening

**If any man hears my voice, and opens the door,
I will come in to him.** *{Revelation 3:20}*

What is your desire this evening? Is it set upon heavenly things? Do you long to enjoy the high doctrine of eternal love? Do you desire liberty in very close communion with God? Do you aspire to know the heights, and depths, and lengths, and breadths? Then you must draw near to Jesus; you must get a clear view of him in his preciousness and completeness: you must view him in his work, in his offices, in his person. He who understands Christ receives an anointing from the Holy One, by which he knows all things. Christ is the great master key of all the chambers of God: there is no treasure house of God which will not open and yield up all its wealth to the soul that lives near to Jesus. Are you saying, "Oh, that he would dwell in my bosom?" "Oh, that he would make my heart his dwelling place for ever?" Open the door, beloved, and he will come into your souls. He has long been knocking, and all with this object, that he may sup with you, and you with him. *He sups with you* because you find the house or the heart, and *you with him* because he brings the provisions. He could not sup with you if it were not in your heart, for you find the house; nor could you sup with him, for you have a bare cupboard, if he did not bring provision with him. Fling wide, then, the portals of your soul. He will come with that love which you long to feel; he will come with that joy into which you cannot work your poor depressed spirit; he will bring the peace which you do not have now; he will come with his flagons of wine and sweet apples of love, and cheer you until you have no other sickness except that of "love overpowering, love divine." Only open the door to him, drive out his enemies, give him the keys of your heart, and he will dwell there for ever. Oh, wondrous love, that brings such a guest to dwell in such a heart!

April 26 — Morning

{Daily Reading: 1 Kings 12:1–13:34} {Quick Study: 1 Kings 21:1–22:53}

This do in remembrance of me. *{1 Corinthians 11:24}*

It seems then, that Christians may forget Christ! There could be no need for this loving exhortation if there were not a fearful supposition that our memories might prove treacherous. Nor is this a mere supposition: it is, alas! too well confirmed in our experience, not as a possibility, but as a lamentable fact. It appears almost impossible that those who have been redeemed by the blood of the dying Lamb, and loved with an everlasting love by the eternal Son of God, should forget that gracious Saviour; but, if startling to the ear, it is, alas! too apparent to the eye to allow us to deny the crime. Forget him who never forgot us! Forget him who poured out his blood for our sins! Forget him who loved us even to the death! Can it be possible? Yes, it is not only possible, but conscience confesses that it is too sadly a fault with all of us, that we permit him to be as a wayfaring man tarrying only for a night. He whom we should make the abiding tenant of our memories is only a visitor in it. The cross where one would think that memory would linger, and unmindfulness would be an unknown intruder, is desecrated by the feet of forgetfulness. Does not your conscience say that this is true? Do you not find yourselves forgetful of Jesus? Some creature steals away your heart, and you are unmindful of him upon whom your affection ought to be set. Some earthly business engrosses your attention when you should fix your eye steadily upon the cross. It is the incessant turmoil of the world, the constant attraction of earthly things which takes away the soul from Christ. While memory too well preserves a poisonous weed, it allows the rose of Sharon to wither. Let us charge ourselves to bind a heavenly forget-me-not about our hearts for Jesus our Beloved, and, whatever else we let slip, let us firmly hold onto him.

April 26 — Evening

Blessed is he who watches. *{Revelation 16:15}*

We die daily," said the apostle. This was the life of the early Christians; they went everywhere with their lives in their hands. We are not today called to pass through the same fearful persecutions: if we were, the Lord would give us grace to bear the test; but the tests of Christian life, at the present moment, though outwardly not so terrible, are yet more likely to overcome us than even those of the fiery age. We have to bear the sneer of the world — that is little; its blandishments, its soft words, its oily speeches, its fawning, its hypocrisy, are far worse. Our danger is lest we grow rich and become proud, lest we give ourselves up to the fashions of this present evil world, and lose our faith. Or if wealth is not the trial, worldly care is quite as mischievous. If we cannot be torn in pieces by the roaring lion, if we may be hugged to death by the bear, the devil could care less which it is, as long as he destroys our love for Christ, and our confidence in him. I fear that the Christian church is far more likely to lose her integrity in these soft and silken days than in those rougher times. We must be awake now, for we traverse the enchanted ground, and are most likely to fall asleep to our own undoing, unless our faith in Jesus is a reality, and our love for Jesus a vehement flame. Many in these days of easy profession are likely to prove to be tares, and not wheat; hypocrites with fair masks on their faces, but not the true born children of the living God. Christian, do not think that these are times in which you can dispense with watchfulness or with holy ardour; you need these things more than ever, and may God the eternal Spirit display his omnipotence in you, so that you may be able to say, in all these softer things, as well as in the rougher, "We are more than conquerors through him who loved us."

April 27 — Morning

{Daily Reading: 1 Kings 14:1–15:34} {Quick Study: 2 Kings 1:1–3:27}

God, even our own God. *{Psalms 67:6}*

It is strange how little use we make of the spiritual blessings which God gives us, but it is stranger still how little use we make of God himself. Although he is "our own God," we apply ourselves very little to him, and ask very little from him. How seldom do we ask counsel at the hands of the Lord! How often do we go about our business, without seeking his guidance! In our troubles how constantly do we strive to bear our burdens ourselves, instead of casting them upon the Lord, so that he may sustain us! This is not because we may not, for the Lord seems to say, "I am yours, soul, come and make use of me as you wish; you may freely come to my storehouse, and the more often the more welcome." It is our own fault if we do not freely use the riches of our God. Then, since you have such a friend, and he invites you, draw from him daily. Never suffer lack while you have a God to go to; never fear or faint while you have God to help you; go to your treasure and take whatever you need — there is all that you can need. Learn the divine skill of making God all things to you. He can supply you with all, or, better still, he can be to you instead of all. Let me urge you, then, to make use of your God. Make use of him *in prayer*. Go to him often, because he is *your* God. Oh, will you fail to use so great a privilege? Flee to him, tell him all your needs. Use him constantly *by faith* at all times. If some dark providence has overshadowed you, use your God as a "sun"; if some strong enemy has attacked you, find in Jehovah a "shield," for he is a sun and shield to his people. If you have lost your way in the mazes of life, use him as a "guide," for he will direct you. Whatever you are, and wherever you are, remember God is just *what* you need, and just *where* you need him, and that he can do *all* you need.

April 27 — Evening

The Lord is King
for ever and ever. *{Psalms 10:16}*

Jesus Christ is no despotic claimant of *divine right*, but he is really and truly the Lord's anointed! "It has pleased the Father that in him should all fulness dwell." God has given to him all power and all authority. As the Son of man, he is now head over all things to his church, and he reigns over heaven, and earth, and hell, with the keys of life and death at his belt. Certain princes have delighted to call themselves kings by the *popular will*, and certainly our Lord Jesus Christ is such in his church. If it could be put to the vote whether he should be King in the church, every believing heart would crown him. Oh, that we could crown him more gloriously than we do! We would count no expense to be wasted that could glorify Christ. Suffering would be pleasure, and loss would be gain, if by it we could surround his brow with brighter crowns, and make him more glorious in the eyes of men and angels. Yes, he shall reign. Long live the King! All hail to you, King Jesus! Go out, oh virgin souls who love your Lord, bow at his feet, strew his way with the lilies of your love, and the roses of your gratitude: "Bring out the royal diadem, and crown him Lord of all." Moreover, our Lord Jesus is King in Zion by *right of conquest*: he has taken and carried by storm the hearts of his people, and has slain their enemies who held them in cruel bondage. In the Red Sea of his own blood, our Redeemer has drowned the Pharaoh of our sins: shall he not be King in Jeshurun? He has delivered us from the iron yoke and heavy curse of the law: shall not the Liberator be crowned? We are his portion, whom he has taken out of the hand of the Amorite with his sword and with his bow: who shall snatch his conquest from his hand? All hail, King Jesus! we gladly submit to your gentle sway! Rule in our hearts for ever, oh lovely Prince of Peace.

April 28 — Morning

{Daily Reading: 1 Kings 16:1–18:46} {Quick Study: 2 Kings 4:1–5:27}

Remember the word to your servant,
upon which you have caused me to hope. *{Psalms 119:49}*

Whatever your special need may be, you may readily find some promise in the Bible suited to it. Are you faint and feeble because your way is rough and you are weary? Here is the promise — "He gives power to the faint." When you read such a promise, take it back to the great Promiser, and ask him to fulfil his own word. Are you seeking after Christ, and thirsting for closer communion with him? This promise shines like a star upon you — "Blessed are those who hunger and thirst after righteousness, for they shall be filled." Take that promise to the throne continually; do not plead anything else, but go to God over and over again with this — "Lord, you have said it, do as you have said." Are you distressed because of sin, and burdened with the heavy load of your iniquities? Listen to these words — "I, even I, am he who blots out your transgressions, and will no more remember your sins." You have no merit of your own to plead why he should pardon you, but plead his written engagements and he will perform them. Are you afraid lest you should not be able to hold on to the end, lest, after having thought yourself to be a child of God, you should prove a castaway? If that is your state, take this word of grace to the throne and plead it: "The mountains may depart, and the hills may be removed, but the covenant of my love shall not depart from you." If you have lost the sweet sense of the Saviour's presence, and are seeking him with a sorrowful heart, remember the promises: "Return to me, and I will return to you"; "For a small moment I have forsaken you, but with great mercies I will gather you." Banquet your faith upon God's own word, and whatever your fears or needs, go to the Bank of Faith with your Father's note in hand, saying, "Remember the word to your servant, upon which you have caused me to hope."

April 28 — Evening

All the house of Israel are impudent and hardhearted. *{Ezekiel 3:7}*

Are there no exceptions? No, not one. Even the favoured nation are thus described. Are the best so bad, then what must the worst be? Come, my heart, consider how far you have a share in this universal accusation, and while considering, be ready to take shame to yourself in which you may have been guilty. The first charge is *impudence*, or hardness of forehead, a lack of holy shame, an unhallowed boldness in evil. Before my conversion, I could sin and feel no compunction, hear of my guilt and yet remain proud, and even confess my iniquity and reveal no inward humiliation on account of it. For a sinner to go to God's house and pretend to pray to him and praise him argues a brazen facedness of the worst kind! Alas! Since the day of my new birth I have doubted my Lord to his face, murmured unblushingly in his presence, worshipped before him in a slovenly manner, and sinned without bewailing myself concerning it. If my forehead were not as adamant, harder than flint, I would have far more holy fear, and a far deeper contrition of spirit. Woe is me, I am one of the impudent house of Israel. The second charge is *hardheartedness*, and I must not venture to plead innocent here. Once I had nothing but a heart of stone, and although through grace I now have a new and fleshy heart, much of my former obduracy remains. I am not affected by the death of Jesus as I ought to be; neither am I moved by the ruin of my fellow men, the wickedness of the times, the chastisement of my Heavenly Father, and my own failures, as I should be. Oh, that my heart would melt at the recital of my Saviour's sufferings and death. Oh, that I were rid of this heavy millstone within me, this hateful body of death. Blessed be the name of the Lord, the disease is not incurable, the Saviour's precious blood is the universal solvent, and it will effectually soften me, even me, until my heart melts as wax before the fire.

April 29 — Morning

{Daily Reading: 1 Kings 19:1–20:43} {Quick Study: 2 Kings 6:1–8:29}

You are my hope in the day of evil. *{Jeremiah 17:17}*

The path of the Christian is not always bright with sunshine; he has his seasons of darkness and of storm. True, it is written in God's word, "Her ways are ways of pleasantness, and all her paths are peace," and it is a great truth that religion is calculated to give a man happiness below as well as bliss above; but experience tells us that if the course of the just is "as the shining light that shines more and more to the perfect day," yet sometimes *that* light is eclipsed. At certain times clouds cover the believer's sun, and he walks in darkness and sees no light. There are many who have rejoiced in the presence of God for a season; they have basked in the sunshine in the earlier stages of their Christian career; they have walked along the "green pastures" by the side of the "still waters," but suddenly they find the glorious sky is clouded; instead of the land of Goshen they have to tread the sandy desert; in the place of sweet waters, they find troubled streams, bitter to their taste, and they say, "Surely, if I were a child of God, this would not happen." Oh! Do not say so, you who are walking in darkness. The best of God's saints must drink the wormwood; the dearest of his children must bear the cross. No Christian has enjoyed perpetual prosperity; no believer can always keep his harp from the willows. Perhaps the Lord allotted you at first a smooth and unclouded path, because you were weak and timid. He tempered the wind to the shorn lamb, but now that you are stronger in the spiritual life, you must enter upon the riper and rougher experience of God's fully grown children. We need winds and tempests to exercise our faith, to tear off the rotten bough of self-dependence, and to root us more firmly in Christ. The day of evil reveals to us the value of our glorious hope.

The Lord takes pleasure in his people. *{Psalms 149:4}*

How comprehensive is the love of Jesus! There is no part of his people's interests which he does not consider, and there is nothing which concerns their welfare which is not important to him. Not merely does he think of you, believer, as an immortal being, but as a mortal being, too. Do not deny it or doubt it: "The very hairs of your head are all numbered." "The steps of a good man are ordered by the Lord: and he delights in his way." It would be a sad thing for us if this mantle of love did not cover all our concerns, for what mischief might come to us in that part of our life which did not come under our gracious Lord's inspection! Believer, rest assured that the heart of Jesus cares about your lowly affairs. The breadth of his tender love is such that you may resort to him in all matters; for in all your afflictions he is afflicted, and just as a father pities his children, so he pities you. The simplest interests of all his saints are entirely borne upon the broad bosom of the Son of God. Oh, what a heart is his, that does not merely comprehend his people, but comprehends also the diverse and innumerable concerns of all those people! Do you think, oh Christian, that you can measure the love of Christ? Think of what his love has brought you — justification, adoption, sanctification, and eternal life! The riches of his goodness are unsearchable; you shall never be able to count them or even conceive of them. Oh, the breadth of the love of Christ! Shall such a love as this have half our hearts? Shall it have a cold love in return? Shall Jesus' marvellous lovingkindness and tender care meet with only a faint response and tardy acknowledgment? Oh, my soul, tune your harp to a glad song of thanksgiving! Go to your rest rejoicing, for you are no desolate wanderer, but a beloved child, watched over, cared for, supplied, and defended by your Lord.

April 30 — Morning

{Daily Reading: 1 Kings 21:1–22:53} {Quick Study: 2 Kings 9:1–10:36}

And all the children of Israel murmured. *{Numbers 14:2}*

There are murmurers among Christians now, as there were in the camp of Israel of old. There are those who, when the rod falls, cry out against the afflictive dispensation. They ask, "Why am I thus afflicted? What have I done to be chastened in this manner?" A word with you, oh murmurer! Why should you murmur against the dispensations of your Heavenly Father? Can he treat you more harshly than you deserve? Consider what a rebel you were once, but he has pardoned you! Surely, if he in his wisdom sees fit now to chasten you, you should not complain. After all, are you punished as harshly as your sins deserve? Consider the corruption which is in your heart, and then will you wonder that there needs to be so much of the rod to beat it out? Weigh yourself, and discern how much dross is mingled with your gold; and do you think the fire is too hot to purge away so much dross as you have? Does that proud rebellious spirit of yours not prove that your heart is not thoroughly sanctified? Are not those murmuring words contrary to the holy submissive nature of God's children? Is the correction not needed? But if you *will* murmur against the chastening, take heed, for it will go hard with murmurers. God always chastises his children twice, if they do not bear the first stroke patiently. But know one thing — "He does not afflict willingly, nor grieve the children of men." All his corrections are sent in love, to purify you, and to draw you nearer to himself. Surely it must help you to bear the chastening with resignation if you are able to recognise your *Father's* hand. For "whom the Lord loves he chastens, and scourges every son whom he receives. If you endure chastening, God deals with you as with sons." "Do not murmur as some of them also murmured and were destroyed by the destroyer."

April 30 — Evening

How precious also are your thoughts
to me, oh God. *{Psalms 139:17}*

Divine omniscience affords no comfort to the ungodly mind, but to the child of God it overflows with consolation. God is always thinking about us, never turns aside his mind from us, has us always before his eyes; and this is precisely as we would have it, for it would be dreadful to exist for a moment beyond the observation of our Heavenly Father. His thoughts are always tender, loving, wise, prudent, far reaching, and they bring to us countless benefits: hence it is a choice delight to remember them. The Lord always thought upon his people: hence their election and the covenant of grace by which their salvation is secured; he always will think upon them: hence their final perseverance by which they shall be brought safely to their final rest. In all our wanderings the watchful glance of the Eternal Watcher is always fixed upon us — we never roam beyond the Shepherd's eye. In our sorrows he observes us incessantly, and not a pang escapes him; in our toils he marks all our weariness, and writes in his book all the struggles of his faithful ones. These thoughts of the Lord encompass us in all our paths, and penetrate the innermost region of our being. Not a nerve or tissue, valve or vessel, of our physical body is uncared for; all the littles of our little world are duly considered by the great God.

Dear reader, is this precious to you? Then cling to it. Never be led astray by those philosophical fools who preach about an impersonal God, and speak of self-existent, self-governing matter. The Lord lives and thinks about us; this is a truth far too precious for us to be lightly robbed of it. The notice of a nobleman is valued so highly that he who has it counts his fortune made; but what is it to be thought of by the King of kings! If the Lord thinks upon us, all is well, and we may rejoice for evermore.

May 1 — Morning

{Daily Reading: 2 Kings 1:1–3:27} {Quick Study: 2 Kings 11:1–12:21}

His cheeks are as a bed of spices,
as sweet flowers. *{Song of Solomon 5:13}*

Lo, the flowery month is come! March winds and April show-ers have done their work, and the earth is all bedecked with beauty. Come, my soul, put on your holiday attire and go out to gather garlands of heavenly thoughts. You know where to go, for to you "the beds of spices" are well known, and you have so often smelled the perfume of "the sweet flowers," that you will go at once to your well Beloved and find all loveliness, all joy in him. That cheek once so rudely smitten with a rod, often bedewed with tears of sympathy and then defiled with spittle — that cheek as it smiles with mercy is as fragrant aromatic to my heart. You did not hide your face from shame and spitting, oh, Lord Jesus, and therefore I will find my dearest delight in praising you. Those cheeks were furrowed by the plough of grief, and crimsoned with red lines of blood from your thorn-crowned temples; such marks of unbounded love can only charm my soul far more than "pillars of perfume." If I may not see all of his face I would behold his cheeks, for the least glimpse of him is exceedingly refreshing to my spiritual sense and yields a variety of delights. In Jesus I not only find fragrance, but a bed of spices; not one flower, but all kinds of sweet flowers. He is to me my rose and my lily, my heart's ease and my cluster of camphire. When he is with me it is May all the year round, and my soul goes out to wash her happy face in the morning dew of his grace, and to solace herself with the singing of the birds of his promises. Precious Lord Jesus, let me in very deed know the blessedness which comes from abiding, unbroken fellowship with you. I am a poor worthless one, whose cheek you have deigned to kiss! Oh, let me kiss you in return with the kisses of my lips.

I am the rose of Sharon. *{Song of Solomon 2:1}*

Whatever there may be of beauty in the material world, Jesus Christ possesses all that in the spiritual world in a tenfold degree. Among flowers, the rose is deemed the sweetest, but Jesus is infinitely more beautiful in the garden of the soul than the rose can be in the gardens of earth. He takes the first place as the fairest among ten thousand. He is the sun, and all others are the stars; the heavens and the day are dark in comparison with him, *for the King in his beauty transcends all.* "I am the rose of *Sharon.*" This was the best and rarest of roses. Jesus is not "the rose" alone, he is "the rose of Sharon," just as he calls his righteousness "gold," and then adds, "the gold of Ophir" — the best of the best. He is positively lovely, and superlatively the loveliest. *There is variety in his charms.* The rose is delightful to the eye, and its scent is pleasant and refreshing; so each of the senses of the soul, whether it is the taste or feeling, the hearing, the sight, or the spiritual smell, finds appropriate gratification in Jesus. *Even the remembrance of his love is sweet.* Take the rose of Sharon, and pull it leaf from leaf, and lay aside the leaves in the jar of memory, and you shall find each leaf fragrant long afterwards, filling the house with perfume. Christ *satisfies the highest taste* of the most educated spirit to the very fullest. The greatest amateur in perfumes is quite satisfied with the rose: and when the soul has arrived at her highest pitch of true taste, she shall still be content with Christ, indeed, she shall be the better able to appreciate him. Heaven itself possesses nothing which excels the rose of Sharon. What emblem can fully picture his beauty? Human speech and earth born things fail to describe him. Earth's choicest charms commingled, feebly picture his abounding preciousness. Blessed rose, bloom in my heart for ever!

May 2 — Morning

{Daily Reading: 2 Kings 4:1–5:27} {Quick Study: 2 Kings 13:1–15:38}

I do not pray that you should take them out of the world. *{John 17:15}*

It is a sweet and blessed event which will occur to all believers in God's own time — the going home to be with Jesus. In a few more years, the Lord's soldiers, who are now fighting "the good fight of faith" will be finished with the conflict, and have entered into the joy of their Lord. But although Christ prays that his people may eventually be with him where he is, he does not ask that they may be taken at once away from this world to heaven. He wishes them to stay here. Yet how frequently does the wearied pilgrim raise the prayer, "Oh, that I had wings like a dove! For then I would fly away and be at rest"; but Christ does not pray like that, he leaves us in his Father's hands, until, like shocks of grain fully ripe, each of us shall be gathered into our Master's garner. Jesus does not plead for our instant removal by death, for to abide in the flesh is needful for others if not profitable for ourselves. He asks that we may be kept from evil, but he never asks for us to be admitted to the inheritance in glory until we are of full age. Christians often want to die when they have any trouble. Ask them why, and they tell you, "Because we wish to be with the Lord." We fear it is not so much because they are longing to be with the Lord, as because they desire to get rid of their troubles; or else they would feel the same wish to die at other times when not under the pressure of trial. They want to go home, not so much for the Saviour's company, but to be at rest. Now it is quite right to desire to depart if we can do it in the same spirit that Paul did, because to be with Christ is far better, but the wish to escape from trouble is a selfish one. Rather, let your care and wish be to glorify God by your life here as long as he pleases, even though it is in the midst of toil, and conflict, and suffering, and leave him to say when "it is enough."

May 2 — Evening

These all died in faith. *{Hebrews 11:13}*

Behold the epitaph of all those blessed saints who fell asleep before the coming of our Lord! It does not matter how they died, whether by old age, or by violent means; this one point, in which they all agree, is the most worthy of record, "These all died in faith." In faith they lived — it was their comfort, their guide, their motive and their support; and in the same spiritual grace they died, ending their life song in the sweet strain in which they had so long continued. They did not die resting in the flesh or upon their own attainments; they made no advance from their first way of acceptance with God, but held to the way of faith to the end. Faith is as precious to die by as to live by.

Dying in faith has distinct reference to the past. They believed the promises which had gone before, and were assured that their sins were blotted out through the mercy of God. Dying in faith has to do with the present. These saints were confident of their acceptance with God, they enjoyed the sunbeams of his love, and rested in his faithfulness. Dying in faith looks *into the future*. They fell asleep, affirming that the Messiah would surely come, and that when he would in the last days appear upon the earth, they would rise from their graves to behold him. To them the pains of death were only the birth pangs of a better state. Take courage, my soul, as you read this epitaph. Your course, through grace, is one of faith, and sight seldom cheers you; this has also been the pathway of the brightest and the best. Faith was the orbit in which these stars of the first magnitude moved all the time of their shining here; and happy are you that it is yours. Look anew tonight to Jesus, the Author and Finisher of your faith, and thank him for giving you like precious faith with souls now in glory.

May 3 — Morning

{Daily Reading: 2 Kings 6:1–8:29} {Quick Study: 2 Kings 16:1–17:41}

In the world you shall have tribulation. *{John 16:33}*

Are you asking the reason for this, believer? Look *upward* to your Heavenly Father, and behold him pure and holy. Do you know that you are one day to be like him? Will you easily be conformed to his image? Will you not require much refining in the furnace of affliction to purify you? Will it be an easy thing to get rid of your corruptions, and make you perfect even as your Father which is in heaven is perfect? Next, Christian, turn your eyes *downward*. Do you know what foes you have beneath your feet? You were once a servant of Satan, and no king will willingly lose his subjects. Do you think that Satan will let you alone? No, he will be always after you, for he "goes about like a roaring lion, seeking whom he may devour." Expect trouble, therefore, Christian, when you look beneath you. Then look *around you*. Where are you? You are in an enemy's country, a stranger and a sojourner. The world is not your friend. If it is, then you are not God's friend, for he who is the friend of the world is the enemy of God. Be assured that you shall find foes everywhere. When you sleep, think that you are resting on the battlefield; when you walk, suspect an ambush in every hedge. Just as mosquitoes are said to bite strangers more than natives, so the trials of earth will be sharpest to you. Lastly, look *within* you, into your own heart and observe what is there. *Sin* and *self* are still within. Ah! If you had no devil to tempt you, no enemies to fight you, and no world to ensnare you, you would still find in yourself evil enough to be a grievous trouble to you, for "the heart is deceitful above all things, and desperately wicked." Expect trouble then, but do not be despondent on account of it, for God is with you to help and to strengthen you. He has said, "I will be with you in trouble; I will deliver you and honour you."

May 3 — Evening

A very present help. *{Psalms 46:1}*

Covenant blessings are not meant to be looked at only, but to be appropriated. Even our Lord Jesus is given to us for our present use. Believer, you do not make use of Christ as you ought to do. When you are in trouble, why do you not tell him all your grief? Has he not a sympathising heart, and can he not comfort and relieve you? No, you are going around to all your friends, except your best friend, and telling your story everywhere except to your Lord. Are you burdened with this day's sins? Here is a fountain filled with blood: use it, saint, use it. Has a sense of guilt returned upon you? The pardoning grace of Jesus may be proven again and again. Come to him at once for cleansing. Do you deplore your weakness? He is your strength: why not lean upon him? Do you feel naked? Come here, soul; put on the robe of Jesus' righteousness. Do not stand looking at it, but wear it. Strip off your own righteousness, and your own fears too: put on the fair white linen, for it was meant to *wear*. Do you feel yourself sick? Pull the night bell of prayer, and call up the Beloved Physician! He will give the cordial that will revive you. You are poor, but then you have "a kinsman, a mighty man of wealth." What! Will you not go to him, and ask him to give you from his abundance, when he has given you this promise, that you shall be a joint heir with him, and has bequeathed all that he is and all that he has to be yours? There is nothing Christ dislikes more than for his people just to make a show thing of him, and not to use him. He loves to be employed by us. The more burdens we put on his shoulders, the more precious he will be to us.

> Let us be simple with him, then,
> Not backward, stiff, or cold,
> As though our Bethlehem could be
> What Sinai was of old.

{Daily Reading: 2 Kings 9:1–10:36} {Quick Study: 2 Kings 18:1–20:21}

Shall a man make gods for himself and they are not gods. *{Jeremiah 16:20}*

One great besetting sin of ancient Israel was idolatry, and the spiritual Israel are vexed with a tendency to the same folly. Remphan's star shines no longer, and the women weep no more for Tammuz, but Mammon still intrudes his golden calf, and the shrines of pride are not forsaken. Self in various forms struggles to subdue the chosen ones under its dominion, and the flesh sets up its altars wherever it can find space for them. Favourite children are often the cause of much sin in believers; the Lord is grieved when he sees us doting upon them above measure; they will live to be as great a curse to us as Absalom was to David, or they will be taken from us to leave our homes desolate. If Christians desire to grow thorns to stuff their sleepless pillows, let them dote on their dear ones.

It is truly said that "they are not gods," for the objects of our foolish love are very doubtful blessings, the solace which they yield us now is dangerous, and the help which they can give us in the hour of trouble is little indeed. Why, then, are we so bewitched with vanities? We pity the poor heathen who adore a god of stone, and yet worship a god of gold. Where is the vast superiority between a god of flesh and one of wood? The principle, the sin, the folly is the same in either case, only that in ours the crime is more aggravated because we have more light, and sin in the face of it. The heathen bows to a false deity, but he has never known the true God; we commit two evils, inasmuch as we forsake the living God and turn to idols. May the Lord purge us all from this grievous iniquity!

> The dearest idol I have known,
> Whate'er that idol be;
> Help me to tear it from your throne,
> And worship only thee.

May 4 — Evening

**Being born again, not of corruptible seed,
but of incorruptible.** *{1 Peter 1:23}*

Peter most earnestly exhorted the scattered saints to love each other "with a pure heart fervently" and he wisely drew his argument, not from the law, from nature, or from philosophy, but from that high and divine nature which God has implanted in his people. Just as some judicious tutor of princes might labour to create and foster in them a kingly spirit and dignified behaviour, finding arguments in their position and descent, so, looking upon God's people as heirs of glory, princes of the royal blood, descendants of the King of kings, earth's truest and oldest aristocracy, Peter says to them, "See that you love one another, because of your noble birth, being born of incorruptible seed; because of your pedigree, being descended from God, the Creator of all things; and because of your immortal destiny, for you shall never pass away, though the glory of the flesh shall fade, and even its existence shall cease." It would be well if, in the spirit of humility, we recognised the true dignity of our regenerated nature, and lived up to it. What is a Christian? If you compare him with a king, he adds priestly sanctity to royal dignity. The king's royalty often lies only in his crown, but with a Christian it is infused into his innermost nature. He is as much above his fellows through his new birth, as a man is above the beast that perishes. Surely he ought to carry himself, in all his dealings, as one who is not of the multitude, but chosen out of the world, distinguished by sovereign grace, written among "the particular people," and who therefore cannot grovel in the dust as others, nor live after the manner of the world's citizens. Let the dignity of your nature, and the brightness of your prospects, oh believers in Christ, constrain you to cleave to holiness, and to avoid the very appearance of evil.

May 5 — Morning

{Daily Reading: 2 Kings 11:1–13:25} {Quick Study: 2 Kings 21:1–23:37}

I will be their God, and they shall be my people. *{2 Corinthians 6:16}*

What a sweet title: "my people!" What a cheering revelation: "their God!" How much of meaning is couched in those two words, "my people!" Here is *speciality*. The whole world is God's; the heaven, even the heaven of heavens is the Lord's, and he reigns among the children of men; but of those whom he has chosen, whom he has purchased for himself, he says what he does not say of others — "my people." In this word there is the idea of *proprietorship*. In a special manner the "Lord's portion is his people; Jacob is the lot of his inheritance." All the nations upon earth are his; the whole world is in his power; yet his people are his chosen, more specially his possession; for he has done more for them than others; he has bought them with his blood; he has brought them near to himself; he has set his great heart upon them; he has loved them with an everlasting love, a love which many waters cannot quench, and which the revolutions of time shall never suffice in the least degree to diminish. Dear friends, can you, by faith, see yourselves in that number? Can you look up to heaven and say, "My Lord and my God: mine by that sweet *relationship* which entitles me to call you Father; mine by that hallowed *fellowship* which I delight to hold with you when you are pleased to reveal yourself to me as you do not do to the world?" Can you read the Book of Inspiration, and find there the indentures of your salvation? Can you read your title written in precious blood? Can you, by humble faith, lay hold of Jesus' garments, and say, "my Christ?" If you can, then God says of you, and of others like you, "my people" for, if God is your God, and Christ your Christ, the Lord has special, particular favour towards you; you are the object of his choice, accepted in his beloved Son.

May 5 — Evening

He who handles a matter wisely shall find good: and whoever trusts in the Lord, is happy. {Proverbs 16:20}

Wisdom is man's true strength; and under its guidance he best accomplishes the purpose of his existence. Wisely handling the matter of life gives to man the richest enjoyment, and presents the noblest occupation for his powers; hence by it he finds good in the fullest sense. Without wisdom, man is as the wild donkey's colt, running here and there, wasting strength which might be profitably employed. Wisdom is the compass by which man is to steer across the trackless waste of life; without it he is a derelict vessel, the sport of winds and waves. A man must be prudent in such a world as this, or he will find no good, but be betrayed into innumerable ills. The pilgrim will severely wound his feet among the briers of the woods of life if he does not choose his steps with the utmost caution. He who is in a wilderness infested with robber bands must handle matters wisely if he wishes to journey safely. If, trained by the Great Teacher, we follow where he leads, we shall find good, even while in this dark abode; there are celestial fruits to be gathered this side of Eden's bowers, and songs of paradise to be sung amid the groves of earth. But where shall this wisdom be found? Many have dreamed of it, but have not possessed it. Where shall we learn it? Let us listen to the voice of the Lord, for he has declared the secret; he has revealed to the sons of men where true wisdom lies, and we have it in the text, "Whoever trusts in the Lord, is happy." *The true way to handle a matter wisely is to trust in the Lord.* This is the sure clue to the most intricate labyrinths of life, follow it and find eternal bliss. He who trusts in the Lord has a diploma for wisdom granted by inspiration: he is happy now, and he will be happier above. Lord, in this sweet eventide walk with me in the garden, and teach me the wisdom of faith.

May 6 — Morning

{Daily Reading: 2 Kings 14:1–15:38} {Quick Study: 2 Kings 24:1–25:30}

We dwell in him. *{1 John 4:13}*

Do you want a house for your soul? Do you ask, "What is the purchase price?" It is something less than proud human nature will like to give. It is without money and without price. Ah! You would like to pay a respectable rent! Would you love to do something to win Christ? Then you cannot have the house, for it is "without price." Will you take my Master's house on a lease for all eternity, with nothing to pay for it, nothing but the ground rent of loving and serving him for ever? Will you take Jesus and "dwell in him?" See, this house is furnished with all you will ever need; it is filled with riches more than you will spend as long as you live. Here you can have intimate communion with Christ and feast on his love; here are cupboards well stocked with food for you to live on for ever; in it, when weary, you can find rest with Jesus; and from it you can look out and see heaven itself. Will you have the house? Ah! If you are homeless, you will say, "I would like to have the house; but may I have it?" Yes; there is the key — the key is, "Come to Jesus." "But," you say, "I am too shabby for such a house." Never mind; there are clothes inside. If you feel guilty and condemned, come; and although the house is too good for you, Christ will make you good enough for the house in due time. He will wash you and cleanse you, and you will yet be able to sing, "We dwell in him." Believer: thrice happy are you to have such a dwelling place! You are greatly privileged, for you have a "strong habitation" in which you are always safe. And "dwelling in him," you have not only a perfect and secure house, but an everlasting one. When this world shall have melted like a dream, our house shall stand, and stand more imperishable than marble, more solid than granite, self-existent as God, for it is God himself — "we dwell in him."

May 6 — Evening

I will wait all the days of my appointed time. *{Job 14:14}*

A little while on earth will make heaven more heavenly. Nothing makes rest so sweet as toil; nothing renders security so pleasant as exposure to alarms. The bitter medicinal cups of earth will give a relish to the new wine which sparkles in the golden bowls of glory. Our battered armour and scarred countenances will render our victory above more illustrious, when we are welcomed to the seats of those who have overcome the world. We would not have full *fellowship with Christ* if we did not sojourn for a while below, for he was baptized with a baptism of suffering among men, and we must be baptized with the same if we wish to share his kingdom. Fellowship with Christ is so honourable that the most grievous sorrow is a light price by which to procure it. Another reason for our lingering here is *for the good of others*. We would not wish to enter heaven until our work is done, and it may be that we are still ordained to minister light to lost souls in the wilderness of sin. Our prolonged stay here is doubtless *for God's glory*. A tried saint, like a well-cut diamond, glitters much in the King's crown. Nothing reflects so much honour on a workman as a protracted and severe trial of his work, and its triumphant endurance of the ordeal without giving way in any part. We are God's workmanship, in whom he will be glorified by our afflictions. It is for the honour of Jesus that we endure the trial of our faith with sacred joy. Let each man surrender his own longings to the glory of Jesus, and feel, "If my lying in the dust would elevate my Lord by so much as an inch, let me still lie among the pots of earth. If to live on earth for ever would make my Lord more glorious, it should be my heaven to be shut out of heaven." Our time is fixed and settled by eternal decree. Let us not be anxious about it, but wait with patience until the gates of pearl shall open.

May 7 — Morning

{Daily Reading: 2 Kings 16:1–17:41} {Quick Study: 1 Chronicles 1:1–2:55}

**Great multitudes followed him, and he
healed them all.** *{Matthew 12:15}*

What a mass of hideous sickness must have thrust itself under the eye of Jesus! Yet we do not read that he was disgusted, but patiently attended to every case. What an extreme variety of evils must have met at his feet! What sickening ulcers and putrefying sores! Yet he was ready for every new shape of the monster evil, and was victor over it in every form. Let the arrow fly from what quarter it might, he quenched its fiery power. The heat of fever, or the cold of dropsy; the lethargy of palsy, or the rage of madness; the filth of leprosy, or the darkness of inflamed eyes — all knew the power of his word, and fled at his command. In every corner of the field he was triumphant over evil and received the homage of delivered captives. He came, he saw, he conquered everywhere. It is even so this morning. Whatever my own case may be, the beloved Physician can heal me; and whatever may be the state of others whom I may remember at this moment in prayer, I may have hope in Jesus that he will be able to heal them from their sins. My child, my friend, my dearest one, I can have hope for each, for all, when I remember the healing power of my Lord; and on my own account, however severe my struggle with sins and infirmities, I may yet be of good cheer. He who on earth walked among the sick still dispenses his grace and works wonders among the sons of men; let me at once go to him very earnestly.

Let me praise him, this morning, as I remember how he performed his spiritual cures, which brought him most renown. It was by taking upon himself our sicknesses. "By his stripes we are healed." The church on earth is full of souls healed by our beloved Physician; and the inhabitants of heaven itself confess that "he healed them all." Come, then, my soul, publish abroad the virtue of his grace, and let it be "to the Lord for a name, for an everlasting sign which shall not be cut off."

May 7 — Evening

Jesus says to him, "Rise, take up your bed, and walk." *{John 5:8}*

Like many others, the impotent man had been waiting for a wonder to be performed, and a sign to be given. Wearily he watched the pool, but either no angel came, or he did not come for him; yet, thinking it to be his only chance, he still waited, and did not know that there was one near him whose word could heal him in a moment. Many are in the same plight: they are waiting for some stirring emotion, remarkable impression, or celestial vision; they wait in vain and watch for nothing. Even supposing that, in a few cases, remarkable signs are seen, yet these are rare, and no man has a right to look for them in his own case; no man especially who feels his impotency to avail himself of the moving of the water even if it came. It is a very sad reflection that tens of thousands are now waiting in the use of means, and ordinances, and vows, and resolutions, and have so waited for time beyond reason, in vain, utterly in vain. Meanwhile these poor souls forget the present Saviour, who invites them to look to him and be saved. He could heal them at once, but they prefer to wait for an angel and a wonder. To trust him is the sure way to every blessing, and he is worthy of the most implicit confidence; but unbelief makes them prefer the cold porches of Bethesda to the warm bosom of his love. Oh, that the Lord may turn his eye upon the multitudes who are in this case tonight; may he forgive the slights which they put upon his divine power, and call them by that sweet, constraining voice, to rise from the bed of despair, and in the energy of faith take up their bed and walk. Oh, Lord, hear our prayer for all such ones at this calm hour of sunset, and before the day breaks may they look and live.

Courteous reader, is there anything in this portion for you?

May 8 — Morning

{Daily Reading: 2 Kings 18:1–20:21} {Quick Study: 1 Chronicles 3:1–5:26}

He who was healed did not know who it was. *{John 5:13}*

Years are short to the happy and healthy; but thirty-eight years of disease must have dragged on for a very weary length of time for the poor impotent man. When Jesus, therefore, healed him by a word, while he lay at the pool of Bethesda, he was delightfully *sensible of a change*. Even so, the sinner who has for weeks and months been paralysed with despair, and has wearily sighed for salvation, is very conscious of the change when the Lord Jesus speaks the word of power, and gives joy and peace in believing. The evil removed is too great to be removed without our discerning it; the life imparted is too remarkable to be possessed and remain inoperative; and the change is too marvellous not to be perceived. Yet the poor man was *ignorant of the author* of his cure; he did not know the sacredness of his person, the offices which he sustained, or the errand which brought him among men. Much ignorance about Jesus may remain in hearts which are yet to feel the power of his blood. We must not hastily condemn men for lack of knowledge; but where we can see the faith which saves the soul, we must believe that salvation has been bestowed. The Holy Spirit makes men penitents long before he makes them divines; and he who believes what he knows, shall soon know more clearly what he believes. Ignorance is, however, an evil; for this poor man was much *tantalised by the Pharisees*, and was quite unable to cope with them. It is good to be able to answer the sceptic; but we cannot do so if we do not know the Lord Jesus clearly and with understanding. The cure for his ignorance, however, soon followed the cure of his infirmity, for he was *visited by the Lord in the temple*; and after that gracious meeting, he was *found testifying* that "it was Jesus who had made him whole." Lord, if you have saved me, show me yourself, so that I may declare you to the sons of men.

May 8 — Evening

Now acquaint yourself with him. *{Job 22:21}*

If we wish to properly "acquaint ourselves with God, and be at peace," we must know him as he has revealed himself, not only in *the unity of his essence and subsistence*, but also in the *plurality of his persons*. God said, "Let us make man in our *own* image" — let man not be content until he knows something about the "us" from whom his being was derived. Endeavour to know the Father; bury your head in his bosom in deep repentance, and confess that you are not worthy to be called his son; receive the kiss of his love; let the ring which is the token of his eternal faithfulness be on your finger; sit at his table and let your heart make merry in his grace. Then press forward and seek to know much of *the Son of God* who is the brightness of his Father's glory, and yet in unspeakable condescension of grace became man for our sakes; know him in the extreme complexity of his nature: eternal God, and yet suffering, finite man; follow him as he walks the waters with the tread of deity, and as he sits upon the well in the weariness of humanity. Do not be satisfied unless you know much about Jesus Christ as your Friend, your Brother, your Husband, your all. Do not forget *the Holy Spirit*; endeavour to obtain a clear view of his nature and character, his attributes, and his works. Behold that Spirit of the Lord, who first of all moved upon chaos, and brought forth order; who now visits the chaos of your soul, and creates the order of holiness. Behold him as the Lord and giver of spiritual life, the Illuminator, the Instructor, the Comforter, and the Sanctifier. Behold him as, like holy unction, he descends upon the head of Jesus, and then afterwards rests upon *you* who are as the skirts of his garments. Such an intelligent, scriptural, and experiential belief in the Trinity in Unity is yours if you truly know God; and such knowledge *brings peace indeed*.

May 9 — Morning

{Daily Reading: 2 Kings 21:1–23:20} {Quick Study: 1 Chronicles 6:1–7:40}

Who has blessed us with all spiritual blessings. *{Ephesians 1:3}*

All the goodness of the past, the present, and the future, Christ bestows upon his people. In the mysterious ages of the past the Lord Jesus was his Father's first elect, and in his *election* he gave us an interest, for we were chosen in him from before the foundation of the world. He had from all eternity the prerogatives of *Sonship*, as his Father's only begotten and well-beloved Son, and he has, in the riches of his grace, by adoption and regeneration, elevated us to sonship also, so that to us he has given "power to become the sons of God." The *eternal covenant*, based upon suretiship and confirmed by an oath, is ours, for our strong consolation and security. In the *everlasting settlements of predestinating wisdom* and omnipotent decree, the eye of the Lord Jesus was always fixed on us; and we may rest assured that in the whole scroll of destiny there is not a line which militates against the interests of his redeemed. The *great betrothal* of the Prince of Glory is ours, for it is to us that he is affianced, as the sacred nuptials shall before long declare to an assembled universe. The *marvellous incarnation* of the God of heaven, with all the amazing condescension and humiliation which attended it, is ours. The bloody sweat, the scourge, the cross, are ours for ever. Whatever blissful consequences flow from *perfect obedience, finished atonement, resurrection, ascension, or intercession*, all are ours by his own gift. Upon his breastplate he is now bearing our names; and in his authoritative pleadings at the throne he remembers us individually and pleads our cause. His *dominion* over principalities and powers, and his absolute majesty in heaven, he employs for the benefit of those who trust in him. His high estate is as much at our service as was his condition of abasement. He who gave himself for us in the depths of woe and death does not withdraw the grant now that he is enthroned in the highest heavens.

May 9 — Evening

Come, my beloved, let us go out into the field . . . let us see if the vine flourishes. {Song of Solomon 7:11–12}

The church was about to engage in earnest labour, and desired her Lord's company in it. She does not say, "I will go," but "let us go." It is blessed working when Jesus is at our side! It is the business of God's people to be trimmers of God's vines. Like our first parents, we are put into the garden of the Lord for usefulness; let us therefore go out into the field. Observe that the church, when she is in her right mind, in all her many labours desires to enjoy communion with Christ. Some imagine that they cannot serve Christ actively, and yet have fellowship with him: they are mistaken. Doubtless it is very easy to fritter away our inward life in outward exercises, and come to complain with the spouse, "They made me keeper of the vineyards; but I have not kept my own vineyard," but there is no reason why this should be the case except for our own folly and neglect. It is certain that a professor may do nothing, and yet grow quite as lifeless in spiritual things as those who are most busy. Mary was not praised for sitting still; but for her *sitting at Jesus' feet*. Even so, Christians are not to be praised for neglecting duties under the pretence of having secret fellowship with Jesus; it is not sitting, but sitting at Jesus' feet which is commendable. Do not think that activity is in itself an evil; it is a great blessing, and a means of grace to us. Paul called it a grace given to him to be allowed to preach; and every form of Christian service may become a personal blessing to those engaged in it. Those who have most fellowship with Christ are not recluses or hermits, who have much time to spare, but indefatigable labourers who are toiling for Jesus, and who, in their toil, have him side by side with them, so that they are workers together with God. Let us remember then, in anything we have to do for Jesus, that we can do it, and should do it in close communion with him.

May 10 — Morning

{Daily Reading: 2 Kings 23:21–25:30} {Quick Study: 1 Chronicles 8:1–10:14}

But now Christ is risen from the dead. *{1 Corinthians 15:20}*

The whole system of Christianity rests upon the fact that "Christ is risen from the dead," for "If Christ is not risen, then our preaching is vain, and your faith is also vain: you are still in your sins." The *divinity* of Christ finds its surest proof in his resurrection, since he was "declared to be the Son of God with power, according to the Spirit of holiness, by the resurrection from the dead." It would not be unreasonable to doubt his deity if he had not risen. Moreover, Christ's *sovereignty* depends upon his resurrection, "For to this end Christ both died, and rose, and revived, so that he might be Lord both of the dead and living." Again, our *justification*, that choice blessing of the covenant, is linked with Christ's triumphant victory over death and the grave; for "He was delivered for our offences, and was raised again for our justification." Indeed, our very *regeneration* is connected with his resurrection, for we are "begotten again to a lively hope by the resurrection of Jesus Christ from the dead." And most certainly our *ultimate resurrection* rests here, for, "If the Spirit of him who raised up Jesus from the dead lives in you, he who raised up Christ from the dead shall also quicken your mortal bodies by his Spirit who lives in you." If Christ is not risen, then we shall not rise; but if he is risen then those who are asleep in Christ have not perished, but in their flesh shall surely behold their God. Thus, the silver thread of resurrection runs through all the believer's blessings, from his regeneration onwards to his eternal glory, and binds them together. How important then will this glorious fact be in his estimation, and how he will rejoice that beyond a doubt it is established, that "now Christ is risen from the dead."

> The promise is fulfill'd, redemption's work is done,
> Justice with mercy's reconciled, for God has raised his Son.

May 10 — Evening

The only begotten of the Father,
full of grace and truth. *{John 1:14}*

Believer, you can say that Christ is *the only begotten of the Father*, as well as the first begotten from the dead. You can say, "He is divine to me, if he is human to all the world beside. He has done that for me which only God could do. He has subdued my stubborn will, melted an adamant heart, opened gates of brass, and snapped bars of iron. He has turned my mourning into laughter for me, and my desolation into joy; he has led my captives captive, and made my heart rejoice with joy unspeakable and full of glory. Let others think as they wish about him, to me he must be the only begotten of the Father: blessed be his name. And he is *full of grace*. Ah! If he had not been then I would never have been saved. He drew me when I struggled to escape from his grace; and when at last I came all trembling like a condemned culprit to his mercy seat he said, 'Your sins which are many are all forgiven: be of good cheer.' And he is *full of truth*. His promises have been true, not one has failed. I bear witness that no servant has ever had such a Master as I have; never has a brother had such a kinsman as he has been to me; never has a spouse had such a husband as Christ has been to my soul; never has a sinner had a better Saviour; never has a mourner had a better comforter than Christ has been to my spirit. I need no one except him. In life he is my life, and in death he shall be the death of death; in poverty Christ is my riches; in sickness he makes my bed; in darkness he is my star, and in brightness he is my sun; he is the manna of the camp in the wilderness, and he shall be the new grain of the host when they come to Canaan. Jesus is to me all grace and no wrath, all truth and no falsehood: and he is *full*, infinitely full of truth and grace. My soul, tonight, with all your might bless 'the only Begotten.' "

May 11 — Morning

{Daily Reading: 1 Chronicles 1:1–2:55} {Quick Study: 1 Chronicles 11:1–12:40}

I am with you always. *{Matthew 28:20}*

It is good there is one who is always the same, and who is always with us. It is good there is one stable rock amidst the billows of the sea of life. Oh my soul, do not set your affections upon rusting, moth-eaten, decaying treasures, but set your heart upon him who abides for ever faithful to you. Do not build your house upon the moving quicksands of a deceitful world, but found your hopes upon this rock, which, amid descending rain and roaring floods, shall stand immovably secure. My soul, I charge you, lay up your treasure in the only secure cabinet; store your jewels where you can never lose them. Put your all in Christ; set all your affections on his person, all your hope in his merit, all your trust in his efficacious blood, all your joy in his presence, and so you may laugh at loss, and defy destruction. Remember that all the flowers in the world's garden fade with time, and the day comes when nothing will be left except the black, cold earth. Death's black extinguisher must soon put out your candle. Oh! How sweet to have sunlight when the candle is gone! The dark flood must soon roll between you and all you have; then wed your heart to him who will never leave you; trust yourself with him who will go with you through the black and surging current of death's stream, and who will land you safely on the celestial shore, and make you sit with him in heavenly places for ever. Go, sorrowing son of affliction, tell your secrets to the Friend who sticks closer than a brother. Trust all your concerns with him who never can be taken from you, who will never leave you, and who will never let you leave him, even "Jesus Christ, the same yesterday, and today, and for ever." "Lo, I am with you always," is enough for my soul to live upon, no matter who may forsake me.

May 11 — Evening

Only be strong and very courageous. *{Joshua 1:7}*

Our God's tender love for his servants makes him concerned for the state of their inward feelings. He desires them to be of good courage. Some esteem it a small thing for a believer to be vexed with doubts and fears, but God does not think so. From this text it is plain that our Master would not have us entangled with fears. He desires to have us without worry, without doubt, without cowardice. Our Master does not think as lightly of our unbelief as we do. When we are desponding we are subject to a grievous malady, not to be trifled with, but to be carried at once to the beloved Physician. Our Lord hates to see our countenance sad. It was a law of Ahasuerus that no one should come into the king's court dressed in mourning: this is not the law of the King of kings, for we may come mourning as we are; but still he wants to have us put off the spirit of heaviness, and put on the garment of praise, for there is much reason to rejoice. The Christian man ought to be of a courageous spirit, in order that he may glorify the Lord by enduring trials in a heroic manner. If he is fearful and fainthearted, *it will dishonour his God.* Besides, *what a bad example it is.* This disease of doubtfulness and discouragement is an epidemic which soon spreads among the Lord's flock. One downcast believer makes twenty souls sad. Moreover, unless your courage is kept up, *Satan will be too much for you.* Let your spirit be joyful in God your Saviour, the joy of the Lord shall be your strength, and no fiend of hell shall make any headway against you: but cowardice throws down the banner. Moreover, *labour is light* to a man with a cheerful spirit; and *success waits upon cheerfulness.* The man who toils, rejoicing in his God, believing with all his heart, has success guaranteed. He who sows in hope shall reap in joy; therefore, dear reader, "Be strong, and very courageous."

And I will reveal myself to him. *{John 14:21}*

The Lord Jesus gives special revelations of himself to his people. Even if Scripture did not declare this, there are many of the children of God who could testify to the truth of it from their own experience. They have had epiphanies of their Lord and Saviour Jesus Christ in a particular manner, such as no mere reading or hearing could afford. In the biographies of eminent saints, you will find many instances recorded in which Jesus has been pleased, in a very special manner to speak to their souls, and to unfold the wonders of his person; yes, their souls have been so steeped in happiness that they have thought themselves to be in heaven, whereas they were not there, although they were almost on the threshold of it — for when Jesus reveals himself to his people, it is heaven on earth; it is paradise in embryo; it is bliss begun. Special revelations of Christ exercise a holy influence on the believer's heart. One effect will be *humility*. If a man says, "I have had such and such spiritual communications, I am a great man," he has never had any communion with Jesus at all; for "God has respect to the lowly: but the proud he knows afar off." He does not need to come near them to know them, and will never give them any visits of love. Another effect will be *happiness*; for in God's presence there are pleasures for evermore. *Holiness* will be sure to follow. A man who has no holiness has never had this manifestation. Some men profess a great deal; but we must not believe anyone unless we see that his deeds answer to what he says. "Do not be deceived; God is not mocked." He will not bestow his favours upon the wicked: for while he will not cast away a perfect man, neither will he respect an evildoer. Thus, there will be three effects of nearness to Jesus — humility, happiness, and holiness. May God give them to you, Christian!

May 12 — Evening

Do not be afraid to go down into Egypt;
for there I will make of you a great nation:
I will go down with you into Egypt; and I will
also surely bring you up again. *{Genesis 46:3–4}*

Jacob must have shuddered at the thought of leaving the land of his father's sojourning, and living among heathen strangers. It was *a new scene, and likely to be a trying one*: who shall venture among courtiers of a foreign monarch without anxiety? Yet the way was *evidently appointed* for him, and therefore he resolved to go. This is frequently the position of believers now — they are called to perils and temptations altogether untried: at such times *let them imitate Jacob's example* by offering sacrifices of prayer to God, and seeking his direction; do not let them take a step until they have waited upon the Lord for his blessing: then they *will have Jacob's companion* to be their friend and helper. How blessed to feel assured that the Lord is with us in all our ways, and condescends to go down into our humiliations and banishments with us! Even beyond the ocean our Father's love beams like the sun in its strength. We cannot hesitate to go where Jehovah promises his presence; even the valley of death grows bright with the radiance of this assurance. Marching onwards with faith in their God, believers *shall have Jacob's promise*. They shall be brought up again, whether it is from the troubles of life or the chambers of death. Jacob's descendants came out of Egypt in due time, and so shall all the faithful pass unscathed through the tribulation of life, and the terror of death. Let us *exercise Jacob's confidence*. *"Do not be afraid,"* is the Lord's command and his divine encouragement to those who at his bidding are launching upon new seas; the divine presence and preservation forbid so much as one unbelieving fear. Without our God we should fear to move; but when he bids us to, it would be dangerous to tarry. Reader, go forward, and do not be afraid.

May 13 — Morning

{Daily Reading: 1 Chronicles 6:1–7:40} {Quick Study: 1 Chronicles 17:1–20:8}

Weeping may endure for a night,
but joy comes in the morning. *{Psalms 30:5}*

Christian! If you are in a night of trial, think of the morning; cheer up your heart with the thought of the coming of your Lord. Be patient, for "Lo! He comes with clouds descending."

Be patient! The Husbandman waits until he reaps his harvest. Be patient; for you know who has said, "Behold, I come quickly; and my reward is with me, to give to every man according as his work shall be." If you are ever so depressed now, remember

> A few more rolling suns, at most,
> Will land you on fair Canaan's coast.

Your head may be crowned with thorny troubles now, but it shall wear a starry crown before long; your hand may be filled with cares — it shall sweep the strings of the harp of heaven soon. Your garments may be soiled with dust now; they shall be white by and by. Wait a little longer. Ah! How despicable our troubles and trials will seem when we look back on them! Looking at them here in the prospect, they seem immense; but when we get to heaven we shall then

> With transporting joys recount, the labours of our feet.

Our trials will then seem light and momentary afflictions. Let us go on boldly; if the night is ever so dark, the morning comes, which is more than they can say who are shut up in the darkness of hell. Do you know what it is thus to live on the future — to live on expectation — to have a foretaste of heaven? Happy believer, to have so sure, so comforting a hope. It may be all dark now, but it will soon be light; it may be all trial now, but it will soon be all happiness. What does it matter though "weeping may endure for a night," when "joy comes in the morning?"

May 13 — Evening

You are my portion, oh Lord. {*Psalms 119:57*}

Look at your possessions, oh believer, and compare your portion with the lot of your fellow men. Some of them have their portion in the field; they are rich, and their harvests yield them a golden increase; but what are harvests compared with your God, who is the God of harvests? What are bursting granaries compared with him, who is the Husbandman, and feeds you with the bread of heaven? Some have their portion in the city; their wealth is abundant, and flows to them in constant streams, until they become a very reservoir of gold; but what is gold compared with your God? You could not live on it; your spiritual life could not be sustained by it. Put it on a troubled conscience, and could it allay its pangs? Apply it to a desponding heart, and see if it could prevent a solitary groan, or give one less grief! But you have God, and in him you have more than gold or riches ever could buy. Some have their portion in what most men love — applause and fame; but ask yourself, is not your God more to you than that? What if ten thousand trumpets should be loud in your applause, would this prepare you to pass the Jordan, or cheer you in prospect of judgment? No, there are griefs in life which wealth cannot alleviate; and there is the deep need of a dying hour, for which no riches can provide. But when you have *God* for your portion, you have more than all else put together. In him every need is met, whether in life or in death. With God for your portion you are rich indeed, for he will supply your need, comfort your heart, assuage your grief, guide your steps, be with you in the dark valley, and then take you home, to enjoy him as your portion for ever. "I have enough," said Esau; this is the best thing a worldly man can say, but Jacob replies, "I have all things," which is a note too high for carnal minds.

May 14 — Morning

{Daily Reading: 1 Chronicles 8:1–10:14} {Quick Study: 1 Chronicles 21:1–23:32}

Joint heirs with Christ. *{Romans 8:17}*

The boundless realms of his Father's universe are Christ's by prescriptive right. As "heir of all things," he is the sole proprietor of the vast creation of God, and he has admitted us to claim all of it as ours, by virtue of that deed of joint heirship which the Lord has ratified with his chosen people. The golden streets of paradise, the pearly gates, the river of life, the transcendent bliss, and the unutterable glory, are, by our blessed Lord, conferred to us for our everlasting possession. All that he has he shares with his people. Then he has placed a royal crown upon the head of his church, appointing her a kingdom, and calling her sons a royal priesthood, a generation of priests and kings. He uncrowned himself so that we might have a coronation of glory; he would not sit upon his own throne until he had procured a place upon it for all who overcome by his blood. Crown the head and the whole body shares the honour. Behold here the reward of every Christian conqueror! Christ's throne, crown, sceptre, palace, treasure, robes, and heritage are yours. Far superior to the jealousy, selfishness, and greed, which allow no participation of their advantages, Christ deems his happiness to be complete when his people share it. "The glory which you gave me I have given them." "These things I have spoken to you, that my joy might remain in you, and that your joy might be full." The smiles of his Father are all the sweeter to him, because his people share them. The honours of his kingdom are more pleasing, because his people appear with him in glory. His conquests are more valuable to him, since they have taught his people to overcome. He delights in his throne, because there is a place on it for them. He rejoices in his royal robes, since his skirts are spread over them. He delights the more in his joy, because he calls them to enter into it.

May 14 — Evening

He shall gather the lambs with his arm,
and carry them in his bosom. *{Isaiah 40:11}*

Who is he of whom such gracious words are spoken? He is THE GOOD SHEPHERD. Why does he carry the lambs in his bosom? Because *he has a tender heart, and any weakness at once melts his heart.* The sighs, the ignorance, the feebleness of the little ones of his flock draw out his compassion. *It is his office*, as a faithful High Priest, to consider the weak. Besides, *he purchased them with blood, they are his property*: he must and will care for *what* cost him so dearly. Then he is *responsible for each lamb*, bound by covenant engagements not to lose one. Moreover, *they are all a part of his glory and reward*.

But how may we understand the expression "He will *carry* them?" Sometimes he carries them by *not permitting them to endure much trial*. Providence deals tenderly with them. Often they are "carried" by being filled with *an unusual degree of love*, so that they bear up and stand firm. Though their knowledge may not be deep, they have great sweetness in what they do know. Frequently he "carries" them by giving them *a very simple faith*, which takes the promise just as it stands, and believingly runs with every trouble straight to Jesus. The simplicity of their faith gives them an unusual degree of confidence, which carries them above the world.

"He carries the lambs in his bosom." Here is *boundless affection.* Would he put them in his bosom if he did not love them much? Here is *tender nearness*: they are so near that they could not possibly be nearer. Here is *hallowed familiarity*: there are precious love passages between Christ and his weak ones. Here is *perfect safety*: in his bosom who can hurt them? They must hurt the shepherd first. Here is *perfect rest and sweetest comfort*. Surely we are not sufficiently sensitive to the infinite tenderness of Jesus!

May 15 — Morning

{Daily Reading: 1 Chronicles 11:1–13:14} {Quick Study: 1 Chronicles 24:1–25:31}

All who believe are justified. *{Acts 13:39}*

The believer in Christ receives a *present* justification. Faith does not produce this fruit eventually, but *now*. So far as justification is the result of faith, it is given to the soul in the moment when it receives Christ, and accepts him as its all in all. Are those who stand before the throne of God justified now? So are we as truly and as clearly justified as those who walk in white and sing melodious praises to celestial harps. The thief upon the cross was justified the moment that he turned the eye of faith to Jesus; and Paul, the aged, after years of service, was no more justified than was the thief with no service at all. We are *today* accepted in the Beloved, *today* absolved from sin, *today* acquitted at the judgment bar of God. Oh! soul transporting thought! There are some clusters of Eshcol's vine which we shall not be able to gather until we enter heaven; but this is a bough which runs over the wall. This is not as the grain of the land, which we can never eat until we cross the Jordan; but this is part of the manna in the wilderness, a portion of our daily nutriment with which God supplies us in our journeying to and fro. We are *now* — even *now* pardoned; even *now* our sins are put away; even *now* we stand accepted in the sight of God, as though we had never been guilty. "There is therefore *now* no condemnation to those who are in Christ Jesus." There is not a sin in the book of God, even *now*, against one of his people. Who dares to lay anything to their charge? There is neither speck, nor spot, nor wrinkle, nor any such thing remaining upon any believer in the matter of justification in the sight of the Judge of all the earth. Let present privilege awaken us to present duty, and now, while life lasts, let us spend and be spent for our sweet Lord Jesus.

May 15 — Evening

Made perfect. *{Hebrews 12:23}*

Remember that there are two kinds of perfection which the Christian needs — the perfection of justification in the person of Jesus, and the perfection of sanctification worked in him by the Holy Spirit. At present, corruption yet remains even in the hearts of the regenerate — experience soon teaches us this. Within us are still lusts and evil imaginations. But I rejoice to know that the day is coming when God shall finish the work which he has begun; and he shall present my soul, not only perfect in Christ, but perfect through the Spirit, without spot or blemish, or any such thing. Can it be true that this poor sinful heart of mine is to become holy even as God is holy? Can it be that this spirit, which often cries, "Oh wretched man that I am! Who shall deliver me from the body of this sin and death?" shall get rid of sin and death — that I shall have no evil things to vex my ears, and no unholy thoughts to disturb my peace? Oh, happy hour! May it be hastened! When I cross the Jordan, the work of sanctification will be finished; but not until that moment shall I even claim perfection in myself. Then my spirit shall have its last baptism in the Holy Spirit's fire. I think I long to die to receive that last and final purification which shall usher me into heaven. No angel shall be more pure than I, for I shall be able to say, in a double sense, "I am clean," through Jesus' blood, and through the Spirit's work. Oh, how should we extol the power of the Holy Spirit in thus making us fit to stand before our Father in heaven! Yet do not let the hope of future perfection make us content with imperfection now. If it does this, our hope cannot be genuine; for a good hope is a purifying thing, even now. The work of grace must be *abiding in us now* or it cannot be *perfected then*. Let us pray to "be filled with the Spirit," so that we may bring forth *increasingly* the fruits of righteousness.

May 16 — Morning

{Daily Reading: 1 Chronicles 14:1–16:43} {Quick Study: 1 Chronicles 26:1–27:34}

Who richly gives to us all things to enjoy. *{1 Timothy 6:17}*

Our Lord Jesus is always giving, and does not for a solitary instant withdraw his hand. As long as there is a vessel of grace not yet full to the brim, the oil shall not be stopped. He is an ever shining sun; he is manna always falling around the camp; he is a rock in the desert, always sending out streams of life from his smitten side; the rain of his grace is always dropping; the river of his bounty is always flowing, and the wellspring of his love is constantly overflowing. Since the King can never die, his grace can never fail. Daily we pick his fruit, and daily his branches bend down to our hand with a fresh supply of mercy. There are seven feast days in his weeks, and as many as are the days, so many are the banquets in his years. Who has ever returned from his door unblessed? Who has ever risen from his table unsatisfied, or from his bosom unemparadised? His mercies are new every morning and fresh every evening. Who can know the number of his benefits, or recount the list of his bounties? Every sand which drops from the glass of time is only the tardy follower of a myriad of mercies. The wings of our hours are covered with the silver of his kindness, and with the yellow gold of his affection. The river of time bears from the mountains of eternity the golden sands of his favour. The countless stars are only as the standard bearers of a more innumerable host of blessings. Who can count the dust of the benefits which he bestows on Jacob, or count the number of the fourth part of his mercies towards Israel? How shall my soul extol him who daily loads us with benefits, and who crowns us with lovingkindness? Oh that my praise could be as ceaseless as his bounty! Oh miserable tongue, how can you be silent? Please wake up lest I call you no more my glory, but my shame. "Awake, psaltery and harp: I myself will awaken very early."

May 16 — Evening

*And he said, "Thus says the Lord, 'Make this valley full
of ditches.' For thus says the Lord, 'You shall not
see wind, neither shall you see rain; yet that valley shall
be filled with water, so that you may drink, both you
and your cattle, and your beasts.' "* {2 Kings 3:16–17}

The armies of the three kings were dying for lack of water:
God was about to send it, and in these words the prophet
announced the coming blessing. Here was *a case of human helplessness*: not a drop of water could all the valiant men procure from the
skies or find in the wells of earth. Thus often the people of the Lord
are at their wits' end; they see the vanity of the creature, and learn
by experience where their help is to be found. Still the people were
to make *a believing preparation for the divine blessing*; they were to
dig the trenches in which the precious liquid would be held. The
church must by her varied agencies, efforts, and prayers, make herself ready to be blessed; she must make the pools, and the Lord will
fill them. This must be done in faith, in the full assurance that the
blessing is about to descend. By and by there was *a singular bestowal
of the needed boon.* Not as in Elijah's case did the shower pour from
the clouds, but in a silent and mysterious manner the pools were
filled. The Lord has his own sovereign modes of action: he is not
tied to manner and time as we are, but does as he pleases among
the sons of men. It is ours thankfully to receive from him, and not
to dictate to him. We must also notice *the remarkable abundance
of the supply* — there was enough for the need of all. And so it is
in the gospel blessing; all the needs of the congregation and of the
entire church shall be met by the divine power in answer to prayer;
and above all this, victory shall be speedily given to the armies of
the Lord.

What am I doing for Jesus? What trenches am I digging? Oh
Lord, make me ready to receive the blessing which you are so willing to bestow.

May 17 — Morning

{*Daily Reading: 1 Chronicles 17:1–20:8*} {*Quick Study: 1 Chronicles 28:1–29:30*}

So walk even as he walked. {*1 John 2:6*}

Why should Christians imitate Christ? They should do it *for their own sakes*. If they desire to be in a healthy state of soul — if they wish to escape the sickness of sin, and enjoy the vigour of growing grace, let Jesus be their model. For their own happiness' sake, if they wish to drink wine on the lees, well refined; if they wish to enjoy holy and happy communion with Jesus; if they wish to be lifted up above the cares and troubles of this world, let them walk even as he walked. There is nothing which can so assist you to walk towards heaven with good speed, as wearing the image of Jesus on your heart to rule all its actions. When, by the power of the Holy Spirit, you are enabled to walk with Jesus in his very footsteps, then you are most happy, and most known to be the sons of God. Peter afar off is both unsafe and uneasy. Next, for *religion's sake*, strive to be like Jesus. Ah! Poor religion, you have been grievously shot at by cruel foes, but you have not been wounded one half so dangerously by your foes as by your friends. Who made those wounds in the fair hand of Godliness? The professor who used the dagger of hypocrisy. The man who with pretences enters the fold, being nothing but a wolf in sheep's clothing, worries the flock more than the lion outside. There is no weapon half as deadly as a Judas kiss. Inconsistent professors injure the gospel more than the sneering critic or the infidel. But, especially for *Christ's own sake*, imitate his example. Christian, do you love your Saviour? Is his name precious to you? Is his cause dear to you? Do you wish to see the kingdoms of the world become his? Is it your desire that he should be glorified? Are you longing that souls should be won to him? If so, *imitate Jesus*; be an "epistle of Christ, known and read by all men."

You are my servant; I have chosen you. *{Isaiah 41:9}*

If we have received the grace of God in our hearts, its practical effect has been to make us God's *servants*. We may be unfaithful servants, we certainly are unprofitable ones, but yet, blessed be his name, we *are* his servants, wearing his livery, dining at his table, and obeying his commands. We were once the servants of sin, but he who made us free has now taken us into his family and taught us obedience to his will. We do not serve our Master perfectly, but we would if we could. Since we hear God's voice saying to us, "You are my servant," we can answer with David, "I am your servant; you have loosened my bonds." But the Lord does not only call us his *servants*, but also his *chosen* ones — "I have chosen you." We have not chosen him first, but he has chosen us. If we are God's servants, we were not always so; to sovereign grace the change must be ascribed. The eye of sovereignty singled us out, and the voice of unchanging grace declared, "I have loved you with an everlasting love." Long before time began or space was created, God had written upon his heart the names of his elect people, had predestinated them to be conformed to the image of his Son, and ordained them heirs of all the fulness of his love, his grace, and his glory. What comfort is here! Has the Lord loved us so long, and will he yet cast us away? He knew how stiffnecked we would be, he understood that our hearts were evil, and yet he made the choice. Ah! Our Saviour is no fickle lover. He does not feel enchanted for a while with some gleams of beauty from his church's eye, and then afterwards cast her off because of her unfaithfulness. No, he married her in old eternity; and it is written concerning Jehovah, "He hates divorce." The eternal choice is a bond upon *our* gratitude and upon *his* faithfulness which neither can disown.

May 18 — Morning

{Daily Reading: 1 Chronicles 21:1–23:32} {Quick Study: 2 Chronicles 1:1–5:14}

**In him dwells all the fulness of the Godhead bodily.
And you are complete in him.** *{Colossians 2:9–10}*

ALL the attributes of Christ, as God and man, are at our disposal. All the fulness of the Godhead, whatever that marvellous term may comprehend, is ours to make us complete. He cannot endow us with the attributes of Deity; but he has done all that can be done, for he has made even his divine power and Godhead subservient to our salvation. His omnipotence, omniscience, omnipresence, immutability, and infallibility, are all combined for our defence. Arise, believer, and behold the Lord Jesus yoking all of his divine Godhead to the chariot of salvation! How vast his grace, how firm his faithfulness, how unswerving his immutability, how infinite his power, how limitless his knowledge! All these are by the Lord Jesus made the pillars of the temple of salvation; and all, without diminution of their infinity, are covenanted to us as our perpetual inheritance. Every drop of the fathomless love of the Saviour's heart is ours; every sinew in the arm of might, every jewel in the crown of majesty, the immensity of divine knowledge, and the sternness of divine justice, all are ours, and shall be employed for us. The whole of Christ, in his adorable character as the Son of God, is by himself given over to us most richly to enjoy. His wisdom is our direction, his knowledge our instruction, his power our protection, his justice our surety, his love our comfort, his mercy our solace, and his immutability our trust. He makes no reserve, but opens the recesses of the Mount of God and invites us to dig in its mines for the hidden treasures. "All, all, all are yours," he says, "be satisfied with favour and full of the goodness of the Lord." Oh! How sweet thus to behold Jesus, and to call upon him with the certain confidence that in seeking the interposition of his love or power, we are only asking for what he has already faithfully promised.

May 18 — Evening

Afterwards. *{Hebrews 12:11}*

How happy are tried Christians, *afterwards*. No calm is more deep than what succeeds a storm. Who has not rejoiced in clear shinings after rain? Victorious banquets are for well-exercised soldiers. After killing the lion we eat the honey; after climbing the Hill Difficulty, we sit down in the arbour to rest; after traversing the Valley of Humiliation, after fighting with Apollyon, the Shining One appears, with the healing branch from the tree of life. Our sorrows, like the passing keels of the vessels upon the sea, leave a silver line of holy light behind them "afterwards." It is peace, sweet, deep peace, which follows the horrible turmoil which once reigned in our tormented, guilty souls. See, then, the happy estate of a Christian! He has his best things last, and he therefore in this world receives his worst things first. But even his worst things are "afterwards" good things, harsh ploughings yielding joyful harvests. Even now he grows rich by his losses, he rises by his falls, he lives by dying, and becomes full by being emptied; if, then, his grievous afflictions yield him so much peaceable fruit in this life, what shall be the full vintage of joy "afterwards" in heaven? If his dark nights are as bright as the world's days, what shall his days be? If even his starlight is more splendid than the sun, what must his sunlight be? If he can sing in a dungeon, how sweetly will he sing in heaven! If he can praise the Lord in the fires, how will he extol him before the eternal throne! If evil is good to him now, what will the overflowing goodness of God be to him *then*? Oh, blessed "afterwards!" Who would not wish to be a Christian? Who would not bear the present cross for the crown which comes afterwards? But herein is work for patience, for the rest is not for today, nor the triumph for the present, but "afterwards." Wait, oh soul, and let patience have her perfect work.

**I have seen servants upon horses, and princes walking
as servants upon the earth.** *{Ecclesiastes 10:7}*

Upstarts frequently usurp the highest places, while the truly great pine in obscurity. This is a riddle in providence whose solution will one day gladden the hearts of the upright; but it is so common a fact that none of us should murmur if it should fall to our own lot. When our Lord was upon earth, although he is the Prince of the kings of the earth, yet he walked the footpath of weariness and service as the Servant of servants: what wonder is it if his followers, who are princes of the blood, should also be looked down upon as inferior and contemptible people? The world is upside down, and therefore, the first are last and the last first. See how the servile sons of Satan lord it in the earth! What a high horse they ride! How they lift up their horn on high! Haman is in the court, while Mordecai sits in the gate; David wanders on the mountains, while Saul reigns in state; Elijah is complaining in the cave while Jezebel is boasting in the palace; yet who would wish to change places with the proud rebels? And who, on the other hand, might not envy the despised saints? When the wheel turns, those who are lowest rise, and the highest sink. Patience, then, believer, eternity will right the wrongs of time.

Let us not fall into the error of letting our passions and carnal appetites ride in triumph, while our nobler powers walk in the dust. Grace must reign as a prince, and make the members of the body instruments of righteousness. The Holy Spirit loves order, and therefore he sets our powers and faculties in due rank and place, giving the highest position to those spiritual faculties which link us with the great King; let us not disturb the divine arrangement, but ask for grace so that we may keep under our body and bring it into subjection. We were not created anew to allow our passions to rule over us, but that we, as kings, may reign in Christ Jesus over the triple kingdom of spirit, soul, and body, to the glory of God the Father.

May 19 — Evening

And he requested for himself
that he might die. *{1 Kings 19:4}*

It was a remarkable thing that the man who was never to die, for whom God had ordained an infinitely better lot, the man who would be carried to heaven in a chariot of fire, and be translated, that he would not see death — should thus pray, "Let me die, I am no better than my fathers." We have here a memorable proof that God does not always answer prayer in kind, although he always does in effect. He gave Elijah something better than what he asked for, and thus really heard and answered him. It was strange that the lion-hearted Elijah should be so depressed by Jezebel's threat as to ask to die, and it was blessedly kind on the part of our Heavenly Father that he did not take his desponding servant at his word. There is a limit to the doctrine of the prayer of faith. We are not to expect that God will give us everything we choose to ask for. We know that we sometimes ask, and do not receive, because we ask amiss. If we ask for what is not promised — if we run counter to the spirit which the Lord would have us cultivate — if we ask contrary to his will, or to the decrees of his providence — if we ask merely for the gratification of our own ease, and without an eye for his glory, we must not expect that we shall receive. Yet, when we ask in faith, nothing doubting, if we do not receive the precise thing asked for, we shall receive an equivalent, and more than an equivalent, for it. As one remarks, "If the Lord does not pay in silver, he will in gold; and if he does not pay in gold, he will in diamonds." If he does not give you precisely what you ask for, he will give you what is tantamount to it, and what you will greatly rejoice to receive in lieu of it. Dear reader, be then much in prayer, and make this evening a time of earnest intercession, but take heed what you ask for.

Marvellous lovingkindness. *{Psalms 17:7}*

When we give our hearts with our alms, we give well, but we must often plead to a failure in this respect — not so our Master and our Lord. His favours are always performed with the love of his heart. He does not send to us the cold meat and the broken pieces from the table of his luxury, but he dips our morsel in his own dish, and seasons our provisions with the spices of his fragrant affections. When he puts the golden tokens of his grace into our palms, he accompanies the gift with such a warm pressure of his hand that the manner of his giving is as precious as the boon itself. He will come into our houses upon his errands of kindness, and he will not act as some austere visitors do in the poor man's cottage, but he sits by our side, not despising our poverty, nor blaming our weakness. Beloved, with what smiles does he speak! What golden sentences drop from his gracious lips! What embraces of affection does he bestow upon us! If he had only given us pennies, the way of his giving would have gilded them; but as it is, the costly alms are set in a golden basket by his pleasant attitude. It is impossible to doubt the sincerity of his charity, for there is a bleeding heart stamped upon the face of all his gifts. He gives liberally and does not chide. There is not one hint that we are burdensome to him; not one cold look for his poor pensioners; but he rejoices in his mercy, and presses us to his heart while he is pouring out his life for us. There is a fragrance in his spikenard which nothing but his heart could produce; there is a sweetness in his honeycomb which could not be in it unless the very essence of his soul's affection had been mingled with it. Oh! The rare communion which such singular heartiness effects! May we continually taste and know the blessedness of it!

May 20 — Evening

I drew them with cords of a man,
with bands of love. *{Hosea 11:4}*

Our Heavenly Father often draws us with the cords of love; but ah! how reluctant we are to run towards him! How slowly do we respond to his gentle impulses! *He draws us to exercise a more simple faith in him*; but we have not yet attained to Abraham's confidence; we do not leave our worldly cares with God, but, like Martha, we encumber ourselves with much serving. Our meagre faith brings leanness into our souls; we do not open our mouths wide, though God has promised to fill them. Does he not this evening draw us to trust him? Can we not hear him say, "Come, my child, and trust me. The veil is torn open; enter into my presence, and approach boldly to the throne of my grace. I am worthy of your fullest confidence; cast your cares on me. Shake yourself from the dust of your cares, and put on your beautiful garments of joy." But, alas! Though called with tones of love to the blessed exercise of this comforting grace, we will not come. At another time *he draws us to closer communion with himself.* We have been sitting on the doorstep of God's house, and he invites us to come into the banqueting hall and dine with him, but we decline the honour. There are secret rooms not yet opened to us; Jesus invites us to enter them, but we hold back. Shame on our cold hearts! We are very poor lovers of our sweet Lord Jesus, not fit to be his servants, much less to be his brides, and yet he has exalted us to be bone of his bone and flesh of his flesh, married to him by a glorious marriage covenant. Herein is love! But it is love which *takes no denial.* If we do not obey the gentle drawings of his love, he will send affliction to drive us into closer intimacy with himself. He will have us closer to him. What foolish children we are to refuse those bands of love, and so bring upon our backs that scourge of small cords, which Jesus knows how to use!

If it is that you have tasted that the Lord is gracious. *{1 Peter 2:3}*

"If" — then, this is not a matter to be taken for granted concerning everyone of the human race. "If" — then there is a possibility and a probability that some may not have tasted that the Lord is gracious. "If" — then this is not a general but a special mercy; and it is needful to enquire whether we know the grace of God by inward experience. There is no spiritual favour which may not be a matter for heart searching.

But while this should be a matter of earnest and prayerful enquiry, no one ought to be content while there is any such thing as an "if" about his having tasted that the Lord is gracious. A jealous and holy distrust of self may give rise to the question even in the believer's heart, but the *continuance* of such a doubt would be an evil indeed. We must not rest without a desperate struggle to clasp the Saviour in the arms of faith, and say, "I know whom I have believed, and I am persuaded that he is able to keep what I have committed to him." Do not rest, oh believer, until you have a full assurance of your interest in Jesus. Let nothing satisfy you until, by the infallible witness of the Holy Spirit bearing witness with your spirit, you are certified that you are a child of God. Oh, do not trifle here; let no "perhaps" and "peradventure" and "if" and "maybe" satisfy your soul. Build on eternal verities, and truly build upon them. Get the sure mercies of David, and surely get them. Let your anchor be cast into what is within the veil, and see to it that your soul is linked to the anchor by a cable that will not break. Advance beyond these dreary "ifs"; do not remain any more in the wilderness of doubts and fears; cross the Jordan of distrust, and enter the Canaan of peace, where the Canaanite still lingers, but where the land does not cease to flow with milk and honey.

There is grain in Egypt. *{Genesis 42:2}*

Famine pinched all the nations, and it seemed inevitable that Jacob and his family would suffer great want; but the God of providence, who never forgets the objects of electing love, had stored a granary for his people by giving the Egyptians warning of the scarcity, and leading them to treasure up the grain of the years of plenty. Little did Jacob expect deliverance from Egypt, but there was the grain in store for him. Believer, though all things are apparently against you, rest assured that God has made a reservation on your behalf; in the scroll of your griefs there is a saving clause. Somehow he will deliver you, and somewhere he will provide for you. The quarter from which your rescue shall arise may be a very unexpected one, but help will assuredly come in your extremity, and you shall magnify the name of the Lord. If men do not feed you, ravens shall; and if earth does not yield wheat, heaven shall drop with manna. Therefore, be of good courage, and rest quietly in the Lord. God can make the sun rise in the west if he pleases, and make the source of distress the channel of delight. The grain in Egypt was all in the hands of the beloved Joseph; he opened or closed the granaries at will. And so the riches of providence are all in the absolute power of our Lord Jesus, who will dispense them liberally to his people. Joseph was abundantly ready to help his own family; and Jesus is unceasing in his faithful care for his brethren. Our business is to go after the help which is provided for us: we must not sit still in despondency, but bestir ourselves. Prayer will bear us soon into the presence of our royal Brother: once before his throne we have only to ask and have: his stores are not exhausted; there still is an abundance of grain: his heart is not hard, he will give the grain to us. Lord, forgive our unbelief, and this evening constrain us to draw largely from your fulness and receive grace for grace.

May 22 — Morning

{Daily Reading: 2 Chronicles 4:1–6:42} {Quick Study: 2 Chronicles 15:1–18:34}

He led them forth by the right way. *{Psalms 107:7}*

Changing experiences often lead the anxious believer to enquire "Why is it thus with me?" I looked for light, but lo, darkness came; for peace, but behold trouble. I said in my heart, "My mountain stands firm, I shall never be moved." Lord, you only have to hide your face, and I am troubled. It was only yesterday that I could read my title clear; today my evidences are dimmed, and my hopes are clouded. Yesterday I could climb to Pisgah's top, and view the landscape, and rejoice with confidence in my future inheritance; today, my spirit has no hopes, but many fears; no joys, but much distress. Is this part of God's plan with me? Can this be the way in which God would bring me to heaven? Yes, it is even so. The eclipse of your faith, the darkness of your mind, the fainting of your hope, all these things are only parts of God's method for making you ripe for the great inheritance upon which you shall soon enter. These trials are for the testing and strengthening of your faith — they are waves that wash you further upon the rock — they are winds which waft your ship the more swiftly towards the desired haven. According to David's words, so it might be said of you, "So he brings them to their desired haven." By honour and dishonour, by evil report and by good report, by plenty and by poverty, by joy and by distress, by persecution and by peace, by all these things the life of your soul is maintained, and by each of these you are helped on your way. Oh believer, do not think that your sorrows are outside of God's plan; they are necessary parts of it. "We must, through much tribulation, enter the kingdom." Learn, then, even to "count it all joy when you fall into various temptations."

> Oh, let my trembling soul be still,
> And wait your wise, your holy will!
> I cannot, Lord, your purpose see,
> Yet all is well since ruled by thee.

May 22 — Evening

Behold, you are fair, my Beloved. *{Song of Solomon 1:16}*

From every point our well Beloved is most fair. Our various experiences are meant by our Heavenly Father to furnish fresh standpoints from which we may view the loveliness of Jesus; how amiable are our trials when they carry us aloft where we may gain clearer views of Jesus than ordinary life could afford us! We have seen him from the top of Amana, from the top of Shenir and Hermon, and he has shone upon us as the sun in its strength; but we have seen him also "from the lions' dens, from the mountains of the leopards," and he has not lost any of his loveliness. From the languishing of a sickbed, from the borders of the grave, we have turned our eyes to our soul's spouse, and he has never been otherwise than "all fair." Many of his saints have looked upon him from the gloom of dungeons, and from the red flames of the stake, yet they have never uttered an ill word about him, but have died extolling his surpassing charms. Oh, it is a noble and pleasant employment to be for ever gazing at our sweet Lord Jesus! Is it not unspeakably delightful to view the Saviour in all his offices, and to perceive him matchless in each? — to shift the kaleidoscope, as it were, and to find fresh combinations of peerless graces? In the manger and in eternity, on the cross and on his throne, in the garden and in his kingdom, among thieves or in the midst of cherubim, he is everywhere "altogether lovely." Examine carefully every little act of his life, and every trait of his character, and he is as lovely in the minute as in the majestic. Judge him however you wish, you cannot censure; weigh him however you please, and he will not be found lacking. Eternity shall not expose the shadow of a spot in our Beloved, but rather, as ages revolve, his hidden glories shall shine forth with yet more inconceivable splendour, and his unutterable loveliness shall more and more ravish all celestial minds.

The Lord will perfect what concerns me. *{Psalms 138:8}*

Most obviously the confidence which the psalmist here expressed was a *divine confidence*. He did not say, "*I* have grace enough to perfect what concerns me — my faith is so steady that it will not stagger — my love is so warm that it will never grow cold — my resolution is so firm that nothing can move it"; no, his dependence was on the Lord alone. If we indulge in any confidence which is not grounded on the Rock of Ages, our confidence is worse than a dream, it will fall upon us, and cover us with its ruins, to our sorrow and confusion. All that nature spins time will unravel, to the eternal confusion of all who are clothed in it. The psalmist was wise, he rested upon nothing short of the *Lord's* work. It is the Lord who has begun the good work within us; it is he who has carried it on; and if he does not finish it, it never will be complete. If there is one stitch in the celestial garment of our righteousness which we are to insert ourselves, then we are lost; but this is our confidence, the Lord who began will perfect. He *has* done it all, *must* do it all, and *will* do it all. Our confidence must not be in what we have done, nor in what we have resolved to do, but entirely in what *the Lord* will do. Unbelief insinuates, "You will never be able to stand. Look at the evil of your heart, you can never conquer sin; remember the sinful pleasures and temptations of the world that come upon you, you will be certainly allured by them and led astray." Oh! Yes, we would indeed perish if left to our own strength. If we had to navigate our frail vessels alone over so rough a sea, we might well give up the voyage in despair; but, thanks be to God, he will perfect what concerns us, and bring us to the desired haven. We can never be too confident when we confide in him alone, and never too much concerned to *have such* a trust.

May 23 — Evening

You have not bought me any sweet cane with money. *{Isaiah 43:24}*

Worshippers at the temple were accustomed to bring presents of sweet perfumes to be burned upon the altar of God: but Israel, in the time of her backsliding, became niggardly, and made very few votive offerings to her Lord: this was an evidence of coldness of heart towards God and his house. Reader, does this never happen with you? Might not the complaint of the text be occasionally, if not frequently, brought against you? Those who are poor in pocket, if rich in faith, will be accepted none the less because their gifts are small; but, poor reader, do you give in fair proportion to the Lord, or is the widow's mite kept back from the sacred treasury? The rich believer should be thankful for the talent entrusted to him, but should not forget his great responsibility, for where much is given much will be required; but, rich reader, are you mindful of your obligations, and rendering to the Lord according to the benefit received? Jesus gave his blood for us, what shall we give to him? We are his, and all that we have, for he has purchased us for himself — can we act as if we were our own? Oh, for more consecration! And to this end, oh, for more love! Blessed Jesus, how good it is of you to accept our sweet cane bought with money! Nothing is too costly as a tribute to your unrivalled love, and yet you do receive with favour the smallest sincere token of affection! You do receive our poor forget-me-nots and love tokens as though they were intrinsically precious, though indeed they are only like the bunch of wild flowers which the child brings to its mother. Never may we grow niggardly towards you, and from this hour may we never hear you complain about us again for withholding the gifts of our love. We will give you the first fruits of our increase, and pay to you tithes of all, and then we will confess "Of your own have we given you."

May 24 — Morning

{Daily Reading: 2 Chronicles 10:1–13:22} {Quick Study: 2 Chronicles 21:1–23:21}

Blessed be God, who has not turned away my prayer. *{Psalms 66:20}*

In looking back upon the character of our prayers, if we do it honestly, we shall be filled with wonder that God has ever answered them. There may be some who think their prayers to be worthy of acceptance — as the Pharisee did; but the true Christian, in a more enlightened retrospect, weeps over his prayers, and if he could retrace his steps he would desire to pray more earnestly. Remember, Christian, how *cold* your prayers have been. When in your prayer closet you should have wrestled as Jacob did; but instead of that, your petitions have been faint and few — far removed from that humble, believing, persevering faith, which cries, "I will not let you go unless you bless me." Yet, wonderful to say, God has heard these cold prayers of yours, and not only heard, but answered them. Reflect also, how *infrequent* have been your prayers, unless you have been in trouble, and *then* you have gone often to the mercy seat: but when deliverance has come, where has been your constant supplication? Yet, although you have ceased to pray as you once did, God has not ceased to bless. When you have neglected the mercy seat, God has not deserted it, but the bright light of the Shekinah has always been visible between the wings of the cherubim. Oh! It is marvellous that the Lord should regard those intermittent spasms of importunity which come and go with our necessities. What a God is he thus to hear the prayers of those who come to him when they have pressing needs, but neglect him when they have received a mercy; who approach him when they are forced to come, but who almost forget to address him when mercies are plentiful and sorrows are few. Let his gracious kindness in hearing such prayers touch our hearts, so that we may henceforth be found "praying always with all prayer and supplication in the Spirit."

May 24 — Evening

**Only let your conversation be as it becomes
the gospel of Christ.** *{Philippians 1:27}*

The word "conversation" does not merely mean our talk and conversation with one another, but the whole course of our life and behaviour in the world. The Greek word signifies the actions and the privileges of citizenship: and thus we are commanded to let our actions, as citizens of the New Jerusalem, be such as becomes the gospel of Christ. What kind of conversation is this? In the first place, *the gospel is very simple*. So Christians should be simple and plain in their habits. There should be about our manner, our speech, our dress, our whole behaviour, that simplicity which is the very soul of beauty. The gospel is *preeminently true*, it is gold without dross; and the Christian's life will be lustreless and valueless without the jewel of truth. The gospel is a very *fearless gospel*; it boldly proclaims the truth, whether men like it or not; we must be equally faithful and unflinching. But the gospel is also *very gentle*. Notice this spirit in its Founder: "He will not break a bruised reed." Some professors are sharper than a thorn hedge; such men are not like Jesus. Let us seek to win others by the gentleness of our words and acts. The gospel is *very loving*. It is the message of the God of love for a lost and fallen race. Christ's last command to his disciples was, "Love one another." Oh, for more real, hearty union and love for all the saints; for more tender compassion towards the souls for the worst and vilest of men! We must not forget that the gospel of Christ is *holy*. It never excuses sin: it pardons it, but only through an atonement. If our life is to resemble the gospel, we must shun, not merely the grosser vices, but everything that would hinder our perfect conformity to Christ. For his sake, for our own sakes, and for the sakes of others, we must strive day by day to let our conversation be more in accordance with his gospel.

{Daily Reading: 2 Chronicles 14:1–17:19} {Quick Study: 2 Chronicles 24:1–25:28}

Do not forsake me, oh Lord. *{Psalms 38:21}*

Frequently we pray that God would not forsake us in the hour of trial and temptation, but we too often forget that we need to use this prayer at *all times*. There is no moment of our life, however holy, when we can do without his constant upholding. Whether in light or in darkness, in communion or in temptation, all of us need the prayer, "Do not forsake me, oh Lord." "Hold me up, and I shall be safe." A little child, while learning to walk, always needs the nurse's aid. The ship left by the pilot drifts at once from her course. We cannot do without continued aid from above; let it then be your prayer today, "Do not forsake me. Father, do not forsake your child, lest he should fall by the hand of the enemy. Shepherd, do not forsake your lamb, lest he should wander from the safety of the fold. Great Husbandman, do not forsake your plant, lest it should wither and die. 'Do not forsake me, oh Lord,' now; and do not forsake me at any moment of my life. Do not forsake me in my joys, lest they should absorb my heart. Do not forsake me in my sorrows, lest I should murmur against you. Do not forsake me in the day of my repentance, lest I should lose the hope of pardon, and fall into despair; and do not forsake me in the day of my strongest faith, lest faith should degenerate into presumption. Do not forsake me, for without you I am weak, but with you I am strong. Do not forsake me, for my path is dangerous, and full of snares, and I cannot do without your guidance. The hen does not forsake her brood, then for evermore cover me with your feathers, and permit me to find my refuge under your wings. 'Do not be far from me, oh Lord, for trouble is near, for there is no one to help.' 'Do not leave me, neither forsake me, oh God of my salvation!' "

> Oh ever in our cleansed breast,
> Bid your Eternal Spirit rest;
> And make our secret soul to be
> A temple pure and worthy to thee.

And they rose up the same hour, and returned to
Jerusalem . . . and they told what things were done in the
way, and how he was known by them. *{Luke 24:33–35}*

When the two disciples had reached Emmaus, and were
refreshing themselves at the evening meal, the mysterious
stranger who had so enchanted them upon the road, took bread
and broke it, made himself known to them, and then vanished
out of their sight. They had constrained him to abide with them,
because the day was far spent; but now, although it was much later,
their love was a lamp to their feet, yes, wings also; they forgot the
darkness, their weariness was all gone, and immediately they journeyed back the eight miles to tell the glad news of a risen Lord, who
had appeared to them by the way. They reached the Christians in
Jerusalem, and were received by a burst of joyful news before they
could tell their own story. These early Christians were all on fire to
speak about Christ's resurrection, and to proclaim what they knew
about the Lord; they made common property of their experiences.
This evening let their example deeply impress us. We too must
bear our witness concerning Jesus. John's account of the sepulchre
needed to be supplemented by Peter; and Mary could still speak
about something more; combined, we have a full testimony from
which nothing can be omitted. Each of us has particular gifts and
special insights; but the one object God has in view is the perfecting of the whole body of Christ. We must, therefore, bring our
spiritual possessions and lay them at the apostle's feet, and make a
distribution to all of what God has given to us. Keep back no part
of the precious truth, but speak about what you know, and testify
what you have seen. Do not let the toil or darkness, or possible
unbelief of your friends, weigh one moment in the scale. Get up
and march to the place of duty, and tell what great things God has
shown to your soul.

Cast your burden upon the Lord,
and he shall sustain you. *{Psalms 55:22}*

Care, even though exercised upon legitimate objects, if carried to excess, has in it the nature of sin. The precept to avoid anxious care is earnestly inculcated by our Saviour, again and again. It is reiterated by the apostles; and it is one which cannot be neglected without involving transgression: for the very essence of anxious care is the imagining that we are wiser than God, and the thrusting of ourselves into his place to do for him what he has undertaken to do for us. We attempt to think of what we imagine he will forget; we labour to take upon ourselves our weary burden, as if he were unable or unwilling to take it for us. Now this disobedience to his plain precept, this unbelief in his Word, this presumption in intruding upon his province, is all sinful. Yet more than this, anxious care often leads to acts of sin. He who cannot calmly leave his affairs in God's hand, but will carry his own burden, is very likely to be tempted to use wrong means to help himself. This sin leads to a forsaking of God as our counsellor, and resorting instead to human wisdom. This is going to the "broken cistern" instead of to the "fountain," a sin which was laid against Israel of old. Anxiety makes us doubt God's lovingkindness, and thus our love for him grows cold; we feel mistrust, and thus grieve the Spirit of God, so that our prayers become hindered, our consistent example marred, and our life one of self-seeking. Thus, lack of confidence in God leads us to wander far from him; but if through simple faith in his promise, we cast each burden as it comes upon him, and are "careful for nothing" because he undertakes to care for us, it will keep us close to him, and strengthen us against much temptation. "You will keep him in perfect peace whose mind is resting on you, because he trusts in you."

May 26 — Evening

Continue in the faith. *{Acts 14:22}*

Perseverance is the badge of true saints. The Christian life is not a *beginning* only in the ways of God, but also a *continuance* in the same as long as life lasts. It is with a Christian as it was with the great Napoleon: he said, "Conquest has made me what I am, and conquest must maintain me." So, under God, dear brother in the Lord, conquest has made you what you are, and conquest must sustain you. Your motto must be, "Excelsior." He only is a true conqueror, and shall be crowned at the last, who continues until war's trumpet is blown no more. Therefore, perseverance is the target of all our spiritual enemies. The *world* does not object to your being a Christian for a time, if she can only tempt you to halt your pilgrimage, and settle down to buy and sell with her in Vanity Fair. The *flesh* will seek to ensnare you, and to prevent your pressing on to glory. "It is weary work being a pilgrim; come, give it up. Am I always to be mortified? Am I never to be indulged? Give me at least a furlough from this constant warfare." *Satan* will make many a fierce attack on your perseverance; it will be the target for all his arrows. He will strive to hinder you *in service*: he will insinuate that you are doing no good; and that you need rest. He will endeavour to make you weary of *suffering*, he will whisper, "Curse God, and die." Or he will attack your *steadfastness*: "What is the good of being so zealous? Be quiet like the rest; sleep like others do, and let your lamp go out like the other virgins do." Or he will assail your *doctrinal sentiments*: "Why do you hold to these denominational creeds? Sensible men are becoming more liberal; they are removing the old landmarks; fall in with the times." Therefore, Christian, hold your shield close to your armour, and cry mightily to God, that by his Spirit you may endure to the end.

May 27 — Morning

{Daily Reading: 2 Chronicles 21:1–24:27} {Quick Study: 2 Chronicles 29:1–30:27}

So Mephibosheth lived in Jerusalem: for he ate continually at the king's table; and was lame in both his feet. *{2 Samuel 9:13}*

Mephibosheth was no great ornament to a royal table, yet he had a continual place at David's meals, because the king could see in his face the features of the beloved Jonathan. Like Mephibosheth, we may cry to the King of Glory, "What is your servant, that you should look upon such a dead dog as I am?" But still the Lord indulges us with a most familiar relationship with himself, because he sees in our faces the remembrance of his dearly beloved Jesus. The Lord's people are *dear for another's sake.* Such is the love which the Father bears to his only begotten, that for his sake he raises his lowly brethren from poverty and banishment, to courtly companionship, noble rank, and royal provision. Their *deformity shall not rob them of their privileges.* Lameness is no bar to sonship; the cripple is as much the heir as if he could run like Asahel. Our right does not limp, though our might may. A king's table is a noble hiding place for lame legs, and at the gospel feast we learn to glory in infirmities, because the power of Christ rests upon us. Yet grievous *disability may mar the person of the best loved saints.* Here is one feasted by David, and yet so lame in both his feet that he could not go up with the king when he fled from the city, and was therefore maligned and injured by his servant Ziba. Saints whose faith is weak, and whose knowledge is slender, are great losers; they are exposed to many enemies, and cannot follow the King wherever he goes. This *disease frequently arises from falls.* Bad nursing in their spiritual infancy often causes converts to fall into a despondency from which they never recover, and sin in other cases brings broken bones. Lord, help the lame to leap like a hart, and satisfy all your people with the food of your table!

May 27 — Evening

**What is your servant, that you should look
upon such a dead dog as I am?** *{2 Samuel 9:8}*

If Mephibosheth was thus humbled by David's kindness, what shall we be in the presence of our gracious Lord? The more grace we have, the less we shall think of ourselves, for grace, like light, reveals our impurity. Eminent saints have scarcely known to what to compare themselves, their sense of unworthiness has been so clear and keen. "I am," says holy Rutherford, "a dry and withered branch, a piece of dead carcass, dry bones, and not able to step over a straw." In another place he writes, "Except for their public remorse for sin, I want nothing of what Judas and Cain had." The very least objects in nature appear to the humbled mind to have a preference above itself, because they have never contracted sin: a dog may be greedy, fierce, or filthy, but it has no conscience to violate, no Holy Spirit to resist. A dog may be a worthless animal, and yet by a little kindness it is soon won to love its master, and is faithful to death; but we forget the goodness of the Lord, and do not follow when he calls. The term "dead dog" is the most expressive of all terms of contempt, but it is not too strong to express the self-abhorrence of instructed believers. They do not affect mock modesty, they mean what they say, they have weighed themselves in the balances of the sanctuary, and found out the vanity of their nature. At best, we are only clay, animated dust, mere walking hillocks; but viewed as sinners, we are monsters indeed. Let it be published in heaven as a wonder, that the Lord Jesus should set his heart's love upon such as we are. Dust and ashes though we are, we must and will "magnify the exceeding greatness of his grace." Could not his heart find rest in heaven? Does he need to come to these tents of Kedar for a spouse, and choose a bride upon whom the sun had looked? Oh heavens and earth, break forth into a song, and give all glory to our sweet Lord Jesus.

May 28 — Morning

{Daily Reading: 2 Chronicles 25:1–27:9} {Quick Study: 2 Chronicles 31:1–33:25}

Whom he justified, those he also glorified. *{Romans 8:30}*

Here is a precious truth for you, believer. You may be poor, or in suffering, or unknown, but for your encouragement take a review of your "calling" and the consequences that flow from it, and especially that blessed result spoken of here. As surely as you are God's child today, so surely shall all your trials soon be at an end, and you shall be rich to all the intents of bliss. Wait a while, and that weary head shall wear the crown of glory, and that hand of labour shall grasp the palm branch of victory. Do not lament your troubles, but rather rejoice that before long you will be where "there shall be neither sorrow, nor crying, neither shall there be any more pain." The chariots of fire are at your door, and a moment will suffice to bear you to the glorified. The everlasting song is almost on your lip. The portals of heaven stand open for you. Do not think that you can fail to enter into rest. If he has called you, nothing can separate you from his love. Distress cannot sever the bond; the fire of persecution cannot burn the link; the hammer of hell cannot break the chain. You are secure; that voice which called you at first, shall yet again call you from earth to heaven, from death's dark gloom to immortality's unuttered splendours. Rest assured, the heart of him who has justified you beats with infinite love towards you. You shall soon be with the glorified, where your portion is; you are only waiting here to be made fit for the inheritance, and when that is done, the wings of angels shall waft you far away, to the mount of peace, and joy, and blessedness, where,

> Far from a world of grief and sin,
> With God eternally shut in,

you shall rest for ever and ever.

May 28 — Evening

I recall this to my mind,
therefore I have hope. *{Lamentations 3:21}*

Memory is frequently the bondslave of despondency. Despairing minds call to remembrance every dark foreboding in the past, and magnify every gloomy feature in the present; thus memory, clothed in sackcloth, presents to the mind a cup of mingled gall and wormwood. There is, however, no necessity for this. Wisdom can readily transform memory into an angel of comfort. That same recollection which in its left hand brings so many gloomy omens, may be trained to bear in its right a wealth of hopeful signs. She does not need to wear a crown of iron, she may encircle her brow with a fillet of gold, all spangled with stars. Thus it was in Jeremiah's experience: in the previous verse memory had brought him to deep humiliation of soul: "My soul has them still in remembrance, and is humbled in me"; and now this same memory restored him to life and comfort. "I recall this to my mind, therefore I have hope." Like a two-edged sword, his memory first killed his pride with one edge, and then slew his despair with the other. As a general principle, if we would exercise our memories more wisely, we might, in our very darkest distress, strike a match which would instantaneously kindle the lamp of comfort. There is no need for God to create a new thing upon the earth in order to restore believers to joy; if they would prayerfully rake the ashes of the past, they would find light for the present; and if they would turn to the book of truth and the throne of grace, their candle would soon shine as it did before. We must remember the loving-kindness of the Lord, and rehearse his deeds of grace. Let us open the volume of memory which is so richly illuminated with memorials of mercy, and we shall soon be happy. Thus, memory may be, as Coleridge calls it, "The bosom spring of joy," and when the Divine Comforter bends it to his service, it may be chief among earthly comforters.

May 29 — Morning

{Daily Reading: 2 Chronicles 28:1–30:27} {Quick Study: 2 Chronicles 34:1–36:23}

You hate wickedness. *{Psalms 45:7}*

"Be angry, and do not sin." There can hardly be goodness in a man if he is not angry at sin; he who loves truth must hate every false way. How our Lord Jesus hated it when the temptation came! Thrice it assailed him in different forms, but he always met it with, "Get behind me, Satan." He hated it in others none the less fervently, because he showed his hate more often in tears of pity than in words of rebuke; yet what language could be more stern, more like Elijah, than the words, "Woe to you, scribes and Pharisees, hypocrites! For you devour widows' houses, and for a pretence make long prayer." He hated wickedness so much that he bled to wound it to the heart; he died that it might die; he was buried that he might bury it in his tomb; and he rose that he might for ever trample it beneath his feet. Christ is in the gospel, and that gospel is opposed to wickedness in every form. Wickedness arrays itself in fine apparel, and imitates the language of holiness; but the precepts of Jesus, like his famous scourge of small cords, chase it out of the temple, and will not tolerate it in the church. So, too, in the heart where Jesus reigns, what a war there is between Christ and wickedness! And when our Redeemer shall come to be our Judge, those thundering words, "Depart, you cursed," which are, indeed, only a prolongation of his life teaching concerning sin, shall reveal his abhorrence of iniquity. As warm as is his love for sinners, so hot is his hatred for sin; as perfect as is his righteousness, so complete shall be the destruction of every form of wickedness. Oh, you glorious champion of right, and destroyer of wrong, for this cause has God, even your God, anointed you with the oil of gladness more than your companions.

May 29 — Evening

**Cursed is the man before the Lord, who rises up
and builds this city Jericho.** *{Joshua 6:26}*

Since he was cursed who rebuilt Jericho, how much more the man who labours to restore Popery among us. In our fathers' days the gigantic walls of Popery fell by the power of their faith, the perseverance of their efforts, and the blast of their gospel trumpets; and now there are some who wish to rebuild that accursed system upon its old foundation. Oh Lord, be pleased to thwart their unrighteous endeavours, and pull down every stone which they build. It should be a serious business with us to be thoroughly purged of every error which may have a tendency to foster the spirit of Popery, and when we have made a clean sweep at home we should seek in every way to oppose its all too rapid spread abroad in the church and in the world. This last can be done in secret by fervent prayer, and in public by audacious testimony. We must warn with judicious boldness those who are inclined towards the errors of Rome; we must instruct the young in gospel truth, and tell them about the black doings of Popery in times past. We must aid in spreading the light more thoroughly through the land, for priests, like owls, hate daylight. Are we doing all we can for Jesus and the gospel? If not, our negligence plays into the hands of the priestcraft. What are we doing to spread the Bible, which is the Pope's bane and poison? Are we casting abroad good, sound gospel writings? Luther once said, "The devil hates goose quills," and, doubtless, he has good reason, for by the Holy Spirit's blessing, skilled writers have done much damage to his kingdom. If the thousands who will read this short word tonight will do all they can to hinder the rebuilding of this accursed Jericho, the Lord's glory shall speed among the sons of men. Reader, what can you do? What will you do?

{Daily Reading: 2 Chronicles 31:1–33:25} {Quick Study: Ezra 1:1–3:13}

Seize the foxes for us, the little foxes that spoil the vines. *{Song of Solomon 2:15}*

A little thorn may cause much suffering. A little cloud may hide the sun. Little foxes spoil the vines; and little sins do mischief to the tender heart. These little sins burrow into the soul, and make it so full of what is hateful to Christ, that he will hold no comforting fellowship and communion with us. A great sin cannot destroy a Christian, but a little sin can make him miserable. Jesus will not walk with his people unless they drive out every known sin. He says, "If you keep my commandments, you shall abide in my love, even as I have kept my Father's commandments and abide in his love." Some Christians very seldom enjoy their Saviour's presence. How is this? Surely it must be an affliction for a tender child to be separated from his father. Are you a child of God, and yet satisfied to go on without seeing your Father's face? What! You, the spouse of Christ, and yet content without his company! Surely you have fallen into a sad state, for the chaste spouse of Christ mourns like a dove without her mate, when he has left her. Ask, then, the question, what has driven Christ from you? He hides his face behind the wall of your sins. That wall may be built up of *little* pebbles, as easily as of large stones. The sea is made of drops; the rocks are made of grains of sand: and the sea which divides you from Christ may be filled with the drops of your little sins; and the rock which has almost wrecked your barque, may have been made by the daily working of the coral insects of your little sins. If you wish to live with Christ, and walk with Christ, and see Christ, and have fellowship with Christ, take heed of "the little foxes that spoil the vines, for our vines have tender grapes." Jesus invites you to go *with him* and take them. He will surely, like Samson, take the foxes at once and easily. Go with him to the hunt.

May 30 — Evening

That from now on we should not serve sin. *{Romans 6:6}*

Christian, what have you to do with sin? *Has it not cost you enough already?* Burnt child, will you play with the fire? What! When you have already been between the jaws of the lion, will you step a second time into his den? Have you not had enough of the old serpent? Did he not once poison all your veins, and will you play upon the hole of the asp, and put your hand upon the cockatrice's den a second time? Oh, do not be so mad! So foolish! Did sin ever yield you real pleasure? Did you find solid satisfaction in it? If so, go back to your old drudgery, and wear the chain again, if it delights you. But inasmuch as sin never gave you what it promised to bestow, but deluded you with lies, do not be snared a second time by the old fowler — be free, and let the remembrance of your ancient bondage forbid you to enter the net again! *It is contrary to the designs of eternal love*, which all have an eye to your purity and holiness; therefore, do not run counter to the purposes of your Lord. Another thought should restrain you from sin. *Christians can never sin cheaply*; they pay a heavy price for iniquity. Transgression destroys peace of mind, obscures fellowship with Jesus, hinders prayer, brings darkness over the soul; therefore, do not be the serf and bondman of sin. There is yet a higher argument: each time you "serve sin" you have *"crucified the Lord afresh, and put him to an open shame."* Can you bear *that* thought? Oh! If you have fallen into any special sin today, it may be my Master has sent this admonition this evening, to bring you back before you have backslidden very far. Turn to Jesus anew; he has not forgotten his love for you; his grace is still the same. With weeping and repentance, come to his footstool, and you shall be once more received into his heart; you shall be set upon a rock again, and your goings shall be established.

May 31 — Morning

{Daily Reading: 2 Chronicles 34:1–36:23} {Quick Study: Ezra 4:1–6:22}

The king himself also passed over the brook Kidron. *{2 Samuel 15:23}*

David passed that gloomy brook when fleeing with his mourning company from his traitorous son. The man after God's own heart was not exempt from trouble, indeed, his life was full of it. He was both the Lord's Anointed, and the Lord's Afflicted. Why then should we expect to escape? At sorrow's gates the noblest of our race have waited with ashes on their heads, why then should we complain as though some strange thing had happened to us?

The KING of kings himself was not favoured with a more cheerful or royal road. He passed over the filthy ditch of Kidron, through which the filth of Jerusalem flowed. God had one Son without sin, but not a single child without the rod. It is a great joy to believe that Jesus has been tempted in all points just as we are. What is our Kidron this morning? Is it a faithless friend, a sad bereavement, a slanderous reproach, a dark foreboding? The King has passed over all these. Is it bodily pain, poverty, persecution, or contempt? Over each of these Kidrons the King has gone before us. "In all our afflictions he was afflicted." The idea that our trials are unique must be banished at once and for ever, for he who is the Head of all saints, knows by experience the grief which we think is so unique. All the citizens of Zion must belong to the *Honourable Company of Mourners,* of which the Prince Emmanuel is Head and Captain.

Notwithstanding the abasement of David, he still returned in triumph to his city, and David's Lord arose victorious from the grave; let us then be of good courage, for we also shall win the day. We shall again with joy draw water out of the wells of salvation, though now for a season we have to pass by the noxious streams of sin and sorrow. Courage, soldiers of the cross, the King himself triumphed after going over Kidron, and so shall you.

May 31 — Evening

Who heals all your diseases. *{Psalms 103:3}*

Humbling as is the statement, yet the fact is certain, that we are all more or less suffering under the disease of sin. What a comfort to know that we have a great Physician who is both able and willing to heal us! Let us think of him for a while tonight. His cures are very *speedy* — there is life in a look at him; his cures are *radical* — he strikes at the centre of the disease; and hence, his cures are *sure* and certain. He never fails, and *the disease never returns*. There is no relapse where Christ heals; no fear that his patients should be merely patched up for a season, he makes new men of them: he also gives them a new heart, and he puts within them a right spirit. He is well skilled in *all* diseases. Physicians generally have some speciality. Although they may know a little about almost all our pains and ills, there is usually one disease which they have studied more than all others; but Jesus Christ is thoroughly acquainted with all of human nature. He is as much at home with one sinner as with another, and never yet did he meet with an out of the way case that was difficult for him. He has had extraordinary complications of strange diseases to deal with, but with one glance of his eye he has known exactly how to treat the patient. He is the only universal doctor; and the medicine he gives is the only universal cure, healing in every instance. Whatever our spiritual malady may be, we should at once resort to this Divine Physician. There is no brokenness of heart which Jesus cannot bind up. "His blood cleanses from all sin." We have only to think of the myriads who have been delivered from all sorts of diseases through the power and virtue of his touch, and we shall joyfully put ourselves in his hands. We trust him, and sin dies; we love him, and grace lives; we wait for him and grace is strengthened; we see him as he is, and grace is perfected for ever.

June 1 — Morning

{Daily Reading: Ezra 1:1–2:70} {Quick Study: Ezra 7:1–8:36}

The evening and the morning were the first day. *{Genesis 1:5}*

Was it so even in the beginning? Did light and darkness divide the realm of time in the first day? Then it is little wonder if I have also changes in my circumstances from the sunshine of prosperity to the midnight of adversity. It will not always be the blaze of noon even in my soul concerns, I must expect at times to mourn the absence of my former joys, and seek my Beloved in the night. Nor am I alone in this, for all the Lord's beloved ones have had to sing the mingled song of judgment and of mercy, of trial and deliverance, of mourning and of delight. It is one of the arrangements of divine providence that day and night shall not cease either in the spiritual or natural creation until we reach the land of which it is written, "There is no night there." What our Heavenly Father ordains is wise and good.

What, then, my soul, is it best for you to do? Learn first *to be content* with this divine order, and be willing, with Job, to receive evil from the hand of the Lord as well as good. Study next, *to make the outgoings of the morning and the evening to rejoice.* Praise the Lord for the sun of joy when it rises, and for the gloom of evening as it falls. There is beauty both in sunrise and sunset, sing of it, and glorify the Lord. Like the nightingale, pour forth your notes at all hours. *Believe that the night is as useful as the day.* The dews of grace fall heavily in the night of sorrow. The stars of promise shine forth gloriously amid the darkness of grief. *Continue your service* under all changes. If in the day your watchword is *labour*, at night exchange it for *watch*. Every hour has its duty; continue in your calling as the Lord's servant until he shall suddenly appear in his glory. My soul, your evening of old age and death is drawing near, do not dread it, for it is part of the day; and the Lord has said, "I will cover him all the day long."

June 1 — Evening

He will make her wilderness like Eden. *{Isaiah 51:3}*

I think I see in a vision a howling wilderness, a great and terrible desert, like the Sahara. I perceive nothing in it to relieve the eye, all around I am wearied with a vision of hot and arid sand, strewn with ten thousand bleaching skeletons of wretched men who have expired in anguish, having lost their way in the pitiless waste. What an appalling sight! How horrible! A sea of sand without a bound, and without an oasis, a cheerless graveyard for a forlorn race! But behold and wonder! Suddenly springing up from the scorching sand I see a plant of renown; and as it grows it buds, the bud expands — it is a rose, and by its side a lily bows its modest head; and, miracle of miracles! As the fragrance of those flowers is diffused the wilderness is transformed into a fruitful field, and all around it blossoms exceedingly, the glory of Lebanon is given to it, the excellency of Carmel and Sharon. Do not call it Sahara, call it Paradise. Do not speak of it any longer as the valley of the shadow of death, for where the skeletons lay bleaching in the sun, behold a resurrection is proclaimed, and up spring the dead, a mighty army, full of life immortal. Jesus is that plant of renown, and his presence makes all things new. Nor is the wonder less in each individual's salvation. Over there I see you, dear reader, cast out, an infant, unswathed, unwashed, defiled with your own blood, left to be food for beasts of prey. But lo, a jewel has been thrown into your bosom by a divine hand, and for its sake you have been pitied and tended to by divine providence, you are washed and cleansed from your defilement, you are adopted into heaven's family, the fair seal of love is upon your forehead, and the ring of faithfulness is on your hand — you are now a prince of God, although you were once an orphan, cast away. Oh, prize exceedingly the matchless power and grace which changes deserts into gardens, and makes the barren heart to sing for joy.

June 2 — Morning

{Daily Reading: Ezra 3:1–5:17} {Quick Study: Ezra 9:1–10:44}

**For the flesh lusts against the Spirit, and
the Spirit against the flesh.** *{Galatians 5:17}*

In every believer's heart there is a constant struggle between the old nature and the new. The old nature is very active, and loses no opportunity of plying all the weapons of its deadly armoury against newborn grace; while on the other hand, the new nature is always on the watch to resist and destroy its enemy. Grace within us will employ prayer, and faith, and hope, and love, to cast out the evil; it uses the "whole armour of God," and wrestles earnestly. These two opposing natures will never cease to struggle as long as we are in this world. The battle of "Christian" with "Apollyon" lasted three hours, but the battle of Christian with himself lasted all the way from the Wicket Gate to the Jordan River. The enemy is so securely entrenched within us that he can never be driven out while we are in this body: but although we are closely beset, and often in severe conflict, we have an almighty helper, even Jesus, the Captain of our salvation, who is always with us, and who assures us that we shall eventually be more than conquerors through him. With such assistance, the newborn nature is more than a match for its foes. Are you fighting with the adversary today? Are Satan, the world, and the flesh all against you? Do not be discouraged nor dismayed. Fight on! For God himself is with you; *Jehovah Nissi* is your banner, and *Jehovah Rophi* is the healer of your wounds. Do not fear, you shall overcome, for who can defeat Omnipotence? Fight on, "looking to Jesus"; and though long and stern is the conflict, sweet will be the victory, and glorious the promised reward.

> From strength to strength go on;
> Wrestle, and fight, and pray,
> Tread all the powers of darkness down,
> And win the well-fought day.

June 2 — Evening

Good Master. *{Matthew 19:16}*

If the young man in the gospel used this title in speaking to our Lord, how much more fitly may I thus address him! He is indeed my Master in both senses, a ruling Master and a teaching Master. I delight to run on his errands, and to sit at his feet. I am both his servant and his disciple, and count it my highest honour to own the double character. If he should ask me why I call him "good," I should have a ready answer. It is true that "there is no one good but one, that is, God," but then he is God, and all the goodness of Deity shines forth in him. In my experience, I have found him good, so good, indeed, that all the good I have has come to me through him. He was good to me when I was dead in sin, for he raised me by his Spirit's power; he has been good to me in all my needs, trials, struggles, and sorrows. Never could there be a better Master, for his service is freedom, his rule is love: I wish I were one thousandth part as good a servant. When he teaches me as my Rabbi, he is unspeakably good, his doctrine is divine, his manner is condescending, his spirit is gentleness itself. No error mingles with his instruction — pure is the golden truth which he brings forth, and all his teachings lead to goodness, sanctifying as well as edifying the disciple. Angels find him a good Master and delight to pay their homage at his footstool. The ancient saints proved him to be a good Master, and each of them rejoiced to sing, "I am your servant, oh Lord!" My own humble testimony must certainly be to the same effect. I will bear this witness before my friends and neighbours, for possibly they may be led by my testimony to seek my Lord Jesus as their Master. Oh, that they would do so! They would never regret so wise a deed. If they would only take his easy yoke, they would find themselves in so royal a service that they would enlist in it for ever.

June 3 — Morning

{Daily Reading: Ezra 6:1–7:28} {Quick Study: Nehemiah 1:1–3:32}

These were potters who lived among plants and hedges: they lived there with the king for his work. *{1 Chronicles 4:23}*

Potters were not the very highest grade of workers, but "the king" needed potters, and therefore they were in royal service, although the material upon which they worked was nothing but clay. We, too, may be engaged in the most menial part of the Lord's work, but it is a great privilege to do anything for "the king"; and therefore we will remain in our calling, hoping that, "Although we have worked among the pots, yet we shall be like the wings of a dove covered with silver, and her feathers with yellow gold." The text tells us about those who *lived among plants and hedges*, having rough, rustic, hedging and ditching work to do. They may have desired to live in the city, amid its life, society, and refinement, but they kept their appointed places, for they also were doing the king's work. The place of our habitation is fixed, and we are not to move from it out of whim and caprice, but seek to serve the Lord in it, by being a blessing to those among whom we reside. These potters and gardeners had *royal company*, for they lived "with the king," and although among hedges and plants, they lived with the king there. No lawful place, or gracious occupation, however humble, can debar us from communion with our divine Lord. In visiting hovels, swarming lodging houses, workhouses, or jails, we may go *with the king*. In all works of faith we may count upon Jesus' fellowship. When we are in his work then we may depend upon his smile. You unknown workers who are occupied for your Lord amid the dirt and wretchedness of the lowest of the low, be of good cheer, for jewels have been found in dunghills before now, earthen pots have been filled with heavenly treasure, and noxious weeds have been transformed into precious flowers. Live with the King to do his work, and when he writes his chronicles your name shall be recorded.

June 3 — Evening

He humbled himself. *{Philippians 2:8}*

Jesus is the great teacher of lowliness of heart. We need daily to learn from him. See the Master taking a towel and washing his disciples' feet! Follower of Christ, will you not humble yourself? See him as the servant of servants, and surely you cannot be proud! Is not this sentence the compendium of his biography, "He humbled himself?" Was he not on earth always stripping off first one robe of honour and then another, until, naked, he was fastened to the cross, and there did he not empty out his innermost self, pouring out his life blood, giving up for all of us, until they laid him penniless in a borrowed grave? How low was our dear Redeemer brought! How then can we be proud? Stand at the foot of the cross, and count the purple drops by which you have been cleansed; see the thorn crown; notice his scourged shoulders, still gushing with encrimsoned rills; see hands and feet given up to the rough iron, and his whole self to mockery and scorn; see the bitterness, and the pangs, and the throes of inward grief, showing themselves in his outward frame; hear the thrilling shriek, "My God, my God, why have you forsaken me?" And if you do not lie prostrate on the ground before that cross, you have never seen it: if you are not humbled in the presence of Jesus, you do not know him. You were so lost that nothing could save you except the sacrifice of God's only begotten. Think of that, and just as Jesus stooped for you, so bow yourself in lowliness at his feet. A sense of Christ's amazing love for us has a greater tendency to humble us than even a consciousness of our own guilt. May the Lord bring us in contemplation to Calvary, then our position will no longer be that of the pompous man of pride, but we shall take the humble place of one who loves much because much has been forgiven him. Pride cannot live beneath the cross. Let us sit there and learn our lesson, and then rise and carry it into practice.

June 4 — Morning

{Daily Reading: Ezra 8:1–9:15} {Quick Study: Nehemiah 4:1–6:19}

The kindness and love of God our Saviour. *{Titus 3:4}*

How sweet it is to see the Saviour communing with his own beloved people! There can be nothing more delightful than, by the Divine Spirit, to be led into this fertile field of delight. Let the mind for an instant consider the history of the Redeemer's love, and a thousand enchanting acts of affection will suggest themselves, all of which have had for their design the weaving of the heart into Christ, and the intertwisting of the thoughts and emotions of the renewed soul with the mind of Jesus. When we meditate upon this amazing love, and behold the all-glorious Kinsman of the church endowing her with all his ancient wealth, our souls may well faint for joy. Who can endure such a weight of love? That partial sense of it which the Holy Spirit is sometimes pleased to afford, is more than the soul can contain; how transporting must be a complete view of it! When the soul shall have understanding to discern all the Saviour's gifts, wisdom by which to estimate them, and time in which to meditate upon them, such as the world to come will afford us, we shall then commune with Jesus in a more intimate manner than at present. But who can imagine the sweetness of such fellowship? It must be one of the things which have not entered into the heart of man, but which God has prepared for those who love him. Oh, to burst open the door of our Joseph's granaries, and see the plenty which he has stored up for us! This will overwhelm us with love. By faith we see, as in a glass darkly, the reflected image of his unbounded treasures, but when we shall actually see the heavenly things themselves, with our own eyes, how deep will be the stream of fellowship in which our soul shall bathe itself! Until then, our loudest sonnets shall be reserved for our loving benefactor, Jesus Christ our Lord, whose love for us is wonderful, surpassing the love of women.

June 4 — Evening

Received up into glory. *{1 Timothy 3:16}*

We have seen our well-beloved Lord in the days of his flesh, humiliated and severely vexed; for he was "despised and rejected by men, a man of sorrows, and acquainted with grief." He whose brightness is as the morning, wore the sackcloth of sorrow as his daily dress: shame was his mantle, and reproach was his vesture. Yet now, inasmuch as he has triumphed over all the powers of darkness upon the bloody tree, our faith sees our King returning with dyed garments from Edom, robed in the splendour of victory. How glorious must he have been in the eyes of seraphs, when a cloud received him out of mortal sight, and he ascended up to heaven! Now he wears the glory which he had with God before the earth ever existed, and yet another glory above all — what he has well earned in the fight against sin, death, and hell. As victor he wears the illustrious crown. Listen how the song swells high! It is a new and sweeter song: "Worthy is the Lamb who was slain, for he has redeemed us to God by his blood!" He wears the glory of an Intercessor who can never fail, of a Prince who can never be defeated, of a Conqueror who has vanquished every foe, of a Lord who has the heart's allegiance of every subject. Jesus wears all the glory which the pomp of heaven can bestow upon him, which ten thousand times ten thousand angels can minister to him. You cannot even in your wildest imagination conceive of his exceeding greatness; yet there will be a further revelation of it when he shall descend from heaven in great power, with all the holy angels — "Then he shall sit upon the throne of his glory." Oh, the splendour of that glory! It will ravish his people's hearts. Nor is this all, for eternity shall sound his praise, "Your throne, oh God, is for ever and ever!" Reader, if you wish to have joy in Christ's glory hereafter, he must be glorious in your sight now. *Is he so?*

June 5 — Morning

{Daily Reading: Ezra 10:1–10:44} {Quick Study: Nehemiah 7:1–8:18}

The Lord shut him in. *{Genesis 7:16}*

Noah was shut in away from all the world by the hand of divine love. The door of electing purpose interposes between us and the world which lies in the wicked one. We are not of the world even as our Lord Jesus was not of the world. We cannot enter into the sin, the gaiety, the pursuits of the multitude; we cannot play in the streets of Vanity Fair with the children of darkness, for our Heavenly Father has shut us in. Noah was shut in *with his God*. "*Come* into the ark," was the Lord's invitation, by which he clearly showed that he himself intended to dwell in the ark with his servant and his family. Thus, all the chosen dwell in God and God in them. Happy are the people who are enclosed in the same circle which contains God in the Trinity of his persons, Father, Son, and Spirit. Let us never be inattentive to that gracious call, "Come, my people, enter into your own rooms, and shut your doors after you, and hide yourself as it were for a little moment until the indignation is passed over." Noah was so shut in that *no evil could reach him*. Floods only lifted him heavenward, and winds only wafted him on his way. Outside of the ark all was ruin, but inside all was rest and peace. Without Christ we perish, but in Christ Jesus there is perfect safety. Noah was so shut in that *he could not even desire to come out*, and those who are in Christ Jesus are in him for ever. They shall go out no more for ever, for eternal faithfulness has shut them in, and infernal malice cannot drag them out. The Prince of the house of David shuts and no man opens; and when once in the last days as Master of the house he shall rise up and shut the door, it will be in vain for mere professors to knock, and cry, "Lord, Lord open to us," for that same door which shuts in the wise virgins will shut out the foolish for ever. Lord, shut me in by your grace.

June 5 — Evening

He who does not love does not know God. *{1 John 4:8}*

The distinguishing mark of a Christian is his confidence in the love of Christ, and the yielding of his affections to Christ in return. First, faith sets her seal upon the man by enabling the soul to say with the apostle, "Christ loved me and gave himself for me." Then love gives the countersign, and stamps upon the heart gratitude and love for Jesus in return. "We love him because he first loved us." In those grand old ages, which are the heroic period of the Christian religion, this double mark was clearly to be seen in all believers in Jesus; they were men who knew the love of Christ, and rested upon it as a man leans upon a staff whose trustiness he has tried. The love which they felt towards the Lord was not a quiet emotion which they hid within themselves in the secret chamber of their souls, and which they only spoke about in their private assemblies when they met on the first day of the week, and sang hymns in honour of Christ Jesus the crucified, but it was a passion with them of such a vehement and all-consuming energy, that it was visible in all their actions, spoken about in their everyday conversation, and was visible in their eyes even in their most common glances. Love for Jesus was a flame which fed upon the core and heart of their being; and, therefore, from its own force burned its way into the outer man, and shone there. Zeal for the glory of King Jesus was the seal and mark of all genuine Christians. Because of their dependence upon Christ's love they *dared* much, and because of their love for Christ they *did* much, and it is the same now. The children of God are ruled in their innermost powers by love — the love of Christ constrains them; they rejoice that divine love is set upon them, they feel it shed abroad in their hearts by the Holy Spirit, which is given to them, and then by force of gratitude they love the Saviour with a pure heart, fervently. My reader, do *you* love him? Before you sleep tonight give an honest answer to a weighty question!

June 6 — Morning

{Daily Reading: Nehemiah 1:1–3:32} {Quick Study: Nehemiah 9:1–11:36}

Behold, I am vile. *{Job 40:4}*

One cheering word, poor lost sinner, for you! You think you must not come to God because you are vile. Now, there is not a saint living on earth who has not been made to feel that he is vile. If Job, and Isaiah, and Paul were all obliged to say "I am vile," oh, poor sinner, will you be ashamed to join in the same confession? If divine grace does not eradicate all sin from the believer, how do you hope to do it yourself? If God loves his people while they are still vile, do you think your vileness will prevent his loving you? Believe on Jesus, you outcast of the world's society! Jesus calls *you*, and such as you are.

> Not the righteous, not the righteous;
> Sinners, Jesus came to call.

Even now say, "You have died for sinners; I am a sinner, Lord Jesus, sprinkle your blood on me"; if you will confess your sin you shall find pardon. If, now, with all your heart, you will say, "I am vile, wash me," you shall be washed *now*. If the Holy Spirit shall enable you from your heart to cry

> Just as I am, without one plea
> But that your blood was shed for me,
> And that you bidd'st me come to thee,
> Oh Lamb of God, I come!

You shall rise from reading this morning's portion with all your sins pardoned; and although you awoke this morning with every sin that man has ever committed on your head, you shall rest tonight accepted in the Beloved; although once degraded with the rags of sin, you shall be adorned with a robe of righteousness, and appear as white as the angels are. For "now," note it, "*Now* is the accepted time." If you "believe on him who justifies the ungodly you are saved." Oh! May the Holy Spirit give you saving faith in him who receives the vilest.

June 6 — Evening

Are they Israelites?
So am I. *{2 Corinthians 11:22}*

We have here A PERSONAL CLAIM, and one that *needs proof.* The apostle knew that *his* claim was indisputable, but there are many people who have no right to the title who still claim to belong to the Israel of God. If we are with confidence declaring, "So am I also an Israelite," let us only say it after having searched our heart in the presence of God. But if we can give proof that we are following Jesus, if we can from the heart say, "I trust him wholly, trust him only, trust him simply, trust him now, and trust him for ever," then the position which the saints of God hold belongs to us — all their enjoyments are our possessions; we may be the very least in Israel, "less than the least of all saints," yet since the mercies of God belong to the saints AS SAINTS, and not as advanced saints, or well-taught saints, we may put in our plea, and say, "Are they Israelites? So am I; therefore the promises are mine, grace is mine, glory will be mine." The claim, rightfully made, is one which will yield untold comfort. When God's people are rejoicing that they are his, what a happiness if they can say, "SO AM I!" When they speak of being pardoned, and justified, and accepted in the Beloved, how joyful to respond, "Through the grace of God, SO AM I." But this claim not only has its enjoyments and privileges, but also its conditions and duties. We must share with God's people in cloud as well as in sunshine. When we hear them spoken of with contempt and ridicule for being Christians, we must come boldly forward and say, "So am I." When we see them working for Christ, giving their time, their talent, their whole heart to Jesus, we must be able to say, "So do I." Oh, let us prove our gratitude by our devotion, and live as those who, having claimed a privilege, are willing to take the responsibility connected with it.

June 7 — Morning

{Daily Reading: Nehemiah 4:1–6:19} {Quick Study: Nehemiah 12:1–13:31}

You who love the Lord hate evil. *{Psalms 97:10}*

You have good reason to "hate evil," for only consider what harm it has already done to you. Oh, what a world of mischief sin has brought into your heart! Sin blinded you so that you could not see the beauty of the Saviour; it made you deaf so that you could not hear the Redeemer's tender invitations. Sin turned your feet into the way of death, and poured poison into the very fountain of your being; it tainted your heart, and made it "deceitful above all things, and desperately wicked." Oh, what a creature you were when evil had done its utmost with you, before divine grace interposed! You were an heir of wrath even as others; you "ran with the multitude to do evil." Such were all of us; but Paul reminds us, "but you are washed, but you are sanctified, but you are justified in the name of the Lord Jesus, and by the Spirit of our God." We have good reason, indeed, for hating evil when we look back and trace its deadly workings. Evil did such mischief to us, that our souls would have been lost had not omnipotent love interfered to redeem us. Even now it is an active enemy, always watching to harm us, and to drag us to perdition. Therefore, "hate evil," oh, Christians, unless you desire trouble. If you wish to strew your path with thorns, and plant nettles in your death pillow, then neglect to "hate evil," but if you wish to live a happy life, and die a peaceful death, then walk in all the ways of holiness, hating evil, even to the end. If you truly love your Saviour, and wish to honour him, then "hate evil." We know of no cure for the love of evil in a Christian like frequent communion with the Lord Jesus. Spend much time with him, and it is impossible for you to be at peace with sin.

> Order my footsteps by your Word,
> And make my heart sincere;
> Let sin have no dominion, Lord,
> But keep my conscience clear.

June 7 — Evening

Be zealous. *{Revelation 3:19}*

If you wish to see souls converted, if you wish to hear the cry that "the kingdoms of this world have become the kingdoms of our Lord"; if you wish to place crowns upon the head of the Saviour, and see his throne lifted high, then be filled with zeal. For, under God, the way of the world's conversion must be by the zeal of the church. Every grace shall do exploits, but this shall be first; prudence, knowledge, patience, and courage will follow in their places, but zeal must lead the vanguard. It is not the extent of your knowledge, though that is useful; it is not the extent of your talent, though that is not to be despised; it is your zeal that shall do great exploits. This zeal is the fruit of the Holy Spirit: it draws its vital force from *the continued operations* of the Holy Spirit in the soul. If our inner life dwindles, if our heart beats slowly before God, we shall not know zeal; but if all is strong and vigorous within, then we can only feel a loving anxiety to see the kingdom of Christ come, and his will done on earth, even as it is in heaven. A deep *sense of gratitude* will nourish Christian zeal. Looking to the hole of the pit from where we were dug, we find abundant reason why we should spend and be spent for God. And zeal is also stimulated by *the thought of the eternal future.* It looks with tearful eyes down to the flames of hell, and it cannot slumber: it looks up with anxious gaze to the glories of heaven, and it can only bestir itself. It feels that time is short compared with the work to be done, and therefore it devotes all that it has to the cause of its Lord. And it is always strengthened *by the remembrance of Christ's example.* He was clothed with zeal as with a cloak. How swift the chariot wheels of duty went with him! He knew no loitering by the way. Let us prove that we are his disciples by showing the same spirit of zeal.

June 8 — Morning

{Daily Reading: Nehemiah 7:1–8:18} {Quick Study: Esther 1:1–2:23}

Many slain fell down there, because the war was of God. *{1 Chronicles 5:22}*

Warrior, fighting under the banner of the Lord Jesus, observe this verse with holy joy, for as it was in the days of old so it is now, if the war is of God the victory is certain. The sons of Reuben, and the Gadites, and the half tribe of Manasseh could barely muster forty-five thousand fighting men, and yet in their war with the Hagarites, they slew "a hundred thousand men," "for they cried to God in the battle, and he answered them, because they put their trust in him." The Lord does not save by many nor by few; it is ours to go out in Jehovah's name even if we are only a handful of men, for the Lord of Hosts is our Captain. They did not neglect buckler, and sword, and bow, neither did they place their trust in these weapons; we must use all fitting means, but our confidence must rest in the Lord alone, for he is the sword and the shield of his people. The great reason for their extraordinary success lay in the fact that "the war was of God." Beloved, in fighting with sin without and within, with doctrinal or practical error, with spiritual wickedness in high places or low places, with demons and the devil's allies, you are waging Jehovah's war, and unless he himself can be worsted, you need not fear defeat. Do not quail before superior numbers, do not shrink from difficulties or impossibilities, do not flinch at wounds or death, strike with the two-edged sword of the Spirit, and the slain shall lie in heaps. The battle is the Lord's and he will deliver his enemies into our hands. With steadfast foot, strong hand, dauntless heart, and flaming zeal, rush to the conflict, and the hosts of evil shall fly like chaff before the gale.

> Stand up! Stand up for Jesus! The strife will not be long;
> This day the noise of battle, the next the victor's song:
> To him that overcomes, a crown of life shall be;
> He with the King of glory shall reign eternally.

June 8 — Evening

Now you shall see whether my word comes true or not. *{Numbers 11:23}*

God had made a positive promise to Moses that for the period of a whole month he would feed the vast host in the wilderness with meat. Moses, being overtaken by a fit of unbelief, looks to the outward means, and is at a loss to know how the promise can be fulfilled. He looked to the creature instead of the Creator. But does the Creator expect the creature to fulfil his promise for him? No; he who makes the promise always fulfils it by his own unaided omnipotence. If he speaks, it is done — done by himself. His promises do not depend for their fulfilment upon the co-operation of the puny strength of man. We can at once perceive the mistake which Moses made. And yet how commonly we do the same! God has promised to supply our needs, and we look to the creature to do what God has promised to do; and then, because we perceive the creature to be weak and feeble, we indulge in unbelief. Why do we look to that quarter at all? Will you look to the north pole to gather fruits ripened in the sun? Truly, you would act no more foolishly if you did this than when you look to the weak for strength, and to the creature to do the Creator's work. Let us, then, put the question on the right footing. The basis of faith is not the sufficiency of the visible means for the performance of the promise, but the all-sufficiency of the invisible God, who will most surely do as he has said. If after clearly seeing that the onus lies with the Lord and not with the creature, we dare to indulge in mistrust, the question of God comes home mightily to us: "Has the Lord's hand waxed short?" May it happen, too, in his mercy, that with the question there may flash upon our souls that blessed declaration, "Now you shall see whether my word comes true or not."

June 9 — Morning

{Daily Reading: Nehemiah 9:1–10:39} {Quick Study: Esther 3:1–5:14}

The Lord has done great things for us, for which we are glad. *{Psalms 126:3}*

Some Christians are sadly prone to *look* on the *dark* side of everything, and to dwell more upon what they have gone through than upon what God has done for them. Ask for their impression of the Christian life, and they will describe their continual conflicts, their deep afflictions, their sad adversities, and the sinfulness of their hearts, yet with scarcely any allusion to the mercy and help which God has given to them. But a Christian whose soul is in a *healthy* state, will come forward joyously, and say, "I will speak, not about myself, but for the honour of my God. He has brought me up out of a horrible pit, and out of the miry clay, and set my feet upon a rock, and established my goings: and he has put a new song in my mouth, even praise to our God. The Lord has done great things for me, for which I am glad." Such an abstract of experience as this is the very best that any child of God can present. It is true that we endure trials, but it is just as true that we are delivered out of them. It is true that we have our corruptions, and mournfully we know this, but it is quite as true that we have an all-sufficient Saviour, who overcomes these corruptions, and delivers us from their dominion. In looking back, it would be wrong to deny that we have been in the Slough of Despond, and have crept along the Valley of Humiliation, but it would be equally wicked to forget that we have been *through* them safely and profitably; we have not remained in them, thanks to our Almighty Helper and Leader, who has brought us "out into a wealthy place." The deeper our troubles, the louder our thanks to God, who has led us through all, and preserved us until now. Our griefs cannot mar the melody of our praise, we account them to be the bass part of our life's song, "He has done great things for us, for which we are glad."

June 9 — Evening

Search the Scriptures. *{John 5:39}*

The Greek word here rendered *search* signifies a strict, close, diligent, curious search, such as men make when they are seeking gold, or hunters when they are in earnest after game. We must not rest content with having given a superficial reading to a chapter or two, but with the candle of the Spirit we must deliberately seek out the hidden meaning of the word. Holy Scripture *requires searching* — much of it can only be learned by careful study. There is milk for babes, but also meat for strong men. The rabbis wisely say that a mountain of matter hangs upon every word, yes, upon every tittle of Scripture. Tertullian exclaims, "I adore the fulness of the Scriptures." No man who merely skims the book of God can profit by it; we must dig and mine until we obtain the hidden treasure. The door of the Word only opens to the key of diligence. The Scriptures *claim searching*. They are the writings of God, bearing the divine stamp and seal — who shall dare to treat them with levity? He who despises them despises the God who wrote them. God forbid that any of us should leave our Bibles to become swift witnesses against us in the great day of account. The Word of God *will repay searching*. God does not ask us to sift a mountain of chaff with here and there a grain of wheat in it, but the Bible is winnowed grain — we have only to open the granary door and find it. Scripture grows upon the student. It is full of surprises. Under the teaching of the Holy Spirit, to the searching eye it glows with splendour of revelation, like a vast temple paved with beaten gold, and roofed with rubies, emeralds, and all manner of gems. There is no merchandise like the merchandise of scriptural truth. Lastly, *the Scriptures reveal Jesus*: "They are what testify about me." No more powerful motive can be urged upon Bible readers than this: he who finds Jesus finds life, heaven, and all things. He is happy who, in searching his Bible, discovers his Saviour.

June 10 — Morning

{Daily Reading: Nehemiah 11:1–12:47} {Quick Study: Esther 6:1–8:17}

We live for the Lord. *{Romans 14:8}*

If God had willed it, each of us might have entered heaven at the moment of conversion. It was not absolutely necessary for our preparation for immortality that we should remain here. It is possible for a man to be taken to heaven, and to be found fit to be a partaker of the inheritance of the saints in light, though he has only just believed in Jesus. It is true that our sanctification is a long and continued process, and we shall not be perfected until we lay aside our bodies and enter within the veil; but nevertheless, had the Lord so willed it, he might have changed us from imperfection to perfection, and have taken us to heaven at once. Why then are we here? Would God keep his children out of paradise a single moment longer than was necessary? Why is the army of the living God still on the battlefield when one charge might give them the victory? Why are his children still wandering here and there through a maze, when a solitary word from his lips would bring them into the centre of their hopes in heaven? The answer is — they are here so that they may *"live for the Lord,"* and may bring others to know his love. We remain on earth as sowers to scatter good seed; as ploughmen to break up the fallow ground; as heralds publishing salvation. We are here as the "salt of the earth," to be a blessing to the world. We are here to glorify Christ in our daily life. We are here as workers for him, and as "workers together with him." Let us see that our life fulfils its purpose. Let us live earnest, useful, holy lives, to "the praise of the glory of his grace." Meanwhile we long to be with him, and daily sing —

> My heart is with him on his throne,
> And ill can brook delay;
> Each moment listening for the voice,
> "Rise up, and come away."

June 10 — Evening

These are they which testify of me. *{John 5:39}*

Jesus Christ is the Alpha and Omega of the Bible. He is the constant theme of its sacred pages; from first to last they testify about him. At the creation we at once discern him as one of the sacred Trinity; we catch a glimpse of him in the promise of the woman's seed; we see him typified in the ark of Noah; we walk with Abraham, as he sees the Messiah's day; we dwell in the tents of Isaac and Jacob, feeding upon the gracious promise; we hear the venerable Israel speaking of Shiloh; and in the numerous types of the law, we find the Redeemer abundantly foreshadowed. Prophets and kings, priests and preachers, all look one way — they all stand as the cherubs did over the ark, desiring to look within, and to read the mystery of God's great propitiation. Still more clearly in the New Testament we find our Lord is the one pervading subject. It is not an ingot here and there, or dust of gold thinly scattered, but here you stand upon a solid floor of gold; for the whole substance of the New Testament is Jesus crucified, and even its closing sentence is bejewelled with the Redeemer's name. We should always read Scripture in this light; we should consider the word to be as a mirror into which Christ looks down from heaven; and then we, looking into it, see his face reflected as in a mirror — darkly, it is true, but still in such a way as to be a blessed preparation for seeing him as we shall see him face to face. This volume contains Jesus Christ's letters to us, perfumed by his love. These pages are the garments of our King, and they all smell of myrrh, and aloes, and cassia. Scripture is the royal chariot in which Jesus rides, and it is paved with love for the daughters of Jerusalem. The Scriptures are the swaddling bands of the holy child Jesus; unroll them and you find your Saviour. The quintessence of the Word of God is Christ.

June 11 — Morning

{Daily Reading: Nehemiah 13:1–13:31} {Quick Study: Esther 9:1–10:3}

We love him because he first loved us. *{1 John 4:19}*

There is no light in the planet but what proceeds from the sun; and there is no true love for Jesus in the heart except what comes from the Lord Jesus himself. All our love for God must spring from this overflowing fountain of the infinite love of God. This must always be a great and certain truth, that we love him for no other reason than because he first loved us. Our love for him *is the fair offspring* of his love for us. Anyone may have cold admiration when studying the works of God, but the warmth of love can only be kindled in the heart by God's Spirit. How great is the wonder that such as we should ever have been brought to love Jesus at all! How marvellous that when we had rebelled against him, he would, by a display of such amazing love, seek to draw us back. No! We would never have had a grain of love towards God unless it had been sown in us by the sweet seed of his love for us. Love, then, has for its parent the love of God shed abroad in the heart: but after it is thus divinely born, it must be *divinely nourished*. Love is an exotic; it is not a plant which will flourish naturally in human soil, it must be watered from above. Love for Jesus is a flower of a delicate nature, and if it received no nourishment except for what could be drawn from the rock of our hearts it would soon wither. Since love comes from heaven, it must feed on heavenly bread. It cannot exist in the wilderness unless it is fed by manna from on high. Love must feed on love. The very soul and life of our love for God is his love for us.

> I love you, Lord, but with no love of mine,
> For I have none to give;
> I love you, Lord; but all the love is yours,
> For by your love I live.
> I am as nothing, and rejoice to be
> Emptied, and lost, and swallowed up in thee.

June 11 — Evening

There he broke the arrows of the bow, the shield, and the sword, and the battle. *{Psalms 76:3}*

Our Redeemer's glorious cry of "It is finished" was the death knell of all the adversaries of his people, the breaking of "the arrows of the bow, the shield, and the sword, and the battle." Behold the hero of Golgotha using his cross as an anvil, and his woes as a hammer, dashing to shivers bundle after bundle of our sins, those poisoned "arrows of the bow"; trampling on every indictment, and destroying every accusation. What glorious blows the mighty Breaker gives with a hammer far more ponderous than the fabled weapon of Thor! How the diabolical darts fly to fragments, and the infernal bucklers are broken like potters' vessels! Behold, he draws from its sheath of hellish workmanship the dread sword of Satanic power! He snaps it across his knee, as a man breaks the dry wood of a fagot, and casts it into the fire. Beloved, no sin of a believer can now be an arrow to mortally wound him, no condemnation can now be a sword to kill him, for the punishment of our sin was borne by Christ, a full atonement was made for all our iniquities by our blessed Substitute and Surety. Who now accuses? Who now condemns? Christ has died, yes rather, has risen again. Jesus has emptied the quivers of hell, has quenched every fiery dart, and broken off the head of every arrow of wrath; the ground is strewn with the splinters and relics of the weapons of hell's warfare, which are only visible to us to remind us of our former danger, and of our great deliverance. Sin has dominion over us no more. Jesus has made an end of it, and put it away for ever. Oh, you enemy, destructions are come to a perpetual end. Talk of all the wondrous works of the Lord, you who make mention of his name, do not keep silence, neither by day, nor when the sun goes to its rest. Bless the Lord, oh my soul.

June 12 — Morning

{Daily Reading: Esther 1:1–3:15} {Quick Study: Job 1:1–2:13}

You are weighed in the balances and are found wanting. *{Daniel 5:27}*

It is good to frequently weigh ourselves in the scale of God's Word. You will find it a holy exercise to read some psalm of David, and, as you meditate upon each verse, to ask yourself, "Can I say this? Have I felt as David felt? Has my heart ever been broken on account of sin as his was when he penned his penitential psalms? Has my soul been full of true confidence in the hour of difficulty as his was when he sang of God's mercies in the cave of Adullam, or in the strongholds of Engedi? Do I take the cup of salvation and call upon the name of the Lord?" Then turn to the life of Christ, and as you read, ask yourselves how far you are conformed to his likeness. Endeavour to discover whether you have the meekness, the humility, the lovely spirit which he constantly inculcated and displayed. Take, then, the epistles, and see whether you can go with the apostle in what he said of his experience. Have you ever cried out as he did — "Oh wretched man that I am! Who shall deliver me from the body of this death?" Have you ever felt his self-abasement? Have you seemed to yourself to be the chief of sinners, and less than the least of all saints? Have you known anything of his devotion? Could you join with him and say, "For me to live is Christ, and to die is gain?" If we thus read God's Word as a test of our spiritual condition, we shall have good reason to stop many a time and say, "Lord, I feel I have never yet been here, oh bring me here! Give me true penitence, such as what I am reading about. Give me real faith; give me warmer zeal; inflame me with more fervent love; grant me the grace of meekness; make me more like Jesus. Let me no longer be 'found wanting,' when weighed in the balances of the sanctuary, lest I am found wanting in the scales of judgment." "Judge yourselves so that you are not judged."

June 12 — Evening

Who has saved us, and called us with a holy calling. {2 Timothy 1:9}

The apostle uses the perfect tense and says, "Who has saved us." Believers in Christ Jesus *are* saved. They are not looked upon as people who are in a hopeful state, and may ultimately be saved, but they *are* already saved. Salvation is not a blessing to be enjoyed upon the deathbed, and to be sung of in a future state above, but a matter to be obtained, received, promised, and enjoyed now. The Christian is perfectly saved *in God's purpose*; God has ordained him to salvation, and that purpose is complete. He is saved also with respect to the *price which has been paid for him*: "It is finished" was the cry of the Saviour before he died. The believer is also perfectly saved *in his covenant head*, for just as he fell in Adam, so he lives in Christ. This complete salvation is accompanied by *a holy calling*. Those whom the Saviour saved upon the cross are in due time effectually called by the power of God the Holy Spirit to holiness: they leave their sins; they endeavour to be like Christ; they choose holiness, not out of any compulsion, but from the stress of a new nature, which leads them to rejoice in holiness just as naturally as they delighted in sin before. God neither chose them nor called them because they were holy, but he called them so that they might be holy, and holiness is the beauty produced by his workmanship in them. The excellencies which we see in a believer are as much the work of God as the atonement itself. Thus the fulness of the grace of God is brought out very sweetly. Salvation must be by grace, because the Lord is its author: and what motive except grace could move him to save the guilty? Salvation must be by grace, because the Lord works in such a manner that our righteousness is for ever excluded. Such is the believer's privilege — *a present salvation*; such is the evidence that he is called to it — *a holy life*.

June 13 — Morning

{Daily Reading: Esther 4:1–7:10} {Quick Study: Job 3:1–7:21}

Whoever will, let him take
the water of life freely. *{Revelation 22:17}*

Jesus says, "Take freely." He wants no payment or preparation. He seeks no recommendation from our virtuous emotions. If you have no good feelings, if you are only willing, you are invited; therefore, come! You have no belief and no repentance, — come to him, and he will give them to you. Come just as you are, and take "freely," without money and without price. He gives himself to needy ones. The drinking fountains at the corners of our streets are valuable institutions; and we can hardly imagine anyone so foolish as to feel for his purse, when he stands before one of them, and to cry, "I cannot drink because I do not have five pounds in my pocket." However poor the man is, there is the fountain, and just as he is he may drink from it. Thirsty passengers, as they go by, whether they are dressed in fustian or in broadcloth, do not look for any warrant for drinking; its being there is their warrant for freely taking its water. The liberality of some good friends has put the refreshing crystal there and we take it, and ask no questions. Perhaps the only people who need to go thirsty through the street where there is a drinking fountain, are the fine ladies and gentlemen who are in their carriages. They are very thirsty, but cannot think of being so vulgar as to get out to drink. It would demean them, they think, to drink at a common drinking fountain: so they ride by with parched lips. Oh, how many are there who are rich in their own good works and therefore cannot come to Christ! "I will not be saved," they say, "in the same way as the prostitute or the swearer." What! Go to heaven in the same way as a chimney sweep? Is there no pathway to glory but the path which led the thief there? I will not be saved that way. Such proud boasters must remain without the living water; but,

WHOEVER WILL, LET HIM
TAKE THE WATER OF LIFE FREELY.

June 13 — Evening

Remove vanity and lies far from me. {*Proverbs 30:8*}

Oh, my God, do not be far from me. {*Psalms 38:21*}

Here we have two great lessons — what to deprecate and what to supplicate. The happiest state of a Christian is the holiest state. Just as there is the most heat nearest to the sun, so there is the most happiness nearest to Christ. No Christian enjoys comfort when his eyes are fixed on vanity — he finds no satisfaction unless his soul is quickened in the ways of God. The world may win happiness elsewhere, but he cannot. I do not blame ungodly men for rushing to their pleasures. Why should I? Let them have their fill. That is all they have to enjoy. A converted wife who despaired about her husband was always very kind to him, for she said, "I fear that this is the only world in which he will be happy, and therefore I have made up my mind to make him as happy as I can in it." Christians must seek their delights in a higher sphere than the insipid frivolities or sinful enjoyments of the world. Vain pursuits are dangerous to renewed souls. We have heard of a philosopher who, while he looked *up* to the stars, fell into a pit; but how deeply do they fall who look *down*. Their fall is fatal. No Christian is safe when his soul is slothful and his God is far from him. Every Christian is always safe with regard to the great matter of his standing in Christ, but he is not safe with regard to his experience in holiness, and communion with Jesus in this life. Satan does not often attack a Christian who is living near to God. When the Christian departs from his God, becomes spiritually starved, and endeavours to feed on vanities, then the devil discovers the hour of his advantage. He may sometimes stand foot to foot with the child of God who is active in his Master's service, but the battle is generally short: he who slips as he goes down into the Valley of Humiliation, every time he takes a false step invites Apollyon to assail him. Oh, for grace to walk humbly with our God!

June 14 — Morning

{Daily Reading: Esther 8:1–10:3} {Quick Study: Job 8:1–10:22}

Delight yourself also in the Lord. *{Psalms 37:4}*

The teaching of these words must seem very surprising to those who are strangers to vital godliness, but to the sincere believer it is only the affirmation of a recognised truth. The life of the believer is here described as a *delight in God*, and we are thus assured of the great fact that true religion overflows with happiness and joy. Ungodly people and mere professors never look upon religion as a joyful thing; to them it is service, duty, or necessity, but never pleasure or delight. If they attend to religion at all, it is either that they may gain by it, or else because they dare not do otherwise. The thought of *delight in religion* is so strange to most men, that no two words in their language stand further apart than "holiness" and "delight." But believers who know Christ understand that delight and faith are so blessedly united that the gates of hell cannot prevail to separate them. Those who love God with all their hearts, find that his ways are ways of pleasantness, and all his paths are peace. Such joys, such brimful delights, such overflowing blessednesses, the saints discover in their Lord, that so far from serving him from custom, they would follow him though all the world casts out his name as evil. We do not fear God because of any compulsion; our faith is no fetter, our profession is no bondage, we are not dragged to holiness, nor driven to duty. No, our piety is our pleasure, our hope is our happiness, our duty is our delight.

Delight and true religion are as allied as root and flower; as indivisible as truth and certainty; they are, in fact, two precious jewels glittering side by side in a setting of gold.

> 'Tis when we taste your love,
> Our joys divinely grow,
> Unspeakable like those above,
> And heaven begins below.

June 14 — Evening

Oh Lord, shame of face belongs to us ... because we have sinned against you. {Daniel 9:8}

A deep sense and clear sight of sin, its heinousness, and the punishment which it deserves, should make us lie low before the throne. We have sinned as Christians. Alas! That it should be so. Favoured as we have been, we have yet been ungrateful: privileged beyond most, we have not brought forth fruit in proportion. Who is there, although he may long have been engaged in the Christian warfare, who will not blush when he looks back upon the past? As for our days before we were regenerated, may they be forgiven and forgotten; but since then, although we have not sinned as before, yet we have sinned against light and against love — light which has really penetrated our minds, and love in which we have rejoiced. Oh, the atrocity of the sin of a pardoned soul! An unpardoned sinner sins cheaply compared with the sin of one of God's own elect ones, who has had communion with Christ and leaned his head upon Jesus' bosom. Look at David! Many will talk about his sin, but I urge you to look at his repentance, and hear his broken bones, as each one of them moans out its dolorous confession! See his tears, as they fall upon the ground, and the deep sighs with which he accompanies the softened music of his harp! We have erred: let us, therefore, seek the spirit of penitence. Look, again, at Peter! We speak much about Peter's denying his Master. Remember, it is written, "He wept bitterly." Have we no denials of our Lord to be lamented with tears? Alas! These sins of ours, before and after conversion, would consign us to the place of inextinguishable fire if it were not for the sovereign mercy which has made us to differ, snatching us like brands from the burning. My soul, bow down under a sense of your natural sinfulness, and worship your God. Admire the grace which saves you — the mercy which spares you — the love which pardons you!

June 15 — Morning

{Daily Reading: Job 1:1–4:21} {Quick Study: Job 11:1–14:22}

And Sarah said, "God has made me to laugh,
so that all who hear will laugh with me." *{Genesis 21:6}*

It was far above the power of nature, and even contrary to its laws, that the aged Sarah should be honoured with a son; and even so it is beyond all ordinary rules that I, a poor, helpless, undone sinner, should find grace to bear about in my soul the indwelling Spirit of the Lord Jesus. I, who once despaired, as well I might, for my nature was as dry, and withered, and barren, and accursed as a howling wilderness, even I have been made to bring forth the fruit of holiness. Well may my mouth be filled with joyous laughter, because of the singular, surprising grace which I have received from the Lord, for I have found Jesus, the promised seed, and he is mine for ever. Today I will lift up psalms of triumph to the Lord who has remembered my low estate, for "my heart rejoices in the Lord; my horn is exalted in the Lord; my mouth is enlarged over my enemies, because I rejoice in your salvation."

I wish to have all those who hear of my great deliverance from hell, and my most blessed visitation from on high, laugh for joy with me. I wish to surprise my family with my abundant peace; I wish to delight my friends with my ever-increasing happiness; I wish to edify the church with my grateful confessions; and even impress the world with the cheerfulness of my daily conversation. Bunyan tells us that Mercy laughed in her sleep, and no wonder when she dreamed of Jesus; my joy shall not stop short of hers while my Beloved is the theme of my daily thoughts. The Lord Jesus is a deep sea of joy: my soul shall dive into it and shall be swallowed up in the delights of his companionship. Sarah looked on her Isaac, and laughed with excess of rapture, and all her friends laughed with her; and you, my soul, look on your Jesus, and bid heaven and earth unite in your joy unspeakable.

June 15 — Evening

He opens, and no man shuts. *{Revelation 3:7}*

Jesus is the keeper of the gates of paradise and before every believing soul he sets an open door, which no man or devil shall be able to close against it. What joy it will be to find that faith in him is the golden key to the everlasting doors. My soul, do you carry this key in your bosom, or are you trusting in some deceitful picklock, which will fail you at last? Hear this parable of the preacher, and remember it. The great King has made a banquet, and he has proclaimed to all the world that no one shall enter except those who bring with them the fairest flower that blooms. The spirits of men advance to the gate by the thousands, and each one brings the flower which he esteems to be the queen of the garden; but they are driven in crowds from the royal presence, and do not enter into the festive halls. Some bear in their hand the deadly nightshade of superstition, or the flaunting poppies of Rome, or the hemlock of self-righteousness, but these are not dear to the King, the bearers are shut out of the pearly gates. My soul, have you gathered the rose of Sharon? Do you wear the lily of the valley in your bosom constantly? If so, when you come up to the gates of heaven you will know its value, for you have only to show this choicest of flowers, and the Porter will open: he will not deny you admission for a moment, for the Porter always opens for that rose. You shall find your way with the rose of Sharon in your hand up to the throne of God himself, for heaven itself possesses nothing that excels its radiant beauty, and of all the flowers that bloom in paradise there is none that can rival the lily of the valley. My soul, get Calvary's blood red rose into your hand by faith, by love wear it, by communion preserve it, by daily watchfulness make it your all in all, and you shall be blessed beyond all bliss, happy beyond a dream. Jesus, be mine for ever, my God, my heaven, my all.

June 16 — Morning

{Daily Reading: Job 5:1–8:22} {Quick Study: Job 15:1–17:16}

And I give to them eternal life,
and they shall never perish. *{John 10:28}*

The Christian should never think or speak lightly of unbelief. For a child of God to mistrust his love, his truth, his faithfulness, must be greatly displeasing to him. How can we ever grieve him by doubting his upholding grace? Christian, it is contrary to every promise of God's precious Word that you should ever be forgotten or left to perish! If it could be so, how could he be true who has said, "Can a woman forget her nursing child, that she should not have compassion on the son of her womb? Yes, they may forget, yet I will never forget you." What would be the value of that promise — " 'The mountains shall depart, and the hills be removed; but my kindness shall not depart from you, neither shall the covenant of my peace be removed,' says the Lord who has mercy on you." Where would be the truth of Christ's words — "I give to my sheep eternal life; and they shall never perish, neither shall any man pluck them out of my hand. My Father, who gave them to me, is greater than all; and no man is able to pluck them out of my Father's hand." Where would the doctrines of grace be? They would all be disproved if one child of God should perish. Where would the veracity of God be, his honour, his power, his grace, his covenant, his oath, if any of those for whom Christ has died, and who have put their trust in him, should nevertheless be cast away? Banish those unbelieving fears which so dishonour God. Arise, shake yourself from the dust, and put on your beautiful garments. Remember it is sinful to doubt his Word in which he has promised you that you shall never perish. Let the eternal life within you express itself in confident rejoicing.

> The gospel bears my spirit up:
> A faithful and unchanging God
> Lays the foundation for my hope,
> In oaths, and promises, and blood.

June 16 — Evening

*The Lord is my light and my salvation;
whom shall I fear? The Lord is the strength of my life;
of whom shall I be afraid?* {Psalms 27:1}

The Lord is my light and my salvation." Here is personal interest, *"my light," "my salvation";* the soul is assured of it, and therefore declares it boldly. Into the soul at the new birth divine light is poured as the precursor of salvation; where there is not enough light to reveal our own darkness and to make us long for the Lord Jesus, there is no evidence of salvation. After conversion our God is our joy, comfort, guide, teacher, and in every sense our light: he is light within, light around, light reflected from us, and light to be revealed to us. Note, it is not said merely that the Lord gives light, but that he is light; nor that he gives salvation, but that he is salvation; he, then, who by faith has laid hold upon God, has all covenant blessings in his possession. This being made sure as a fact, the argument drawn from it is put in the form of a question, *"Whom shall I fear?"* A question which is its own answer. The powers of darkness are not to be feared, for the Lord, our light, destroys them; and the damnation of hell is not to be dreaded by us, for the Lord is our salvation. This is a very different challenge from that of boastful Goliath, for it rests, not upon the conceited vigour of an arm of flesh, but upon the real power of the omnipotent I AM. *"The Lord is the strength of my life."* Here is a third glowing epithet, to show that the writer's hope was fastened with a threefold cord which could not be broken. We may well accumulate terms of praise where the Lord lavishes deeds of grace. Our life derives all its strength from God; and if he deigns to make us strong, we cannot be weakened by all the machinations of the adversary. *"Of whom shall I be afraid?"* The bold question looks into the future as well as the present. "If God is for us," who can be against us, either now or in time to come?

June 17 — Morning

{Daily Reading: Job 9:1–12:25} {Quick Study: Job 18:1–21:34}

Help, Lord. *{Psalms 12:1}*

*T*he prayer itself is remarkable, for it is *short*, but *seasonable, sententious*, and *suggestive*. David mourned the fewness of faithful men, and therefore lifted up his heart in supplication — when the creature failed, he fled to the Creator. He evidently felt his own weakness, or he would not have cried for help; but at the same time he intended honestly to exert himself for the cause of truth, for the word "help" is inapplicable where we ourselves do nothing. There is much of *directness, clearness of perception*, and *distinctness of utterance* in this petition of two words; much more, indeed, than in the long rambling outpourings of certain professors. The psalmist runs directly to his God, with a well-considered prayer; he knows what he is seeking, and where to seek it. Lord, teach us to pray in the same blessed manner.

The occasions for the use of this prayer are frequent. In providential afflictions how suitable it is for tried believers who find all helpers failing them. Students, in *doctrinal difficulties*, may often obtain aid by lifting up this cry of "Help, Lord," to the Holy Spirit, the great Teacher. Spiritual warriors in *inward conflicts* may send to the throne for reinforcements, and this will be a model for their request. Workers in *heavenly labour* may thus obtain grace in time of need. Seeking sinners, in *doubts and alarms,* may offer up the same weighty supplication; in fact, in all these cases, times, and places, this will be sufficient for needy souls. "Help, Lord," will suit us living and dying, suffering or labouring, rejoicing or sorrowing. In him our help is found, let us not be slack to cry to him.

The answer to the prayer is certain, if it is sincerely offered through Jesus. The Lord's character assures us that he will not leave his people; his relationship as Father and Husband guarantee us his aid; his gift of Jesus is a pledge of every good thing; and his sure promise stands, "Do not fear, I WILL HELP YOU."

June 17 — Evening

**Then Israel sang this song, "Spring up,
oh well; sing to it."** *{Numbers 21:17}*

The well of Beer in the wilderness was famous, because it was *the subject of a promise*: "That is the well of which the Lord spoke to Moses, 'Gather the people together, and I will give them water.' " The people needed water, and it was promised by their gracious God. We need fresh supplies of heavenly grace, and in the covenant the Lord has pledged himself to give all we require. The well next became *the cause for a song*. Before the water gushed forth, cheerful faith prompted the people to sing; and as they saw the crystal fount bubbling up, the music grew still more joyous. In like manner, we who believe the promise of God should rejoice in the prospect of divine revivals in our souls, and as we experience them our holy joy should overflow. Are we thirsting? Let us not murmur, but sing. Spiritual thirst is bitter to bear, but we need not bear it — the promise indicates a well; let us be of good heart, and look for it. Moreover, the well was *the centre of prayer*. "Spring up, oh well." What God has engaged to give, we must enquire after, or we show that we have neither desire nor faith. This evening let us ask that the Scripture we have read, and our devotional exercises, may not be an empty formality, but a channel of grace for our souls. Oh, that God the Holy Spirit would work in us with all his mighty power, filling us with all the fulness of God. Lastly, the well was *the object of effort*. "The nobles of the people dug it with their staves." The Lord would have us active in obtaining grace. Our staves are poorly suited for digging in the sand, but we must use them to the utmost of our ability. Prayer must not be neglected; the assembling of ourselves together must not be forsaken; ordinances must not be slighted. The Lord will give us his peace most plenteously, but not in a way of idleness. Let us, then, bestir ourselves to seek him in whom are all our fresh springs.

June 18 — Morning

{Daily Reading: Job 13:1–16:22} {Quick Study: Job 22:1–24:25}

Your Redeemer. *{Isaiah 54:5}*

Jesus, the Redeemer, is altogether ours and ours for ever. All the *offices* of Christ are held on our behalf. He is king for us, priest for us, and prophet for us. Whenever we read a new title of the Redeemer, let us appropriate him as ours under that name as much as under any other. The shepherd's staff, the father's rod, the captain's sword, the priest's mitre, the prince's sceptre, the prophet's mantle, all are ours. Jesus has no dignity which he will not employ for our exaltation, and no prerogative which he will not exercise for our defence. His fulness of *Godhead* is our unfailing, inexhaustible treasure house.

His *manhood* also, which he took upon him for us, is ours in all its perfection. To us our gracious Lord communicates the spotless virtue of a stainless character; to us he gives the meritorious efficacy of a devoted life; on us he bestows the reward procured by obedient submission and incessant service. He makes the unsullied garment of his life our covering beauty; the glittering virtues of his character our ornaments and jewels; and the superhuman meekness of his death our boast and glory. He bequeaths us his manger, from which to learn how God came down to man; and his cross to teach us how man may go up to God. All his thoughts, emotions, actions, utterances, miracles, and intercessions, were for us. He trod the road of sorrow on our behalf, and has bequeathed to us as his heavenly legacy the full results of all the labours of his life. He is now as much ours as he ever was; and he does not blush to acknowledge himself as "*our* Lord Jesus Christ," though he is the blessed and only Potentate, the King of kings, and Lord of lords. Christ everywhere and every way is our Christ, for ever and ever most richly to enjoy. Oh, my soul, by the power of the Holy Spirit! Call him this morning, "Your Redeemer."

June 18 — Evening

I have come into my garden, my sister, my spouse. *{Song of Solomon 5:1}*

The heart of the believer is Christ's garden. He bought it with his precious blood, and he enters it and claims it as his own. A garden *implies separation*. It is not the open common; it is not a wilderness; it is walled around, or hedged in. Oh, that we could see the wall of separation between the church and the world made broader and stronger. It makes one sad to hear Christians saying, "Well, there is no harm in this; there is no harm in that," thus getting as near to the world as possible. Grace is at a low ebb in that soul which can even raise the question of how far it may go in worldly conformity. A garden is *a place of beauty*, it far surpasses the wild uncultivated lands. The genuine Christian must seek to be more excellent in his life than the best moralist, because Christ's garden ought to produce the best flowers in all the world. Even the best is poor compared with Christ's deservings; let us not put him off with withering and dwarf plants. The rarest, richest, choicest lilies and roses ought to bloom in the place which Jesus calls his own. The garden is *a place of growth*. The saints are not to remain undeveloped, always mere buds and blossoms. We should grow in grace, and in the knowledge of our Lord and Saviour Jesus Christ. Growth should be rapid where Jesus is the gardener, and the Holy Spirit the dew from above. A garden is *a place of retirement*. So the Lord Jesus Christ would have us reserve our souls as a place in which he can reveal himself, as he does not to the world. Oh, that Christians were more retired, that they kept their hearts more closely set apart for Christ! We often worry and trouble ourselves, like Martha, with much serving, so that we do not have the room for Christ that Mary had, and do not sit at his feet as we should. May the Lord grant the sweet showers of his grace to water his garden today.

June 19 — Morning

{Daily Reading: Job 17:1–20:29} {Quick Study: Job 25:1–28:28}

And they were all filled with the Holy Spirit. *{Acts 2:4}*

The blessings of today would be rich if all of us were filled with the Holy Spirit. It would be impossible to overestimate the consequences of this sacred filling of the soul. Life, comfort, light, purity, power, peace; and many other precious blessings are inseparable from the Spirit's benign presence. As sacred *oil*, he anoints the head of the believer, sets him apart for the priesthood of saints, and gives him grace to execute his office properly. As the only truly purifying *water* he cleanses us from the power of sin and sanctifies us to holiness, working in us to will and to do of the Lord's good pleasure. As the *light*, he first showed us our lost estate, and now he reveals the Lord Jesus to us and in us, and guides us in the way of righteousness. Enlightened by his pure celestial ray, we are no more darkness but light in the Lord. As *fire*, he both purges us from dross, and sets our consecrated nature ablaze. He is the sacrificial flame by which we are enabled to offer our whole souls as a living sacrifice to God. As heavenly *dew*, he removes our barrenness and enriches our lives. Oh, that he would drop from above upon us at this early hour! Such morning dew would be a sweet commencement for the day. As the *dove*, with wings of peaceful love he broods over his church and over the souls of believers, and as a Comforter he dispels the cares and doubts which mar the peace of his beloved. He descends upon the chosen as upon the Lord in Jordan, and bears witness to their sonship by working in them a filial spirit by which they cry, "Abba, Father." As the *wind*, he brings the breath of life to men; blowing where he wishes he performs the quickening operations by which the spiritual creation is animated and sustained. Oh, that we might feel his presence today and every day.

June 19 — Evening

*My Beloved is mine, and I am his: he feeds among
the lilies. Until the daybreak, and the shadows flee away,
return, my Beloved, and be like a roe or a young hart upon
the mountains of Bether.* {Song of Solomon 2:16–17}

Surely if there is a happy verse in the Bible it is this — "My Beloved is mine, and I am his." It is so peaceful, so full of assurance, so overrunning with happiness and contentment that it might well have been written by the same hand which penned the twenty-third Psalm. Yet though the prospect is exceedingly fair and lovely — earth cannot show its superior — it is not entirely a sunlit landscape. There is a cloud in the sky which casts a shadow over the scene. Listen, "Until the daybreak, and the shadows flee away."

There is a word, too, about the "mountains of Bether," or, "the mountains of division," and to our love, anything like division is bitterness. Beloved, this may be your present state of mind; you do not doubt your salvation; you know that Christ is yours, but you are not feasting with him. You understand your vital interest in him, so that you have no shadow of a doubt of your being his, and of his being yours, but still his left hand is not under your head, nor does his right hand embrace you. A shadow of sadness is cast over your heart, perhaps by affliction, certainly by the temporary absence of your Lord, so even while exclaiming, "I am his," you are forced to drop to your knees, and to pray, "until the daybreak, and the shadows flee away, return, my Beloved."

"Where is he?" asks the soul. And the answer comes, "He feeds among the lilies." If we wish to find Christ, we must have fellowship with his people, we must come to the ordinances with his saints. Oh, for an evening glimpse of him! Oh, to sup with him tonight!

June 20 — Morning

{Daily Reading: Job 21:1–24:25} {Quick Study: Job 29:1–31:40}

For, lo, I will command, and I will sift the house of Israel
among all nations, just as grain is sifted in a sieve, yet shall
the least grain not fall upon the earth. *{Amos 9:9}*

Every sifting comes by *divine command and permission*. Satan must have consent before he can lay a finger upon Job. Indeed, more, in some sense our siftings are *directly the work of heaven*, for the text says, "I will sift the house of Israel." Satan, like a drudge, may hold the sieve, hoping to destroy the grain; but the overruling hand of the Master is accomplishing the purity of the grain by the very process which the enemy intended to be destructive. Precious, but much sifted grain of the Lord's floor, be comforted by the blessed fact that the Lord directs both flail and sieve for his own glory, and for your eternal profit.

The Lord Jesus will surely use the fan which is in his hand, and will *divide the precious from the vile*. All are not Israel who are of Israel; the heap on the barn floor is not clean grain, and hence the winnowing process must be performed. In the sieve, true weight alone has power. Husks and chaff being devoid of substance must fly before the wind, and only solid grain will remain.

Observe the *complete safety of the Lord's wheat*; even the least grain has a promise of preservation. God himself sifts, and therefore it is stern and terrible work; he sifts them in all places, "Among all nations"; he sifts them in the most effective manner, "just as grain is sifted in a sieve"; and yet for all this, not the smallest, lightest, or most shrivelled grain, is permitted to fall to the ground. Every individual believer is precious in the sight of the Lord; a shepherd would not lose one sheep, nor a jeweller one diamond, nor a mother one child, nor a man one limb of his body, nor will the Lord lose one of his redeemed people. However insignificant we may be, if we are the Lord's, we may rejoice that we are preserved in Christ Jesus.

June 20 — Evening

Immediately they left their nets,
and followed him. *{Mark 1:18}*

When they heard the call of Jesus, Simon and Andrew obeyed at once without demur. If we would always, punctually and with resolute zeal, put in practice what we hear upon the spot, or at the first fitting occasion, our attendance to the means of grace, and our reading of good books, could not fail to enrich us spiritually. He will not lose his loaf who has taken care at once to eat it, neither can he be deprived of the benefit of the doctrine who has already acted upon it. Most readers and hearers become stirred so far as to purpose to amend; but, alas! the proposal is a blossom which has not been pollinated, and therefore no fruit comes from it; they wait, they waver, and then they forget, until, like the ponds in nights of frost, when the sun shines by day, they are only thawed in time to be frozen again. That fatal *tomorrow* is blood red with the murder of fair resolutions; it is the slaughter house of the innocents. We are very concerned that our little book of "Evening Readings" should not be fruitless, and therefore we pray that readers may not be readers only, but doers, of the word. *The practice of truth is the most profitable reading of it.* Should the reader be impressed with any duty while perusing these pages, let him hasten to fulfil it before the holy glow has departed from his soul, and let him leave his nets, and all that he has, sooner than to be found rebellious to the Master's call. Do not give place to the devil by delay! Hurry on while opportunity and quickening are in happy conjunction. Do not be caught in your own nets, but break the meshes of worldliness, and get away to where glory calls you. Happy is the writer who shall meet with readers resolved to carry out his teachings: his harvest shall be a hundredfold, and his Master shall have great honour. Oh that such might be our reward upon these brief meditations and hurried hints. Grant it, oh Lord, to your servant!

June 21 — Morning

{Daily Reading: Job 25:1–29:25} {Quick Study: Job 32:1–34:37}

You are fairer than the children of men. *{Psalms 45:2}*

The entire person of Jesus is only as one gem, and his life is all along only one impression of the seal. He is altogether complete; not only in his various parts, but as a gracious, all-glorious whole. His character is not a mass of fair colours mixed confusedly, nor a heap of precious stones laid carelessly one upon another; he is a picture of beauty and a breastplate of glory. In him, all the "things of good repute" are in their proper places, and assist in adorning each other. Not one feature in his glorious person attracts attention at the expense of others; but he is perfectly and altogether lovely.

Oh, Jesus! Your power, your grace, your justice, your tenderness, your truth, your majesty, and your immutability make up such a man, or rather such a God-man, as neither heaven nor earth has seen elsewhere. Your infancy, your eternity, your sufferings, your triumphs, your death, and your immortality, are all woven in one gorgeous tapestry, without seam or rent. You are music without discord; you are many, and yet not divided; you are all things, and yet not diverse. As all the colours blend into one resplendent rainbow, so all the glories of heaven and earth meet in you, and unite so wondrously, that there is no one like you in all things; indeed, if all the virtues of the most excellent were bound in one bundle, they could not rival you, oh mirror of all perfection. You have been anointed with the holy oil of myrrh and cassia, which your God has reserved for you alone; and as for your fragrance, it is as the holy perfume, the like of which no one else can ever make, even with the art of the apothecary; each spice is fragrant, but the compound is divine.

> Oh, sacred symmetry! Oh, rare connection
> Of many perfects, to make one perfection!
> Oh, heavenly music, where all parts do meet
> In one sweet strain, to make one perfect sweet!

June 21 — Evening

The foundation of God stands firm. *{2 Timothy 2:19}*

The foundation upon which our faith rests is this, that "God was in Christ reconciling the world to himself, not imputing their trespasses to them." The great fact on which genuine faith relies is, that "the Word was made flesh and lived among us," and that "Christ also has suffered for sin, the just for the unjust, so that he might bring us to God"; "who himself bore our sins in his own body on the tree"; "for the chastisement of our peace was upon him, and by his stripes we are healed." In one word, the great pillar of the Christian's hope is *substitution*. The vicarious sacrifice of Christ for the guilty, Christ being made sin for us so that we might be made the righteousness of God in him, Christ offering up a true and proper expiatory and substitutionary sacrifice in the room, place, and stead of as many as the Father gave him, who are known to God by name, and are recognised in their own hearts by their trusting in Jesus — this is the cardinal fact of the gospel. If this foundation would be removed, what could we do? But it stands firm as the throne of God. We know it; we rest on it; we rejoice in it; and our delight is to hold it, to meditate upon it, and to proclaim it, while we desire to be actuated and moved by gratitude for it in every part of our life and conduct. In these days a direct attack is made upon the doctrine of the atonement. Men cannot bear substitution. They gnash their teeth at the thought of the Lamb of God bearing the sin of man. But we, who know by experience the preciousness of this truth, will proclaim it in defiance of them confidently and unceasingly. We will neither dilute it nor change it, nor fritter it away in any shape or fashion. It shall still be Christ, a *positive substitute*, bearing human guilt and suffering in the place of men. We cannot, dare not, give it up, for it is our life, and despite every controversy we feel that "nevertheless the foundation of God stands firm."

June 22 — Morning

{Daily Reading: Job 30:1–33:33} {Quick Study: Job 35:1–37:24}

He shall build the temple of the Lord; and he shall bear the glory. *{Zechariah 6:13}*

Christ himself is the builder of his spiritual temple, and he has built it on the mountains of his unchangeable affection, his omnipotent grace, and his infallible truthfulness. But as it was in Solomon's temple, so in this; the materials need to be prepared. There are the "cedars of Lebanon," but they are not framed for the building; they are not cut down, and shaped, and made into those planks of cedar, whose odoriferous beauty shall make glad the courts of the Lord's house in Paradise. There are also the rough stones still in the quarry, they must be hewn there, and squared. All this is Christ's own work. Each individual believer is being prepared, and polished, and made ready for his place in the temple; but Christ's own hand performs the preparation work. Afflictions cannot sanctify, unless they are used by him for this end. Our prayers and efforts cannot make us ready for heaven, apart from the hand of Jesus, who properly fashions our hearts.

As in the building of Solomon's temple, "There was neither hammer, nor axe, nor any tool of iron, heard in the house," because all was brought perfectly ready for the exact spot it was to occupy — it is so with the temple which Jesus builds; the preparation is all done on earth. When we reach heaven, there will be no sanctifying us there, no squaring us with affliction, no planing us with suffering. No, we must be made fit here — all *that* Christ will do beforehand; and when he has done it, we shall be ferried by a loving hand across the stream of death, and brought to the heavenly Jerusalem, to abide as eternal pillars in the temple of our Lord.

> Beneath his eye and care,
> The edifice shall rise,
> Majestic, strong, and fair,
> And shine above the skies.

June 22 — Evening

That those things which cannot be
shaken may remain. *{Hebrews 12:27}*

We have many things in our possession at the present moment which can be shaken, and it ill becomes a Christian man to set much stock in them, for there is nothing stable beneath these rolling skies; change is written upon all things. Yet, we have certain "things which *cannot* be shaken," and I invite you this evening to think of them, that if the things which can be shaken should all be taken away, you may derive real comfort from the things that cannot be shaken, which will remain. Whatever your losses have been, or may be, you enjoy present salvation. You are standing at the foot of his cross, trusting alone in the merit of Jesus' precious blood, and no rise or fall of the markets can interfere with your salvation in him; no breaking of banks, no failures and bankruptcies can touch that. Then you are *a child of God* this evening. God is your Father. No change of circumstances can ever rob you of that. Although by losses brought to poverty, and stripped bear, you can say, "He is my Father still. In my Father's house are many mansions; therefore I will not be troubled." You have another permanent blessing, namely, *the love of Jesus Christ.* He who is God and man loves you with all the strength of his affectionate nature — nothing can affect *that.* The fig tree may not blossom, and the flocks may cease from the field, it does not matter to the man who can sing, "My Beloved is mine, and I am his." We cannot lose our best portion and richest heritage. Whatever troubles come, let us play the man; let us show that we are not such little children as to be cast down by what may happen in this poor fleeting state of time. Our country is Emmanuel's land, our hope is above the sky, and therefore, calm as the summer's ocean; we will see the wreck of everything earthborn, and yet rejoice in the God of our salvation.

June 23 — Morning

{Daily Reading: Job 34:1–37:24} {Quick Study: Job 38:1–39:30}

Ephraim is a cake not turned. {Hosea 7:8}

A cake not turned is *uncooked on one side*; and so Ephraim was, in many respects, untouched by divine grace: though there was some partial obedience, there was very much rebellion left. My soul, I charge you, see whether this is your case. Are you thorough in the things of God? Has grace gone through the very centre of your being so as to be felt in its divine operations in all your powers, your actions, your words, and your thoughts? Your aim and prayer should be to be sanctified, spirit, soul, and body. Although you may not yet be perfectly sanctified, yet it must be universal in its action. There must not be the appearance of holiness in one place and reigning sin in another, or else you, too, will be like a cake not turned.

A cake not turned is *soon burnt on the side nearest the fire*, and although no man can have too much religion, there are some who seem burnt black with bigoted zeal for that part of truth which they have received, or are charred to a cinder with a vainglorious Pharisaic ostentation of those religious performances which suit their humour. The assumed appearance of superior sanctity frequently accompanies a total absence of all vital godliness. The saint in public is a devil in private. He deals in flour by day and in soot by night. The cake which is burned on one side, is dough on the other.

If it is so with me, oh Lord, turn me! Turn my unsanctified nature to the fire of your love and let it feel the sacred glow, and let my burnt side cool a little while I learn my own weakness and lack of heat when I am removed from your heavenly flame. Do not let me be found to be a double-minded man, but one entirely under the powerful influence of reigning grace; for I well know if I am left like a cake unturned, and am not on both sides the subject of your grace, I must be consumed for ever amid everlasting burnings.

June 23 — Evening

Waiting for the adoption. *{Romans 8:23}*

Even in this world saints are God's children, but men cannot discover them to be so, except by certain moral characteristics. The adoption is not revealed, the children are not yet openly declared. Among the Romans a man might adopt a child, and keep it private for a long time: but there was a second adoption in public; when the child was brought before the constituted authorities its former garments were taken off, and the father who took it to be his child gave him clothing suitable for his new station in life. "Beloved, now we are the sons of God, and it does not yet appear what we shall be." We are not yet arrayed in the apparel befitting the royal family of heaven; we are wearing in this flesh and blood just what we wore as the sons of Adam; but we know that "when *he* shall appear" who is the "firstborn among many brethren," we shall be like him, we shall see him as he is. Can you not imagine that a child taken from the lowest ranks of society, and adopted by a Roman senator, would say to himself, "I long for the day when I shall be publicly adopted. Then I shall take off these plebeian garments, and be robed as befitting my senatorial rank?" Happy in what he has received, for that very reason he groans to get the fulness of what is promised to him. So it is with us today. We are waiting until we shall put on our proper garments, and shall be revealed as the children of God. We are young nobles, and have not yet worn our coronets. We are young brides, and the marriage day is not yet come, and by the love our Spouse bears for us, we are led to long and sigh for the bridal morning. Our very happiness makes us groan after more; our joy, like a swollen spring, longs to well up like an Iceland geyser, leaping to the skies, and it heaves and groans within our spirit to desire for a time and place to reveal itself to men.

June 24 — Morning

{Daily Reading: Job 38:1–40:24} {Quick Study: Job 40:1–42:17}

A certain woman of the company lifted up her
voice, and said to him, "Blessed is the womb
that bore you, and the breasts which nursed you."
But he said, "Yes rather, blessed are those who
hear the Word of God, and keep it." *{Luke 11:27–28}*

It is fondly imagined by some that it must have involved very special privileges to have been the mother of our Lord, because they supposed that she had the benefit of looking into his very heart in a way in which we cannot hope to do. There may be an appearance of plausibility in the supposition, but not much. We do not know that Mary knew more than others; what she did know she did well to lay up in her heart; but she does not appear from anything we read in the evangelists to have been a better-instructed believer than any other of Christ's disciples. All that she knew we also may discover. Do you wonder that we should say so? Here is a text to prove it: "The secret of the Lord is with those who fear him, and he will show them his covenant." Remember the Master's words — "Henceforth I do not call you servants; for the servant does not know what his Lord does: but I have called you friends; for all things that I have heard from my Father I have made known to you." So blessedly does this Divine Revealer of secrets tell us his heart, that he keeps back nothing which is profitable for us; his own assurance is, "If it were not so, I would have told you." Does he not today show himself to us as he does not do to the world? It is even so; and therefore we will not ignorantly cry out, "Blessed is the womb that bore you," but we will intelligently bless God that, having heard the Word and kept it, we have first of all as true a communion with the Saviour as his mother had, and in the second place as true an acquaintance with the secrets of his heart as she can be supposed to have obtained. Happy soul to be thus privileged!

June 24 — Evening

Shadrach, Meshach, and Abednego, answered
and said "...let be it known to you, oh king, that
we will not serve your gods." *{Daniel 3:16–18}*

The narrative of the manly courage and marvellous deliverance of the three holy children, or rather champions, is well calculated to excite in the minds of believers firmness and steadfastness in upholding the truth in the teeth of tyranny and in the very jaws of death. Let young Christians especially learn from their example, both in matters of faith in religion, and matters of uprightness in business, never to sacrifice their consciences. Lose all rather than lose your integrity, and when all else is gone, still hold firmly to a clear conscience as the rarest jewel which can adorn the bosom of a mortal. Do not be guided by the will-o'-the-wisp of policy, but by the pole star of divine authority. Follow the right at all costs. When you see no present advantage, walk by faith and not by sight. Do God the honour to trust him when it comes to matters of loss for the sake of principle. See whether he will be your debtor! See if he does not even in this life prove his word that "godliness, with contentment, is great gain," and that those who "seek first the kingdom of God and his righteousness, shall have all these things added to them." Should it happen that, in the providence of God, you are a loser by conscience, you shall find that if the Lord does not pay you back in the silver of earthly prosperity, he will discharge his promise in the gold of spiritual joy. Remember that a man's life does not consist in the abundance of his possessions. To wear a guileless spirit, to have a heart void of offence, to have the favour and smile of God, is greater riches than the mines of Ophir could yield, or the traffic of Tyre could win. "Better is a dinner of herbs where love is, than a stalled ox and inward contention with it." An ounce of heart's ease is worth a ton of gold.

June 25 — Morning

{Daily Reading: Job 41:1–42:17} {Quick Study: Psalms 1:1–9:20}

Go up into the high mountain. *{Isaiah 40:9}*

Our knowledge of Christ is somewhat like climbing one of our Welsh mountains. When you are at the base you see very little: the mountain itself appears to be only one half as high as it really is. Confined in a little valley, you discover scarcely anything but the rippling brooks as they descend into the stream at the foot of the mountain. Climb the first rising knoll, and the valley lengthens and widens beneath your feet. Go higher, and you see the country for four or five miles around, and you are delighted with the widening prospect. Mount still higher, and the scene enlarges; until at last, when you are on the summit, and look east, west, north, and south, you see almost all of England lying before you. Over there is a forest in some distant county, perhaps two hundred miles away, and here the sea, and there a shining river and the smoking chimneys of a manufacturing town, or the masts of the ships in a busy port. All these things please and delight you, and you say, "I could not have imagined that so much could be seen at this elevation." Now, the Christian life is much the same. When we first believe in Christ we see very little of him. The higher we climb the more we discover of his beauties. But who has ever gained the summit? Who has known all the heights and depths of the love of Christ which surpasses knowledge? Paul, when grown old, sitting grey haired, shivering in a dungeon in Rome, could say with greater emphasis than we can, "I know whom I have believed," for each experience had been like the climbing of a hill, each trial had been like ascending another summit, and his death seemed like gaining the top of the mountain, from which he could see all of the faithfulness and the love of him to whom he had committed his soul. Climb up, dear friend, into the high mountain.

June 25 — Evening

The dove found no rest for the sole of her foot. *{Genesis 8:9}*

Reader, can you find rest apart from the ark, Christ Jesus? Then be assured that your religion is vain. Are you satisfied with anything short of a conscious knowledge of your union and interest in Christ? Then woe to you. If you profess to be a Christian, yet find full satisfaction in worldly pleasures and pursuits, your profession is false. If your soul can stretch herself at rest, and find the bed long enough, and the coverlet broad enough to cover her in the chambers of sin, then you are a hypocrite, and far enough from any proper thoughts of Christ or perception of his preciousness. But if, on the other hand, you feel that if you could indulge in sin without punishment, yet it would be a punishment in itself; and that if you could have the whole world, and abide in it for ever, it would be quite enough misery not to be parted from it; for your God — your God — is what your soul craves after; then be of good courage, you are a child of God. With all your sins and imperfections, take this for your comfort: if your soul has no rest in sin, you are not as the sinner is! If you are still crying after and craving after something better, Christ has not forgotten you, for you have not quite forgotten him. The believer cannot do without his Lord; words are inadequate to express his thoughts of him. We cannot live on the sands of the wilderness, we want the manna which drops from on high; our skin bottles of creature confidence cannot yield us a drop of moisture, but we drink of the Rock which follows us, and that Rock is Christ. When you feed on him your soul can sing, "He has satisfied my mouth with good things, so that my youth is renewed like the eagle's," but if you do not have him, your bursting wine vat and well-filled barn can give you no sort of satisfaction: rather lament over them in the words of wisdom, "Vanity of vanities, all is vanity!"

June 26 — Morning

{Daily Reading: Psalms 1:1–9:20} {Quick Study: Psalms 10:1–18:50}

Have you become like us? *{Isaiah 14:10}*

What must be the apostate professor's doom when his naked soul appears before God? How will he bear that voice, "Depart, you cursed; you have rejected me, and I reject you; you have played the prostitute, and departed from me: I also have banished you for ever from my presence, and will not have mercy upon you." What will be this wretch's shame on the last great day when, before assembled multitudes, the apostate shall be unmasked? See the profane, and sinners who never professed religion, lifting themselves up from their beds of fire to point at him. "There he is," one says, "Will he preach the gospel in hell?" "There he is," says another, "He rebuked me for cursing, and was a hypocrite himself!" "Aha!" says another, "here comes a psalm-singing Methodist — one who was always at his meeting; he is the man who boasted of his being sure of everlasting life; and here he is!" No greater eagerness will ever be seen among satanic tormentors, than in that day when demons drag the hypocrite's soul down to perdition. Bunyan pictures this with massive but awful grandeur of poetry when he speaks of the back way to hell. Seven demons bound the wretch with nine cords, and dragged him from the road to heaven, in which he had professed to walk, and thrust him through the back door into hell. Mind that back way to hell, professors! "Examine yourselves, whether you are in the faith." Look well to your state; see whether you are in Christ or not. It is the easiest thing in the world to give a lenient verdict when oneself is to be tried; but oh, be just and true here. Be just to all, but be rigorous to yourself. Remember, if it is not a rock on which you build, when the house shall fall, great will be the fall of it. Oh, may the Lord give you sincerity, constancy, and firmness; and in no day, however evil, may you be led to turn aside.

*Having escaped the corruption that is in
the world through lust. {2 Peter 1:4}*

Banish for ever all thought of indulging the flesh if you wish to live in the power of your risen Lord. It would be bad if a man who is alive in Christ should dwell in the corruption of sin. "Why do you seek the living among the dead?" said the angel to Magdalene. Should the living dwell in the sepulchre? Should divine life be immured in the charnel house of fleshly lust? How can we partake of the cup of the Lord and yet drink the cup of demons? Surely, believer, you are delivered from open lusts and sins: have you also escaped from the more secret and delusive lime twigs of the satanic fowler? Have you come forth from the lust of pride? Have you escaped from slothfulness? Have you completely escaped from carnal security? Are you seeking day by day to live above worldliness, the pride of life, and the ensnaring vice of avarice? Remember, it is for this that you have been enriched with the treasures of God. If you are indeed the chosen of God, and beloved by him, do not allow all the lavish treasure of grace to be wasted upon you. Follow after holiness; it is the Christian's crown and glory. An unholy church! It is useless to the world, and of no esteem among men. It is an abomination, hell's laughter, heaven's abhorrence. The worst evils which have ever come upon the world have been brought upon her by an unholy church. Oh, Christian, the vows of God are upon you. You are God's priest: act as such. You are God's king: reign over your lusts. You are God's chosen: do not associate with wickedness. Heaven is your portion: live like a heavenly spirit, so shall you prove that you have true faith in Jesus, for there cannot be faith in the heart unless there is holiness in the life.

Lord, I desire to live as one
Who bears a blood-bought name,
As one who fears but grieving thee,
And knows no other shame.

June 27 — Morning

{Daily Reading: Psalms 10:1–17:15} {Quick Study: Psalms 19:1–24:10}

Only you shall not go very far away. *{Exodus 8:28}*

This is a crafty word from the lip of the archtyrant Pharaoh. If the poor enslaved Israelites must needs go out of Egypt, then he bargains with them that it shall not be very far away; not too far for them to escape the terror of his arms, and the observation of his spies. In the same way, the world does not love the nonconformity of nonconformity, or the dissidence of dissent; it wishes to have us be more charitable and not carry matters with too severe a hand. Death to the world and burial with Christ are experiences which carnal minds treat with ridicule, and hence the ordinance which sets them forth is almost universally neglected, and even condemned. Worldly wisdom recommends the path of compromise, and talks of "moderation." According to this carnal policy, purity is admitted to be very desirable, but we are warned against being too precise; truth is of course to be followed, but error is not to be severely denounced. "Yes," says the world, "be spiritually minded by all means, but do not deny yourself a little carefree companionship, an occasional ball, and a Christmas visit to a theatre. What is the good of decrying a thing when it is so fashionable, and everyone does it?" Multitudes of professors yield to this cunning advice, to their own eternal ruin. If we wish to follow the Lord completely, we must immediately go into the wilderness of separation, and leave the Egypt of the carnal world behind us. We must leave its maxims, its pleasures, and its religion too, and go far away to the place where the Lord calls his sanctified ones. When the town is on fire, our house cannot be too far from the flames. When the plague is abroad, a man cannot be too far from its haunts. The farther from a viper the better, and the farther from worldly conformity the better. To all true believers let the trumpet call be sounded, "Come out from among them, be separate."

June 27 — Evening

**Let every man remain in the same calling in which
he was called.** *{1 Corinthians 7:20}*

Some people have the foolish notion that the only way in which they can live for God is by becoming ministers, missionaries, or Bible women. Alas! How many would be excluded from any opportunity of magnifying the Most High if this were the case. Beloved, it is not office, it is earnestness; it is not position, it is grace which will enable us to glorify God. God is most surely glorified in that cobbler's stall, where the godly worker, as he plies the awl, sings about the Saviour's love, indeed, glorified far more than in many a cathedral where official religiousness performs its scanty duties. The name of Jesus is glorified by the poor unlearned delivery boy as he drives his horse, and blesses his God, or speaks to his fellow labourer by the roadside, as much as by the popular divine who, throughout the country, like Boanerges, is thundering out the gospel. God is glorified by our serving him in our proper vocations. Take care, dear reader, that you do not forsake the path of duty by leaving your occupation, and take care you do not dishonour your profession while in it. Think little of yourselves, but do not think too little of your callings. Every lawful trade may be sanctified by the gospel to noblest ends. Turn to the Bible, and you will find the most menial forms of labour connected either with most daring deeds of faith, or with people whose lives have been illustrious for holiness. Therefore, be contented with your calling. Whatever God has made your position, or your work, remain in that, unless you are quite sure that he calls you to something else. Let your first care be to glorify God to the utmost of your power where you are. Fill your present sphere to his praise, and if he needs you in another he will show it to you. This evening lay aside vexatious ambition, and embrace peaceful content.

{Daily Reading: Psalms 18:1–22:31} {Quick Study: Psalms 25:1–30:12}

Looking to Jesus. *{Hebrews 12:2}*

It is always the Holy Spirit's work to turn our eyes away from self to Jesus; but Satan's work is just the opposite of this, for he is constantly trying to make us look at ourselves instead of Christ. He insinuates, "Your sins are too great for pardon; you have no faith; you do not repent enough; you will never be able to continue to the end; you do not have the joy of his children; you have such a wavering hold of Jesus." All these are thoughts about self, and we shall never find comfort or assurance by looking within. But the Holy Spirit turns our eyes entirely away from self: he tells us that we are nothing, but that "Christ is all in all." Remember, therefore, it is not *your hold* on Christ that saves you — it is Christ; it is not *your joy* in Christ that saves you — it is Christ; it is not even faith in Christ, though that is the instrument — it is Christ's blood and merits; therefore, do not look so much to your hand with which you are grasping Christ, but to Christ; do not look to your hope, but to Jesus, the source of your hope; do not look to your faith, but to Jesus, the author and finisher of your faith. We shall never find happiness by looking at our prayers, our doings, or our feelings; it is what *Jesus* is, not what we are, that gives rest to the soul. If we wish to quickly overcome Satan and have peace with God, it must be by "looking to Jesus." Keep your eyes simply on him; let his death, his sufferings, his merits, his glories, his intercession, be fresh upon your mind; when you awaken in the morning look to him; when you lie down at night look to him. Oh! Do not let your hopes or fears come between you and Jesus; follow closely after him, and he will never fail you.

> My hope is built on nothing less
> Than Jesus' blood and righteousness:
> I dare not trust the sweetest frame,
> But wholly lean on Jesus' name.

June 28 — Evening

But Aaron's rod swallowed up their rods. *{Exodus 7:12}*

This incident is an instructive emblem of the sure victory of the divine handiwork over all opposition. Whenever a divine principle is planted in the heart, although the devil may fashion a counterfeit, and produce swarms of opponents, as truly as God is in the work, it will swallow up all its foes. If God's grace takes possession of a man, the world's magicians may throw down all their rods; and every rod may be as cunning and poisonous as a serpent, but Aaron's rod will swallow up their rods. The sweet attractions of the cross will woo and win the man's heart, and he who lived only for this deceitful earth will now have an eye for the upper spheres, and a wing to mount into celestial heights. When grace has won the day the worldling seeks the world to come. The same fact is to be observed in the life of the believer. What multitudes of foes has our faith had to meet! Our old sins — the devil threw them down before us, and they turned to serpents. What hosts of them! Ah, but the cross of Jesus destroys them all. Faith in Christ makes short work of all our sins. Then the devil has launched forth another host of serpents in the form of worldly trials, temptations, unbelief; but faith in Jesus is more than a match for them, and overcomes them all. The same absorbing principle shines in the faithful service of God! With an enthusiastic love for Jesus difficulties are surmounted, sacrifices become pleasures, sufferings are honours. But if religion is thus a consuming passion in the heart, then it follows that there are many people who profess religion but do not have it; for what they have will not bear this test. Examine yourself, my reader, on this point. Aaron's rod *proved* its heaven-given power. Is your religion doing so? If Christ is anything, he must be everything. Oh, do not rest until love and faith in Jesus are the master passions of your soul!

June 29 — Morning

{Daily Reading: Psalms 23:1–30:12} {Quick Study: Psalms 31:1–35:28}

Also those who sleep in Jesus, God will bring with him. *{1 Thessalonians 4:14}*

Let us not imagine that *the soul* sleeps in insensibility. "Today you shall be with me in paradise," is the whisper of Christ to every dying saint. They "sleep in Jesus," but their souls are before the throne of God, praising him day and night in his temple, singing hallelujahs to him who washed them from their sins in his blood. The body sleeps in its lonely bed of earth, beneath the coverlet of grass. But what is this sleep? The idea connected with sleep is *"rest,"* and that is the thought which the Spirit of God would convey to us. Sleep makes each night a Sabbath for the day. Sleep closes the door of the soul, and bids all intruders tarry for a while, so that the life within may enter its summer garden of ease. The toil-worn believer quietly sleeps, just as does the weary child when it slumbers on its mother's breast. Oh! Happy are those who die in the Lord; they rest from their labours, and their works follow them. Their quiet repose shall never be broken until God shall rouse them to give them their full reward. Guarded by angel watchers, curtained by eternal mysteries, they sleep on, the heirs of glory, until the fulness of time shall bring the fulness of redemption. What an awakening shall be theirs! They were laid in their last resting place, weary and worn, but they shall not rise as such. They went to their rest with the furrowed brow, and the wasted features, but they wake up in beauty and glory. The shrivelled seed, so destitute of form and comeliness, rises from the dust a beautiful flower. The winter of the grave gives way to the spring of redemption and the summer of glory. Blessed is death, since it, through the divine power, disrobes us of this work day garment, to clothe us with the wedding garment of incorruption. Blessed are those who "sleep in Jesus."

June 29 — Evening

However, in the business of the ambassadors of the princes of Babylon, who were sent to him to enquire about the wonder that was done in the land, God left him, to try him, so that he might know all that was in his heart. *{2 Chronicles 32:31}*

Hezekiah was growing so inwardly great, and priding himself so much upon the favour of God, that self-righteousness crept in, and through his carnal security, the grace of God was for a time, in its more active operations, withdrawn. Here is quite enough to account for his folly with the Babylonians; for if the grace of God should leave the best Christian, there is enough of sin in his heart to make him the worst of transgressors. If left to yourselves, you who are warmest for Christ would cool down like Laodicea into sickening lukewarmness; you who are sound in the faith would be white with the leprosy of false doctrine; you who now walk before the Lord in excellency and integrity would reel to and fro, and stagger with a drunkenness of evil passion. Like the moon, we borrow our light; bright as we are when grace shines on us, we are darkness itself when the Sun of Righteousness withdraws himself. *Therefore, let us cry to God never to leave us.* "Lord, do not take your Holy Spirit from us! Do not withdraw your indwelling grace from us! Have you not said, 'I the Lord do keep it; I will water it every moment: lest any harm it, I will keep it night and day?' Lord, keep us everywhere. Keep us when in the valley, so that we do not murmur against your humbling hand; keep us when on the mountain, so that we do not grow giddy through being lifted up; keep us in youth, when our passions are strong; keep us in old age, when becoming conceited with our wisdom, we may therefore prove to be greater fools than the young and giddy; keep us when we come to die, lest, at the very last, we should deny you! Keep us living, keep us dying, keep us labouring, keep us suffering, keep us fighting, keep us resting, keep us everywhere, for everywhere we need you, oh our God!"

June 30 — Morning

{Daily Reading: Psalms 31:1–35:28} {Quick Study: Psalms 36:1–41:13}

And the glory which you gave to me
I have given to them. {John 17:22}

Behold the superlative liberality of the Lord Jesus, for he has given us his all. Although a tithe of his possessions would have made a universe of angels rich beyond all thought, yet he was not content until he had given us all that he had. It would have been surprising grace if he had allowed us to eat the crumbs of his bounty beneath the table of his mercy; but he will do nothing by halves, he makes us sit with him and share the feast. Had he given us some small pension from his royal coffers, we would have had cause to love him eternally; but no, he wishes to have his bride as rich as himself, and he will not have a glory or a grace in which she shall not share. He has not been content with less than making us joint heirs with himself, so that we might have equal possessions. He has emptied all his estate into the coffers of the church, and has all things in common with his redeemed. There is not one room in his house the key of which he will withhold from his people. He gives them full liberty to take all that he has to be their own; he loves for them to freely use his treasure, and to appropriate as much as they can possibly carry. The boundless fulness of his all-sufficiency is as free to the believer as the air he breathes. Christ has put the flagon of his love and grace to the believer's lip, and bidden him drink on for ever; for if he could drain it, he is welcome to do so, and since he cannot exhaust it, he is bidden to drink abundantly, for it is all his own. What truer proof of fellowship can heaven or earth afford?

> When I stand before the throne
> Dressed in beauty not my own;
> When I see thee as thou art,
> Love thee with unsinning heart;
> Then, Lord, shall I fully know —
> Not until then — how much I owe.

June 30 — Evening

*Ah, Lord God, behold, you have made the heaven and
the earth by your great power and outstretched arm, and
there is nothing too hard for you. {Jeremiah 32:17}*

At the very time when the Chaldeans surrounded Jerusalem,
and when the sword, famine and pestilence had desolated the
land, Jeremiah was commanded by God to purchase a field, and
have the deed of transfer legally sealed and witnessed. This was a
strange purchase for a rational man to make. Prudence could not
justify it, for it was buying with scarcely a probability that the buyer
could ever enjoy the possession. But it was enough for Jeremiah
that his God had bidden him, for he well knew that God will be
justified in his actions by their results. He reasoned thus: "Ah, Lord
God! You can make this plot of ground of use to me; you can rid
this land of these oppressors; you can make me yet sit under my
vine and my fig tree in the heritage which I have bought; for you
made the heavens and the earth, and there is nothing too hard for
you." This gave a majesty to the early saints, that they dared to do
at God's command things which carnal reason would condemn.
Whether it is a Noah who is to build a ship on dry land, an Abraham who is to offer up his only son, a Moses who is to despise
the treasures of Egypt, or a Joshua who is to besiege Jericho seven
days, using no weapons but the blasts of rams' horns, they all act
upon God's command, contrary to the dictates of carnal reason;
and the Lord gives them a rich reward as the result of their obedient
faith. Oh that we had in the religion of these modern times a more
potent infusion of this heroic faith in God. If we would venture
more upon the naked promise of God, we would enter a world
of wonders to which we are now strangers. Let Jeremiah's place of
confidence be ours — nothing is too hard for the God who created
the heavens and the earth.

{Daily Reading: Psalms 36:1–39:13} {Quick Study: Psalms 42:1–49:20}

In summer and in winter it shall be. *{Zechariah 14:8}*

The streams of living water which flow from Jerusalem are not dried up by the parching heats of sultry midsummer any more than they were frozen by the cold winds of blustering winter. Rejoice, oh my soul, that you are spared to testify of the faithfulness of the Lord. The seasons change and you change, but your Lord remains for evermore the same, and the streams of his love are as deep, as broad and as full as ever. The heats of business cares and scorching trials make me need the cooling influences of the river of his grace; I may go at once and drink to the full from the inexhaustible fountain, for in summer and in winter it pours forth its flood. The upper springs are never scanty, and blessed be the name of the Lord, the lower springs cannot fail either. Elijah found that Cherith dried up, but Jehovah was still the same God of providence. Job said his brethren were like deceitful brooks, but he found his God an overflowing river of consolation. The Nile is the great confidence of Egypt, but its floods are variable; our Lord is always the same. By turning the course of the Euphrates, Cyrus took the city of Babylon, but no power, human or infernal, can divert the current of divine grace. The tracks of ancient rivers have been found all dry and desolate, but the streams which take their rise on the mountains of divine sovereignty and infinite love shall always be full to the brim. Generations melt away, but the course of grace is unaltered. The river of God may sing with greater truth than the brook in the poem —

> Men may come, and men may go,
> But I go on for ever.

How happy are you, my soul, to be led beside such still waters! Never wander to other streams, lest you hear the Lord's rebuke, "What have you to do in the way of Egypt to drink of the muddy river?"

July 1 — Evening

**The voice of the Lord God walking in the garden
in the cool of the day.** *{Genesis 3:8}*

My soul, now that the cool of the day has come, retire a while and listen to the voice of your God. He is always ready to speak with you when you are prepared to hear. If there is any reluctance to commune it is not on his part, but altogether on your own, for he stands at the door and knocks, and if his people will only open he rejoices to enter. But in what state is my heart, which is my Lord's garden? May I venture to hope that it is well-trimmed and watered, and is bringing forth fruit fit for him? If not, he will have much to reprove, but still I pray for him to come to me, for nothing can so certainly bring my heart into a right condition as the presence of the Sun of Righteousness, who brings healing in his wings. Come, therefore, oh Lord, my God, my soul invites you earnestly, and waits for you eagerly. Come to me, oh Jesus, my well Beloved, and plant fresh flowers in my garden, such as I see blooming in such perfection in your matchless character! Come, oh my Father, who is the Husbandman, and deal with me in your tenderness and prudence! Come, oh Holy Spirit, and bedew my whole nature, as the herbs are now moistened with the evening dews. Oh that God would speak to me. Speak, Lord, for your servant hears! Oh that he would walk with me; I am ready to give up my whole heart and mind to him, and every other thought is hushed. I am only asking what he delights to give. I am sure that he will condescend to have fellowship with me, for he has given me his Holy Spirit to abide with me for ever. Sweet is the cool twilight, when every star seems like the eye of heaven, and the cool wind is as the breath of celestial love. My Father, my older Brother, my sweet Comforter, speak now in lovingkindness, for you have opened my ear and I am not rebellious.

July 2 — Morning

{Daily Reading: Psalms 40:1–45:17} {Quick Study: Psalms 50:1–57:11}

Our hearts shall rejoice in him. *{Psalms 33:21}*

Blessed is the fact that Christians can rejoice even in the deepest distress; although trouble may surround them, they still sing; and, like many birds, they sing best in their cages. The waves may roll over them, but their souls soon rise to the surface and see the light of God's countenance; they have a buoyancy about them which keeps their head always above the water, and helps them to sing amid the tempest, "God is with me still." To whom shall the glory be given? Oh! To *Jesus* — it is all by Jesus. Trouble does not necessarily bring consolation with it to the believer, but the presence of the Son of God in the fiery furnace with him fills his heart with joy. He is sick and suffering, but Jesus visits him and makes his bed for him. He is dying, and the cold chilly waters of Jordan are gathering around him up to the neck, but Jesus puts his arms around him, and cries, "Do not fear, beloved; to die is to be blessed; the waters of death have their fountain head in heaven; they are not bitter, they are sweet as nectar, for they flow from the throne of God." As the departing saint wades through the stream, and the billows gather around him, and heart and flesh fail him, the same voice sounds in his ears, "Do not fear; I am with you; do not be dismayed; I am your God." As he nears the borders of the infinite unknown, and is almost frightened to enter the realm of shades, Jesus says, "Do not fear, it is your Father's good pleasure to give you the kingdom." Thus strengthened and consoled, the believer is not afraid to die; no, he is even willing to depart, for since he has seen Jesus as the morning star, he longs to gaze upon him as the sun in its strength. Truly, the presence of Jesus is all the heaven we desire. He is at once

> The glory of our brightest days;
> The comfort of our nights.

July 2 — Evening

*I will cry to you, oh Lord my rock; do not be silent
to me: lest, if you are silent to me, I become like
those who go down into the pit. {Psalms 28:1}*

A cry is the natural expression of sorrow, and a suitable utterance when all other modes of appeal fail us; but the cry must alone be directed to the Lord, for to cry to man is to waste our entreaties upon the air. When we consider the readiness of the Lord to hear, and his ability to aid, we shall see good reason for directing all our appeals at once to the God of our salvation. It will be in vain to call to the rocks in the day of judgment, but our Rock attends to our cries.

"Do not be silent to me." Mere formalists may be content without answers to their prayers, but genuine supplicants cannot; they are not satisfied with the results of prayer itself in calming the mind and subduing the will — they must go further, and obtain actual replies from heaven, or they cannot rest; and they long to receive those replies at once, they dread even a little of God's silence. God's voice is often so terrible that it shakes the wilderness; but his silence is equally full of awe to an eager supplicant. When God seems to close his ear, we must not therefore close our mouths, but rather cry with more earnestness; for when our note grows shrill with eagerness and grief, he will not long deny us a hearing. What a dreadful case we should be in if the Lord would become silent to our prayers for ever? *"Lest, if you are silent to me, I become like those who go down into the pit."* Deprived of the God who answers prayer, we would be in a more pitiable plight than the dead in the grave, and would soon sink to the same level as the lost in hell. We must have answers to prayer: ours is an urgent case of dire necessity; surely the Lord will speak peace to our agitated minds, for he never can find it in his heart to permit his own elect to perish.

{*Daily Reading: Psalms 46:1–51:19*} {*Quick Study: Psalms 58:1–66:20*}

The ill favoured, lean cows ate up the seven healthy, fat cows. {*Genesis 41:4*}

Pharaoh's dream has too often been my waking experience. My days of sloth have ruinously destroyed all that I had achieved in times of zealous industry; my seasons of coldness have frozen all the genial glow of my periods of fervency and enthusiasm; and my fits of worldliness have thrown me back from my advances in the divine life. I need to beware of lean prayers, lean praises, lean duties, and lean experiences, for these will eat up the fat of my comfort and peace. If I neglect prayer for even a short time, I lose all the spirituality which I had achieved; if I draw no fresh supplies from heaven, the old grain in my granary is soon consumed by the famine which rages in my soul. When the caterpillars of indifference, the cankerworms of worldliness, and the palmerworms of self-indulgence, lay my heart completely desolate, and make my soul languish, all my former fruitfulness and growth in grace avails me nothing whatever. How anxious should I be to have no lean fleshed days, no ill favoured hours! If every day I journeyed towards the goal of my desires I would soon reach it, but backsliding leaves me still far off from the prize of my high calling, and robs me of the advances which I had so laboriously made. The only way in which all my days can be as the "fat cows," is to feed them in the right meadow, to spend them with the Lord, in his service, in his company, in his fear, and in his way. Why should not every year be richer than the past, in love, and usefulness, and joy? — I am nearer the celestial hills, I have had more experience with my Lord, and should be more like him. Oh Lord, keep far from me the curse of leanness of soul; let me not have to cry, "My leanness, my leanness, woe to me!" But may I be well fed and nourished in your house, so that I may praise your name.

July 3 — Evening

If we suffer, then we shall also reign
with him. *{2 Timothy 2:12}*

We must not imagine that we are suffering for Christ, and with Christ, if we are not in Christ. Beloved friend, are you trusting in Jesus only? If not, whatever you may have to mourn over on earth, you are not "suffering with Christ," and have no hope of reigning with him in heaven. Neither are we to conclude that all of a Christian's sufferings are sufferings with Christ, for *it is essential that he is called by God to suffer*. If we are rash and imprudent, and run into positions for which neither providence nor grace has outfitted us, we ought to question whether we are not rather sinning than communing with Jesus. If we let passion take the place of judgment, and self-will reign instead of scriptural authority, we shall fight the Lord's battles with the devil's weapons, and if we cut our own fingers we must not be surprised. Again, *in troubles which come upon us as the result of sin, we must not dream that we are suffering with Christ*. When Miriam spoke evil of Moses, and the leprosy polluted her, she was not suffering for God. Moreover, suffering which God accepts must have *God's glory as its goal*. If I suffer so that I may earn a name, or win applause, I shall get no other reward than that of the Pharisee. It is necessary also *that love for Jesus, and love for his elect, be always the mainspring of all our patience. We must display the Spirit of Christ* in meekness, gentleness, and forgiveness. Let us search and see if we truly *suffer with Jesus*. And if we do thus suffer, what is our "light affliction" compared with *reigning with him*? Oh, it is so blessed to be in the furnace with Christ, and such an honour to stand in the pillory with him, that if there would be no future reward, we might count ourselves happy in present honour; but when the reward is so eternal, so infinitely more than we had any right to expect, shall we not take up the cross with alacrity, and go on our way rejoicing?

July 4 — Morning

{Daily Reading: Psalms 52:1–59:17} {Quick Study: Psalms 67:1–72:20}

Sanctify them through your truth. *{John 17:17}*

Sanctification begins in regeneration. The Spirit of God infuses into man that new living principle by which he becomes "a new creature" in Christ Jesus. This work, which begins in the new birth, is carried on in two ways — mortification, by which the lusts of the flesh are subdued and kept under; and vivification, by which the life which God has put within us is made to be a well of water springing up to everlasting life. This is carried on every day in what is called "perseverance," by which the Christian is preserved and continued in a gracious state, and is made to abound in good works to the praise and glory of God; and it culminates or comes to perfection, in "glory," when the soul, being thoroughly purged, is caught up to dwell with holy beings at the right hand of the majesty on high. But while the Spirit of God is thus the author of sanctification, yet there is a visible agency employed which must not be forgotten. "Sanctify them," said Jesus, "through your *truth*: your word is truth." The passages of Scripture which prove that the instrument of our sanctification is the Word of God are very many. The Spirit of God brings to our minds the precepts and doctrines of truth, and applies them with power. These are heard in the ear, and being received in the heart, they work in us to will and to do God's good pleasure. The truth is the sanctifier, and if we do not hear or read the truth, we shall not grow in sanctification. We only progress in sound living as we progress in sound understanding. "Your word is a lamp to my feet and a light to my path." Do not say of any error, "It is a mere matter of opinion." No man indulges an error of judgment, without sooner or later tolerating an error in practice. Firmly hold to the truth, for by so holding the truth you shall be sanctified by the Spirit of God.

July 4 — Evening

He who has clean hands, and a pure heart;
who has not lifted up his soul to vanity,
nor sworn deceitfully. *{Psalms 24:4}*

Outward practical holiness is a very precious mark of grace. It is to be feared that many professors have perverted the doctrine of justification by faith in such a way as to treat good works with contempt; if so, they will receive everlasting contempt at the last great day. If our hands are not clean, let us wash them in Jesus' precious blood, and so let us lift up pure hands to God. But *"clean hands"* will not suffice, unless they are connected with *"a pure heart."* True religion is heart work. We may wash the outside of the cup and the platter as long as we please, but if the inward parts are filthy, we are altogether filthy in the sight of God, for our hearts are more truly ourselves than our hands are; the very life of our being lies in the inner nature, and hence the imperative need of purity within. The pure in heart shall see God, all others are only blind bats.

The man who is born for heaven *"has not lifted up his soul to vanity."* All men have their joys, by which their souls are lifted up; the worldling lifts up his soul in carnal delights, which are mere empty vanities; but the saint loves more substantial things; like Jehoshaphat, he is lifted up in the ways of the Lord. He who is content with husks, will be counted with the swine. Does the world satisfy you? Then you have your reward and portion in this life; make much of it, for you shall know no other joy.

"Nor sworn deceitfully." The saints are men of honour still. The Christian man's word is his only oath; but that is as good as twenty oaths of other men. False speaking will shut any man out of heaven, for a liar shall not enter into God's house, whatever may be his professions or doings. Reader, does the text before us condemn you, or do you hope to ascend into the hill of the Lord?

July 5 — Morning

{Daily Reading: Psalms 60:1–66:20} {Quick Study: Psalms 73:1–77:20}

Called to be saints. *{Romans 1:7}*

We are very apt to regard the apostolic saints as if they were "saints" in a more special manner than the other children of God. All are "saints" whom God has called by his grace, and sanctified by his Spirit; but we are apt to look upon the *apostles* as extraordinary beings, scarcely subject to the same weaknesses and temptations as ourselves. Yet in so doing we are forgetful of this truth, that the nearer a man lives to God the more intensely he has to mourn over his own evil heart; and the more his Master honours him in his service, the more also the evil of the flesh vexes and teases him day by day. The fact is, if we had seen the apostle Paul, we would have thought him to be remarkably like the rest of the chosen family: and if we had talked with him, we would have said, "We find that his experience and ours are much the same. He is more faithful, more holy, and more deeply taught than we are, but he has the very same trials to endure. Indeed, in some respects he is more severely tried than we are." Do not, then, look upon the ancient saints as being exempt either from infirmities or sins; and do not regard them with that mystic reverence which will almost make us idolaters. Their holiness is attainable even by us. We are "called to be saints" by that same voice which constrained them to their high vocation. It is a Christian's duty to force his way into the inner circle of saintship; and if these saints were superior to us in their attainments, as they certainly were, let us follow them; let us emulate their ardour and holiness. We have the same light that they had, the same grace is accessible to us, and why should we rest satisfied until we have equalled them in heavenly character? They lived *with* Jesus, they lived *for* Jesus, therefore they grew *like* Jesus. Let us live by the same Spirit as they did, "looking to Jesus," and our saintship will soon be apparent.

July 5 — Evening

*Trust in the Lord for ever: for in the Lord Jehovah
is everlasting strength. {Isaiah 26:4}*

Seeing that we have such a God to trust in, let us rest upon him with all our weight; let us resolutely drive out all unbelief, and endeavour to get rid of doubts and fears, which so much mar our comfort; since there is no excuse for fear where God is the foundation of our trust. A loving parent would be severely grieved if his child could not trust him; and how ungenerous, how unkind is our conduct when we put so little confidence in our Heavenly Father who has never failed us, and who never will. It would be well if doubting was banished from the household of God; but it is to be feared that old Unbelief is as nimble nowadays as when the psalmist asked, "Is his mercy completely gone for ever? Will he be no more favourable?" David had not made any very lengthy trial of the mighty sword of the giant Goliath, and yet he said, "There is none like it." He had tried it once in the hour of his youthful victory, and it had proven itself to be of the right metal, and therefore he always praised it afterwards; even so should we speak well of our God, there is no one like him in the heaven above or the earth beneath; " 'To whom then will you liken me, or shall I be equal?' says the Holy One." There is no rock like the Rock of Jacob, our enemies themselves being judges. So far from allowing doubts to live in our hearts, we will take the whole detestable crew, as Elijah did the prophets of Baal, and slay them at the brook; and for a stream to kill them by, we will select the sacred torrent which streams from our Saviour's wounded side. We have been in many trials, but we have always been in a position where we could find in our God all that we needed. Let us then be encouraged to trust in the Lord for ever, assured that his everlasting strength will be, as it has been, our help and support.

July 6 — Morning

{Daily Reading: Psalms 67:1–71:24} {Quick Study: Psalms 78:1–83:18}

Whoever listens to me shall live safely, and shall be
secure without fear of evil. *{Proverbs 1:33}*

Divine love is rendered conspicuous when it shines in the midst
of judgments. Fair is that lone star which smiles through the
rifts of the thunder clouds; bright is the oasis which blooms in the
wilderness of sand; so fair and so bright is love in the midst of wrath.
When the Israelites provoked the Most High by their continued
idolatry, he punished them by withholding both dew and rain, so
that their land was visited by a severe famine; but while he did this,
he took care that his own chosen ones should be secure. If all other
brooks are dry, yet there shall be one reserved for Elijah; and when
that fails, God shall still preserve for him a place of sustenance; no,
not only so, the Lord had not simply one "Elijah," but he had a
remnant according to the election of grace, who were hidden by fifties in a cave. And although the whole land was subject to famine,
yet these fifties in the cave were fed, and fed from Ahab's table too
by his faithful, God-fearing steward, Obadiah. Let us draw from
this the inference, that come what may, God's people are safe. Let
convulsions shake the solid earth, let the skies themselves be torn
apart, yet amid the wreck of worlds the believer shall be as secure
as in the calmest hour of rest. If God cannot save his people *under*
heaven, he will save them *in* heaven. If the world becomes too hot
to hold them, then heaven shall be the place of their reception and
their safety. Then be confident, when you hear of wars, and rumours
of wars. Let no agitation distress you, but be secure without fear
of evil. Whatever comes upon the earth, you, beneath the broad
wings of Jehovah, shall be secure. Fortify yourself with his promise;
rest in his faithfulness, and bid defiance to the blackest future, for
there is nothing direful in it for you. Your sole concern should be
to show forth to the world the blessedness of listening to the voice
of wisdom.

July 6 — Evening

How many are my iniquities and sins? {*Job 13:23*}

Have you ever really weighed and considered how great the sin of God's people is? Think how heinous your own transgression is, and you will find that not only does a sin here and there tower up like an alp, but that your iniquities are heaped upon each other, as in the old fable of the giants who piled Pelian upon Ossa, mountain upon mountain. What an aggregate of sin there is in the life of one of the most sanctified of God's children! Attempt to multiply this, the sin of one only, by the multitude of the redeemed, "a number which no man can number," and you will have some conception of the great mass of the guilt of the people for whom Jesus shed his blood. But we arrive at a more adequate idea of the magnitude of sin by the greatness of the remedy provided. It is the blood of Jesus Christ, God's only and well-beloved Son. God's Son! Angels cast their crowns before him! All the choral symphonies of heaven surround his glorious throne. "God over all, blessed for ever. Amen." And yet he takes upon himself the form of a servant, and is scourged and pierced, bruised and torn, and at last slain; since nothing but the blood of the incarnate Son of God could make atonement for our offences. No human mind can adequately estimate the infinite value of the divine sacrifice, for great as is the sin of God's people, the atonement which takes it away is immeasurably greater. Therefore, the believer, even when sin rolls like a black flood, and the remembrance of the past is bitter, can yet stand before the blazing throne of the great and holy God, and cry, "Who is he who condemns? It is Christ who died; yes rather, who has risen again." While the remembrance of his sin fills him with shame and sorrow, he at the same time makes it a foil to show the brightness of mercy — guilt is the dark night in which the fair star of divine love shines with serene splendour.

July 7 — Morning

{Daily Reading: Psalms 72:1–77:20} {Quick Study: Psalms 84:1–91:16}

Brethren, pray for us. *{1 Thessalonians 5:25}*

This one morning in the year we reserved to refresh the reader's memory upon the subject of prayer for ministers, and we do most earnestly implore every Christian household to grant the fervent request of the text first uttered by an apostle and now repeated by us. Brethren, our work is solemnly momentous, involving weal or woe to thousands; we are engaged with souls for God on eternal business, and our word is either a savour of life to life, or of death to death. A very heavy responsibility rests upon us, and it will be no small mercy if at the last we are found clear of the blood of all men. As officers in Christ's army, we are the special target for the enmity of men and demons; they watch for our faltering, and labour to take us by the heels. Our sacred calling involves us in temptations from which you are exempt, above all, it too often draws us away from our personal enjoyment of truth into a ministerial and official consideration of it. We meet with many knotty cases, and our wits are at a *non plus*; we observe very sad backslidings, and our hearts are wounded; we see millions perishing, and our spirits sink. We wish to profit you by our preaching; we desire to be blest to your children; we long to be useful both to saints and sinners; therefore, dear friends, intercede for us with our God. We are miserable men if we lack the aid of your prayers, but we are happy if we live in your supplications. You do not look to us but to our Master for spiritual blessings, and yet how many times has he given those blessings through his ministers; ask then, again and again, that we may be the earthen vessels into which the Lord may put the treasure of the gospel. We, the whole company of missionaries, ministers, city missionaries, and students, do in the name of Jesus beseech you:

"BRETHREN, PRAY FOR US."

July 7 — Evening

When I passed by you, I said to you, "Live." *{Ezekiel 16:6}*

Saved one, consider gratefully this mandate of mercy. Note that this fiat of God is *majestic*. In our text, we perceive a sinner with nothing in him but sin, expecting nothing but wrath; but the eternal Lord passes by in his glory; he looks, he pauses, and he pronounces the solitary but royal word, "Live." There speaks a God. Who but he could venture thus to deal with life and dispense it with a single syllable? Again, this fiat is *manifold*. When he says "Live," it includes many things. Here is judicial life. The sinner is ready to be condemned, but the Mighty One says, "Live," and he rises pardoned and absolved. It is spiritual life. We did not know Jesus — our eyes could not see Christ, our ears could not hear his voice — Jehovah said "Live," and we were quickened who were dead in trespasses and sins. Moreover, it includes glory life, which is the perfection of spiritual life. "I said to you, 'Live' ": and that word rolls on through all the years of time until death comes, and in the midst of the shadows of death, the Lord's voice is still heard, "Live!" In the morning of the resurrection it is that very same voice which is echoed by the archangel, "Live," and as holy spirits rise to heaven to be blest for ever in the glory of their God, it is in the power of this same word, "Live." Note again, that it is an *irresistible* mandate. Saul of Tarsus is on the road to Damascus to arrest the saints of the living God. A voice is heard from heaven and a light is seen greater than the brightness of the sun, and Saul is crying out, "Lord, what will you have me to do?" This mandate is a mandate of *free grace*. When sinners are saved, it is only and solely because God *will* do it to magnify his free, unpurchased, unsought grace. Christians, see your position, debtors to grace; show your gratitude by earnest, Christlike lives, and as God has bidden you live, see to it that you live in earnest.

July 8 — Morning

{Daily Reading: Psalms 78:1–80:19} {Quick Study: Psalms 92:1–102:28}

Please tell me where your great strength lies. *{Judges 16:6}*

Where does the secret strength of faith lie? It lies in the food it feeds on; for faith studies *what the promise is* — an emanation of divine grace, an overflowing of the great heart of God; and faith says, "My God could not have given this promise, except from love and grace; therefore it is quite certain his Word will be fulfilled." Then faith thinks, "*Who gave* this promise?" It does not consider so much its greatness, as, "Who is the author of it?" She remembers that it is God who cannot lie — God omnipotent, God immutable; and therefore concludes that the promise must be fulfilled; and forward she advances in this firm conviction. She remembers *why the promise was given* — namely, for God's glory, and she feels perfectly sure that God's glory is safe, that he will never stain his own banner nor mar the lustre of his own crown; and therefore the promise must and will stand. Then faith also considers the amazing *work of Christ* as being a clear proof of the Father's intention to fulfil his Word. "He who did not spare his own Son, but freely delivered him up for us all, how shall he not with him also freely give us all things?" Moreover faith looks back upon *the past*, for her battles have strengthened her, and her victories have given her courage. She remembers that God never has failed her; no, that he never once failed any of his children. She remembers times of great peril, when deliverance came; hours of awful need, when as her day her strength was found, and she cries, "No, I never will be led to think that he can change and leave his servant now. So far the Lord has helped me, and he will help me still." Thus faith views each promise in its connection with the promise giver, and, because she does so, can with assurance say, "Surely goodness and mercy shall follow me all the days of my life!"

July 8 — Evening

Lead me in your truth, and teach me: for you are the God of my salvation; I wait on you all the day. {Psalms 25:5}

When the believer has begun with trembling feet to walk in the way of the Lord, he asks to be still led onward like a little child upheld by his parent's helping hand, and he craves to be further instructed in the alphabet of truth. Experiential teaching is the burden of this prayer. David knew much, but he felt his ignorance, and desired to be still in the Lord's school: over four times in two verses he applies for a scholarship in the college of grace. It would be well for many professors if instead of following their own devices, and cutting out new paths of thought for themselves, they would enquire for the good old ways of God's own truth, and beseech the Holy Spirit to give them sanctified understandings and teachable spirits. *"For you are the God of my salvation."* The three in one Jehovah is the author and perfecter of salvation for his people. Reader, is he the God of *your* salvation? Do you find in the Father's election, in the Son's atonement, and in the Spirit's quickening, all the grounds of your eternal hopes? If so, you may use this as an argument for obtaining further blessings; if the Lord has ordained to save you, surely he will not refuse to instruct you in his ways. It is a happy thing when we can address the Lord with the confidence which David here reveals, it gives us great power in prayer, and comfort in trial. *"I wait on you all the day."* Patience is the fair handmaid and daughter of faith; we cheerfully wait when we are certain that we shall not wait in vain. It is our duty and our privilege to wait upon the Lord in service, in worship, in expectancy, in trust all the days of our life. Our faith will be a tried faith, and if it is of the true kind, it will endure continued trial without yielding. We shall not grow weary of waiting upon God if we remember how long and how graciously he once waited for us.

Do not forget all his benefits. *{Psalms 103:2}*

It is a delightful and profitable occupation to see the hand of God in the lives of ancient saints, and to observe his goodness in delivering them, his mercy in pardoning them, and his faithfulness in keeping his covenant with them. But would it not be even more interesting and profitable for us to see the hand of God in our own lives? Ought we not to look upon our own history as being at least as full of God, as full of his goodness and of his truth, as much a proof of his faithfulness and veracity, as the lives of any of the saints who have gone before? We do our Lord an injustice when we suppose that he performed all his mighty acts, and showed himself strong for those in the early time, but does not perform wonders or lay bear his arm for the saints who are upon the earth now. Let us review our own lives. Surely in these we may discover some happy incidents, refreshing to ourselves and glorifying to our God. Have you had no *deliverances*? Have you passed through no rivers, supported by the divine presence? Have you walked through no fires unharmed? Have you had no revelations? Have you had no *choice favours*? The God who gave Solomon the desire of his heart, has he never listened to you and answered your requests? That God of lavish bounty of whom David sang, "Who satisfies your mouth with good things," has he never satiated *you* with fatness? Have you never been made to lie down in green pastures? Have you never been led by the still waters? Surely the goodness of God has been the same to us as to the saints of old. Let us, then, weave his mercies into a song. Let us take the pure gold of thankfulness, and the jewels of praise and make them into another crown for the head of Jesus. Let our souls give forth music as sweet and as exhilarating as came from David's harp, while we praise the Lord whose mercy endures for ever.

July 9 — Evening

And God divided the light
from the darkness. *{Genesis 1:4}*

A believer has two principles at work within him. In his natural estate he was subject to one principle only, which was darkness; now light has entered, and the two principles disagree. Note the apostle Paul's words in the seventh chapter of Romans: "I find then a law, that, when I would do good, evil is present with me. For I delight in the law of God after the inward man: but I see another law in my members, warring against the law of my mind, and bringing me into captivity to the law of sin, which is in my members." What is the reason for this state of things? "The Lord divided the light from the darkness." Darkness, by itself, is quiet and undisturbed, but when the Lord sends in light, there is a conflict, for the one is in opposition to the other: a conflict which will never cease until the believer is altogether light in the Lord. If in the individual Christian there is a division *inwardly*, there is certain to be a division *outwardly*. As soon as the Lord gives light to any man, he proceeds to separate himself from the darkness around; he secedes from a merely worldly religion of outward ceremonies, for nothing short of the gospel of Christ will satisfy him now, and he withdraws himself from worldly society and frivolous amusements, and seeks the company of the saints, for "We know we have passed from death to life, because we love the brethren." The light gathers to itself, and the darkness to itself. What God has divided, let us never try to unite, but as Christ went outside the camp, bearing his reproach, so let us come out from the ungodly, and be a particular people. He was holy, harmless, undefiled, separate from sinners; and, as he was, so we are to be nonconformists to the world, dissenting from all sin, and distinguished from the rest of mankind by our likeness to our Master.

July 10 — Morning

{Daily Reading: Psalms 88:1–91:16} {Quick Study: Psalms 107:1–110:7}

Fellow citizens with the saints. *{Ephesians 2:19}*

What is meant by our being citizens in heaven? It means that *we are under heaven's government.* Christ the King of heaven reigns in our hearts; our daily prayer is, "Your will be done on earth as it is in heaven." The proclamations issued from the throne of glory are freely received by us: the decrees of the Great King we cheerfully obey. Then as citizens of the New Jerusalem, *we share heaven's honours.* The glory which belongs to beatified saints belongs to us, for we are already sons of God, already princes of the imperial blood; already we wear the spotless robe of Jesus' righteousness; already we have angels for our servants, saints for our companions, Christ for our Brother, God for our Father, and a crown of immortality for our reward. We share the honours of citizenship, for we have come to the general assembly and church of the firstborn whose names are written in heaven. As citizens, we have *common rights to all the property of heaven.* Ours are its gates of pearl and walls of chrysolite; ours the azure light of the city that needs no candle nor light of the sun; ours the river of the water of life, and the twelve manner of fruits which grow on the trees planted on its banks; there is nothing in heaven that does not belong to us. "Things present, or things to come," all are ours. Also as citizens of heaven we *enjoy its delights.* Do they rejoice there over sinners who repent — prodigals who have returned? So do we. Do they chant the glories of triumphant grace? We do the same. Do they cast their crowns at Jesus' feet? Such honours as we have we cast there, too. Are they charmed with his smile? It is no less sweet to us who live below. Do they look forward, waiting for his second advent? We also look and long for his appearing. If we are thus *citizens of heaven*, then let our walk and actions be consistent with our high dignity.

July 10 — Evening

**And the evening and the morning
were the first day.** *{Genesis 1:5}*

The evening was "darkness" and the morning was "light," and yet *the two together are called by the name that is given to the light alone!* This is somewhat remarkable, but it has an exact analogy in spiritual experience. In every believer there is darkness and light, and yet he is not to be named a sinner because there is sin in him, but he is to be named a saint because he possesses some degree of holiness. This will be a most comforting thought to those who are mourning their infirmities, and who ask, "Can I be a child of God while there is so much darkness in me?" Yes; for you, like the day, do not take your name from the evening, but from the morning; and you are spoken of in the Word of God as if you were even now perfectly holy as you will be soon. You are called the child of light, though there is still darkness in you. You are named after what is the predominating quality in the sight of God, which will one day be the only principle remaining. Observe that *the evening comes first.* Naturally we are darkness first in order of time, and the gloom is often first in our mournful apprehension, driving us to cry out in deep humiliation, "God be merciful to me, a sinner." The place of the morning is second, it dawns when grace overcomes nature. It is a blessed aphorism of John Bunyan, "What is last, lasts for ever." What is first, yields in due time to the last; but nothing comes after the last. So that though you are naturally darkness, when once you become light in the Lord, there is no evening to follow; "your sun shall no more go down." The first day in this life is an evening and a morning; but the second day, when we shall be with God, for ever, shall be a day with no evening, but one, sacred, high, eternal noon.

July 11 — Morning

{Daily Reading: Psalms 92:1–100:5} {Quick Study: Psalms 111:1–118:29}

After you have suffered for a little while, he will make you perfect, establish, strengthen, settle you. *{1 Peter 5:10}*

You have seen the arch of heaven as it spans the plain: glorious are its colours, and rare its hues. It is beautiful, but, alas, it passes away, and lo, it is gone. The fair colours give way to the fleecy clouds, and the sky is no longer brilliant with the tints of heaven. It is not *established*. How can it be? A glorious show made up of transitory sun beams and passing rain drops, how can it abide? The graces of the Christian character must not resemble the rainbow in its transitory beauty, but, on the contrary, must be established, settled and abiding. Seek, oh believer, so that every good thing you have may be an abiding thing. May your character not be a writing upon the sand, but an inscription upon the rock! May your faith be no "baseless fabric of a vision," but may it be built of material able to endure that awful fire which shall consume the wood, hay, and stubble of the hypocrite. May you be rooted and grounded in love. May your convictions be deep, your love real, your desires earnest. May your whole life be so settled and established that all the blasts of hell, and all the storms of earth shall never be able to move you. But notice how this blessing of being "established in the faith" is gained. The apostle's words point us to *suffering* as the means employed — *"After you have suffered for a little while."* It is of no use to hope that we shall be well rooted if no rough winds pass over us. Those old gnarlings on the root of the oak tree, and those strange twistings of the branches, all tell of the many storms that have swept over it, and they are also indicators of the depth into which the roots have forced their way. So the Christian is made strong, and firmly rooted by all the trials and storms of life. Then do not shrink from the tempestuous winds of trial, but take comfort, believing that by their rough discipline God is fulfilling this benediction in you.

July 11 — Evening

Tell your children about it, and let your children tell their children, and their children the next generation. {Joel 1:3}

In this simple way, by God's grace, a living testimony for truth is always to be kept alive in the land — the beloved of the Lord are to hand down their witness for the gospel, and the covenant to their heirs, and these again to their next descendants. This is our *first* duty; we are to begin at the family hearth: he is a bad preacher who does not commence his ministry at home. The heathen are to be sought by all means, and the highways and hedges are to be searched, but home has a prior claim, and woe to those who reverse the order of the Lord's arrangements. To teach our children is a *personal* duty; we cannot delegate it to Sunday School teachers, or other friendly aids; these can assist us, but cannot deliver us from the sacred obligation; proxies and sponsors are wicked devices in this case: mothers and fathers must, like Abraham, command their households in the fear of God, and talk with their offspring concerning the wondrous works of the Most High. Parental teaching is a *natural* duty — who are so qualified to attend to the child's well being as those who are his parents? To neglect the instruction of our offspring is worse than brutish. Family religion is *necessary* for the nation, for the family itself, and for the church of God. By a thousand plots popery is covertly advancing in our land, and one of the most effectual means for resisting its inroads is left almost neglected, namely, the instruction of children in the faith. Oh that parents would awaken to a sense of the importance of this matter. It is a pleasant duty to talk about Jesus to our sons and daughters, and the more so because it has often proven to be an *accepted* work, for God has saved the children through the parents' prayers and admonitions. May every house into which this volume shall come honour the Lord and receive his smile.

July 12 — Morning

{Daily Reading: Psalms 101:1–105:45} {Quick Study: Psalms 119}

Sanctified by God the Father. *{Jude 1:1}*
Sanctified in Christ Jesus. *{1 Corinthians 1:2}*
Through sanctification of the Spirit. *{1 Peter 1:2}*

Note the union of the Three Divine Persons in all their gracious acts. How unwisely do those believers talk who make preferences in the Persons of the Trinity; who think of Jesus as if he were the embodiment of everything lovely and gracious, while the Father they regard as severely just, but destitute of kindness. Equally wrong are those who magnify the decree of the Father, and the atonement of the Son, so as to depreciate the work of the Spirit. In deeds of grace none of the Persons of the Trinity act apart from the rest. They are as united in their deeds as in their essence. In their love towards the chosen they are one, and in the actions which flow from that great central source they are still undivided. Especially notice this in the matter of sanctification. While we may without mistake speak of sanctification as the work of the Spirit, yet we must take heed that we do not view it as if the Father and the Son had no part in it. It is correct to speak of sanctification as the work of the Father, of the Son, and of the Spirit. Still Jehovah says, "Let *us* make man in our own image after our likeness," and thus we are "*his* workmanship, created in Christ Jesus to good works, which God has before ordained that we should walk in them." See the value which God sets upon real holiness, since the Three Persons in the Trinity are represented as co-working to produce a church without "spot, or wrinkle, or any such thing." And you, believer, as the follower of Christ, must also set a high value on holiness — upon purity of life and godliness of conversation. Value the blood of Christ as the foundation of your hope, but never speak disparagingly of the work of the Spirit which is your fitness for the inheritance of the saints in light. Today let us so live as to reveal the work of the Triune God in us.

July 12 — Evening

His heavenly kingdom. *{2 Timothy 4:18}*

That city of the great King is a place of *active service*. Ransomed spirits serve him day and night in his temple. They never cease to fulfil the good pleasure of their King. They always "rest," as far as ease and freedom from care is concerned; and never "rest" in the sense of indolence or inactivity. Jerusalem the golden is the place of communion with all the people of God. We shall sit with Abraham, Isaac, and Jacob, in eternal fellowship. We shall hold good conversations with the noble host of the elect, all reigning with him who by his love and his potent arm has brought them safely home. We shall not sing solos, but in chorus we shall praise our King. Heaven is a place of *realised victory*. Whenever, Christian, you have achieved a victory over your lusts — whenever after hard struggling, you have laid a temptation dead at your feet — you have in that hour a foretaste of the joy that awaits you when the Lord shall shortly tread Satan under your feet, and you shall find yourself more than conqueror through him who has loved you. Paradise is a place of *security*. When you enjoy the full assurance of faith, you have the pledge of that glorious security which shall be yours when you are a perfect citizen of the heavenly Jerusalem. Oh my sweet home, Jerusalem, oh happy harbour of my soul! Thanks, even now, to him whose love has taught me to long for you; but louder thanks in eternity, when I shall possess you.

> My soul has tasted of the grapes,
> And now it longs to go
> Where my dear Lord his vineyard keeps
> And all the clusters grow.
>
> Upon the true and living vine,
> My famished soul would feast,
> And banquet on the fruit divine,
> An everlasting guest.

July 13 — Morning

{Daily Reading: Psalms 106:1–107:43} {Quick Study: Psalms 120:1–131:3}

God said to Jonah, "Is it right for you to be angry?" *{Jonah 4:9}*

Anger is not always or necessarily sinful, but it has such a tendency to run wild that whenever it displays itself, we should be quick to question its character, with this enquiry, "Is it right for you to be angry?" It may be that we can answer, "YES." Very frequently anger is the madman's firebrand, but sometimes it is Elijah's fire from heaven. We are right to be angry with sin, because of the wrong which it commits against our good and gracious God; or with ourselves because we remain so foolish after so much divine instruction; or with others when the sole cause of anger is the evil which they do. He who is not angry at transgression becomes a partaker in it. Sin is a loathsome and hateful thing, and no renewed heart can patiently endure it. God himself is angry with the wicked every day, and it is written in his Word, "You who love the Lord, hate evil."

Far more frequently it is to be feared that our anger is not commendable or even justifiable, and then we must answer, "NO." Why should we be fretful with children, passionate with servants, and angry with companions? Is such anger honourable to our Christian profession, or glorifying to God? Is it not the old evil heart seeking to gain dominion, and should we not resist it with all the might of our newborn nature? Many professors give way to temper as though it were useless to attempt resistance; but let the believer remember that he must be a conqueror in every point, or else he cannot be crowned. If we cannot control our tempers, what has grace done for us? Someone told Mr. Jay that grace was often grafted on a crab stump. "Yes," he said, "but the fruit will not be crabs." We must not make natural infirmity an excuse for sin, but we must flee to the cross and pray to the Lord to crucify our tempers, and renew us in gentleness and meekness after his own image.

July 13 — Evening

**When I cry to you, then my enemies shall turn back:
I know this; for God is for me.** *{Psalms 56:9}*

It is impossible for any human speech to express the full meaning of this delightful phrase, *"God is for me."* He was "for us" before the worlds were made; he was "for us," or he would not have given his well-beloved Son; he was "for us" when he struck the only begotten Son, and laid the full weight of his wrath upon him — he was "for *us*," although he was against *him*; he was "for us," when we were ruined in the fall — he loved us notwithstanding all; he was "for us," when we were rebels against him, and with a high hand were bidding him defiance; he was "for us," or he would not have brought us humbly to seek his face. He has been "for us" in many struggles; we have been summoned to encounter hosts of dangers; we have been assailed by temptations from without and within — how could we have remained unharmed to this hour if he had not been "for us?" He is "for us," with all the infinity of his being; with all the omnipotence of his love; with all the infallibility of his wisdom; arrayed in all his divine attributes, he is "for us" — eternally and immutably "for us"; "for us" when the blue skies shall be rolled up like a worn out vesture; "for us" throughout eternity. And because he is "for us," the voice of prayer will always ensure his help. *"When I cry to you, then my enemies shall be turned back."* This is no uncertain hope, but a well-grounded assurance — *"I know this."* I will direct my prayer to you, and will look up for the answer, assured that it will come, and that my enemies shall be defeated, "for God is for me." Oh believer, how happy are you to have the King of kings on your side! How safe with such a Protector! How sure is your cause when pleaded by such an Advocate! If God is for you, who can be against you?

July 14 — Morning

{Daily Reading: Psalms 108:1–118:29} {Quick Study: Psalms 132:1–139:24}

If you lift up your tool upon it, you have polluted it. *{Exodus 20:25}*

God's altar was to be built of unhewn stones, so that no trace of human skill or labour might be seen upon it. Human wisdom delights to trim and arrange the doctrines of the cross into a system more artificial and more congenial with the depraved tastes of fallen nature; instead, however, of improving the gospel, carnal wisdom pollutes it until it becomes another gospel, and not the truth of God at all. All alterations and amendments of the Lord's own Word are defilements and pollutions. The proud heart of man is very anxious to have a hand in the justification of the soul before God; preparations for Christ are dreamed up, humblings and repentings are trusted in, good works are cried up, natural ability is much vaunted, and by all means the attempt is made to lift up human tools upon the divine altar. It would be well if sinners should remember that so far from perfecting the Saviour's work, their carnal confidences only pollute and dishonour it. The Lord alone must be exalted in the work of atonement, and not a single mark of man's chisel or hammer will be endured. There is an inherent blasphemy in seeking to add to what Christ Jesus in his dying moments declared to be finished, or to improve what the Lord Jehovah finds to be perfect satisfaction. Trembling sinner, away with your tools, and fall upon your knees in humble supplication; and accept the Lord Jesus to be the altar of your atonement, and rest in him alone.

Many professors may take warning from this morning's text concerning the doctrines which they believe. There is among Christians far too much inclination to square and reconcile the truths of revelation; this is a form of irreverence and unbelief, let us strive against it, and receive truth as we find it; rejoicing that the doctrines of the Bible are unhewn stones, and so are all the more fit to build an altar for the Lord.

July 14 — Evening

As it began to dawn, Mary Magdalene came . . .
to see the sepulchre. *{Matthew 28:1}*

Let us learn from Mary Magdalene how to obtain fellowship with the Lord Jesus. Notice how she sought him. She sought the Saviour *very early* in the morning. If you can wait for Christ, and be patient in the hope of having fellowship with him at some distant time, you will never have fellowship at all; for the heart that is fitted for communion is a hungering and a thirsting heart. She sought him also with *very great boldness*. Other disciples fled from the sepulchre, for they trembled and were amazed; but it is said Mary "stood" at the sepulchre. If you wish to have Christ with you, seek him boldly. Let nothing hold you back. Defy the world. Press on where others flee. She sought Christ *faithfully* — she stood *at the sepulchre*. Some find it hard to stand by a living Saviour, but she stood by a dead one. Let us seek Christ in this way, cleaving to the very least thing that has to do with him, remaining faithful though all others should forsake him. Note further, she sought Jesus *earnestly* — she stood *"weeping."* Those tear droppings were as spells that led the Saviour captive, and made him come out and show himself to her. If you desire Jesus' presence, weep after it! If you cannot be happy unless he comes and says to you, "You are my beloved," you will soon hear his voice. Lastly, she sought the Saviour *only*. What did she care for angels, she turned herself back from them; her search was only for her Lord. If Christ is your one and only love, if your heart has cast out all rivals, you will not lack the comfort of his presence for long. Mary Magdalene sought like this *because she loved much*. Let us arouse ourselves to the same intensity of affection; let our heart, like Mary's, be full of Christ, and our love, like hers, will be satisfied with nothing short of himself. Oh Lord, reveal yourself to us this evening!

July 15 — Morning

{Daily Reading: Psalms 119:1–119:176} {Quick Study: Psalms 140:1–150:6}

**The fire shall always be burning upon the altar;
it shall never go out.** *{Leviticus 6:13}*

Keep the altar of *private prayer* burning. This is the very life of all piety. The sanctuary and family altars borrow their fires here, therefore let this burn well. Secret devotion is the very essence, evidence, and barometer, of vital and experiential religion.

Burn the fat of your sacrifices here. Let your times of prayer be, if possible, regular, frequent, and undisturbed. Effectual prayer avails much. Have you nothing to pray for? Let us suggest the church, the ministry, your own soul, your children, your relatives, your neighbours, your country, and the cause of God and truth throughout the world. Let us examine ourselves on this important matter. Do we engage with lukewarmness in private devotion? Is the fire of devotion burning dimly in our hearts? Do the chariot wheels drag heavily? If so, let us be alarmed at this sign of decay. Let us go with weeping, and ask for the Spirit of grace and of supplications. Let us set apart special seasons for extraordinary prayer. For if this fire should be smothered beneath the ashes of a worldly conformity, it will dim the fire on the family altar, and lessen our influence both in the church and in the world.

The text will also apply to *the altar of the heart*. This is a golden altar indeed. God loves to see the hearts of his people glowing towards himself. Let us give to God our hearts, all blazing with love, and seek his grace, so that the fire may never be quenched; for it will not burn if the Lord does not keep it burning. Many foes will attempt to extinguish it; but if the unseen hand behind the wall pours the sacred oil on it, it will blaze higher and higher. Let us use texts of Scripture as fuel for our heart's fire, they are live coals; let us attend sermons, but above all, let us be much alone with Jesus.

July 15 — Evening

He appeared first to Mary Magdalene. *{Mark 16:9}*

Jesus "appeared first to Mary Magdalene," probably not only on account of her great love and persevering seeking, but because, as the context intimates, *she had been a special trophy of Christ's delivering power.* Learn from this, that the greatness of our sin before conversion should not make us imagine that we may not be especially favoured with the very highest grade of fellowship. She was one who had left all to become a *constant attendant on the Saviour.* He was her first, her chief object. Many who were on Christ's side did not take up Christ's cross; *she* did. *She spent her substance in relieving his needs.* If we wish to see much of Christ, let us *serve* him. Tell me who are those who sit most often under the banner of his love, and drink the deepest draughts from the cup of communion, and I am sure they will be those who give most, who serve best, and who abide closest to the bleeding heart of their dear Lord. But notice *how* Christ revealed himself to this sorrowing one — by a *word*, "Mary." It needed only one word *in his voice*, and at once she knew him, and *her heart owned allegiance by another word*, her heart was too full to say any more. That one word would naturally be the most fitting for the occasion. It implies obedience. She said, *"Master."* There is no state of mind in which this confession of allegiance will be too cold. No, when your spirit glows most with the heavenly fire, then you will say, "I am your servant, you have loosened my bonds." If you can say, "Master," if you feel that his will is your will, then you stand in a happy, holy place. He must have said, "Mary," or else you could not have said, "Rabboni." See, then, from all this, how Christ honours those who honour him, how love draws our Beloved, how it needs only one word of his to turn our weeping to rejoicing; how his presence makes the heart's sunshine.

July 16 — Morning

{Daily Reading: Psalms 120:1–131:3} {Quick Study: Proverbs 1:1–4:27}

They gathered manna every morning. *{Exodus 16:21}*

Labour to maintain a sense of your entire dependence upon the Lord's good will and pleasure for the continuance of your richest enjoyments. Never try to live on the old manna, nor seek to find help in Egypt. All must come from Jesus, or you are undone for ever. Old anointings will not suffice to impart unction to your spirit; your head must have fresh oil poured upon it from the golden horn of the sanctuary, or it will cease from its glory. Today you may be upon the summit of the mount of God, but he who has put you there must keep you there, or you will sink far more speedily than you dream. Your mountain only stands firm when he settles it in its place; if he hides his face, you will soon be troubled. If the Saviour should see fit, there is not a window through which you see the light of heaven which he could not darken in an instant. Joshua bade the sun stand still, but Jesus can shroud it in total darkness. He can withdraw the joy of your heart, the light of your eyes, and the strength of your life; in his hand your comforts lie, and at his will they can depart from you. Our Lord is determined that we shall feel and recognise this hourly dependence on him, for he only permits us to pray for "daily bread," and only promises that "as our days our strength shall be." Is it not best for us that it should be so, that we may often resort to his throne, and constantly be reminded of his love? Oh how rich the grace which supplies us so continually, and does not refrain itself because of our ingratitude! The golden shower never ceases, the cloud of blessing always tarries above our habitation. Oh, Lord Jesus, we wish to bow at your feet, conscious of our utter inability to do anything without you, and in every favour which we are privileged to receive, we wish to adore your blessed name and acknowledge your inexhaustible love.

July 16 — Evening

*You shall arise and have mercy upon Zion:
for the time to favour her, yes, the set time
is come. For your servants take pleasure in
her stones, and favour its dust. {Psalms 102:13–14}*

A selfish man in trouble is exceedingly hard to comfort, because the springs of his comfort lie entirely within himself, and when he is sad all his springs are dry. But a large-hearted man full of Christian philanthropy has other springs from which to supply himself with comfort besides those which lie within. He can go to his God first of all, and there find abundant help; and he can find reasons for consolation in things relating to the world at large, to his country, and, above all, to the church. David in this psalm was exceedingly sorrowful; he wrote, "I am like an owl in the desert. I watch, and am as a sparrow alone upon the house top." The only way in which he could comfort himself was in the reflection that God would arise and have mercy upon Zion: though *he* was sad, yet Zion should prosper; however low his own estate, yet Zion should arise. Christian man! Learn to comfort yourself in God's gracious dealing towards the church. What is so dear to your Master, should it not be dear above all else to you? Even though your way is dark, can you not cheer your heart with the triumphs of his cross and the spread of his truth? Our own personal troubles are forgotten while we look, not only upon what God *has* done, and is doing for Zion, but on the glorious things he *will yet do* for his church. Try this remedy, oh believer, whenever you have a sad heart and a heavy spirit: forget yourself and your little concerns, and seek the welfare and prosperity of Zion. When you bend your knee in prayer to God, do not limit your petition to the narrow circle of your own life, tried though it is, but send out your longing prayers for the church's prosperity, "Pray for the peace of Jerusalem," and your own soul shall be refreshed.

July 17 — Morning

{Daily Reading: Psalms 132:1–138:8} {Quick Study: Proverbs 5:1–9:18}

Knowing, beloved brethren, your election by God. *{1 Thessalonians 1:4}*

Many people want to know their election before they look to Christ, but they cannot learn it like this, it is only to be discovered by "looking to Jesus." If you desire to ascertain your own election — after the following manner, you shall assure your heart before God. Do you feel yourself to be a lost, guilty sinner? Go immediately to the cross of Christ, and tell Jesus so, and tell him that you have read in the Bible, "He who comes to me, I will in no wise cast out." Tell him that he has said, "This is a faithful saying, and worthy of all acceptance, that Christ Jesus came into the world to save sinners." Look to Jesus and believe on him, and you shall make proof of your election directly, for as surely as you believe, you are elect. If you will give yourself wholly up to Christ and trust him, then you are one of God's chosen ones; but if you stop and say, "I want to know first whether I am elect," you do not know what you are asking. Go to Jesus, no matter how guilty, just as you are. Leave all curious enquiry about election alone. Go straight to Christ and hide in his wounds, and you shall know your election. The assurance of the Holy Spirit shall be given to you, so that you shall be able to say, "I know whom I have believed, and I am persuaded that he is able to keep what I have committed to him." Christ was at the everlasting council: he can tell you whether you were chosen or not; but you cannot find it out in any other way. Go and put your trust in him, and his answer will be — "I have loved you with an everlasting love, therefore with lovingkindness I have drawn you." There will be no doubt about his having chosen you, when you have chosen *him*.

Sons we are through God's election,
Who in Jesus Christ believe.

July 17 — Evening

Let none of them escape. *{1 Kings 18:40}*

When the prophet Elijah had received the answer to his prayer, and the fire from heaven had consumed the sacrifice in the presence of all the people, he called upon the assembled Israelites to take the priests of Baal, and sternly cried, "Let none of them escape." He took them all down to the brook Kishon, and killed them there. So it must be with our sins — they are all doomed, not one must be preserved. Our darling sin must die. Do not spare it for its much crying. Strike, though it is as dear as an Isaac. Strike, for God struck at sin when it was laid upon his own Son. With stern unflinching purpose you must condemn to death that sin which was once the idol of your heart. Do you ask how you are to accomplish this? Jesus will be your power. You have grace to overcome sin given to you in the covenant of grace; you have strength to win the victory in the crusade against inward lusts, because Christ Jesus has promised to be with you even to the end. If you wish to triumph over darkness, set yourself in the presence of the Sun of Righteousness. There is no place so well adapted for the exposure of sin, and recovery from its power and guilt, as the immediate presence of God. Job never knew how to get rid of sin half so well as he did when his eye of faith rested upon God, and then he abhorred himself, and repented in dust and ashes. The fine gold of the Christian is often becoming tarnished. We need the sacred fire to consume the dross. Let us flee to our God, he is a consuming fire; he will not consume our spirit, but our sins. Let the goodness of God stir us up to a sacred jealousy, and to a holy revenge against those iniquities which are hateful in his sight. Go out to battle with Amalek, in his strength, and utterly destroy the accursed crew: let none of them escape.

July 18 — Morning

{Daily Reading: Psalms 139:1–143:12} {Quick Study: Proverbs 10:1–12:28}

They shall go last with their standards. *{Numbers 2:31}*

The camp of Dan brought up the rear when the armies of Israel were on the march. The Danites occupied *the last place*, but what did the position matter, since they were as truly part of the host as were the tribes in the vanguard; they followed the same fiery cloudy pillar, they ate from the same manna, drank from the same spiritual Rock, and journeyed to the same inheritance. Come, my heart, cheer up, although last and least; it is your privilege to be in the army, and to fare as they fare who lead the vanguard. Someone must be the least in honour and esteem, someone must do menial work for Jesus, and why should not I? In a poor village, among an ignorant peasantry; or in a back street, among degraded sinners, I will work on, and "go last with my standard."

The Danites occupied *a very useful place*. Stragglers have to be picked up upon the march, and lost property has to be gathered from the field. Fiery spirits may dash forward over untrodden paths to learn fresh truth, and win more souls to Jesus; but some of a more conservative spirit may be well engaged in reminding the church of her ancient faith, and restoring her fainting sons. Every position has its duties, and the slowly moving children of God will find their particular state one in which they may be eminently a blessing to the whole host.

The rear guard is *a place of danger*. There are foes behind us as well as before us. Attacks may come from any quarter. We read that Amalek attacked Israel, and killed some of the stragglers. The experienced Christian will find much work for his weapons in aiding those poor doubting, desponding, wavering, souls, who are lacking in faith, knowledge, and joy. These must not be left unaided, and therefore it is the business of well-taught saints to bear their standards among the last. My soul, tenderly watch to help those who are among the last today.

July 18 — Evening

They shall neither jostle each other;
each one shall walk in his path. *[Joel 2:8]*

Locusts always keep their rank, and although their number is legion, they do not crowd each other, so as to throw their columns into confusion. This remarkable fact in natural history shows how thoroughly the Lord has infused the spirit of order into his universe, since the smallest animate creatures are as much controlled by it as are the rolling spheres or the seraphic messengers. It would be wise for believers to be ruled by the same influence in all their spiritual life. *In their Christian graces* no one virtue should usurp the sphere of another, or eat out the vitals of the rest for its own support. Affection must not smother honesty, courage must not elbow weakness out of the field, modesty must not jostle energy, and patience must not slaughter resolution. So also with *our duties*, one must not interfere with another; public usefulness must not injure private piety; church work must not push family worship into a corner. It is wrong to offer God one duty stained with the blood of another. Each thing is beautiful in its season, but not otherwise. It was to the Pharisee that Jesus said, "You ought to have done this, and not to have left the other undone." The same rule applies to *our personal position*, we must take care to know our place, take it, and stay in it. We must minister as the Spirit has given us ability, and not intrude upon our fellow servant's domain. Our Lord Jesus taught us not to covet the high places, but to be willing to be the least among the brethren. May an envious, ambitious spirit be far from us, let us feel the force of the Master's command, and do as he bids us, keeping rank with the rest of the host. Tonight let us see whether we are keeping the unity of the Spirit in the bonds of peace, and let our prayer be such that, in all the churches of the Lord Jesus, peace and order may prevail.

July 19 — Morning

{Daily Reading: Psalms 144:1–150:6} {Quick Study: Proverbs 13:1–15:33}

The Lord our God has shown us his glory. *{Deuteronomy 5:24}*

God's great design in all his works is the revealing of his own glory. Any aim less than this would be unworthy of himself. But how shall the glory of God be revealed to such fallen creatures as we are? Man's eye is not single, he always has a side glance towards his own honour, has too high an estimate of his own powers, and so is not qualified to behold the glory of the Lord. It is clear, then, that self must stand out of the way, so that there may be room for God to be exalted; and this is the reason why he brings his people often into straits and difficulties, so that, being made conscious of their own folly and weakness, they may be fitted to behold the majesty of God when he comes forth to work their deliverance. He whose life is one even and smooth path, will see very little of the glory of the Lord, for he has few occasions of self-emptying, and hence, very little fitness for being filled with the revelation of God. Those who navigate little streams and shallow creeks, know very little about the God of tempests; but those who "do business in great waters," these see his "wonders in the deep." Among the huge Atlantic waves of bereavement, poverty, temptation, and reproach, we learn the power of Jehovah, because we feel the littleness of man. Thank God, then, if you have been led by a rough road: it is this which has given you your experience of God's greatness and lovingkindness. Your troubles have enriched you with a wealth of knowledge to be gained by no other means: your trials have been the cleft of the rock in which Jehovah has set you, as he did his servant Moses, so that you might behold his glory as it passed by. Praise God that you have not been left to the darkness and ignorance which continued prosperity might have involved, but that in the great fight of affliction you have been rendered capable for the outshinings of his glory in his wonderful dealings with you.

July 19 — Evening

*He shall not break a bruised reed, and he shall
not quench smoking flax. {Matthew 12:20}*

What is weaker than the bruised reed or the smoking flax? A *reed* that grows in the fen or marsh, only let the wild duck light upon it, and it snaps; only let the foot of man brush against it, and it is bruised and broken; every wind that flits across the river moves it to and fro. You can conceive of nothing more frail or brittle, or whose existence is more in jeopardy, than a bruised reed. Then look at the smoking flax — what is it? It has a spark within it, it is true, but it is almost smothered; an infant's breath might blow it out; nothing has a more precarious existence than its flame. *Weak things* are described here, yet Jesus says about them, "I shall not break a bruised reed; and I shall not quench smoking flax." Some of God's children are made strong to do mighty works for him; God has his Samsons here and there who can pull up Gaza's gates, and carry them to the top of the hill; he has a few mighties who are lionlike men, but the majority of his people are a timid, trembling race. They are like starlings, frightened at every passerby; a little fearful flock. If temptation comes, they are taken like birds in a snare; if trial threatens, they are ready to faint; their frail skiff is tossed up and down by every wave, they are drifted along like a sea bird on the crest of the billows — weak things, without strength, without wisdom, without foresight. Yet, weak as they are, and *because* they are so weak, they have this promise made especially for them. Herein is grace and graciousness! Herein is love and lovingkindness! How it opens to us the compassion of Jesus — so gentle, tender, considerate! We need never shrink back from *his* touch. We need never fear a harsh word from *him*; although he might well chide us for our weakness, he does not rebuke. Bruised reeds shall receive no blows from him, and the smoking flax no dampening frowns.

July 20 — Morning

{Daily Reading: Proverbs 1:1–3:35} {Quick Study: Proverbs 16:1–19:29}

The guarantee of our inheritance. *{Ephesians 1:14}*

Oh! What enlightenment, what joys, what consolation, what delight of heart is experienced by that man who has learned to feed on Jesus, and on Jesus alone. Yet the realisation which we have of Christ's preciousness is, in this life, imperfect at the best. As an old writer says, "It is only a taste!" We have tasted "that the Lord is gracious," but we do not yet know *how* good and gracious he is, although what we know of his sweetness makes us long for more. We have enjoyed the firstfruits of the Spirit, and they have set us hungering and thirsting for the fulness of the heavenly vintage. We groan within ourselves, waiting for the adoption. *Here* we are like Israel in the wilderness, who had only one cluster from Eshcol, *there* we shall be in the vineyard. Here we see the small manna falling, like coriander seed, but there we shall eat the bread of heaven and the old grain of the kingdom. We are only beginners now in spiritual education; for although we have learned the first letters of the alphabet, we cannot read words yet, much less can we put sentences together; but as one says, "He who has been in heaven only five minutes, knows more than the general assembly of divines on earth." We have many ungratified desires at present, but soon every wish shall be satisfied; and all our powers shall find the sweetest employment in that eternal world of joy. Oh, Christian, anticipate heaven for a few years. Within a very little time you shall be rid of all your trials and your troubles. Your eyes now suffused with tears shall weep no longer. You shall gaze in unutterable rapture upon the splendour of him who sits upon the throne. Indeed, more, you shall sit upon his throne. The triumph of his glory shall be shared by you; his crown, his joy, his paradise, these shall be yours, and you shall be co-heir with him who is the heir of all things.

July 20 — Evening

*And now what have you to do in the way of Egypt,
to drink the waters of Sihor?* {Jeremiah 2:18}

By various miracles, by different mercies, by strange deliverances Jehovah had proven himself to be worthy of Israel's trust. Yet they broke down the hedges with which God had enclosed them as a sacred garden; they forsook their own true and living God, and followed after false gods. Constantly the Lord reproved them for this infatuation, and our text contains one instance of God's expostulating with them, "What have you to do in the way of Egypt, to drink the waters of the muddy river?" — for so it may be translated. "Why do you wander afar and leave your own cool stream from Lebanon? Why do you forsake Jerusalem to turn aside to Noph and to Tahapanes? Why are you so strangely set on mischief, that you cannot be content with the good and healthful, but would follow after what is evil and deceitful?" Is there not here a word of expostulation and warning to the Christian? Oh true believer, called by grace and washed in the precious blood of Jesus, you have tasted of better drink than the muddy river of this world's pleasure can give you; you have had fellowship with Christ; you have obtained the joy of seeing Jesus, and leaning your head upon his bosom. After that, are you now content with the trifles, the songs, the honours, the merriment of this earth? Have you eaten the bread of angels, and can you now live on husks? Good Rutherford once said, "I have tasted of Christ's own manna, and it has put my mouth out of taste for the brown bread of this world's joys." I think it should be so with you. If you are wandering after the waters of Egypt, oh return quickly to the one living fountain: the waters of Sihor may be sweet to the Egyptians, but they will prove only bitterness to you. What have *you* to do with them? *Jesus asks you this question* this evening — what will you answer him?

July 21 — Morning

{Daily Reading: Proverbs 4:1–7:27} {Quick Study: Proverbs 20:1–22:29}

The daughter of Jerusalem has shaken
her head at you. *{Isaiah 37:22}*

Reassured by the Word of the Lord, the poor trembling citizens of Zion grew bold, and shook their heads at Sennacherib's boastful threats. Strong faith enables the servants of God to look with calm contempt upon their most haughty foes. *We know that our enemies are attempting impossibilities.* They seek to destroy the eternal life, which cannot die while Jesus lives; to overthrow the citadel, against which the gates of hell shall not prevail. They kick against the goads to their own wounding, and rush upon the bosses of Jehovah's buckler to their own hurt.

We know their weakness. What are they but men? And what is man but a worm? They roar and swell like waves of the sea, foaming out their own shame. When the Lord arises, they shall fly as chaff before the wind, and be consumed as crackling thorns. Their utter powerlessness to do damage to the cause of God and his truth, may make the weakest soldiers in Zion's ranks laugh them to scorn.

Above all, *we know that the Most High is with us*, and when he dresses himself in arms, where are his enemies? If he comes forth from his place, the potsherds of the earth will not long contend with their Maker. His rod of iron shall dash them in pieces like a potter's vessel, and their very remembrance shall perish from the earth. Away, then, all fears, the kingdom is safe in the King's hands. Let us shout for joy, for the Lord reigns, and his foes shall be as straw for the dunghill.

> As true as God's own Word is true;
> Nor earth, nor hell, with all their crew,
> Against us shall prevail.
> A jest, and byword, are they grown;
> God is with us, we are his own,
> Our victory cannot fail.

July 21 — Evening

Why am I mourning? *{Psalms 42:9}*

Can you answer this, believer? Can you find any reason why you are so often mourning instead of rejoicing? Why yield to gloomy anticipations? Who told you that the night would never end in day? Who told you that the sea of circumstances would ebb out until there would be nothing left but long leagues of the mud of horrible poverty? Who told you that the winter of your discontent would proceed from frost to frost, from snow, and ice, and hail, to deeper snow, and yet more heavy tempest of despair? Do you not know that day follows night, that flood comes after ebb, that spring and summer succeed winter? Hope then! Hope always! For God does not fail you. Do you not know that your God loves you in the midst of all this? Mountains, when hidden by darkness, are just as real as in the day, and God's love is as true to you now as it was in your bright moments. No father always chastens: your Lord hates the rod as much as you do; he only cares to use it for that reason which should make you willing to receive it, namely, that it works your lasting good. You shall yet climb Jacob's ladder with the angels, and behold him who sits at its top — your covenant God. You shall yet, amidst the splendours of eternity, forget the trials of time, or only remember them to bless the God who led you through them, and worked out your lasting good by them. Come, sing in the midst of tribulation. Rejoice even while passing through the furnace. Make the wilderness to blossom like the rose! Cause the desert to ring with your exulting joys, for these light afflictions will soon be over, and then "for ever with the Lord," your bliss shall never wane.

> Faint not nor fear, his arms are near,
> He changes not, and you are dear;
> Only believe and you shall see,
> That Christ is all in all to thee.

July 22 — Morning

{Daily Reading: Proverbs 8:1–11:31} {Quick Study: Proverbs 23:1–25:28}

I am married to you. *{Jeremiah 3:14}*

Christ Jesus is joined to his people in marriage union. In love he espoused his church as a chaste virgin, long before she fell under the yoke of bondage. Full of burning affection he toiled, like Jacob for Rachel, until all of her purchase money had been paid, and now, having sought her by his Spirit, and brought her to know and love him, he awaits the glorious hour when their mutual bliss shall be consummated at the marriage supper of the Lamb. Not yet has the glorious Bridegroom presented his betrothed, perfected and complete, before the Majesty of heaven; not yet has she actually entered upon the enjoyment of her dignities as his wife and queen: she is as yet a wanderer in a world of woe, a dweller in the tents of Kedar; but she is even now the bride, the spouse of Jesus, dear to his heart, precious in his sight, written on his hands, and united with his person. On earth he exercises towards her all the affectionate offices of a husband. He makes rich provision for her needs, pays all her debts, allows her to assume his name, and to share in all his wealth. Nor will he ever act otherwise towards her. He will never mention the word divorce, for "he hates putting away." Death must sever the conjugal tie between the most loving mortals, but it cannot divide the links of this immortal marriage. In heaven they do not marry, but are as the angels of God; yet there is this one marvellous exception to the rule, for in heaven Christ and his church shall celebrate their joyous nuptials. Since this affinity is more lasting, it is more intimate than earthly wedlock. Let the love of husband be ever so pure and fervent, it is only a faint picture of the flame which burns in the heart of Jesus. Surpassing all human union is that mystical cleaving to the church, for which Christ left his Father, and became one flesh with her.

July 22 — Evening

Behold the Man! *{John 19:5}*

If there is one place where our Lord Jesus most fully becomes the joy and comfort of his people, it is the place he plunged deepest into the depths of woe. Come here, gracious souls, and behold the Man in the garden of Gethsemane; behold his heart so brimming with love that he cannot hold it in — so full of sorrow that it must find a vent. Behold the bloody sweat as it distils from every pore of his body, and falls upon the ground. Behold the Man as they drive the nails into his hands and feet. Look up, repenting sinners, and see the sorrowful image of your suffering Lord. See him, as the ruby drops stand on the thorn crown, and adorn with priceless gems the diadem of the King of Misery. Behold the Man when all his bones are out of joint, and he is poured out like water and brought into the dust of death; God has forsaken him, and hell surrounds him. Behold and see, was there ever sorrow like his sorrow which he experienced? All you who pass by draw near and look upon this spectacle of grief, unique, unparalleled, a wonder to men and angels, a prodigy unmatched. Behold the Emperor of Woe who had no equal or rival in his agonies! Gaze upon him, oh mourners, for if there is not consolation in a crucified Christ there is no joy in heaven or earth. If in the ransom price of his blood there is no hope, oh harps of heaven, there is no joy in you, and the right hand of God shall know no pleasures for evermore. We have only to sit more continually at the foot of the cross to be less troubled with our doubts and woes. We have only to see *his* sorrows, and we shall be ashamed to mention *our* sorrows. We have only to gaze into his wounds to heal our own. If we wish to live properly it must be by the contemplation of his death; if we wish to rise to dignity, it must be by considering his humiliation and his sorrow.

July 23 — Morning

{Daily Reading: Proverbs 12:1–15:33} {Quick Study: Proverbs 26:1–29:27}

Even you were as one of them. *{Obadiah 1:11}*

Brotherly kindness was due from Edom to Israel in the time of need, but instead of it, the men of Esau joined in with Israel's foes. Special stress in the sentence before us is laid upon the word *you*; as when Caesar cried to Brutus, "and *you* Brutus"; a bad action may be all the worse, because of the person who has committed it. When we sin, who are the chosen favourites of heaven, we sin with an emphasis; ours is a crying offence, because we are so particularly indulged. If an angel should lay his hand upon us when we are doing evil, he need not use any other rebuke than the question, "What! Is it *you*? What are *you* doing here?" Much forgiven, much delivered, much instructed, much enriched, much blessed, shall we dare to put forth our hand to evil? God forbid!

A few minutes of confession may be beneficial to you, gentle reader, this morning. Have you never been as the wicked? At an evening party certain men laughed at uncleanness, and the joke was not altogether offensive to your ear, *even you were as one of them.* When harsh things were spoken concerning the ways of God, you were bashfully silent; and so, to onlookers, *you were as one of them.* When worldlings were bartering in the market, and driving hard bargains, were you not as one of them? When they were pursuing vanity with a hunter's foot, were you not as greedy for gain as they were? Could any difference be discerned between you and them? *Is there any difference?* Here we come to close quarters. Be honest with your own soul, and make sure that you are a new creature in Christ Jesus; but when this is sure, walk jealously, lest any should again be able to say, "Even you were as one of them." You would not desire to share their eternal doom, why then be like them here? Do not be intimately associated with them, lest you share in their ruin. Side with the afflicted people of God, and not with the world.

July 23 — Evening

The blood of Jesus Christ his Son
cleanses us from all sin. *{1 John 1:7}*

Cleanses," says the text — not "*shall* cleanse." There are multitudes who think that as a dying hope they may look forward to pardon. Oh! How infinitely better to have cleansing now than to depend on the mere possibility of forgiveness when I come to die. Some imagine that a sense of pardon is an attainment only obtainable after many years of Christian experience. But forgiveness of sin is a *present* thing — a privilege for this day, a joy for this very hour. The moment a sinner trusts Jesus he is fully forgiven. The text, being written in the present tense, also indicates continuance; it was "cleanses" yesterday, it is "cleanses" today, it will be "cleanses" tomorrow: it will be always so with you, Christian, until you cross the river; every hour you may come to this fountain, for it still cleanses. Notice, likewise, the *completeness* of the cleansing, "The blood of Jesus Christ his Son cleanses us from *all sin*" — not only from sin, but "from *all* sin." Reader, I cannot tell you the exceeding sweetness of this word, but I pray God the Holy Spirit to give you a taste of it. We have many sins against God. Whether the bill is little or great, the same receipt can discharge one as well as the other. The blood of Jesus Christ is as blessed and divine a payment for the transgressions of blaspheming Peter as for the shortcomings of loving John; our iniquity is gone, all gone at once, and all gone for ever. Blessed completeness! What a sweet theme to dwell upon as one gives himself to sleep.

> Sins against a holy God;
> Sins against his righteous laws;
> Sins against his love, his blood;
> Sins against his name and cause;
> Sins immense as is the sea —
> From them all he cleanses me.

Stand still, and see the salvation of the Lord. *{Exodus 14:13}*

These words contain God's command to the believer when he is reduced to great straits and brought into extraordinary difficulties. He cannot retreat; he cannot go forward; he is shut up on the right hand and on the left; what is he to do now? The Master's word to him is, "Stand still." It will be well for him if at such times he listens only to his Master's word, for other evil advisers come with their suggestions. *Despair* whispers, "Lie down and die; give it all up." But God would have us put on a cheerful courage, and even in our worst times, rejoice in his love and faithfulness. *Cowardice* says, "Retreat; go back to the worldling's way of action; you cannot play the Christian's part, it is too difficult. Relinquish your principles." But, however much Satan may urge this course upon you, you cannot follow it if you are a child of God. His divine fiat has bidden you to go from strength to strength, and so you shall, and neither death nor hell shall divert you from your course. What if for a while you are called to stand still, yet this is only to renew your strength for some greater advance in due time. *Precipitancy* cries, "Do something. Stir yourself; to stand still and wait, is sheer idleness." We must be doing something at once — we must do it so we think — instead of looking to the Lord, who will not only do something but will do everything. *Presumption* boasts, "If the sea is before you, march into it and expect a miracle." But Faith listens neither to Presumption, nor to Despair, nor to Cowardice, nor to Precipitancy, but it hears God say, "Stand still," and immovable as a rock it stands. "*Stand* still" — keep the posture of an upright man, ready for action, expecting further orders, cheerfully and patiently awaiting the directing voice; and it will not be long before God shall say to you, as distinctly as Moses said it to the people of Israel, "Go forward."

July 24 — Evening

His camp is very great. *{Joel 2:11}*

Consider, my soul, the mightiness of the Lord who is your glory and defence. He is a man of war; Jehovah is his name. All *the forces of heaven* are at his beck and call, legions wait at his door, cherubim and seraphim, watchers and holy ones, principalities and powers, are all attentive to his will. If our eyes were not blinded by the ophthalmia of the flesh, we should see horses of fire and chariots of fire all around the Lord's beloved. *The powers of nature* are all subject to the absolute control of the Creator: stormy wind and tempest, lightning and rain, and snow, and hail, and the soft dews and cheering sunshine, come and go at his decree. He loosens the bands of Orion, and binds the sweet influences of the Pleiades. Earth, sea, and air, and the places under the earth, are the barracks for Jehovah's great armies; space is his camping ground, light is his banner, and flame is his sword. When he goes out to war, famine ravages the land, pestilence strikes the nations, hurricane sweeps the sea, tornado shakes the mountains, and earthquake makes the solid world to tremble. As for *animate creatures,* they all acknowledge his dominion, and from the great fish which swallowed the prophet, down to "all manner of flies," which plagued the field of Zoan, all are his servants, and like the palmerworm, the caterpillar, and the cankerworm, are squadrons of his great army, for his camp is very great. My soul, see to it that you are at peace with this mighty King, yes, more, be sure to enlist under his banner, for to war against him is madness, and to serve him is glory. Jesus, Emmanuel, God with us, is ready to receive recruits for the army of the Lord: if I am not already enlisted let me go to him before I sleep, and beg to be accepted through his merits; and if I am already a soldier of the cross, as I hope I am, let me be of good courage; for the enemy is powerless compared with my Lord, whose camp is very great.

July 25 — Morning

{Daily Reading: Proverbs 20:1–22:29} {Quick Study: Ecclesiastes 1:1–4:16}

**He left his garment in her hand, and fled,
and escaped.** *{Genesis 39:12}*

In contending with certain sins there remains no mode of victory but by flight. The ancient naturalists wrote much of basilisks, whose eyes fascinated their victims and rendered them easy targets; so the mere gaze of wickedness puts us in solemn danger. He who wishes to be safe from acts of evil must flee from even any opportunities for it. A covenant must be made with our eyes not even to look upon the cause of temptation, for such sins only need a spark to begin with and a blaze follows in an instant. Who would wantonly enter the leper's prison and sleep amid its horrible corruption? He only who desires to be leprous himself would thus court contagion. If the mariner knew how to avoid a storm, he would do anything rather than run the risk of weathering it. Cautious pilots have no desire to try to see how near the quicksand they can sail, or how often they may touch a rock without springing a leak; their aim is to keep as nearly as possible in the middle of a safe channel.

Today I may be exposed to great peril, let me have the serpent's wisdom to keep out of it and avoid it. The wings of a dove may be of more use to me today than the jaws of a lion. It is true I may be an apparent loser by declining evil company, but I had better leave my cloak than lose my character; it is not needful that I should be rich, but it is imperative upon me to be pure. No ties of friendship, no chains of beauty, no flashings of talent, no shafts of ridicule must turn me from the wise resolve to flee from sin. I must resist the devil and he will flee from me, but I must flee the lusts of the flesh, or they will surely overcome me. Oh, God of holiness, preserve your Josephs, so that Madam Bubble does not bewitch them with her vile suggestions. May the horrible trinity of the world, the flesh, and the devil, never overcome us!

July 25 — Evening

In their affliction they will seek me early. *{Hosea 5:15}*

Losses and adversities are frequently the means which the great Shepherd uses to bring home his wandering sheep; like fierce dogs they worry the wanderers back to the fold. There is no making lions tame if they are too well fed; they must be brought down from their great strength, and their stomachs must be lowered, and then they will submit to the tamer's hand; and often we have seen the Christian rendered obedient to the Lord's will by scarcity of food and hard labour. When rich and increased in goods many professors carry their heads much too loftily, and speak very boastfully. Like David, they flatter themselves, "My mountain stands firm; I shall never be moved." When the Christian grows wealthy, is in good repute, has good health, and a happy family, he too often admits Mr. Carnal Security to feast at his table, and then if he is a true child of God there is a rod preparing for him. Wait a while, and it may be you will see his substance melt away as a dream. There goes a portion of his estate — how soon the acres change hands. That debt, that dishonoured bill — how fast his losses roll in; where will they end? It is a blessed sign of divine life if when these embarrassments occur one after another he begins to be distressed about his backslidings, and returns to his God. Blessed are the waves that wash the mariner upon the rock of salvation! Losses in business are often sanctified to our soul's enriching. If the chosen soul will not come to the Lord full handed, it shall come empty. If God, in his grace, finds no other means of making us honour him among men, he will cast us into the deep; if we fail to honour him on the pinnacle of riches, he will bring us into the valley of poverty. Yet do not faint, heir of sorrow, when you are thus rebuked, rather recognise the loving hand which chastens, and say, "I will arise, and go to my Father."

July 26 — Morning

{Daily Reading: Proverbs 23:1–26:28} {Quick Study: Ecclesiastes 5:1–8:17}

Giving all diligence, add to your faith virtue;
and to virtue knowledge, etc. *{2 Peter 1:5–6}*

If you wish to enjoy the eminent grace of the full assurance of faith, under the blessed Spirit's influence, and assistance, do what the Scripture tells you, *"Give diligence."* Take care that your *faith* is of the right kind — that it is not a mere belief of doctrine, but a simple faith, depending on Christ, and on Christ alone. Give diligent heed to your *courage*. Plead with God that he would give you the face of a lion, so that you may, with a consciousness of right, go on boldly. Study well the Scriptures, and get *knowledge*; for a knowledge of doctrine will tend very much to confirm faith. Try to understand God's Word; let it dwell in your heart richly.

When you have done this, "Add to your knowledge *temperance.*" Take heed to your body: be temperate without. Take heed to your soul: be temperate within. Get temperance of lip, life, heart, and thought. Add to this, by God's Holy Spirit, *patience*; ask him to give you that patience which endures affliction, which, when it is tried, shall come forth as gold. Array yourself with patience, so that you may not murmur nor be depressed in your afflictions. When that grace is won look to *godliness*. Godliness is something more than religion. Make God's glory your object in life; live in his sight; dwell close to him; seek for fellowship with him; and you have "godliness"; and to that add *brotherly love*. Have a love for all the saints: and add to that a *love*, which opens its arms to all men, and loves their souls. When you are adorned with these jewels, and just in proportion as you practise these heavenly virtues, you will come to know by clearest evidence "your calling and election." "Give diligence," if you wish to have assurance, for lukewarmness and doubting very naturally go hand in hand.

July 26 — Evening

That he may set him with princes. {Psalms 113:8}

Our spiritual privileges are of the highest order. "Among princes" *is the place of select society.* "Truly our fellowship is with the Father, and with his Son Jesus Christ." Speaking of select society, there is no one like this! "We are a chosen generation, a particular people, a royal priesthood." "We are come to the general assembly and church of the firstborn, whose names are written in heaven." The saints *have courtly audience*: princes have admittance to royalty when common people must stand afar off. The child of God has free access to the inner courts of heaven. "For through him we both have access by one Spirit to the Father." "Let us come boldly," says the apostle, "*to the throne* of the heavenly grace." Among princes there is *abundant wealth*, but what is the abundance of princes compared with the riches of believers? for "all things are yours, and you are Christ's, and Christ is God's." "He who did not spare his own Son, but delivered him up for us all, how shall he not with him also freely give us all things?" Princes have *particular power*. A prince of heaven's empire has great influence: he wields a sceptre in his own domain; he sits upon Jesus' throne, for "He has made us kings and priests to God, and we shall reign for ever and ever." We reign over the united kingdom of time and eternity. Princes, again, have *special honour*. We may look down upon all earth born dignity from the eminence upon which grace has placed us. For what is human grandeur to this, "He has raised us up together, and made us sit together in heavenly places in Christ Jesus?" We share the honour of Christ, and compared with this, earthly splendours are not worth a thought. Communion with Jesus is a richer gem than ever glittered in any imperial diadem. Union with the Lord is a coronet of beauty outshining all the blaze of imperial pomp.

July 27 — Morning

{Daily Reading: Proverbs 27:1–31:31} {Quick Study: Ecclesiastes 9:1–12:14}

Exceedingly great and precious promises. *{2 Peter 1:4}*

If you wish to know by experience the preciousness of the promises, and enjoy them in your own heart, *meditate much upon them.* There are promises which are like grapes in the winepress; if you will tread them the juice will flow. Thinking over the hallowed words will often be the prelude to their fulfilment. While you are musing upon them, the boon which you are seeking will silently come to you. Many a Christian who has thirsted for the promise has found the favour which it ensured gently distilling into his soul even while he has been considering the divine record; and he has rejoiced that he ever was led to lay the promise close to his heart.

But besides *meditating* upon the promises, *seek in your soul to receive them as being the very Words of God.* Speak to your soul thus, "If I were dealing with a man's promise, I would carefully consider the ability and the character of the man who had covenanted with me. So with the promise of God; my eye must not be so much fixed upon the greatness of the mercy — that may stagger me; as upon the greatness of the Promiser — that will cheer me. My soul, it is God, even your God, God who cannot lie, who speaks to you. This Word of his which you are now considering is as true as his own existence. He is an unchangeable God. He has not altered the thing which has gone out of his mouth, nor called back one single consolatory sentence. Nor does he lack any power; it is the God who made the heavens and the earth who has spoken thus. Nor can he fail in wisdom concerning the time when he will bestow the favours, for he knows when it is best to give and when better to withhold. Therefore, seeing that it is the Word of a God so true, so immutable, so powerful, so wise, I will and must believe the promise." If we thus meditate upon the promises, and consider the Promiser, we shall experience their sweetness, and obtain their fulfilment.

July 27 — Evening

Who shall lay anything to the charge of God's elect? {Romans 8:33}

Most blessed challenge! How unanswerable it is! Every sin of the elect was laid upon the great Champion of our salvation, and by the atonement carried away. There is no sin in God's book against his people: he sees no sin in Jacob, neither iniquity in Israel; they are justified in Christ for ever. When the guilt of sin was taken away, the punishment of sin was removed. For the Christian there is no stroke from God's angry hand — no, not so much as a single frown of punitive justice. The believer may be chastised by his Father, but God the Judge has nothing to say to the Christian, except, "I have absolved you: you are acquitted." For the Christian there is no penal death in this world, much less any second death. He is completely freed from all the punishment as well as the guilt of sin, and the power of sin is removed, too. It may stand in our way, and agitate us with perpetual warfare; but sin is a conquered foe to every soul in union with Jesus. There is no sin which a Christian cannot overcome if he will only rely upon his God to do it. Those who wear the white robe in heaven overcame through the blood of the Lamb, and we may do the same. No lust is too mighty, no besetting sin too strongly entrenched; we can overcome through the power of Christ. Do believe it, Christian, that your sin is a condemned thing. It may kick and struggle, but it is doomed to die. God has written condemnation across its brow. Christ has crucified it, "nailing it to his cross." Go now and mortify it, and the Lord help you to live for his praise, for sin with all its guilt, shame, and fear, is gone.

> Here's pardon for transgressions past,
> It matters not how black their cast;
> And, oh my soul, with wonder view,
> For sins to come here's pardon too.

July 28 — Morning

{Daily Reading: Ecclesiastes 1:1–4:16} {Quick Study: Song of Solomon 1:1–8:14}

I was so foolish and ignorant; I was like a beast before you. *{Psalms 73:22}*

Remember this is the confession of the man after God's own heart; and in telling us his inner life, he writes, "I was so foolish and ignorant." The word *foolish,* here, means more than it signifies in ordinary language. David, in a former verse of the psalm, writes, "I was envious at *the foolish* when I saw the prosperity of the wicked," which shows that the folly he intended had sin in it. He puts himself down as being thus "foolish," and adds a word which is to give intensity to it: "I was so foolish." *How foolish* he could not tell. It was a sinful folly, a folly which was not to be excused by frailty, but to be condemned because of its perverseness and wilful ignorance, for he had been envious of the present prosperity of the ungodly, forgetful of the dreadful end awaiting all such. And are we better than David that we should call ourselves wise? Do we profess that we have attained perfection, or to have been so chastened that the rod has taken all our wilfulness out of us? Ah, this would be pride indeed! If *David* was foolish, how foolish would *we* be in our own esteem if we could only see ourselves! Look back, believer: think of your doubting God when he has been so faithful to you — think of your foolish outcry of "Not so, my Father," when he crossed his hands in affliction to give you the larger blessing. Think of the many times when you have read his providences in the dark, misinterpreted his dispensations, and groaned out, "All these things are against me," when they are all working together for your good! Think how often you have chosen sin because of its pleasure, when indeed, that pleasure was a root of bitterness to you! Surely if we know our own heart we must plead guilty to the indictment of a sinful folly; and conscious of this "foolishness," we must make David's consequent resolve our own — *"You shall guide me with your counsel."*

July 28 — Evening

Who went about doing good. {*Acts 10:38*}

Few words, but yet it is an exquisite miniature of the Lord Jesus Christ. There are not many touches, but they are the strokes of a master's pencil. Of the Saviour and only of the Saviour is it true in the fullest, broadest, and most unqualified sense. "He went about doing good." From this description it is evident that he did good *personally*. The evangelists constantly tell us that he touched the leper with his own finger, that he anointed the eyes of the blind, and that in cases where he was asked to speak the word only at a distance, he did not usually comply, but went himself to the sick bed, and there personally performed the cure. A lesson for us, if we wish to do good, to do it ourselves. Give alms with your own hand; a kind look, or word, will enhance the value of the gift. Speak to a friend about his soul; your loving appeal will have more influence than a whole library of tracts. Our Lord's mode of doing good exhibits his *incessant activity*! He did not only the good which came close to hand, but he "went about" on his errands of mercy. Throughout the whole land of Judea there was scarcely a village or a hamlet which was not gladdened by the sight of him. How this reproves the creeping, loitering manner in which many professors serve the Lord. Let us gird up the loins of our mind, and do not be weary in well doing. Does not the text imply that Jesus Christ *went out of his way to do good?* "He went *about* doing good." He was never deterred by danger or difficulty. He sought out the objects of his gracious intentions. So must we. If old plans will not work, we must try new ones, for fresh experiments sometimes achieve more than regular methods. Christ's *perseverance*, and the *unity* of his purpose, are also hinted at, and the practical application of the subject may be summed up in the words, "He has left us an example that we should follow his steps." {*1 Peter 2:21*}

July 29 — Morning

{Daily Reading: Ecclesiastes 5:1–8:17} {Quick Study: Isaiah 1:1–4:6}

Nevertheless I am continually with you. *{Psalms 73:23}*

Nevertheless, — as if, notwithstanding all the foolishness and ignorance which David had just been confessing to God, not one atom the less was it true and certain that David was saved and accepted, and that the blessing of being constantly in God's presence was undoubtedly his. Fully conscious of his own lost estate, and of the deceitfulness and vileness of his nature, yet, by a glorious outburst of faith, he sings "nevertheless I am continually with you." Believer, you are forced to enter into Asaph's confession and acknowledgment, endeavour in like spirit to say "nevertheless, since I belong to Christ I am continually with God!" By this is meant continually upon his *mind*, he is always thinking of me for my good. Continually before his *eye* — the eye of the Lord never sleeps, but is perpetually watching over my welfare. Continually in his *hand*, so that no one shall be able to pluck me from there. Continually on his *heart*, worn there as a memorial, even as the high priest bore the names of the twelve tribes upon his heart for ever. You always think of me, oh God. The heart of your love continually yearns towards me. You are always making providence work for my good. You have set me as a signet upon your arm; your love is as strong as death, many waters cannot quench it; neither can the floods drown it. Surprising grace! You see me in Christ, and though in myself abhorred, you behold me as wearing Christ's garments, and washed in his blood, and thus I stand accepted in your presence. I am thus continually in your favour — "continually with you." Here is comfort for the tried and afflicted soul; vexed with the tempest within — look at the calm without. *"Nevertheless"* — oh, say it in your heart, and take the peace it gives. "Nevertheless I am continually with you."

July 29 — Evening

All whom the Father gives to me
shall come to me. {John 6:37}

This declaration involves *the doctrine of election*: there are some whom the Father gave to Christ. It involves *the doctrine of effectual calling*: these who are given must and shall come; however stoutly they may set themselves against it, yet they shall be brought out of darkness into God's marvellous light. It teaches us *the indispensable necessity of faith*; for even those who are given to Christ are not saved unless they come to Jesus. Even *they* must come, for there is no other way to heaven but by the door, Christ Jesus. All whom the Father gives to our Redeemer *must come to him*, therefore no one can come to heaven unless they come to Christ.

Oh, the power and majesty which rest in the words *"shall come"*! He does not say they have power to come, nor they may come if they wish, but they *"shall come."* The Lord Jesus does by his messengers, his Word, and his Spirit, sweetly and graciously compel men to come in so that they may eat his marriage supper; and he does this, not by any violation of the free agency of man, but by the power of his grace. I may exercise power over another man's will, and yet that other man's will may be perfectly free, because the constraint is exercised in a manner accordant with the laws of the human mind. Jehovah Jesus knows how, by irresistible arguments addressed to the understanding, by mighty reasons appealing to the affections, and by the mysterious influence of his Holy Spirit operating upon all the powers and passions of the soul, so to subdue the whole man, that whereas he was once rebellious, he yields cheerfully to his government, subdued by sovereign love. But how shall those be known whom God has chosen? By this result: that they willingly and joyfully accept Christ, and come to him with simple and sincere faith, resting upon him as all their salvation and all their desire. Reader, have you thus come to Jesus?

July 30 — Morning

{Daily Reading: Ecclesiastes 9:1–12:14} {Quick Study: Isaiah 5:1–7:25}

And when he thought about it, he wept. *{Mark 14:72}*

It has been thought by some that as long as Peter lived, the fountain of his tears began to flow whenever he remembered his denying his Lord. It is not unlikely that it was so, for his sin was very great, and grace in him had afterwards a perfect work. This same experience is common to all the redeemed family according to the degree in which the Spirit of God has removed the natural heart of stone. We, like Peter, remember *our boastful promise*: "Though all men shall forsake you, yet I will not." We eat our own words with the bitter herbs of repentance. When we think of what we vowed we would be, and of what we have been, we may weep whole showers of grief. He thought about *his denying his Lord.* The place in which he did it, the little cause which led him into such heinous sin, the oaths and blasphemies with which he tried to confirm his falsehood, and the dreadful hardness of heart which drove him to do so again and yet again. Can we, when we are reminded of our sins, and their exceeding sinfulness, remain stolid and stubborn? Will we not make our house a Bochim, and cry to the Lord for renewed assurances of pardoning love? May we never look at sin with a dry eye, lest before long we have a tongue parched in the flames of hell. Peter also thought about *his Master's look of love.* The Lord followed up the cock's warning voice with an admonitory look of sorrow, pity, and love. That glance was never out of Peter's mind as long as he lived. It was far more effectual than ten thousand sermons would have been without the Spirit. The penitent apostle would be sure to weep when he remembered the *Saviour's full forgiveness*, which restored him to his former place. To think that we have offended so kind and good a Lord is more than sufficient reason for being constant weepers. Lord, strike our rocky hearts, and make the waters flow.

July 30 — Evening

He who comes to me I will in no wise cast out. *{John 6:37}*

No limit is set to *the duration* of this promise. It does not merely say, "I will not cast out a sinner at his first coming," but, "I will in no wise cast out." The original reads, "I will *not, not* cast out," or "I will never, never cast out." The text means that Christ will not *at first* reject a believer; and that just as he will not do it at first, so he will not *to the last*.

But suppose the believer sins after coming? "If any man sins we have an advocate with the Father, Jesus Christ the righteous." But suppose that believers backslide? "I will heal their backsliding, I will love them freely: for my anger is turned away from him." But believers may fall under temptation! "God is faithful, who will not allow you to be tempted more than you are able; but will with the temptation also make a way to escape, so that you may be able to bear it." But the believer may fall into sin as David did! Yes, but he will "purge them with hyssop, and they shall be clean; he will wash them and they shall be whiter than snow"; "I will cleanse them from all their iniquities."

> Once in Christ, in Christ for ever,
> Nothing from his love can sever.

"I give to my sheep," he says, "eternal life; and they shall never perish, neither shall any man pluck them out of my hand." What do you say to this, oh trembling feeble mind? Is this not a precious mercy, that coming to Christ, you do not come to one who will treat you well for a little while, and then send you about your business? However, he will receive you and make you his bride, and you shall be his for ever. No longer receive the spirit of bondage again to fear, but the spirit of adoption by which you shall cry, "Abba, Father!" Oh, the grace of these words: "I will in no wise cast out!"

July 31 — Morning

{Daily Reading: Song of Solomon 1:1–8:14} {Quick Study: Isaiah 8:1–12:6}

I am in them. *{John 17:23}*

If such is the union which subsists between our souls and the person of our Lord, how deep and broad is the channel of our communion! This is no narrow pipe through which a thread-like stream may wind its way, it is a channel of amazing depth and breadth, along whose glorious length a ponderous volume of living water may roll its floods. Behold, he has set before us an open door, let us not be slow to enter. This city of communion has many pearly gates, every individual gate is of one pearl, and each gate is thrown open to the uttermost so that we may enter, assured of welcome. If there would be only one small loophole through which to talk with Jesus, it would be a high privilege to thrust a word of fellowship through the narrow door; how much we are blessed in having so large an entrance! Had the Lord Jesus been far away from us, with many a stormy sea between, we should have longed to send a messenger to him to carry him our loves, and bring us tidings from his Father's house; but see his kindness, he has built his house next door to ours, indeed, more, he takes lodging with us, and tabernacles in poor humble hearts, so that he may have perpetual communion with us. Oh, how foolish must we be, if we do not live in habitual communion with him. When the road is long, and dangerous, and difficult, we need not wonder that friends seldom meet each other, but when they live together, shall Jonathan forget his David? A wife may when her husband is upon a journey, live for many days without conversing with him, but she could never endure to be separated from him if she knew him to be in one of the rooms of her own house. Why, believer, do you not sit at his banquet of wine? Seek your Lord, for he is near; embrace him, for he is your brother. Hold him close, for he is your Husband; and press him to your heart, for he is of your own flesh.

July 31 — Evening

**And these are the singers…they were employed in
that work day and night.** *{1 Chronicles 9:33}*

It was so well ordered in the temple that the sacred chant never
ceased: the singers continually praised the Lord, whose mercy
endures for ever. Just as mercy did not cease to rule either by day
or by night, so neither did music hush its holy ministry. My heart,
there is a lesson sweetly taught to you in the ceaseless song of Zion's
temple, you too are a constant debtor, and see to it that your gratitude, like love, never fails. God's praise is constant in heaven, which
is to be your final dwelling place, learn to practise the eternal hallelujah. Around the earth as the sun scatters its light, its beams
awaken grateful believers to tune their morning hymn, so that by
the priesthood of the saints perpetual praise is kept up at all hours,
they swathe our globe in a mantle of thanksgiving, and encompass
it with a golden belt of song.

The Lord always deserves to be praised for what he is in himself,
for his works of creation and providence, for his goodness towards
his creatures, and especially for the transcendent act of redemption,
and all the marvellous blessing flowing from it. It is always beneficial to praise the Lord; it cheers the day and brightens the night; it
lightens toil and softens sorrow; and over earthly gladness it sheds
a sanctifying radiance which makes it less liable to blind us with its
glare. Have we not something to sing about at this moment? Can
we not weave a song out of our present joys, or our past deliverances, or our future hopes? Earth yields her summer fruits: the hay
is housed, the golden grain invites the sickle, and the sun tarrying
long to shine upon a fruitful earth shortens the interval of darkness
so that we may lengthen the hours of devout worship. By the love
of Jesus, let us be stirred up to close the day with a psalm of sanctified gladness.

August 1 — Morning

{Daily Reading: Isaiah 1:1–4:6} {Quick Study: Isaiah 13:1–17:14}

Now let me go to the field,
and glean ears of grain. *{Ruth 2:2}*

Downcast and troubled Christian, come and glean today in the broad field of promise. Here is an abundance of precious promises, which exactly meet your needs. Take this one: "He will not break the bruised reed, nor quench the smoking flax." Does that not suit your case? A reed, helpless, insignificant, and weak, a bruised reed, out of which no music can come; weaker than weakness itself; a reed, and that reed is bruised, yet, he will not break you; but on the contrary, will restore and strengthen you. You are like the smoking flax: no light, no warmth, can come from you; but he will not quench you; he will blow with his sweet breath of mercy until he fans you into a flame. Would you glean another ear? "Come to me all you who labour and are heavy laden, and I will give you rest." What soft words! Your heart is tender, and the Master knows it, and therefore he speaks so gently to you. Will you not obey him, and come to him even now? Take another ear of grain: "Do not fear, you worm Jacob, I will help you, says the Lord and your Redeemer, the Holy One of Israel." How can you fear with such a wonderful assurance as this? You may gather ten thousand such golden ears as these! "I have blotted out your sins like a cloud, and like a thick cloud your transgressions." Or this, "Though your sins are as scarlet, they shall be as white as snow; though they are red like crimson, they shall be as wool." Or this, "The Spirit and the Bride say, 'Come, and let him who is thirsty come, and whoever wishes, let him take the water of life freely.' " Our Master's field is very rich; behold the handfuls. See, there they lie before you, poor timid believer! Gather them up, make them your own, for Jesus bids you to take them. Do not be afraid, only believe! Grasp these sweet promises, thresh them out by meditation and feed on them with joy.

August 1 — Evening

You crown the year with your goodness. *{Psalms 65:11}*

All the year round, every hour of every day, God is richly blessing us; both when we sleep and when we are awake his mercy waits upon us. The sun may leave us a legacy of darkness, but our God never ceases to shine upon his children with beams of love. Like a river, his lovingkindness is always flowing, with a fulness inexhaustible as his own nature. Like the atmosphere which constantly surrounds the earth, and is always ready to support the life of man, the benevolence of God surrounds all his creatures; in it, as in their element, they live, and move, and have their being. Yet as the sun on summer days gladdens us with beams more warm and bright than at other times, and as rivers are in certain seasons swollen by the rain, and as the atmosphere itself is sometimes fraught with more fresh, more bracing, or more balmy influences than before, so it is with the mercy of God; it has its golden hours; its days of overflow, when the Lord magnifies his grace before the sons of men. Among the blessings of the lower springs, *the joyous days of harvest* are a special season of excessive favour. It is the glory of autumn that the ripe gifts of providence are then abundantly bestowed; it is the mellow season of realisation, whereas all before was only hope and expectation. Great is the joy of harvest. Happy are the reapers who fill their arms with the liberality of heaven. The psalmist tells us that the harvest is the crowning of the year. Surely these crowning mercies call for crowning thanksgiving! Let us render it by the *inward emotions of gratitude.* Let our hearts be warmed; let our spirits remember, meditate, and think upon this goodness of the Lord. Then let us *praise him with our lips,* and laud and magnify his name from whose bounty all this goodness flows. Let us glorify God by yielding *our gifts* to his cause. A practical proof of our gratitude is a special thank offering to the Lord of the harvest.

August 2 — Morning

{Daily Reading: Isaiah 5:1–9:21} {Quick Study: Isaiah 18:1–21:17}

Who works all things after the counsel of his own will. *{Ephesians 1:11}*

Our belief in God's wisdom supposes and necessitates that he has a settled purpose and plan in the work of salvation. What would *creation* have been without his design? Is there a fish in the sea, or a fowl in the air, which was left to chance for its formation? No, in every bone, joint, and muscle, sinew, gland, and blood vessel, you see the presence of a God working everything according to the design of infinite wisdom. And shall God be present in creation, ruling over all, and not in *grace*? Shall the new creation have the fickle genius of free will to preside over it when divine counsel rules the old creation? Look at *Providence*! Who does not know that no sparrow falls to the ground without your Father knowing it? Even the hairs of your head are all numbered. God weighs the mountains of our grief in scales, and the hills of our tribulation in balances. And shall there be a God in providence and not in grace? Shall the shell be ordained by wisdom and the kernel be left to blind chance? No, he knows the end from the beginning. He sees in its appointed place, not merely the corner stone which he has laid in fair colours, in the blood of his dear Son, but he beholds in their ordained position each of the chosen stones taken out of the quarry of nature, and polished by his grace; he sees everything from corner to cornice, from basement to roof, from foundation to pinnacle. He has in his mind a clear knowledge of every stone which shall be laid in its prepared place, and how vast the edifice shall be, and when the top stone shall be brought forth with shoutings of "Grace! Grace! to it." At the last it shall be clearly seen that in every chosen vessel of mercy, Jehovah did as he willed with his own; and that in every part of the work of grace he accomplished his purpose, and glorified his own name.

August 2 — Evening

So she gleaned in the field until the evening. *{Ruth 2:17}*

Let me learn from Ruth, the gleaner. As she went out to gather the ears of grain, so must I go forth into the fields of prayer, meditation, the ordinances, and hearing the word to gather spiritual food. *The gleaner gathers her portion ear by ear*; her gains are little by little: so I must be content to search for single truths, if there is no abundance of them. Every ear helps to make a bundle, and every gospel lesson assists in making us wise to salvation. *The gleaner keeps her eyes open*: if she stumbled among the stubble in a dream, she would have no load to carry home rejoicingly in the evening. I must be watchful in religious exercises lest they become unprofitable to me; I fear I have lost much already — oh that I may rightly estimate my opportunities, and glean with greater diligence. *The gleaner stoops for all she finds*, and so must I. High spirits criticize and object, but lowly minds glean and receive benefit. A humble heart is a great help towards profitably hearing the gospel. The engrafted soul-saving word is not received except with meekness. A stiff back makes a bad gleaner; down, master pride, you are a vile robber, not to be endured for a moment. *What the gleaner gathers she holds*: if she dropped one ear to find another, the result of her day's work would be only scant; she is as careful to retain as to obtain, and so at last her gains are great. How often do I forget all that I hear; the second truth pushes the first out of my head, and so my reading and hearing end in much ado about nothing! Do I duly feel the importance of storing up the truth? A hungry belly makes the gleaner wise; if there is no grain in her hand, there will be no bread on her table; she labours under the sense of necessity, and hence her tread is nimble and her grasp is firm; I have even a greater necessity, Lord, help me to feel it, that it may urge me onward to glean in fields which yield so plenteous a reward for diligence.

{Daily Reading: Isaiah 10:1–14:32} {Quick Study: Isaiah 22:1–24:23}

The Lamb is its light. *{Revelation 21:23}*

Quietly contemplate the Lamb as the light of heaven. Light in Scripture is the emblem of *joy*. The joy of the saints in heaven is comprised in this: *Jesus* chose us, loved us, bought us, cleansed us, robed us, kept us, and glorified us: we are here entirely through the Lord Jesus. Each one of these thoughts shall be to them like a cluster of the grapes of Eshcol. Light is also the cause of *beauty*. Nothing of beauty is left when light is gone. Without light no radiance flashes from the sapphire, no peaceful ray proceeds from the pearl; and thus all the beauty of the saints above comes from Jesus. As planets, they reflect the light of the Sun of Righteousness; they live as beams proceeding from the central orb. If he withdrew, they must die; if his glory were veiled, their glory must expire. Light is also the emblem of *knowledge*. In heaven our knowledge will be perfect, but the Lord Jesus himself will be the fountain of it. Dark providences, never understood before, will then be clearly seen, and all that puzzles us now will become plain to us in the light of the Lamb. Oh what unfoldings there will be and what glorifying of the God of love! Light also means *manifestation*. Light reveals. In this world it does not yet appear what we shall be. God's people are a hidden people, but when Christ receives his people into heaven, he will touch them with the wand of his own love, and change them into the image of his revealed glory. They were poor and wretched, but what a transformation! They were stained with sin, but one touch of his finger, and they are bright as the sun, and clear as crystal. Oh what a manifestation! All this proceeds from the exalted Lamb. Whatever there may be of effulgent splendour, Jesus shall be the centre and soul of it all. Oh, to be present and to see him in his own light, the King of kings, and Lord of lords!

August 3 — Evening

But as he went. *{Luke 8:42}*

Jesus is passing through the throng to the house of Jairus, to raise the ruler's dead daughter; but he is so profuse in goodness that he works another miracle while upon the road. While yet this rod of Aaron bears the blossom of an unaccomplished wonder, it yields the ripe almonds of a perfect work of mercy. It is enough for us, if we have just one purpose, immediately to go and accomplish it; it would be imprudent to expend our energies by the way. Hastening to the rescue of a drowning friend, we cannot afford to exhaust our strength upon another in similar danger. It is enough for a tree to yield one sort of fruit, and for a man to fulfil his own particular calling. But our Master knows no limit of power or boundary of mission. He is so prolific in grace, that like the sun which shines as it rolls onward in its orbit, his path is radiant with lovingkindness. He is a swift arrow of love, which not only reaches its ordained target, but perfumes the air through which it flies. Virtue is constantly emanating from Jesus, just as sweet odours exude from flowers; and it always will flow from him, just as water flows from a sparkling fountain. What delightful encouragement this truth affords us! If our Lord is so ready to heal the sick and bless the needy, then, my soul, do not be slow to put yourself in his way, so that he may smile on you. Do not be slack in asking, if he is so abundant in bestowing. Give earnest heed to his word now, and at all times, so that Jesus may speak to your heart through it. Where he is to be found there make your destination, so that you may obtain his blessing. When he is present to heal, may he not heal you? But surely he is present even now, for he always comes to hearts which need him. And do you not need him? Ah, *he* knows how much! Oh, Son of David, turn your eye and look upon the distress which is now before you, and make your supplicant whole.

August 4 — Morning

{Daily Reading: Isaiah 15:1–21:17} {Quick Study: Isaiah 25:1–27:13}

The people who know their God
shall be strong. *{Daniel 11:32}*

Every believer understands that to know God is the highest and best form of knowledge; and this spiritual knowledge is a source of strength to the Christian. It strengthens his *faith*. Believers are constantly spoken of in the Scriptures as being people who are enlightened and taught by the Lord; they are said to "have an unction from the Holy One," and it is the Spirit's particular office to lead them into all truth, and all this for the increase and the fostering of their faith. Knowledge strengthens *love*, as well as faith. Knowledge opens the door, and then through that door we see our Saviour. Or, to use another similitude, knowledge paints the portrait of Jesus, and when we see that portrait then we love him. We cannot love a Christ whom we do not know, at least, in some degree. If we know very little about the excellencies of Jesus, what he has done for us, and what he is doing now, we cannot love him much; but the more we know him, the more we shall love him. Knowledge also strengthens *hope*. How can we hope for a thing if we do not know about its existence? Hope may be the telescope, but until we receive instruction, our ignorance stands in the front of the telescope, and we can see nothing whatever; knowledge removes the interposing object, and when we look through the bright telescope we discern the glory to be revealed, and anticipate it with joyous confidence. Knowledge supplies us reasons for *patience*. How shall we have patience unless we know something about the sympathy of Christ, and understand the good which is to come out of the correction which our Heavenly Father sends us? Nor is there one single grace of the Christian which, under God, will not be fostered and brought to perfection by holy knowledge. How important, then, is it that we should grow not only in grace, but in the "knowledge" of our Lord and Saviour Jesus Christ.

August 4 — Evening

I struck you with blight and with mildew and with hail in all the labours of your hands. *{Haggai 2:17}*

How destructive is the hail to the standing crops, beating out the precious grain upon the ground! How grateful ought we to be when the grain is spared so terrible a ruin! Let us offer to the Lord thanksgiving. Even more to be dreaded are those mysterious destroyers — smut, bunt, rust, and mildew. These turn the ear into a mass of soot, or render it putrid, or dry up the grain, and all in a manner so beyond all human control that the farmer is compelled to cry, "This is the finger of God." Innumerable minute fungi cause the mischief, and if it were not for the goodness of God, the rider on the black horse would soon scatter famine over the land. Infinite mercy spares the food of men, but in view of the active agents which are ready to destroy the harvest, we are very wisely taught to pray, "Give us this day our daily bread." The curse is abroad; we have constant need for the blessing. When blight and mildew come they are chastisements from heaven, and men must learn to bear the rod, and the one who has appointed it.

Spiritually, mildew is no uncommon evil. When our work is most promising this blight appears. We hoped for many conversions, and lo! a general apathy, an abounding worldliness, or a cruel hardness of heart! There may be no open sin in those for whom we are labouring, but there is a deficiency of sincerity and decision sadly disappointing our desires. We learn our dependence upon the Lord from this, and the need of prayer that no blight may fall upon our work. Spiritual pride or sloth will soon bring upon us the dreadful evil, and only the Lord of the harvest can remove it. Mildew may even attack our own hearts, and shrivel our prayers and religious exercises. May it please the great Husbandman to avert so serious a calamity. Shine, blessed Sun of Righteousness, and drive the blights away.

August 5 — Morning

{Daily Reading: Isaiah 22:1–26:21} {Quick Study: Isaiah 28:1–31:9}

**We know that all things work together for good
to those who love God.** *{Romans 8:28}*

Upon some points a believer is absolutely sure. He knows, for instance, that God sits in the stern part of the vessel when it rocks most. He believes that an invisible hand is always on the world's tiller, and that wherever providence may drift, Jehovah steers it. That reassuring knowledge prepares him for everything. He looks over the raging waters and sees the spirit of Jesus treading the billows, and he hears a voice saying, "It is I, do not be afraid." He knows, too, that God is always wise, and, knowing this, he is confident that there can be no accidents, no mistakes; that nothing can occur which ought not to arise. He can say, "If I should lose all I have, it is better that I should lose than have, if God so wills: the worst calamity is the wisest and the kindest thing that could befall me if God ordains it." "We know that all things work together for good to those who love God." The Christian does not merely hold this as a theory, but *he knows it* as a matter of fact. Everything *has* worked for good until now; the poisonous drugs mixed in proper proportions have worked the cure; the sharp cuts of the lancet have cleansed out the proud flesh and facilitated the healing. So far, every event has worked out the most divinely blessed results; and so, believing that God rules all, that he governs wisely, that he brings good out of evil, the believer's heart is assured, and he is enabled calmly to meet each trial as it comes. The believer can in the spirit of true resignation pray, "Send me what you will, my God, as long as it comes from you; there never came a poor portion from your table for any of your children."

> Say not my soul, "From where can God relieve my care?"
> Remember that Omnipotence has servants everywhere.
> His method is sublime, his heart profoundly kind,
> God never is before his time, and never is behind.

August 5 — Evening

Shall your brethren go to war, and shall you sit here? {Numbers 32:6}

Kindred has its obligations. The Reubenites and Gadites would have been unbrotherly if they had claimed the land which had been conquered, and had left the rest of the people to fight for their portions alone. We have received much by means of the efforts and sufferings of the saints in years gone by, and if we do not make some return to the church of Christ by giving her our best energies, we are unworthy to be enrolled in her ranks. Others are combating the errors of the age manfully, or excavating perishing ones from amid the ruins of the fall, and if we fold our hands in idleness we had need to be warned, lest the curse of Meroz fall upon us. The Master of the vineyard says, "Why do you stand here all the day idle?" What is the idler's excuse? Personal service for Jesus becomes all the more the duty of all because it is cheerfully and abundantly rendered by some. The toils of devoted missionaries and fervent ministers shame us if we sit still in indolence. Shrinking from trial is the temptation of those who are at ease in Zion: they would try to escape the cross and yet wear the crown; to them the question for this evening's meditation is very applicable. If the most precious are tried in the fire, are we to escape the crucible? If the diamond must be vexed upon the wheel, are we to be made perfect without suffering? Who has commanded the wind to cease from blowing because our bark is on the deep? Why should we be treated better than our Lord? The firstborn felt the rod, and why not the younger brother? It is a cowardly pride which would choose a downy pillow and a silken couch for a soldier of the cross. Wiser far is he who, being first resigned to the divine will, grows by the energy of grace to be pleased with it, and so learns to gather lilies at the foot of the cross, and, like Samson, to find honey in the lion.

August 6 — Morning

{Daily Reading: Isaiah 27:1–31:9} {Quick Study: Isaiah 32:1–35:10}

Watchman, what of the night? *{Isaiah 21:11}*

What enemies are abroad? Errors are a numerous horde, and new ones appear every hour: against what heresy am I to be on my guard? Sins creep from their lurking places when the darkness reigns; I must myself mount the watch tower, and watch and pray. Our heavenly Protector foresees all the attacks which are about to be made upon us, and when as yet the evil designed for us is only in the desire of Satan, he prays for us so that our faith does not fail, when we are sifted as wheat. Continue oh gracious Watchman, to forewarn us about our foes, and for Zion's sake do not hold your peace.

"Watchman, what of the night?" *What weather is coming* for the church? Are the clouds lowring, or is it all clear and fair overhead? We must care for the church of God with anxious love; and now that Popery and infidelity are both threatening, let us observe the signs of the times and prepare for conflict.

"Watchman, what of the night?" *What stars are visible?* What precious promises suit our present case? You sound the alarm, give us the consolation, also. Christ, the pole star, is always fixed in his place, and all the stars are secure in the right hand of their Lord.

But watchman, *when is the morning coming?* The Bridegroom tarries. Are there no signs of his coming forth as the Sun of Righteousness? Has not the morning star arisen as the pledge of day? When will the day dawn, and the shadows flee away? Oh, Jesus, if you do not come in person to your waiting church today, yet come in Spirit to my sighing heart, and make it sing for joy.

> Now all the earth is bright and glad
> > With the fresh morn;
> But all my heart is cold, and dark and sad:
> Sun of the soul, let me behold your dawn!
> > Come, Jesus, Lord,
> Oh quickly come, according to your word.

August 6 — Evening

Let the whole earth be filled with his glory;
Amen, and Amen. *{Psalms 72:19}*

This is a large petition. To intercede for a whole city needs a stretch of faith, and there are times when a prayer for one man is enough to stagger us. But how far reaching was the psalmist's dying intercession! How comprehensive! How sublime! "Let the whole earth be filled with his glory." It does not exempt a single country however crushed by the foot of superstition; it does not exclude a single nation however barbarous. For the cannibal as well as for the civilized, for all climes and races this prayer is uttered: it encompasses the whole circle of the earth, and omits no son of Adam. We must be up and doing for our Master, or we cannot honestly offer such a prayer. The petition is not asked with a sincere heart unless we endeavour, as God shall help us, to extend the kingdom of our Master. Are there not some who *neglect* both to plead and to labour? Reader, is it *your* prayer? Turn your eyes to Calvary. Behold the Lord of Life nailed to a cross, with the thorn crown upon his brow, with bleeding head, and hands, and feet. What! Can you look upon this miracle of miracles, the death of the Son of God, without feeling within your heart a marvellous adoration that language can never express? And when you feel the blood applied to your conscience, and know that he has blotted out your sins, *you are not a man* unless you spring up from your knees and cry, "Let the whole earth be filled with his glory; Amen, and Amen." Can you bow before the Crucified in loving homage, and not wish to see your Monarch master of the world? Away with you if you can pretend to love your Prince, and do not desire to see him as the universal ruler. Your piety is worthless unless it leads you to wish that the same mercy which has been extended to you may bless the whole world. Lord, it is harvest time, put in your sickle and reap.

August 7 — Morning

{Daily Reading: Isaiah 32:1–37:38} {Quick Study: Isaiah 36:1–39:8}

The upright love you. *{Song of Solomon 1:4}*

Believers love Jesus with a deeper affection than they dare to give to any other being. They would sooner lose father and mother than part with Christ. They hold all earthly comforts with a loose hand, but they carry him firmly locked in their hearts. They voluntarily deny themselves for his sake, but they are not to be driven to deny *him*. It is scant love which the fire of persecution can dry up; the true believer's love is a deeper stream than this. Men have laboured to divide the faithful from their Master, but their attempts have been fruitless in every age. Neither crowns of honour, nor frowns of anger, have untied this more than Gordian knot. This is no everyday attachment which the world's power may at length dissolve. Neither man nor devil have found a key which opens this lock. Never has the craft of Satan been more at fault than when he has exercised it in seeking to tear asunder this union of two divinely welded hearts. It is written, and nothing can blot out the sentence, *"The upright love you."* The intensity of the love of the upright, however, is not so much to be judged by what it appears to be as by what the upright long for. It is our daily lament that we cannot love enough. Oh, that our hearts were capable of holding more, and reaching farther. Like Samuel Rutherford, we sigh and cry, "Oh, for as much love as would go all around the earth, and over heaven — yes, the heaven of heavens, and ten thousand worlds — that I might let it all out upon fair, fair, only fair Christ." Alas! Our longest reach is only a handbreadth of love, and our affection is only as a drop in a bucket compared with his deserts. Measure our love by our intentions, and it is high indeed; it is thus, we trust, our Lord judges it. Oh, that we could give all the love in all hearts in one great mass, a gathering together of all loves to him who is altogether lovely!

August 7 — Evening

Satan hindered us. *{1 Thessalonians 2:18}*

Since the first hour in which goodness came into conflict with evil, it has never ceased to be true in spiritual experience, that Satan hinders us. From all points of the compass, all along the line of battle, in the vanguard and in the rear, at the dawn of day and in the midnight hour, Satan hinders us. If we toil in the field, he tries to break the ploughshare; if we build the wall, he labours to throw down the stones; if we wish to serve God in suffering or in conflict — everywhere Satan hinders us. He hinders us when we are first coming to Jesus Christ. We had fierce conflicts with Satan when we first looked to the cross and lived. Now that we are saved, he endeavours to hinder the completeness of our personal character. You may be congratulating yourself, "I have so far walked consistently; no man can challenge my integrity." Beware of boasting, for your virtue will yet be tried; Satan will direct his engines against that very virtue for which you are the most famous. If so far you have been a firm believer, your faith will be attacked before long; if you have been meek as Moses, expect to be tempted to speak unadvisedly with your lips. The birds will peck at your ripest fruit, and the wild boar will dash his tusks at your choicest vines. Satan is sure to hinder us when we are earnest in prayer. He checks our importunity, and weakens our faith in order that, if possible, we may miss the blessing. Nor is Satan less vigilant in obstructing Christian effort. There was never a revival of religion without a revival of his opposition. As soon as Ezra and Nehemiah begin to labour, Sanballat and Tobiah are stirred up to hinder them. What then? We are not alarmed because Satan hinders us, for it is a proof that we are on the Lord's side, and are doing the Lord's work, and in his strength we shall win the victory, and triumph over our adversary.

August 8 — Morning

{Daily Reading: Isaiah 38:1–42:25} {Quick Study: Isaiah 40:1–43:28}

They weave the spider's web. *{Isaiah 59:5}*

See the spider's web, and behold in it a most suggestive picture of the hypocrite's religion. *It is meant to catch his prey*: the spider fattens himself on flies, and the Pharisee has his reward. Foolish people are easily entrapped by the loud professions of pretenders, and even the more judicious cannot always escape. Philip baptized Simon Magus, whose guileful declaration of faith was so soon exploded by the stern rebuke of Peter. Custom, reputation, praise, advancement, and other flies, are the small game which hypocrites take in their nets. A spider's web is *a marvel of skill*: look at it and admire the cunning hunter's wiles. Is not a deceiver's religion equally wonderful? How does he make so barefaced a lie appear to be a truth? How can he make his tinsel answer so well the purpose of gold? A spider's web *comes all from the creature's own body*. The bee gathers her wax from flowers, the spider sucks no flowers, and yet she spins out her material to any length. Even so hypocrites find their trust and hope within themselves; their anchor was forged on their own anvil, and their cable twisted by their own hands. They lay their own foundation, and hew out the pillars of their own house, disdaining to be debtors to the sovereign grace of God. But a spider's web is *very frail*. It is intricately wrought, but not enduringly manufactured. It is no match for the servant's broom, or the traveller's staff. The hypocrite needs no battery of Armstrongs to blow his hope to pieces, a mere puff of wind will do it. Hypocritical cobwebs will soon come down when the broom of destruction begins its purifying work. Which reminds us of one more thought, namely, that such cobwebs *are not to be endured in the Lord's house*: he will see to it that they and those who spin them shall be destroyed for ever. Oh my soul, be resting on something better than a spider's web. Make the Lord Jesus your eternal hiding place.

August 8 — Evening

All things are possible for him who believes. *{Mark 9:23}*

Many professing Christians are always doubting and fearing, and they forlornly think that this is the necessary state of believers. This is a mistake, for "all things are possible for him who believes"; and it is possible for us to mount into a state in which a doubt or a fear shall be only as a bird flitting across the soul, but never lingering there. When you read of the high and sweet communions enjoyed by favoured saints, you sigh and murmur in the chamber of your heart, "Alas! these are not for me." Oh, climber, if you only have faith, you shall yet stand upon the sunny pinnacle of the temple, for "all things are possible for him who believes." You hear of exploits which holy men have done for Jesus; what they have enjoyed of him; how much they have been like him; how they have been able to endure great persecutions for his sake; and you say, "Ah! As for me, I am only a worm; I can never attain to this." But there is nothing which one saint was, that you may not be. There is no elevation of grace, no attainment of spirituality, no clearness of assurance, no post of duty, which is not open to you if you only have the power to believe. Lay aside your sackcloth and ashes, and rise to the dignity of your true position; you are little in Israel because you wish to be so, not because there is any necessity for it. It is not fitting that you should grovel in the dust, oh child of a King. Ascend! The golden throne of assurance is waiting for you! The crown of communion with Jesus is ready to bedeck your brow. Wrap yourself in scarlet and fine linen, and fare sumptuously every day; for if you believe, you may eat the fat of the kidneys of wheat; your land shall flow with milk and honey, and your soul shall be satisfied as with marrow and fatness. Gather golden sheaves of grace, for they await you in the fields of faith. *"All things are possible for him who believes."*

August 9 — Morning

{Daily Reading: Isaiah 43:1–46:13} {Quick Study: Isaiah 44:1–48:22}

The city has no need of the sun, neither of the moon, to shine in it. *{Revelation 21:23}*

Up there in the better world, the inhabitants are independent of all creature comforts. They have no need of clothing; their white robes never wear out, neither shall they ever be defiled. They need no medicine to heal diseases, "for the inhabitant shall not say, I am sick." They need no sleep to refresh their bodies — they do not rest day or night, but unweariedly praise him in his temple. They need no social relationship to minister comfort, and whatever happiness they may derive from association with their fellows is not essential to their bliss, for their Lord's company is enough for their greatest desires. They need no teachers there; they doubtless commune with one another concerning the things of God, but they do not require this by way of instruction; they shall all be taught by the Lord. Ours are the alms at the King's gate, but they feast at the table itself. Here we lean upon the friendly arm, but there they lean upon their Beloved and upon him alone. Here we must have the help of our companions, but there they find all they need in Christ Jesus. Here we look to the food which perishes, and to the clothing which decays before the moth, but there they find everything in God. We use the bucket to fetch water from the well, but there they drink from the fountain head, and put their lips down to the living water. Here the angels bring us blessings, but we shall need no messengers from heaven then. They shall need no Gabriels there to bring their love notes from God, for there they shall see *him* face to face. Oh! What a blessed time shall that be when we shall have mounted above every second cause and shall rest upon the bare arm of God! What a glorious hour when God, and not his creatures; the Lord, and not his works, shall be our daily joy! Our souls shall then have attained the perfection of bliss.

August 9 — Evening

He appeared first to Mary Magdalene, out of
whom he had cast seven demons. *{Mark 16:9}*

Mary of Magdala was *the victim of a fearful evil.* She was possessed by not one demon only, but seven. These dreadful inmates caused much pain and pollution to the poor body in which they had found a lodging. Hers was a hopeless, horrible case. She could not help herself, neither could any human help avail. But Jesus passed that way, and unsought, and probably even resisted by the poor demoniac, he uttered the word of power, and Mary of Magdala became *a trophy of the healing power of Jesus.* All the seven demons left her, left her never to return, forcibly ejected by the Lord of all. What a blessed deliverance! What a happy change! From delirium to delight, from despair to peace, from hell to heaven! Immediately she became *a constant follower of Jesus*, catching his every word, following his various steps, sharing his toilsome life; and by this she became *his generous helper*, first among that band of healed and grateful women who ministered to him from their substance. When Jesus was lifted up in crucifixion, Mary remained *the sharer of his shame*: we find her first watching from afar, and then drawing near to the foot of the cross. She could not die on the cross with Jesus, but she stood as near it as she could, and when his blessed body was taken down, she watched to see how and where it was laid. She was *the faithful and watchful believer*, last at the sepulchre where Jesus slept, first at the grave from where he arose. Her holy fidelity made her *a favoured beholder of her beloved Rabboni*, who deigned to call her by her name, and to make her *his messenger of good news* to the trembling disciples and Peter. Thus, grace found her a maniac and made her a minister, cast out demons and gave her to see angels, delivered her from Satan, and united her for ever to the Lord Jesus. May I also be such a miracle of grace!

Christ, who is our life. {*Colossians 3:4*}

Paul's marvellously rich expression indicates that Christ is the *source* of our life. "He has quickened you who were dead in trespasses and sins." That same voice which brought Lazarus out of the tomb raised us to newness of life. He is now the *substance* of our spiritual life. It is by his life that we live; he is in us, the hope of glory, the spring of our actions, the central thought which moves every other thought. *Christ is the sustenance of our life.* What can the Christian feed upon except Jesus' flesh and blood? "This is the bread which comes down from heaven, that a man may eat of it, and not die." Oh, way-worn pilgrims, in this wilderness of sin you never have a morsel to satisfy the hunger of your spirits, unless you find it in him! *Christ is the solace of our life.* All our true joys come from him; and in times of trouble, his presence is our consolation. There is nothing worth living for except him; and his lovingkindness is better than life! *Christ is the object of our life.* Just as the ship speeds towards the port, so the believer hurries towards the haven of his Saviour's bosom. Just as the arrow flies to its goal, so the Christian runs towards the perfecting of his fellowship with Christ Jesus. Just as the soldier fights for his captain, and is crowned in his captain's victory, so the believer contends for Christ, and gets his triumph out of the triumphs of his Master. "For him to live is Christ." *Christ is the model for our life.* Where there is the same life within, there will, there must be, to a great extent, the same developments without; and if we live in close fellowship with the Lord Jesus we shall grow to be like him. We shall set him before us as our divine example, and we shall try to tread in his footsteps, until he shall become *the crown of our life in glory.* Oh! How safe, how honoured, how happy is the Christian, since Christ is our life!

August 10 — Evening

The Son of Man has power on earth to forgive sins. *{Matthew 9:6}*

Behold one of the great Physician's mightiest skills: he has power to forgive sin! While he lived here below, before the ransom had been paid, before the blood had been literally sprinkled on the mercy seat, he had power to forgive sin. Has he not power to do it now that he has died? What power must dwell in him who to the utmost farthing has faithfully discharged the debts of his people! He has boundless power now that he has finished transgression and made an end of sin. If you doubt it, see him rising from the dead! Behold him in ascending splendour raised to the right hand of God! Hear him pleading before the eternal Father, pointing to his wounds, urging the merit of his sacred passion! What power to forgive is here! "He has ascended on high, and received gifts for men." "He is exalted on high to give repentance and remission of sins." The most crimson sins are removed by the crimson of his blood. At this moment, dear reader, whatever your sinfulness, Christ has power to pardon, power to pardon *you*, and millions such as you are. A word will speak it. He has nothing more to do to win your pardon; all the atoning work is done. He can, in answer to your tears, forgive your sins today, and make you know it. He can breathe into your soul at this very moment a peace with God which surpasses all understanding, which shall spring from perfect remission of your mass of iniquities. Do you believe that? I trust you believe it. May you experience now the power of Jesus to forgive sin! Waste no time in applying to the Physician of souls, but hurry to him with words like these:

> Jesus! Master! hear my cry;
> Save me, heal me with a word;
> Fainting at your feet I lie,
> You my whisper'd plaint have heard.

August 11 — Morning

{Daily Reading: Isaiah 52:1–57:21} {Quick Study: Isaiah 52:1–57:21}

Oh, that I were as in months past. *{Job 29:2}*

Numbers of Christians can view the past with pleasure, but regard the present with dissatisfaction; they look back upon the days which they have passed in communing with the Lord as being the sweetest and the best they have ever known, but concerning the present, it is clad in a sable garb of gloom and dreariness. Once they lived near to Jesus, but now they feel that they have wandered from him, and they say, "Oh, that I were as in months past!" They complain that they have lost their evidences, or that they have no present peace of mind, or that they have no enjoyment in the means of grace, or that conscience is not so tender, or that they have not so much zeal for God's glory. The causes of this mournful state of things are numerous. It may arise through a comparative *neglect of prayer*, for a neglected prayer closet is the beginning of all spiritual decline. Or it may be the result of *idolatry*. The heart has been occupied with something else, more than with God; the affections have been set on the things of earth, instead of the things of heaven. A jealous God will not be content with a divided heart; he must be loved first and best. He will withdraw the sunshine of his presence from a cold, wandering heart. Or the cause may be found in *self-confidence* and *self-righteousness*. Pride is busy in the heart, and self is exalted instead of lying low at the foot of the cross. Christian, if you are not now as you "were in months past," do not rest satisfied with *wishing* for a return of former happiness, but go at once to seek your Master, and tell him your sad state. Ask for his grace and strength to help you to walk more closely with him; humble yourself before him, and he will lift you up, and yet again permit you to enjoy the light of his countenance. Do not sit down to sigh and lament; while the beloved Physician lives there is hope, indeed there is a certainty of recovery for the worst cases.

August 11 — Evening

Everlasting consolation. *{2 Thessalonians 2:16}*

"Consolation." There is music in the word; like David's harp, it charms away the evil spirit of melancholy. It was a distinguished honour to Barnabas to be called "the son of consolation"; indeed, it is one of the illustrious names of one greater than Barnabas, for the Lord Jesus is "the consolation of Israel." "*Everlasting* consolation" — here is the cream of all, for the eternity of comfort is its crown and glory. What is this "everlasting consolation?" It includes a sense of pardoned sin. A Christian man has received in his heart the witness of the Spirit that his iniquities are put away like a cloud, and his transgressions like a thick cloud. If sin is pardoned, is not that an everlasting consolation? Next, the Lord gives his people an abiding sense of acceptance in Christ. The Christian knows that God looks upon him as standing in union with Jesus. Union to the risen Lord is a consolation of the most abiding order; it is, in fact, everlasting. Let sickness prostrate us, have we not seen hundreds of believers as happy in the weakness of disease as they would have been in the strength of hale and blooming health? Let death's arrows pierce us to the heart, our comfort does not die, for have not our ears very often heard the songs of saints as they have rejoiced because the living love of God was shed abroad in their hearts in dying moments? Yes, a sense of acceptance in the Beloved is an everlasting consolation. Moreover, the Christian has a conviction of his security. God has promised to save those who trust in Christ: the Christian does trust in Christ, and he believes that God will be as good as his word, and will save him. He feels that he is safe by virtue of his being bound up with the person and work of Jesus.

August 12 — Morning

{Daily Reading: Isaiah 58:1–63:19} {Quick Study: Isaiah 58:1–62:12}

The Lord reigns, let the earth rejoice. *{Psalms 97:1}*

There is no reason for anxiety as long as this blessed sentence is true.

On earth the Lord's power just as easily controls the rage of the wicked as the rage of the sea; his love as easily refreshes the poor with mercy as the earth with showers. Majesty gleams in flashes of fire amid the tempest's horrors, and the glory of the Lord is seen in its grandeur in the fall of empires, and the crash of thrones. In all our conflicts and tribulations, we may behold the hand of the divine King.

> God is God; he sees and hears all our troubles, all our tears.
> Soul, forget not, 'mid your pains, God o'er all for ever reigns.

In hell, evil spirits confess, with misery, his undoubted supremacy. When permitted to roam abroad, it is with a chain at their heel; the bit is in the mouth of behemoth, and the hook in the jaws of leviathan. Death's darts are under the Lord's lock, and the grave's prisons have divine power as their warden. The terrible vengeance of the Judge of all the earth makes fiends cower down and tremble, even as dogs in the kennel fear the hunter's whip.

> Fear not death, nor Satan's thrusts, God defends who in him trusts;
> Soul, remember, in your pains, God o'er all for ever reigns.

In heaven no one doubts the sovereignty of the King Eternal, but all fall on their faces to do him homage. Angels are his courtiers, the redeemed are his favourites, and all delight to serve him day and night. May we soon reach the city of the great King!

> For this life's long night of sadness
> He will give us peace and gladness.
> Soul, remember, in your pains,
> God o'er all for ever reigns.

August 12 — Evening

The rainbow shall be seen in the cloud. *{Genesis 9:14}*

The rainbow, the symbol of the covenant with Noah, is typical of our Lord Jesus, who is the Lord's witness to the people. When may we *expect to see the token of the covenant*? The rainbow is only to be seen painted upon a *cloud*. When the sinner's conscience is dark with clouds, when he remembers his past sin, and mourns and laments before God, then Jesus Christ is revealed to him as the covenant rainbow, displaying all the glorious hues of the divine character and betokening peace. To the believer, when his trials and temptations surround him, it is sweet to behold the person of our Lord Jesus Christ — to see him bleeding, living, rising, and pleading for us. God's rainbow is hung over the cloud of our sins, our sorrows, and our woes, to prophesy deliverance. Nor does a *cloud* alone give a rainbow, there must be *the crystal drops* to reflect the light of the sun. So our sorrows must not only threaten, but they must really fall upon us. There would have been no Christ for us if the vengeance of God had been merely a threatening cloud: punishment must fall in terrible drops upon the Surety. Until there is a *real* anguish in the sinner's conscience, there is no Christ for him; until the chastisement which he feels becomes grievous, he cannot see Jesus. But there must also be a *sun*; for clouds and drops of rain do not make rainbows unless the sun shines. Beloved, our God, who is as the sun to us, always shines, but we do not always see him — clouds hide his face; but no matter what drops may be falling, or what clouds may be threatening, if *he* only shines there will be a rainbow at once. It is said that when we see the rainbow the shower is over. It is certain that when Christ comes, our troubles are gone; when we see Jesus, our sins vanish, and our doubts and fears subside. When Jesus walks the waters of the sea, how profound the calm!

August 13 — Morning

{Daily Reading: Isaiah 64:1–66:24} {Quick Study: Isaiah 63:1–66:24}

The cedars of Lebanon which he has planted. *{Psalms 104:16}*

Lebanon's cedars are emblematic of the Christian, in that *they owe their planting entirely to the Lord*. This is quite true of every child of God. He is not planted by man, nor self-planted, but planted by God. The mysterious hand of the divine Spirit dropped the living seed into a heart which he had himself prepared for its reception. Every true heir of heaven owns the great Husbandman as his planter. Moreover, the cedars of Lebanon *are not dependent upon man for their watering*; they stand on the lofty rock, unmoistened by human irrigation; and yet our Heavenly Father supplies them. Thus it is with the Christian who has learned to live by faith. He is independent of man, even in temporal things; for his continued maintenance he looks to the Lord his God, and to him alone. The dew of heaven is his portion, and the God of heaven is his fountain. Again, the cedars of Lebanon *are not protected by any mortal power*. They owe nothing to man for their preservation from stormy wind and tempest. They are God's trees, kept and preserved by him, and by him alone. It is precisely the same with the Christian. He is not a hothouse plant, sheltered from temptation; he stands in the most exposed position; he has no shelter, no protection, except this, that the broad wings of the eternal God always cover the cedars which he himself has planted. Like cedars, believers are *full of sap*, having vitality enough to be ever green, even amid winter's snows. Lastly, the flourishing and majestic condition of the cedar *is to the praise of God only*. The Lord, even the Lord alone has been everything to the cedars, and, therefore David very sweetly puts it in one of the psalms, "Praise the Lord, fruitful trees and all cedars." In the believer there is nothing that can magnify man; he is planted, nourished, and protected by the Lord's own hand, and to him let all the glory be ascribed.

August 13 — Evening

And I will remember my covenant. *{Genesis 9:15}*

See the form of the promise. God does not say, "And when you shall look upon the rainbow, and *you* shall remember my covenant, *then* I will not destroy the earth," but it is gloriously put, not upon *our* memory, which is fickle and frail, but upon *God's* memory, which is infinite and immutable. "The rainbow shall be in the cloud; and I will look upon it, so that I may remember the everlasting covenant." Oh! It is not *my* remembering God, it is God's remembering *me* which is the basis of my safety; it is not my laying hold of his covenant, but his covenant's laying hold on me. Glory be to God! All of the bulwarks of salvation are secured by divine power, and even the minor towers, which we may imagine might have been left to man, are guarded by almighty strength. Even the *remembrance* of the covenant is not left to our memories, for *we* might forget, but our Lord cannot forget the saints whom he has engraven on the palms of his hands. It is with us as with Israel in Egypt; the blood was upon the lintel and the two side posts, but the Lord did not say, "When *you* see the blood I will pass over you," but "When *I* see the blood I will pass over you." My looking to Jesus brings me joy and peace, but it is God's looking to Jesus which secures my salvation and that of all his elect, since it is impossible for our God to look at Christ, our bleeding Surety, and then to be angry with us for sins already punished in him. No, it is not left with us even to be saved by remembering the covenant. There is no linsey woolsey here — not a single thread of the creature mars the fabric. It is not *of* man, neither *by* man, but by the Lord alone. We *should* remember the covenant, and we *shall* do it, through divine grace; but the hinge of our safety does not hang there — it is God's remembering *us*, not our remembering *him*; and hence the covenant is *an everlasting covenant.*

August 14 — Morning

{Daily Reading: Jeremiah 1:1–3:25} {Quick Study: Jeremiah 1:1–3:25}

You, Lord, have made me glad
through your work. *{Psalms 92:4}*

Do you believe that your sins are forgiven, and that Christ has made a full atonement for them? Then what a joyful Christian *you ought to be*! How you should live above the common trials and troubles of the world! Since sin is forgiven, can it matter what happens to you now? Luther said, "Strike, Lord, strike, for my sin is forgiven; if you have forgiven me, strike as hard as you wish"; and in a similar spirit you may say, "Send sickness, poverty, losses, crosses, persecution, whatever you wish, *you have forgiven me*, and my soul is glad." Christian, if you are thus saved, while you are glad, *be grateful and loving*. Cling to that cross which took your sin away; serve him who served you. "I beseech you therefore, by the mercies of God, that you present your bodies a living sacrifice, holy, acceptable to God, which is your reasonable service." Do not let your zeal evaporate in some little ebullition of song. Show your love in expressive tokens. Love the brethren of him who loved you. If there is a Mephibosheth anywhere who is lame or halt, help him for Jonathan's sake. If there is a poor tried believer, weep with him, and bear his cross for the sake of him who wept for you and carried your sins. Since you are thus forgiven freely for Christ's sake, go and tell others the joyful news of pardoning mercy. Do not be content with this unspeakable blessing for yourself alone, but proclaim everywhere the account of the cross. Holy gladness and holy boldness will make you a good preacher, and all the world will be a pulpit for you to preach in. Cheerful holiness is the most forcible of sermons, but the Lord must give it to you. Seek it this morning before you go into the world. When it is the Lord's work in which we rejoice, we need not to be afraid of being too glad.

August 14 — Evening

I know their sorrows. *{Exodus 3:7}*

The child is cheered as he sings, "This my father knows"; and shall not we be comforted as we discern that our dear Friend and tender soul-husband knows all about us?

1. *He is the Physician*, and if he knows all, there is no need that the patient should know. Hush, oh silly, fluttering, prying, peeping, and suspecting heart! What you do not know now, you shall know hereafter, and meanwhile Jesus, the beloved Physician, knows your soul in adversities. Why does the patient need to analyze all the medicine, or evaluate all the symptoms? This is the Physician's work, not mine; it is my business to trust, and his to prescribe. If he shall write his prescription in uncouth characters which I cannot read, I will not be uneasy on that account, but rely upon his unfailing skill to make all plain in the result, however mysterious in the working.

2. *He is the Teacher*, and his knowledge is to serve us instead of our own; we are to obey, not to judge: "The servant does not know what his lord does." Shall the architect explain his plans to every labourer on the works? If he knows his own intent, is it not enough? The vessel on the wheel cannot guess to what pattern it shall be conformed, but if the potter understands his craft, what does the ignorance of the clay matter? My Lord must not be cross-examined any more by one so ignorant as I am.

3. *He is the Head.* All understanding centres there. What judgment has the arm? What comprehension has the foot? All the power to know lies in the head. Why should the member have a brain of its own when the head fulfils for it every intellectual office? Here, then, must the believer rest his comfort in sickness, not that he himself can see the end, but that Jesus knows all. Sweet Lord, be for ever eye, and soul, and head for us, and let us be content to know only what you choose to reveal.

August 15 — Morning

{Daily Reading: Jeremiah 4:1–6:30} {Quick Study: Jeremiah 4:1–6:30}

Isaac went out to meditate in the field in the evening. *{Genesis 24:63}*

Very admirable was his occupation. If those who spend so many hours in idle company, light reading, and useless pastimes, could learn wisdom, they would find more profitable company and more interesting engagements in meditation than in the vanities which now have such charms for them. We should all know more, live nearer to God, and grow in grace, if we were more alone. Meditation chews the cud and extracts the real nutriment from the mental food gathered elsewhere. When Jesus is the theme, meditation is sweet indeed. Isaac found Rebecca while engaged in private musings; many others have found their best Beloved there.

Very admirable was the choice of place. In the field we have a study hung all around with texts for thought. From the cedar to the hyssop, from the soaring eagle down to the chirping grasshopper, from the blue expanse of heaven to a drop of dew, all things are full of teaching, and when the eye is divinely opened, that teaching flashes upon the mind far more vividly than from written books. Our little rooms are neither so healthy, so suggestive, so agreeable, or so inspiring as the fields. Let us count nothing common or unclean, but feel that all created things point to their Maker, and the field will at once be hallowed.

Very admirable was the time. The time of sunset as it draws a veil over the day, befits that repose of the soul when earthborn cares yield to the joys of heavenly communion. The glory of the setting sun excites our wonder, and the solemnity of approaching night awakens our awe. If the business of this day will permit it, it will be well, dear reader, if you can spare an hour to walk in the field in the evening, but if not, the Lord is in the town, too, and will meet with you in your bedroom or in the crowded street. Let your heart go out to meet him.

And I will give you a heart of flesh. *{Ezekiel 36:26}*

A heart of flesh is known by its *tenderness concerning sin*. To have indulged a foul imagination, or to have allowed a wild desire to tarry even for a moment, is quite enough to make a heart of flesh grieve before the Lord. The heart of stone calls a great iniquity nothing, but not so the heart of flesh.

> If to the right or left I stray,
> That moment, Lord, reprove;
> And let me weep my life away,
> For having grieved your love.

The heart of flesh is *tender towards God's will*. My Lord Will-Be-Will is a great blusterer, and it is hard to subject him to God's will; but when the heart of flesh is given, the will quivers like an aspen leaf in every breath of heaven, and bows like a willow in every breeze of God's Spirit. The natural will is cold, hard iron, which is not to be hammered into form, but the renewed will, like molten metal, is soon moulded by the hand of grace. In the fleshy heart there is a *tenderness of the affections*. The hard heart does not love the Redeemer, but the renewed heart burns with affection towards him. The hard heart is selfish and coldly demands, "Why should I weep for sin? Why should I love the Lord?" But the heart of flesh says, "Lord, you know that I love you; help me to love you more!" Many are the privileges of this renewed heart; it is here the Spirit dwells, "it is here that Jesus rests." It is fitted to receive every spiritual blessing, and every blessing comes to it. It is prepared to yield every heavenly fruit to the honour and praise of God, and therefore the Lord delights in it. A tender heart is the best defence against sin, and the best preparation for heaven. A renewed heart stands on its watchtower looking for the coming of the Lord Jesus. Have you this heart of flesh?

August 16 — Morning

{Daily Reading: Jeremiah 7:1–10:25} {Quick Study: Jeremiah 7:1–10:25}

Give to the Lord the glory due to his name. *{Psalms 29:2}*

God's glory is the result of his nature and acts. He is glorious in his character, for there is such a store of everything that is holy, and good, and lovely in God, that he must be glorious. The actions which flow from his character are also glorious; but while he intends that they should reveal to his creatures his goodness, and mercy, and justice, he is equally concerned that the glory associated with them should be given only to himself. Nor is there anything in ourselves in which we may glory; for who makes us to differ from another? And what have we that we did not receive from the God of all grace? Then how careful ought we to be to *walk humbly before the Lord!* The moment we glorify ourselves, since there is only room for one glory in the universe, we set ourselves up as rivals to the Most High. Shall the insect of an hour glorify itself against the sun which warmed it into life? Shall the potsherd exalt itself above the man who fashioned it upon the wheel? Shall the dust of the desert strive with the whirlwind? Or the drops of the ocean struggle with the tempest? Give to the Lord, all you righteous, give to the Lord glory and strength; give to him the honour that is due to his name. Yet it is, perhaps, one of the hardest struggles of the Christian life to learn this sentence — "Not to us, not to us, but to your name be glory." It is a lesson which God is always teaching us, and teaching us sometimes by most painful discipline. Let a Christian begin to boast, "I can do all things," without adding "through Christ who strengthens me," and before long he will have to groan, "I can do nothing," and bemoan himself in the dust. When we do anything for the Lord, and he is pleased to accept our doings, let us lay our crown at his feet, and exclaim, "Not I, but the grace of God which was with me!"

August 16 — Evening

Ourselves also, who have the
firstfruits of the Spirit. {*Romans 8:23*}

Present possession is declared. At this present moment we have the firstfruits of the Spirit. We have repentance, that gem of the first water; faith, that priceless pearl; hope, the heavenly emerald; and love, the glorious ruby. We are already made "new creatures in Christ Jesus," by the effectual working of God the Holy Spirit. This is called the firstfruit because *it comes first*. As the wave sheaf was the first of the harvest, so the spiritual life, and all the graces which adorn that life, are the first operations of the Spirit of God in our souls. *The firstfruits were the pledge of the harvest.* As soon as the Israelite had plucked the first handful of ripe ears, he looked forward with glad anticipation to the time when the wagon would creak beneath the sheaves. So, brethren, when God gives us things which are pure, lovely, and of good report, as the work of the Holy Spirit, these are to us the prognostications of the coming glory. *The firstfruits were always holy to the Lord,* and our new nature, with all its powers, is a consecrated thing. The new life is not ours that we should ascribe its excellence to our own merit; it is Christ's image and creation, and is ordained for his glory. But *the firstfruits were not the harvest,* and the works of the Spirit in us at this moment are not the consummation — the perfection is yet to come. We must not boast that we have attained, and so reckon the wave sheaf to be all the produce of the year: we must hunger and thirst after righteousness, and pant for the day of full redemption. Dear reader, this evening open your mouth wide, and God will fill it. Let the boon in present possession excite in you a sacred avarice for more grace. Groan within yourself for higher degrees of consecration, and your Lord will grant them to you, for he is able to do exceedingly and abundantly above what we ask or even think.

{Daily Reading: Jeremiah 11:1–14:22} {Quick Study: Jeremiah 11:1–15:21}

The mercy of God. *{Psalms 52:8}*

Meditate a little on this mercy of the Lord. It is *tender mercy*. With gentle, loving touch, he heals the broken in heart, and binds up their wounds. He is as gracious in the manner of his mercy as in the matter of it. It is *great mercy*. There is nothing little in God; his mercy is like himself — it is infinite. You cannot measure it. His mercy is so great that it forgives great sins to great sinners, after great lengths of time, and then gives great favours and great privileges, and raises us up to great enjoyments in the great heaven of the great God. It is *undeserved mercy*, as indeed all true mercy must be, for deserved mercy is only a misnomer for justice. There was no right on the sinner's part to the kind consideration of the Most High; had the rebel been doomed at once to eternal fire he would have richly merited the doom, and if delivered from wrath, sovereign love alone has found a reason, for there was nothing in the sinner himself. It is *rich mercy*. Some things are great, but have little efficacy in them, but this mercy is a cordial to your drooping spirits; a golden ointment to your bleeding wounds; a heavenly bandage to your broken bones; a royal chariot for your weary feet; a bosom of love for your trembling heart. It is *manifold mercy*. As Bunyan says, "All the flowers in God's garden are double." There is no single mercy. You may think you have only one mercy, but you shall find it to be a whole cluster of mercies. It is *abounding mercy*. Millions have received it, yet far from it being exhausted; it is as fresh, as full, and as free as ever. It is *unfailing mercy*. It will never leave you. If mercy is your friend, mercy will be with you in temptation to keep you from yielding; with you in trouble to prevent you from sinking; with you in living to be the light and life of your countenance; and with you in dying to be the joy of your soul when earthly comfort is ebbing quickly.

August 17 — Evening

This sickness is not to death. *{John 11:4}*

From our Lord's words we learn that there is a limit to sickness. Here is a "to" within which its ultimate end is restrained, and beyond which it cannot go. Lazarus might pass through death, but death was not to be the ultimatum of his sickness. In all sickness, the Lord says to the waves of pain, "So far shall you go, but no farther." His fixed purpose is not the destruction, but the instruction of his people. Wisdom hangs up the thermometer at the furnace mouth, and regulates the heat.

1. *The limit is encouragingly comprehensive.* The God of providence has limited the time, manner, intensity, repetition, and effects of all our sicknesses; each throb is decreed, each sleepless hour predestined, each relapse ordained, each depression of spirit foreknown, and each sanctifying result eternally purposed. Nothing great or small escapes the ordaining hand of him who numbers the hairs of our head.

2. *This limit is wisely adjusted* to our strength, to the end designed, and to the grace apportioned. Affliction does not come haphazardly — the weight of every stroke of the rod is accurately measured. He who made no mistakes in balancing the clouds and meting out the heavens, commits no errors in measuring out the ingredients which compose the medicine for souls. We cannot suffer too much nor be relieved too late.

3. *The limit is tenderly appointed.* The knife of the heavenly surgeon never cuts deeper than is absolutely necessary. "He does not afflict willingly, nor grieve the children of men." A mother's heart cries, "Spare my child"; but no mother is more compassionate than our gracious God. When we consider how hard mouthed we are, it is a wonder that we are not driven with a sharper bit. The thought is full of consolation, that he who has fixed the bounds of our habitation, has also fixed the bounds of our tribulation.

August 18 — Morning

{Daily Reading: Jeremiah 15:1–18:23} {Quick Study: Jeremiah 16:1–20:18}

Strangers are come into the sanctuaries of the Lord's house. *{Jeremiah 51:51}*

In this account the faces of the Lord's people were covered with shame, for it was a terrible thing that men should intrude into the Holy Place reserved for the priests alone. Everywhere around us we see a similar cause for sorrow. How many ungodly men are now being educated with the view of entering into the ministry! What a crying sin is that solemn lie by which our whole population is nominally comprehended in a National Church! How fearful it is that ordinances should be pressed upon the unconverted, and that among the more enlightened churches of our land there should be such laxity of discipline. If the thousands who will read this portion shall all take this matter before the Lord Jesus today, he will interfere and avert the evil which otherwise will come upon his church. To adulterate the church is to pollute a well, to pour water upon fire, to sow a fertile field with stones. May we all have grace to maintain in our own proper way the purity of the church, as being an assembly of believers, and not a nation, an unsaved community of unconverted men.

Our zeal must, however, begin at home. Let us examine *ourselves* concerning our right to eat at the Lord's table. Let us see to it that we have on our wedding garment, lest we ourselves should be intruders in the Lord's sanctuaries. Many are called, but few are chosen; the way is narrow, and the gate is strait. Oh, for grace to come to Jesus in the manner, with the faith of God's elect. He who struck Uzzah for touching the ark is very jealous of his two ordinances; as a true believer I may approach them freely, as an alien I must not touch them lest I die. Heart searching is the duty of all who are baptized or come to the Lord's table. "Search me, oh God, and know my way, try me and know my heart."

August 18 — Evening

And they gave to him wine mingled with myrrh to drink: but he refused it. {Mark 15:23}

A golden truth is couched in the fact that the Saviour put the myrrhed wine cup from his lips. On the heights of heaven the Son of God stood of old, and as he looked down upon our globe he measured the long descent to the utmost depths of human misery; he added up the sum total of all the agonies which expiation would require, and did not abate a jot. He solemnly determined that to offer a sufficient atoning sacrifice he must go the whole way, from the highest to the lowest, from the throne of highest glory to the cross of deepest woe. This myrrhed cup, with its stupefying influence, would have kept him from the utmost limit of misery, therefore he refused it. He would not stop short of all he had undertaken to suffer for his people. Ah, how many of us have pined after reliefs from our grief which would have been injurious to us! Reader, did you never pray for a discharge from hard service or suffering with a petulant and wilful eagerness? Providence has taken from you the desire of your eyes with a stroke. Say, Christian, if it had been said, "If you so desire it, that loved one of yours shall live, but God will be dishonoured," could you have put away the temptation, and said, "Your will be done?" Oh, it is sweet to be able to say, "My Lord, if for other reasons I need not suffer, yet if I can honour you more by suffering, and if the loss of my earthly all will bring you glory, then so let it be. I refuse the comfort, if it stands in the way of your honour." Oh, that we thus walked more in the footsteps of our Lord, cheerfully enduring trial for his sake, promptly and willingly putting away the thought of self and comfort when it would interfere with our finishing the work which he has given us to do. Great grace is needed, but great grace is provided.

August 19 — Morning

{Daily Reading: Jeremiah 19:1–22:30} {Quick Study: Jeremiah 21:1–24:10}

He shall stand and feed in the strength of the Lord. *{Micah 5:4}*

Christ's reign in his church is that of a *Shepherd King*. He has supremacy, but it is the superiority of a wise and tender shepherd over his needy and loving flock; he commands and receives obedience, but it is the willing obedience of the well-cared-for sheep, rendered joyfully to their beloved Shepherd, whose voice they know so well. He rules by the force of love and the energy of goodness.

His reign is *practical in its character*. It is said, "He shall *stand and feed*." The great Head of the church is actively engaged in providing for his people. He does not sit down upon the throne in empty state, or hold a sceptre without wielding it in government. No, he stands and feeds. The expression "feed," in the original, is like an analogous one in the Greek, which means "to shepherdize," to do everything expected of a shepherd: to guide, to watch, to preserve, to restore, to tend, as well as to feed.

His reign is *continual in its duration*. It is said, "*He shall stand and feed*"; not "He shall feed now and then, and leave his position"; not, "He shall one day grant a revival, and then next day leave his church to barrenness." His eyes never slumber, and his hands never rest; his heart never ceases to beat with love, and his shoulders are never weary of carrying his people's burdens.

His reign is *effectually powerful in its action*; "He shall feed in the strength of Jehovah." Wherever Christ is, there is God; and whatever Christ does is the act of the Most High. Oh! It is a joyful truth to consider that he who stands today representing the interests of his people is very God of very God, to whom every knee shall bow. Happy are we who belong to such a Shepherd, whose humanity communes with us, and whose divinity protects us. Let us worship and bow down before him as the people of his pasture.

August 19 — Evening

**Pull me out of the net that they have secretly laid
for me: for you are my strength.** *{Psalms 31:4}*

Our spiritual foes are from the serpent's brood, and seek to
ensnare us by subtlety. The prayer before us supposes the possibility of the believer being caught like a bird. So deftly does the
fowler do his work, that simple ones are soon surrounded by the
net. The text asks that even out of Satan's meshes the captive one
may be delivered; this is a proper petition, and one which can be
granted: from between the jaws of the lion, and out of the belly of
hell, eternal love can rescue the saint. It may need a sharp *pull* to
save a soul from the net of temptations, and a mighty pull to extri-
cate a man from the snares of malicious cunning, but the Lord is
equal to every emergency, and the most skilfully placed nets of the
hunter shall never be able to hold his chosen ones. Woe to those
who are so clever at net laying; those who tempt others shall be
destroyed themselves.

"For you are my strength." What an inexpressible sweetness is to
be found in these few words! How joyfully may we encounter toils,
and how cheerfully may we endure sufferings, when we can lay hold
upon celestial strength. Divine power will tear apart all the toils of
our enemies, confound their politics, and frustrate their knavish
tricks; he is a happy man who has such matchless might engaged
upon his side. Our own strength would be of little service when
embarrassed in the nets of base cunning, but the Lord's strength is
always available; we only have to invoke it, and we shall find it near
at hand. If by faith we are depending alone upon the strength of
the mighty God of Israel, we may use our holy reliance as a plea in
supplication.

> Lord, evermore your face we seek:
> Tempted we are, and poor, and weak;
> Keep us with lowly hearts, and meek.
> Let us not fall. Let us not fall.

August 20 — Morning

{Daily Reading: Jeremiah 23:1–25:38} {Quick Study: Jeremiah 25:1–28:17}

The sweet psalmist of Israel. *{2 Samuel 23:1}*

Among all the saints whose lives are recorded in Holy Writ, David possesses an experience of the most striking, varied, and instructive character. In his history we meet with trials and temptations not to be found, as a rule, in other saints of ancient times, and hence he is all the more a suggestive type of our Lord. David knew the trials of all ranks and conditions of men. Kings have their troubles, and David wore a crown: the peasant has his cares, and David handled a shepherd's crook: the wanderer has many hardships, and David abode in the caves of Engedi: the captain has his difficulties, and David found the sons of Zeruiah too hard for him. The psalmist was also tried in his friends; his counsellor Ahithophel forsook him, "He who eats bread with me, has lifted up his heel against me." His worst foes were those of his own household: his children were his greatest affliction. The temptations of poverty and wealth, of honour and reproach, of health and weakness, all tried their power upon him. He had temptations from without to disturb his peace, and from within to mar his joy. David no sooner escaped from one trial than he fell into another; no sooner emerged from one time of despondency and alarm, than he was again brought into the lowest depths, and all God's waves and billows rolled over him. It is probably for this reason that David's psalms are so universally the delight of experienced Christians. Whatever our frame of mind, whether ecstasy or depression, David has exactly described our emotions. He was an able master of the human heart, because he had been tutored in the best of all schools — the school of heart-felt, personal experience. As we are instructed in the same school, as we mature in grace and in years, we increasingly appreciate David's psalms, and find them to be "green pastures." My soul, let David's experience cheer and counsel you today.

August 20 — Evening

And they fortified Jerusalem up to the broad wall. *{Nehemiah 3:8}*

Well-fortified cities have broad walls, and so had Jerusalem in her glory. The New Jerusalem must, in like manner, be surrounded and preserved by a broad wall of nonconformity to the world, and separation from its customs and spirit. The tendency of these days is to break down the holy barrier, and make the distinction between the church and the world merely nominal. Professors are no longer strict and puritanical, questionable literature is read on all hands, frivolous pastimes are currently indulged, and a general laxity threatens to deprive the Lord's particular people of those sacred singularities which separate them from sinners. It will be a bad day for the church and the world when the proposed amalgamation shall be complete, and the sons of God and the daughters of men shall be as one: then another deluge of wrath shall be ushered in. Beloved reader, let it be your aim in heart, in word, in dress, in action to maintain the broad wall, remembering that the friendship of this world is enmity against God.

The broad wall afforded a pleasant place of *resort* for the inhabitants of Jerusalem, from which they could command prospects of the surrounding country. This reminds us of the Lord's exceedingly broad commandments, in which we walk at liberty in communion with Jesus, overlooking the scenes of earth, and looking out towards the glories of heaven. Separated from the world, and denying ourselves all ungodliness and fleshly lusts, we are nevertheless not in prison, nor restricted within narrow bounds; indeed, we walk at liberty, because we keep his precepts. Come, reader, this evening walk with God in his statutes. As friend met friend upon the city wall, so meet your God in the way of holy prayer and meditation. You have a right to traverse the bulwarks of salvation, for you are a freeman of the royal city, a citizen of the metropolis of the universe.

August 21 — Morning

{Daily Reading: Jeremiah 26:1–28:17} {Quick Study: Jeremiah 29:1–31:40}

He who waters shall be himself
also watered. *{Proverbs 11:25}*

We are here taught the great lesson, that to get, we must give; that to accumulate, we must scatter; that to make ourselves happy, we must make others happy; and that in order to become spiritually vigorous, we must seek the spiritual good of others. In watering others, we are ourselves watered. How? Our efforts to be useful *bring out our powers for usefulness.* We have latent talents and dormant faculties which are brought to light by exercise. Our strength for labour is hidden even from ourselves, until we go out to fight the Lord's battles or to climb the mountains of difficulty. We do not know what tender sympathies we possess until we try to dry the widow's tears and soothe the orphan's grief. We often find in attempting to teach others that we *gain instruction for ourselves.* Oh, what gracious lessons some of us have learned at sick beds! We went to teach the Scriptures, we came away blushing that we knew so little about them. In our conversation with poor saints, we are taught the way of God more perfectly for ourselves and get a deeper insight into divine truth. So that watering others *makes us humble.* We discover how much grace there is where we had not looked for it; and how much the poor saint may outstrip us in knowledge. Our own *comfort is also increased* by our working for others. We endeavour to cheer them, and the consolation gladdens our own heart. Like the two men in the snow; one chafed the other's limbs to keep him from dying, and in so doing kept his own blood in circulation and saved his own life. The poor widow of Sarepta gave from her meagre supply for the prophet's needs, and from that day she never again knew what want was. Give then, and it shall be given to you, good measure, pressed down, and running over.

August 21 — Evening

**I did not say to the seed of Jacob,
"You seek me in vain."** *{Isaiah 45:19}*

We may gain much solace by considering what God has *not* said. What he has said is inexpressibly full of comfort and delight; what he has *not* said is scarcely less rich in consolation. It was one of these *"said nots"* which preserved the kingdom of Israel in the days of Jeroboam the son of Joash, for "the Lord has not said that he would blot out the name of Israel from under heaven." *{2 Kings 14:27}* In our text we have an assurance that God *will* answer prayer, because he has "*not* said to the seed of Israel, 'You seek me in vain.' " You who write bitter things against yourselves should remember that, let your doubts and fears say what they wish, if *God* has not cut you off from mercy, there is no room for despair: even the voice of conscience is of little weight if it is not seconded by the voice of God. Tremble at what God *has* said! But do not allow your vain imaginings to overwhelm you with despondency and sinful despair. Many timid people have been vexed by the suspicion that there may be something in God's decree which shuts *them* out from hope, but here is a complete refutation to that troublesome fear, for no true seeker can be decreed to wrath. "I have not spoken in secret, in a dark place of the earth; I have not said," even in the secret of my unsearchable decree, "You seek me in vain." God has clearly revealed that he *will* hear the prayer of those who call upon him, and that declaration cannot be contravened. He has so firmly, so truthfully, so righteously spoken, that there can be no room for doubt. He does not reveal his mind in unintelligible words, but he speaks plainly and positively, "Ask, and you shall receive." Believe, oh trembler, this sure truth — that prayer must and shall be heard, and that never, even in the secrets of eternity, has the Lord said to any living soul, "You seek me in vain."

August 22 — Morning

{Daily Reading: Jeremiah 29:1–31:40} {Quick Study: Jeremiah 32:1–35:19}

I charge you, oh daughters of Jerusalem,
if you find my beloved, that you tell him that
I am sick with love. *{Song of Solomon 5:8}*

Such is the language of the believer panting after present fellow-ship with Jesus, *he is sick with love for his Lord.* Gracious souls are never perfectly at ease unless they are in a state of nearness to Christ; for when they are away from him they lose their peace. The nearer to him, the nearer to the perfect calm of heaven; the nearer to him, the fuller the heart is, not only of peace, but of life, and vigour, and joy, for these all depend on constant communion with Jesus. What the sun is to the day, what the moon is to the night, what the dew is to the flower, such is Jesus Christ to us. What food is to the hungry, clothing to the naked, the shadow of a great rock to the traveller in a weary land, such is Jesus Christ to us. There-fore, if we are not consciously one with him, little marvel if our spirit cries in the words of the Song, "I charge you, oh you daugh-ters of Jerusalem, if you find my beloved, tell him that I am sick with love." *This earnest longing after Jesus has a blessing attending it:* "Blessed are those who hunger and thirst after righteousness"; and therefore, supremely blessed are those who thirst after the Righ-teous One. Blessed is that hunger, since it comes from God: if I may not have the full-blown blessedness of being filled, I wish to seek the same blessedness in its sweet bud pining in emptiness and eagerness until I am filled with Christ. If I may not feed on Jesus, it shall be next door to heaven to hunger and thirst after him. There is a hallowedness about that hunger, since it sparkles among the beatitudes of our Lord. But the blessing *involves a promise.* Such hungry ones *"shall be filled"* with what they are desiring. If Christ thus causes us to long after himself, he will certainly satisfy those longings; and when he does come to us, as come he will, *oh, how sweet it will be!*

August 22 — Evening

The unsearchable riches of Christ. *{Ephesians 3:8}*

My Master has riches beyond the count of arithmetic, the measurement of reason, the dream of imagination, or the eloquence of words. They are *unsearchable!* You may look, and study, and weigh, but Jesus is a greater Saviour than you think him to be when your thoughts are at the greatest. My Lord is more ready to pardon than you are to sin, more able to forgive than you to transgress. My Master is more willing to supply your needs than you are to confess them. Never tolerate low thoughts about my Lord Jesus. When you put the crown on his head, you will only crown him with silver when he deserves gold. *My Master has riches of happiness to bestow upon you now.* He can make you to lie down in green pastures, and lead you beside still waters. There is no music like the music of his pipe, when he is the Shepherd and you are the sheep, and you lie down at his feet. There is no love like his, neither earth nor heaven can match it. To know Christ and to be found in him — oh! This is life, this is joy, this is marrow and fatness, wine on the lees well refined. My Master does not treat his servants churlishly; he gives to them as a king gives to a king; he gives them two heavens — a heaven below in serving him here, and a heaven above in delighting in him for ever. *His unsearchable riches will be best known in eternity.* He will give to you on the way to heaven all you need; your place of defence shall be the munitions of rocks, your food shall be given to you, and your waters shall be sure; but it is there, THERE, where you shall hear the song of those who triumph, the shout of those who feast, and shall have a face to face view of the glorious and Beloved One. The unsearchable riches of Christ! This is the tune for the minstrels of earth, and the song for the harpers of heaven. Lord, teach us more and more about Jesus, and we will proclaim the good news to others.

August 23 — Morning

{Daily Reading: Jeremiah 32:1–33:26} {Quick Study: Jeremiah 36:1–39:18}

The voice of weeping shall be heard no more. *{Isaiah 65:19}*

The glorified weep no more, for *all outward causes of grief are gone.* There are no broken friendships, nor blighted prospects in heaven. Poverty, famine, peril, persecution, and slander, are unknown there. No pain distresses, no thought of death or bereavement saddens. They weep no more, for *they are perfectly sanctified.* No "evil heart of unbelief" prompts them to depart from the living God; they are without fault before his throne, and are fully conformed to his image. Well may they cease to mourn who have ceased to sin. They weep no more, because *all fear of change is past.* They know that they are eternally secure. Sin is shut out, and they are shut in. They dwell within a city which shall never be stormed; they bask in a sun which shall never set; they drink from a river which shall never run dry; they pick fruit from a tree which shall never wither. Countless cycles may revolve, but eternity shall not be exhausted, and while eternity endures, their immortality and blessedness shall co-exist with it. They are for ever with the Lord. They weep no more, because *every desire is fulfilled.* They cannot wish for anything which they do not already possess. Eye and ear, heart and hand, judgment, imagination, hope, desire, will, all the faculties, are completely satisfied; and imperfect as our present ideas are of the things which God has prepared for those who love him, yet we know enough, by the revelation of the Spirit, that the saints above are supremely blessed. The joy of Christ, which is an infinite fulness of delight, is in them. They bathe themselves in the bottomless, shoreless sea of infinite beatitude. That same joyful rest remains for us. It may not be far distant. Before long the weeping willow shall be exchanged for the palm branch of victory, and sorrow's dewdrops will be transformed into the pearls of everlasting bliss. "Therefore, comfort one another with these words."

August 23 — Evening

That Christ may dwell in your hearts
by faith. *{Ephesians 3:17}*

Beyond measure it is desirable that we, as believers, should have the person of Jesus constantly before us, to inflame our love towards him, and to increase our knowledge of him. I wish that my readers were all entered as diligent scholars in Jesus' college, students of *Corpus Christi* or the body of Christ, resolved to attain to a good degree in the learning of the cross. But to have Jesus always near, the heart must be full of him, welling up with his love, even to overflowing; hence the apostle prays "that Christ may *dwell in your hearts.*" See how near he wants Jesus to be! You cannot get a subject closer to you than to have it in the heart itself. *"That he may dwell"*; not that he may call upon you sometimes, as a casual visitor enters into a house and stays for a night, but that he may *dwell*; that Jesus may become the Lord and Tenant of your innermost being, never more to go out.

Observe the words — that he may dwell *in your heart*, that best room of the house of manhood; not in your thoughts alone, but in your affections; not merely in the mind's meditations, but in the heart's emotions. We should pant after love for Christ of a most abiding character, not a love that flames up and then dies out into the darkness of a few embers, but a constant flame, fed by sacred fuel, like the fire upon the altar which never went out. This can only be accomplished by faith. Faith must be strong, or love will not be fervent; the root of the flower must be healthy, or we cannot expect the bloom to be sweet. Faith is the lily's root, and love is the lily's bloom. Now, reader, Jesus cannot be in your heart's love unless you have a firm hold on him by your heart's faith; and, therefore, pray that you may always trust Christ in order that you may always love him. If love is cold, be sure that faith is drooping.

August 24 — Morning

{Daily Reading: Jeremiah 34:1–36:32} {Quick Study: Jeremiah 40:1–45:5}

The breaker is come up before them. *{Micah 2:13}*

Inasmuch as Jesus has gone before us, things do not remain as they would have been had he never passed that way. He has *conquered every foe* who obstructed the way. Cheer up now oh faint-hearted warrior. Not only has Christ travelled the road, but he has killed your enemies. Do you dread sin? He has nailed it to his cross. Do you fear death? He has been the death of Death. Are you afraid of hell? He has barred it against the advent of any of his children; they shall never see the gulf of perdition. Whatever foes may be before the Christian, they are all overcome. There are lions, but their teeth are broken; there are serpents, but their fangs are extracted; there are rivers, but they are bridged or fordable; there are flames, but we wear that matchless garment which renders us invulnerable to fire. The sword that has been forged against us is already blunted; the instruments of war which the enemy is preparing have already lost their point. God has taken away in the person of Christ all the power that anything can have to harm us. Well then, the army may safely march on, and you may go joyously along your journey, for all your enemies are conquered beforehand. What shall you do but march on to take the prey? They are beaten, they are vanquished; all you have to do is to divide the spoil. You shall, it is true, often engage in combat; but your fight shall be with a vanquished foe. His head is broken; he may attempt to injure you, but his strength shall not be sufficient for his malicious design. Your victory shall be easy, and your treasure shall be beyond all count.

> Proclaim aloud the Saviour's fame,
> Who bears *the Breaker's* wond'rous name;
> Sweet name; and it becomes him well,
> Who breaks down earth, sin, death, and hell.

August 24 — Evening

If fire breaks out, and catches in thorns, so that
the stacks of grain, or the standing grain, or the field,
is consumed by it; he who kindled the fire
shall surely make restitution. {Exodus 22:6}

But what restitution can he make who casts abroad the fire-brands of error, or the coals of lasciviousness, and sets men's souls ablaze with the fire of hell? The guilt is beyond estimate, and the result is irretrievable. If such an offender is forgiven, what grief it will cause him in retrospect, since he cannot undo the mischief which he has done! A bad example may kindle a flame which years of amended character cannot quench. To burn the food of man is bad enough, but how much worse to destroy the soul! It may be useful to us to reflect how far we may have been guilty in the past, and to enquire whether, even in the present, there may not be evil in us which has a tendency to bring damage to the souls of our relatives, friends, or neighbours.

The fire of strife is a terrible evil when it breaks out in a Christian church. Where converts were multiplied, and God was glorified, jealousy and envy do the devil's work most effectually. Where the golden grain was being housed, to reward the toil of the great Boaz, the fire of enmity comes in and leaves little else but smoke and a heap of blackness. Woe to those by whom offences come! May they never come through us, for although we cannot make restitution, we shall certainly be the chief sufferers if we are the chief offenders. Those who feed the fire deserve just censure, but he who first kindles it is most to blame. Discord usually takes first hold upon the thorns; it is nurtured among the hypocrites and base professors in the church, and away it goes among the righteous, blown by the winds of hell, and no one knows where it may end. Oh, Lord and giver of peace, make us peacemakers, and never let us aid and abet the men of strife, or even unintentionally cause the least division among your people.

August 25 — Morning

{Daily Reading: Jeremiah 37:1–40:16} {Quick Study: Jeremiah 46:1–49:39}

His fruit was sweet to my taste. *{Song of Solomon 2:3}*

Faith, in the Scripture, is spoken of under the emblem of all the senses. It is *sight*: "Look to me and be saved." It is *hearing*: "Hear, and your soul shall live." Faith is *smelling*: "All your garments smell of myrrh, and aloes, and cassia"; "your name is as ointment poured out." Faith is spiritual *touch*. By this faith the woman came behind and touched the hem of Christ's garment, and by this we handle the things of the good word of life. Faith is equally the spirit's *taste*. "How sweet are your words to my taste! Yes, sweeter than honey to my lips." "Unless a man eats my flesh," says Christ, *"and drinks my blood, there is no life in him."*

This *"taste"* is faith *in one of its highest operations.* One of the first performances of faith is *hearing.* We hear the voice of God, not with the outward ear alone, but with the inward ear; we hear it as God's Word, and we believe it to be so; that is the "hearing" of faith. Then our mind *looks* upon the truth as it is presented to us; that is to say, we understand it, we perceive its meaning; that is the "seeing" of faith. Next we discover its preciousness; we begin to admire it, and find how fragrant it is; that is faith in its *"smell."* Then we appropriate the mercies which are prepared for us in Christ; that is faith in its *"touch."* Hence follow the enjoyments, peace, delight, communion; which are faith in its "taste." Any one of these acts of faith is saving. To hear Christ's voice as the sure voice of God in the soul will save us; but what gives true enjoyment is the aspect of faith when Christ, by holy taste, is received into us, and made, by inward and spiritual apprehension of his sweetness and preciousness, to be the food of our souls. It is then we sit "under his shadow with great delight," and find his fruit sweet to our taste.

August 25 — Evening

If you believe with all your heart, you may. *{Acts 8:37}*

These words may answer your scruples, devout reader, concerning *the ordinances*. Perhaps you say, "I should be afraid to be baptized; it is such a solemn thing to avow myself to be dead with Christ, and buried with him. I should not feel at liberty to come to the Master's table; I should be afraid of eating and drinking damnation to myself, not discerning the Lord's body." Ah! Poor trembler, Jesus has given you liberty, do not be afraid. If a stranger came to your house, he would stand at the door, or wait in the hall; he would not dream of intruding unbidden into your parlour — he is not at home: but your child makes himself very free around the house; and so it is with the child of God. A stranger may not intrude where a child may venture. When the Holy Spirit has given you to feel the spirit of adoption, you may come to Christian ordinances without fear. The same rule holds good for the *Christian's inward privileges*. You think, poor seeker, that you are not allowed to rejoice with joy unspeakable and full of glory; if you are permitted to get inside Christ's door, or sit at the end of his table, you will be well content. Ah! But you shall not have less privileges than the very greatest. God makes no difference in his love for his children. A child is a child to him; he will not make him a hired servant; but he shall feast upon the fatted calf, and shall have the music and the dancing as much as if he had never gone astray. When Jesus comes into the heart, he issues a general licence to be glad in the Lord. No chains are worn in the court of King Jesus. Our admission into full privileges may be gradual, but it is sure. Perhaps our reader is saying, "I wish I could enjoy the promises, and walk at liberty in my Lord's commands." "If you believe with all your heart, you may." Loosen the chains from off your neck, oh captive daughter, for Jesus makes you free.

August 26 — Morning

{Daily Reading: Jeremiah 41:1–44:30} {Quick Study: Jeremiah 50:1–52:34}

He has commanded his covenant for ever. *{Psalms 111:9}*

The Lord's people delight in the covenant itself. It is an unfailing source of consolation to them as often as the Holy Spirit leads them into its banqueting house and waves its banner of love. They delight to contemplate *the antiquity* of that covenant, remembering that before the daystar knew its place, or planets ran their courses, the interests of the saints were made secure in Christ Jesus. It is particularly pleasing to them to remember *the certainty* of the covenant, while meditating upon "the sure mercies of David." They delight to celebrate it as "signed, and sealed, and ratified, in all things ordered well." It often makes their hearts dilate with joy to think of its *immutability,* as a covenant which neither time nor eternity, life nor death, shall ever be able to violate — a covenant as old as eternity and as everlasting as the Rock of Ages. They rejoice also to feast upon *the fulness* of this covenant, for they see in it all things provided for them. God is their portion, Christ their companion, the Spirit their Comforter, earth their lodge, and heaven their home. They see in it an inheritance reserved and entailed to every soul possessing an interest in its ancient and eternal deed of gift. Their eyes sparkled when they saw it as a treasure trove in the Bible; but oh! how their souls were gladdened when they saw in the last will and testament of their divine Kinsman, that it was bequeathed to them! More especially it is the pleasure of God's people to contemplate *the graciousness* of this covenant. They see that the law was made void because it was a covenant of works and depended upon merit, but this they perceive to be enduring because grace is the basis, grace the condition, grace the strain, grace the bulwark, grace the foundation, grace the top stone. The covenant is a treasury of wealth, a granary of food, a fountain of life, a storehouse of salvation, a charter of peace, and a haven of joy.

*The people, when they saw him, were greatly amazed,
and running to him greeted him. {Mark 9:15}*

How great the difference between Moses and Jesus! When the prophet of Horeb had been forty days upon the mountain, he underwent a kind of transfiguration, so that his countenance shone with exceeding brightness, and he put a veil over his face, for the people could not endure to look upon his glory. Not so our Saviour. He had been transfigured with a greater glory than that of Moses, and yet, it is not written that the people were blinded by the blaze of his countenance, but rather they were amazed, and running to him they greeted him. The glory of the law repels, but the greater glory of Jesus attracts. Though Jesus is holy and just, yet blended with his purity there is so much of truth and grace, that sinners run to him amazed by his goodness, fascinated by his love; they greet him, become his disciples, and take him to be their Lord and Master. Reader, it may be that just now you are blinded by the dazzling brightness of the law of God. You feel its claims on your conscience, but you cannot keep it in your life. Not that you find fault with the law, on the contrary, it commands your profoundest esteem, still in no way are you drawn to God by it; you are rather hardened in heart, and are verging towards desperation. Ah, poor heart! Turn your eye from Moses, with all his repelling splendour, and look to Jesus, resplendent with milder glories. Behold his flowing wounds and thorn-crowned head! He is the Son of God, and by it he is greater than Moses, but he is the Lord of love, and by it more tender than the lawgiver. He bore the wrath of God, and in his death revealed more of God's justice than Sinai on a blaze, but that justice is now vindicated, and henceforth it is the guardian of believers in Jesus. Look, sinner, to the bleeding Saviour, and as you feel the attraction of his love, flee into his arms, and you shall be saved.

August 27 — Morning

{Daily Reading: Jeremiah 45:1–48:47} {Quick Study: Lamentations 1:1–5:22}

How long will it be before they believe me? *{Numbers 14:11}*

*S*trive with all diligence to keep out that monster unbelief. It so dishonours Christ, that he will withdraw his visible presence if we insult him by indulging it. It is true it is a weed, the seeds of which we can never entirely extract from the soil, but we must aim at its root with zeal and perseverance. Among hateful things it is the most to be abhorred. Its injurious nature is so venomous that he who exercises it and he upon whom it is exercised are both harmed by it. In your case, oh believer! it is most wicked, for the mercies of your Lord in the past, increase your guilt in doubting him now. When you do distrust the Lord Jesus, he may well cry out, "Behold, I am pressed under you, as a cart is pressed that is full of sheaves." This is crowning his head with thorns of the sharpest kind. It is very cruel for a well-beloved wife to mistrust a kind and faithful husband. The sin is needless, foolish, and unwarranted. Jesus has never given the slightest ground for suspicion, and it is hard to be doubted by those to whom our conduct is uniformly affectionate and true. Jesus is the Son of the Highest, and has unbounded wealth; it is shameful to doubt Omnipotence and distrust All-Sufficiency. The cattle on a thousand hills will suffice for our most hungry feeding, and the granaries of heaven are not likely to be emptied by our eating. If Christ would be only a cistern, we might soon exhaust his fulness, but who can drain a fountain? Myriads of spirits have drawn their supplies from him, and not one of them has murmured at the scantiness of his resources. Away, then, with this lying traitor unbelief, for his only errand is to cut the bonds of communion and make us mourn an absent Saviour. Bunyan tells us that unbelief has "as many lives as a cat": if so, let us kill one life now, and continue the work until the whole nine are gone. Down with you, you traitor, my heart abhors you.

August 27 — Evening

*Into your hand I commit my spirit: you have
redeemed me, oh Lord God of truth.* {Psalms 31:5}

These words have been frequently used by holy men in their hour of departure. We may profitably consider them this evening. The object of the faithful man's solicitude in life and death is not his body or his estate, but his spirit; this is his choice treasure — if this is safe, all is well. What is this mortal state compared with the soul? The believer commits his soul to the hand of his God; it came from him, it is his own, he has sustained it in the past, he is able to keep it, and it is most fitting that he should receive it. All things are safe in Jehovah's hands; what we entrust to the Lord will be secure, both now and in that day of days towards which we are hastening. It is peaceful living, and glorious dying, to repose in the care of heaven. At all times we should commit our all to Jesus' faithful hand; then, though life may hang on a thread, and adversities may multiply as the sands of the sea, our soul shall dwell at ease, and delight itself in quiet resting places.

"You have redeemed me, oh Lord God of truth." Redemption is a solid basis for confidence. David had not known Calvary as we have done, but temporal redemption cheered him; and shall not eternal redemption yet more sweetly console us? Past deliverances are strong pleas for present assistance. What the Lord has done he will do again, for he does not change. He is faithful to his promises, and gracious to his saints; he will not turn away from his people.

> Though you slay me I will trust,
> Praise you even from the dust,
> Prove, and tell it as I prove,
> Your unutterable love.
>
> You may chasten and correct,
> But you never can neglect;
> Since the ransom price is paid,
> On your love my hope is stay'd.

August 28 — Morning

{Daily Reading: Jeremiah 49:1–50:46} {Quick Study: Ezekiel 1:1–6:14}

Oil for the light. *{Exodus 25:6}*

My soul, how much you need this, for your lamp will not long continue to burn without it. Your wick will smoke and become an offence if light is gone, and it will be gone if oil is absent. You have no oil well springing up in your human nature, and therefore you must go to those who sell and buy for yourself, or like the foolish virgins, you will have to cry, "My lamp is gone out." Even the consecrated lamps could not give light without oil; though they shone in the tabernacle they needed to be fuelled, though no rough winds blew upon them they were required to be trimmed, and your need is equally as great. Under the most happy circumstances you cannot give light for another hour unless fresh oil of grace is given to you.

It was not just any oil that might be used in the Lord's service; neither the petroleum which exudes so plentifully from the earth, nor the produce of fishes, nor that extracted from nuts would be accepted; only one oil was selected, and that was the best olive oil. Pretended grace from natural goodness, fancied grace from priestly hands, or imaginary grace from outward ceremonies will never serve the true saint of God; he knows that the Lord would not be pleased with rivers of such oil. He goes to the olive press of Gethsemane, and draws his supplies from him who was crushed in it. The oil of gospel grace is pure and free from lees and dregs, and hence the light which is fed by it is clear and bright. Our churches are the Saviour's golden candelabra, and if they are to be lights in this dark world, they must have much holy oil. Let us pray for ourselves, our ministers, and our churches, so that they may never lack oil for the light. Truth, holiness, joy, knowledge, and love, these are all beams of the sacred light, but we cannot shine forth unless in private we receive oil from God the Holy Spirit.

August 28 — Evening

Sing, oh barren. *{Isaiah 54:1}*

Although we have brought forth some fruit for Christ, and have a joyful hope that we are "plants of his own right hand planting," yet there are times when we feel very barren. Prayer is lifeless, love is cold, faith is weak, each grace in the garden of our heart languishes and droops. We are like flowers in the hot sun, requiring the refreshing shower. In such a condition what are we to do? The text is addressed to us in just such a state. *"Sing, oh barren, break forth and cry aloud."* But what can I sing about? I cannot talk about the present, and even the past looks full of barrenness. Ah! I *can* sing of *Jesus Christ.* I can speak of visits which the Redeemer has previously paid to me; or if not of these, I can magnify the great love by which he loved his people when he came from the heights of heaven for their redemption. I will go to the cross again. Come, my soul, you once were heavy laden, and you lost your burden there. Go to Calvary again. Perhaps that very cross which gave you life may give you fruitfulness. What is my barrenness? It is the platform for his fruit-creating power. What is my desolation? It is the black setting for the sapphire of his everlasting love. I will go in poverty, I will go in helplessness, I will go in all my shame and backsliding, I will tell him that I am still his child, and in confidence in his faithful heart, even I, the barren one, will sing and cry aloud.

Sing, believer, for it will cheer your own heart, and the hearts of other desolate ones. Sing on, for now that you are really ashamed of being barren, you will be fruitful soon; now that God makes you *loath* to be without fruit he will soon cover you with clusters. The experience of our barrenness is painful, but the Lord's visitations are delightful. A sense of our own poverty drives us to Christ, and that is the place we need to be, for in him our fruit is found.

August 29 — Morning

{Daily Reading: Jeremiah 51:1–52:34} {Quick Study: Ezekiel 7:1–10:22}

Have mercy upon me, oh God. *{Psalms 51:1}*

When Dr. Carey was suffering from a dangerous illness, the enquiry was made, "If this sickness should prove fatal, what passage would you select as the text for your funeral sermon?" He replied, "Oh, I feel that such a poor sinful creature is unworthy to have anything said about him; but if a funeral sermon must be preached, let it be from the words, 'Have mercy upon me, oh God, according to your lovingkindness; according to the multitude of your tender mercies blot out my transgressions.' " In the same spirit of humility he directed in his will that the following inscription and nothing more should be cut on his gravestone: —

WILLIAM CAREY, BORN AUGUST 17th, 1761:
DIED —
A wretched, poor, and helpless worm,
On your kind arms I fall.

Only on the footing of free grace can the most experienced and most honoured of the saints approach their God. The best of men are conscious above all others that they are men at the best. Empty boats float high, but heavily laden vessels are low in the water; mere professors can boast, but true children of God cry for mercy upon their unprofitableness. We have need that the Lord should have mercy upon our good works, our prayers, our preachings, our alms givings, and our holiest things. The blood was not only sprinkled upon the doorposts of Israel's dwelling houses, but upon the sanctuary, the mercy seat, and the altar, because as sin intrudes into our holiest things, the blood of Jesus is needed to purify them from defilement. If mercy is needed to be exercised towards our duties, what shall be said of our sins? How sweet the remembrance that inexhaustible mercy is waiting to be gracious to us, to restore our backslidings, and make our broken bones rejoice!

August 29 — Evening

All the days of his separation he shall eat
nothing that is made of the vine tree, from
the kernels even to the husk. {Numbers 6:4}

Nazarites had taken, among other vows, one which debarred them from the use of wine. In order that they might not violate the obligation, they were forbidden to drink the vinegar of wine or strong liquors, and to make the rule still more clear, they were not to touch the unfermented juice of grapes, nor even to eat the fruit either fresh or dried. In order, altogether, to secure the integrity of the vow, they were not even allowed anything that had to do with the vine; they were, in fact, to avoid the appearance of evil. Surely this is a lesson to the Lord's separated ones, teaching them to come away from sin in every form, to avoid not merely its grosser shapes, but even its spirit and similitude. Strict walking is much despised in these days, but rest assured, dear reader, it is both the safest and the happiest. He who yields a point or two to the world is in fearful peril; he who eats the grapes of Sodom will soon drink the wine of Gomorrah. A little crevice in the sea bank in Holland lets in the sea, and the gap speedily swells until a province is drowned. Worldly conformity, in any degree, is a snare to the soul, and makes it more and more liable to commit presumptuous sins. Moreover, just as the Nazarite who drank grape juice could not be quite sure whether it might not have endured a degree of fermentation, and consequently could not be clear in heart that his vow was intact, so the yielding, temporizing Christian cannot wear a conscience void of offence, but must feel that the inward monitor is in doubt of him. We need not doubt about doubtful things; they are wrong for us. We must not dally with tempting things, but flee from them quickly. Better to be sneered at as a Puritan than to be despised as a hypocrite. Careful walking may involve much self-denial, but it has pleasures of its own which are more than a sufficient reward.

August 30 — Morning

{Daily Reading: Lamentations 1:1–2:22} {Quick Study: Ezekiel 11:1–15:8}

Wait on the Lord. *{Psalms 27:14}*

It may seem an easy thing to *wait*, but it is one of the postures which a Christian soldier only learns after many years of teaching. Marching and quick marching are much easier for God's warriors than standing still. There are hours of perplexity when the most willing spirit, anxiously desirous to serve the Lord, does not know what part to take. Then what shall it do? Vex itself by despair? Flee back in cowardice, turn to the right hand in fear, or rush forward in presumption? No, but simply wait. *Wait in prayer*, however. Call upon God, and spread the case before him; tell him your difficulty, and plead his promise of aid. In dilemmas between one duty and another, it is sweet to be humble as a child, and *wait with simplicity of soul* upon the Lord. It is sure to be well with us when we feel and know our own folly, and are heartily willing to be guided by the will of God. But *wait in faith*. Express your unstaggering confidence in him; for unfaithful, untrusting waiting is only an insult to the Lord. Believe that if he keeps you waiting even until midnight, he will still come at the right time; the vision shall come and shall not tarry. *Wait in quiet patience*, not rebelling because you are under the affliction, but blessing your God for it. Never murmur against the second cause, as the children of Israel did against Moses; never wish you could go back to the world again, but accept the case as it is, and put it as it stands, simply and with your whole heart, without any self-will, into the hand of your covenant God, saying, "Now, Lord, not my will, but yours be done. I do not know what to do; I am brought to extremities, but I will wait until you shall part the floods, or drive back my foes. I will wait, if you keep me many a day, for my heart is fixed upon you alone, oh God, and my spirit waits for you in the full conviction that you will yet be my joy and my salvation, my refuge and my strong tower."

August 30 — Evening

Heal me, oh Lord, and I shall be healed. {Jeremiah 17:14}
I have seen his ways, and will heal him. *{Isaiah 57:18}*

It is the sole prerogative of God to remove spiritual disease. Natural disease may be instrumentally healed by men, but even then the honour is to be given to God who gives virtue to medicine, and bestows power to the human frame to cast off disease. As for spiritual sicknesses, these remain with the great Physician alone; he claims it as his prerogative, "I kill and I make alive, I wound and I heal"; and one of the Lord's choice titles is Jehovah Rophi, "the Lord who heals you." "I will heal you of your wounds," is a promise which could not come from the lip of man, but only from the mouth of the eternal God. On this account the psalmist cried to the Lord, "Oh Lord, heal me, for my bones are severely vexed," and again, "Heal my soul, for I have sinned against you." For this, also, the godly praise the name of the Lord, saying, "He heals all our diseases." He who made man can restore man; he who was at first the creator of our nature can recreate it. What a transcendent comfort it is that in the person of Jesus "dwells all the fulness of the Godhead bodily!" My soul, whatever your disease may be, this great Physician can heal you. If he is God, there can be no limit to his power. Come then with the blind eye of darkened understanding, come with the limping foot of wasted energy, come with the maimed hand of weak faith, the fever of an angry temper, or the ague of shivering despondency, come just as you are, for he who is God can certainly heal you of your plague. No one shall restrain the healing virtue which proceeds from Jesus our Lord. Legions of demons have been made to recognise the power of the beloved Physician, and never once has he been baffled. All his patients have been cured in the past and shall be in the future, and you shall be one among them, my friend, if you will only rest yourself on him tonight.

August 31 — Morning

{Daily Reading: Lamentations 3:1–5:22} {Quick Study: Ezekiel 16:1–19:14}

They shall trust on my arm. *{Isaiah 51:5}*

In seasons of severe trial, the Christian has nothing on earth that he can trust in, and is therefore compelled to cast himself on his God alone. When his vessel is on its beam ends, and no human deliverance can avail, he must simply and entirely trust himself to the providence and care of God. Happy storm that wrecks a man on such a rock as this! Oh, blessed hurricane that drives the soul to God and God alone! There is no room for our God sometimes because of the multitude of our friends; but when a man is so poor, so friendless, so helpless that he has nowhere else to turn, he flees into his Father's arms, and is blessedly embraced! When he is burdened with troubles so pressing and so painful that he cannot tell them to anyone except his God, he may be thankful for them; for he will learn more about his Lord then than at any other time. Oh, tempest-tossed believer, it is a happy trouble that drives you to your Father! Now that you have only your God to trust in, see that you put your full confidence in him. Do not dishonour your Lord and Master by unworthy doubts and fears; but be strong in faith, giving glory to God. Show the world that your God is worth ten thousand worlds to you. Show rich men how rich you are in your poverty when the Lord God is your Helper. Show the strong man how strong you are in your weakness when underneath you are the everlasting arms. Now is the time for feats of faith and valiant exploits. Be strong and very courageous, and the Lord your God shall certainly, as surely as he built the heavens and the earth, glorify himself in your weakness, and magnify his might in the midst of your distress. The grandeur of the arch of heaven would be spoiled if the sky were supported by a single visible column, and your faith would lose its glory if it rested on anything discernible by the carnal eye. May the Holy Spirit give rest to you in Jesus this closing day of the month.

August 31 — Evening

If we walk in the light, as he is in the light. *{1 John 1:7}*

As he is in the light! Can we ever attain to this? Shall we ever be able to walk as clearly in the light as he is whom we call "Our Father," of whom it is written, "God is light, and in him is no darkness at all?" Certainly, this is the model which is set before us, for the Saviour himself said, "Be perfect, even as your Father who is in heaven is perfect"; and although we may feel that we can never rival the perfection of God, yet we are to seek after it, and never to be satisfied until we attain to it. The youthful artist, as he grasps his early pencil, can hardly hope to equal Raphael or Michelangelo, but still, if he did not have a noble *beau ideal* before his mind, he would only attain to something very common and ordinary. But what is meant by the expression that the Christian is to walk in light as God is in the light? We conceive it to suggest *likeness*, but not *degree*. We are as truly in the light, we are as heartily in the light, we are as sincerely in the light, as honestly in the light, although we cannot be there in the same measure. I cannot dwell in the sun, it is too bright a place for my residence, but I can *walk* in the light of the sun; and so, although I cannot attain that perfection of purity and truth which belongs to the Lord of hosts by nature as the infinitely good, yet I can set the Lord always before me, and by the help of the indwelling Spirit, strive after conformity to his image. That famous old commentator, John Trapp, says, "We may be in the light as God is in the light for *quality*, but not for *equality*." We are to have the same light, and are as truly to have it and walk in it as God does, though, as for equality with God in his holiness and purity, that must be left until we cross the Jordan and enter into the perfection of the Most High. Notice that the blessings of sacred fellowship and perfect cleansing are bound up with walking in the light.

September 1 — Morning

{Daily Reading: Ezekiel 1:1–4:17} {Quick Study: Ezekiel 20:1–22:31}

You shall guide me with your counsel, and afterwards receive me to glory. *{Psalms 73:24}*

The psalmist felt his need for divine guidance. He had just been discovering the foolishness of his own heart, and unless he should be constantly led astray by it, he resolved that God's counsel should henceforth guide him. A sense of our own folly is a great step towards being wise, when it leads us to rely on the wisdom of the Lord. The blind man leans on his friend's arm and reaches home in safety, and so we should give ourselves up implicitly to divine guidance, doubting nothing; assured that although we cannot see, it is always safe to trust the all-seeing God. *"You shall,"* is a blessed expression of confidence. He was sure that the Lord would not decline the condescending task. There is a word for you, oh believer; rest in it. Be assured that your God will be your Counsellor and Friend; he shall guide you; he will direct all your ways. In his written Word you have this assurance partly fulfilled, for holy Scripture is his counsel to you. We are happy to have God's Word always to guide us! Where would the mariner be without his compass? And where would the Christian be without his Bible? This is the unerring chart, the map in which every shoal is described, and all the channels from the quicksands of destruction to the haven of salvation mapped and marked by one who knows all the way. Blessed be you, oh God, that we may trust you to guide us now, and guide us even to the end! After this guidance through life, the psalmist anticipates a divine reception at last — *"and afterwards receive me to glory."* What a thought for you, believer! Himself will receive *you* to glory — *you!* Wandering, erring, straying, yet he will bring you safe at last *to glory!* This is your portion; live on it today, and if perplexities should surround you, go in the strength of this text straight to the throne.

September 1 — Evening

Trust in him at all times. *{Psalms 62:8}*

Faith is as much the rule for temporal as for spiritual life; we ought to have faith in God for our earthly affairs as well as for our heavenly business. It is only as we learn to trust in God for the supply of all our daily need that we shall live above the world. We are not to be idle, *that* would show we did *not* trust in God, who is always working, but in the devil, who is the father of idleness. We are not to be imprudent or rash; that would be trusting in chance, and not the living God, who is a God of economy and order. Acting in all prudence and uprightness, we are to rely simply and entirely upon the Lord at all times.

Let me commend to you a life of trust in God in temporal things. Trusting in God, you will not be compelled to mourn because you have used sinful means to grow rich. Serve God with integrity, and if you achieve no success, at least no sin will lie upon your conscience. Trusting God, you will not be guilty of self-contradiction. He who trusts in craft, sails this way today and that way the next, like a vessel tossed about by the fickle wind; but he who trusts in the Lord is like a vessel propelled by steam, she cuts through the waves, defies the wind, and makes one bright silvery straightforward track to her destined haven. Be a man with living principles within; never bow to the varying customs of worldly wisdom. Walk in your path of integrity with steadfast steps, and show that you are invincibly strong in the strength which confidence in God alone can confer. Thus you will be delivered from anxious care, you will not be troubled with evil tidings, your heart will be fixed, trusting in the Lord. How pleasant to float along the stream of providence! There is no more blessed way of living than a life of dependence upon a covenant-keeping God. We have no care, for he cares for us; we have no troubles, because we cast our burdens upon the Lord.

September 2 — Morning

{Daily Reading: Ezekiel 5:1–9:11} {Quick Study: Ezekiel 23:1–24:27}

But Simon's wife's mother lay sick with a fever, and immediately they told him about her. *{Mark 1:30}*

Very interesting is this little peep into the house of the apostolic fisherman. We see at once that household joys and cares are no hindrance to the full exercise of ministry, indeed, that since they furnish an opportunity for personally witnessing the Lord's gracious work upon one's own flesh and blood, they may even instruct the teacher better than any other earthly discipline. Papists and other sects may decry marriage, but true Christianity and household life agree well together. Peter's house was probably a poor fisherman's hut, but the Lord of Glory entered it, lodged in it, and performed a miracle in it. Should our little book be read this morning in some very humble cottage, let this fact encourage the residents to seek the company of King Jesus. God is more often in little huts than in rich palaces. Jesus is looking around your room now, and is waiting to be gracious to you. Into Simon's house sickness had entered, fever in a deadly form had prostrated his mother-in-law, and as soon as Jesus came they told him about the sad affliction, and he hurried to the patient's bed. Have you any sickness in the house this morning? You will find Jesus by far the best Physician, go to him at once and tell him all about the matter. Immediately lay the case before him. It concerns one of his people, and therefore will not be trivial to him. Observe that at once the Saviour restored the sick woman; no one can heal as he does. We may not be sure that the Lord will *at once* remove all disease from those we love, but we may know that believing prayer for the sick is far more likely to be followed by restoration than anything else in the world; and where this does not avail, we must meekly bow to his will by whom life and death are determined. The tender heart of Jesus waits to hear our griefs, let us pour them into his patient ear.

September 2 — Evening

Unless you see signs and wonders, you will not believe. *{John 4:48}*

Acraving after marvels was a symptom of the sickly state of men's minds in our Lord's day; they refused solid nourishment, and pined after mere wonder. The gospel which they so greatly needed they would not have; the miracles which Jesus did not always choose to give they eagerly demanded. Many nowadays must see signs and wonders, or they will not believe. Some have said in their heart, "I must feel deep horror of soul, or I never will believe in Jesus." But what if you never should feel it, as probably you never may? Will you go to hell out of spite against God, because he will not treat you like someone else? One has said to himself, "If I had a dream, or if I could feel a sudden shock from something, then I would believe." Thus you undeserving mortals dream that my Lord is to be dictated to by you! You are beggars at his gate, asking for mercy, and must you draw up rules and regulations concerning how he shall give that mercy? Do you think that he will submit to this? My Master is of a generous spirit, but he has a very royal heart, he spurns all dictation, and maintains his sovereignty of action. Why, dear reader, if such is your case, do you crave for signs and wonders? Is not the gospel its own sign and wonder? Is not this a miracle of miracles, that "God so loved the world that he gave his only begotten Son, that whoever believes in him might not perish?" Surely that precious word, "Whoever will, let him come and take the water of life freely" and that solemn promise, "He who comes to me, I will in no wise cast out," are better than signs and wonders! A truthful Saviour ought to be believed. He is truth itself. Why will you ask for proof of the veracity of one who cannot lie? The demons themselves declared him to be the Son of God; will you not trust him?

September 3 — Morning

{Daily Reading: Ezekiel 10:1–13:23} {Quick Study: Ezekiel 25:1–28:26}

You whom my soul loves. *{Song of Solomon 1:7}*

It is well to be able, without any "if" or "but," to say to the Lord Jesus — *"You whom my soul loves."* Many can only say of Jesus that they *hope* they love him; they *trust* they love him; but only a poor and shallow experience will be content to stay here. No one ought to give any rest to his spirit until he feels quite sure about a matter of such vital importance. We ought not to be satisfied with a superficial *hope* that Jesus loves us, and with a bare trust that we love him. The old saints did not generally speak with "buts," and "ifs," and "hopes," and "trusts," but they spoke positively and plainly. "I know whom I have believed," says Paul. "I know that my Redeemer lives," says Job. Get positive knowledge of your love of Jesus, and do not be satisfied until you can speak of your interest in him as a reality, which you have made sure by having received the witness of the Holy Spirit, and his seal upon your soul by faith.

True love for Christ is in every case the Holy Spirit's work, and must be performed in the heart by him. He is the *efficient cause* of it; but the logical reason why we love Jesus lies in *himself*. Why do we love Jesus? *Because he first loved us*. *Why* do we love Jesus? Because he *"gave himself for us."* We have life through his death; we have peace through his blood. Though he was rich, yet *for our sakes* he became poor. *Why* do we love Jesus? Because of the *excellency of his person*. We are filled with a sense of his beauty! An admiration of his charms! A consciousness of his infinite perfection! His greatness, goodness, and loveliness, in one resplendent ray, combine to enchant the soul until it is so ravished that it exclaims, "Yes, he is altogether lovely." Blessed love is this — a love which binds the heart with chains more soft than silk, and yet more firm than adamant!

September 3 — Evening

The Lord tries the righteous. *{Psalms 11:5}*

All events are under the control of Providence; consequently all the trials of our outward life are traceable at once to the great First Cause. Out of the golden gate of God's ordinance the armies of trial march forth in array, clad in their iron armour, and armed with weapons of war. All providences are doors to trial. Even our mercies, like roses, have their thorns. Men may be drowned in seas of prosperity as well as in rivers of affliction. Our mountains are not too high, and our valleys are not too low for temptations: trials lurk on all roads. Everywhere, above and beneath, we are beset and surrounded with dangers. Yet no shower falls unpermitted from the threatening cloud; every drop has its order before it hastens to the earth. The trials which come from God are sent to prove and strengthen our graces, and so at once to illustrate the power of divine grace, to test the genuineness of our virtues, and to add to their energy. Our Lord in his infinite wisdom and superabundant love, sets so high a value upon his people's faith that he will not screen them from those trials by which faith is strengthened. You would never have possessed the precious faith which now supports you if the trial of your faith had not been like fire. You are a tree that never would have rooted so well if the wind had not rocked you to and fro, and made you take firm hold upon the precious truths of the covenant grace. Worldly ease is a great foe to faith; it loosens the joints of holy valour, and snaps the sinews of sacred courage. The balloon never rises until the cords are cut; affliction does this sharp service for believing souls. While the wheat sleeps comfortably in the husk it is useless to man, it must be threshed out of its resting place before its value can be known. Thus it is well that Jehovah tries the righteous, for it causes them to grow rich towards God.

September 4 — Morning

{Daily Reading: Ezekiel 14:1–16:63} {Quick Study: Ezekiel 29:1–32:32}

I will; be clean. *{Mark 1:41}*

Primeval darkness heard the Almighty fiat, "light be," and immediately light was, and the word of the Lord Jesus is equal in majesty to that ancient word of power. Redemption like creation has its word of might. Jesus speaks and it is done. Leprosy yielded to no human remedies, but it fled at once at the Lord's "I will." The disease exhibited no hopeful signs or tokens of recovery, nature contributed nothing to its own healing, but the unaided word effected the entire work on the spot and for ever. The sinner is in a plight more miserable than the leper; let him imitate his example and go to Jesus, "beseeching him and kneeling down to him." Let him exercise what little faith he has, even though it should go no further than "Lord, if you will, you can make me clean"; and there is no room for doubt concerning the result of the application. Jesus heals all who come, and casts out no one. In reading the narrative in which our morning's text occurs, it is worthy of devout notice that Jesus touched the leper. This unclean person had broken through the regulations of the ceremonial law and pressed into the house, but Jesus so far from chiding him broke through the law himself in order to meet him. He made an exchange with the leper, for while he cleansed him, he contracted by that touch a levitical defilement. Even so, Jesus Christ was made sin for us, although in himself he knew no sin, so that we might be made the righteousness of God in him. Oh that poor sinners would go to Jesus, believing in the power of his blessed substitutionary work, and they would soon learn the power of his gracious touch. That hand which multiplied the loaves, which saved sinking Peter, which upholds afflicted saints, which crowns believers, that same hand will touch every seeking sinner, and in a moment make him clean. The love of Jesus is the source of salvation. He loves, he looks, he touches us, WE LIVE.

September 4 — Evening

**You shall have just balances, just weights,
a just ephah, and a just hin.** *{Leviticus 19:36}*

Weights and scales and measures were to be all according to the standard of justice. Surely no Christian man will need to be reminded of this in his business, for if righteousness should be banished from all the world, it would find a shelter in believing hearts. There are, however, other balances which weigh moral and spiritual things, and these often need examining. We will call in the officer tonight.

The balances in which we weigh our own and other men's characters, are they quite accurate? Do we not turn our own ounces of goodness into pounds, and other people's bushels of excellence into pecks? See to weights and measures here, Christian. The scales in which we measure our trials and troubles, are they according to standard? Paul, who had more to suffer than we have, called his afflictions light, and yet we often consider ours to be heavy — surely something must be amiss with the weights! We must see to this matter, lest we get reported to the court above for unjust dealing. Those weights with which we measure our doctrinal belief, are they quite fair? The doctrines of grace should have the same weight with us as the precepts of the Word, no more and no less; but it is to be feared that with many one scale or the other is unfairly weighted. It is a grand matter to give just measure in truth. Christian, be careful here. Those measures in which we estimate our obligations and responsibilities look rather small. When a rich man gives no more to the cause of God than the poor contribute, is that a just ephah and a just hin? When ministers are half starved, is that honest dealing? When the poor are despised, while ungodly rich men are held in admiration, is that a just balance? Reader, we might lengthen the list, but we prefer to leave it as your evening's work to find and destroy all unrighteous balances, weights, and measures.

September 5 — Morning

{Daily Reading: Ezekiel 17:1–19:14} {Quick Study: Ezekiel 33:1–36:38}

Woe is me, that I sojourn in Mesech, that I live in the tents of Kedar. *{Psalms 120:5}*

As a Christian you have to live in the midst of an ungodly world, and it is of little use for you to cry "Woe is me." Jesus did not pray that you should be taken out of the world, and what he did not pray for, you need not desire. Better far in the Lord's strength to meet the difficulty, and glorify him in it. The enemy is always on the watch to detect inconsistency in your conduct; be therefore very *holy*. Remember that the eyes of all are upon you, and that more is expected from you than from other men. Strive to give no occasion for blame. Let your goodness be the only fault they can discover in you. Like Daniel, compel them to say of you, "We shall not find any occasion against this Daniel, except we find it against him concerning the law of his God." Seek to be *useful* as well as consistent. Perhaps you think, "If I were in a more favourable position I might serve the Lord's cause, but I cannot do any good where I am"; but the worse the people are among whom you live, the more need they have of your exertions; if they are crooked, the more needful that you should set them straight; and if they are perverse, the more need you have to turn their proud hearts to the truth. Where should the physician be but where there are many sick? Where is honour to be won by the soldier but in the hottest fire of the battle? And when you are weary of the strife and sin that meets you on every hand, consider that all the saints have endured the same trial. They were not carried on beds of down to heaven, and you must not expect to travel more easily than they did. They had to risk their lives in the high places of the field, and you will not be crowned until you also have endured hardness as a good soldier of Jesus Christ. Therefore, "stand firm in the faith, behave like men, and be strong."

September 5 — Evening

Have you entered into the springs of the sea? *{Job 38:16}*

Some things in nature must remain a mystery to the most intelligent and enterprising investigators. Human knowledge has bounds beyond which it cannot pass. Universal knowledge is for God alone. If this is so in the things which are seen and temporal, I may rest assured that it is even more so in matters spiritual and eternal. Why, then, have I been torturing my brain with speculations as to destiny and will, fixed fate, and human responsibility? I am no more able to comprehend these deep and dark truths than to find out the depth which couches beneath, from which old ocean draws her watery stores. Why am I so curious to know the reason for my Lord's providences, the motive of his actions, the intentions of his visitations? Shall I ever be able to clasp the sun in my fist, and hold the universe in my palm? Yet these are as a drop in a bucket compared with the Lord my God. Do not let me strive to understand the infinite, but spend my strength in love. What I cannot gain by intellect I can possess by affection, and let that satisfy me. I cannot penetrate the heart of the sea, but I can enjoy the healthful breezes which sweep over its bosom, and I can sail over its blue waves with propitious winds. If I could enter the springs of the sea, the feat would serve no useful purpose either to myself or to others, it would not save the sinking ship, or give back the drowned mariner to his weeping wife and children; neither would my solving deep mysteries avail me a single whit, for the least love for God, and the simplest act of obedience to him, are better than the most profound knowledge. My Lord, I leave the infinite to you, and pray you to put far from me such a love for the tree of knowledge as might keep me from the tree of life.

September 6 — Morning

{Daily Reading: Ezekiel 20:1–21:32} {Quick Study: Ezekiel 37:1–39:29}

In the midst of a crooked and perverse nation, among whom you shine as lights in the world. *{Philippians 2:15}*

We use lights to *reveal*. A Christian man should so shine in his life, that a person could not live with him a week without knowing the gospel. His conversation should be such that all who are around him should clearly perceive whose he is, and whom he serves; and should see the image of Jesus reflected in his daily actions. Lights are intended for *guidance*. We are to help those around us who are in the dark. We are to hold forth to them the Word of life. We are to point sinners to the Saviour, and the weary to a divine resting place. Men sometimes read their Bibles and fail to understand them; we should be ready, like Philip, to instruct the enquirer in the meaning of God's Word, the way of salvation, and the life of godliness. Lights are also used for *warning*. On our rocks and shoals a lighthouse is sure to be erected. Christian men should know that there are many false lights shown everywhere in the world, and therefore the right light is needed. The wreckers of Satan are always abroad, tempting the ungodly to sin under the name of pleasure; they hoist the wrong light, it is our responsibility to put up the true light upon every dangerous rock, to point out every sin, and tell what it leads to, so that we may be clear of the blood of all men, shining as lights in the world. Lights also have a very *cheering* influence, and so have Christians. A Christian ought to be a comforter, with kind words on his lips, and sympathy in his heart; he should carry sunshine wherever he goes, and diffuse happiness around him.

Gracious Spirit dwell with me; I myself would gracious be,
And with words that help and heal would your life in mine reveal,
And with actions bold and meek
Would for Christ my Saviour speak.

September 6 — Evening

If you are led by the Spirit, you are not under the law. {Galatians 5:18}

He who looks at his own character and position from a legal point of view, will not only despair when he comes to the *end* of his reckoning, but if he is a wise man he will despair at the *beginning*; for if we are to be judged on the basis of the law, no living flesh shall be justified. How blessed to know that we dwell in the domains of grace and not of law! When thinking of my state before God the question is not, "Am I perfect in myself before the law?" but, "Am I perfect in Christ Jesus?" That is a very different matter. We need not enquire, "Am I without sin naturally?" but, "Have I been washed in the fountain opened for sin and for uncleanness?" It is not "Am I in myself well pleasing to God?" but it is "Am I accepted in the Beloved?" The Christian views his evidences from the top of Sinai, and grows alarmed concerning his salvation; it would be far better if he read his title by the light of Calvary. "Why," he says, "my faith has unbelief in it, it is not able to save me." Suppose he had considered *the object* of his faith instead of his faith, then he would have said, "There is no failure in *him*, and therefore I am safe." He sighs over his hope: "Ah! my hope is marred and dimmed by an anxious care about present things; how can I be accepted?" Had he regarded *the basis* of his hope, he would have seen that the promise of God stands sure, and that whatever our doubts may be, the oath and promise never fail. Ah! believer, it is safer always for you to be led by the Spirit into gospel liberty than to wear legal fetters. Judge yourself by what *Christ* is rather than by what *you* are. Satan will try to mar your peace by reminding you of your sinfulness and imperfections: you can only meet his accusations by faithfully adhering to the gospel and refusing to wear the yoke of bondage.

September 7 — Morning

{Daily Reading: Ezekiel 22:1–24:27} {Quick Study: Ezekiel 40:1–42:20}

And when they could not come near to him for
the crowd, they uncovered the roof where he was:
and when they had broken it up, they let down the
bed on which the sick of the palsy lay. *{Mark 2:4}*

Faith is full of inventions. The house was full, a crowd blocked the door, but faith found a way of getting at the Lord and placing the palsied man before him. If we cannot get sinners where Jesus is by ordinary methods we must use extraordinary ones. It seems, according to Luke 5:19, that a tiling had to be removed, which would make dust and cause a measure of danger to those below, but where the case is very urgent we must not mind running some risks and shocking some proprieties. Jesus was there to heal, and therefore fall what might, faith ventured all so that her poor paralysed charge might have his sins forgiven. Oh that we had more daring faith among us! Can we not, dear reader, seek it this morning for ourselves and for our fellow workers, and will we not try today to perform some gallant act for the love of souls and the glory of the Lord?

The world is constantly inventing; genius serves all the purposes of human desire: cannot faith invent too, and reach by some new means the outcasts who lie perishing around us? It was the presence of Jesus which stirred up victorious courage in the four bearers of the palsied man: is not the Lord among us now? Have we seen his face for ourselves this morning? Have we felt his healing power in our own souls? If so, then through door, through window, or through roof, let us, breaking through all impediments, labour to bring poor souls to Jesus. All means are good and decorous when faith and love are truly set on winning souls. If hunger for bread can break through stone walls, surely hunger for souls is not to be hindered in its efforts. Oh Lord, make us eager to suggest methods of reaching your poor sin sick ones, and bold to carry them out whatever the risk.

September 7 — Evening

**There is sorrow on the sea;
it cannot be quiet.** *{Jeremiah 49:23}*

Little do we know what sorrow may be upon the sea at this moment. We are safe in our quiet home, but far away on the salt sea the hurricane may be cruelly seeking for the lives of men. Hear how the death fiends howl among the cordage; how every timber creaks as the waves beat like battering rams upon the vessel! God help you, poor drenched and wearied ones! My prayer goes up to the great Lord of sea and land, that he will make the storm a calm, and bring you to your desired haven! Nor ought I to offer prayer alone, I should try to benefit those hardy men who risk their lives so constantly. Have I ever done anything for them? What can I do? How often does the boisterous sea swallow up the mariner! Thousands of corpses lie where pearls lie deep. There is death sorrow on the sea, which is echoed in the long wail of widows and orphans. The salt of the sea is in many eyes of mothers and wives. Remorseless billows, you have devoured the love of women, and the mainstay of households. What a resurrection shall there be from the caverns of the deep when the sea gives up her dead! Until then there will be sorrow on the sea. As if in sympathy with the woes of earth, the sea is for ever fretting along a thousand shores, wailing with a sorrowful cry like her own birds, booming with a hollow crash of unrest, raving with uproarious discontent, chafing with hoarse wrath, or jangling with the voices of ten thousand murmuring pebbles. The roar of the sea may be joyous to a rejoicing spirit, but to the son of sorrow the wide, wide ocean is even more forlorn than the wide, wide world. This is not our rest, and the restless billows tell us so. There is a land where there is no more sea — our faces are steadfastly set towards it; we are going to the place of which the Lord has spoken. Until then, we cast our sorrows on the Lord who trod the sea of old, and who makes a way for his people through its depths.

{Daily Reading: Ezekiel 25:1–28:26} {Quick Study: Ezekiel 43:1–45:25}

Your fruit comes from me. *{Hosea 14:8}*

Our fruit comes from our God as a result of *union*. The fruit of the branch is directly traceable to the root. Sever the connection, the branch dies, and no fruit is produced. By virtue of our union with Christ we bring forth fruit. Every bunch of grapes has been first in the root, it has passed through the stem, and flowed through the sap vessels, and fashioned itself externally into fruit, but it was first in the stem; so also every good work was first in Christ, and then is brought forth in us. Oh Christian, prize this precious union to Christ; for it must be the source of all the fruitfulness which you can hope to know. If you were not joined to Jesus Christ, you would be a barren bough indeed.

Our fruit comes from God as a result of *spiritual providence*. When the dew drops fall from heaven, when the cloud looks down from on high, and is about to distil its liquid treasure, when the bright sun swells the berries of the cluster, each heavenly boon may whisper to the tree and say, "Your fruit comes from me." The fruit owes much to the root — that is essential to fruitfulness — but it owes very much also to external influences. How much we owe to God's grace — providence! in which he provides us constantly with quickening, teaching, consolation, strength, or whatever else we need. To this we owe all our usefulness or virtue.

Our fruit comes from God as a result of *wise husbandry*. The gardener's sharp-edged knife promotes the fruitfulness of the tree, by thinning the clusters, and by cutting off superfluous shoots. So it is, Christian, with that pruning which the Lord gives to you. "My Father is the husbandman. Every branch in me that does not bear fruit he takes away; and every branch that bears fruit he purges, so that it may bring forth more fruit." Since our God is the author of our spiritual graces, let us give to him all the glory of our salvation.

September 8 — Evening

*The exceeding greatness of his power towards us
who believe according to the working of his
mighty power, which he performed in Christ,
when he raised him from the dead. {Ephesians 1:19–20}*

In the resurrection of Christ, as in our salvation, there was exerted nothing less than a *divine power*. What shall we say of those who think that conversion is performed by the free will of man, and is due to his own improvement of disposition? When we shall see the dead rise from the grave by their own power, then we may expect to see ungodly sinners by their own free will turning to Christ. It is not the Word preached, nor the Word read in itself; all quickening power proceeds from the Holy Spirit. This power was *irresistible*. All the soldiers and the high priests could not keep the body of Christ in the tomb; Death himself could not hold Jesus in his bonds: even thus irresistible is the power exerted on the believer when he is raised to newness of life. No sin, no corruption, no demons in hell nor sinners upon earth, can stop the hand of God's grace when it intends to convert a man. If God omnipotently says, "You shall," man shall not say, "I will not." Notice that the power which raised Christ from the dead was *glorious*. It reflected honour upon God and resulted in dismay in the hosts of evil. So there is great glory to God in the conversion of every sinner. It was *everlasting power*. "Christ being raised from the dead dies no more; death has no more dominion over him." So we, being raised from the dead, do not go back to our dead works nor to our old corruptions, but we live for God. "Because he lives we live also." "For we are dead, and our life is hidden with Christ in God." "Just as Christ was raised up from the dead by the glory of the Father, even so we also should walk in newness of life." Lastly, in the text, note *the union of the new life with Jesus*. The same power which raised the Head works life in the members. What a blessing to be quickened together with Christ!

September 9 — Morning

{Daily Reading: Ezekiel 29:1–32:32} {Quick Study: Ezekiel 46:1–48:35}

I will answer you, and show you great and
mighty things which you do not know. *{Jeremiah 33:3}*

There are different translations of these words. One version renders it, "I will show you great and fortified things." Another, "Great and reserved things." Now, there are reserved and special things in Christian experience: all the developments of spiritual life are not equally easy to attain. There are the common experiences and feelings of repentance, and faith, and joy, and hope, which are enjoyed by the entire family; but there is an upper realm of rapture, of communion, and conscious union with Christ, which is far from being the common dwelling place of believers. We do not all have the high privilege of John, to lean upon Jesus' bosom; nor of Paul, to be caught up into the third heaven. There are heights in experiential knowledge of the things of God which the eagle's eye of acumen and philosophical thought has never seen: God alone can bear us there; but the chariot in which he takes us up, and the fiery steeds with which that chariot is drawn, are prevailing prayers. Prevailing prayer is victorious over the God of mercy, "By his strength he had power with God: yes, he had power over the angel, and prevailed: he wept, and made supplication to him: he found him in Bethel, and there he spoke with us." Prevailing prayer takes the Christian to Carmel, and enables him to cover heaven with clouds of blessing, and earth with floods of mercy. Prevailing prayer bears the Christian aloft to Pisgah, and shows him the reserved inheritance; it elevates us to Tabor and transfigures us, until in the likeness of his Lord, as he is, so are we also in this world. If you wish to reach to something higher than ordinary grovelling experience, look to the Rock that is higher than you, and gaze with the eye of faith through the window of importunate prayer. When you open the window on your side, it will not be bolted on the other.

September 9 — Evening

> And all around the throne were twenty-four seats:
> and upon the seats I saw twenty-four elders sitting,
> clothed in white raiment. *{Revelation 4:4}*

These representatives of the saints in heaven are said to be *all around the throne.* In the passage in Canticles, where Solomon sings of the king sitting at his table, some render it "a round table." From this, some expositors, I think, without straining the text, have said, "There is an equality among the saints." That idea is conveyed by the equal nearness of the twenty-four elders. The condition of glorified spirits in heaven is that of nearness to Christ, clear vision of his glory, constant access to his court, and familiar fellowship with his person: nor is there any difference in this respect between one saint and another, but all the people of God, apostles, martyrs, ministers, or private and obscure Christians, shall all be seated *near the throne,* where they shall for ever gaze upon their exalted Lord, and be satisfied with his love. They shall all be near to Christ, all ravished with his love, all eating and drinking at the same table with him, all equally beloved as his favourites and friends, even if not all equally rewarded as servants.

Let believers on earth imitate the saints in heaven in their nearness to Christ. Let us on earth be as the elders are in heaven, sitting around the throne. May Christ be the object of our thoughts, the centre of our lives. How can we endure to live at such a distance from our Beloved? Lord Jesus, draw us nearer to yourself. Say to us, "Abide in me, and I in you"; and permit us to sing, "His left hand is under my head, and his right hand embraces me."

> Oh lift me higher, nearer you,
> And as I rise more pure and meet,
> Oh let my soul's humility
> Make me lie lower at your feet;
> Less trusting self, the more I prove
> The blessed comfort of your love.

September 10 — Morning

{Daily Reading: Ezekiel 33:1–36:38} {Quick Study: Daniel 1:1–3:30}

**And he goes up into a mountain, and calls to him
those he himself wanted: and they came to him.** *{Mark 3:13}*

Here was sovereignty. Impatient spirits may fret and fume, because they are not called to the highest places in the ministry; but reader rejoice that Jesus calls those he himself wanted. If he shall leave me to be a doorkeeper in his house, I will cheerfully bless him for his grace in permitting me to do anything in his service. The call of Christ's servants comes from above. Jesus stands on the mountain, for evermore above the world in holiness, earnestness, love and power. Those whom he calls must go up the mountain to him, they must seek to rise to his level by living in constant communion with him. They may not be able to mount to classic honours, or attain scholastic eminence, but they must like Moses go up into the mount of God and have intimate communion with the unseen God, or they will never be suitable to proclaim the gospel of peace. Jesus went apart to hold high fellowship with the Father, and we must enter into the same divine companionship if we wish to bless our fellow men. No wonder that the apostles were clothed with power when they came down fresh from the mountain where Jesus was. This morning we must endeavour to ascend the mount of communion, so that there we may be ordained to the lifework for which we are set apart. Let us not see the face of man today until we have seen Jesus. Time spent with him is time well spent. We too shall cast out demons and work wonders if we go down into the world girded with that divine energy which Christ alone can give. It is of no use going to the Lord's battle until we are armed with heavenly weapons. We *must* see Jesus, this is essential. At the mercy seat we will linger until he shall reveal himself to us as he does not to the world, and until we can truthfully say, "We were with him in the Holy Mount."

September 10 — Evening

Evening wolves. *{Habakkuk 1:8}*

While preparing the present volume, this particular expression recurred to me so frequently, that in order to be rid of its constant importunity I determined to give a page to it. The evening wolf, infuriated by a day of hunger, was more fierce and ravenous than he would have been in the morning. May not the furious creature represent our doubts and fears after a day of distraction of mind, losses in business, and perhaps unkind tauntings from our fellow men? How our thoughts howl in our ears, "Where is your God now?" How voracious and greedy they are, swallowing up all suggestions of comfort, and remaining as hungry as before. Great Shepherd, kill these evening wolves, and bid your sheep lie down in green pastures, undisturbed by insatiable unbelief. How similar the fiends of hell are to evening wolves, for when the flock of Christ is in a cloudy and dark day, and their sun seems to be going down, they hasten to tear and to devour. They will scarcely attack the Christian in the daylight of faith, but in the gloom of soul conflict they fall upon him. Oh you who have laid down your life for the sheep, preserve them from the fangs of the wolf.

False teachers who craftily and industriously hunt for the precious life, devouring men by their falsehoods, are as dangerous and detestable as evening wolves. Darkness is their element, deceit is their character, destruction is their end. We are most in danger from them when they wear the sheep's skin. Blessed is he who is kept from them, for thousands are made the prey of grievous wolves that enter within the fold of the church.

What a wonder of grace it is when fierce persecutors are converted, for then the wolf dwells with the lamb, and men of cruel ungovernable dispositions become gentle and teachable. Oh Lord, convert many such: for such we will pray tonight.

September 11 — Morning

{Daily Reading: Ezekiel 37:1–39:29} {Quick Study: Daniel 4:1–6:28}

Be separate. *{2 Corinthians 6:17}*

The Christian, while in the world, is not to be of the world. He should be distinguished from it in *the great object of his life*. To him, "to live" should be "Christ." Whether he eats, or drinks, or whatever he does, he should do all for God's glory. You may lay up treasure; but lay it up in heaven, where neither moth nor rust corrupts, where thieves do not break through or steal. You may strive to be rich; but make it your ambition to be "rich in faith" and good works. You may have pleasure; but when you are merry, sing psalms and make melody in your hearts to the Lord. In your *spirit*, as well as in your aim, you should differ from the world. Waiting humbly before God, always conscious of his presence, delighting in communion with him, and seeking to know his will, you will prove that you are of the heavenly race. And you should be separate from the world in your *actions*. If a thing is right, though you lose by it, it must be done; if it is wrong, though you would gain by it, you must scorn the sin for your Master's sake. You must have no fellowship with the unfruitful works of darkness, but rather reprove them. Walk worthy of your high calling and dignity. Remember, oh Christian, that you are a son of the King of kings. Therefore, keep yourself unspotted from the world. Do not soil the fingers which are soon to sweep celestial strings; do not let these eyes become the windows of lust which are soon to see the King in his beauty — do not let those feet be defiled in miry places, which are soon to walk the golden streets — do not let those hearts be filled with pride and bitterness which are before long to be filled with heaven, and to overflow with ecstatic joy.

> Then rise my soul! and soar away, above the thoughtless crowd;
> Above the pleasures of the gay, and splendours of the proud;
> Up where eternal beauties bloom, and pleasures all divine;
> Where wealth, that never can consume, and endless glories shine.

September 11 — Evening

Lead me, oh Lord, in your righteousness because of my enemies. *{Psalms 5:8}*

Very bitter is the enmity of the world against the people of Christ. Men will forgive a thousand faults in others, but they will magnify the most trivial offence in the followers of Jesus. Instead of vainly regretting this, let us turn it to good account, and since so many are watching for our halting, let this be a special motive for walking very carefully before God. If we live carelessly, the lynx-eyed world will soon see it, and with its hundred tongues it will spread the story, exaggerated and emblazoned by the zeal of slander. They will shout triumphantly, "Aha! So would we have it! See how these Christians act! They are hypocrites to a man." Thus will much damage be done to the cause of Christ, and much insult offered to his name. The cross of Christ is in itself an offence to the world; let us take heed that we add no offence of our own. It is "to the Jews a stumblingblock": let us be careful that we put no stumblingblocks where there are enough already. "To the Greeks it is foolishness": let us not add our folly to give point to the scorn with which the worldly wise deride the gospel. How jealous should we be of ourselves! How rigid with our consciences! In the presence of adversaries who will misrepresent our best deeds, and impugn our motives where they cannot censure our actions, how circumspect should we be! Pilgrims travel as suspected people through Vanity Fair. Not only are we under surveillance, but there are more spies than we know about. The espionage is everywhere, at home and abroad. If we fall into the enemies' hands we may sooner expect generosity from a wolf, or mercy from a fiend, than anything like patience with our infirmities from men who spice their infidelity towards God with scandals against his people. Oh Lord, always lead us, lest our enemies trip us up!

September 12 — Morning

{Daily Reading: Ezekiel 40:1–42:20} {Quick Study: Daniel 7:1–9:27}

God is jealous. *{Nahum 1:2}*

Your Lord is very jealous of your love, oh believer. Did he choose you? He cannot bear that you should choose another. Did he buy you with his own blood? He cannot endure that you should think that you are your own, or that you belong to this world. He loved you with such a love that he would not stay in heaven without you; he would sooner die than that you should perish, and he cannot endure that anything should stand between your heart's love and himself. *He is very jealous of your trust.* He will not permit you to trust in an arm of flesh. He cannot bear that you should hew out broken cisterns, when the overflowing fountain is always free to you. When we lean upon him, he is glad, but when we transfer our dependence to another, when we rely upon our own wisdom, or the wisdom of a friend — worst of all, when we trust in any works of our own, he is displeased, and will chasten us so that he may bring us to himself. *He is also very jealous of our company.* There should be no one with whom we converse so much as with Jesus. To abide in him only, this is true love; but to commune with the world, to find sufficient solace in our carnal comforts, to prefer even the companionship of our fellow Christians to secret communion with him, this is grievous to our jealous Lord. He wishes to have us abide in him, and enjoy constant fellowship with himself; and many of the trials which he sends us are for the purpose of weaning our hearts from the creature, and fixing them more closely upon himself. Let this jealousy which would keep us near to Christ *be also a comfort* to us, for if he loves us so much as to care thus about our love we may be sure that he will allow nothing to harm us, and will protect us from all our enemies. Oh that we may have grace today to keep our hearts in sacred chastity for our Beloved alone, with sacred jealousy shutting our eyes to all the fascinations of the world!

September 12 — Evening

I will sing of mercy and judgment. *{Psalms 101:1}*

Faith triumphs in trial. When reason is thrust into the inner prison, with her feet bound firm in the stocks, faith makes the dungeon walls ring with her merry notes as she cries, "I will sing of mercy and of judgment. To you, oh Lord, I will sing." Faith pulls the black mask from the face of trouble, and discovers the angel beneath. Faith looks up at the cloud, and sees that

> 'Tis big with mercy and shall break
> In blessings on her head.

There is a subject for song even in the judgments of God towards us. For, first, the trial is *not as heavy as it might have been*; next, the trouble is *not as severe as we deserved to have borne*; and our affliction is *not as crushing as the burden which others have to carry*. Faith sees that in her worst sorrow there is nothing penal; there is not a drop of God's wrath in it; it is all sent in love. Faith discerns love gleaming like a jewel on the heart of an angry God. Faith says of her grief, "This is a badge of honour, for the child must feel the rod"; and then she sings of the sweet result of her sorrows, because they work her spiritual good. "Indeed more," says Faith, "these light afflictions, which are only for a moment, work out for me a far more exceeding and eternal weight of glory." So Faith rides forth on the black horse, conquering and to conquer, trampling down carnal reason and fleshly sense, and chanting notes of victory amid the thickest of the fray.

> All I meet I find assists me in my path to heavenly joy:
> Where, though trials now attend me, trials never more annoy.
> Blest there with a weight of glory, still the path I'll ne'er forget,
> But, exulting, cry, it led me to my blessed Saviour's seat.

September 13 — Morning

{Daily Reading: Ezekiel 43:1–45:25} {Quick Study: Daniel 10:1–12:13}

Who passing through the valley of Baca make it a well, the rain also fills the pools. *{Psalms 84:6}*

This teaches us that the *comfort* obtained by one may often prove serviceable to another; just as wells would be used by the company who came after. We read some book full of consolation, which is like Jonathan's rod, dropping with honey. Ah! we think our brother has been here before us, and dug this well for us as well as for himself. Many a "Night of Weeping," "Midnight Harmonies," an "Eternal Day," a "Crook in the Lot," a "Comfort for Mourners," has been a well dug by a pilgrim for himself, but has proven quite as useful to others. We notice this especially in the Psalms, such as that beginning, "Why are you cast down, oh my soul?" Travellers have been delighted to see the footprint of man on a barren shore, and we love to see the waymarks of pilgrims while passing through the vale of tears.

The pilgrims dig the well, but, strange enough, it fills from the top instead of the bottom. We use the means, but the blessing does not spring from the means. We dig a well, but heaven fills it with rain. The horse is prepared for the day of battle, but safety is from the Lord. The means are connected with the end, but they do not by themselves produce it. See here the rain fills the pools, so that the wells become useful as reservoirs for the water; labour is not lost, but yet it does not supersede divine help.

Grace may well be compared to rain for its purity, for its refreshing and vivifying influence, for its coming alone from above, and for the sovereignty with which it is given or withheld. May our readers have showers of blessing, and may the wells they have dug be filled with water! Oh, what are means and ordinances without the smile of heaven! They are as clouds without rain, and pools without water. Oh, God of love, open the windows of heaven and pour us out a blessing!

September 13 — Evening

This Man receives sinners. *{Luke 15:2}*

Observe *the condescension* of this fact. This Man, who towers above all other men, holy, harmless, undefiled, and separate from sinners — *this* Man receives sinners. This Man, who is none other than the eternal God, before whom angels veil their faces — *this* Man receives sinners. It needs an angel's tongue to describe such a mighty stoop of love. That any of us should be willing to seek after the lost is nothing wonderful — they are of our own race; but that he, the offended God, against whom the transgression has been committed, should take upon himself the form of a servant, and bear the sin of many, and should then be willing to receive the vilest of the vile, this is marvellous.

"This Man receives sinners"; not, however, that they may remain sinners, but he receives them so that he may pardon their sins, justify them, cleanse their hearts by his purifying Word, preserve their souls by the indwelling of the Holy Spirit, and enable them to serve him, to show forth his praise, and to have communion with him. Into his heart's love he receives sinners, takes them from the dunghill, and wears them as jewels in his crown; plucks them as brands from the burning, and preserves them as costly monuments of his mercy. None are so precious in Jesus' sight as the sinners for whom he died. When Jesus receives sinners, he does not have some outdoor reception place, no casual ward where he charitably entertains them as men do passing beggars, but he opens the golden gates of his royal heart, and receives the sinner right into himself — yes, he admits the humble penitent into personal union and makes him a member of his body, of his flesh, and of his bones. There was never such a reception as this! This fact is still most sure this evening, he is still receiving sinners: oh that sinners would receive him.

September 14 — Morning

{Daily Reading: Ezekiel 46:1–48:35} {Quick Study: Hosea 1:1–6:11}

There were also other little ships with him. *{Mark 4:36}*

Jesus was the Lord High Admiral of the sea that night, and his presence preserved the whole convoy. It is well to sail with Jesus, even though it is in a little ship. When we sail in Christ's company, we may not be sure of fair weather, for great storms may toss the vessel which carries the Lord himself, and we must not expect to find the sea less boisterous around our little boat. If we go with Jesus we must be content to fare as he fares; and when the waves are rough for him, they will be rough for us. It is by tempest and tossing that we shall come to land, as he did before us.

When the storm swept over Galilee's dark lake, all faces gathered blackness, and all hearts dreaded shipwreck. When all creature help was useless, the slumbering Saviour arose, and with a word, transformed the riot of the tempest into the deep quiet of a calm; then were the little vessels at rest as well as the one that carried the Lord. Jesus is the star of the sea; and although there is sorrow upon the sea, when Jesus is on it there is joy, too. May our hearts make Jesus their anchor, their rudder, their lighthouse, their life boat, and their harbour. His church is the Admiral's flagship, let us attend her movements, and cheer her officers with our presence. He himself is the great attraction; let us always follow in his wake, obey his signals, steer by his chart, and never fear while he is within hail. Not one ship in the convoy shall be shipwrecked; the great Commodore will steer every barque in safety to the desired haven. By faith we will slip our cable for another day's cruise, and sail forth with Jesus into a sea of tribulation. Winds and waves will not spare us, but they all obey him; and, therefore, whatever squalls may occur without, faith shall feel a blessed calm within. He is always in the centre of the weather-beaten company: let us rejoice in him. His vessel has reached the haven, and so shall ours.

September 14 — Evening

*I acknowledged my sin to you, and I have not
hidden my iniquity. I said, "I will confess
my transgressions to the Lord"; and you forgave
the iniquity of my sin. {Psalms 32:5}*

David's grief for sin was bitter. Its effects were visible upon his outward frame: "his bones waxed old"; "his moisture was turned into the drought of summer." He could find no remedy until he made a full confession before the throne of the heavenly grace. He tells us that for a time he kept silence, and his heart became more and more filled with grief: like a mountain stream whose outlet is dammed up, his soul was swollen with torrents of sorrow. He made excuses; he endeavoured to divert his thoughts, but it was all to no avail; like a festering sore his anguish gathered, and since he would not use the lancet of confession, his spirit was full of torment, and knew no rest. At last it came to this, that he must return to his God in humble penitence, or die outright; so he hastened to the mercy seat, and there unrolled the volume of his iniquities before the all-seeing One, acknowledging all the evil of his ways in language such as you read in the fifty-first and other penitential psalms. Having done this, a work so simple and yet so difficult for pride, he received at once the token of divine forgiveness; the bones which had been broken were made to rejoice, and he came forth from his prayer closet to sing the blessedness of the man whose transgression is forgiven. See the value of a grace-worked confession of sin! It is to be prized above all price, for in every case where there is a genuine, gracious confession, mercy is freely given, not because the repentance and confession deserve mercy, but for *Christ's sake*. Blessed be God, there is always healing for the broken heart; the fountain is always flowing to cleanse us from our sins. Truly, oh Lord, you are a God "ready to pardon!" Therefore, we will acknowledge our iniquities.

September 15 — Morning

{Daily Reading: Daniel 1:1–3:30} {Quick Study: Hosea 7:1–14:9}

He shall not be afraid of bad news. *{Psalms 112:7}*

Christian, you ought not to dread the arrival of bad news; because if you are distressed by them, *how do you differ from other men?* Other men do not have your God to flee to; they have never proven his faithfulness as you have done, and it is no wonder if they are bowed down with alarm and cowed with fear: but you profess to be of another spirit; you have been begotten again to a lively hope, and your heart lives in heaven and not on earthly things; now, if you are seen to be distracted as other men, what is the value of that grace which you profess to have received? Where is the dignity of that new nature which you claim to possess?

Again, if you should be filled with alarm, as others are, *you would, doubtlessly, be led into the sins so common to others under trying circumstances.* The ungodly, when they are overtaken by bad news, rebel against God; they complain, and think that God deals harshly with them. Will you fall into that same sin? Will you provoke the Lord as they do?

Moreover, unconverted men often resort to wrong means in order to escape from difficulties, and you will be sure to do the same if your mind yields to the present pressure. Trust in the Lord, and wait patiently for him. Your wisest course is to do as Moses did at the Red Sea, "Stand still and see the salvation of God." For if you are afraid when you hear bad news, you will be unable to meet the trouble with that calm composure which nerves for duty, and sustains under adversity. How can you glorify God if you play the coward? Saints have often sung God's high praises in the fires, but will your doubting and desponding, as if you had no one to help you, magnify the Most High? Then take courage, and relying in sure confidence upon the faithfulness of your covenant God, "Do not let your heart be troubled, neither let it be afraid."

September 15 — Evening

A people near to him. *{Psalms 148:14}*

The dispensation of the old covenant was one of distance. When God appeared even to his servant Moses, he said, "Do not draw near: take off your shoes from your feet"; and when he revealed himself upon Mount Sinai, to his own chosen and separated people, one of the first commands was, "You shall set bounds around the mount." Both in the sacred worship of the tabernacle and the temple, the thought of distance was always prominent. The mass of the people did not even enter the outer court. Into the inner court no one except the priests might dare to intrude; while into the innermost place, or the holy of holies, the high priest only entered once in the year. It was as if the Lord in those early ages wished to teach man that sin was so utterly loathsome to him that he must treat men as lepers put outside the camp; and when he came nearest to them, he still made them feel the distance of the separation between a holy God and an impure sinner. When the gospel came, we were placed on quite another footing. The word "Go" was exchanged for "Come"; distance was made to give place to nearness, and we who were previously far off, were made near by the blood of Jesus Christ. Incarnate Deity has no wall of fire around him. "Come to me, all you who labour and are heavy laden, and I will give you rest," is the joyful proclamation of God as he appears in human flesh. He does not now keep the leper at a distance because of his leprosy, but Jesus himself suffers the penalty for his defilement. What a state of safety and privilege is this nearness to God through Jesus! Do you know it by experience? If you know it, are you living in the power of it? Marvellous is this nearness, yet it is to be followed by a time of greater nearness still, when it shall be said, "The tabernacle of God is with men, and he dwells among them." Hasten it, oh Lord.

{Daily Reading: Daniel 4:1–6:28} {Quick Study: Joel 1:1–3:21}

Partakers of the divine nature. *{2 Peter 1:4}*

To be a partaker of the divine nature is not, of course, to become God. That cannot be. The essence of Deity is not to be participated in by the creature. Between the creature and the Creator there must always be a gulf fixed in respect of essence; but just as the first man Adam was made in the image of God, so we, by the renewal of the Holy Spirit, are in a yet more divine sense made in the image of the Most High, and are partakers of the divine nature. We are, by grace, made like God. "God is love"; we become love — "He who loves is born from God." God is truth; we become true, and we love what is true: God is good, and he makes us good by his grace, so that we become the pure in heart who shall see God. Moreover, we become partakers of the divine nature in even a higher sense than this — in fact, in as lofty a sense as can be conceived, short of our being absolutely divine. Do we not become members of the body of the divine person of Christ? Yes, the same blood which flows in the head flows in the hand: and the same life which quickens Christ quickens his people, for "You are dead, and your life is hidden with Christ in God." Indeed, as if this were not enough, we are married to Christ. He has betrothed us to himself in righteousness and in faithfulness, and he who is joined to the Lord is one spirit. Oh! Marvellous mystery! We look into it, but who shall understand it? One with Jesus — so one with him that the branch is not more one with the vine than we are a part of the Lord, our Saviour, and our Redeemer! While we rejoice in this, let us remember that those who are made partakers of the divine nature will reveal their high and holy relationship in their conduct with others, and make it evident by their daily walk and conversation that they have escaped the corruption that is in the world through lust. Oh, for more divine holiness of life!

September 16 — Evening

Am I a sea, or a whale, that you set a watch over me? *{Job 7:12}*

This was a strange question for Job to ask the Lord. He felt himself to be too insignificant to be so strictly watched and chastened, and he hoped that he was not so unruly as to need to be so restrained. The enquiry was natural from one surrounded with such insupportable miseries, but after all, it is capable of a very humbling answer. It is true man is not the sea, but he is even more troublesome and unruly. The sea obediently respects its boundary, and although it is only a belt of sand, it does not leap over the limit. Mighty as it is, it hears the divine *go only so far*, and when it is most raging with tempest it respects the word; but self-willed man defies heaven and oppresses earth, neither is there any end to this rebellious rage. The sea, obedient to the moon, ebbs and flows with ceaseless regularity, and thus renders an active as well as a passive obedience; but man, restless beyond his sphere, sleeps within the lines of duty, indolent where he should be active. He will neither come nor go at the divine command, but sullenly prefers to do what he should not, and to leave undone what is required of him. Every drop in the ocean, every beaded bubble, and every yeasty foam flake, every shell and pebble, feel the power of law, and yield or move at once. Oh, that our nature were only one thousandth part as much conformed to the will of God! We call the sea fickle and false, but how constant it is! Since our fathers' days, and the old time before them, the sea resides where it was, beating on the same cliffs to the same tune; we *know* where to find it, it does not forsake its bed, and does not change in its ceaseless roar; but where is man — vain, fickle man? Can the wise man guess by what folly he will next be seduced from his obedience? We need more watching than the billowy sea, and are far more rebellious. Lord, rule us for your own glory. Amen.

September 17 — Morning

{Daily Reading: Daniel 7:1–9:27} {Quick Study: Amos 1:1–5:27}

Bring him to me. *{Mark 9:19}*

Despairingly the poor disappointed father turned away from the disciples to their Master. His son was in the worst possible condition, and all means had failed, but the miserable child was soon delivered from the evil one when the parent in faith obeyed the Lord Jesus' word, "Bring him to me." Children are a precious gift from God, but much anxiety comes with them. They may be a great joy or a great bitterness to their parents; they may be filled with the Spirit of God, or possessed with the spirit of evil. In all cases, the Word of God gives us one prescription for the curing of all their ills, "Bring him to me." Oh, for more agonizing prayer on their behalf while they are still babes! Sin is there, let our prayers begin to attack it. Our cries for our offspring should precede those cries which betoken their actual advent into a world of sin. In the days of their youth we shall see sad tokens of that dumb and deaf spirit which will neither pray properly, nor hear the voice of God in the soul, but Jesus still commands, "Bring them to me." When they are grown up they may wallow in sin and foam with enmity against God; then when our hearts are breaking we should remember the great Physician's words, "Bring them to me." Never must we cease to pray until they cease to breathe. No case is hopeless while Jesus lives.

The Lord sometimes permits his people to be driven into a corner so that they may know by experience how necessary he is to them. Ungodly children, when they show us our own powerlessness against the depravity of their hearts, drive us to flee to the strong for strength, and this is a great blessing to us. Whatever our morning's need may be, let it like a strong current bear us to the ocean of divine love. Jesus can soon remove our sorrow, he delights to comfort us. Let us hasten to him while he waits to meet us.

September 17 — Evening

Encourage him. *{Deuteronomy 1:38}*

God employs his people to encourage one another. He did not say to an angel, "Gabriel, my servant Joshua is about to lead my people into Canaan — go, encourage him." God never works needless miracles; if his purposes can be accomplished by ordinary means, he will not use miraculous agency. Gabriel would not have been half so well fitted for the work as Moses. A brother's sympathy is more precious than an angel's embassy. The angel, swift of wing, had better known the Master's bidding than the people's temper. An angel had never experienced the hardness of the road, nor seen the fiery serpents, nor had he led the stiffnecked multitude in the wilderness as Moses had done. We should be glad that God usually works for man by man. It forms a bond of brotherhood, and being mutually dependent on one another, we are fused more completely into one family. Brethren, take the text as God's message to you. Labour to help others, and especially strive to *encourage* them. Speak cheerfully to the young and anxious enquirer, lovingly try to remove stumblingblocks out of his way. When you find a spark of grace in the heart, kneel down and blow it into a flame. Leave the young believer to discover the roughness of the road by degrees, but tell him of the strength which dwells in God, of the sureness of the promise, and of the charms of communion with Christ. Aim to comfort the sorrowful, and to animate the desponding. Speak a word in season to him who is weary, and encourage those who are fearful to go on their way with gladness. God encourages *you* by his promises; Christ encourages *you* as he points to the heaven he has won for you, and the Spirit encourages *you* as he works in you to will and to do his own will and pleasure. Imitate divine wisdom, and encourage others, according to the word of this evening.

September 18 — Morning

{Daily Reading: Daniel 10:1–12:13} {Quick Study: Amos 6:1–9:15}

**If we live in the Spirit, let us also
walk in the Spirit.** *{Galatians 5:25}*

The two most important things in our holy religion are the *life of faith* and the *walk of faith*. He who shall rightly understand these is not far from being a master in experiential theology, for they are vital points to a Christian. You will never find true faith unattended by true godliness; on the other hand, you will never discover a truly holy life which does not have as its root a living faith upon the righteousness of Christ. Woe to those who seek after the one without the other! There are some who cultivate faith and forget holiness; these may be very high in orthodoxy, but they shall be very deep in condemnation, for they hold the truth in unrighteousness; and there are others who have strained after holiness of life, but have denied the faith, like the Pharisees of old, of whom the Master said, they were "whitewashed sepulchres." We must have faith, for this is the foundation; we must have holiness of life, for this is the superstructure. Of what service is the mere foundation of a building to a man in the day of tempest? Can he hide himself in it? He needs a house to cover him, as well as a foundation for that house. Even so, we need the superstructure of spiritual life if we wish to have comfort in the day of doubt. But do not seek a holy life without faith, for that would be to erect a house which can afford no permanent shelter, because it has no foundation on a rock. Let faith and life be put together, and, like the two abutments of an arch, they will make our piety enduring. Like light and heat streaming from the same sun, they are equally full of blessing. Like the two pillars of the temple, they are for glory and for beauty. They are two streams from the fountain of grace; two lamps lit with holy fire; two olive trees watered by heavenly care. Oh, Lord, give us today life within, and it will reveal itself to your glory.

September 18 — Evening

And they follow me. *{John 10:27}*

We should follow our Lord as unhesitatingly as sheep follow their shepherd, for *he has a right to lead us wherever he pleases.* We are not our own, we are bought with a price — let us recognise the rights of the redeeming blood. The soldier follows his captain, the servant obeys his master, how much more must we follow our Redeemer, to whom we are a purchased possession. We are not true to our profession of being Christians if we question the bidding of our Leader and Commander. Submission is our duty, complaining is our folly. Often might our Lord say to us as he said to Peter, "What is that to you? Follow me." Wherever Jesus may lead us, *he goes before us.* If we do not know where we are going, we know *with whom* we go. With such a companion, who will dread the perils of the road? The journey may be long, but his everlasting arms will carry us to the end. The presence of Jesus is the assurance of eternal salvation; because he lives, we shall live also. We should follow Christ in simplicity and faith, because *the paths in which he leads us all end in glory and immortality.* It is true they may not be *smooth* paths — they may be covered with sharp flinty trials, but they lead to the "city which has foundations, whose builder and maker is God." "All the paths of the Lord are mercy and truth to such as keep his covenant." Let us put full trust in our Leader, since we know that, come prosperity or adversity, sickness or health, popularity or contempt, his purpose shall be worked out, and that purpose shall be pure, unmingled good to every heir of mercy. We shall find it sweet to go up the bleak side of the hill with Christ; and when rain and snow blow into our faces, his dear love will make us far more blest than those who sit at home and warm their hands at the world's fire. To the top of Amana, to the dens of lions, or to the hills of leopards, we will follow our Beloved. Precious Jesus, draw us, and we will run after you.

September 19 — Morning

{Daily Reading: Hosea 1:1–6:11} {Quick Study: Obadiah 1–21}

The liberty by which Christ has made us free. *{Galatians 5:1}*

This "liberty" makes us *free* to heaven's charter — *the Bible.* Here is a choice passage, believer, "When you pass through the rivers, I will be with you." You are free to that. Here is another: "Although the mountains shall depart, and the hills be removed, but my kindness shall not depart from you"; you are free to that. You are a welcome guest at the table of the promises. Scripture is a never-failing treasury filled with boundless stores of grace. It is the bank of heaven; you may draw from it as much as you please, without restraint or hindrance. Come in faith and you are welcome to all *covenant blessings.* There is not a promise in the Word which shall be withheld. In the depths of tribulations let this freedom comfort you; amidst waves of distress let it cheer you; when sorrows surround you let it be your solace. This is your Father's love token; you are free to it at all times. You are also *free to the throne of grace.* It is the believer's privilege to have access at all times to his Heavenly Father. Whatever our desires, our difficulties, our needs, we are at liberty to spread all before him. It does not matter how much we may have sinned, we may ask and expect pardon. It means nothing how poor we are, we may plead his promise that he will provide all needful things. We have permission to approach his throne at all times — in midnight's darkest hour, or in noontime's most burning heat. Exercise your right, oh believer, and live up to your privilege. You are free to all that is treasured up *in Christ* — wisdom, righteousness, sanctification, and redemption. It does not matter what your need is, for there is fulness of supply in Christ, and it is there *for you.* Oh what a "freedom" is yours! Freedom from condemnation, freedom to the promises, freedom to the throne of grace, and, at last, freedom to enter heaven!

September 19 — Evening

For this child I prayed. *{1 Samuel 1:27}*

Devout souls delight to look upon those mercies which they have obtained in answer to supplication, for they can see God's special love in them. When we can name our blessings *Samuel*, that is, "asked of God," they will be as dear to us as her child was to Hannah. Peninnah had many children, but they came as common blessings unsought in prayer: Hannah's one heaven-given child was far dearer, because he was the fruit of earnest pleadings. How sweet was that water to Samson which he found at "the well of him who prayed!" Quassia cups turn all waters bitter, but the cup of prayer puts a sweetness into the draughts it brings. Did we pray for the conversion of our children? How doubly sweet, when they are saved, to see in them our own petitions fulfilled! Better to rejoice over them as the fruit of our pleadings than as the fruit of our bodies. Have we sought from the Lord some choice spiritual gift? When it comes to us it will be wrapped up in the gold cloth of God's faithfulness and truth, and so be doubly precious. Have we petitioned for success in the Lord's work? How joyful is the prosperity which comes flying upon the wings of prayer! It is always best to bring blessings into our house in the legitimate way, by the door of prayer; then they are blessings indeed, and not temptations. Even when prayer is not speedily answered, the blessings grow all the richer for the delay; the child Jesus was all the more lovely in the eyes of Mary when she found him after having sought him sorrowing. What we win by prayer we should dedicate to God, as Hannah dedicated Samuel. The gift came from heaven, let it go to heaven. Prayer brought it, gratitude sang over it, let devotion consecrate it. Here will be a special occasion for saying, "Of your own I have given to you." Reader, is prayer your element or your weariness? Which?

September 20 — Morning

{Daily Reading: Hosea 7:1–14:9} {Quick Study: Jonah 1:1–4:11}

The sword of the Lord, and of Gideon. *{Judges 7:20}*

Gideon ordered his men to do two things: covering up a torch in an earthen pitcher, he ordered them, at an appointed signal, to break the pitcher and let the light shine, and then to sound with the trumpet, crying, "The sword of the Lord, and of Gideon! The sword of the Lord, and of Gideon!" This is precisely what all Christians must do. First, *you must shine*; break the pitcher which conceals your light; throw aside the bushel which has been hiding your candle, and shine. Let your light shine before men; let your good works be such, that when men look upon you, they shall know that you have been with Jesus. Then *there must be the sound*, the blowing of the trumpet. There must be active exertions for the ingathering of sinners by proclaiming Christ crucified. Take the gospel to them; carry it to their door; put it in their way; do not allow them to escape from it; blow the trumpet right up against their ears. Remember that the true war cry of the church is Gideon's watchword, "*The sword of the Lord, and of Gideon!*" God must do it, it is his own work. But we are not to be idle; instrumentality is to be used — "The sword of the Lord, and of Gideon!" If we only cry, "The sword of the Lord!" we shall be guilty of an idle presumption; and if we shout, "The sword of Gideon!" alone, we shall display idolatrous reliance on an arm of flesh: we must blend the two in practical harmony, "The sword of the Lord, and of Gideon!" We can do nothing by ourselves, but we can do everything by the help of our God; let us, therefore, in his name determine to go out personally and serve with our flaming torch of holy example, and with our trumpet tones of earnest declaration and testimony, and God shall be with us, and Midian shall be put to confusion, and the Lord of hosts shall reign for ever and ever.

September 20 — Evening

In the evening do not withhold your hand. *{Ecclesiastes 11:6}*

In *the evening of the day* opportunities are plentiful: men return from their labour, and the zealous soul winner finds time to tell abroad the love of Jesus. Have I no evening work for Jesus? If I do not have, let me no longer withhold my hand from a service which requires abundant labour. Sinners are perishing for lack of knowledge; he who loiters may find his skirts crimson with the blood of souls. Jesus gave both his hands to the nails; how can I keep back one of mine from his blessed work? Night and day he toiled and prayed for me; how can I give a single hour to the pampering of my flesh with luxurious ease? Up, idle heart; stretch out your hand to work, or uplift it to pray; heaven and hell are in earnest, let me be so, and this evening sow good seed for the Lord my God.

The evening of life also has its calls. Life is so short that a morning of manhood's vigour and an evening of decay make up the sum of it. To some it seems long, but a pound note is a great sum of money to a poor man. Life is so brief that no man can afford to lose a day. It has been well said that if a great king should bring us a great heap of gold, and bid us take as much as we could count in a day, we would make a long day of it; we would begin early in the morning, and in the evening we would not withhold our hand; but to win souls is a far nobler work, how is it that we stop doing it so soon? Some are spared to a long evening of ripe old age; if such is my case, let me use such talents as I still retain, and to the last hour serve my blessed and faithful Lord. By his grace I will die in harness, and lay down my charge only when I lay down my body. Age may instruct the young, cheer the faint, and encourage the desponding; if eventide has less of vigorous heat, it should have more of calm wisdom, therefore in the evening I will not withhold my hand.

{Daily Reading: Joel 1:1–3:21} {Quick Study: Micah 1:1–7:20}

I will rejoice over them to do them good. *{Jeremiah 32:41}*

How heart cheering to the believer is the delight which God has in his saints! We cannot see any reason in ourselves why the Lord should take pleasure in us; we cannot take delight in ourselves, for we often have to groan, being burdened; conscious of our sinfulness, and deploring our unfaithfulness. We fear that God's people cannot take much delight in us, for they must perceive so much of our imperfections and our follies that they may rather lament our infirmities than admire our graces. But we love to dwell upon this transcendent truth, this glorious mystery: that just as the bridegroom rejoices over the bride, so the Lord rejoices over us. We do not read anywhere that God delights in the cloud-capped mountains, or the sparkling stars, but we do read that he delights in the habitable parts of the earth, and that his delights are with the sons of men. We do not find it written that even angels give his soul delight; nor does he say, concerning cherubim and seraphim, "You shall be called Hephzibah, for the Lord delights in you"; but he does say all that to poor fallen creatures like ourselves, debased and depraved by sin, but saved, exalted, and glorified by his grace. In what strong language he expresses his delight in his people! Who could have conceived of the Eternal One as bursting forth into a song? Yet it is written, "He will rejoice over you with joy, he will rest in his love, he will joy over you with singing." As he looked upon the world he had made, he said, "It is very good"; but when he beheld those who are the purchase of Jesus' blood, his own chosen ones, it seemed as if the great heart of the Infinite could not restrain itself any longer, but overflowed in divine exclamations of joy. Should we not utter our grateful response to such a marvellous declaration of his love, and sing, "I will rejoice in the Lord, I will joy in the God of my salvation?"

September 21 — Evening

Do not gather my soul with sinners. *{Psalms 26:9}*

Fear made David pray thus, for something whispered, "Perhaps, after all, you may be gathered with the wicked." That fear, although marred by unbelief, springs, in the main, from holy anxiety, arising from the memory of past sin. Even the pardoned man will enquire, "What if at the end my sins should be remembered, and I should be left out of the catalogue of the saved?" He remembers his present unfruitfulness — so little grace, so little love, so little holiness, and looking forward to the future, he considers his weakness and the many temptations which beset him, and he fears that he may fall and become a prey to the enemy. A sense of sin and present evil, and his prevailing corruptions, compel him to pray, in fear and trembling, "Do not gather my soul with sinners." Reader, if you have prayed this prayer, and if your character is correctly described in the Psalm from which it is taken, you do not need to be afraid that you shall be gathered with sinners. Do you have the two virtues which David had — the outward walking in integrity, and the inward trusting in the Lord? Are you resting upon Christ's sacrifice, and can you come to the altar of God with humble hope? If so, rest assured, you never shall be gathered with the wicked, for that calamity is impossible. The gathering at the judgment is like to like. "Gather together first the tares, and bind them in bundles to burn them: but gather the wheat into my barn." If you are *like* God's people, then you shall be *with* God's people. You cannot be gathered with the wicked, for you are too dearly bought. Redeemed by the blood of Christ, you are his for ever, and where he is, there must his people be. You are loved too much to be cast away with reprobates. Shall one dear to Christ perish? Impossible! Hell cannot hold you! Heaven claims you! Trust in your Surety and do not fear!

September 22 — Morning

{Daily Reading: Amos 1:1–5:27} {Quick Study: Nahum 1:1–3:19}

Let Israel rejoice in him. *{Psalms 149:2}*

Be glad of heart, oh believer, but take care that your gladness has its spring *in the Lord*. You have many reasons for gladness in your God, for you can sing with David, "God, my exceeding joy." Be glad that the Lord reigns, that Jehovah is King! Rejoice that he sits upon the throne, and rules all things! Every attribute of God should become a fresh ray in the sunlight of our gladness. Since he is *wise,* that should make us glad, knowing as we do our own foolishness. Since he is *mighty*, that should cause us to rejoice who tremble at our weakness. Since he is *everlasting*, that should always be a theme of joy when we know that we wither as the grass. Since he is *unchanging*, that should perpetually yield us a song, since *we* change every hour. Since he is full of grace and is overflowing with it, he has given to us this grace in the covenant. It is ours to cleanse us, keep us, sanctify us, perfect us, and bring us to glory — all this should tend to make us glad in him. This gladness in God is like a deep river; we have only as yet touched its brink, we know a little of its clear sweet, heavenly streams, but onward the depth is greater, and the current more impetuous in its joy. The Christian feels that he may delight himself not only in what God is, but also in all that God *has done* in the past. The psalms show us that God's people in olden times were accustomed to think much of God's actions, and to have a song concerning each of them. So let God's people now rehearse the deeds of the Lord! Let them tell of his mighty acts, and "sing to the Lord, for he has triumphed gloriously." Nor let them ever cease to sing, for as new mercies flow to them day by day, so should their gladness in the Lord's loving acts in providence and in grace show itself in continued thanksgiving. Be glad, oh children of Zion, and rejoice in the Lord your God.

September 22 — Evening

*When my heart is overwhelmed: lead me to
the rock that is higher than I.* {Psalms 61:2}

Most of us know what it is to be overwhelmed in heart; emptied as when a man wipes a dish and turns it upside down; submerged and thrown on our beam ends like a vessel mastered by the storm. Discoveries of inward corruption will do this, if the Lord permits the great deep of our depravity to become troubled and cast up mire and dirt. Disappointments and heartbreaks will do this when billow after billow rolls over us, and we are like a broken shell hurled to and fro by the surf. Blessed be God; in such times we are not without an all-sufficient solace, our God is the harbour of weatherbeaten sails, the hospice of forlorn pilgrims. He is higher than we are, his mercy is higher than our sins, his love is higher than our thoughts. It is pitiful to see men putting their trust in something lower than themselves; but our confidence is fixed upon an exceedingly high and glorious Lord. He is a Rock since he does not change, and a high Rock, because the tempests which overwhelm us roll far beneath at his feet; he is not disturbed by them, but rules them at his will. If we get under the shelter of this lofty Rock we may defy the hurricane; all is calm under the lee of that towering cliff. Alas! Such is the confusion in which the troubled mind is often cast, that we need piloting to this divine shelter. Hence the prayer of the text. Oh, Lord, our God, by your Holy Spirit teach us the way of faith, lead us into your rest. The wind blows us out to sea, the helm does not answer to our puny hand; you and you alone can steer us over the bar between those sunken rocks, safe into the fair haven. How dependent we are upon you — we need you to bring us to you. To be wisely directed and steered into safety and peace is your gift, and yours alone. Tonight be pleased to deal well with your servants.

{Daily Reading: Amos 6:1–Obadiah 1:21} {Quick Study: Habakkuk 1:1–3:19}

Accepted in the Beloved. *{Ephesians 1:6}*

What a state of privilege! It includes our *justification* before God, but the term "acceptance" in the Greek means more than that. It signifies that we are the objects of *divine complacence*, indeed, even of *divine delight.* How marvellous that we, worms, mortals, sinners, should be the objects of divine love! But it is only *"in the Beloved."* Some Christians seem to be accepted in their own experience, at least, that is their apprehension. When their spirit is lively, and their hopes bright, they think God accepts them, for they feel so high, so heavenly minded, so drawn above the earth! But when their souls cleave to the dust, they are the victims of the fear that they are no longer accepted. If they could only see that all their high joys do not exalt them, and all their low despondencies do not really depress them in their Father's sight, but that they stand accepted in one who never alters, in one who is always the beloved of God, always perfect, always without spot or wrinkle, or any such thing, how much happier they would be, and how much more they would honour the Saviour! Rejoice then, believer, in this: you are accepted "in the Beloved." You look within, and you say, "There is nothing acceptable *here!*" But look at Christ, and see that everything is acceptable *there*. Your sins trouble you; but God has cast your sins behind his back, and you are accepted in the Righteous One. You have to fight with corruption, and to wrestle with temptation, but you are already accepted in him who has overcome the powers of evil. The devil tempts you; be of good cheer, he cannot destroy you, for you are accepted in him who has broken Satan's head. Know by full assurance your glorious standing. Even glorified souls are not more accepted than you are. They are only accepted in heaven "in the Beloved," and you are even now accepted in Christ after the same manner.

September 23 — Evening

Jesus said to him,
"If you can believe." {*Mark 9:23*}

Acertain man had a demoniac son who was afflicted with a dumb spirit. The father, having seen the futility of the endeavours of the disciples to heal his child, had little or no faith in Christ, and therefore, when he was bidden to bring his son to him, he said to Jesus, "If you can do anything, have compassion on us, and help us." Now there was an "if" in the question, but the poor trembling father had put the "if" in the wrong place: Jesus Christ, therefore, without commanding him to retract the "if," kindly puts it in its legitimate position. "No, truly," he seemed to say, "there should be no 'if' about my power, nor concerning my willingness, the 'if' lies somewhere else." "*If you can believe,* all things are possible to him who believes." The man's trust was strengthened, he offered a humble prayer for an increase of faith, and instantly Jesus spoke the word, and the demon was cast out, with an injunction never to return. There is a lesson here which we need to learn. We, like this man, often see that there is an "if" somewhere, but we are perpetually blundering by putting it in the wrong place. "*If*" Jesus can help me — "*if*" he can give me grace to overcome temptation — "*if*" he can give me pardon — "*if*" he can make me successful? No, "*if*" you can believe, he both can and will. You have misplaced your "if." If you can confidently trust, just as all things are possible for Christ, so shall all things be possible for you. Faith stands in God's power, and is robed in God's majesty; it wears the royal apparel, and rides on the King's horse, for it is the grace which the King delights to honour. Girding itself with the glorious might of the all-working Spirit, it becomes, in the omnipotence of God, mighty to do, to dare, and to suffer. All things, without limit, are possible to him who believes. My soul, can you believe your Lord tonight?

September 24 — Morning

{Daily Reading: Jonah 1:1–4:11} {Quick Study: Zephaniah 1:1–3:20}

For I was ashamed to require from the
king a band of soldiers and horsemen to help us
against the enemy in the way: because we had spoken
to the king, saying, "The hand of our God is upon all
those for good who seek him; but his power and his
wrath is against all those who forsake him." *{Ezra 8:22}*

A convoy on many accounts would have been desirable for the pilgrim band, but a holy shamefacedness would not allow Ezra to seek one. He feared lest the heathen king should think his professions of faith in God to be mere hypocrisy, or imagine that the God of Israel was not able to preserve his own worshippers. He could not bring his mind to lean on an arm of flesh in a matter so evidently of the Lord, and therefore the caravan set out with no visible protection, guarded by him who is the sword and shield of his people. It is to be feared that few believers feel this holy jealousy for God; even those who in a measure walk by faith, occasionally mar the lustre of their life by craving aid from man. It is a most blessed thing to have no props and no buttresses, but to stand upright on the Rock of Ages, upheld by the Lord alone. Would any believers seek state endowments for their church, if they remembered that the Lord is dishonoured by their asking for Caesar's aid? As if the Lord could not supply the needs of his own cause! Should we run so hastily to friends and relatives for assistance, if we remembered that the Lord is magnified by our implicit reliance upon his solitary arm? My soul, wait only upon God. "But," one says, "are not means to be used?" Assuredly they are; but our fault seldom lies in their neglect; far more frequently it springs out of foolishly believing in them instead of believing in God. Few run too far in neglecting the creature's arm; but very many sin greatly in making too much of it. Learn, dear reader, to glorify the Lord by leaving means untried, if by using them you would dishonour the name of the Lord.

September 24 — Evening

I sleep, but my heart
is awake. *{Song of Solomon 5:2}*

Paradoxes abound in Christian experience, and here is one — the spouse was asleep, and yet she was awake. He only can read the believer's riddle who has ploughed with the heifer of his experience. The two points in this evening's text are — a mournful sleepiness and a hopeful wakefulness. I *sleep*. Through sin that dwells in us we may become lax in holy duties, slothful in religious exercises, dull in spiritual joys, and altogether supine and careless. This is a shameful state for one in whom the quickening Spirit dwells; and it is dangerous to the highest degree. Even wise virgins sometimes slumber, but it is high time for all to shake off the bands of sloth. It is to be feared that many believers lose their strength as Samson lost his locks, while sleeping on the lap of carnal security. With a perishing world around us, to sleep is cruel; with eternity so near at hand, it is madness. Yet none of us are as much awake as we should be; a few thunder claps would do us all good, and it may be, unless we soon bestir ourselves, we shall have them in the form of war, or pestilence, or personal bereavements and losses. Oh that we may leave for ever the couch of fleshly ease, and go forth with flaming torches to meet the coming Bridegroom! *My heart awakens*. This is a happy sign. Life is not extinct, though sadly smothered. When our renewed heart struggles against our natural heaviness, we should be grateful to sovereign grace for keeping a little vitality within the body of this death. Jesus will hear our hearts, will help our hearts, will visit our hearts; for the voice of the wakeful heart is really the voice of our Beloved, saying, "Open to me." Holy zeal will surely unbar the door.

> Oh lovely attitude! He stands
> With melting heart and laden hands;
> My soul forsakes her every sin;
> And lets the heavenly stranger in.

Just, and the justifier of him
who believes. *{Romans 3:26}*

Being justified by faith, we have peace with God. Conscience accuses no longer. Judgment now decides for the sinner instead of against him. Memory looks back upon past sins, with deep sorrow for the sin, but yet with no dread of any penalty to come; for Christ has paid the debt of his people to the last jot and tittle, and received the divine receipt; and unless God can be so unjust as to demand double payment for one debt, no soul for whom Jesus died as a substitute can ever be cast into hell. It seems to be one of the very principles of our enlightened nature to believe that God is just; we feel that it must be so, and this gives us our terror at first; but is it not marvellous that this very same belief that God is just, becomes afterwards the pillar of our confidence and peace! If God is just, I, a sinner, alone and without a substitute, must be punished; but Jesus stands in my place and is punished for me; and now, if God is just, I, a sinner, standing in Christ, can never be punished. God must change his nature before one soul for whom Jesus was a substitute can ever by any possibility suffer the lash of the law. Therefore, Jesus having taken the place of the believer — having rendered a full equivalent to divine wrath for all that his people ought to have suffered as the result of sin, the believer can shout with glorious triumph, "Who shall lay anything to the charge of God's elect?" Not God, for he has justified; not Christ, for he has died, "yes rather has risen again." My hope does not live because I am not a sinner, but because I am a sinner for whom Christ died; my trust is not that I am holy, but that being unholy, *he* is my righteousness. My faith does not rest upon what I am, or shall be, or feel, or know, but in what Christ is, in what he has done, and in what he is now doing for me. On the lion of justice the fair maid of hope rides like a queen.

September 25 — Evening

Who is made to us wisdom by God. *{1 Corinthians 1:30}*

Man's intellect seeks after rest, and by nature seeks it apart from the Lord Jesus Christ. Men of education are apt, even when converted, to look upon the simplicities of the cross of Christ with too little reverent and loving an eye. They are snared in the old net in which the Greeks were taken, and have a hankering to mix philosophy with revelation. The temptation with a man of refined thought and high education is to depart from the simple truth of Christ crucified, and to invent, as the term is, a more *intellectual* doctrine. This led the early Christian churches into Gnosticism, and bewitched them with all sorts of heresies. This is the root of Neology, and the other fine things which in days gone by were so fashionable in Germany, and are now so ensnaring to certain classes of divines. Whoever you are, good reader, and whatever your education may be, if you are the Lord's, be assured you will find no rest in philosophizing divinity. You may receive this dogma from one great thinker, or that dream from another profound reasoner, but what the chaff is to the wheat, that will these be to the pure Word of God. All that reason, when best guided, can find out is only the A B C of truth, and even that lacks certainty, while in Christ Jesus there is treasured up all the fulness of wisdom and knowledge. All attempts on the part of Christians to be content with systems such as Unitarian and Broad Church thinkers would approve of, must fail; true heirs of heaven must come back to the grand simple reality which makes the plough boy's eye flash with joy, and gladdens the pious pauper's heart — "Jesus Christ came into the world to save sinners." Jesus satisfies the most elevated intellect when he is believingly received, but apart from him the mind of the regenerate finds no rest. "The fear of the Lord is the beginning of knowledge." "All those who do his commandments have a good understanding."

The myrtle trees that were in the valley. *{Zechariah 1:8}*

The vision in this chapter describes the condition of Israel in Zechariah's day; but being interpreted in its aspect towards *us*, it describes the church of God as we find it now in the world. The church is compared to a myrtle grove flourishing in a valley. It is *hidden*, unobserved, secreted; courting no honour and attracting no observation from the careless gazer. The church, like her Head, has a glory, but it is concealed from carnal eyes, for the time of her breaking forth in all her splendour is not yet come. The idea of *tranquil security* is also suggested to us: for the myrtle grove in the valley is still and calm, while the storm sweeps over the mountain summits. Tempests spend their force upon the craggy peaks of the Alps, but down where the stream flows which makes the city of our God glad, the myrtles flourish by the still waters, all unshaken by the impetuous wind. How great is the inward tranquillity of God's church! Even when opposed and persecuted, she has a peace which the world does not give, and which, therefore, it cannot take away: the peace of God which passes all understanding keeps the hearts and minds of God's people. Does the metaphor not forcibly picture the peaceful, *perpetual growth* of the saints? The myrtle does not shed her leaves, she is always green; and the church in her worst time still has a blessed verdure of grace about her; indeed, she has sometimes exhibited *most* verdure when her winter has been harshest. She has prospered most when her adversities have been most severe. Hence the text *hints at victory*. The myrtle is the emblem of peace, and a significant token of *triumph*. The brows of conquerors were bound with myrtle and with laurel; and is not the church always victorious? Is not every Christian more than a conqueror through him who loved him? Living in peace, do not the saints fall asleep in the arms of victory?

September 26 — Evening

*Howl, fir tree, for the cedar
is fallen. {Zechariah 11:2}*

When in the forest there is heard the crash of a falling oak, it is a sign that the woodman is abroad, and every tree in the whole company may tremble lest tomorrow the sharp edge of the axe should find it out. We are all like trees marked for the axe, and the fall of one should remind us that for everyone, whether great as the cedar, or humble as the fir, the appointed hour is stealing on apace. I trust we do not, by often hearing of death, become callous to it. May we never be like the birds in the steeple, which build their nests when the bells are tolling, and sleep quietly when the solemn funeral peals are startling the air. May we regard death as the most weighty of all events, and be sobered by its approach. It ill behooves us to sport while our eternal destiny hangs on a thread. The sword is out of its scabbard — let us not trifle; it is furbished, and the edge is sharp — let us not play with it. He who does not prepare for death is more than an ordinary fool, he is a madman. When the voice of God is heard among the trees of the garden, let fig tree and sycamore and elm and cedar alike hear the sound of it.

Be ready, servant of Christ, for your Master comes suddenly, when an ungodly world least expects him. See to it that you are faithful in his work, for the grave shall soon be dug for you. Be ready, parents, see that your children are brought up in the fear of God, for they must soon be orphans; be ready, men of business, take care that your affairs are correct, and that you serve God with all your hearts, for the days of your terrestrial service will soon be ended, and you will be called to give an account for the deeds done in the body, whether they are good or whether they are evil. May we all prepare for the tribunal of the great King with a care which shall be rewarded with the gracious commendation, "Well done, good and faithful servant."

September 27 — Morning

{Daily Reading: Zephaniah 1:1–Haggai 2:23} {Quick Study: Zechariah 5:1–8:23}

**Happy are you, oh Israel; who is like you,
oh people saved by the Lord!** *{Deuteronomy 33:29}*

He who affirms that Christianity makes men miserable, is himself an utter stranger to it. It would be strange indeed, if it made us wretched, for see *to what a position it exalts us!* It makes us sons of God. Do you suppose that God will give all the happiness to his enemies, and reserve all the mourning for his own family? Shall his foes have mirth and joy, and shall his homeborn children inherit sorrow and wretchedness? Shall the sinner, who has no part in Christ, call himself rich in happiness, and shall we go mourning as if we were penniless beggars? No, we will rejoice in the Lord always, and glory in our inheritance, for we "have not received the spirit of bondage again to fear; but we have received the spirit of adoption, by which we cry, 'Abba, Father.' " The rod of chastisement must rest upon us in our measure, but it works for us the comforting fruits of righteousness; and therefore by the aid of the divine Comforter, we, the "people saved by the Lord," will joy in the God of our salvation. We are married to Christ; and shall our great Bridegroom permit his spouse to linger in constant grief? Our hearts are knit to him: we are his members, and although for a while we may suffer as our Head once suffered, yet we are even now blessed with heavenly blessings in him. We have the pledge of our inheritance in the comforts of the Spirit, which are neither few nor small. Heirs of joy for ever, we have foretastes of our portion. There are streaks of the light of joy to herald our eternal sunrising. Our riches are beyond the sea; our city with firm foundations lies on the other side of the river; gleams of glory from the spirit world cheer our hearts, and urge us onward. Truly it is said of us, "Happy are you, oh Israel; who is like you, oh people saved by the Lord?"

September 27 — Evening

My beloved put in his hand by the hole of the door,
and my heart was moved for him. *{Song of Solomon 5:4}*

Knocking was not enough, for my heart was too full of sleep, too cold and ungrateful to arise and open the door, but the touch of his effectual grace has made my soul bestir itself. Oh, the longsuffering of my Beloved, to tarry when he found himself shut out, and me asleep upon the bed of sloth! Oh, the greatness of his patience, to knock and knock again, and to add his voice to his knockings, beseeching me to open to him! How could I have refused him! Base heart, blush and be confounded! But what greatest kindness of all is this, that he becomes his own porter and unbars the door himself. Thrice blessed is the hand which condescends to lift the latch and turn the key. Now I see that nothing but my Lord's own power can save such a naughty mass of wickedness as I am; ordinances fail, even the gospel has no effect upon me, until his hand is stretched out. Now, also, I perceive that his hand is good where all else is unsuccessful, he can open when nothing else will. Blessed be his name, I feel his gracious presence even now. Well may my heart move for him, when I think of all that he has suffered for me, and of my ungenerous return. I have allowed my affections to wander. I have set up rivals. I have grieved him. Sweetest and dearest of all beloveds, I have treated you as an unfaithful wife treats her husband. Oh, my cruel sins, my cruel self. What can I do? Tears are a poor show of my repentance, my whole heart boils with indignation at myself. Wretch that I am, to treat my Lord, my All in All, my exceedingly great joy, as though he were a stranger. Jesus, you forgive freely, but this is not enough, prevent my unfaithfulness in the future. Kiss away these tears, and then purge my heart and bind it with sevenfold cords to yourself, never to wander any more.

September 28 — Morning

{Daily Reading: Zechariah 1:1–7:14} {Quick Study: Zechariah 9:1–11:17}

The Lord looks from heaven;
he sees all the sons of men. *{Psalms 33:13}*

Perhaps no figure of speech represents God in a more gracious light than when he is spoken of as stooping from his throne, and coming down from heaven to attend to the needs and to behold the woes of mankind. We love him, who, when Sodom and Gomorrah were full of iniquity, would not destroy those cities until he had made a personal visit to them. We cannot help pouring out our heart in affection for our Lord who inclines his ear from the highest glory, and puts it to the lip of the dying sinner, whose failing heart longs after reconciliation. How can we not love him when we know that he numbers the very hairs of our heads, marks our path, and orders our ways? This great truth is especially brought near to our heart, when we remember how attentive he is, not merely to the temporal interests of his creatures, but to their spiritual concerns. Although leagues of distance lie between the finite creature and the infinite Creator, still there are links uniting both. When you weep a tear, do not think that God does not see; for, "Just as a father pities his children, so the Lord pities those who fear him." Your sigh is able to move the heart of Jehovah; your whisper can incline his ear to you; your prayer can restrain his hand; your faith can move his arm. Do not think that God sits on high taking no account of you. Remember that however poor and needy you are, still the Lord thinks about you. For the eyes of the Lord run to and fro throughout the whole earth, to show himself strong on behalf of those whose hearts are perfect towards him.

> Oh! Then repeat the truth that never tires;
> No God is like the God my soul desires;
> He at whose voice heaven trembles, even he,
> *Great as he is, knows how to stoop to me.*

September 28 — Evening

Go again seven times. *{1 Kings 18:43}*

Success is certain when the Lord has promised it. Although you may have pleaded month after month without any evidence of an answer, it is not possible that the Lord should be deaf when his people are earnest in a matter which concerns his glory. The prophet on the top of Carmel continued to wrestle with God, and never for a moment gave way to a fear that he should be denied his request in Jehovah's courts. Six times the servant returned, but on each occasion no word was spoken but "Go again." We must not dream of unbelief, but hold to our faith even to seventy times seven. Faith sends expectant hope to look from Carmel's brow, and if nothing is seen, she sends again and again. So far from being crushed by repeated disappointment, faith is motivated to plead more fervently with her God. She is humbled, but not abashed: her groans are deeper, and her sighings more vehement, but she never relaxes her hold or restrains her hand. It would be more agreeable to flesh and blood to have a speedy answer, but believing souls have learned to be submissive, and to find it good to wait *for* as well as *upon* the Lord. Delayed answers often set the heart searching itself, and so lead to contrition and spiritual reformation: deadly blows are thus struck at our corruption, and the chambers of imagery are cleansed. The great danger is lest men should faint, and miss the blessing. Reader, do not fall into that sin, but continue in prayer and watching. At last the little cloud was seen, the sure forerunner of torrents of rain, and even so with you, the token for good shall surely be given, and you shall rise as a prevailing prince to enjoy the mercy you have sought. Elijah was a man of like passions with us: his power with God did not lie in his own merits. If his believing prayer availed so much, why not yours? Plead the precious blood with unceasing importunity, and it shall be with you according to your desire.

September 29 — Morning

{Daily Reading: Zechariah 8:1–14:21} {Quick Study: Zechariah 12:1–14:21}

Behold, if the leprosy has covered all his flesh, he shall pronounce him clean who has the plague. *{Leviticus 13:13}*

This regulation appears strange enough, yet there was wisdom in it, for the throwing out of the disease proved that the constitution was sound. This morning it may be well for us to see the typical teaching of so singular a rule. We, too, are lepers, and may read the law of the leper as applicable to ourselves. When a man sees himself to be altogether lost and ruined, covered all over with the defilement of sin, and no part free from pollution; when he disclaims all righteousness of his own, and pleads guilty before the Lord, then he is clean through the blood of Jesus, and the grace of God. Hidden, unfelt, unconfessed iniquity is the true leprosy, but when sin is seen and felt it has received its death blow, and the Lord looks with eyes of mercy upon the soul afflicted with it. Nothing is more deadly than self-righteousness, or more hopeful than contrition. We must confess that we are "nothing else but sin," for no confession short of this will be the whole truth, and if the Holy Spirit is at work in us, convicting us of sin, there will be no difficulty about making such an acknowledgment — it will spring spontaneously from our lips. What comfort does the text afford to those under a deep sense of sin! Sin mourned and confessed, however black and foul, shall never shut a man out from the Lord Jesus. Whoever comes to him, he will in no wise cast out. Although dishonest as the thief, although unchaste as the woman who was a sinner, though fierce as Saul of Tarsus, although cruel as Manasseh, although rebellious as the prodigal, the great heart of love will look upon the man who feels himself to have no soundness in him, and will pronounce him clean, when he trusts in Jesus crucified. Come to him, then, poor heavy laden sinner,

> Come needy, come guilty, come loathsome and bare;
> You cannot come too filthy — come just as you are.

September 29 — Evening

*I found him whom my soul loves: I held him,
and would not let him go. {Song of Solomon 3:4}*

Does Christ receive us when we come to him, notwithstanding all our past sinfulness? Does he never chide us for having tried all other refuges first? And is there no one on earth like him? Is he the best of all the good, the fairest of all the fair? Oh, then let us praise him! Daughters of Jerusalem, extol him with timbrel and harp! Down with your idols, up with the Lord Jesus. Now let the standards of pomp and pride be trampled underfoot, but let the cross of Jesus, which the world frowns and scoffs at, be lifted on high. Oh, for a throne of ivory for our King Solomon! Let him be set on high for ever, and let my soul sit at his footstool, and kiss his feet, and wash them with my tears. Oh, how precious is Christ! How can it be that I have thought so little of him? How is it that I can go elsewhere for joy or comfort when he is so full, so rich, so satisfying. Fellow believer, make a covenant with your heart so that you will never depart from him, and ask your Lord to ratify it. Bid him to set you as a signet upon his finger, and as a bracelet upon his arm. Ask him to bind you to him, as the bride decks herself with ornaments, and as the bridegroom puts on his jewels. I would live in Christ's heart; my soul would eternally abide in the clefts of that rock. The sparrow has made a house, and the swallow a nest for herself where she may lay her young, even your altars, oh Lord of hosts, my King and my God; and so too would I make my nest, my home, in you, and may the soul of your turtledove never go forth from you again, but may I nestle close to you, oh Jesus, my true and only rest.

> When my precious Lord I find,
> All my ardent passions glow;
> Him with cords of love I bind,
> Hold and will not let him go.

September 30 — Morning

{Daily Reading: Malachi 1:1–4:6} {Quick Study: Malachi 1:1–4:6}

Sing out the honour of his name,
make his praise glorious. *{Psalms 66:2}*

It is not left to our own option whether we shall praise God or not. Praise is God's most righteous due, and every Christian, as the recipient of his grace, is bound to praise God from day to day. It is true we have no authoritative rubric for daily praise; we have no commandment prescribing certain hours of song and thanksgiving: but the law written upon the heart teaches us that it is right to praise God; and the unwritten mandate comes to us with as much force as if it had been recorded on the tables of stone, or handed to us from the top of thundering Sinai. Yes, it is the Christian's *duty* to praise God. It is not only a pleasurable exercise, but it is the absolute obligation of his life. Do not think, you who are always mourning, that you are guiltless in this respect, or imagine that you can discharge your duty to your God without songs of praise. You are bound by the bonds of his love to bless his name as long as you live, and his praise should continually be in your mouth, for you are blessed, in order that you may bless him; "I have formed this people for myself, they shall show forth my praise"; and if you do not praise God, you are not bringing forth the fruit which he, as the Divine Husbandman, has a right to expect from your hands. Do not let your harp then hang upon the willows, but take it down, and strive, with a grateful heart, to bring forth its loudest music. Arise and chant his praise. With every morning's dawn, lift up your notes of thanksgiving, and let every setting sun be followed with your song. Girdle the earth with your praises; surround it with an atmosphere of melody, and God himself will listen from heaven and accept your music.

Even so I love you, and will love, and in your praise will sing,
Because you are my loving God, and my redeeming King.

September 30 — Evening

A living dog is better than
a dead lion. *{Ecclesiastes 9:4}*

Life is a precious thing, and in its humblest form it is superior to death. This truth is eminently certain in spiritual things. It is better to be the least in the kingdom of heaven than the greatest out of it. The lowest degree of grace is superior to the noblest development of unregenerate nature. Where the Holy Spirit implants divine life in the soul, there is a precious deposit which none of the refinements of education can equal. The thief on the cross excels Caesar on his throne; Lazarus among the dogs is better than Cicero among the senators; and the most unlettered Christian is in the sight of God superior to Plato. Life is the badge of nobility in the realm of spiritual things, and men without it are only coarser or finer specimens of the same lifeless material, needing to be quickened, for they are dead in trespasses and sins.

A living, loving, gospel sermon, however unlearned in matter and uncouth in style, is better than the finest discourse devoid of unction and power. A living dog keeps better watch than a dead lion, and is of more service to his master; and so the poorest spiritual preacher is infinitely to be preferred to the exquisite orator who has no wisdom except that of words, no energy except that of sound. The same holds true for our prayers and other religious exercises; if we are quickened in them by the Holy Spirit, they are acceptable to God through Jesus Christ, though we may think them to be worthless things; while our grand performances in which our hearts were absent, like dead lions, are mere carrion in the sight of the living God. Oh, for living groans, living sighs, living despondencies, rather than lifeless songs and dead calms. Anything is better than death. The snarlings of the dog of hell will at least keep us awake, but dead faith and dead profession, what greater curses can a man have? Quicken us, quicken us, oh Lord!

October 1 — Morning

{Daily Reading: Matthew 1:1–4:25} {Quick Study: Matthew 1:1–4:25}

**Pleasant fruits, new and old, which I have laid up
for you, oh my beloved.** *{Song of Solomon 7:13}*

The spouse desires to give to Jesus all that she produces. Our heart has "all manner of pleasant fruits," both "old and new," and they are laid up for our Beloved. At this rich autumnal season of fruit, let us survey our stores. We have *new* fruits. We desire to feel new life, new joy, new gratitude; we wish to make new resolves and carry them out by new labours; our heart blossoms with new prayers, and our soul is pledging herself to new efforts. But we have some *old* fruits, too. There is our first love: a choice fruit is that! And Jesus delights in it. There is our first faith: that simple faith by which, having nothing, we became possessors of all things. There is our joy when first we knew the Lord: let us revive it. We have our old remembrances of the promises. How faithful God has been! In sickness, how softly he made our bed! In deep waters, how placidly he buoyed us up! In the flaming furnace, how graciously he delivered us. Old fruits, indeed! We have many of them, for his mercies have been more than the hairs of our head. Old sins we must regret, but then we have had repentances which he has given to us, by which we have wept our way to the cross, and learned the merit of his blood. We have fruits, this morning, both new and old; but here is the point — *they are all laid up for Jesus*. Truly, those are the best and most acceptable services in which Jesus is the solitary aim of the soul, and his glory, without any admixture whatever, the end of all our efforts. Let our many fruits be laid up only for our Beloved; let us display them when he is with us, and not hold them up before the gaze of men. Jesus, we will turn the key in our garden door, and no one shall enter to rob you of one good fruit from the soil which you have watered with your bloody sweat. Our all shall be yours, yours only, oh Jesus, our Beloved!

October 1 — Evening

He will give grace and glory. *{Psalms 84:11}*

Jehovah is bounteous in his nature; to give is his delight. His gifts are precious beyond measure, and are as freely given as the light of the sun. He gives grace to his elect because he wills it, to his redeemed because of his covenant, to the called because of his promise, to believers because they seek it, to sinners because they need it. He gives grace abundantly, seasonably, constantly, readily, sovereignly; doubly enhancing the value of the boon by the manner of its bestowal. Grace in all its forms he freely renders to his people: comforting, preserving, sanctifying, directing, instructing, assisting grace, he generously pours into their souls without ceasing, and he always will do so, whatever may occur. Sickness may befall us, but the Lord will give grace; poverty may happen to us, but grace will surely be afforded; death must come but grace will light a candle at the darkest hour. Reader, how blessed it is as years roll around, and the leaves begin again to fall, to enjoy such an unfading promise as this, "The Lord will give grace."

The little conjunction *and* in this verse is a diamond rivet binding the present with the future: grace and glory always go together. God has married them, and no one can divorce them. The Lord will never deny a soul glory to whom he has freely given to live upon his grace; indeed, glory is nothing more than grace in its Sunday dress, grace in full bloom, grace like autumn fruit, mellow and perfected. How soon we may have glory no one can tell! It may be before this month of October has run out we shall see the Holy City; but whether the interval is longer or shorter, we shall be glorified before long. Glory, the glory of heaven, the glory of eternity, the glory of Jesus, the glory of the Father, the Lord will surely give to his chosen. Oh, rare promise of a faithful God!

Two golden links of one celestial chain:
Who owns grace shall surely glory gain.

October 2 — Morning

{Daily Reading: Matthew 5:1–6:34} {Quick Study: Matthew 5:1–7:29}

The hope which is laid up for you in heaven. *{Colossians 1:5}*

Our hope in Christ for the future is the mainspring and the mainstay of our joy here. It will animate our hearts to think often of heaven, for all that we can desire is promised there. Here we are weary and toilworn, but over there is the land of *rest* where the sweat of labour shall no more bedew the worker's brow, and fatigue shall be for ever banished. To those who are weary and spent, the word "rest" is full of heaven. We are always in the field of battle; we are so tempted within, and so molested by foes without, that we have little or no peace; but in heaven we shall enjoy the *victory*, when the banner shall be waved aloft in triumph, and the sword shall be sheathed, and we shall hear our Captain say, "Well done, good and faithful servant." We have suffered bereavement after bereavement, but we are going to the land of the *immortal* where graves are unknown things. Here sin is a constant grief to us, but there we shall be perfectly *holy*, for by no means shall anything enter into that kingdom which defiles. Hemlock does not spring up in the furrows of celestial fields. Oh! Is it not joy, that you are not to be in banishment for ever, that you are not to be eternally in this wilderness, but shall soon inherit Canaan? Nevertheless, let it never be said of us that we are dreaming about the *future* and forgetting the *present*, let the future sanctify the present to highest uses. Through the Spirit of God the hope of heaven is the most potent force for the product of virtue; it is a fountain of joyous effort, it is the corner stone of cheerful holiness. The man who has this hope in him goes about his work with vigour, for the joy of the Lord is his strength. He fights against temptation with ardour, for the hope of the next world repels the fiery darts of the adversary. He can labour without present reward, for he looks for a reward in the world to come.

October 2 — Evening

A man greatly beloved. *{Daniel 10:11}*

Child of God, do you hesitate to appropriate this title? Ah! Has your unbelief made you forget that *you* are greatly beloved, too? Must you not have been greatly beloved, to have been bought with the precious blood of Christ, as a lamb without blemish and without spot? When God struck his only begotten Son for you, what was this but being greatly beloved? You lived in sin, and rioted in it, must you not have been greatly beloved for God to have borne so patiently with you? You were called by grace and led to a Saviour, and made a child of God and an heir of heaven. All this proves, does it not, a very great and superabounding love? Since that time, whether your path has been rough with troubles, or smooth with mercies, it has been full of proofs that you are a man greatly beloved. If the Lord has chastened you, yet not in anger; if he has made you poor, yet in grace you have been rich. The more unworthy you feel yourself to be, the more evidence you have that nothing except unspeakable love could have led the Lord Jesus to save such a soul as yours. The more demerit you feel, the clearer is the display of the abounding love of God in having chosen you, and called you, and made you an heir of bliss. Now, if there is such love between God and us let us live in the influence and sweetness of it, and use the privilege of our position. Do not let us approach our Lord as though we were strangers, or as though he were unwilling to hear us — for we are greatly beloved by our loving Father. "He who did not spare his own Son, but delivered him up for us all, how shall he not with him also freely give us all things?" Come boldly, oh believer, for despite the whisperings of Satan and the doubtings of your own heart, you are greatly beloved. Meditate on the exceeding greatness and faithfulness of divine love this evening, and so go to your bed in peace.

October 3 — Morning

{Daily Reading: Matthew 7:1–9:38} {Quick Study: Matthew 8:1–11:30}

Are they not all ministering spirits, sent forth to minister for those who shall be heirs of salvation? *{Hebrews 1:14}*

Angels are the unseen attendants of the saints of God; they bear us up in their hands, lest we dash our foot against a stone. Loyalty to their Lord leads them to take a deep interest in the children of his love; they rejoice over the return of the prodigal to his father's house below, and they welcome the advent of the believer to the King's palace above. In olden times the sons of God were favoured with their visible appearance, and to this day, although unseen by us, heaven is still opened, and the angels of God ascend and descend upon the Son of man, so that they may visit the heirs of salvation. Seraphim still fly with live coals from off the altar to touch the lips of men greatly beloved. If our eyes could be opened, we would see horses of fire and chariots of fire around the servants of the Lord; for we have come to an innumerable company of angels, who are all watchers and protectors of the royal seed. Spenser's line is no poetic fiction, where he sings —

> How oft do they with golden pinions cleave
> The flitting skies, like flying pursuivant
> Against foul fiends to aid us militant!

To what dignity are the chosen elevated when the brilliant courtiers of heaven become their willing servants! Into what communion we are raised since we have fellowship with spotless celestials! How well we are defended since all the twenty thousand chariots of God are armed for our deliverance! To whom do we owe all this? Let the Lord Jesus Christ be for ever endeared to us, for through him we are made to sit in heavenly places far above principalities and powers. His camp is all around those who fear him; he is the true Michael whose foot is upon the dragon. All hail, Jesus! You angel of Jehovah's presence, to you this family offers its morning vows.

October 3 — Evening

He himself has suffered
being tempted. *{Hebrews 2:18}*

It is a commonplace thought, and yet it tastes like nectar to the weary heart — Jesus was tempted as I am. You have heard that truth many times: have you grasped it? He was tempted with the very same sins into which we fall. Do not disassociate Jesus from our common manhood. It is a dark room which you are going through, but Jesus went through it before. It is a sharp fight which you are waging, but Jesus has stood foot to foot with the same enemy. Let us be of good cheer, Christ has borne the load before us, and the blood stained footsteps of the King of glory may be seen along the road which we travel at this hour. There is something sweeter yet — Jesus was tempted, but Jesus never sinned. Then, my soul, it is not needful for you to sin, for Jesus was a man, and if one man endured these temptations and did not sin, then in his power his members may also cease from sin. Some beginners in the divine life think that they cannot be tempted without sinning, but they are mistaken; there is no sin in *being tempted*, but there *is* sin in *yielding to temptation*. Herein is comfort for the severely tempted ones. There is still more to encourage them if they reflect that the Lord Jesus, though tempted, gloriously triumphed, and just as he overcame, so surely shall his followers also, for Jesus is the representative man for his people; the Head has triumphed, and the members share in the victory. Fears are needless, for Christ is with us, armed for our defence. Our place of safety is the bosom of the Saviour. Perhaps we are tempted just now, in order to drive us nearer to him. Blessed is any wind that blows us into the port of our Saviour's love! Happy wounds, which make us seek the beloved Physician. You tempted ones, come to your tempted Saviour, for he can be touched with the feeling of your infirmities, and will help every tried and tempted one.

October 4 — Morning

{Daily Reading: Matthew 10:1–11:30} {Quick Study: Matthew 12:1–13:58}

At evening time it shall be light. *{Zechariah 14:7}*

Oftentimes we look forward with forebodings to the *time of old age*, forgetful that at eventide it shall be light. To many saints, old age is the choicest season in their lives. A balmier air fans the mariner's cheek as he nears the shore of immortality, fewer waves ruffle his sea, quiet reigns, deep, still, and solemn. From the altar of age the flashes of the fire of youth are gone, but the more real flame of earnest feeling remains. The pilgrims have reached the land Beulah, that happy country, whose days are as the days of heaven upon earth. Angels visit it, celestial breezes blow over it, flowers of paradise grow in it, and the air is filled with seraphic music. Some dwell here for years, and others come to it only a few hours before their departure, but it is an Eden on earth. We may well long for the time when we shall recline in its shady groves and be satisfied with hope until the time of fruition comes. The setting sun seems larger than when aloft in the sky, and a splendour of glory tinges all the clouds which surround its going down. Pain does not break the calm of the sweet twilight of age, for strength made perfect in weakness bears up with patience under it all. Ripe fruits of choice experience are gathered as the rare repast of life's evening, and the soul prepares itself for rest.

The Lord's people shall also enjoy light *in the hour of death*. Unbelief laments; the shadows fall, the night is coming, existence is ending. "Ah no," cries faith, "the night is far spent, the true day is at hand." Light is come, the light of immortality, the light of a Father's countenance. Gather up your feet into the bed, see the waiting bands of spirits! Angels waft you away. Farewell, beloved one, you are gone, you wave your hand. Ah, now it is light. The pearly gates are open, the golden streets shine in the jasper light. We cover our eyes, but you behold the unseen; adieu, brother, you have light at eventide, such as we do not yet have.

October 4 — Evening

If any man sins, we have an advocate with the Father, Jesus Christ the righteous. *{1 John 2:1}*

"If any man sins, we *have* an advocate." Yes, although we sin, we still have him. John does not say, "If any man sins he has forfeited his advocate," but "we *have* an advocate," sinners though we are. All the sin that a believer ever did, or can be allowed to commit, cannot destroy his interest in the Lord Jesus Christ, as his advocate. The name here given to our Lord is suggestive. *"Jesus."* Ah! Then he is an advocate such as we need, for Jesus is the name of one whose business and delight it is to save. "They shall call his name Jesus, for *he shall save* his people from their sins." His sweetest name implies his success. Next, it is "Jesus *Christ*" — Christos, the anointed. This shows *his authority* to plead. The Christ has a right to plead, for he is the Father's own appointed advocate and elected priest. If he were of our choosing he might fail, but if God has laid help upon one who is mighty, we may safely lay our trouble where God has laid his help. He is Christ, and therefore authorized; he is Christ, and therefore *qualified*, for the anointing has fully fitted him for his work. He can plead so as to move the heart of God and prevail. What words of tenderness, what sentences of persuasion will the anointed use when he stands up to plead for me! One more letter of his name remains, "Jesus Christ *the righteous.*" This is not only his character BUT his plea. It is his character, and if the Righteous One is my advocate, then my cause is good, or he would not have espoused it. It is his plea, for he meets the charge of unrighteousness against me by the plea that *he* is righteous. He declares himself my substitute and puts his obedience to my account. My soul, you have a friend well fitted to be your advocate, he can only succeed; leave yourself entirely in his hands.

October 5 — Morning

{Daily Reading: Matthew 12:1–12:50} {Quick Study: Matthew 14:1–16:28}

**He arose, and ate and drank, and went in the strength
of that food forty days and forty nights.** *{1 Kings 19:8}*

All the strength supplied to us by our gracious God is meant for service, not for wantonness or boasting. When the prophet Elijah found the cake baked on the coals, and the cruse of water placed at his head, as he lay under the juniper tree, he was no gentleman to be gratified with dainty fare so that he might stretch himself at his ease; far otherwise, he was commissioned to go forty days and forty nights in the strength of it, journeying towards Horeb, the mount of God. When the Master invited the disciples to "Come and dine" with him, after the feast was concluded he said to Peter, "Feed my sheep"; further adding, "Follow me." Even thus it is with us; we eat the bread of heaven, so that we may expend our strength in the Master's service. We come to the passover, and eat the paschal lamb with loins girded, and staff in hand, so as to start off at once when we have satisfied our hunger. Some Christians are for living *on* Christ, but are not so anxious to live *for* Christ. Earth should be a preparation for heaven; and heaven is the place where saints feast most and work most. They sit down at the table of our Lord, and they serve him day and night in his temple. They eat heavenly food and render perfect service. Believer, in the strength you daily gain from Christ, labour for him. Some of us have yet to learn much concerning the purpose of our Lord in giving us his grace. We are not to retain the precious grains of truth as the Egyptian mummy held the wheat for ages, without giving it an opportunity to grow: we must sow and water it. Why does the Lord send down the rain upon the thirsty earth, and give the genial sunshine? Is it not so that these may all help the fruits of the earth to yield food for man? Even so, the Lord feeds and refreshes our souls so that we may afterwards use our renewed strength in the promotion of his glory.

October 5 — Evening

**He who believes and is baptized
shall be saved.** *{Mark 16:16}*

Mr. MacDonald asked the inhabitants of the island of St. Kilda how a man must be saved. An old man replied, "We shall be saved if we repent, and forsake our sins, and turn to God." "Yes," said a middle aged female, "and with a true heart, too." "Indeed," rejoined a third, "and with prayer"; and, a fourth added, "It must be the prayer of the heart." "And we must be diligent, too," said a fifth, "in keeping the commandments." Thus, each having contributed his mite, feeling that a very decent creed had been made up, they all looked and listened for the preacher's approbation, but they had aroused his deepest pity. The carnal mind always maps out for itself a way in which self can work and become great, but the Lord's way is quite the reverse. Believing and being baptized are no matters of merit to be gloried in — they are so simple that boasting is excluded, and free grace bears the palm branch. It may be that the reader is unsaved — what is the reason? Do you think the way of salvation as laid down in the text to be dubious? How can that be when God has pledged his own word for its certainty? Do you think it is too easy? Why, then, do you not attend to it? Its ease leaves those without excuse who neglect it. To believe is simply to trust, to depend, to rely upon Christ Jesus. To be baptized is to submit to the ordinance which our Lord fulfilled at Jordan, to which the converted ones submitted at Pentecost, to which the jailer yielded obedience the very night of his conversion. The outward sign does not save, but it represents our death, burial, and resurrection with Jesus, and, like the Lord's Supper, is not to be neglected. Reader, do you believe in Jesus? Then, dear friend, dismiss your fears, you shall be saved. Are you still an unbeliever, then remember there is only one door, and if you will not enter by it you will perish in your sins.

October 6 — Morning

{Daily Reading: Matthew 13:1–14:36} {Quick Study: Matthew 17:1–20:34}

Whoever drinks of the water that I shall give him shall never thirst. *{John 4:14}*

He who is a believer in Jesus finds enough in his Lord to satisfy him now, and to make him content for evermore. The believer is not the man whose days are weary for lack of comfort, and whose nights are long from absence of heart cheering thought, for he finds in religion such a spring of joy, such a fountain of consolation, that he is content and happy. Put him in a dungeon and he will find good company; place him in a barren wilderness, he will eat the bread of heaven; drive him away from friendship, he will meet the "friend that sticks closer than a brother." Blast all his gourds, and he will find shadow beneath the Rock of Ages; sap the foundation of his earthly hopes, but his heart will still be fixed, trusting in the Lord. The heart is as insatiable as the grave until Jesus enters it, and then it is a cup full to overflowing. There is such a fulness in Christ that he alone is the believer's all. The true saint is so completely satisfied with the all-sufficiency of Jesus that he thirsts no more — except it is for deeper draughts of the living fountain. In that sweet manner, believer, you shall thirst; it shall not be a thirst of pain, but of loving desire; you will find it a sweet thing to be panting after a fuller enjoyment of Jesus' love. One in days of yore said, "I have been sinking my bucket down into the well very often, but now my thirst after Jesus has become so insatiable, that I long to put the well itself to my lips, and drink right on." Is this the feeling of your heart now, believer? Do you feel that all your desires are satisfied in Jesus, and that you have no need now, but to know more of him, and to have closer fellowship with him? Then come continually to the fountain, and take from the water of life freely. Jesus will never think you take too much, but will always welcome you, saying, "Drink, yes, drink abundantly, oh beloved."

October 6 — Evening

He had married an
Ethiopian woman. *{Numbers 12:1}*

What a strange choice for Moses, but how much more strange the choice of him who is a prophet like Moses, and greater than he was! Our Lord, who is as fair as the lily, has entered into marriage union with one who confesses herself to be black, because the sun has looked upon her. It is the wonder of angels that the love of Jesus should be set upon poor, lost, guilty men. Each believer must, when filled with a sense of Jesus' love, be also overwhelmed with astonishment that such love should be lavished on an object so utterly unworthy of it. Knowing as we do our secret guiltiness, unfaithfulness, and black-heartedness, we are dissolved in grateful admiration of the matchless freeness and sovereignty of grace. Jesus must have found the cause of his love in his own heart, he could not have found it in us, for it is not there. Even since our conversion we have been black, though grace has made us comely. Holy Rutherford said of himself what we must each subscribe to — "His relationship to me is, that I am sick, and he is the Physician of whom I stand in need. Alas! How often I play fast and loose with Christ! He binds, I loosen; he builds, I tear down; I quarrel with Christ, and he agrees with me twenty times a day!" Most tender and faithful Husband of our souls, pursue your gracious work of conforming us to your image, until you shall present even us poor Ethiopians to yourself, without spot, or wrinkle, or any such thing. Moses met with opposition because of his marriage, and both himself and his spouse were the subjects of an evil eye. Can we wonder if this vain world opposes Jesus and his spouse, and especially when great sinners are converted? For this is always the Pharisee's ground of objection, "This man receives sinners." Still the old cause for the quarrel is revived, "Because he had married an Ethiopian woman."

October 7 — Morning

{Daily Reading: Matthew 15:1–17:27} {Quick Study: Matthew 21:1–22:46}

Why have you afflicted your servant? *{Numbers 11:11}*

Our Heavenly Father sends us frequent troubles *to try our faith*. If our faith is worth anything, it will stand the test. Gilt is afraid of fire, but gold is not: the paste gem dreads to be touched by the diamond, but the true jewel fears no test. It is a poor faith which can only trust God when friends are true, the body full of health, and the business profitable; but that is true faith which holds by the Lord's faithfulness when friends are gone, when the body is sick, when spirits are depressed, and the light of our Father's countenance is hidden. A faith which can say, in the direst trouble, "Although he kills me, yet I will trust in him," is heaven-born faith. The Lord afflicts his servants *to glorify himself*, for he is greatly glorified in the graces of his people, which are his own handiwork. When "tribulation works patience; and patience, experience; and experience, hope," the Lord is honoured by these growing virtues. We would never know the music of the harp if the strings were left untouched; nor enjoy the juice of the grape if it were not trodden in the winepress; nor discover the sweet perfume of cinnamon if it were not pressed and beaten; nor feel the warmth of fire if the coals were not utterly consumed. The wisdom and power of the great Workman are discovered by the trials through which his vessels of mercy are permitted to pass. Present afflictions *tend also to heighten future joy*. There must be shades in the picture to bring out the beauty of the lights. Could we be so supremely blessed in heaven, if we had not known the curse of sin and the sorrow of earth? Will not peace be sweeter after conflict, and rest more welcome after toil? Will not the memory of past sufferings enhance the bliss of the glorified? There are many other comforting answers to the question with which we opened our brief meditation, let us muse upon it all day long.

October 7 — Evening

Now on whom do you trust? *{Isaiah 36:5}*

Reader, this is an important question. Listen to the Christian's answer, and see if it is yours. "On whom do you trust?" "I trust," says the Christian, "in a triune God. I trust *the Father*, believing that he has chosen me from before the foundations of the world; I trust him to provide for me in providence, to teach me, to guide me, to correct me if needs be, and to bring me home to his own house where the many mansions are. I trust *the Son*. Very God of very God is he — the man Christ Jesus. I trust in him to take away all my sins by his own sacrifice, and to adorn me with his perfect righteousness. I trust him to be my Intercessor, to present my prayers and desires before his Father's throne, and I trust him to be my Advocate at the last great day, to plead my cause, and to justify me. I trust him for what he is, for what he has done, and for what he has promised yet to do. And I trust *the Holy Spirit* — he has begun to save me from my inbred sins; I trust him to drive them all out; I trust him to curb my temper, to subdue my will, to enlighten my understanding, to check my passions, to comfort my despondency, to help my weakness, to illuminate my darkness. I trust him to dwell in me as my life, to reign in me as my King, to sanctify me wholly, spirit, soul, and body, and then to take me up to live with the saints in light for ever."

Oh, blessed trust! To trust him whose power will never be exhausted, whose love will never wane, whose kindness will never change, whose faithfulness will never fail, whose wisdom will never be nonplussed, and whose perfect goodness can never know a diminution! Happy are you, reader, if this trust is yours! So trusting, you shall enjoy sweet peace now, and glory hereafter, and the foundation of your trust shall never be removed.

October 8 — Morning

{Daily Reading: Matthew 18:1–20:34} {Quick Study: Matthew 23:1–25:46}

Launch out into the deep, and let down your nets for a draught. *{Luke 5:4}*

We learn from this narrative, *the necessity of human agency*. The draught of fishes was miraculous, yet neither the fisherman nor his boat, nor his fishing tackle were ignored — all were used to take the fishes. So in the saving of souls, God works by means; and while the present economy of grace shall stand, God will be pleased by the foolishness of preaching to save those who believe. When God works without instruments, doubtless he is glorified; but he has himself selected the plan of instrumentality as being that by which he is most magnified in the earth. *Means by themselves are utterly unavailing.* "Master, we have toiled all the night and have caught nothing." What was the reason for this? Were they not fishermen plying their special calling? Truly, they were not raw hands; they understood the work. Had they gone about the toil unskilfully? No. Had they lacked industry? No, they had toiled. Had they lacked perseverance? No, they had *toiled all the night*. Was there a deficiency of fish in the sea? Certainly not, for as soon as the Master came, they swam to the net in shoals. What, then, is the reason? Is it because there is no power in the means by themselves apart from the presence of Jesus? "Without him we can do nothing." But with Christ we can do all things. *Christ's presence confers success.* Jesus sat in Peter's boat, and his will, by a mysterious influence, drew the fish to the net. When Jesus is lifted up in his church, his presence is the church's power — the shout of a King is in the midst of her. "I, if I am lifted up, will draw all men to me." Let us go out this morning on our work of soul fishing, looking up in faith, and around us in solemn anxiety. Let us toil until night comes, and we shall not labour in vain, for he who bids us to let down the net, will fill it with fishes.

October 8 — Evening

Praying in the Holy Spirit. *{Jude 1:20}*

Note the grand characteristic of true prayer — *"In the Holy Spirit."* The seed of acceptable devotion must come from heaven's storehouse. Only the prayer which comes from God can go back to God. We must shoot the Lord's arrows back to him. That desire which he writes upon our heart will move his heart and bring down a blessing, but the desires of the flesh have no power with him.

Praying in the Holy Spirit is praying in *fervency*. Cold prayers ask the Lord not to hear them. Those who do not plead with fervency, do not plead at all. You may as well speak of lukewarm fire as of lukewarm prayer — it is essential that it is red hot. It is praying *perseveringly*. The true supplicant gathers force as he proceeds, and grows more fervent when God delays to answer. The longer the gate is closed, the more vehemently does he use the knocker, and the longer the angel lingers the more resolved he is that he will never let him go without the blessing. Beautiful in God's sight is tearful, agonizing, unconquerable importunity. It means praying *humbly*, for the Holy Spirit never puffs us up with pride. It is his office to convict of sin, and so to bow us down in contrition and brokenness of spirit. We shall never sing *Gloria in excelsis* except we pray to God *De profundis*: out of the depths must we cry, or we shall never behold glory in the highest. It is *loving* prayer. Prayer should be perfumed with love, saturated with love — love for our fellow saints, and love for Christ. Moreover, it must be a prayer full of *faith*. A man prevails only as he believes. The Holy Spirit is the author of faith, and strengthens it, so that we pray believing God's promise. Oh, that this blessed combination of excellent graces, priceless and sweet as the spices of the merchant, might be fragrant within us because the Holy Spirit is in our hearts! Most blessed Comforter, exert your mighty power within us, helping our infirmities in prayer.

October 9 — Morning

{Daily Reading: Matthew 21:1–22:46} {Quick Study: Matthew 26:1–28:20}

Able to keep you from falling. *{Jude 1:24}*

In some sense the path to heaven is very safe, but in other respects there *is no road so dangerous.* It is beset with difficulties. One false step (and how easy it is to take that if grace is absent), and down we go. What a slippery path some of us have to tread! How many times have we to exclaim with the psalmist, "My feet were almost gone, my steps had almost slipped." If we were strong, sure-footed mountaineers, this would not matter so much; but in ourselves, *how weak we are!* On the best roads *we soon falter,* on the smoothest paths we quickly stumble. These feeble knees of ours can scarcely support our tottering weight. A straw may throw us, and a pebble can wound us; we are mere children tremblingly taking our first steps in the walk of faith, our Heavenly Father holds us by the arms or we would soon fall down. Oh, if we are kept from falling, how must we bless the patient power which watches over us day by day! Think, how prone we are to sin, how apt to choose danger, how strong is our tendency to cast ourselves down, and these reflections will make us sing more sweetly than we have ever done, "Glory be to him, who is able to keep us from falling." *We have many foes* who try to push us down. The road is rough and we are weak, but in addition to this, enemies lurk in ambush, who rush out when we least expect them, and labour to trip us up, or hurl us down the nearest precipice. Only an almighty arm can preserve us from these unseen foes, who are seeking to destroy us. Such an arm is engaged for our defence. He is faithful who has promised, and he is able to keep us from falling, so that with a deep sense of our utter weakness, we may cherish a firm belief in our perfect safety, and say, with joyful confidence,

> Against me earth and hell combine,
> But on my side is power divine;
> Jesus is all, and he is mine!

October 9 — Evening

But he answered her not a word. *{Matthew 15:23}*

Genuine seekers who as yet have not obtained the blessing, may take comfort from the account before us. The Saviour did not at once bestow the blessing, even though the woman had great faith in him. He intended to give it, but he waited a while. "He answered her not a word." Were not her prayers good? Never better in the world. Was not her case needy? Sorrowfully needy. Did she not *feel* her need sufficiently? She felt it overwhelmingly. Was she not earnest enough? She was intensely so. Had she no faith? She had such a high degree of it that even Jesus wondered, and said, "Oh woman, great is your faith." See then, although it is true that faith brings peace, yet it does not always bring it instantaneously. There may be certain reasons calling for the trial of faith, rather than the reward of faith. Genuine faith may be in the soul like a hidden seed, but as yet it may not have budded and blossomed into joy and peace. A painful silence from the Saviour is the grievous trial of many a seeking soul, but heavier still is the affliction of a harsh, cutting reply such as this, "It is not fitting to take the children's bread, and to cast it to dogs." Many in waiting upon the Lord find immediate delight, but this is not the case with all. Some, like the jailer, are in a moment turned from darkness to light, but others are plants of slower growth. A deeper sense of sin may be given to you instead of a sense of pardon, and in such a case you will have need of patience to bear the heavy blow. Ah! poor heart, although Christ beats and bruises you, or even kills you, trust him; although he should give you an angry word, believe in the love of his heart. Do not, I beseech you, give up seeking or trusting my Master, because you have not yet obtained the conscious joy which you long for. Cast yourself on him, and perseveringly depend even where you cannot rejoicingly hope.

October 10 — Morning

{Daily Reading: Matthew 23:1–24:51} {Quick Study: Mark 1:1–3:35}

Faultless before the presence of his glory. *{Jude 1:24}*

Turn over in your mind that wondrous word, *faultless*! We are far off from it now; but since our Lord never stops short of perfection in his work of love, we shall reach it one day. The Saviour who will keep his people to the end, will also present them at last to himself as "a glorious church, not having spot, or wrinkle, or any such thing, but holy and without blemish." All the jewels in the Saviour's crown are of the first water and without a single flaw. All the maids of honour who attend the Lamb's wife are pure virgins without spot or stain. But how will Jesus make us faultless? He will wash us from our sins in his own blood until we are white and fair as God's purest angel; and we shall be clothed in his righteousness, that righteousness which makes the saint who wears it positively faultless; yes, perfect in the sight of God. We shall be unblameable and unreproveable even in his eyes. His law will not only have no charge against us, but it will be magnified in us. Moreover, the work of the Holy Spirit within us will be altogether complete. He will make us so perfectly holy, that we shall have no lingering tendency to sin. Judgment, memory, will — every power and passion shall be emancipated from the thraldom of evil. We shall be holy even as God is holy, and in his presence we shall dwell for ever. Saints will not be out of place in heaven, their beauty will be as great as that of the place prepared for them. Oh, the rapture of that hour when the everlasting doors shall be lifted up, and we, being made fit for the inheritance, shall dwell with the saints in light. Sin gone, Satan shut out, temptation past for ever, and ourselves "faultless" before God — this will be heaven indeed! Let us be joyful now as we rehearse the song of eternal praise so soon to roll forth in full chorus from all the bloodwashed host; let us copy David's exultings before the ark as a prelude to our ecstasies before the throne.

October 10 — Evening

*And I will deliver you out of the hand of
the wicked, and I will redeem you out of
the hand of the terrible.* {Jeremiah 15:21}

Note the glorious personality of the promise. *I* will, *I* will. The
Lord Jehovah himself interposes to deliver and redeem his
people. He pledges himself personally to rescue them. His own arm
shall do it, so that he may have the glory. Here, not a word is said
of any effort of our own which may be needed to assist the Lord.
Neither our strength nor our weakness is taken into account, but
the lone *I*, like the sun in the heavens, shines out resplendent in
all-sufficiency. Why then do we calculate our forces, and consult
with flesh and blood to our grievous wounding? Jehovah has power
enough without borrowing from our puny arm. Peace, you unbelieving thoughts, be still, and know that the Lord reigns. Nor is
there a hint concerning secondary means and causes. The Lord says
nothing about friends and helpers: he undertakes the work alone,
and feels no need of human arms to aid him. Vain are all our look-
ings around to companions and relatives; they are broken reeds
if we lean upon them — often unwilling when able, and unable
when they are willing. Since the promise comes alone from God,
it would be well to wait only upon him; and when we do so, our
expectation never fails us. Who are the wicked that we should fear
them? The Lord will utterly consume them; they are to be pitied
rather than feared. As for terrible ones, they are only terrors to
those who have no God to flee to, for when the Lord is on our side,
whom shall we fear? If we run into sin to please the wicked, we have
cause to be alarmed, but if we maintain our integrity, the rage of
tyrants shall be overruled for our good. When the fish swallowed
Jonah, he found him a morsel which he could not digest; and when
the world devours the church, it is glad to be rid of it again. In all
times of fiery trial, in patience let us possess our souls.

October 11 — Morning

{Daily Reading: Matthew 25:1–26:75} {Quick Study: Mark 4:1–5:43}

**Let us lift up our heart with our hands to
God in the heavens.** *{Lamentations 3:41}*

The act of prayer teaches us our unworthiness, which is a very salutary lesson for such proud beings as we are. If God gave us favours without constraining us to pray for them we would never know how poor we are, but a true prayer is an inventory of needs, a catalogue of necessities, a revelation of hidden poverty. While it is an application to divine wealth, it is a confession of human emptiness. The most healthy state of a Christian is to be always empty in self and constantly depending upon the Lord for supplies; to be always poor in self and rich in Jesus; weak as water personally, but mighty through God to do great exploits; and hence the use of prayer, because, while it adores God, it lays the creature where it should be, in the very dust. Prayer is, in itself, apart from the answer which it brings, a great benefit to the Christian. As the runner gains strength for the race by daily exercise, so for the great race of life we acquire energy by the hallowed labour of prayer. Prayer plumes the wings of God's young eaglets, so that they may learn to mount above the clouds. Prayer girds the loins of God's warriors, and sends them forth to combat with their sinews braced and their muscles firm. An earnest pleader comes out of his prayer closet, even as the sun arises from the chambers of the east, rejoicing like a strong man to run his race. Prayer is that uplifted hand of Moses which routs the Amalekites more than the sword of Joshua; it is the arrow shot from the room of the prophet foreboding defeat to the Syrians. Prayer girds human weakness with divine strength, turns human folly into heavenly wisdom, and gives to troubled mortals the peace of God. We do know what prayer can do! We thank you, great God, for the mercy seat, a choice proof of your marvellous lovingkindness. Help us to use it properly throughout this day!

October 11 — Evening

**Whom he predestinated, those
he also called.** *{Romans 8:30}*

In Second Timothy are these words — "Who has saved us, and called us with a *holy* calling." *{2 Timothy 1:9}* Now, here is a touch-stone by which we may try our calling. It is "a holy calling, not according to our works, but according to his own purpose and grace." This calling forbids all trust in our own doings, and conducts us to Christ alone for salvation, but it afterwards purges us from dead works to serve the living and true God. Just as he who has called you is holy, so must you be holy. If you are living in sin, you are not called, but if you are truly Christ's, you can say, "Nothing pains me so much as sin; I desire to be rid of it; Lord, help me to be holy." Is this the panting of your heart? Is this the tenor of your life towards God, and his divine will? Again, in Philippians, we are told of "the *high* calling of God in Christ Jesus." *{Philippians 3:13–14}* Then is your calling a high calling? Has it ennobled your heart, and set it upon heavenly things? Has it elevated your hopes, your tastes, your desires? Has it raised up the constant tenor of your life, so that you spend it with God and for God? We find another test in Hebrews — "Partakers of the *heavenly* calling." *{Hebrews 3:1}* Heavenly calling means a call *from* heaven. If man alone calls you, you are uncalled. Is your calling from God? Is it a call *to* heaven as well as from heaven? Unless you are a stranger here, and heaven your home, you have not been called with a heavenly calling; for those who have been so called, declare that they look for a city which has foundations, whose Builder and Maker is God, and they themselves are strangers and pilgrims upon the earth. Is your calling thus holy, high, heavenly? Then, beloved, you have been called by God, for such is the calling by which God calls his people.

October 12 — Morning

{Daily Reading: Matthew 27:1–28:20} {Quick Study: Mark 6:1–7:37}

I will meditate on your precepts. *{Psalms 119:15}*

There are times when solitude is better than society, and silence is wiser than speech. We would be better Christians if we were more alone, waiting upon God, and gathering through meditation on his Word spiritual strength for labour in his service. We ought to meditate *on the things of God, because we thus get the real nutriment from them.* Truth is something like the cluster of the vine: if we wish to have wine from it, we must bruise it; we must press and squeeze it many times. The bruiser's feet must come down joyfully upon the bunches, or else the juice will not flow; and they must tread the grapes well, or else much of the precious liquid will be wasted. So we must, by meditation, tread the clusters of truth, if we wish to get the wine of consolation from it. Our bodies are not nourished by merely taking food into the mouth, but the process which really supplies the muscle, and the nerve, and the sinew, and the bone, is the process of digestion. It is by digestion that the outward food becomes assimilated with the inner life. Our souls are not nourished merely by listening a while to this, and then to that, and then to the other part of divine truth. Hearing, reading, marking, and learning, all require inwardly digesting to complete their usefulness, and the inward digesting of the truth lies for the most part in meditating upon it. Why is it that some Christians, although they hear many sermons, make very slow advances in the divine life? Because they neglect their prayer closets, and do not thoughtfully meditate on God's Word. They love the wheat, but they do not grind it; they wish to have the grain, but they will not go out into the fields to gather it; the fruit hangs upon the tree, but they will not pick it; the water flows at their feet, but they will not stoop to drink it. From such folly deliver us, oh Lord, and let this be our resolve this morning, "I will meditate on your precepts."

The Comforter, who is
the Holy Spirit. *{John 14:26}*

This age is specifically the dispensation of the Holy Spirit, in which Jesus cheers us, not by his personal presence, as he shall do by and by, but by the indwelling and constant abiding of the Holy Spirit, who is for evermore the Comforter of the church. It is his office to console the hearts of God's people. He convicts of sin; he illuminates and instructs; but still the main part of his work lies in making glad the hearts of the renewed, in confirming the weak, and lifting up all those who are bowed down. He does this by revealing Jesus to them. The Holy Spirit consoles, but Christ *is the consolation.* If we may use the illustration, the Holy Spirit is the Physician, but Jesus is the medicine. *He* heals the wound, but it is by applying the holy ointment of Christ's name and grace. He does not take from his own things, but from the things of Christ. So if we give to the Holy Spirit the Greek name of *Paraclete*, as we sometimes do, then our heart confers on our blessed Lord Jesus the title of *Paraclesis.* If the one is the Comforter, the other is the Comfort. Now, with such rich provision for his needs, why should the Christian be sad and desponding? The Holy Spirit has graciously engaged to be your Comforter: do you imagine, oh you weak and trembling believer, that he will be negligent in his sacred trust? Can you suppose that he has undertaken what he cannot or will not perform? If it is his special work to strengthen you, and to comfort you, do you suppose he has forgotten his business, or that he will fail in the loving office which he sustains towards you? No, do not think so harshly of the tender and blessed Spirit whose name is "the Comforter." He delights to give the oil of joy for mourning, and the garment of praise for the spirit of heaviness. Trust in him, and he will surely comfort you until the house of mourning is closed for ever, and the marriage feast has begun.

October 13 — Morning

{Daily Reading: Mark 1:1–3:35} {Quick Study: Mark 8:1–9:50}

Godly sorrow works repentance. *{2 Corinthians 7:10}*

Genuine, spiritual mourning for sin is *the work of the Spirit of God*. Repentance is too choice a flower to grow in nature's garden. Pearls grow naturally in oysters, but penitence never shows itself in sinners except divine grace works it in them. If you have one particle of real hatred for sin, God must have given it to you, for human nature's thorns never produced a single fig. "What is born of the flesh is flesh."

True repentance *has a distinct reference to the Saviour*. When we repent of sin, we must have one eye upon sin and another upon the cross, or it will be better still if we fix both our eyes upon Christ and see our transgressions only, in the light of his love.

True sorrow for sin is *eminently practical*. No man may say he hates sin, if he lives in it. Repentance makes us see the evil of sin, not merely as a theory, but from experience — as a burnt child dreads fire. We shall be as much afraid of it, as a man who has recently been stopped and robbed is afraid of the thief upon the highway; and we shall shun it — shun it in everything — not in great things only, but in little things, as men shun little vipers as well as large snakes. True mourning for sin will make us very jealous over our tongue, lest it should say a wrong word; we shall be very watchful over our daily actions, lest in anything we offend, and each night we shall close the day with painful confessions of shortcoming, and each morning awaken with anxious prayers, that today God would hold us up that we may not sin against him.

Sincere repentance is *continual*. Believers repent until their dying day. This dropping well is not intermittent. Every other sorrow yields to time, but this dear sorrow grows with our growth, and it is so sweet a bitter, that we thank God we are permitted to enjoy and to suffer with it until we enter our eternal rest.

October 13 — Evening

Love is as strong as death. *{Song of Solomon 8:6}*

Whose love can this be which is as mighty as the conqueror of monarchs, the destroyer of the human race? Would it not sound like satire if it were applied to my poor, weak, and scarcely living love for Jesus my Lord? I do love him, and perhaps by his grace, I could even die for him, but as for my love in itself, it can scarcely endure a scoffing jest, much less a cruel death. Surely it is my Beloved's love which is here spoken of — the love of Jesus, the matchless lover of souls. His love was indeed stronger than the most terrible death, for it endured the trial of the cross triumphantly. It was a lingering death, but love survived the torment; a shameful death, but love despised the shame; a penal death, but love bore our iniquities; a forsaken, lonely death, from which the eternal Father hid his face, but love endured the curse, and gloried over all. Never was there such a love, never was there such a death. It was a desperate duel, but love bore the palm branch of victory. What then, my heart? Have you no emotions excited within you at the contemplation of such heavenly affection? Yes, my Lord, I long, I pant to feel your love flaming like a furnace within me. Come yourself and excite the ardour of my spirit.

> For every drop of crimson blood
> Thus shed to make me live,
> Oh why, why have not I
> A thousand lives to give?

Why should I despair of loving Jesus with a love as strong as death? He deserves it: I desire it. The martyrs felt such love, and they were only flesh and blood, then why not I? They mourned their weakness, and yet out of weakness were made strong. Grace gave them all their unflinching constancy — there is the same grace for me. Jesus, lover of my soul, shed abroad such love, even your love in my heart, this evening.

October 14 — Morning

{Daily Reading: Mark 4:1–5:43} {Quick Study: Mark 10:1–11:33}

I count all things loss for the excellency of the knowledge of Christ Jesus my Lord. *{Philippians 3:8}*

Spiritual knowledge of Christ will be a *personal* knowledge. I cannot know Jesus through another person's acquaintance with him. No, I must know him *myself*; I must know him on my own account. It will be an *intelligent* knowledge — I must know *him*, not as the visionary dreams of him, but as the Word reveals him. I must know his natures, divine and human. I must know his offices — his attributes — his works — his shame — his glory. I must meditate upon him until I "comprehend with all saints what is the breadth, and length, and depth, and height; and know the love of Christ, which surpasses knowledge." It will be an *affectionate* knowledge of him; indeed, if I know him at all, I must love him. An ounce of heart knowledge is worth a ton of head learning. Our knowledge of him will be a *satisfying* knowledge. When I know my Saviour, my mind will be full to the brim — I shall feel that I have what my spirit panted after. "This is that bread of which if a man eats he shall never hunger." At the same time it will be an exciting knowledge; the more I know of my Beloved, the more I shall want to know. The higher I climb, the loftier will be the summits which invite my eager footsteps. I shall want all the more as I get more. Like the miser's treasure, my gold will make me covet more. To conclude, this knowledge of Christ Jesus will be a most *happy* one; in fact, so elevating, that sometimes it will completely bear me up above all trials, and doubts, and sorrows; and it will, while I enjoy it, make me something more than "Man who is born of woman, who is of few days, and full of trouble"; for it will engulf me with the immortality of the ever-living Saviour, and gird me with the golden belt of his eternal joy. Come, my soul, sit at Jesus' feet and learn about him all this day.

October 14 — Evening

And do not be conformed
to this world. {Romans 12:2}

If a Christian can possibly be saved while he conforms to this world, at any rate it must be so as by fire. Such a bare salvation is almost as much to be dreaded as desired. Reader, do you wish to leave this world in the darkness of a desponding deathbed, and enter heaven as a shipwrecked mariner climbs the rocks of his native country? Then be worldly; be mixed up with Mammonites, and refuse to go outside the camp bearing Christ's reproach. But do you wish to have a heaven below as well as a heaven above? Do you wish to comprehend with all saints what are the heights and depths, and know the love of Christ which surpasses knowledge? Do you wish to receive an abundant entrance into the joy of your Lord? Then come out from among them, and be separate, and do not touch the unclean thing. Do you wish to attain the full assurance of faith? You cannot gain it while you commune with sinners. Do you wish to flame with vehement love? Your love will be dampened by the drenchings of godless society. You cannot become a great Christian — you may be a babe in grace, but you never can be a perfect man in Christ Jesus while you yield yourself to the worldly maxims and modes of business of men of the world. It is wrong for an heir of heaven to be a great friend with the heirs of hell. It looks bad when a courtier is too intimate with his king's enemies. Even small inconsistencies are dangerous. Little thorns make great blisters, little moths destroy fine garments, and little frivolities and little rogueries will rob religion of a thousand joys. Oh professor, too little separated from sinners, you do not know what you lose by your conformity to the world. It cuts the tendons of your strength, and makes you creep where you ought to run. Then, for your own comfort's sake, and for the sake of your growth in grace, if you are a Christian, be a Christian, and be a marked and distinct one.

October 15 — Morning

{Daily Reading: Mark 6:1–7:37} {Quick Study: Mark 12:1–13:37}

**But who may abide the day
of his coming?** *{Malachi 3:2}*

His first coming was without external pomp or show of power, and yet in truth there were few who could abide its testing might. Herod and all Jerusalem with him were stirred at the news of the wondrous birth. Those who supposed themselves to be waiting for him showed the fallacy of their professions by rejecting him when he came. His life on earth was a winnowing fan, which tried the great heap of religious profession, and few enough could abide the process. But what will his second advent be? What sinner can endure to think of it? "He shall strike the earth with the rod of his mouth, and with the breath of his lips he shall kill the wicked." When in his humiliation he only said to the soldiers, "I am he," they fell backwards; what will be the terror of his enemies when he shall more fully reveal himself as the *"I am"*? His death shook earth and darkened heaven, what shall be the dreadful splendour of that day in which as the living Saviour, he shall summon the quick and dead before him? Oh, that the terrors of the Lord would persuade men to forsake their sins and kiss the Son lest he is angry! Though a lamb, he is yet the lion of the tribe of Judah, tearing the prey in pieces; and though he does not break the bruised reed, yet he will break his enemies with a rod of iron, and dash them in pieces like a potter's vessel. Not one of his foes shall bear up before the tempest of his wrath, or hide themselves from the sweeping hail of his indignation; but his beloved bloodwashed people look for his appearing with joy, and hope to abide it without fear: to them he sits as a refiner even now, and when he has tried them they shall come forth as gold. Let us search ourselves this morning and make our calling and election sure, so that the coming of the Lord may cause no dark forebodings in our mind. Oh, for grace to cast away all hypocrisy, and to be found by him being sincere and without rebuke in the day of his appearing.

October 15 — Evening

**But you shall redeem the firstborn of a donkey
with a lamb: and if you do not redeem him,
then you shall break his neck.** *{Exodus 34:20}*

Every firstborn creature must be the Lord's, but since the donkey was unclean, it could not be presented in sacrifice. What then? Should it be allowed to go free from the universal law? By no means. God permits no exceptions. The donkey is his due, but he will not accept it; he will not abate the claim, but yet he cannot be pleased with the victim. No way of escape remained except redemption — the creature must be saved by the substitution of a lamb in its place; or if not redeemed, it must die. My soul, here is a lesson for you. That unclean animal is yourself; you are justly the property of the Lord who made you and preserves you, but you are so sinful that God will not and cannot accept you; and it has come to this, the Lamb of God must stand in your place, or you must die eternally. Let all the world know of your gratitude to that spotless Lamb who has already bled for you, and so redeemed you from the fatal curse of the law. Must it not sometimes have been a question with the Israelite which should die, the donkey or the lamb? Would the good man not pause to estimate and compare? Assuredly there was no comparison between the value of the soul of man and the life of the Lord Jesus, and yet the Lamb dies, and man the donkey is spared. My soul, admire the boundless love of God to you and others of the human race. Worms are bought with the blood of the Son of the Highest! Dust and ashes redeemed with a price far above silver and gold! What a doom would have been mine had not a plenteous redemption been found! The breaking of the neck of the donkey was only a momentary penalty, but who shall measure the wrath to come to which no limit can be imagined? Inestimably dear is the glorious Lamb who has redeemed us from such a doom.

October 16 — Morning

{Daily Reading: Mark 8:1–9:50} {Quick Study: Mark 14:1–16:20}

Jesus says to them, "Come and dine." *{John 21:12}*

In these words the believer is invited to a holy *nearness to Jesus*. "Come and dine," implies the same table, the same food; indeed, and sometimes it means to sit side by side, and lean our head upon the Saviour's bosom. It is being brought into the banqueting house, where the banner of redeeming love is waving. "Come and dine," gives us a vision of *union with Jesus*, because the only food that we can feast upon when we dine with Jesus is *himself*. Oh, what union is this! It is a depth which reason cannot fathom, that we thus feed upon Jesus. "He who eats my flesh, and drinks my blood, lives in me, and I in him." It is also an invitation to enjoy *fellowship with the saints*. Christians may differ on a variety of points, but they have all one spiritual appetite; and if we cannot all *feel* alike, we can all *feed* alike on the bread of life sent down from heaven. At the table of fellowship with Jesus we are one bread and one cup. As the loving cup goes around we pledge one another heartily in it. Get nearer to Jesus, and you will find yourself linked more and more in spirit to all who are like yourself, supported by the same heavenly manna. If we were more near to Jesus we should be more near to one another. We likewise see in these words the *source of strength* for every Christian. To look at Christ is to live, but for strength to serve him you must "come and dine." We labour under much unnecessary weakness on account of neglecting this precept of the Master. None of us needs to put ourselves on a strict diet; on the contrary, we should fatten on the marrow and fatness of the gospel so that we may be strengthened by it, and bring every power to bear in the Master's service. Thus, then, if you wish to experience *nearness* to Jesus, *union* with Jesus, *love* for his people and *strength from Jesus*, "come and dine" with him by faith.

October 16 — Evening

The fountain of life is with you. *{Psalms 36:9}*

There are times in our spiritual experience when human counsel or sympathy, or religious ordinances, fail to comfort or help us. Why does our gracious God permit this? Perhaps it is because we have been living too much without him, and he therefore takes away everything upon which we have been in the habit of depending, so that he may drive us to himself. It is a blessed thing to live at the fountain head. While our water bottles are full, we are content, like Hagar and Ishmael, to go into the wilderness; but when those are dry, nothing will serve us except, "Oh God, you see me." We are like the prodigal; we love the swine troughs and forget our Father's house. Remember, we can make swine troughs and husks even out of the forms of religion; they are blessed things, but we may put them in God's place, and then they are of no value. Anything becomes an idol when it keeps us away from God: even the brazen serpent is to be despised as "Nehushtan," if we worship it instead of God. The prodigal was never safer than when he was driven to his father's heart, because he could find sustenance nowhere else. Our Lord favours us with a famine in the land so that it may make us seek after himself all the more. The best position for a Christian is living wholly and directly on God's grace — still abiding where he stood at first — "Having nothing, and yet possessing all things." Let us never for a moment think that our standing is in our sanctification, our mortification, our graces, or our feelings, but know that because Christ offered a full atonement, therefore we are saved; for we are complete in him. Having nothing of our own to trust in, but resting upon the merits of Jesus — his passion and holy life furnish us with the only sure basis for confidence. Beloved, when we are brought to a thirsting condition, we are sure to turn to the fountain of life with eagerness.

October 17 — Morning

{Daily Reading: Mark 10:1–11:33} {Quick Study: Luke 1:1–2: 52}

And David said in his heart, "I shall now perish one day by the hand of Saul." *{1 Samuel 27:1}*

The thought of David's heart at this time was a *false* thought, because he certainly had no basis for thinking that God's anointing him by Samuel was intended to be left as an empty meaningless act. On not one occasion had the Lord deserted his servant; he had been placed in perilous positions very often, but not one instance had occurred in which divine intervention had not delivered him. The trials to which he had been exposed had been varied; they had not assumed one form only, but many — yet in every case he who sent the trial had also graciously ordained a way of escape. David could not put his finger upon any entry in his diary, and say of it, "Here is evidence that the Lord will forsake me," for the entire tenor of his past life proved the very reverse. He should have argued from what God *had* done for him, that God would still be his defender. But is it not just in the same way that *we* doubt God's help? Is it not *mistrust without a cause*? Have we ever had the shadow of a reason to doubt our Father's goodness? Have his lovingkindnesses not been marvellous? Has he *once* failed to justify our trust? Ah, no! Our God has not left us at any time. We have had dark nights, but the star of love has shone forth amid the blackness; we have been in stern conflicts, but over our head he has held aloft the shield of our defence. We have gone through many trials, but never to our detriment, always to our advantage; and the conclusion from our past experience is that he who has been with us in six troubles will not forsake us in the seventh. What we have known of our faithful God proves that he will keep us to the end. Let us not, then, reason contrary to evidence. How can we ever be so faithless as to *doubt* our God? Lord, throw down the Jezebel of our unbelief, and let the dogs devour it.

October 17 — Evening

He shall gather the lambs
with his arm. *{Isaiah 40:11}*

Our good Shepherd has in his flock a variety of experiences, some are strong in the Lord, and others are weak in faith, but he is impartial in his care for all his sheep, and the weakest lamb is as dear to him as the most advanced of the flock. Lambs are accustomed to lag behind, prone to wander, and apt to grow weary, but from all the danger of these infirmities the Shepherd protects them with his arm of power. He finds newborn souls, like young lambs, ready to perish — he nourishes them until life becomes vigorous; he finds weak minds ready to faint and die — he consoles them and renews their strength. He gathers all the little ones, for it is not the will of our Heavenly Father that anyone of them should perish. What a quick eye he must have to see them all! What a tender heart to care for them all! What a far reaching and potent arm, to gather them all! In his lifetime on earth he was a great gatherer of the weak, and now that he dwells in heaven, his loving heart yearns towards the meek and contrite, the timid and feeble, the fearful and fainting here below. How gently he gathered me to himself, to his truth, to his blood, to his love, to his church! With what effectual grace he compelled me to come to himself! Since my first conversion, how frequently has he restored me from my wanderings, and once again folded me within the circle of his everlasting arm! The best of all is, that he does it all himself personally, not delegating the task of love, but condescending himself to rescue and preserve his most unworthy servant. How shall I love him enough or serve him worthily? I would gladly make his name great to the ends of the earth, but what can my feebleness do for him? Great Shepherd, add to your mercies this one other, a heart to love you more truly as I ought.

October 18 — Morning

{Daily Reading: Mark 12:1–13:37} {Quick Study: Luke 3:1–4:44}

Your paths drop fatness. *{Psalms 65:11}*

Many are "the paths of the Lord" which "drop fatness," but a special one is the *path of prayer*. No believer, who is much in the prayer closet, will have need to cry, "My leanness, my leanness; woe to me." Starving souls live at a distance from the mercy seat, and become like the parched fields in times of drought. Prevalence with God in wrestling prayer is sure to make the believer strong — if not happy. The nearest place to the gate of heaven is the throne of the heavenly grace. Much alone, and you will have much assurance; little alone with Jesus, your religion will be shallow, polluted with many doubts and fears, and not sparkling with the joy of the Lord. Since the soul-enriching path of prayer is open to the very weakest saint; since no high attainments are required; since you are not bidden to come because you are an advanced saint, but freely invited if you are a saint at all; see to it, dear reader, that you are often in the way of private devotion. Be much on your knees, for so Elijah drew the rain upon famished Israel's fields.

There is another special path dropping with fatness to those who walk in it, it is the secret walk of *communion*. Oh! The delights of fellowship with Jesus! Earth has no words which can describe the holy calm of a soul leaning on Jesus' bosom. Few Christians understand it, they live in the lowlands and seldom climb to the top of Nebo: they live in the outer court, they do not enter the holy place, they do not take up the privilege of priesthood. At a distance they see the sacrifice, but they do not sit down with the priest to eat it, and to enjoy the fat of the burnt offering. But, reader, always sit under the shadow of Jesus; come up to that palm tree, and take hold of its branches; let your Beloved be to you as the apple tree among the trees of the forest, and you shall be satisfied as with marrow and fatness. Oh Jesus, visit us with your salvation!

October 18 — Evening

Behold, to obey is better than sacrifice. *{1 Samuel 15:22}*

Saul had been commanded to utterly kill all the Amalekites and their cattle. Instead of doing so, he preserved the king, and allowed his people to take the best of the oxen and of the sheep. When called to account for this, he declared that he did it with a view of offering sacrifice to God; but Samuel met him at once with the assurance that sacrifices were no excuse for an act of direct rebellion. The sentence before us is worthy to be printed in letters of gold, and to be hung up before the eyes of the present idolatrous generation, who are very fond of the fineries of will-worship, but utterly neglect the laws of God. May you remember that to keep strictly in the path of your Saviour's command is better than any outward form of religion; and to listen to his precept with an attentive ear is better than to bring the fat of rams, or any other precious thing to lay upon his altar. If you are failing to keep the least of Christ's commands to his disciples, I beseech you be disobedient no longer. All the pretensions you make of attachment to your Master, and all the devout actions which you may perform, are no compensation for disobedience. "To obey," even in the slightest and smallest thing, "is better than sacrifice," however pompous. Do not speak of Gregorian chants, sumptuous robes, incense, and banners; the first thing which God requires of his child is obedience; and even though you should give your body to be burned, and all your goods to feed the poor, yet if you do not listen to the Lord's precepts, all your formalities shall be worthless. It is a blessed thing to be as teachable as a little child, but it is a much more blessed thing when one has been taught the lesson, to carry it out to the letter. How many adorn their temples and decorate their priests, but refuse to obey the word of the Lord! My soul, never be a party to their plans.

October 19 — Morning

{Daily Reading: Mark 14:1–16:20} {Quick Study: Luke 5:1–7:50}

Babes in Christ. *{1 Corinthians 3:1}*

Are you mourning, believer, because you are so weak in the divine life: because your faith is so little, your love so feeble? Cheer up, for you have cause for gratitude. Remember that *in some things you are equal to the greatest and most fully grown Christian.* You are as much bought with blood as he is. You are as much an adopted child of God as any other believer. An infant is as truly a child of his parents as is the fully grown man. You are as completely justified, for your justification is not a thing of degrees: your little faith has made you completely clean. You have as much right to the precious things of the covenant as the most advanced believers, for your right to covenant mercies lies not in your growth, but in the covenant itself; and your faith in Jesus is not the measure, but the token of your inheritance in him. You are as rich as the richest, if not in enjoyment, yet in real possession. The smallest star that gleams is set in heaven; the faintest ray of light has affinity with the great orb of day. In the family register of glory the small and the great are written with the same pen. You are as dear to your Father's heart as the greatest in the family. Jesus is very tender over you. You are like the smoking flax; a rougher spirit would say, "Put out that smoking flax, it fills the room with an offensive odour!" But *he* will not quench the smoking flax. You are like a bruised reed; and any less tender hand than that of the Chief Musician would tread upon you or throw you away, but *he* will never break the bruised reed. Instead of being downcast by reason of what you are, you should triumph in Christ. Am I very little in Israel? Yet in Christ I am made to sit in heavenly places. Am I poor in faith? Still in Jesus I am heir of all things. Though "less than nothing I can boast, and vanity confess." Yet, if the root of the matter is in me I will rejoice in the Lord, and glory in the God of my salvation.

October 19 — Evening

God, my Maker, who gives songs
in the night. *{Job 35:10}*

Any man can sing in the day. When the cup is full, man draws inspiration from it. When wealth rolls in abundance around him, any man can praise the God who gives a plenteous harvest or sends home a loaded argosy. It is easy enough for an Aeolian harp to whisper music when the winds blow — the difficulty is for music to swell forth when no wind is stirring. It is easy to sing when we can read the notes by daylight; but he is skilful who sings when there is not a ray of light to read by — who sings from his heart. No man can make a song in the night by himself; he may attempt it, but he will find that a song in the night must be divinely inspired. Let all things go well, I can weave songs, fashioning them wherever I go out of the flowers that grow upon my path; but put me in a desert, where no green thing grows, and how shall I frame a hymn of praise to God? How shall a mortal man make a crown for the Lord where no jewels are? Only let this voice be clear, and this body full of health, and I can sing God's praise: silence my tongue, lay me upon the bed of languishing, and how shall I then chant God's high praises, unless he himself gives me the song? No, it is not in man's power to sing when all is adverse, unless an altar coal shall touch his lip. It was a divine song, which Habakkuk sang, when in the night he said, "Although the fig tree shall not blossom, neither shall fruit be on the vines; the labour of the olive shall fail, and the fields shall yield no food; the flock shall be cut off from the fold, and there shall be no herd in the stalls: yet I will rejoice in the Lord, I will joy in the God of my salvation." Then, since our Maker gives *songs in the night*, let us wait upon him for the music. Oh you Chief Musician, let us not remain songless because affliction is upon us, but tune our lips to the melody of thanksgiving.

October 20 — Morning

{Daily Reading: Luke 1:1–1:80} {Quick Study: Luke 8:1–9:62}

Grow up into him in all things. *{Ephesians 4:15}*

Many Christians remain stunted and dwarfed in spiritual things, so as to present the same appearance year after year. No upspringing of advanced and refined feeling is revealed in them. They *exist* but do not *"grow up into him in all things."* But should we rest content with being in the "green blade," when we might advance to "the ear," and eventually ripen into the "full grain in the ear"? Should we be satisfied to believe in Christ, and to say, "I am safe," without wishing to know in our own experience more of the fulness which is to be found in him? It should not be so; we should, as good traders in heaven's market, covet to be enriched in the knowledge of Jesus. It is all very well to keep other men's vineyards, but we must not neglect our own spiritual growth and ripening. Why should it always be winter time in our hearts? We must have our seedtime, it is true, but oh for a spring time — yes, a summer season, which shall give promise of an early harvest. If we wish to ripen in grace, we must live near to Jesus — in his presence — ripened by the sunshine of his smiles. We must hold sweet communion with him. We must leave the distant view of his face and come near, as John did, and pillow our head on his heart; then we shall find ourselves advancing in holiness, in love, in faith, in hope — yes, in every precious gift. Just as the sun rises first on mountain tops and gilds them with its light, and presents one of the most charming sights to the eye of the traveller; so it is one of the most delightful contemplations in the world to see the glow of the Spirit's light on the head of some saint, who has risen up in spiritual stature, like Saul, above his companions, until, like a mighty snow capped Alp, he reflects first among the chosen, the beams of the Sun of Righteousness, and bears the sheen of his effulgence high aloft for all to see, and seeing it, to glorify his Father who is in heaven.

October 20 — Evening

Do not hold back. {Isaiah 43:6}

Although this message was sent to the south, and referred to the seed of Israel, it may profitably be a summons to ourselves. We are naturally backward in all good things, and it is a lesson of grace to learn to go forward in the ways of God. Reader, are you unconverted, but do you desire to trust in the Lord Jesus? Then *do not hold back*. Love invites you, the promises secure you success, the precious blood prepares the way. Do not let sins or fears hinder you, but come to Jesus just as you are. Do you long to pray? Do you wish to pour out your heart before the Lord? *Do not hold back*. The mercy seat is prepared for those who need mercy; a sinner's cries will prevail with God. You are invited, indeed, you are commanded to pray, therefore come with boldness to the throne of grace.

Dear friend, are you already saved? *Then do not hold back* from union with the Lord's people. Do not neglect the ordinances of baptism and the Lord's Supper. You may be of a timid disposition, but you must strive against it, lest it lead you into disobedience. There is a sweet promise made to those who confess Christ — by no means miss it, lest you come under the condemnation of those who deny him. If you have talents *do not hold back* from using them. Do not hoard your wealth, do not waste your time; do not let your abilities rust or your influence be unused. Jesus did not hold back; imitate him by being foremost in self-denials and self-sacrifices. *Do not hold back* from close communion with God, from boldly appropriating covenant blessings, from advancing in the divine life, from prying into the precious mysteries of the love of Christ. Neither, beloved friend, be guilty of keeping others back by your coldness, harshness, or suspicions. For Jesus' sake go forward yourself, and encourage others to do the same. Hell and the beleaguered bands of superstition and infidelity are forward for the fight. Oh soldiers of the cross, do not hold back.

October 21 — Morning

{Daily Reading: Luke 2:1–3:38} {Quick Study: Luke 10:1–11:54}

The love of Christ constrains us. *{2 Corinthians 5:14}*

How much do you owe to my Lord? Has he ever done anything for you? Has he forgiven your sins? Has he covered you with a robe of righteousness? Has he set your feet upon a rock? Has he established your goings? Has he prepared heaven for you? Has he prepared you for heaven? Has he written your name in his book of life? Has he given you countless blessings? Has he laid up for you a store of mercies, which eye has not seen nor ear heard? Then do something for Jesus worthy of his love. Do not give a mere wordy offering to a dying Redeemer. How will you feel when your Master comes, if you have to confess that you *did* nothing for him, but kept your love shut up, like a stagnant pool, neither flowing forth to his poor or to his work. Away with such love as that! What do men think of a love which never shows itself in action? Why, they say, "Open rebuke is better than secret love." Who will accept a love so weak that it does not motivate you to a single deed of self-denial, of generosity, of heroism, or zeal! Think how *he* has loved you, and given himself for you! Do you know the power of that love? Then let it be like a rushing mighty wind to your soul to sweep out the clouds of your worldliness, and clear away the mists of sin. "For Christ's sake" may this be the tongue of fire that shall sit upon you: "for Christ's sake" may this be the divine rapture, the heavenly impulse to bear you aloft from earth, the divine spirit that shall make you bold as lions and swift as eagles in your Lord's service. Love should give wings to the feet of service, and strength to the arms of labour. Fixed on God with a constancy that is not to be shaken, resolute to honour him with a determination that is not to be turned aside, and pressing on with an ardour never to be wearied, let us reveal the constraints of love for Jesus. May the divine magnet draw us heavenward towards itself.

October 21 — Evening

Why are you troubled? And why do thoughts arise in your hearts? {Luke 24:38}

Oh Jacob, why do you say, and oh Israel, why do you speak that my way is hidden from the Lord, and my judgment is passed over from my God?" The Lord cares for all things, and the lowliest creatures share in his universal providence, but his particular providence is over his saints. "The angel of the Lord camps all around those who fear him." "Precious shall their blood be in his sight." "Precious in the sight of the Lord is the death of his saints." "We know that all things work together for good to those who love God, to those who are the called according to his purpose." Let the fact that, while he is the Saviour of all men, he is especially the Saviour of those who believe, cheer and comfort you. You are his particular care; his regal treasure which he guards as the apple of his eye; his vineyard over which he watches day and night. "The very hairs of your head are all numbered." Let the thought of his special love *for you* be a spiritual pain killer, a dear quietus to your woe: "I will never leave *you*, nor forsake *you*." God says that as much to you as to any saint of old. "Do not fear, I am your shield, and your exceedingly great reward." We lose much consolation by the habit of reading his promises for the whole church, instead of applying them directly to ourselves. Believer, grasp the divine word with a personal, appropriating faith. Think that you hear Jesus say, "I have prayed for *you* that your faith does not fail." Think that you see him walking on the waters of your trouble, for he is there, and he is saying, "Do not fear, it is I; do not be afraid." Oh, those sweet words of Christ! May the Holy Spirit make you feel that they are spoken to *you*; forget others for a while — accept the voice of Jesus as addressed to you, and say, "Jesus whispers consolation; I cannot refuse it; I will sit under his shadow with great delight."

October 22 — Morning

{Daily Reading: Luke 4:1–5:39} {Quick Study: Luke 12:1–13:35}

I will love them freely. *{Hosea 14:4}*

This sentence is a body of divinity in miniature. He who understands its meaning is a theologian, and he who can dive into its fulness is a true master in Israel. It is a condensation of the glorious message of salvation which was delivered to us in Christ Jesus our Redeemer. The sense hinges upon the word "freely." This is the glorious, the suitable, the divine way by which love streams from heaven to earth, a spontaneous love flowing forth to those who neither deserved it, purchased it, nor sought after it. It is, indeed, the only way in which God can love such as we are. The text is a death blow to all sorts of fitness: "I will love them *freely.*" Now, if there were any fitness necessary in us, then he would not love us freely, at least, this would be a mitigation and a drawback to the freeness of it. But it stands, "I will love you freely." We complain, "Lord, my heart is so hard." "I will love you *freely.*" "But I do not feel my need of Christ as I could wish." "I will not love you because you feel your need; I will love you freely." "But I do not feel that softening of spirit which I could desire." Remember, the softening of spirit is not a condition, for there are no conditions; the covenant of grace has no conditions at all; so that we without any fitness may venture upon the promise of God which was made to us in Christ Jesus, when he said, "He who believes on him is not condemned." It is blessed to know that the grace of God is free to us at all times, without preparation, without fitness, without money, and without price! "I will love them freely." These words *invite backsliders to return*: indeed, the text was especially written for such — "I will heal their backsliding; I will love them freely." Backslider! Surely the generosity of the promise will at once break your heart, and you will return, and seek your injured Father's face.

October 22 — Evening

**He shall take of mine, and shall
show it to you.** *{John 16:15}*

There are times when all the promises and doctrines of the Bible are of no avail, unless a gracious hand shall apply them to us. We are thirsty, but too faint to crawl to the water brook. When a soldier is wounded in battle it is of little use for him to know that there are those at the hospital who can bind up his wounds, and medicines there to ease all the pains which he now suffers: what he needs is to be carried there, and to have the remedies applied. It is thus with our souls, and to meet this need there is one, even the Spirit of truth, who takes the things of Jesus, and applies them to us. Do not think that Christ has placed his joys on heavenly shelves so that we may climb up to them for ourselves, but he draws near, and sheds his peace abroad in our hearts. Oh Christian, if you are tonight labouring under deep distresses, your Father does not give you promises and then leave you to draw them up from the Word like buckets from a well, but the promises he has written in the Word he will write anew on your heart. He will reveal his love to you, and by his blessed Spirit dispel your cares and troubles. Know, oh mourner, that it is God's prerogative to wipe every tear from the eye of his people. The good Samaritan did not say, "Here is the wine, and here is the oil for you"; he actually poured in the oil and the wine. So Jesus not only gives you the sweet wine of the promise, but holds the golden chalice to your lips, and pours the life blood into your mouth. The poor, sick, wayworn pilgrim is not merely strengthened to walk, but he is borne on eagles' wings. Glorious gospel! which provides everything for the helpless, which draws near to us when we cannot reach after it — brings us grace before we seek for grace! Here is as much glory in the giving as in the gift. Happy are the people who have the Holy Spirit to bring Jesus to them.

October 23 — Morning

{Daily Reading: Luke 6:1–7:50} {Quick Study: Luke 14:1–16:31}

Will you also go away? *{John 6:67}*

Many have forsaken Christ, and have walked no more with him; *but what reason have* YOU *to make a change?* Has there been any reason for it in the *past?* Has not Jesus proven himself to be all-sufficient? He appeals to you this morning — "Have I been a wilderness to you?" When your soul has simply trusted Jesus, have you ever been confounded? Have you not up until now found your Lord to be a compassionate and generous friend to you, and has not simple faith in him given you all the peace your spirit could desire? Can you so much as dream of a better friend than he has been to you? Then do not change the old and tried for new and false. As for *the present,* can that compel you to leave Christ? When we are hard beset with this world, or with the severer trials within the church, we find it a most blessed thing to pillow our head upon the bosom of our Saviour. This is the joy we have today that we are saved in him; and if this joy is satisfying, why should we think of changing? Who barters gold for dross? We will not abandon the sun until we find a better light, nor leave our Lord until a brighter lover shall appear; and, since this can never be, we will hold him with a grasp immortal, and bind his name as a seal upon our arm. As for *the future,* can you suggest anything which can arise that shall render it necessary for you to mutiny, or desert the old flag to serve under another captain? We do not think so. If life is long — he does not change. If we are poor, what is better than to have Christ who can make us rich? When we are sick, what more do we want than Jesus to make our bed in our sickness? When we die, is it not written that "neither death, nor life, nor things present, nor things to come, shall be able to separate us from the love of God, which is in Christ Jesus our Lord!" We say with Peter, "Lord, to whom shall we go?"

October 23 — Evening

Why do you sleep? Rise and pray,
lest you enter into temptation. {Luke 22:46}

When is the Christian most liable to sleep? Is it not *when his temporal circumstances are prosperous?* Have you not found it to be so? When you had daily troubles to take to the throne of grace, were you not more wakeful than you are now? Easy roads make sleepy travellers. Another dangerous time occurs *when all goes pleasantly in spiritual matters.* Christian did not go to sleep when lions were in the way, or when he was wading through the river, or when he was fighting with Apollyon, but when he had climbed halfway up the Hill Difficulty, and came to a delightful arbour, he sat down, and immediately fell asleep, to his great sorrow and loss. The Enchanted Ground is a place of balmy breezes, laden with fragrant odours and soft influences, all tending to lull pilgrims to sleep. Remember Bunyan's description: "Then they came to an arbour, warm, and promising much refreshment to the weary pilgrims; for it was finely fashioned overhead, beautified with greens, and furnished with benches and settles. It had also in it a soft couch, where the weary might recline. The arbour was called the Slothful's Friend, and was made on purpose to allure, if it might be, some of the pilgrims to take up their rest there when weary." Depend upon it, it is in easy places that men shut their eyes and wander into the dreamy land of forgetfulness. Old Erskine wisely remarked, "I like a roaring devil better than a sleeping devil." There is no temptation half so dangerous as not being tempted. The distressed soul does not sleep; it is after we enter into peaceful confidence and full assurance that we are in danger of slumbering. The disciples fell asleep after they had seen Jesus transfigured on the mountain top. Take heed, joyous Christian, prosperous times are close neighbours to temptations: be as happy as you wish, only be watchful.

October 24 — Morning

{Daily Reading: Luke 8:1–9:62} {Quick Study: Luke 17:1–18:43}

The trees of the Lord are full of sap. *{Psalms 104:16}*

Without sap the tree cannot flourish or even exist. *Vitality* is essential to a Christian. There must be *life* — a vital principle infused into us by God the Holy Spirit, or we cannot be trees of the Lord. The mere name of being a Christian is only a dead thing, we must be filled with the spirit of divine life. This life is *mysterious*. We do not understand the circulation of the sap, by what force it rises, and by what power it descends again. So the life within us is a sacred mystery. Regeneration is accomplished by the Holy Spirit entering into man and becoming man's life; and this divine life in a believer afterwards feeds upon the flesh and blood of Christ and is thus sustained by divine food, but who shall explain to us from where it comes and where it goes? What a secret thing the sap is! The roots go searching through the soil with their little spongioles, but we cannot see them suck out the various gases, or transmute the mineral into the vegetable; this work is done down in the dark. Our root is Christ Jesus, and our life is hidden in him; this is the secret of the Lord. The source of the Christian life is as secret as the life itself. How *permanently active* is the sap in the cedar! In the Christian the divine life is always full of energy — not always in fruit bearing, but in inward operations. Are not every one of the believer's *graces* in constant motion? But his life never ceases to palpitate within. He is not always working for God, but his heart is always living upon him. As the sap *reveals itself in producing the foliage and fruit of the tree,* so with a truly healthy Christian, his grace is externally revealed in his walk and conversation. If you talk with him, he cannot help speaking about Jesus. If you notice his actions you will see that he has been with Jesus. He has so much sap within, that it must fill his conduct and conversation with life.

October 24 — Evening

He began to wash the disciples' feet. *{John 13:5}*

The Lord Jesus loves his people so much, that every day he is still doing for them much that is analogous to washing their soiled feet. He accepts their poorest actions; he feels their deepest sorrow; he hears their slenderest wish, and he forgives their every transgression. He is still their servant as well as their Friend and Master. He not only performs majestic deeds for them, as wearing the mitre on his brow, and the precious jewels glittering on his breastplate, and standing up to plead for them, but humbly, patiently, he still goes around among his people with the basin and the towel. He does this when he puts away from us day by day our constant infirmities and sins. Last night, when you bowed the knee, you mournfully confessed that much of your conduct was not worthy of your profession; and even tonight, you must mourn afresh that you have fallen again into the very same folly and sin from which special grace delivered you long ago; and yet Jesus will have great patience with you; he will hear your confession of sin; he will say, "I will, be clean"; he will again apply the blood of sprinkling, and speak peace to your conscience, and remove every spot. It is a great act of eternal love when Christ once and for all absolves the sinner, and puts him into the family of God; but what condescending patience there is when the Saviour with much longsuffering bears the often recurring follies of his wayward disciple; day by day, and hour by hour, washing away the multiplied transgressions of his erring but yet beloved child! To dry up a flood of rebellion is something marvellous, but to endure the constant dropping of repeated offences — to bear with a perpetual trying of patience, this is divine indeed! While we find comfort and peace in our Lord's daily cleansing, its legitimate influence upon us will be to increase our watchfulness, and quicken our desire for holiness. *Is it so?*

October 25 — Morning

{Daily Reading: Luke 10:1–11:54} {Quick Study: Luke 19:1–20:47}

For the truth's sake, which dwells in us,
and shall be with us for ever. *{2 John 1:2}*

Once the truth of God obtains an entrance into the human heart and subdues the whole man to itself, no human or infernal power can dislodge it. We do not entertain it as a guest but as the master of the house — this is a *Christian necessity*, he is no Christian who does not believe this. Those who feel the vital power of the gospel, and know the might of the Holy Spirit as he opens, applies, and seals the Lord's Word, would sooner be torn to pieces than be torn away from the gospel of their salvation. What a thousand mercies are wrapped up in the assurance that the truth will be with us for ever; will be our living support, our dying comfort, our rising song, our eternal glory; this is a *Christian privilege*, without it our faith would be worthless. Some truths we outgrow and leave behind, for they are only rudiments and lessons for beginners, but we cannot thus deal with divine truth, for though it is sweet food for babes, it is in the highest sense strong meat for men. The truth that we are sinners is painfully with us to humble us and make us watchful; the more blessed truth that whoever believes on the Lord Jesus shall be saved, abides with us as our hope and joy. Experience, so far from loosening our hold on the doctrines of grace, has knit us to them more and more firmly; our grounds and motives for believing are now more strong, more numerous than ever, and we have reason to expect that it will be so until in death we hold the Saviour in our arms.

Wherever this abiding love of truth can be discovered, we are bound to exercise our love. No narrow circle can contain our gracious sympathies, wide as the election of grace must be our communion of heart. Much of error may be mingled with received truth. Let us war with the error but still love the brother for the measure of truth which we see in him; above all let us love and spread the truth ourselves.

October 25 — Evening

*She gleaned in the field after the reapers: and she
happened to come upon a part of the field
belonging to Boaz, who was of the
family of Elimelech. {Ruth 2:3}*

She *happened.* Yes, it seemed nothing but an accident, but how divinely it was overruled! Ruth had gone out with her mother's blessing, under the care of her mother's God, to humble but honourable toil, and the providence of God was guiding her every step. Little did she know that amid the sheaves she would find a husband, that he should make her the joint owner of all those broad acres, and that she, a poor foreigner, should become one of the progenitors of the great Messiah. God is very good to those who trust in him, and often surprises them with unlooked for blessings. Little do we know what may happen to us tomorrow, but this sweet fact may cheer us, that no good thing shall be withheld. Chance is banished from the faith of Christians, for they see the hand of God in everything. The trivial events of today or tomorrow may involve consequences of the highest importance. Oh Lord, deal as graciously with your servants as you did with Ruth.

How blessed would it be, if, in wandering in the field of meditation tonight, we should happen to come upon the place where our near Kinsman will reveal himself to us! Oh Spirit of God, guide us to him. We would sooner glean in his field than bear away the whole harvest from any other. Oh for the footsteps of his flock, which may conduct us to the green pastures where he dwells! This is a weary world when Jesus is away — we could better do without sun and moon than without him — but how divinely fair all things become in the glory of his presence! Our souls know the virtue which dwells in Jesus, and can never be content without him. We will wait in prayer tonight until we should happen to come upon a part of the field belonging to Jesus where he will reveal himself to us.

October 26 — Morning

{Daily Reading: Luke 12:1–13:35} {Quick Study: Luke 21:1–22:71}

"You looked for much, and, lo, it came to little; and
when you brought it home, I blew upon it. Why?"
says the Lord of hosts. "Because my house is in
ruins, and each of you runs to his own house." *{Haggai 1:9}*

Churlish souls stint their contributions to the ministry and missionary operations, and call such saving good economy; little
do they dream that they are thus impoverishing themselves. Their
excuse is that they must care for their own families, and they forget
that to neglect the house of God is the sure way to bring ruin upon
their own homes. Our God has a method in providence by which
he can prosper our endeavours beyond our expectation, or can
defeat our plans to our confusion and dismay; by a turn of his hand
he can steer our vessel in a profitable channel, or run it aground
in poverty and bankruptcy. It is the teaching of Scripture that the
Lord enriches the generous and leaves the miserly to find out that
withholding tends to poverty. In a very wide sphere of observation,
I have noticed that the most generous Christians of my acquaintance have been always the most happy, and almost invariably the
most prosperous. I have seen the generous giver rise to wealth of
which he never dreamed; and I have as often seen the mean, ungenerous churl descend to poverty by the very parsimony by which
he thought to rise. Men trust good stewards with larger and larger
sums, and so it frequently is with the Lord; he gives by cartloads to
those who give by bushels. Where wealth is not bestowed the Lord
makes the little much by the contentment which the sanctified
heart feels in a portion of which the tithe has been dedicated to the
Lord. Selfishness looks first at home, but godliness seeks first the
kingdom of God and his righteousness, yet in the long run selfishness is loss, and godliness is great gain. It needs faith to act towards
our God with an open hand, but surely he deserves it from us; and
all that we can do is a very poor acknowledgment of our amazing
indebtedness to his goodness.

October 26 — Evening

All the rivers run into the sea; yet the sea is not full; to the place from where the rivers come, there they return again. {Ecclesiastes 1:7}

Everything under the heavens is on the move; time knows nothing of rest. The solid earth is a rolling ball, and the great sun itself is a star obediently fulfilling its course around some greater luminary. Tides move the sea, winds stir the airy ocean, friction wears the rock: change and death rule everywhere. The sea is not a miser's storehouse for a wealth of waters, for as by one force the waters flow into it, by another they are lifted from it. Men are born only to die: everything is hurry, worry, and vexation of spirit. Friend of the unchanging Jesus, what a joy it is to reflect upon your changeless heritage; your sea of bliss which will be for ever full, since God himself shall pour eternal rivers of pleasure into it. We seek an abiding city beyond the skies, and we shall not be disappointed.

The passage before us may well teach us about gratitude. Father Ocean is a great receiver, but he is a generous distributor. What the rivers bring to him he returns to the earth in the form of clouds and rain. That man is out of sync with the universe who takes all but gives nothing back. To give to others is only sowing seed for ourselves. He who is so good a steward as to be willing to use his substance for his Lord, shall be entrusted with more. Friend of Jesus, are you rendering to him according to the benefit received? Much has been given to you, what is your fruit? Have you done all? Can you not do more? To be selfish is to be wicked. Suppose the ocean gave up none of its watery treasure, it would bring ruin upon our race. God forbid that any of us should follow the ungenerous and destructive policy of living for ourselves. Jesus did not please himself. All fulness dwells in him, but from his fulness we have all received. Oh, for Jesus' spirit, that henceforth we may not live for ourselves!

It is a faithful saying. *{2 Timothy 2:11}*

Paul has four of these *"faithful sayings."* The first is: "This is a faithful saying, and worthy of all acceptance, that Christ Jesus came into the world to save sinners." *{1 Timothy 1:15}* The next is: "Godliness is profitable for all things, having the promise of the life that now is, and of what is to come. 'This is a faithful saying, and worthy of all acceptance.'" *{1 Timothy 4:8–9}* The third is: "It is a faithful saying — If we suffer with him we shall also reign with him"; *{2 Timothy 2:11}* and the fourth is: "This is a faithful saying, that those who have believed in God might be careful to maintain good works." *{Titus 3:8}* We may trace a connection between these faithful sayings. The first one lays the foundation of our eternal salvation in the free grace of God, as shown to us in the mission of the great Redeemer. The next affirms the double blessedness which we obtain through this salvation — the blessings of the upper and lower springs — of time and of eternity. The third shows one of the duties to which the chosen people are called; we are ordained to suffer for Christ with the promise that "if we suffer, we shall also reign with him." The last describes the active form of Christian service, bidding us diligently to maintain good works. Thus, we have the root of salvation in free grace; next, the privileges of that salvation in the life which now is, and in what is to come; and we have also the two great branches of suffering with Christ and serving with Christ, loaded with the fruits of the Spirit. Treasure up these faithful sayings. Let them be the guides of our life, our comfort, and our instruction. The apostle of the Gentiles proved them to be faithful, they are still faithful, not one word shall fall to the ground; they are worthy of all acceptance, let us accept them now, and prove their faithfulness. Let these four faithful sayings be written on the four corners of my house.

October 27 — Evening

We are all as an unclean thing. *{Isaiah 64:6}*

The believer is a new creature, he belongs to a holy generation and a particular people — the Spirit of God is in him, and in all respects he is far removed from the natural man; but for all that the Christian is still a sinner. He is so from the imperfection of his nature, and will continue to be so until the end of his earthly life. The black fingers of sin soil our fairest robes. Sin mars our repentance, before the great Potter has finished it, upon the wheel. Selfishness defiles our tears, and unbelief tampers with our faith. The best thing we ever did apart from the merit of Jesus only swelled the number of our sins; for when we have been most pure in our own sight, yet, like the heavens, we are not pure in God's sight; and just as he charged his angels with folly, even more he must charge us with it, even in our most angelic frames of mind. The song which thrills to heaven, and seeks to emulate seraphic strains, has human discords in it. The prayer which moves the arm of God is still a bruised and battered prayer, and only moves that arm because the sinless One, the great Mediator, has stepped in to take away the sin of our supplication. The most golden faith or the purest degree of sanctification to which a Christian ever attained on earth, has still so much alloy in it as to be only worthy of the flames, when considered by itself. Every night we look in the mirror we see a sinner, and need confess, "We are all as an unclean thing, and all our righteousnesses are as filthy rags." Oh, how precious is the blood of Christ to such hearts as ours! How priceless a gift is his perfect righteousness! And how bright is the hope of perfect holiness hereafter! Even now, though sin dwells in us, *its power is broken*. It has no dominion; it is a broken-backed snake; we are in bitter conflict with it, but we only have to deal with a vanquished foe. In just a little while we shall enter victoriously into the city where nothing defiles.

I have chosen you out of the world. *{John 15:19}*

Here is distinguishing grace and discriminating regard; for some are made the special objects of divine affection. Do not be afraid to dwell upon this high doctrine of election. When your mind is most heavy and depressed, you will find it to be a bottle of the richest cordial. Those who doubt the doctrines of grace, or who cast them into the shade, miss the richest clusters of Eshcol; they lose the wines on the lees well refined, the fat things full of marrow. There is no balm in Gilead comparable to it. If the honey in Jonathan's stick when only touched enlightened *the eyes*, this is honey which will enlighten *your heart* to love and learn the mysteries of the kingdom of God. Eat, and do not fear gluttony; live upon this choice dainty, and do not fear that it will be too delicate a diet. Food from the King's table will not harm any of his courtiers. Desire to have your mind enlarged, so that you may comprehend more and more the eternal, everlasting, discriminating love of God. When you have mounted as high as election, abide on its sister mount, the covenant of grace. Covenant engagements are the munitions of stupendous rock behind which we lie entrenched; covenant engagements with the Surety, Christ Jesus, are the quiet resting places of trembling spirits.

> His oath, his covenant, his blood,
> Support me in the raging flood;
> When every earthly prop gives way,
> This still is all my strength and stay.

If Jesus undertook to bring me to glory, and if the Father promised that he would give me to the Son to be a part of the infinite reward of the travail of his soul; then, my soul, you are safe until God himself shall be unfaithful, until Jesus shall cease to be the truth. When David danced before the ark, he told Michal that election made him do so. Come, my soul, exult before the God of grace and leap for joy of heart.

October 28 — Evening

**His head is as the most fine gold, his locks are bushy,
and black as a raven.** *{Song of Solomon 5:11}*

Comparisons all fail to describe the Lord Jesus, but the spouse uses the best within her reach. By *the head* of Jesus we may understand his deity, "for the head of Christ is God" and then the ingot of purest gold is the best conceivable metaphor, but all too poor to describe one so precious, so pure, so dear, so glorious. Jesus is not a grain of gold, but a vast globe of it, a priceless mass of treasure such as earth and heaven cannot excel. The creatures are mere iron and clay, they all shall perish like wood, hay, and stubble, but the ever-living Head of the creation of God shall shine on for ever and ever. In him is no mixture, nor smallest taint of alloy. He is for ever infinitely holy and altogether divine. *The bushy locks* depict his manly vigour. There is nothing effeminate in our Beloved. He is the manliest of men. Bold as a lion, laborious as an ox, swift as an eagle. Every conceivable and inconceivable beauty is to be found in him, although once he was despised and rejected by men.

> His head the finest gold;
> With secret sweet perfume,
> His curled locks hang all as black
> As any raven's plume.

The glory of his head is not shorn away, he is eternally crowned with peerless majesty. *The black hair* indicates youthful freshness, for Jesus has the dew of his youth upon him. Others grow languid with age, but he is for ever a priest as was Melchizedek; others come and go, but he remains as God upon his throne, world without end. We will behold him tonight and adore him. Angels are gazing upon him — his redeemed must not turn away their eyes from him. Where else is there such a Beloved? Oh for an hour's fellowship with him! Away, oh intruding cares! Jesus draws me, and I run after him.

October 29 — Morning

{Daily Reading: Luke 19:1–20:47} {Quick Study: John 3:1–5:47}

Therefore after this manner pray:
Our Father who is in heaven etc. *{Matthew 6:9}*

This prayer begins where all true prayer must commence, with the spirit of *adoption*, "Our Father." There is no acceptable prayer until we can say, "I will arise, and go to my Father." This child-like spirit soon perceives the grandeur of the Father "in heaven," and ascends to *devout adoration*, "Hallowed be your name." The child lisping, "Abba, Father," grows into the cherub crying, "Holy, Holy, Holy." There is only a step from rapturous worship to the *glowing missionary spirit*, which is a sure outgrowth of filial love and reverent adoration — "Your kingdom come, your will be done on earth as it is in heaven." Next follows the heartfelt *expression of dependence* upon God — "Give us today our daily bread." Being further illuminated by the Spirit, he discovers that he is not only dependent, but sinful, hence he *entreats for mercy*, "Forgive us our debts as we forgive our debtors": and being pardoned, having the righteousness of Christ imputed, and knowing his acceptance with God, he humbly *supplicates for holy perseverance*, "Do not lead us into temptation." The man who is really forgiven is anxious not to offend again; the possession of justification leads to an anxious desire for sanctification. "Forgive us our debts," that is justification; "Do not lead us into temptation, but deliver us from evil," that is sanctification in its negative and positive forms. As the result of all this, there follows a *triumphant ascription of praise*, "Yours is the kingdom, the power, and the glory, for ever and ever, Amen." We rejoice that *our* King reigns in providence and shall reign in grace, from the river even to the ends of the earth, and of his dominion there shall be no end. Thus, from a sense of adoption, up to fellowship with our reigning Lord, this short model of prayer conducts the soul. Lord, teach us thus to pray.

October 29 — Evening

But their eyes were restrained so that they
did not know him. *{Luke 24:16}*

The disciples ought to have known Jesus, they had heard his voice so often, and gazed upon that marred face so frequently, that it is a wonder that they did not recognise him. Yet is it not so with you also? You have not seen Jesus recently. You have been to his table, and you have not met him there. You are in a dark trouble this evening, and though he plainly says, "It is I, do not be afraid," yet you cannot discern him. Alas! Our eyes are restrained. We know his voice; we have looked into his face; we have leaned our head upon his bosom, and yet, though Christ is very near to us, we are saying, "Oh, that I knew where I might find him!" We should know Jesus, for we have the Scriptures to reflect his image, and yet how possible it is for us to open that precious book and have no glimpse of the well Beloved! Dear child of God, are you in that state? Jesus feeds among the lilies of the Word, and you walk among those lilies, and yet you do not see him. He is accustomed to walk through the glades of Scripture, and to commune with his people, as the Father did with Adam in the cool of the day, and yet you are in the garden of Scripture, but cannot see him, although he is always there. And why do we not see him? It must be ascribed in our case, as in the case of the disciples, to unbelief. They evidently did not expect to see Jesus, and therefore they did not know him. To a great extent in spiritual things we get what we expect from the Lord. Faith alone can bring us to see Jesus. Make it your prayer, "Lord, open my eyes, so that I may see my Saviour present with me." It is a blessed thing to *want* to see him; but oh! it is better far to gaze upon him. To those who seek him he is kind; but to those who find him, he is dear beyond expression!

October 30 — Morning

{Daily Reading: Luke 21:1–22:71} {Quick Study: John 6:1–7:53}

I will praise you, oh Lord. *{Psalms 9:1}*

Praise should always follow answered prayer just as the mist of earth's gratitude rises when the sun of heaven's love warms the ground. Has the Lord been gracious to you, and inclined his ear to the voice of your supplication? Then praise him as long as you live. Let the ripe fruit drop upon the fertile soil from which it drew its life. Do not deny a song to him who has answered your prayer and given you the desire of your heart. To be silent over God's mercies is to incur the guilt of ingratitude; it is to act as basely as the nine lepers, who after they had been cured of their leprosy, did not return to give thanks to the healing Lord. To forget to praise God is to refuse to benefit ourselves; for praise, like prayer, is one great means of promoting the growth of the spiritual life. It helps to remove our burdens, to excite our hope, to increase our faith. It is a healthful and invigorating exercise which quickens the pulse of the believer, and nerves him for fresh enterprises in his Master's service. To bless God for mercies received is also the way to benefit our fellow men; "the humble shall hear of it and be glad." Others who have been in similar circumstances shall take comfort if we can say, "Oh! Magnify the Lord with me, and let us exalt his name together; this poor man cried, and the Lord heard him." Weak hearts will be strengthened, and drooping saints will be revived as they listen to our "songs of deliverance." Their doubts and fears will be rebuked, as we teach and admonish one another in psalms and hymns and spiritual songs. They too shall "sing in the ways of the Lord," when they hear us magnify his holy name. Praise is the most heavenly of Christian duties. The angels do not pray, but they do not cease to praise both day and night; and the redeemed, clothed in white robes, with palm branches in their hands, are never weary of singing the new song, "Worthy is the Lamb."

October 30 — Evening

You who dwell in the gardens, the
companions listen for your voice —
let me hear it. *{Song of Solomon 8:13}*

My sweet Lord Jesus well remembers the garden of Gethsemane, and although he has left that garden, he now dwells in the garden of his church; there he intimately reveals himself to those who keep his blessed company. That voice of love with which he speaks to his beloved is more musical than the harps of heaven. There is a depth of melodious love within it which leaves all human music far behind. Tens of thousands on earth, and millions above, are indulged with its harmonious accents. Some whom I well know, and whom I greatly envy, are at this moment listening to the beloved voice. Oh, if only I were a partaker of their joys! It is true some of these are poor, others bedridden, and some near the gates of death, but oh my Lord, I would cheerfully starve with them, pine with them, or die with them, if I might only hear your voice. Once I often heard it, but I have grieved your Spirit. Return to me in compassion, and once again say to me, "I am your salvation." No other voice can make me content; I know your voice, and cannot be deceived by another, oh please let me hear it. I do not know what you will say, neither do I make any condition, oh my Beloved, only let me hear you speak, and if it is a rebuke I will bless you for it. Perhaps to cleanse my dull ears I may need an operation very grievous to the flesh, but whatever it costs I do not turn from the one consuming desire, let me hear your voice. Bore my ears afresh; pierce my ear with your harshest notes, only do not permit me to continue deaf to your calls. Tonight, Lord, grant your unworthy one his desire, for I am yours, and you have bought me with your blood. You have opened my eyes to see you, and the sight has saved me. Lord, open my ears. I have read your heart, now let me hear your lips.

October 31 — Morning

{Daily Reading: Luke 23:1–24:53} {Quick Study: John 8:1–10:42}

Renew a right spirit within me. *{Psalms 51:10}*

A backslider, if there is a spark of life left in him, will groan after restoration. In this renewal the same exercise of grace is required as at our conversion. We needed repentance then; we certainly need it now. We needed faith so that we might come to Christ at first; only the same grace can bring us to Jesus now. We needed a word from the Most High, a word from the lips of the loving One, to end our fears then; we shall soon discover, when under a sense of present sin, that we need it now. No man can be renewed without as real and true a revelation of the Holy Spirit's energy as he felt at first, because the work is as great, and flesh and blood are as much in the way now as they ever were. Let your personal weakness, oh Christian, be a reason to make you pray earnestly to your God for help. Remember, David when he felt himself to be powerless, did not fold his arms or close his lips, but he hastened to the mercy seat with "renew a right spirit within me." Do not let the doctrine that you, by yourself, can do nothing, make you sleep; but let it be a goad in your side to drive you with an awful earnestness to Israel's strong Helper. Oh, that you may have grace to plead with God, as though you pleaded for your very life — "Lord, renew a right spirit within me." He who *sincerely* prays to God to do this, will prove his honesty by using the means through which God works. Be much in prayer; live much upon the Word of God; kill the lusts which have driven your Lord from you; be careful to watch over the future uprisings of sin. The Lord has his own appointed ways; sit by the wayside and you will be ready when he passes by. Continue in all those blessed ordinances which will foster and nourish your dying graces; and, knowing that all the power must proceed from him, do not cease to cry, "Renew a right spirit within me."

October 31 — Evening

**I knew you in the wilderness, in the land
of great drought.** *{Hosea 13:5}*

Yes, Lord, you indeed knew me in my *fallen state*, and you even then chose me for yourself. When I was loathsome and self-abhorred, you received me as your child, and you satisfied my craving wants. Blessed for ever be your name for this free, rich, abounding mercy. Since then, *my inward experience* has often been a wilderness; but you have still honoured me as your beloved, and poured streams of love and grace into me to gladden me, and make me fruitful. Yes, when my *outward circumstances* have been at the worst, and I have wandered in a land of drought, your sweet presence has solaced me. Men have not known me when scorn has awaited me, but you have known my soul in adversities, for no affliction dims the lustre of your love. Most gracious Lord, I magnify you for all your faithfulness to me in trying circumstances, and I deplore that I should at any time have forgotten you and been exalted in heart, when I have owed all to your gentleness and love. Have mercy upon your servant in this thing!

My soul, if Jesus thus acknowledged you in your low estate, be sure that you honour both himself and his cause now that you are in your prosperity. Do not be lifted up by your worldly successes being ashamed of the truth or of your poor church. Follow Jesus into the wilderness: bear the cross with him when the heat of persecution grows hot. He loved you, oh my soul, in your poverty and shame — never be so treacherous as to be ashamed of him. Oh, for more shame at the thought of being ashamed of my best Beloved! Jesus, my soul cleaves to you.

> I'll turn to you in days of light,
> As well as nights of care,
> You brightest amid all that's bright!
> You fairest of the fair!

November 1 — Morning

{Daily Reading: John 1:1–3:36} {Quick Study: John 11:1–12:50}

The church in your house. *{Philemon 1:2}*

Is there a church in this house? Are parents, children, friends, servants, all members of it? Or are some still unconverted? Let us pause here and let the question go around — *Am I a member of the church in this house?* How would father's heart leap for joy, and mother's eyes fill with holy tears if from the oldest to the youngest all were saved! Let us pray for this great mercy until the Lord shall grant it to us. Probably it had been the dearest object of Philemon's desires to have all his household saved; but it was not at first granted to him in its fulness. He had a wicked servant, Onesimus, who, having wronged him, ran away from his service. His master's prayers followed him, and at last, as God would have it, Onesimus was led to hear Paul preach; his heart was touched, and he returned to Philemon, not only to be a faithful servant, but a beloved brother, adding another member to the church in Philemon's house. Is there an unconverted servant or child absent this morning? Make special supplication that such may, on their return to their home, gladden all hearts with good news of what grace has done! Is there one present? Let him partake in the same earnest entreaty.

If there is such a church in our house, let us order it well, and let all act as in the sight of God. Let us move in the common affairs of life with studied holiness, diligence, kindness, and integrity. More is expected of a church than of an ordinary household; family worship must, in such a case, be more devout and hearty; internal love must be more warm and unbroken, and external conduct must be more sanctified and Christlike. We need not fear that the smallness of our number will put us out of the list of churches, for the Holy Spirit has here enrolled a family church in the inspired book of remembrance. As a church let us now draw near to the great head of the one universal church, and let us beseech him to give us grace to shine before men to the glory of his name.

November 1 — Evening

And did not know until the flood came,
and took them all away: so also shall the coming
of the Son of Man be. {Matthew 24:39}

Universal was the doom, neither rich nor poor escaped: the learned and the illiterate, the admired and the abhorred, the religious and the profane, the old and the young, all sank in one common ruin. Some had doubtlessly ridiculed the patriarch — where now are their merry jests? Others had threatened him for his zeal which they counted madness — where were their boastings and harsh speeches now? The critic who judged the old man's work is drowned in the same sea which covers his sneering companions. Those who spoke patronizingly of the good man's fidelity to his convictions, but did not share in them, have sunk to rise no more, and the workers who for pay helped to build the wondrous ark, are all lost also. The flood swept them *all* away, and made no single exception. Even so, outside of Christ, final destruction is certain for every man born of woman; no rank, possession, or character shall suffice to save a single soul who has not believed in the Lord Jesus. My soul, behold this wide spread judgment and tremble.

How marvellous was the general apathy! They were all eating and drinking, marrying and giving in marriage, until the awful morning dawned. There was not one wise man upon earth outside of the ark. Folly duped the whole race, folly as to self-preservation — the most foolish of all follies. Folly in doubting the most true God — the most malignant of fooleries. Strange, my soul, is it not? All men are negligent about their souls until grace gives them reason, then they leave their madness and act like rational beings, but not until then.

All, blessed be God, were safe in the ark, no ruin entered there. From the huge elephant down to the tiny mouse all were safe. The timid hare was equally secure with the courageous lion, the helpless cony as safe as the laborious ox. All are safe in Jesus. My soul, are you in him?

November 2 — Morning

{Daily Reading: John 4:1–5:47} {Quick Study: John 13:1–14:31}

I am the Lord, I do not change. *{Malachi 3:6}*

It is well for us that, amidst all the variableness of life, there is One whom change cannot affect; One whose heart can never alter, and on whose brow mutability can make no furrows. All other things have changed — all things are changing. The sun itself grows dim with age; the world is waxing old; the folding up of the worn out vesture has commenced; the heavens and earth must soon pass away; they shall perish, they shall wax old as does a garment; but there is only One who has immortality, of whose years there is no end, and in whose person there is no change. The delight which the mariner feels, when, after having been tossed about for many a day, he steps again upon the solid shore, is the same satisfaction of a Christian when, amidst all the changes of this troubled life, he rests the foot of his faith upon this truth — *"I am the Lord, I do not change."*

The stability which the anchor gives the ship when it has at last obtained a firm hold, is similar to the Christian's hope when it fixes itself upon this glorious truth. With God "is no variableness, neither shadow of turning." Whatever his attributes were of old, they are now; his power, his wisdom, his justice, his truth, are all unchanged. He has always been the refuge of his people, their stronghold in the day of trouble, and he is still their sure Helper. He is unchanged in his *love*. He has loved his people with "an everlasting love"; he loves them now as much as he ever did, and when all earthly things shall have melted in the last conflagration, his love will still wear the dew of its youth. Precious is the assurance that he does not change! The wheel of providence revolves, but its axle is eternal love.

> Death and change are busy ever,
> Man decays, and ages move;
> But his mercy wanes never;
> God is wisdom, God is love.

November 2 — Evening

*Horror has taken hold upon me because of the
wicked who forsake your law.* {Psalms 119:53}

My soul, do you feel this holy shuddering at the sins of others? For otherwise you lack inward holiness. David's cheeks were wet with rivers of waters because of prevailing unholiness; Jeremiah desired eyes like fountains so that he might lament the iniquities of Israel, and Lot was vexed with the conduct of the men of Sodom. Those upon whom the mark was set in Ezekiel's vision were those who sighed and cried for the abominations of Jerusalem. It can only grieve gracious souls to see what pains men take to go to hell. They know the evil of sin by experience, and they are alarmed to see others flying like moths into its blaze. Sin makes the righteous shudder, because it violates a holy law, which it is in every man's highest interest to keep; it pulls down the pillars of the commonwealth. Sin in others horrifies a believer, because it reminds him of the baseness of his own heart: when he sees a transgressor he cries with the saint mentioned by Bernard, "He fell today, and I may fall tomorrow." Sin to a believer is horrible, because it crucified the Saviour; he sees in every iniquity the nails and spear. How can a saved soul see that cursed kill-Christ sin without abhorrence? Say, my heart, do you sensibly join in all this? It is an awful thing to insult God to his face. The good God deserves better treatment, the great God claims it, the just God will have it, or repay his adversary to his face. An awakened heart trembles at the audacity of sin, and stands alarmed at the contemplation of its punishment. How monstrous a thing is rebellion! How direful a doom is prepared for the ungodly! My soul, never laugh at sin's fooleries, lest you come to smile at sin itself. It is your enemy, and your Lord's enemy — view it with detestation, for only by so doing can you prove your possession of holiness, without which no man can see the Lord.

November 3 — Morning

{Daily Reading: John 6:1–8:59} {Quick Study: John 15:1–17:26}

Behold, he prays. *{Acts 9:11}*

Prayers are instantly noticed in heaven. The moment Saul began to pray the Lord heard him. Here is comfort for the distressed but praying soul. Oftentimes a poor broken hearted one bends his knee, but can only utter his wailing in the language of sighs and tears; yet that groan has made all the harps of heaven thrill with music; that tear has been caught by God and treasured in the lachrymatory of heaven. "You put my tears into your bottle," implies that they are caught as they flow. The supplicant, whose tears precede his words, will be well understood by the Most High. He may only look up with misty eye; but "prayer is the falling of a tear." Tears are the diamonds of heaven; sighs are a part of the music of Jehovah's court, and are numbered with "the sublimest strains that reach the Majesty on high." Do not think that your prayer, however weak or trembling, will not be noticed. Jacob's ladder is lofty, but our prayers shall lean upon the Angel of the covenant and so climb its starry rungs. Our God not only *hears* prayer but also *loves* to hear it. "He does not forget the cry of the humble." Truly, he does not regard high looks and lofty words; he does not care for the pomp and pageantry of kings; he does not listen to the swell of martial music; he does not regard the triumph and pride of man; but wherever there is a heart full of sorrow, or a lip quivering with agony, or a deep groan, or a penitential sigh, the heart of Jehovah is open; he writes it down in the registry of his memory; he puts our prayers, like rose leaves, between the pages of his book of remembrance, and when the volume is opened at last, there shall be a precious fragrance rising up from it.

> Faith asks no signal from the skies,
> To show that prayers accepted rise,
> Our Priest is in his holy place,
> And answers from the throne of grace.

November 3 — Evening

**Their prayer came up to his holy dwelling place,
even to heaven.** *{2 Chronicles 30:27}*

Prayer is the never-failing resort of the Christian in any case, in every plight. When you cannot use your sword you may take the weapon of all prayer. Your powder may be damp, your bow-string may be relaxed, but the weapon of all prayer need never be out of order. Leviathan laughs at the javelin, but he trembles at prayer. Sword and spear need furbishing, but prayer never rusts, and when we think it is most blunt it cuts the best. Prayer is an open door which no one can shut. Demons may surround you on all sides, but the way upward is always open, and as long as that road is unobstructed, you will not fall into the enemy's hand. We can never be taken by blockade, escalade,[1] mine, or storm, as long as heavenly helps can come down to us by Jacob's ladder to relieve us in the time of our necessities. Prayer is never out of season: in summer and in winter its merchandise is precious. Prayer gains audience with heaven in the dead of night, in the midst of business, in the heat of noonday, in the shadows of evening. In every condition, whether of poverty, or sickness, or obscurity, or slander, or doubt, your covenant God will welcome your prayer and answer it from his holy place. Nor is prayer ever *futile*. True prayer is always true power. You may not always get what you ask for, but you shall always have your real needs supplied. When God does not answer his children according to the letter, he does so according to the spirit. If you ask for coarse flour, will you be angered because he gives you the finest flour? If you seek bodily health, should you complain if instead he makes your sickness turn to the healing of spiritual maladies? Is it not better to have the cross sanctified than removed? This evening, my soul, do not forget to offer your petition and request, for the Lord is ready to grant you your desires.

1. Escalade: scaling of walls with ladders.
    (*Oxford English Dictionary*)

November 4 — Morning

{Daily Reading: John 9:1–10:42} {Quick Study: John 18:1–19:42}

For my strength is made perfect
in weakness. *{2 Corinthians 12:9}*

A primary qualification for serving God with any amount of success, and for doing God's work well and triumphantly, is a sense of our own weakness. When God's warrior marches out to battle, strong in his own might, when he boasts, "I know that I shall conquer, my own right arm and my conquering sword shall get the victory for me," defeat is not far off. God will not go with that man who marches in his own strength. He who counts on victory thus has counted wrongly, for " 'It is not by might, nor by power, but by my Spirit,' says the Lord of hosts." Those who go out to fight, boasting about their prowess, shall return with their bright banners trailing in the dust, and their armour stained with disgrace. Those who serve God must serve him in his own way, and in his strength, or he will never accept their service. God can never honour what a man does when he is unaided by divine strength. He casts away the mere fruits of the earth; he will only reap that grain which was sown from heaven, watered by grace, and ripened by the sun of divine love. God will empty out all that you have before he will put his own into you; he will first clean out your granaries before he will fill them with the finest of the wheat. The river of God is full of water; but not one drop of it flows from earthly springs. God will have no strength used in his battles but the strength which he himself imparts. Are you mourning over your own weakness? Take courage, for there must be a consciousness of weakness before the Lord will give you victory. Your emptiness is only the preparation for your being filled, and your casting down is only the making ready for your lifting up.

> When I am weak then I am strong,
> Grace is my shield and Christ my song.

In your light we shall see light. *{Psalms 36:9}*

No lips can describe the love of Christ to the heart until Jesus himself shall speak within. Descriptions all fall flat and tame unless the Holy Spirit fills them with life and power; until our Emmanuel reveals himself within, the soul does not see him. If you wish to see the sun, would you gather together the common means of illumination, and seek in that way to see the orb of day? No, the wise man knows that the sun must reveal itself, and only by its own blaze can that mighty lamp be seen. It is so with Christ. "Blessed are you, Simon Barjona," he said to Peter, "for flesh and blood has not revealed this to you." Purify flesh and blood by any educational process you may select, elevate mental faculties to the highest degree of intellectual power, yet none of these can reveal Christ. The Spirit of God must come with power, and overshadow the man with his wings, and then in that mystic holy of holies the Lord Jesus must display himself to the sanctified eye, as he does not to the totally blind sons of men. Christ must be his own mirror. The great mass of this bleary-eyed world can see nothing of the ineffable glories of Emmanuel. He stands before them without form or comeliness, a root out of a dry ground, rejected by the vain and despised by the proud. Only where the Spirit has touched the eye with eye salve, quickened the heart with divine life, and educated the soul to a heavenly taste, only there is he understood. "To you who believe he is precious"; to you he is the chief cornerstone, the rock of your salvation, your all in all; but to others he is "a stone of stumbling and a rock of offence." Happy are those to whom our Lord reveals himself, for his promise to such is that he will *make his abode with them*. Oh Jesus, our Lord, our heart is open, come in, and go out no more for ever. Show yourself to us now! Favour us with a glimpse of your all conquering charms.

November 5 — Morning

{Daily Reading: John 11:1–12:50} {Quick Study: John 20:1–21:25}

No weapon that is formed against you
shall prosper. *{Isaiah 54:17}*

Today is notable in English history for two great deliverances performed by God for us. On this day the plot of the Papists to destroy our Houses of Parliament was discovered in 1605.

> While for our princes they prepare
> In caverns deep a burning snare,
> He shot from heaven a piercing ray,
> And the dark treachery brought to day.

And secondly — today is the anniversary of the landing of King William III, at Torbay, by which the hope of popish ascendancy was quashed, and religious liberty was secured in 1688.

Today ought to be celebrated, not by the Saturnalia of striplings, but by the songs of saints. Our Puritan forefathers most devoutly made it a special time of thanksgiving. There is extant a record of the annual sermons preached by Matthew Henry on this day. Our Protestant feeling, and our love of liberty, should make us regard its anniversary with holy gratitude. Let our hearts and lips exclaim, "We have heard with our ears, and our fathers have told us the wondrous things which you did in their day, and in the old time before them." You have made this nation the home of the gospel; and when the foe has risen against her, you have shielded her. Help us to offer repeated songs for repeated deliverances. Grant us more and more a hatred of Antichrist, and hasten on the day of her entire extinction. Until then and for ever, we believe the promise, "No weapon that is formed against you shall prosper." Should it not be laid upon the heart of every lover of the gospel of Jesus on this day to plead for the overturning of false doctrines and the extension of divine truth? Would it not be well to search our own hearts, and turn out any of the popish lumber of self-righteousness which may lie concealed in it?

November 5 — Evening

Be thankful to him,
and bless his name. *{Psalms 100:4}*

Our Lord wishes to have all his people rich in high and happy thoughts concerning his blessed person. Jesus is not content that his brethren should think lowly of him; it is his pleasure that his espoused ones should be delighted with his beauty. We are not to regard him as a bare necessity, like bread and water, but as a luxurious delicacy, as a rare and ravishing delight. To this end he has revealed himself as the "pearl of great price" in its peerless beauty, as the "bundle of myrrh" in its refreshing fragrance, as the "rose of Sharon" in its lasting perfume, as the "lily" in its spotless purity.

As a help to high thoughts of Christ, remember the high estimation that Christ has in heaven, where things are measured by the right standard. Think how God esteems the only begotten Son, his unspeakable gift to us. Consider what the angels think of him, as they count it their highest honour to veil their faces at his feet. Consider what the bloodwashed think of him, as day without night they sing his well-deserved praises. High thoughts of Christ will enable us to act consistently in our relationship towards him. The more loftily we see Christ enthroned, and the more lowly we are when bowing before the foot of the throne, the more truly shall we be prepared to act our part towards him. Our Lord Jesus desires us to think well of him, so that we may submit cheerfully to his authority. High thoughts of him increase our love. Love and esteem go together. Therefore, believer, think much of your Master's excellencies. Study him in his primeval glory, before he took upon himself your nature! Think of the mighty love which drew him from his throne to die upon the cross! Admire him as he conquers all the powers of hell! See him risen, crowned, and glorified! Bow before him as the Wonderful, the Counsellor, the Mighty God, for only thus will your love for him be what it should be.

November 6 — Morning

{Daily Reading: John 13:1–16:33} {Quick Study: Acts 1:1–3:26}

I will pour water upon him who is thirsty. *{Isaiah 44:3}*

When a believer has fallen into a low, sad state of feeling, he often tries to lift himself out of it by chastening himself with dark and doleful fears. Such is not the way to rise from the dust, but to continue in it. You may as well chain the eagle's wing to make it mount, as doubt in order to increase our grace. It is not the law, but the gospel which saves the seeking soul at first; and it is not a legal bondage, but gospel liberty which can restore the fainting believer afterwards. Slavish fear does not restore the backslider to God, but the sweet wooings of love allure him to Jesus' bosom. Are you this morning thirsting for the living God, and unhappy because you cannot find him to the delight of your heart? Have you lost the joy of religion, and is this your prayer, "Restore to me the joy of your salvation"? Are you conscious also that you are barren, like the dry ground; that you are not bringing forth the fruit for God which he has a right to expect from you; that you are not as useful in the church, or in the world, as your heart desires to be? Then here is exactly the promise which you need, "I will pour water upon him who is thirsty." You shall receive the grace you so much require, and you shall have it to the uttermost reach of your needs. Water refreshes the thirsty: you shall be refreshed; your desires shall be gratified. Water quickens sleeping vegetable life: your life shall be quickened by fresh grace. Water swells the buds and makes the fruits ripen; you shall have fructifying grace: you shall be made fruitful in the ways of God. Whatever good quality there is in divine grace, you shall enjoy it to the full. All the riches of divine grace you shall receive in plenty; you shall be as it were drenched with it: and as sometimes the meadows become flooded by the bursting rivers, and the fields are turned into pools, so shall you be — the thirsty land shall be springs of water.

November 6 — Evening

Saying, "This is the blood of the testament which God has commanded you." *{Hebrews 9:20}*

There is a strange power about the very name of blood, and the sight of it is always affecting. A kind heart cannot bear to see a sparrow bleed, and unless familiarised by use, turns away with horror at the slaughter of a beast. As for the blood of men, it is a consecrated thing: it is murder to shed it in wrath, it is a dreadful crime to squander it in war. Is this solemnity occasioned by the fact that the blood is the life, and its being pouring out the token of death? We think so. When we rise to contemplate the blood of the Son of God, our awe is yet more increased, and we shudder as we think of the guilt of sin, and the terrible penalty which the Sin Bearer endured. Blood, always precious, is priceless when it streams from Emmanuel's side. The blood of Jesus seals the *covenant* of grace, and makes it for ever sure. Covenants of old were made by sacrifice, and the everlasting covenant was ratified in the same manner. Oh, the delight of being saved upon the sure foundation of divine engagements which cannot be dishonoured! Salvation by the works of the law is a frail and broken vessel whose shipwreck is sure; but the covenant vessel fears no storms, for the blood ensures the whole. The blood of Jesus made his *testament* valid. Wills are of no power unless the testators die. In this light the soldier's spear is a blessed aid to faith, since it proved our Lord to be really dead. There can be no doubt about that matter, and we may boldly appropriate the legacies which he has left for his people. Happy are those who see their title to heavenly blessings assured to them by a dying Saviour. But has this blood no voice for us? Does it not bid us to sanctify ourselves to him by whom we have been redeemed? Does it not call us to newness of life, and incite us to entire consecration to the Lord? Oh that the power of the blood might be known, and felt in us tonight!

November 7 — Morning

{Daily Reading: John 17:1–18:40} {Quick Study: Acts 4:1–5:42}

**Behold, I have engraven you upon
the palms of my hands.** *{Isaiah 49:16}*

No doubt a part of the wonder which is concentrated in the word *Behold,* is heightened by the unbelieving lamentation of the preceding sentence. Zion said, "The Lord has forsaken me, and my God has forgotten me." How amazed the divine mind seems to be at this wicked unbelief! What can be more astounding than the unfounded doubts and fears of God's favoured people? The Lord's loving word of rebuke should make us blush; he cries, "How can I have forgotten you, when I have engraven you upon the palms of my hands? How dare you doubt my constant remembrance, when the memorial is set upon my very flesh?" Oh, unbelief, how strange a marvel you are! We do not know which most to wonder about, the faithfulness of God or the unbelief of his people. He keeps his promise a thousand times, and yet the next trial makes us doubt him. He never fails; he is never a dry well; he is never as a setting sun, a passing meteor, or a melting vapour; and yet we are as continually vexed with anxieties, molested with suspicions, and disturbed with fears, as if our God were the mirage of the desert. "Behold," *is a word intended to heighten admiration*. Here, indeed, we have a theme for marvelling. Heaven and earth may well be astonished that rebels should obtain so great a nearness to the heart of infinite love as to be written upon the palms of his hands. "I have engraven *you*." It does not say, "Your name." The name is there, but that is not all: "I have engraven *you*." See the fulness of this! I have engraven your person, your image, your case, your circumstances, your sins, your temptations, your weaknesses, your needs, your works; I have engraven *you*, everything about you, all that concerns you; I have put you altogether there. Will you ever say again that your God has forsaken you when he has engraven *you* upon his own palms?

November 7 — Evening

And you shall be witnesses to me. *{Acts 1:8}*

In order to learn how to discharge your duty as a witness for Christ, look at his example. He is always witnessing: by the well of Samaria, or in the temple of Jerusalem: by the lake of Gennesaret, or on the mountain's brow. He is witnessing night and day; his mighty prayers are as vocal to God as his daily services. He witnesses under all circumstances; Scribes and Pharisees cannot shut his mouth; even before Pilate he witnesses a good confession. He witnesses so clearly, and distinctly that there is no mistake in him. Christian, make your life a clear testimony. Be as the brook in which you may see every stone at the bottom — not as the muddy creek, of which you only see the surface — but clear and transparent, so that your heart's love for God and man may be visible to all. You need not *say*, "I am true": *be* true. Do not boast of integrity, but *be* upright. So shall your testimony be such that men cannot help seeing it. Never, for fear of feeble man, restrain your witness. Your lips have been warmed with a coal from off the altar; let them speak like heaven-touched lips should. "In the morning sow your seed, and in the evening do not withhold your hand." Do not watch the clouds, do not consult the wind — in season and out of season witness for the Saviour, and if it shall come to pass that for Christ's sake and the gospel's you shall endure suffering in any form, do not shrink, but rejoice in the honour thus conferred upon you, that you are counted worthy to suffer with your Lord; and joy also in this — that your sufferings, your losses, and persecutions shall make you a platform, from which the more vigorously and with greater power you shall witness for Christ Jesus. Study your great Exemplar, and be filled with his Spirit. Remember that you need much teaching, much upholding, much grace, and much humility, if your witnessing is to be for your Master's glory.

November 8 — Morning

{Daily Reading: John 19:1–21:25} {Quick Study: Acts 6:1–7:60}

As you have received
Christ Jesus the Lord. *{Colossians 2:6}*

The life of faith is represented as *receiving — an act which implies the very opposite of anything like merit.* It is simply the acceptance of a gift. As the earth drinks in the rain, as the sea receives the streams, as night accepts light from the stars, so we, giving nothing, partake freely of the grace of God. The saints are not, by nature, wells, or streams, they are only cisterns into which the living water flows; they are empty vessels into which God pours his salvation. The idea of receiving implies *a sense of realisation,* making the matter a *reality.* One cannot very well receive a shadow; we receive what is substantial: so it is in the life of faith, Christ becomes real to us. While we are without faith, Jesus is a mere name to us — a person who lived a long while ago, so long ago that his life is only a history to us now! By an act of faith Jesus becomes a real person in the consciousness of our heart. But receiving also means *grasping or getting possession of.* The thing which I receive becomes my own: I appropriate for myself what is given. When I receive Jesus, he becomes *my* Saviour, so much mine that neither life nor death shall be able to rob me of him. All this is to receive Christ — to take him as God's free gift; to realise him in my heart, and to appropriate him as mine.

Salvation may be described as the blind receiving sight, the deaf receiving hearing, the dead receiving life; but we have not only received these blessings, we have received CHRIST JESUS himself. It is true that he gave us life from the dead. He gave us pardon for sin; he gave us imputed righteousness. These are all precious things, but we are not content with them; we have received *Christ himself.* The Son of God has been poured into us, and we have received him, and appropriated him. What a heartful Jesus must be, for heaven itself cannot contain him!

November 8 — Evening

The Master says, "Where is the guest room, where I shall eat the Passover with my disciples?" {Mark 14:14}

Jerusalem at the time of the Passover was one great inn; each householder had invited his own friends, but no one had invited the Saviour, and he had no dwelling of his own. It was by his own supernatural power that he found himself an upper room in which to keep the feast. It is so even today — Jesus is not received among the sons of men except only where by his supernatural power and grace he makes the heart anew. All doors are open enough to the prince of darkness, but Jesus must clear a way for himself or lodge in the streets. It was through the mysterious power exerted by our Lord that the householder raised no question, but at once cheerfully and joyfully opened his guest room. Who he was, and what he was, we do not know, but he readily accepted the honour which the Redeemer proposed to confer upon him. In like manner it is still discovered who the Lord's chosen are, and who are not; for when the gospel comes to some, they fight against it, and will not have it, but where men receive it, welcoming it, this is a sure indication that there is a secret work going on in the soul, and that God has chosen them for eternal life. Are you willing, dear reader, to receive Christ? Then there is no difficulty in the way; Christ will be your guest; his own power is working with you, making you willing. What an honour to entertain the Son of God! The heaven of heavens cannot contain him, and yet he condescends to find a house within our hearts! We are not worthy that he should come under our roof, but what an unutterable privilege when he condescends to enter! for then he makes a feast, and causes us to feast with him upon royal dainties, we sit at a banquet where the food is immortal, and give immortality to those who eat it. Blessed among the sons of Adam is he who entertains the angels' Lord.

November 9 — Morning

{Daily Reading: Acts 1:1–3:26} {Quick Study: Acts 8:1–9:43}

So walk in him. *{Colossians 2:6}*

If we have received Christ himself in our innermost hearts, our new life will reveal its intimate acquaintance with him by a *walk of faith in him*. Walking implies action. Our religion is not to be confined to our prayer closet; we must carry out into practical effect what we believe. If a man walks in Christ, then he so acts as Christ would act; for Christ being in him, his hope, his love, his joy, his life, he is the reflection of the image of Jesus; and men say of that man, "He is like his Master; he lives like Jesus Christ." Walking signifies *progress*. "So walk in him"; proceed from grace to grace, run forward until you reach the uttermost degree of knowledge that a man can attain concerning our Beloved. Walking implies *continuance*. There must be a perpetual abiding in Christ. How many Christians think that in the morning and evening they ought to come into the company of Jesus, and may then give their hearts to the world all the day: but this is poor living; we should always be with him, treading in his steps and doing his will. Walking also implies *habit*. When we speak of a man's walk and conversation, we mean his habits, the constant tenor of his life. Now, if we sometimes enjoy Christ, and then forget him; sometimes call him ours, and immediately lose our hold, that is not a habit; we do not *walk* in him. We must keep to him, cling to him, never let him go, but live and have our being in him. "Just as you have received Christ Jesus the Lord, so walk in him"; persevere in the same way in which you have begun, and, just as at the first Christ Jesus was the trust of your faith, the source of your life, the principle of your action, and the joy of your spirit, so let him be the same until life's end; the same when you walk through the valley of the shadow of death, and enter into the joy and the rest which remain for the people of God. Oh Holy Spirit, enable us to obey this heavenly precept.

November 9 — Evening

*His place of defence shall be the munitions
of rocks: bread shall be given to him; his waters
shall be sure.* {*Isaiah 33:16*}

Do you doubt, oh Christian, do you doubt if God will fulfil his promise? Shall the munitions of rock be carried by storm? Shall the storehouses of heaven fail? Do you think that your Heavenly Father, although he knows that you have need of food and clothing, will still forget you? When not a sparrow falls to the ground without your Father's knowledge, and the very hairs of your head are all numbered, will you mistrust and doubt him? Perhaps your affliction will continue upon you until you dare to trust your God, and then it shall end. There are very many who have been tried and severely vexed until at last they have been driven in sheer desperation to exercise faith in God, and the moment of their faith has been the instant of their deliverance; they have seen whether God would keep his promise or not. Oh, I beseech you, doubt him no longer! Do not please Satan, and do not grieve yourself by indulging any more those hard thoughts of God. Do not think it a light matter to doubt Jehovah. Remember, it is a *sin*; and not a little sin either, but criminal in the highest degree. The angels never doubted him, nor the demons either: we alone, out of all the beings that God has created, dishonour him by unbelief, and tarnish his honour by mistrust. Shame upon us for this! Our God does not deserve to be so basely suspected; in our past life we have proven him to be true and faithful to his word, and with so many instances of his love and of his kindness as we have received, and are daily receiving from his hands, it is base and inexcusable that we allow a doubt to rest within our heart. May we henceforth wage constant war against doubts about our God — enemies to our peace and to his honour; and with an unstaggering faith believe that what he has promised he will also perform. "Lord, I believe, help my unbelief."

November 10 — Morning

{Daily Reading: Acts 4:1–6:15} {Quick Study: Acts 10:1–12:25}

The eternal God is your refuge. *{Deuteronomy 33:27}*

The word *refuge* may be translated "mansion," or "abiding place," which gives the thought that *God is our abode, our home.* There is a fulness and sweetness in the metaphor, for our home is dear to our hearts, although it is the humblest cottage, or the scantiest attic; and far dearer is our blessed God, in whom we live, and move, and have our being. It is at home that we *feel safe*: we shut the world out and dwell in quiet security. So when we are with our God we "fear no evil." He is our shelter and retreat, our abiding refuge. At home, *we take our rest*; it is there we find repose after the fatigue and toil of the day. And so our hearts find rest in God, when, wearied with life's conflict, we turn to him, and our soul dwells at ease. At home, also, we *let our hearts loose*; we are not afraid of being misunderstood, nor of our words being misconstrued. So when we are with God we can commune freely with him, laying open all our hidden desires; for if the "secret of the Lord is with those who fear him," the secrets of those who fear him ought to be, and must be, with their Lord. Home, too, is the place of our *truest and purest happiness*: and it is in God that our hearts find their deepest delight. We have joy in him which far surpasses all other joy. *It is also for home that we work and labour.* The thought of it gives strength to bear the daily burden, and quickens the fingers to perform the task; and in this sense we may also say that God is our home. Love for him strengthens us. We think of him in the person of his dear Son; and a glimpse of the suffering face of the Redeemer constrains us to labour in his cause. We feel that we must work, for we have brethren yet to be saved, and we have our Father's heart to make glad by bringing home his wandering sons; we wish to fill with holy mirth the sacred family among whom we dwell. Happy are those who have thus the God of Jacob for their refuge!

November 10 — Evening

It is enough for the disciple that he be like his master. *{Matthew 10:25}*

No one will dispute this statement, for it would be unseemly for the servant to be exalted above his master. When our Lord was on earth, what was the treatment he received? Were his claims acknowledged, his instructions followed, his perfections worshipped by those whom he came to bless? No; "He was despised and rejected by men." His place was outside the camp: his occupation was bearing the cross. Did the world yield him solace and rest? "Foxes have holes, and the birds of the air have nests; but the Son of man has nowhere to lay his head." This inhospitable country afforded him no shelter: it cast him out and crucified him. If you are a follower of Jesus, and maintain a consistent, Christlike walk and conduct then you must expect men to watch closely your spiritual life and development. They will treat it as they treated the Saviour — they will despise it. Do not imagine that worldlings will admire you, or that the more holy and the more like Christ you are, the more peaceably people will act towards you. When they did not prize the polished gem, why should they value the jewel in the rough? "If they have called the Master of the house Beelzebub, how much more shall they call those of his household?" If we were more like Christ, we would be more hated by his enemies. It would be a sad dishonour for a child of God to be the world's favourite. It is a very bad omen to hear a wicked world clap its hands and shout "Well done" to the Christian man. He may begin to look at his character, and wonder whether he has not been doing wrong, when the unrighteous give him their approbation. Let us be true to our Master, and have no friendship with a blind and base world which scorns and rejects him. Far be it from us to seek a crown of honour where our Lord found a coronet of thorns.

November 11 — Morning

{Daily Reading: Acts 7:1–8:40} {Quick Study: Acts 13:1–15:41}

Underneath are the everlasting arms. *{Deuteronomy 33:27}*

God — the eternal God — is himself our support at all times, and especially when we are sinking in deep trouble. There are times when the Christian *sinks very low in humiliation.* Under a deep sense of his great sinfulness, he is humbled before God until he scarcely knows how to pray, because he appears, in his own sight, so worthless. Well, child of God, remember that when you are at your worst and lowest, yet "underneath" you "are everlasting arms." Sin may drag you ever so low, but Christ's great atonement is still under all. You may have descended into the deeps, but you cannot have fallen so low as "the uttermost"; and to the uttermost he saves. Again, the Christian sometimes sinks very deeply in *severe trial from without.* Every earthly prop is cut away. What then? Still underneath him are "the everlasting arms." He cannot fall so deep in distress and affliction but the covenant grace of an ever-faithful God will still encircle him. The Christian may be sinking under *trouble from within through* fierce conflict, but even then he cannot be brought so low as to be beyond the reach of the "everlasting arms" — they are underneath him; and, while thus sustained, all Satan's efforts to harm him avail nothing.

This assurance of support is a comfort to any *weary but earnest worker* in the service of God. It implies a promise of strength for each day, grace for each need, and power for each duty. And, further, *when death comes,* the promise shall still hold good. When we stand in the midst of Jordan, we shall be able to say with David, "I will fear no evil, for you are with me." We shall descend into the grave, but we shall go no lower, for the eternal arms prevent our further fall. All through life, and at its close, we shall be upheld by the "everlasting arms" — arms that neither flag nor lose their strength, for "the everlasting God does not faint, neither is weary."

November 11 — Evening

He shall choose our inheritance for us. *{Psalms 47:4}*

Believer, if your inheritance is a lowly one you should be satisfied with your earthly portion; for you may rest assured that it is the best *for you*. Unerring wisdom ordained your lot, and selected the safest and best condition for you. A ship of large tonnage is to be brought up the river; now, in one part of the stream there is a sandbank; should someone ask, "Why does the captain steer through the deep part of the channel and deviate so much from a straight line?" His answer would be, "Because I would not get my vessel into the harbour at all if I did not keep to the deep channel." So, it may be, you would run aground and suffer shipwreck, if your Divine Captain did not steer you into the depths of affliction where waves of trouble follow each other in quick succession. Some plants die if they have too much sunshine. It may be that you are planted where you get very little, you are put there by the loving Husbandman, because only in that situation will you bring forth fruit to perfection. Remember this, had any other condition been better for you than the one in which you are, divine love would have put you there. You are placed by God in the most suitable circumstances, and if you had the choosing of your lot, you would soon cry, "Lord, choose my inheritance for me, for by my self-will I am pierced through with many sorrows." Be content with such things as you have, since the Lord has ordered all things for your good. Take up your own daily cross; it is the burden best suited for your shoulder, and will prove most effective to make you perfect in every good word and work to the glory of God. Down busy self, and proud impatience, it is not for you to choose, but for the Lord of love!

> Trials must and will befall —
> But with humble faith to see
> Love inscribed upon them all;
> This is happiness to me.

November 12 — Morning

{Daily Reading: Acts 9:1–10:48} {Quick Study: Acts 16:1–18:28}

The trial of your faith. *{1 Peter 1:7}*

Untried faith may be true faith, but it is sure to be little faith, and it is likely to remain dwarfish as long as it is without trials. Faith never prospers so well as when all things are against her: tempests are her trainers, and lightnings are her illuminators. When a calm reigns on the sea, spread the sails as you wish, the ship does not move to its harbour; for on a slumbering ocean the keel sleeps, too. Let the winds rush howling forth, and let the waters lift themselves up, then, though the vessel may rock, and her deck may be washed with waves, and her mast may creak under the pressure of the full and swelling sail, it is then that she makes headway towards her desired haven. No flowers wear so lovely a blue as those which grow at the foot of the frozen glacier; no stars gleam so brightly as those which glisten in the polar sky; no water tastes so sweet as what springs amid the desert sand; and no faith is so precious as what lives and triumphs in adversity. Tried faith brings experience. You could not have believed your own weakness had you not been compelled to pass through the rivers; and you would never have known God's strength had you not been supported amid the flood waters. Faith increases in solidity, assurance, and intensity, the more it is exercised with tribulation. Faith is precious, and its trial is precious, too.

Do not let this, however, discourage those who are young in faith. You will have trials enough without seeking them: the full portion will be measured out to you in due time. Meanwhile, if you cannot yet claim the result of long experience, thank God for what grace you have; praise him for that degree of holy confidence which you have attained: walk according to that rule, and you shall yet have more and more of the blessing of God, until your faith shall remove mountains and conquer impossibilities.

November 12 — Evening

**And it came to pass in those days, that he
went out into a mountain to pray, and continued
all night in prayer to God.** *{Luke 6:12}*

If anyone who was born of woman might have lived without prayer, it was our spotless, perfect Lord, and yet no one was ever so much in supplication as he! Such was his love for his Father that he loved much to be in communion with him: such was his love for his people that he desired to be much in intercession for them. *The fact* of this eminent prayerfulness of Jesus is a lesson for us — he has given us an example that we may follow in his steps. *The time* he chose was admirable, it was the hour of silence, when the crowd would not disturb him; the time of inaction, when all except himself had ceased to labour; and the season when slumber made men forget their woes, and cease their applications to him for relief. While others found rest in sleep, he refreshed himself with prayer. *The place* was also well selected. He was alone where no one would intrude, where no one could observe: thus he was free from Pharisaic ostentation and being interrupted. Those dark and silent hills were a fitting oratory for the Son of God. Heaven and earth in midnight stillness heard the groans and sighs of the mysterious Being in whom both worlds were blended. *The continuance* of his pleadings is remarkable; the long watches were not too long; the cold wind did not chill his devotions; the grim darkness did not darken his faith, or loneliness check his importunity. We cannot watch with him one hour, but he watched for us whole nights. *The occasion* for this prayer is notable; it was after his enemies had been enraged — prayer was his refuge and solace; it was before he sent forth the twelve apostles — prayer was the gate of his enterprise, the herald of his new work. Should we not learn from Jesus to resort to special prayer when we are under particular trial, or contemplate fresh endeavours for the Master's glory? Lord Jesus, teach us to pray.

{Daily Reading: Acts 11:1–13:52} {Quick Study: Acts 19:1–20:38}

The branch cannot bear fruit by itself. *{John 15:4}*

How did you begin to bear fruit? It happened when you came to Jesus and cast yourselves on his great atonement, and rested on his finished righteousness. Ah! What fruit you had then! Do you remember those early days? Then indeed the vine flourished, the tender grape appeared, the pomegranates budded forth, and the beds of spices gave forth their sweet smell. Have you declined since then? If you have, we charge you to remember that time of love, and repent, and do your first works. *Be most in those engagements which you have by experience proven to draw you nearest to Christ,* because it is from him that all your fruits proceed. Any holy exercise which will bring you to him will help you to bear fruit. The sun is, no doubt, a great worker in fruit creating among the trees of the orchard: and Jesus is still more so among the trees of his garden of grace. When have you been the most fruitless? Has it not been when you have lived farthest from the Lord Jesus Christ, when you have slackened in prayer, when you have departed from the simplicity of your faith, when your graces have engrossed your attention instead of your Lord, when you have said, "My mountain stands firm, I shall never be moved"; and have forgotten where your strength lies — has it not been *then* that your fruit has ceased? Some of us have been taught that we have nothing without Christ, by terrible abasements of heart before the Lord; and when we have seen the utter barrenness and death of all creature power, we have cried in anguish, "From him all my fruit must be found, for no fruit can ever come from me." We are taught, by past experience, that the more simply we depend upon the grace of God in Christ, and wait upon the Holy Spirit, the more we shall bring forth fruit for God. Oh! to trust Jesus for fruit as well as for life.

November 13 — Evening

Men ought always to pray. *{Luke 18:1}*

If *men* ought always to pray and not to faint, how much more *Christian men* must. Jesus has sent his church into the world on the same errand upon which he himself came, and this mission includes intercession. What if I say that the church is the world's priest? Creation is dumb, but the church is to find a mouth for it. It is the church's high privilege to pray with acceptance. The door of grace is always open for her petitions, and they never return empty handed. The veil was torn *for her*, the blood was sprinkled upon the altar *for her*, God constantly invites *her* to ask for what she needs. Will she refuse the privilege which angels might envy? Is she not the bride of Christ? May she not go in to her King at every hour? Shall she allow the precious privilege to be neglected? The church always has need for prayer. There are always some in her midst who are declining, or falling into open sin. There are lambs to be prayed for, so that they may be carried in Christ's bosom; the strong, lest they grow presumptuous; and the weak, lest they become despairing. If we kept up prayer meetings twenty-four hours a day, all the days in the year, we might never be without a special subject for supplication. Are we ever without the sick and the poor, the afflicted and the wavering? Are we ever without those who seek the conversion of relatives, the reclaiming of backsliders, or the salvation of the depraved? No, with congregations constantly gathering, with ministers always preaching, with millions of sinners lying dead in trespasses and sins; in a country over which the darkness of Romanism is certainly descending; in a world full of idols, cruelties, devilries, if the church does not pray, how shall she excuse her base neglect of the commission of her loving Lord? Let the church be constant in supplication; let every private believer cast his mite of prayer into the treasury.

November 14 — Morning

{Daily Reading: Acts 14:1–16:40} {Quick Study: Acts 21:1–23:35}

I will cut off those who worship
and who swear by the Lord, and who
swear by Malcham. *{Zephaniah 1:5}*

Such people thought themselves safe because they were with both parties: they went with the followers of Jehovah, and bowed at the same time to Malcham. But duplicity is abominable with God, and his soul hates hypocrisy. The idolater who distinctly gives himself to his false god has one sin less than he who brings his polluted and detestable sacrifice to the temple of the Lord, while his heart is with the world and its sins. To hold with the hare and run with the hounds is a dastard's policy. In the common matters of daily life, a double-minded man is despised, but in religion he is loathsome to the last degree. The penalty pronounced in the verse before us is terrible, but it is well deserved; for how should divine justice spare the sinner, who knows the right, approves it, and professes to follow it, and all the while loves the evil, and gives it dominion in his heart?

My soul, search yourself this morning, and see whether you are guilty of double dealing. You profess to be a follower of Jesus — do you truly love him? Is your heart right with God? Are you of the family of old Father Honest, or are you a relative of Mr. By-Ends? A name to live is of little value if I am indeed dead in trespasses and sins. To have one foot on the land of truth, and another on the sea of falsehood will involve a terrible fall and a total ruin. Christ will be all or nothing. God fills the whole universe, and hence there is no room for another god; then if he reigns in my heart, there will be no room for another reigning power. Do I rest alone on Jesus crucified, and live for him alone? Is it my desire to do so? Is my heart set upon so doing? If so, blessed be the mighty grace which has led me to salvation; and if not so, oh Lord, pardon my sad offence, and unite my heart to fear your name.

November 14 — Evening

And Laban said, "It must not be so done in our country, to give the younger before the firstborn." {Genesis 29:26}

We do not excuse Laban for his dishonesty, but we do not scruple to learn from the custom which he quoted as his excuse. There are some things which must be taken in order, and if we wish to win the second we must secure the first. The second may be the more lovely in our eyes, but the rule of the heavenly country must stand, and the elder must be married first. For instance, many men desire the beautiful and well-favoured Rachel of joy and peace in believing, but they must first be wedded to the tender-eyed Leah of repentance. Everyone falls in love with happiness, and many would cheerfully serve twice seven years to enjoy it, but according to the rule of the Lord's kingdom, the Leah of real holiness must be beloved by our soul before the Rachel of true happiness can be attained. Heaven does not stand first but second, and only by persevering to the end can we win a portion in it. The cross must be carried before the crown can be worn. We must follow our Lord in his humiliation, or we shall never rest with him in glory.

My soul, what do you say; are you so vain as to hope to break through the heavenly rule? Do you hope for reward without labour, or honour without toil? Dismiss the idle expectation, and be content to take the ill favoured things for the sake of the sweet love of Jesus, who will reward you for all. In such a spirit, labouring and suffering, you will find bitters grow sweet, and hard things easy. Like Jacob, your years of service will seem to you only a few days for the love you have for Jesus; and when the dear hour of the wedding feast shall come, all your toils shall be as though they had never been — an hour with Jesus will make up for ages of pain and labour.

> Jesus, to win yourself so fair,
> Your cross I will with gladness bear:
> Since so the rules of heaven ordain,
> The first I'll wed the next to gain.

November 15 — Morning

{Daily Reading: Acts 17:1–19:41} {Quick Study: Acts 24:1–26:32}

The Lord's portion is his people. *{Deuteronomy 32:9}*

How are they his? By his own sovereign *choice*. He chose them, and set his love upon them. This he did altogether apart from any goodness in them at the time, or any goodness which he foresaw in them. He had mercy on whom he would have mercy, and ordained a chosen company to eternal life; thus, therefore, they are his by his unconstrained election.

They are not only his by choice, but by *purchase*. He has bought and paid for them to the utmost farthing, hence there can be no dispute about his title. Not with corruptible things, as with silver and gold, but with the precious blood of the Lord Jesus Christ, the Lord's portion has been fully redeemed. There is no mortgage on his estate; no suits can be raised by opposing claimants, the price was paid in open court, and the church is the Lord's freehold for ever. See the blood mark upon all the chosen, invisible to human eye, but known to Christ, for "the Lord knows those who are his"; he does not forget any of those whom he has redeemed from among men; he counts the sheep for whom he laid down his life, and remembers well the church for which he gave himself.

They are also his by *conquest*. What a battle he had in us before we would be won! How long he laid siege to our hearts! How often he sent us terms of capitulation! But we barred our gates, and fenced our walls against him. Do we not remember that glorious hour when he carried our hearts by storm? When he placed his cross against the wall, and scaled our ramparts, planting on our strongholds the blood red flag of his omnipotent mercy? Yes, we are, indeed, the conquered captives of his omnipotent love. Thus chosen, purchased, and subdued, the rights of our divine possessor are inalienable: we rejoice that we never can be our own; and we desire, day by day, to do *his* will, and to show forth *his* glory.

November 15 — Evening

Strengthen, oh God, what you
have done for us. *{Psalms 68:28}*

It is our wisdom, as well as our necessity, to beseech God continually to strengthen what he has done in us. It is because of their neglect in this that many Christians may blame themselves for those trials and afflictions of spirit which arise from unbelief. It is true that Satan seeks to flood the fair garden of the heart and make it a scene of desolation, but it is also true that many Christians leave open the sluice gates themselves, and let in the dreadful deluge through carelessness and lack of prayer to their strong Helper. We often forget that the Author of our faith must be the Preserver of it also. The lamp which was burning in the temple was never allowed to go out, but it had to be daily replenished with fresh oil; in like manner, our faith can only live by being sustained with the oil of grace, and we can only obtain this from God himself. We shall prove to be foolish virgins, if we do not secure the needed sustenance for our lamps. He who built the world upholds it, or it would fall in one tremendous crash; he who made us Christians must maintain us by his Spirit, or our ruin will be speedy and final. Let us, then, evening by evening, go to our Lord for the grace and strength we need. We have a strong argument to plead, for it is *his own work of grace* which we ask him to strengthen — *"what you have done for us."* Do you think he will fail to protect and sustain *that?* Only let your faith take hold of his strength, and all the powers of darkness, led on by the master fiend of hell, cannot cast a cloud or shadow over your joy and peace. Why faint when you may be strong? Why suffer defeat when you may conquer? Oh! Take your wavering faith and drooping graces to him who can revive and replenish them, and earnestly pray, "Strengthen, oh God, what you have done for us."

November 16 — Morning

{Daily Reading: Acts 20:1–22:30} {Quick Study: Acts 27:1–28:31}

"The Lord is my portion,"
says my soul. {Lamentations 3:24}

It is not "The Lord is *partly* my portion," nor "The Lord is *in* my portion"; but he himself makes up the sum total of my soul's inheritance. Within the circumference of that circle lies all that we possess or desire. The *Lord* is my portion. Not his grace merely, nor his love, nor his covenant, but Jehovah himself. He has chosen us for his portion, and we have chosen him for ours. It is true that the Lord must first choose our inheritance for us, or else we shall never choose it for ourselves; but if we are really called according to the purpose of electing love, we can sing —

> Lov'd of my God for him again
> With love intense I burn;
> Chosen of him before time began,
> I choose him in return.

The Lord is our *all-sufficient* portion. God fills himself; and if God is all-sufficient in himself, he must be all-sufficient for us. It is not easy to satisfy man's desires. When he dreams that he is satisfied, immediately he awakens to the perception that there is something more needed, and immediately the horse leech in his heart cries, "Give, give." But all that we can wish for is to be found in our divine portion, so that we ask, "Whom have I in heaven but you? And there is no one upon earth that I desire besides you." Well may we "delight ourselves in the Lord" who makes us to drink from the river of his pleasures. Our faith stretches her wings and mounts like an eagle into the heaven of divine love as to her proper dwelling place. "The lines have fallen to us in pleasant places; yes, we have a goodly heritage." Let us rejoice in the Lord always; let us show to the world that we are a happy and a blessed people, and thus induce them to exclaim, "We will go with you, for we have heard that God is with you."

November 16 — Evening

Your eyes shall see the King in his beauty. *{Isaiah 33:17}*

The more you know about Christ the less you will be satisfied with superficial views of him; and the more deeply you study his transactions in the eternal covenant, his engagements on your behalf as the eternal Surety, and the fulness of his grace which shines in all his offices, the more truly you will see the King in his beauty. Be much in such outlooks. Long more and more to see Jesus. *Meditation and contemplation* are often like windows of agate, and gates of carbuncle, through which we see the Redeemer. Meditation puts the telescope to the eye, and enables us to see Jesus better than we could have seen him if we had lived in the days of his flesh. Oh, that our conversation were more in heaven, and that we were more taken up with the person, the work and the beauty of our incarnate Lord. More meditation, and the beauty of the King would flash upon us with more resplendence. Beloved, it is very probable that we shall have such a sight of our glorious King as we never had before, *when we come to die.* Many saints in dying have looked up from amidst the stormy waters, and have seen Jesus walking on the waves of the sea, and heard him say, "It is I, do not be afraid." Ah, yes! When the tenement begins to shake, and the clay falls away, we see Christ through the rifts, and between the rafters the sunlight of heaven comes streaming in. But if we want to see face to face the "King in his beauty" *we must go to heaven* for the sight, or the King must come here in person. Oh, that he would come on the wings of the wind! He is our Husband, and we are widowed by his absence; he is our dear and fair Brother, and we are lonely without him. Thick veils and clouds hang between our souls and their true life: when shall the day break and the shadows flee away? Oh, long expected day, begin!

November 17 — Morning

{Daily Reading: Acts 23:1–25:27} {Quick Study: Romans 1:1–3:31}

To whom be glory for ever. Amen. *{Romans 11:36}*

To whom be glory for ever." This should be *the single* desire of the Christian. All other wishes must be subservient and tributary to this one. The Christian may wish for prosperity in his business, but only as far as it may help him to promote this — "To him be glory for ever." He may desire to attain more gifts and more graces, but it should only be that "To him may be glory for ever." You are not acting as you ought to do when you are moved by any other motive than a single eye for your Lord's glory. As a Christian, you are "of God, and through God," then live "for God." Let nothing ever set your heart beating so mightily as love for him. Let this ambition fire your soul; may this be the foundation of every enterprise upon which you enter, and this your sustaining motive whenever your zeal cools; make God your *only* object. Depend upon it, where self begins sorrow begins; but if God is my supreme delight and only object,

> To me 'tis equal whether love ordain
> My life or death — appoint me ease or pain.

Let your desire for God's glory be a *growing* desire. You blessed him in your youth, do not be content with such praises as you gave him then. Has God prospered you in business? Give him more just as he has given you more. Has God given you experience? Praise him by stronger faith than you exercised at first. Does your knowledge grow? Then sing more sweetly. Do you enjoy happier times than you once had? Have you been restored from sickness, and has your sorrow been turned into peace and joy? Then give him more music; put more coals and more sweet frankincense into the censer of your praise. Practically in your life give him honour, putting the "Amen" to this doxology to your great and gracious Lord, by your own individual service and increasing holiness.

November 17 — Evening

He who splits wood shall be
endangered by it. *{Ecclesiastes 10:9}*

Oppressors may get their will over poor and needy men as easily as they can split logs of wood, but they had better mind, for it is a dangerous business, and a splinter from a tree has often killed the woodman. Jesus is persecuted in every injured saint, and he is mighty to avenge his beloved ones. Success in treading down the poor and needy is a thing to tremble about: if there is no danger to persecutors now there will be great danger in the future.

To split wood is a common everyday business, and yet it has its dangers; so then, reader, there are dangers connected with your calling and daily life which it will be well for you to be aware of. We do not refer to hazards by flood and field, or by disease and sudden death, but to perils of a spiritual kind. Your occupation may be as humble as log splitting, and yet the devil can tempt you in it. You may be a domestic servant, a farm labourer, or a mechanic, and you may be greatly screened from temptations to the grosser vices, and yet some secret sin may do you harm. Those who live at home, and do not mingle with the rough world, may still be endangered by their very seclusion. Nowhere is he safe who thinks himself so. Pride may enter a poor man's heart; avarice may reign in a cottager's bosom; uncleanness may venture into the quietest home; and anger, and envy, and malice may insinuate themselves into the most rural abode. Even in speaking a few words to an employee we may sin; a little purchase at a shop may be the first link in a chain of temptations; the mere looking out of a window may be the beginning of evil. Oh Lord, how exposed we are! How shall we be secured! It is too hard for us to look after ourselves: only you yourself are able to preserve us in such a world of evils. Spread your wings over us, and we, like little chicks, will cower down beneath you, and feel ourselves to be safe!

November 18 — Morning

{Daily Reading: Acts 26:1–28:31} {Quick Study: Romans 4:1–5:21}

A spring shut up, a fountain sealed. *{Song of Solomon 4:12}*

In this metaphor, which has reference to the inner life of a believer, we have very plainly the idea of *secrecy*. It is a spring *shut up*: just as there were springs in the east, over which an edifice was built, so that no one could reach them except those who knew the secret entrance; so is the heart of a believer when it is renewed by grace: there is a mysterious life within which no human skill can touch. It is a secret which no other man knows; indeed, which the very man who is the possessor of it cannot tell to his neighbour. The text includes not only secrecy, but *separation*. It is not the common spring, of which every passerby may drink, it is one kept and preserved from all others; it is a fountain bearing a particular mark — a king's royal seal, so that all can perceive that it is not a common fountain, but a fountain owned by a proprietor, and placed especially by itself alone. So it is with the spiritual life. The chosen of God were separated in the eternal decree; they were separated by God in the day of redemption; and they are separated by the possession of a life which others do not have; and it is impossible for them to feel at home with the world, or to delight in its pleasures. There is also the idea of *sacredness*. The spring shut up is preserved for the use of some special person: and such is the Christian's heart. It is a spring kept for Jesus. Every Christian should feel that he has God's seal upon him — and he should be able to say with Paul, "From henceforth do not let any man trouble me, for I bear in my body the marks of the Lord Jesus." Another idea is prominent — it is that of *security*. Oh! How sure and safe is the inner life of the believer! If all the powers of earth and hell could combine against it, that immortal principle must still exist, for he who gave it pledged his life for its preservation. And who "is he who shall harm you," when God is your protector?

November 18 — Evening

You are from everlasting. *{Psalms 93:2}*

Christ is EVERLASTING. Of him we may sing with David, "Your throne, oh God, is for ever and ever." Rejoice, believer, in Jesus Christ, the same yesterday, today, and for ever. Jesus always *was*. The Babe born in Bethlehem was united to the Word, which was in the beginning, by whom all things were made. The title by which Christ revealed himself to John on Patmos was, "Him who is, and who was, and who is to come." If he were not God from everlasting, we could not so devoutly love him; we could not feel that he had any share in the eternal love which is the fountain of all covenant blessings; but since he was from all eternity with the Father, we trace the stream of divine love to himself equally with his Father and the blessed Spirit. Just as our Lord always *was*, so also he is for evermore. Jesus is not dead; "He always lives to make intercession for us." Resort to him in all your times of need, for he is still waiting to bless you. Moreover, Jesus our Lord always *shall be*. If God should spare your life to fulfil your full seventy years, you will find that his cleansing fountain is still opened, and his precious blood has not lost its power; you shall find that the Priest who filled the healing fount with his own blood, lives to purge you from all iniquity. When only your last battle remains to be fought, you shall find that the hand of your conquering Captain has not grown feeble — the living Saviour shall cheer the dying saint. When you enter heaven you shall find him there bearing the dew of his youth; and through eternity the Lord Jesus shall still remain the perennial spring of joy, and life, and glory to his people. May you draw Living waters from this sacred well! Jesus always was, he always is, he always shall be. He is eternal in all his attributes, in all his offices, in all his might, and willingness to bless, comfort, guard, and crown his chosen people.

November 19 — Morning

{Daily Reading: Romans 1:1–3:31} {Quick Study: Romans 6:1–8:39}

Avoid foolish questions. *{Titus 3:9}*

Our days are few, and are far better spent in doing good than in disputing over matters which are, at best, of minor importance. The old schoolmen did a world of mischief by their incessant discussion of subjects of no practical importance; and our churches suffer much from petty wars over abstruse points and unimportant questions. After everything has been said that can be said, neither party is any the wiser, and therefore the discussion no more promotes knowledge than love, and it is foolish to sow in so barren a field. Questions upon points where Scripture is silent; upon mysteries which belong to God alone; upon prophecies of doubtful interpretation; and upon mere modes of observing human ceremonies, are all foolish, and wise men avoid them. Our business is neither to ask nor answer foolish questions, but to avoid them altogether; and if we observe the apostle's precept to be careful to maintain good works, *{Titus 3:8}* we shall find ourselves far too much occupied with profitable business to take much interest in unworthy, contentious, and needless strivings.

There are, however, some questions which are the reverse of foolish, which we must not avoid, but fairly and honestly meet, such as these: Do I believe in the Lord Jesus Christ? Am I renewed in the spirit of my mind? Am I not walking after the flesh, but after the Spirit? Am I growing in grace? Does my conduct honour the doctrine of God my Saviour? Am I looking for the coming of the Lord, and watching as a servant should do who expects his master? What more can I do for Jesus? Such enquiries as these urgently demand our attention; and if we have been at all given to disputes, let us now turn our critical abilities to a service so much more profitable. Let us be peacemakers, and endeavour to lead others both by our precept and example, to "avoid foolish questions."

November 19 — Evening

Oh, that I knew where I might find him! *{Job 23:3}*

In Job's uttermost extremity he cried after the Lord. The longing desire of an afflicted child of God is once more to see his Father's face. His first prayer is not, "Oh, that I might be healed of the disease which now festers in every part of my body!" nor even "Oh, that I might see my children restored from the jaws of the grave, and my property once more brought from the hand of the spoiler!" but the first and uppermost cry is, "Oh, that I knew where I might find HIM, who is my God! That I might come even to his seat!" God's children run home when the storm comes on. It is the heaven-born instinct of a gracious soul to seek shelter from all ills beneath the wings of Jehovah. "He who has made his refuge God," might serve as the title of a true believer. A hypocrite, when afflicted by God, resents the infliction, and, like a slave, would run from the master who has scourged him; but not so the true heir of heaven, he kisses the hand which struck him, and seeks shelter from the rod in the bosom of the God who frowned upon him. Job's desire to commune with God was intensified by the failure of all other sources of consolation. The patriarch turned away from his sorry friends, and looked up to the celestial throne, just as a traveller turns from his empty skin bottle, and hurries with all speed to the well. He bids farewell to earth born hopes, and cries, "Oh, that I knew where I might find my God!" Nothing teaches us so much the preciousness of the Creator, as when we learn the emptiness of all besides. Turning away with bitter scorn from earth's hives, where we find no honey, but many sharp stings, we rejoice in him whose faithful word is sweeter than honey or the honeycomb. In every trouble we should first seek to realise God's presence with us. Only let us enjoy his smile, and we can bear our daily cross with a willing heart for his dear sake.

November 20 — Morning

{Daily Reading: Romans 4:1–7:25} {Quick Study: Romans 9:1–11:36}

Oh Lord, you have pleaded the causes of my soul. *{Lamentations 3:58}*

Observe how *positively* the prophet speaks. He does not say, "I hope, I trust, I sometimes think, that God has pleaded the causes of my soul"; but he speaks of it as a matter of fact not to be disputed. "You *have* pleaded the causes of my soul." Let us, by the aid of the gracious Comforter, shake off those doubts and fears which so much mar our peace and comfort. May this be our prayer, that we may stop using the harsh croaking voice of surmise and suspicion, and may be able to speak with the clear, melodious voice of full assurance. Notice how *gratefully* the prophet speaks, ascribing all the glory to God alone! You perceive there is not a word concerning himself or his own pleadings. He does not ascribe his deliverance in any measure to any man, much less to his own merit; but it is *"you"* — "Oh Lord, you have pleaded the causes of my soul; *you* have redeemed my life." A grateful spirit should always be cultivated by the Christian; and especially after deliverances we should prepare a song for our God. Earth should be a temple filled with the songs of grateful saints, and every day should be a censor smoking with the sweet incense of thanksgiving. How *joyful* Jeremiah seems to be while he records the Lord's mercy. How triumphantly he lifts up the strain! He has been in the low dungeon, and is even now none other than the weeping prophet; and yet in the very book which is called "Lamentations," clear as the song of Miriam when she struck her fingers against the tambourine, shrill as the note of Deborah when she met Barak with shouts of victory, we hear the voice of Jeremiah going up to heaven — "You have pleaded the causes of my soul; you have redeemed my life." Oh, children of God, seek after a vital experience of the Lord's lovingkindness, and when you have it, speak positively about it; sing gratefully; shout triumphantly.

November 20 — Evening

*The conies are only a feeble folk, yet they make
their houses in the rocks. {Proverbs 30:26}*

Conscious of their own natural defencelessness, the conies resort to burrows in the rocks, and are secure from their enemies. My heart, be willing to gather a lesson from these feeble folk. You are as weak and as exposed to peril as the timid cony, be as wise to seek a shelter. My best security is within the munitions of an immutable Jehovah, where his unalterable promises stand like giant walls of rock. It will be well with you, my heart, if you can always hide yourself in the bulwarks of his glorious attributes, all of which are guarantees of safety for those who put their trust in him. Blessed be the name of the Lord, I have done so, and have found myself like David in Adullam, safe from the cruelty of my enemy; now I do not have to find out the blessedness of the man who puts his trust in the Lord, for long ago, when Satan and my sins pursued me, I fled to the cleft of the rock Christ Jesus, and in his riven side I found a delightful resting place. My heart, run to him anew tonight, whatever your present grief may be; Jesus feels for you; Jesus consoles you; Jesus will help you. No monarch in his impregnable fortress is more secure than the cony in his rocky burrow. The master of ten thousand chariots is not one whit better protected than the little dweller in the mountain's cleft. In Jesus the weak are strong, and the defenceless are safe; they could not be more strong if they were giants, or more safe if they were in heaven. Faith gives to men on earth the protection of the God of heaven. They cannot need or wish for more. The conies cannot build a castle, but they avail themselves of what is there already: I cannot make myself a refuge, but Jesus has provided it, his Father has given it, his Spirit has revealed it, and lo, again tonight I enter it, and am safe from every foe.

November 21 — Morning

{Daily Reading: Romans 8:1–10:21} {Quick Study: Romans 12:1–14:23}

Do not grieve the Holy Spirit. *{Ephesians 4:30}*

All that the believer has must come from Christ, but it comes solely through the channel of the Spirit of grace. Moreover, just as all blessings thus flow to you through the Holy Spirit, so also no good thing can come out of you in holy thought, devout worship, or gracious act, apart from the sanctifying operation of the same Spirit. Even if the good seed is sown in you, yet it lies dormant unless he works in you to will and to do of his own good pleasure. Do you desire to speak for Jesus — how can you unless the Holy Spirit touches your tongue? Do you desire to pray? Alas! What dull work it is unless the Spirit makes intercession for you! Do you desire to subdue sin? Would you be holy? Would you imitate your Master? Do you desire to rise to superlative heights of spirituality? Are you wanting to be made like the angels of God, full of zeal and ardour for the Master's cause? You cannot without the Spirit — "Without me you can do nothing." Oh, branch of the vine, you can have no fruit without the sap! Oh, child of God, you have no life within you apart from the life which God gives you through his Spirit! Then let us not grieve him or provoke him to anger by our sin. Let us not quench him in one of his faintest motions in our soul; let us foster every suggestion, and be ready to obey every prompting. If the Holy Spirit is indeed so mighty, let us attempt nothing without him; let us begin no project, and carry on no enterprise, and conclude no transaction, without imploring his blessing. Let us give to him the due homage of feeling our entire weakness apart from him, and then depending alone upon him, having this for our prayer, "Open my heart and my whole being to your incoming, and uphold me with your free Spirit when I shall have received that Spirit in my inward being."

November 21 — Evening

*Lazarus was one of those who sat
at the table with him. {John 12:2}*

He is to be envied. It was well to be Martha and serve, but better to be Lazarus and commune. There are times for each purpose, and each is appropriate in its season, but none of the trees of the garden yield such clusters as the vine of fellowship. To sit with Jesus, to hear his words, to see his acts, and receive his smiles, was such a favour as must have made Lazarus as happy as the angels. When it has been our happy lot to feast with our Beloved in his banqueting hall, we would not have given half a sigh for all the kingdoms of the world, if so much breath could have bought them.

He is to be imitated. It would have been a strange thing if Lazarus had not been at the table where Jesus was, for he had been dead, and Jesus had raised him. For the risen one to be absent when the Lord who gave him life was at his house, would have been ungrateful indeed. We too were once dead, yes, and like Lazarus stinking in the grave of sin; Jesus raised us, and by his life we live — can we be content to live at a distance from him? Do we omit to remember him at his table, where he deigns to feast with his brethren? Oh, this is cruel! It behooves us to repent, and do as *he* has bidden us, for his least wish should be law to us. To have lived without constant communion with one of whom the Jews said, "Behold how he loved him," would have been disgraceful to Lazarus, is it excusable in us whom Jesus has loved with an everlasting love? To have been cold to him who wept over his lifeless corpse, would have shown great brutishness in Lazarus. What does it say about us over whom the Saviour has not only wept, but bled? Come, brethren, who read this portion, let us return to our heavenly Bridegroom, and ask for his Spirit so that we may be on terms of closer intimacy with him, and henceforth sit at the table with him.

Israel served for a wife, and for a wife he kept sheep. *{Hosea 12:12}*

Jacob, while expostulating with Laban, thus describes his own toil, "I have been with you these twenty years. I did not bring to you what was torn by beasts: I bore the loss of it; you required it from my hand, whether stolen by day, or stolen by night. Thus I was; in the day the drought consumed me, and the frost by night; and my sleep departed from my eyes." Even more toilsome than this was the life of our Saviour here below. He watched over all his sheep until he gave in as his last account, "Of all those whom you have given me I have lost none." His hair was wet with dew, and his locks with the drops of the night. Sleep departed from his eyes, for all night he was in prayer wrestling for his people. One night Peter must be pleaded for; immediately, another claims his tearful intercession. No shepherd sitting beneath the cold skies, looking up to the stars, could ever utter such complaints because of the hardness of his toil as Jesus Christ might have brought, if he had chosen to do so, because of the sternness of his service in order to procure his spouse —

> Cold mountains and the midnight air,
> Witnessed the fervour of his prayer;
> The desert his temptations knew,
> His conflict and his victory, too.

It is sweet to dwell upon the spiritual parallel of Laban having required all the sheep from Jacob's hand. If they were torn by beasts, Jacob must make it good; if any of them died, he must stand as surety for all of them. Was not the toil of Jesus for his church the toil of one who was under suretiship obligations to bring every believing one safely to the hand of him who had committed them to his charge? Look upon toiling Jacob, and you see a representation of him of whom we read, "He shall feed his flock like a shepherd."

November 22 — Evening

The power of his resurrection. *{Philippians 3:10}*

The doctrine of a risen Saviour is exceedingly precious. The resurrection is the corner stone of the entire building of Christianity. It is the keystone of the arch of our salvation. It would take a volume to describe all the streams of living water which flow from this one sacred source, the resurrection of our dear Lord and Saviour Jesus Christ; but to *know* that he has risen, and to have fellowship with him as such — communing with the risen Saviour by possessing a risen life — seeing him leave the tomb by leaving the tomb of worldliness ourselves, this is even still more precious. The doctrine is the basis for the experience, but just as the flower is more lovely than the root, so is the experience of fellowship with the risen Saviour more lovely than the doctrine itself. I would have you *believe* that Christ rose from the dead so as to sing of it, and derive all the consolation which it is possible for you to extract from this well-ascertained and well-witnessed fact; but I beseech you, do not rest contented even there. Though you cannot, like the disciples, see him visibly, yet I ask you to aspire to see Christ Jesus by the eye of faith; and though, like Mary Magdalene, you may not "touch" him, yet you may be privileged to converse with him, and to know that he is risen, you yourselves being risen in him to newness of life. To know a crucified Saviour as having crucified all my sins, is a high degree of knowledge; but to know a risen Saviour as having justified me, and to realise that he has bestowed upon me new life, having given to me to be a new creature through his own newness of life, this is a noble kind of experience: short of it, no one ought to rest satisfied. May you both "know him, and the power of his resurrection." Why should souls who are quickened with Jesus, wear the grave clothes of worldliness and unbelief? Rise, for the Lord is risen.

Fellowship with him. *{1 John 1:6}*

When we were united by faith to Christ, we were brought into such complete fellowship with him, that we were made one with him, and his interests and ours became mutual and identical. We have fellowship with Christ in his *love*. What he loves we love. He loves the saints — so do we. He loves sinners — so do we. He loves the poor perishing race of man, and pants to see earth's deserts transformed into the garden of the Lord — so do we. We have fellowship with him in his *desires*. He desires the glory of God — we also labour for the same. He desires that the saints may be with him where he is — we desire to be with him there, too. He desires to drive out sin — behold, we fight under his banner. He desires that his Father's name may be loved and adored by all his creatures — we pray daily, "Let your kingdom come. Your will be done on earth, even as it is in heaven." We have fellowship with Christ in his *sufferings*. We are not nailed to the cross, nor do we die a cruel death, but when he is reproached, we are reproached; and a very sweet thing it is to be blamed for his sake, to be despised for following the Master, to have the world against us. The disciple should not be above his Lord. In our measure we commune with him in his *labours*, ministering to men by the word of truth and by deeds of love. Our food and our drink, like his, is to do the will of him who has sent us and to finish his work. We have also fellowship with Christ in his *joys*. We are happy in his happiness, we rejoice in his exaltation. Have you ever tasted that joy, believer? There is no purer or more thrilling delight to be known this side of heaven than that of having Christ's joy fulfilled in us, that our joy may be full. His *glory* awaits us to complete our fellowship, for his church shall sit with him upon his throne, as his well-beloved bride and queen.

November 23 — Evening

Go up into the high mountain. *{Isaiah 40:9}*

Each believer should be thirsting for God, for the living God, and longing to climb the hill of the Lord, and see him face to face. We ought not to rest content in the mists of the valley when the summit of Tabor awaits us. My soul thirsts to drink deep from the cup which is reserved for those who reach the mountain's brow, and bathe their brows in heaven. How pure are the dews of the hills, how fresh is the mountain air, how rich the fare of the dwellers aloft, whose windows look into the New Jerusalem! Many saints are content to live like men in coal mines, who do not see the sun; they eat dust like the serpent when they might taste the ambrosial food of angels; they are content to wear the miner's garb when they might put on King's robes; tears mar their faces when they might anoint them with celestial oil. I am convinced that many a believer pines in a dungeon when he might walk on the palace roof, and view the goodly land and Lebanon. Rise up, oh believer, from your low condition! Cast away your sloth, your lethargy, your coldness, or whatever interferes with your chaste and pure love for Christ, your soul's Husband. Make him the source, the centre, and the circumference of all your soul's range of delight. What enchants you into such folly as to remain in a pit when you may sit on a throne? Do not live in the lowlands of bondage now that mountain liberty is conferred upon you. Do not rest any longer satisfied with your dwarfish attainments, but press forward to things more sublime and heavenly. Aspire to a higher, a nobler, a fuller life. Upward to heaven! Nearer to God!

> When will you come to me, Lord?
> Oh come, my Lord most dear!
> Come near, come nearer, nearer still,
> I'm blest when you are near.

The glorious Lord will be to us a place of broad rivers and streams. *{Isaiah 33:21}*

Broad rivers and streams produce fertility, and abundance in the land. Places near broad rivers are remarkable for the variety of their plants and their plentiful harvests. God is all this to his church. Having God she has *abundance*. What can she ask for that he will not give her? What need can she mention which he will not supply? "In this mountain the Lord of Hosts shall make to all people a feast of fat things." Do you need the bread of life? It drops like manna from the sky. Do you need refreshing streams? The Rock follows you, and that Rock is Christ. If you suffer any need it is your own fault; if you are constrained you are not constrained in him, but in your own heart. Broad rivers and streams also point to *commerce*. Our glorious Lord is to us a place of heavenly merchandise. Through our Redeemer we have commerce with the past; the wealth of Calvary, the treasures of the covenant, the riches of the ancient days of election, the stores of eternity, all come to us down the broad stream of our gracious Lord. We have commerce, too, with the future. What galleys, laden to the water's edge, come to us from the millennium! What visions we have of the days of heaven upon earth! Through our glorious Lord we have commerce with angels; communion with the bright spirits washed in blood, who sing before the throne; indeed, better still, we have fellowship with the Infinite One. Broad rivers and streams are especially intended to portray the idea of *security*. Rivers were of old a defence. Oh! Beloved, what a defence is God to his church! The devil cannot cross this broad river of God. How he wishes he could turn the current, but do not fear, for God abides immutably the same. Satan may worry, but he cannot destroy us; no galley with oars shall invade our river, neither shall a gallant ship pass by it.

November 24 — Evening

Yet a little sleep, a little slumber, a little folding of the hands to sleep: so shall your poverty come as one who travails; and your need as an armed man. *{Proverbs 24:33–34}*

The worst of sluggards only ask for a little slumber; they would be indignant if they were accused of thorough idleness. A little folding of the hands to sleep is all they crave, and they have a multitude of reasons to show that this indulgence is a very proper one. Yet by these littles the day ebbs away, and the time for labour is all gone, and the field is overgrown with thorns. It is by little procrastinations that men ruin their souls. They have no intention to delay for years — a few months will bring the more convenient season — tomorrow if you will, they will attend to serious things; but the present hour is so occupied and altogether so unsuitable, that they beg to be excused. Like sands from an hour glass, time passes, life is wasted by driblets, and seasons of grace lost by little slumbers. Oh, to be wise, to catch the flying hour, to use the moments on the wing! May the Lord teach us this sacred wisdom, for otherwise a poverty of the worst kind awaits us, eternal poverty which shall lack even a drop of water, and beg for it in vain. Like a traveller steadily pursuing his journey, poverty overtakes the slothful, and ruin over-throws the undecided: each hour brings the dreaded pursuer nearer; he does not pause by the way, for he is on his Master's business and must not tarry. Just as an armed man enters with authority and power, so shall poverty come to the idle, and death to the impenitent, and there will be no escape. Oh, that men were now wise, and would seek diligently for the Lord Jesus, or before the solemn day shall dawn when it will be too late to plough and to sow, too late to repent and believe. In harvest, it is vain to lament that the seedtime was neglected. As yet, faith and holy decision are timely. May we obtain them tonight.

November 25 — Morning

{Daily Reading: 1 Corinthians 5:1–9:27} {Quick Study: 1 Corinthians 7:1–8:13}

To preach deliverance to the captives. *{Luke 4:18}*

No one except Jesus can give deliverance to captives. Real liberty only comes from him. It is a liberty *righteously bestowed*; for the Son, who is heir of all things, has a right to make men free. The saints honour the justice of God, which now secures their salvation. It is a liberty which has been *dearly purchased*. Christ speaks it by his power, but he bought it with his blood. He makes you free, but it is by his own bonds. You go free, because he bore your burden for you: you are set at liberty, because he has suffered in your place. But, though dearly purchased, *he freely gives it*. Jesus asks nothing of us as a preparation for this liberty. He finds us sitting in sackcloth and ashes, and invites us to put on the beautiful array of freedom; he saves us just as we are, and all without our help or merit. When Jesus sets free, the liberty is *perpetually entailed*; no chains can ever bind again. Let the Master say to me, "Captive, I have delivered you," and it is done for ever. Satan may plot to enslave us, but if the Lord is on our side, whom shall we fear? The world, with its temptations, may seek to ensnare us, but mightier is he who is for us than all those who are against us. The machinations of our own deceitful hearts may harass and annoy us, but he who has begun the good work in us will carry it on and perfect it to the end. The foes of God and the enemies of man may gather their hosts together, and come with concentrated fury against us, but if God acquits, who is he who condemns? The eagle is not more free which mounts to his nest high up in the rocks, and afterwards outsoars the clouds, than the soul which Christ has delivered. If we are no more under the law, but free from its curse, let our liberty be *practically exhibited* in our serving God with gratitude and delight. "I am your servant, and the son of your handmaid: you have loosened my bonds." "Lord, what will you have me to do?"

November 25 — Evening

For he says to Moses, "I will have mercy on whom I will have mercy, and I will have compassion on whom I will have compassion." {Romans 9:15}

In these words the Lord in the plainest manner claims the right to give or to withhold his mercy according to his own sovereign will. Just as the prerogative of life and death is vested in the monarch, so the Judge of all the earth has a right to spare or condemn the guilty, as may seem best in his sight. Men by their sins have forfeited all claim upon God; they deserve to perish for their sins — and if they all do so, they have no reason to complain. If the Lord steps in to save any, he may do so if the ends of justice are not thwarted; but if he judges it best to leave the condemned to suffer the righteous sentence, no one may arraign him at their judgment bar. Foolish and impudent are all those discourses about the rights of men to be all placed on the same footing; ignorant, if not worse, are those contentions against discriminating grace, which are only the rebellions of proud human nature against the crown and sceptre of Jehovah. When we are brought to see our own utter ruin and fallen state, and the justice of the divine verdict against sin, we no longer object to the truth that the Lord is not bound to save us; we do not murmur if he chooses to save others, as though he were doing us an injury, but feel that if he deigns to look upon us, it will be his own free act of undeserved goodness, for which we shall for ever bless his name.

How shall those who are the subjects of divine election sufficiently adore the grace of God? They have no room for boasting, for sovereignty most effectually excludes it. The Lord's will alone is glorified, and the very notion of human merit is cast out to everlasting contempt. There is no more humbling doctrine in Scripture than that of election, none more conducive to gratitude, and, consequently, none more sanctifying. Believers should not be afraid of it, but adoringly rejoice in it.

November 26 — Morning

{Daily Reading: 1 Corinthians 10:1–13:13} {Quick Study: 1 Corinthians 9:1–11:34}

Whatever your hand finds to do, do it with your might. *{Ecclesiastes 9:10}*

W hatever your hand finds to do," refers to works that are *possible*. There are many things which our heart finds to do which we never shall do. It is well it is in our *heart*; but if we wish to be eminently useful, we must not be content with forming schemes in our heart, and talking about them; we must practically carry out *"whatever our hand finds to do."* One good deed is worth more than a thousand brilliant theories. Let us not wait for large opportunities, or for a different kind of work, but do just the things we "find to do" day by day. We have no other time in which to live. The past is gone; the future has not arrived; we never shall have any time but the *present* time. Then do not wait until your experience has ripened into maturity before you attempt to serve God. Endeavour now to bring forth fruit. Serve God now, but be careful regarding the way in which you perform what you find to do — *"do it with your might."* Do it *promptly*; do not fritter away your life in thinking of what you intend to do tomorrow as if that could compensate for the idleness of today. No man ever served God by doing things tomorrow. If we honour Christ and are blessed, it is by the things which we do *today*. Whatever you do for Christ, throw your whole soul into it. Do not give Christ a little slurred labour, done as a matter of course now and then; but when you do serve him, do it with heart, and soul, and strength.

But where is the might of a Christian? It is not in himself, for he is perfect weakness. His might lies in the Lord of Hosts. Then let us seek his help; let us proceed with prayer and faith, and when we have done what our "hand finds to do," let us wait upon the Lord for his blessing. Whatever we do like this will be well done, and will not fail in its objective.

November 26 — Evening

They shall rejoice, and shall see the plummet
in the hand of Zerubbabel. *{Zechariah 4:10}*

Small things marked the beginning of the work in the hand of Zerubbabel, but no one might despise it, for the Lord had raised up one who would persevere until the headstone should be brought forth with shoutings. *The plummet was in good hands.* Here is the comfort of every believer in the Lord Jesus; let the work of grace be ever so small in its beginnings, the plummet is in good hands, a Master Builder greater than Solomon has undertaken the raising of the heavenly temple, and he will not fail nor be discouraged until the topmost pinnacle shall be raised. If the plummet would be in the hand of any mere human being, we might fear for the building, but the pleasure of the Lord shall prosper in Jesus' hand. The works did not proceed irregularly, and without care, for *the Master's hand carried a good instrument.* Had the walls been hurriedly constructed without due superintendence, they might have been out of the perpendicular; but the plummet was used by the chosen overseer. Jesus is always watching the erection of his spiritual temple, so that it may be built securely and well. We are for haste, but Jesus is for judgment. He will use the plummet, and what is out of line must come down, every stone of it. Hence the failure of many a flattering work, the overthrow of many a glittering profession. It is not for us to judge the Lord's church, since Jesus has a steady hand, and a true eye, and can use the plummet well. Do we not rejoice to see judgment left to him?

The plummet was in active use — it was in the builder's hand; a sure indication that he meant to push on the work to completion. Oh, Lord Jesus, how would we indeed be glad if we could see you at your great work. Oh, Zion, the beautiful, your walls are still in ruins! Rise, you glorious Builder, and make her desolations to rejoice at your coming.

Joshua the high priest standing before the angel of the Lord. *{Zechariah 3:1}*

In Joshua *the high priest* we see a picture of each and every child of God, who has been made near by the blood of Christ, and has been taught to minister in holy things, and enter into what is within the veil. Jesus has made us priests and kings to God, and even here upon earth we exercise the priesthood of consecrated living and hallowed service. But this high priest is said to be "*standing* before the angel of the Lord," that is, standing to minister. This should be the perpetual position of every true believer. Every place is now God's temple, and his people can as truly serve him in their daily employments as well as in his house. They are to be always "ministering," offering the spiritual sacrifice of prayer and praise, and presenting themselves a "living sacrifice." But notice where it is that Joshua stands to minister, it is *before the angel* of Jehovah. It is only through a mediator that we poor defiled ones can ever become priests to God. I present what I have before the messenger, the angel of the covenant, the Lord Jesus; and through him my prayers find acceptance wrapped up in his prayers; my praises become sweet as they are bound up with bundles of myrrh, and aloes, and cassia from Christ's own garden. If I can bring him nothing but my tears, he will put them with his own tears in his own bottle for he once wept; if I can only bring him my groans and sighs, he will accept these as an acceptable sacrifice, for he once was broken in heart, and sighed heavily in spirit. I myself, standing in him, am accepted in the Beloved; and all my polluted works, though in themselves only objects of divine abhorrence, are so received, that God smells a sweet savour. He is content and I am blessed. See, then, the position of the Christian — "a priest — standing — before the angel of the Lord."

November 27 — Evening

The forgiveness of sins, according to the riches of his grace. {Ephesians 1:7}

Could there be a sweeter word in any language than that word "forgiveness," when it sounds in a guilty sinner's ear, like the silver notes of jubilee to the captive Israelite? Blessed, for ever blessed be that dear star of pardon which shines into the condemned cell, and gives the perishing a gleam of hope amid the midnight of despair! Can it be possible that sin, such sin as mine, can be forgiven, forgiven altogether, and for ever? Hell is my portion as a sinner — there is no possibility of my escaping from it while sin remains upon me — can the load of guilt be uplifted, the crimson stain removed? Can the adamantine stones of my prison house ever be loosened from their footings, or the doors be lifted from their hinges? Jesus tells me that I may yet be pardoned. For ever blessed is the revelation of atoning love which not only tells me that pardon is possible, but that it is secured for all who rest in Jesus. I have believed in the appointed propitiation, even Jesus crucified, and therefore my sins are at this moment, and for ever, forgiven by virtue of his substitutionary pains and death. What joy this is! What bliss to be a perfectly pardoned soul! My soul dedicates all her powers to him who by his own unpurchased love became my surety, and worked out for me redemption through his blood. What riches of grace does free forgiveness exhibit! To forgive at all, to forgive fully, to forgive freely, to forgive for ever! Here is a constellation of wonders; and when I think of how great my sins were, how dear were the precious drops which cleansed me from them, and how gracious was the method by which pardon was sealed home to me, I am in a maze of wondering worshipping affection. I bow before the throne which absolves me, I clasp the cross which delivers me, I now serve the incarnate God all my days, through whom I am a pardoned soul tonight.

November 28 — Morning

{Daily Reading: 2 Corinthians 1:1–4:18} {Quick Study: 1 Corinthians 15:1–16:24}

For I rejoiced greatly, when the brethren came
and testified of the truth that is in you,
even as you walk in the truth. *{3 John 1:3}*

The truth was in Gaius, and Gaius walked in the truth. If the first had not been the case, the second could never have occurred; and if the second could not be said about him the first would have been a mere pretence. Truth must enter into the soul, penetrate and saturate it, or else it is of no value. Doctrines held as a matter of creed are like bread in the hand, which ministers no nourishment to the body; but doctrine accepted by the heart is like digested food, which, by assimilation, sustains and builds up the body. In us truth must be a living force, an active energy, and an indwelling reality, a part of the woof and warp of our being. If it is *in us*, we cannot henceforth part with it. A man may lose his garments or his limbs, but his inward parts are vital, and cannot be torn away without absolute loss of life. A Christian can die, but he cannot deny the truth. Now it is a rule of nature that the inward affects the outward, as light shines from the centre of the lantern through the glass: when, therefore, the truth is kindled within, its brightness soon beams forth in the outward life and conversation. It is said that the food of certain worms colours the cocoons of silk which they spin: and just so the nutriment upon which a man's inward nature lives gives a tinge to every word and deed proceeding from him. To walk in the truth results in a life of integrity, holiness, faithfulness, and simplicity — the natural product of those principles of truth which the gospel teaches, and which the Spirit of God enables us to receive. We may judge the secrets of the soul by their presence in the man's conversation. Let us today, oh gracious Spirit, be ruled and governed by your divine authority, so that nothing false or sinful may reign in our hearts, lest it extends its malignant influence to our daily walk among men.

November 28 — Evening

Seeking the wealth of his people. *{Esther 10:3}*

Mordecai was a true patriot, and therefore, being exalted to the highest position under Ahasuerus, he used his eminence to promote the prosperity of Israel. In this he was a type of Jesus, who, upon his throne of glory, does not seek his own, but spends his power for his people. It would be well if every Christian would be a Mordecai to the church, striving according to his ability for its prosperity. Some are placed in positions of affluence and influence, let them honour their Lord in the high places of the earth, and testify for Jesus before great men. Others have what is far better, namely, close fellowship with the King of kings, let them be sure to plead daily for the weak of the Lord's people, the doubting, the tempted, and the comfortless. It will redound to their honour if they make much intercession for those who are in darkness and dare not approach the mercy seat. Instructed believers may serve their Master greatly if they lay out their talents for the general good, and impart their wealth of heavenly learning to others, by teaching them the things of God. The very least in our Israel may at least seek the welfare of his people; and if he can give no more, his desire shall be acceptable. It is at once the most Christlike and the most happy course for a believer to cease from living for himself. He who blesses others cannot fail to be blessed himself. On the other hand, to seek our own personal greatness is a wicked and unhappy plan for life, its way will be grievous and its end will be fatal.

Now is the time to ask you, my friend, whether you are to the best of your ability seeking the wealth of the church in your neighbourhood? I trust you are not doing it mischief by bitterness and scandal, nor weakening it by your neglect. Friend, unite with the Lord's poor, bear their cross, do them all the good you can, and you shall not miss your reward.

November 29 — Morning

{Daily Reading: 2 Corinthians 5:1–8:24} {Quick Study: 2 Corinthians 1:1–4:18}

You shall not go up and down as a talebearer among
your people....You shall surely rebuke your neighbour,
and not tolerate sin in him. *{Leviticus 19:16–17}*

Talebearing emits a threefold poison; for it injures the teller, the hearer, and the person concerning whom the tale is told. Whether the report is true or false, we are by this precept of God's Word forbidden to spread it. The reputations of the Lord's people should be very precious in our sight, and we should count it shame to help the devil to dishonour the church and the name of the Lord. Some tongues need a bridle rather than a spur. Many glory in pulling down their brethren, as if by it they raised themselves up. Noah's wise sons cast a mantle over their father, and he who exposed him earned a fearful curse. We may ourselves one of these dark days need forbearance and silence from our brethren; let us render it cheerfully to those who require it now. Let this be our family rule, and our personal bond — DO NOT SPEAK EVIL OF ANY MAN.

The Holy Spirit, however, permits us to censure sin, and prescribes the way in which we are to do it. It must be done by rebuking our brother to his face, not by railing behind his back. This course is manly, brotherly, Christlike, and under God's blessing will be useful. Does the flesh shrink from it? Then we must lay the greater stress upon our conscience, and apply ourselves to the work, lest by tolerating sin in our friend we ourselves become partakers of it. Hundreds have been saved from gross sins by the timely, wise, affectionate warnings of faithful ministers and brethren. Our Lord Jesus has set us a gracious example of how to deal with erring friends in his warning given to Peter, the prayer with which he preceded it, and the gentle way in which he bore with Peter's boastful denial that he needed such a caution.

November 29 — Evening

Spices for anointing oil. *{Exodus 35:8}*

Much use was made of this anointing oil under the law, and what it represents is of primary importance under the gospel. The Holy Spirit, who anoints us for all holy service, is indispensable to us if we would serve the Lord acceptably. Without his aid our religious services are only a vain oblation, and our inward experience is a dead thing. Whenever our ministry is without unction, what miserable stuff it becomes! Nor are the prayers, praises, meditations, and efforts of private Christians one bit superior. A holy anointing is the soul and life of piety, its absence the most grievous of all calamities. To go before the Lord without anointing is as though some common Levite had thrust himself into the priest's office — his ministry would rather have been sins than services. May we never venture upon hallowed exercises without sacred anointings. They drop upon us from our glorious Head; from his anointing we who are as the skirts of his garments partake of a plenteous unction.

Choice spices were compounded with rarest art by the apothecary to form the anointing oil, to show forth to us how rich are all the influences of the Holy Spirit. All good things are found in the divine Comforter. Matchless consolation, infallible instruction, immortal quickening, spiritual energy, and divine sanctification all lie compounded with other excellencies in that sacred eye salve, the heavenly anointing oil of the Holy Spirit. It imparts a delightful fragrance to the character and person of the man upon whom it is poured. Nothing like it can be found in all the treasuries of the rich, or the secrets of the wise. It is not to be imitated. It comes alone from God, and it is freely given, through Jesus Christ, to every waiting soul. Let us seek it, for we may have it, may have it this very evening. Oh Lord, anoint your servants.

November 30 — Morning

{Daily Reading: 2 Corinthians 9:1–13:14} {Quick Study: 2 Corinthians 5:1–9:15}

And Amaziah said to the man of God, "But what shall
we do about the hundred talents which I have given to the
army of Israel?" And the man of God answered, "The Lord
is able to give you much more than this." *{2 Chronicles 25:9}*

A very important question this seemed to be to the king of Judah, and possibly it is of even more weight with the tried and tempted Christian. To lose money is never pleasant, and when it involves principle, the flesh is not always ready to make the sacrifice. "Why lose what may be so usefully employed? May not the truth itself be bought too dearly? What shall we do without it? Remember the children, and our small income!" All these things and a thousand more would tempt the Christian to put forth his hand to unrighteous gain, or stop himself from carrying out his conscientious convictions, when they involve serious loss. All men cannot view these matters in the light of faith; and even with the followers of Jesus, the doctrine of "we must live" has quite sufficient weight.

The Lord is able to give you much more than this is a very satisfactory answer to the anxious question. Our Father holds the purse strings, and what we lose for his sake he can repay a thousand fold. It is ours to obey his will, and we may rest assured that he will provide for us. The Lord will be no man's debtor at the last. Saints know that a grain of heart's ease is of more value than a ton of gold. He who wraps a threadbare coat over a good conscience has gained a spiritual wealth far more desirable than any he has lost. God's smile and a dungeon are enough for a true heart; his frown and a palace would be hell to a gracious spirit. Let the worst come to the worst, let all the talents go, we have not lost our treasure, for that is above, where Christ sits at the right hand of God. Meanwhile, even now, the Lord makes the meek to inherit the earth, and he withholds no good thing from those who walk uprightly.

Michael and his angels fought against the dragon;
and the dragon and his angels fought. *{Revelation 12:7}*

War always will rage between the two great sovereignties until one or the other will be crushed. Peace between good and evil is an impossibility; the very pretence of it would, in fact, be the triumph of the powers of darkness. *Michael will always fight*; his holy soul is vexed with sin, and will not endure it. Jesus will always be the dragon's foe, and that not in a quiet sense, but actively, vigorously, with full determination to exterminate evil. All his servants, whether angels in heaven or messengers on earth, will and must fight; they are born to be warriors — at the cross they enter into covenant never to make truce with evil; they are a warlike company, firm in defence and fierce in attack. The duty of every soldier in the army of the Lord is daily, with all his heart, and soul, and strength, to fight against the dragon.

The dragon and his angels will not decline the fray; they are incessant in their onslaughts, sparing no weapon, fair or foul. We are foolish to expect to serve God without opposition: the more zealous we are, the more sure we are to be assailed by the hosts of hell. The church may become slothful, but her great antagonist never is; his restless spirit never permits the war to pause; he hates the woman's seed, and would try to devour the church if he could. The servants of Satan are greatly energized by the old dragon's energy, and are usually an active race. War rages all around, and to dream of peace is dangerous and futile.

Glory be to God, we know the end of the war. The great dragon shall be cast out and for ever destroyed, while Jesus and those who are with him shall receive the crown. Let us sharpen our swords tonight, and pray to the Holy Spirit to nerve our arms for the conflict. Never was a battle so important, never was a crown so glorious. Every man to his post, oh warriors of the cross, and may the Lord tread Satan under your feet shortly!

December 1 — Morning

{Daily Reading: Galatians 1:1–3:29} {Quick Study: 2 Corinthians 10:1–13:14}

You have made summer and winter. *{Psalms 74:17}*

My soul begin this wintry month with your God. The cold snows and the piercing winds all remind you that he keeps his covenant with day and night, and tend to assure you that he will also keep that glorious covenant which he has made with you in the person of Christ Jesus. He who is true to his Word in the revolutions of the seasons of this poor sin-polluted world will not prove unfaithful in his dealings with his own well-beloved Son.

Winter in the soul is by no means a comfortable season, and if it is upon you just now it will be very painful to you: but there is this comfort, namely, that *the Lord* makes it. He sends the sharp blasts of adversity to nip the buds of expectation: he scatters the hoarfrost like ashes over the once-verdant meadows of our joy: he casts forth his ice like morsels freezing the streams of our delight. He does it all, he is the great Winter King, and rules in the realms of frost, and therefore you cannot murmur. Losses, crosses, heaviness, sickness, poverty, and a thousand other ills, are of the Lord's sending, and come to us with wise design. Frosts kill noxious insects, and put a bound to raging diseases; they break up the clods, and sweeten the soul. Oh, that such good results would always follow our winters of affliction!

How we prize the fire just now! How pleasant is its cheerful glow! Let us in the same manner prize our Lord, who is the constant source of warmth and comfort in every time of trouble. Let us draw near to him, and in him find joy and peace in believing. Let us wrap ourselves in the warm garments of his promises, and go forth to labours which befit the season, for it would be bad to be like the sluggard who will not plough because of the cold; for he shall beg in summer and have nothing.

December 1 — Evening

Oh, that men would praise the Lord for his
goodness, and for his wonderful works
to the children of men. *{Psalms 107:8}*

If we complained less, and praised more, we should be happier, and God would be more glorified. Let us daily praise God for *common mercies* — common as we frequently call them, and yet so priceless, that when deprived of them we are ready to perish. Let us bless God for eyes to see the sun, for health and strength to walk outside, for bread to eat, and for clothes to wear. Let us praise him that we are not cast out among the hopeless, or confined among the guilty; let us thank him for liberty, for friends, for family associations and comforts; let us praise him, in fact, for everything which we receive from his bounteous hand, for we deserve little, and yet are most plentifully endowed. But, beloved, the sweetest and the loudest note in our songs of praise should be of *redeeming love*. God's redeeming acts towards his chosen are for ever the favourite themes of their praise. If we know what redemption means, let us not withhold our sonnets of thanksgiving. We have been redeemed from the power of our corruptions, uplifted from the depth of sin in which we were naturally plunged. We have been led to the cross of Christ — our shackles of guilt have been broken off; we are no longer slaves, but children of the living God, and can anticipate the time when we shall be presented before the throne without spot or wrinkle or any such thing. Even now by faith we wave the palm branch and wrap ourselves with the fair linen which is to be our everlasting array, and shall we not unceasingly give thanks to the Lord our Redeemer? Child of God, can you be silent? Awake, awake, oh heirs of glory, and lead your captives captive, as you cry with David, "Bless the Lord, oh my soul: and all that is within me, bless his holy name." Let the new month begin with new songs.

December 2 — Morning

{Daily Reading: Galatians 4:1–6:18} {Quick Study: Galatians 1:1–6:18}

You are all fair, my love. *{Song of Solomon 4:7}*

The Lord's admiration of his church is very wonderful, and his description of her beauty is very glowing. She is not merely *fair*, but "*all* fair." He views her in himself, washed in his sin-atoning blood and clothed in his meritorious righteousness, and he considers her to be full of comeliness and beauty. No wonder that such is the case, since it is only his own perfect excellency that he admires; for the holiness, glory, and perfection of his church are his own glorious garments on the back of his own well-beloved spouse. She is not simply pure, or well proportioned; she is positively lovely and fair! She has actual merit! Her deformities of sin are removed; but more, she has through her Lord obtained a meritorious righteousness by which an actual beauty is conferred upon her. Believers have a positive righteousness given to them when they become "accepted in the Beloved." *{Ephesians 1:6}* Nor is the church barely lovely, she is *superlatively* so. Her Lord styles her, "You fairest among women." She has a real worth and excellence which cannot be rivalled by all the nobility and royalty of the world. If Jesus could exchange his elect bride for all the queens and empresses of earth, or even for the angels in heaven, he would not, for he puts her first and foremost — "fairest among women." Like the moon, she far outshines the stars. Nor is this an opinion which he is ashamed of, for he invites all men to hear it. He sets a "behold" before it, a special note of exclamation, inviting and arresting attention. "*Behold*, you are fair, my love; *behold*, you are fair." *{Song of Solomon 4:1}* He publishes his opinion abroad even now, and one day from the throne of his glory he will affirm its truth before the assembled universe. "Come, oh blessed of my Father," *{Matthew 25:34}* will be his solemn affirmation of the loveliness of his elect.

December 2 — Evening

Behold, all is vanity. *{Ecclesiastes 1:14}*

Nothing can satisfy the entire man but the Lord's love and the Lord's own self. Saints have tried to anchor in other harbours, but they have been driven out of such fatal refuges. Solomon, the wisest of men, was permitted to make experiments for us all, and to do for us what we must not dare to do for ourselves. Here is his testimony in his own words: "So I was great, and increased more than all that were before me in Jerusalem: also my wisdom remained with me. And whatever my eyes desired I did not keep from them, I did not withhold my heart from any joy; for my heart rejoiced in all my labour: and this was my portion of all my labour. Then I looked on all the works that my hands had done, and on the labour that I had laboured to do: and, behold, all was vanity and vexation of spirit, and there was no profit under the sun." "Vanity of vanities, all is vanity." What! Was the whole of it vanity? Oh, favoured monarch, is there nothing in all your wealth? Nothing in that wide dominion reaching from the river even to the sea? Nothing in Palmyra's[1] glorious palaces? Nothing in the house of the forest of Lebanon? In all your music and dancing, and wine and luxury, is there nothing? "Nothing," he says, "but weariness of spirit." This was his verdict when he had trodden the whole round of pleasure. To embrace our Lord Jesus, to dwell in his love, and be fully assured of union with him — this is all in all. Dear reader, you need not try other ways of life in order to see whether they are better than the Christian's: if you roam over the whole wide world, you will see no sights like a sight of the Saviour's face; if you could have all the comforts of life, if you lost your Saviour, you would be wretched; but if you win Christ, then if you should rot in a dungeon, then you would find it a paradise; if you should live in obscurity, or die with famine, then you will still be satisfied with favour and full of the goodness of the Lord.

1. Palmyra was in ancient times an important city of central Syria. See http://en.wikipedia.org/wiki/Palmyra.

December 3 — Morning

{Daily Reading: Ephesians 1:1–3:21} {Quick Study: Ephesians 1:1–6:24}

There is no spot in you. *{Song of Solomon 4:7}*

Having pronounced his church positively full of beauty, our Lord confirms his praise by a precious negative, "There is no spot in you." As if the thought occurred to the Bridegroom that the carping world would insinuate that he had only mentioned her comely parts, and had purposely omitted those features which were deformed or defiled, he sums up all by declaring her universally and entirely fair, and utterly devoid of stain. A spot may soon be removed, and is the very least thing that can disfigure beauty, but even from this little blemish the believer is delivered in his Lord's sight. If he had said there is no hideous scar, no horrible deformity, no deadly ulcer, we might even then have marvelled; but when he testifies that she is free from the slightest spot, all these other forms of defilement are included, and the depth of wonder is increased. If he had only promised to remove all spots by and by, we should have had eternal reason for joy; but when he speaks of it as already done, who can restrain the most intense emotions of satisfaction and delight? Oh my soul, here is marrow and fatness for you; eat your full, and be satisfied with royal dainties.

Christ Jesus has no quarrel with his spouse. She often wanders from him, and grieves his Holy Spirit, but he does not allow her faults to affect his love. He sometimes chides, but it is always in the tenderest manner, with the kindest intentions: it is "my love" even then. There is no remembrance of our follies, he does not cherish ill thoughts of us, but he pardons and loves just as well after the offence as before it. It is well for us it is so, for if Jesus were as mindful of injuries as we are, how could he commune with us? Many a time a believer will put himself out of humour with the Lord for some slight turn in providence, but our precious Husband knows our silly hearts too well to take any offence at our poor manners.

December 3 — Evening

The Lord mighty in battle. *{Psalms 24:8}*

Well may our God be glorious in the eyes of his people, seeing that he has performed such wonders for them, in them, and by them. *For them*, the Lord Jesus upon Calvary routed every foe, breaking all the weapons of the enemy in pieces by his finished work of satisfactory obedience; by his triumphant resurrection and ascension he completely overturned the hopes of hell, leading captives captive, making a show of our enemies openly, triumphing over them by his cross. Every arrow of guilt which Satan might have shot at us is broken, for who can lay anything to the charge of God's elect? Vain are the sharp swords of infernal malice, and the perpetual battles of the serpent's seed, for in the midst of the church the lame take the prey, and the feeblest warriors are crowned.

The saved may well adore their Lord for his conquests *in them*, since the arrows of their natural hatred are snapped, and the weapons of their rebellion broken. What victories has grace won in our evil hearts! How glorious is Jesus when the will is subdued, and sin dethroned! As for our remaining corruptions, they shall sustain an equally sure defeat, and every temptation, and doubt, and fear, shall be utterly destroyed. In the Salem of our peaceful hearts, the name of Jesus is great beyond compare: he has won our love, and he shall wear it. Even thus securely may we look for victories *by us*. We are more than conquerors through him who loved us. We shall cast down the powers of darkness which are in the world, by our faith, and zeal, and holiness; we shall win sinners to Jesus, we shall overturn false systems, we shall convert nations, for God is with us, and no one shall stand before us. This evening let the Christian warrior chant the war song, and prepare for tomorrow's fight. Greater is he who is in us than he who is in the world.

December 4 — Morning

{Daily Reading: Ephesians 4:1–6:24} {Quick Study: Philippians 1:1–4:23}

I have many people in this city. *{Acts 18:10}*

This should be a great encouragement to try to do good, since God has among the vilest of the vile, the most reprobate, the most debauched and drunken, an elect people who must be saved. When you take the Word to them, you do so because God has ordained you to be the messenger of life to their souls, and *they must* receive it, for so the decree of predestination runs. They are as much redeemed by blood as the saints before the eternal throne. They are Christ's property, and yet perhaps they are lovers of the ale house, and haters of holiness; but if Jesus Christ purchased them he will have them. God is not unfaithful to forget the price which his Son has paid. He will not permit his substitution to be in any case an ineffectual, dead thing. Tens of thousands of redeemed ones are not regenerated yet, but regenerated they must be; and this is our comfort when we go forth to them with the quickening Word of God.

Indeed, more, these ungodly ones are prayed for by Christ before the throne. "Neither do I pray for these alone," says the great Intercessor, "but for *those also who shall believe* on me through their word." Poor, ignorant souls, they know nothing about prayer for themselves, but Jesus prays for them. Their names are on his breastplate, and before long they must bend their stubborn knee, breathing the penitential sigh before the throne of grace. "The time of figs is not yet." The predestinated moment has not struck; but, when it comes, *they shall obey*, for God will have his own; *they must*, for the Spirit is not to be withstood when he comes forth with fulness of power — *they must* become the willing servants of the living God. "My people shall be willing in the day of my power." "He shall justify many." "He shall see the travail of his soul." "I will divide to him a portion with the great, and he shall divide the spoil with the strong."

December 4 — Evening

Even we ourselves groan within ourselves,
waiting for the adoption, that is, the
redemption of our body. *{Romans 8:23}*

This groaning is universal among the saints: to a greater or lesser extent we all feel it. It is not the groan of murmuring or complaint: it is rather the note of desire than of distress. Having received an earnest, we desire our entire portion; we are sighing that our entire manhood, in its trinity of spirit, soul, and body, may be set free from the last vestige of the fall; we long to put off corruption, weakness, and dishonour, and to wrap ourselves in incorruption, in immortality, in glory, in the spiritual body which the Lord Jesus will bestow upon his people. We long for the manifestation of our adoption as the children of God. "We groan," but it is *"within ourselves."* It is not the hypocrite's groan, by which he wishes to make men believe that he is a saint because he is wretched. Our sighs are sacred things, too hallowed for us to tell publicly. We keep our longings for our Lord alone. Then the apostle says we are *"waiting,"* by which we learn that we are not to be petulant, like Jonah or Elijah, when they said, "Let me die"; nor are we to whimper and sigh for the end of life because we are tired of work, nor wish to escape from our present sufferings until the will of the Lord is done. We are to groan for glorification, but we are to wait patiently for it, knowing that what the Lord appoints is best. Waiting implies being ready. We are to stand at the door expecting the Beloved to open it and take us away to himself. This "groaning" is a *test*. You may judge a man by what he groans after. Some men groan after wealth — they worship Mammon; some groan continually under the troubles of life — they are merely impatient; but the man who sighs after God, who is uneasy until he is made like Christ, that is the blessed man. May God help us to groan for the coming of the Lord, and the resurrection which he will bring to us.

December 5 — Morning

{Daily Reading: Philippians 1:1–4:23} {Quick Study: Colossians 1:1–4:18}

Ask, and it shall be given to you. *{Matthew 7:7}*

We know of a place in England still existing, where a dole of bread is served to every passerby who chooses to ask for it. Whoever the traveller may be, he has only to knock at the door of St. Cross Hospital, and there is the dole of bread for him. Jesus Christ so loves sinners that he has built a St. Cross Hospital, so that whenever a sinner is hungry, he has only to knock and have his needs supplied. Indeed, he has done better; he has attached to this Hospital of the Cross a bath; and whenever a soul is black and filthy, it only has to go there and be washed. The fountain is always full, always efficacious. No sinner ever went into it and found that it could not wash away his stains. Sins which were scarlet and crimson have all disappeared, and the sinner has been whiter than snow. As if this were not enough, there is attached to this Hospital of the Cross a wardrobe, and a sinner making application simply as a sinner, may be clothed from head to foot; and if he wishes to be a soldier, he may not merely have clothes for ordinary wear, but armour which shall cover him from the sole of his foot to the crown of his head. If he asks for a sword, he shall have that given to him, and a shield, too. Nothing that is good for him shall be denied to him. He shall have spending money as long as he lives, and he shall have an eternal heritage of glorious treasure when he enters into the joy of his Lord.

If all these things are to be had by merely knocking at mercy's door, oh my soul, knock hard this morning, and ask large things from your generous Lord. Do not leave the throne of grace until all your needs have been spread before the Lord, and until by faith you have a comforting assurance that they shall be all supplied. No bashfulness need retard when Jesus invites. No unbelief should hinder when Jesus promises. No cold heartedness should restrain when such blessings are to be obtained.

December 5 — Evening

And the Lord showed me four carpenters. *{Zechariah 1:20}*

In the vision described in this chapter, the prophet saw four terrible horns. They were pushing this way and that way, dashing down the strongest and the mightiest; and the prophet asked, "What are these?" The answer was, "These are the horns which have scattered Israel." He saw before him a representation of those powers which had oppressed the church of God. There were four horns; for the church is attacked from all quarters. Well might the prophet have felt dismayed; but suddenly there appeared before him *four carpenters.* He asked, "What shall these do?" These are the men whom God has found to break those horns in pieces. *God will always find men for his work*, and he will find them at the right time. The prophet did not see the carpenters *first*, when there was nothing to do, but first the "horns," and then the "carpenters." Moreover, the Lord finds *enough men*. He did not find *three* carpenters, but *four*; there were four horns, and there must be four workmen. God finds *the right men*; not four men with pens to write; not four architects to draw plans; but four carpenters to do rough work. Rest assured, you who tremble for the ark of God, that when the "horns" grow troublesome, the "carpenters" will be found. You need not fret concerning the weakness of the church of God at any moment; there may be growing up in obscurity the valiant reformer who will shake the nations: Chrysostoms may come forth from our Ragged Schools, and Augustines from the thickest darkness of London's poverty. The Lord knows where to find his servants. He has in ambush a multitude of mighty men, and at his word they shall spring up to the battle; "for the battle is the Lord's," and he shall have the victory. Let us remain faithful to Christ, and he, at the right time, will raise up for us a defence, whether it is in the day of our personal need, or in the season of peril to his church.

December 6 — Morning

{Daily Reading: Colossians 1:1–4:18} {Quick Study: 1 Thessalonians 1:1–5: 28}

As is the heavenly, so also are those
who are heavenly. *{1 Corinthians 15:48}*

The head and members are of one nature, and not like that monstrous image which Nebuchadnezzar saw in his dream. The head was of fine gold, but the belly and thighs were of brass, the legs of iron, and the feet, part of iron and part of clay. Christ's mystical body is no absurd combination of opposites; the members were mortal, and therefore Jesus died; the glorified Head is immortal, and therefore the body is immortal, too, for thus the record stands, "Because I live, you shall live also." As is our loving Head, such is the body, and every member in particular. A chosen Head and chosen members; an accepted Head, and accepted members; a living Head, and living members. If the Head is pure gold, all the parts of the body are of pure gold, also. Thus, there is a double union of nature as a basis for the closest communion. Pause here, devout reader, and see if you can, without ecstatic amazement, contemplate the infinite condescension of the Son of God in thus exalting your wretchedness into blessed union with his glory. You are so lowly that in remembrance of your mortality, you may say to corruption, "You are my father," and to the worm, "You are my sister"; and yet in Christ you are so honoured that you can say to the Almighty, "Abba, Father," and to the incarnate God, "You are my Brother and my Husband." Surely if relationships to ancient and noble families make men think highly of themselves, *we* have someone more glorious than the heads of them all. Let the poorest and most despised believer lay hold upon this privilege; do not let a senseless indolence make him negligent to trace his pedigree, and let him allow no foolish attachment to present vanities to occupy his thoughts to the exclusion of this glorious, this heavenly honour of union with Christ.

December 6 — Evening

Wrapped around the chest with
a golden band. *{Revelation 1:13}*

"One like the Son of Man" appeared to John in Patmos, and the beloved disciple noted that he wore a band of gold. *A band*, for Jesus never was unclothed while upon earth, but always stood ready for service, and now before the eternal throne he does not suspend his holy ministry, but as a priest is wrapped around with "the embroidered band of the ephod." It is good for us that he has not ceased to fulfil his offices of love for us, since this is one of our choicest safeguards that he always lives to make intercession for us. Jesus is never an idler; his garments are never loose as though his offices were ended; he diligently carries on the cause of his people. *A golden band* is to reveal the superiority of his service, the royalty of his person, the dignity of his state, the glory of his reward. No longer does he cry out of the dust, but he pleads with authority, a King as well as a Priest. Our cause is safe enough in the hands of our enthroned Melchizedek.

Our Lord presents all his people with an example. We must never untie our bands. This is not the time for lying down at ease, it is the time of service and warfare. We need to bind the band of truth more and more tightly around our waist. It is a golden band, and so will be our richest ornament, and we greatly need it, for a heart that is not well braced up with the truth as it is in Jesus, and with the fidelity which is wrought by the Spirit, will be easily entangled with the things of this life, and tripped up by the snares of temptation. It is in vain that we possess the Scriptures unless we bind them around us like a band, surrounding our entire nature, keeping each part of our character in order, and giving compactness to our whole man. If in heaven Jesus does not untie the band, much less may we upon earth. Stand, therefore, having your loins clothed with truth.

December 7 — Morning

{Daily Reading: 1 Thessalonians 1:1–5:28} {Quick Study: 2 Thessalonians 1:1–3:18}

God has chosen the base things
of the world. *{1 Corinthians 1:28}*

Walk the streets by moonlight, if you dare, and you will see sinners then. Watch when the night is dark, and the wind is howling, and the picklock is grating in the door, and you will see sinners then. Go to that jail, and walk through the wards, and see the men with heavy overhanging brows, men whom you would not like to meet at night, and there are sinners there. Go to the reformatories, and see those who have betrayed a rampant juvenile depravity, and you will see sinners there. Go across the seas to the place where a man will gnaw a bone upon which is reeking human flesh, and there is a sinner there. Go wherever you wish, you do not need to ransack earth to find sinners, for they are common enough; you may find them in every lane and street of every city, and town, and village, and hamlet. It is for such that Jesus died. If you will select for me the grossest specimen of humanity, if he is born of woman, I will still have hope for him, because Jesus Christ is come to seek and to save *sinners*. Electing love has selected some of the worst to be made the best. Grace turns pebbles of the brook into jewels for the royal crown. He transforms worthless dross into pure gold. Redeeming love has set apart many of the worst of mankind to be the reward of the Saviour's passion. Effectual grace calls forth many of the vilest of the vile to sit at the table of mercy, and therefore let no one despair.

Reader, by that love looking out of Jesus' tearful eyes, by that love streaming from those bleeding wounds, by that faithful love, that strong love, that pure, disinterested, and abiding love; by the heart and by the love of the Saviour's compassion, we admonish you do not turn away as though it was nothing to you; but believe on him and you shall be saved. Trust your soul with him and he will bring you to his Father's right hand in everlasting glory.

December 7 — Evening

I have become all things to all men, so that by
all means I might save some. {1 Corinthians 9:22}

Paul's great object was not merely to instruct and to improve, but to save. Anything short of this would have disappointed him; he wanted to have men renewed in heart, forgiven, sanctified, in fact, *saved*. Have our Christian labours been aimed at anything below this great point? Then let us amend our ways, for of what avail will it be at the last great day to have taught and moralized men if they appear before God unsaved? Our skirts will be blood red if through life we have sought inferior objects, and forgotten that men needed to be saved. Paul knew the ruin of man's natural state, and did not try to educate him, but to save him; he saw men sinking to hell, and did not talk of refining them, but of saving from the wrath to come. To accomplish their salvation, he gave himself up with untiring zeal to telling abroad the gospel, to warning and beseeching men to be reconciled to God. His prayers were importunate and his labours incessant. To save souls was his consuming passion, his ambition, and his calling. He became a servant to all men, toiling for his race, feeling a woe within him if he did not preach the gospel. He laid aside his preferences to prevent prejudice; he submitted his will in things indifferent, and if men would only receive the gospel, he raised no questions about forms or ceremonies: the gospel was the one all-important business with him. If he might save some he would be content. This was the crown for which he strove, the sole and sufficient reward of all his labours and self-denials. Dear reader, have you and I lived to win souls at this noble rate? Are we possessed with the same all absorbing desire? If not, why not? Jesus died for sinners, can we not live for them? Where is our tenderness? Where is our love for Christ, if we do not seek his honour in the salvation of men? Oh, that the Lord would saturate us through and through with an undying zeal for the souls of men.

December 8 — Morning

{Daily Reading: 2 Thessalonians 1:1–3:18} {Quick Study: 1 Timothy 1:1–6:21}

You have a few names even in Sardis which have not defiled their garments; and they shall walk with me in white: for they are worthy. *{Revelation 3:4}*

We may understand this to refer to *justification.* "They shall walk in white"; that is, they shall enjoy a constant sense of their own justification by faith; they shall understand that the righteousness of Christ is imputed to them, that they have all been washed and made whiter than the newly fallen snow.

Again, it refers to *joy and gladness:* for white robes were holiday dresses among the Jews. Those who have not defiled their garments shall have their faces always bright; they shall understand what Solomon meant when he said, "Go your way, eat your bread with joy, and drink your wine with a merry heart. Let your garments be always white, for God has accepted your works." He who is accepted by God shall wear white garments of joy and gladness, while he walks in sweet communion with the Lord Jesus. Where do so many doubts, so much misery, and mourning come from? It is because so many believers defile their garments with sin and error, and hence they lose the joy of their salvation, and the comforting fellowship of the Lord Jesus, they do not walk here below in white.

The promise also refers to *walking in white before the throne of God.* Those who have not defiled their garments here shall most certainly walk in white up there, where the white-robed hosts sing perpetual hallelujahs to the Most High. They shall possess joys inconceivable, happiness beyond a dream, bliss which imagination does not know, blessedness which even the stretch of desire has not reached. The "undefiled in the way" shall have all this — not by merit, nor by works, but by grace. They shall walk with Christ in white, for he has made them "worthy." In his sweet company they shall drink from the living fountains of waters.

December 8 — Evening

You, oh God, have provided from your
goodness for the poor. *{Psalms 68:10}*

All God's gifts are prepared gifts laid up in store for needs which he foresaw. He anticipates our needs; and from the fulness which he has treasured up in Christ Jesus, he provides from his goodness for the poor. You may trust him for all the necessities that can occur, for he has infallibly foreknown everyone of them. He can say of us in all conditions, "I knew that you would be this and that." A man goes on a journey across the desert, and when he has made a day's advance, and pitched his tent, he discovers that he needs many comforts and necessities which he has not brought in his baggage. "Ah!" he says, "I did not foresee this: if I had this journey to go again, I would bring these things with me, so necessary for my comfort." But God has noted with prescient eye all the requirements of his poor, wandering children, and when those needs occur, supplies are ready. It is goodness which he has prepared for the poor in heart, goodness and goodness only. "My grace is sufficient for you." "As your days, so shall your strength be."

Reader, is your heart heavy this evening? God knew it would be; the comfort which your heart needs is treasured in the sweet assurance of the text. You are poor and needy, but he has thought upon you, and has the exact blessing which you require in store for you. Plead the promise, believe it and obtain its fulfilment. Do you feel that you never were so consciously vile as you are now? Behold, the crimson fountain is still open, with all its former efficacy, to wash your sin away. Never shall you come into such a position that Christ cannot aid you. No pinch shall ever arrive in your spiritual affairs in which Jesus Christ shall not be equal to the emergency, for your history has all been foreknown and provided for in Jesus.

December 9 — Morning

{Daily Reading: 1 Timothy 1:1–6:21} {Quick Study: 2 Timothy 1:1–4:22}

**Therefore the Lord will wait so that he
may be gracious to you.** *{Isaiah 30:18}*

God often DELAYS IN ANSWERING PRAYER. We have several instances of this in sacred Scripture. Jacob did not get the blessing from the angel until near the dawn of day — he had to wrestle all night for it. The poor woman of Syrophenicia was answered not a word for a long while. Paul prayed to the Lord *three times* that "the thorn in the flesh" might be taken from him, and he received no assurance that it should be taken away, but instead a promise was given that God's grace would be sufficient for him. If you have been knocking at the gate of mercy, and have received no answer, shall I tell you why the mighty Maker has not opened the door and let you in? Our Father has reasons particular to himself for keeping us waiting. Sometimes it is to show his power and his sovereignty, so that men may know that Jehovah has a right to give or to withhold. More frequently the delay is for our profit. You are perhaps kept waiting in order that your desires may be more fervent. God knows that delay will quicken and increase desire, and that if he keeps you waiting you will see your need more clearly, and will pray more earnestly; and so that you will prize the mercy all the more for its long tarrying. There may also be something wrong in you which needs to be removed, before the joy of the Lord is given. Perhaps your views of the Gospel plan are confused, or you may be placing too much reliance on yourself, instead of trusting simply and entirely in the Lord Jesus. Or God makes you tarry a while so that he may more fully display the riches of his grace to you at last. Your prayers are all filed in heaven, and if not immediately answered they are certainly not forgotten, but in a little while shall be fulfilled to your delight and satisfaction. Do not let despair make you silent, but continue fervently in earnest supplication.

December 9 — Evening

My people shall dwell in quiet resting places. *{Isaiah 32:18}*

Peace and rest do not belong to the unregenerate, they are the particular possession of the Lord's people, and of them only. The God of Peace gives perfect peace to those whose hearts are resting upon him. Before man fell, his God gave him the flowery bowers of Eden as his quiet resting places; alas! how soon sin blighted the fair abode of innocence. In the day of universal wrath when the flood swept away a guilty race, the chosen family were quietly secured in the resting place of the ark, which floated them from the old condemned world into the new earth of the rainbow and the covenant, herein typifying Jesus, the ark of our salvation. Israel rested safely beneath the blood-sprinkled habitations of Egypt when the destroying angel struck the firstborn; and in the wilderness the shadow of the pillar of cloud, and the flowing rock, gave the weary pilgrims sweet repose. At this hour we rest in the promises of our faithful God, knowing that his words are full of truth and power; we rest in the doctrines of his Word, which are consolation itself; we rest in the covenant of his grace, which is a haven of delight. More highly favoured are we than David in Adullam, or Jonah beneath his gourd, for no one can invade or destroy our shelter. The person of Jesus is the quiet resting place of his people, and when we draw near to him in the breaking of the bread, in the hearing of the Word, the searching of the Scriptures, prayer, or praise, we find any form of approach to him to be the return of peace to our spirits.

> I hear the words of love, I gaze upon the blood,
> I see the mighty sacrifice, and I have peace with God.
> 'Tis everlasting peace, sure as Jehovah's name,
> 'Tis stable as his steadfast throne, for evermore the same:
> The clouds may go and come, and storms may sweep my sky,
> This blood-sealed friendship changes not, the cross is ever nigh.

December 10 — Morning

{Daily Reading: 2 Timothy 1:1–4:22} {Quick Study: Titus 1:1–3:15}

So we shall always be with the Lord. *{1 Thessalonians 4:17}*

Even the sweetest visits from Christ, how short they are — and how transitory! One moment our eyes see him, and we rejoice with joy unspeakable and full of glory, but again a little time and we do not see him, for our Beloved withdraws himself from us; like a roe or a young hart he leaps over the mountains of division; he is gone to the land of spices, and feeds no more among the lilies.

> If today he deigns to bless us with a sense of pardoned sin,
> He tomorrow may distress us, make us feel the plague within.

Oh, how sweet the prospect of the time when we shall not behold him at a distance, but see him face to face: when he shall not be as a wayfaring man tarrying only for a night, but shall eternally enfold us in the bosom of his glory. We shall not see him for a little season, but

> Millions of years our wondering eyes,
> Shall o'er our Saviour's beauties rove;
> And myriad ages we'll adore,
> The wonders of his love.

In heaven there shall be no interruptions from care or sin; no weeping shall dim our eyes; no earthly business shall distract our happy thoughts; we shall have nothing to hinder us from gazing for ever on the Sun of Righteousness with unwearied eyes. Oh, if it is so sweet to see him now and then, how sweet to gaze on that blessed face for ever, and never have a cloud rolling between, and never have to turn one's eyes away to look on a world of weariness and woe! Blest day, when will you dawn? Rise, oh unsetting sun! The joys of sense may leave us as soon as they will, for this shall make glorious amends. If to die is only to enter into uninterrupted communion with Jesus, then death is indeed gain, and the black drop is swallowed up in a sea of victory.

December 10 — Evening

Whose heart the Lord opened. *{Acts 16:14}*

In Lydia's conversion there are many points of interest. It was brought about by *providential circumstances*. She was a seller of purple, of the city of Thyatira, but just at the right time for hearing Paul we find her at Philippi; providence, which is the handmaid of grace, led her to the right place. Again, *grace was preparing her soul for the blessing* — grace preparing for grace. She did not know the Saviour, but as a Jewess, she knew many truths which were excellent stepping stones to a knowledge of Jesus. Her conversion took place in the use of the means. On the Sabbath she went when prayer was accustomed to be made, and there prayer was heard. Never neglect the means of grace; God *may* bless us when we are not in his house, but we have the greater reason to hope that he will when we are in communion with his saints. Observe the words, "Whose heart *the Lord* opened." She did not open her own heart. Her prayers did not do it; Paul did not do it. The Lord himself must open the heart, to receive the things which make for our peace. He alone can put the key into the hole of the door and open it, and get admittance for himself. Just as he is the heart's Master so he is the heart's Maker. The first outward evidence of the opened heart was *obedience*. As soon as Lydia had believed in Jesus, she was baptized. It is a sweet sign of a humble and broken heart, when the child of God is willing to obey a command which is not essential for his salvation, which is not forced upon him by a selfish fear of condemnation, but is a simple act of obedience and of communion with his Master. The next evidence was *love*, revealing itself in acts of grateful kindness to the apostles. Love for the saints has always been a mark of the true convert. Those who do nothing for Christ or his church, give very sorry evidence of an "opened" heart. Lord, for evermore give me an opened heart.

December 11 — Morning

{Daily Reading: Titus 1:1–Philemon 1:25} {Quick Study: Philemon 1–25}

He who calls you is faithful, who also will do it. *{1 Thessalonians 5:24}*

Heaven is a place where we shall never sin; where we shall cease our constant watch against an indefatigable enemy, because there will be no tempter to ensnare our feet. There the wicked cease from troubling, and the weary are at rest. Heaven is the "undefiled inheritance"; it is the land of perfect holiness, and therefore of complete security. But do the saints not even on earth sometimes taste the joys of blissful security? The doctrine of God's Word is that all who are in union with the Lamb are safe; that all the righteous shall hold on their way; that those who have committed their souls to the keeping of Christ shall find him to be a faithful and immutable preserver. Sustained by such a doctrine we can enjoy security even on earth; not that high and glorious security which renders us free from every slip, but that holy security which arises from the sure promise of Jesus that no one who believes in him shall ever perish, but shall be with him where he is. Believer, let us often reflect with joy on the doctrine of the perseverance of the saints, and honour the faithfulness of our God by a holy confidence in him.

May our God bring home to you a sense of your safety in Christ Jesus! May he assure you that your name is engraved on his hand; and whisper in your ear the promise, "Do not fear, I am with you." Look upon him, the great Surety of the covenant, as faithful and true, and, therefore, bound and engaged to present you, the weakest of the family, with all the chosen race, before the throne of God; and in such a sweet contemplation you will drink the juice of the spiced wine of the Lord's pomegranate, and taste the dainty fruits of Paradise. You will have a foretaste of the enjoyments which ravish the souls of the perfect saints above, if you can believe with unstaggering faith that "he who calls you is faithful, who also will do it."

December 11 — Evening

You serve the Lord Christ. *{Colossians 3:24}*

To what choice order of officials was this word spoken? To kings who proudly boast a divine right? Ah, no! Too often they serve themselves or Satan, and forget the God whose tolerance permits them to wear their mimic majesty for their little hour. Then the apostle speaks to those so called "right reverend fathers in God," the bishops, or "the venerable the archdeacons"? No, indeed, Paul knew nothing of these mere inventions of man. Not even to pastors and teachers, or to the wealthy and esteemed among believers, was this word spoken, but to servants, indeed, and to slaves. Among the toiling multitudes, the journeymen, the day labourers, the domestic servants, the drudges of the kitchen, the apostle found, as we still find, some of the Lord's chosen, and to them he says, "Whatever you do, do it heartily, as to the Lord, and not to men; knowing that you shall receive the reward of the inheritance from the Lord: for you serve the Lord Christ." This saying ennobles the weary routine of earthly employments, and sheds a halo around the most humble occupations. To wash feet may be servile, but to wash his feet is royal work. To untie the shoe lace is poor employment, but to untie the great Master's shoe is a princely privilege. The shop, the barn, the scullery, and the smithy become temples when men and women do all to the glory of God! Then "divine service" is not a thing for a few hours and a few places, but all life becomes holiness to the Lord, and every place and thing, as consecrated as the tabernacle and its golden lampstand.

> Teach me, my God and King, in all things you to see;
> And what I do in anything to do it as to thee.
> All may of you partake, nothing can be so mean,
> Which with this tincture, for your sake,
>   will not grow bright and clean.
> A servant with this clause makes drudgery divine;
> Who sweeps a room, as for your laws,
>   makes that and the action fine.

December 12 — Morning

{Daily Reading: Hebrews 1:1–4:16} {Quick Study: Hebrews 1:1–2:18}

His ways are everlasting. *{Habakkuk 3:6}*

What he has done at one time, he will do yet again. Man's ways are variable, but God's ways are everlasting. There are many reasons for this most comforting truth: among them are the following — the Lord's ways are *the result of wise deliberation*; he orders all things according to the counsel of his own will. Human action is frequently the hasty result of passion, or fear, and is followed by regret and alteration; but nothing can take the Almighty by surprise, or happen otherwise than what he has foreseen. His ways are *the outgrowth of an immutable character*, and in them the fixed and settled attributes of God are clearly to be seen. Unless the Eternal One himself can undergo change, his ways, which are himself in action, must remain for ever the same. Is he eternally just, gracious, faithful, wise, and tender? — then his ways must always be distinguished for the same excellencies. Beings act according to their nature: when those natures change, their conduct varies also; but since God cannot know the shadow of a turning, his ways will remain everlastingly the same. Moreover, there is no external cause which could reverse the divine ways, since they are *the embodiment of irresistible might*. The earth is said, by the prophet, to be cleft with rivers, mountains tremble, the deep lifts up its hands, and sun and moon stand still, when Jehovah marches forth for the salvation of his people. Who can stop his hand, or say to him, "What are you doing?" But it is not might alone which gives stability; God's ways are *the manifestation of the eternal principles of right*, and therefore can never pass away. Wrong breeds decay and involves ruin, but the true and the good have a vitality about them which ages cannot diminish.

This morning let us go to our Heavenly Father with confidence, remembering that Jesus Christ is the same yesterday, today, and for ever, and in him the Lord is always gracious to his people.

December 12 — Evening

They have dealt treacherously against the Lord. {Hosea 5:7}

Believer, here is a sorrowful truth! You are the beloved of the Lord, redeemed by blood, called by grace, preserved in Christ Jesus, accepted in the Beloved, on your way to heaven, and yet, "you have dealt treacherously" with God, your best friend; treacherously with Jesus, whose you are; treacherously with the Holy Spirit, by whom you have been quickened to eternal life! How treacherous you have been in the matter of vows and promises. Do you remember the love of your espousals, that happy time — the springtime of your spiritual life? Oh, how closely you clung to your Master then, saying, "He shall never charge me with indifference; my feet shall never grow slow in the way of his service; I will not allow my heart to wander after other loves; in him is every store of indescribable sweetness. I give all up for my Lord Jesus' sake." Has it been so? Alas! If conscience speaks, it will say, "He who promised so well has performed most poorly. Prayer has frequently been slurred — it has been short, but not sweet; brief, but not fervent. Communion with Christ has been forgotten. Instead of a heavenly mind, there have been carnal cares, worldly vanities and thoughts of evil. Instead of service, there has been disobedience; instead of fervency, lukewarmness; instead of patience, petulance; instead of faith, confidence in an arm of flesh; and as a soldier of the cross there has been cowardice, disobedience, and desertion, to a very shameful degree." "You have dealt treacherously." Treachery towards Jesus! What words shall be used in denouncing it? Words little avail: let our penitent thoughts execrate and condemn the sin which is so surely in us. Treacherous to your wounds, oh Jesus! Forgive us, and let us not sin again! How shameful to be treacherous towards him who never forgets us, but who today stands with our names engraved on his breastplate before the eternal throne.

Salt without prescribing how much. *{Ezra 7:22}*

Salt was used in every offering made by fire to the Lord, and from its preserving and purifying properties it was the grateful emblem of divine grace in the soul. It is worthy of our attentive regard that, when Artaxerxes gave salt to Ezra the priest, he set no limit to the quantity, and we may be quite certain that when the King of kings distributes grace among his royal priesthood, the supply is not cut short by *him*. We are often constrained in ourselves, but never in the Lord. He who chooses to gather much manna will find that he may have as much as he desires. There is no such famine in Jerusalem that the citizens should eat their bread by weight and drink their water by measure. Some things in the economy of grace are measured; for instance, our vinegar and gall are given to us with such exactness that we never have a single drop too much, but of the salt of grace no stint is made — "Ask what you wish and it shall be given to you." Parents need to lock up the fruit cupboard, and the candy jars, but there is no need to keep the salt box under lock and key, for few children will eat too greedily from that. A man may have too much money, or too much honour, but he cannot have too much grace. When Jeshurun became fat in the flesh, he kicked against God, but there is no fear of a man's becoming too full of grace: a *plethora* of grace is impossible. More wealth brings more care, but more grace brings more joy. Increased wisdom is increased sorrow, but abundance of the Spirit is fulness of joy. Believer, go to the throne for a large supply of heavenly salt. It will season your afflictions, which are unsavoury without salt; it will preserve your heart which corrupts if salt is absent, and it will kill your sins even as salt kills slugs. You need much; seek much, and have much.

December 13 — Evening

I will make your windows of agates. *{Isaiah 54:12}*

The church is most instructively symbolised by a building erected by heavenly power, and designed by divine skill. Such a spiritual house must not be dark, for the Israelites had light in their dwellings; there must therefore be windows to let the light in and to allow the inhabitants to gaze out. These windows are *precious* as agates: the ways in which the church sees her Lord and heaven, and spiritual truth in general, are to be held in the highest esteem. Agates are *not the most transparent* of gems, they are only semi-pellucid at the best:

> Our knowledge of that life is small,
> Our eye of faith is dim.

Faith is one of these precious agate windows, but alas! it is often so misty and clouded that we only see darkly, and mistaken much in what we do see. Yet if we cannot gaze through windows of diamonds and know even as we are known, it is a glorious thing to see the altogether lovely One, even though the glass is hazy as the agate. *Experience* is another of these dim but precious windows, yielding to us a subdued religious light, in which we see the sufferings of the Man of Sorrows, through our own afflictions. Our weak eyes could not endure windows of transparent glass to let in the Master's glory, but when they are dimmed with weeping, the beams of the Sun of Righteousness are tempered, and shine through the windows of agate with a soft radiance inexpressibly soothing to tempted souls. *Sanctification*, as it conforms us to our Lord, is another agate window. Only as we become heavenly can we comprehend heavenly things. The pure in heart see a pure God. Those who are like Jesus see him as he is. Because we are so little like him, the window is only agate; because we are somewhat like him, it is agate. We thank God for what we have, and long for more. When shall we see God and Jesus, and heaven and truth, face to face?

December 14 — Morning

{Daily Reading: Hebrews 8:1–10:39} {Quick Study: Hebrews 5:1–7:28}

They go from strength to strength. *{Psalms 84:7}*

They go from *strength to strength*. There are various renderings of these words, but all of them contain the idea of progress.

Our own good translation of the Authorised Version is enough for us this morning. "They go from strength to strength." That is, they grow stronger and stronger. Usually, if we are walking, we go from strength to weakness; we start fresh and in good order for our journey, but by and by the road is rough, and the sun is hot, we sit down by the wayside, and then again painfully pursue our weary way. But the Christian pilgrim, having obtained fresh supplies of grace, is as vigorous after years of toilsome travel and struggle as when he first set out. He may not be quite so elated and buoyant, nor perhaps quite so hot and hasty in his zeal as he once was, but he is much stronger in all that constitutes real power, and travels, if more slowly, far more surely. Some grey-haired veterans have been as firm in their grasp of truth, and as zealous in diffusing it, as they were in their younger days; but, alas, it must be confessed it is often otherwise, for the love of many waxes cold and iniquity abounds, but this is their own sin and not the fault of the promise which still holds good: "The youths shall faint and be weary, and the young men shall utterly fall, but those who wait upon the Lord shall renew their strength; they shall mount up with wings as eagles, they shall run and not be weary, and they shall walk and not faint." Fretful spirits sit down and trouble themselves about the future. "Alas!" they say, "we go from affliction to affliction." Very true, oh you of little faith, but then you go from strength to strength, also. You shall never find a bundle of affliction which does not have bound up in the midst of it sufficient grace. God will give the strength of ripe manhood with the burden allotted to full grown shoulders.

December 14 — Evening

I am crucified with Christ. {*Galatians 2:20*}

The Lord Jesus Christ acted in what he did as a great public representative person, and his dying upon the cross was the virtual dying of all his people. Then all his saints rendered to justice what was due, and made an expiation to divine vengeance for all their sins. The apostle of the Gentiles delighted to think that as one of Christ's chosen people, he died upon the cross in Christ. He did more than believe this doctrinally, he accepted it confidently, resting his hope upon it. He believed that by virtue of Christ's death, he had satisfied divine justice, and found reconciliation with God. Beloved, what a blessed thing it is when the soul can, as it were, stretch itself upon the cross of Christ, and feel, "I am dead; the law has slain me, and I am therefore free from its power, because in my Surety I have borne the curse, and in the person of my Substitute all that the law could do, by way of condemnation, has been executed upon me, for I am crucified with Christ."

But Paul meant even more than this. He not only believed in Christ's death, and trusted in it, but he actually felt its power in himself in causing the crucifixion of his old corrupt nature. When he saw the pleasures of sin, he said, "I cannot enjoy these: I am dead to them." Such is the experience of every true Christian. Having received Christ, he is to this world as one who is utterly dead. Yet, while conscious of death to the world, he can, at the same time, exclaim with the apostle, "Nevertheless, I live." He is fully alive to God. The Christian's life is a matchless riddle. No worldling can comprehend it; even the believer himself cannot understand it. Dead, yet alive! Crucified with Christ, and yet at the same time risen with Christ in newness of life! Union with the suffering, bleeding Saviour, and death to the world and sin, are soul-cheering things. Oh, for more enjoyment of them!

December 15 — Morning

{Daily Reading: Hebrews 11:1–13:25} {Quick Study: Hebrews 8:1–10:39}

Orpah kissed her mother-in-law;
but Ruth clung to her. *{Ruth 1:14}*

Both of them had an affection for Naomi, and therefore set out with her upon her return to the land of Judah. But the hour of test came; Naomi most unselfishly set before each of them the trials which awaited them, and told them if they cared for ease and comfort to return to their Moabitish friends. At first both of them declared that they would cast in their lot with the Lord's people; but upon still further consideration, Orpah with much grief and a respectful kiss left her mother-in-law, and her people, and her God, and went back to her idolatrous friends, while Ruth with all her heart gave herself up to the God of her mother-in-law. It is one thing to love the ways of the Lord when all is fair, and quite another to cleave to them under all discouragements and difficulties. The kiss of outward profession is very cheap and easy, but the practical cleaving to the Lord, which must show itself in holy decision for truth and holiness, is not so small a matter. How does the case stand with us, is our heart fixed upon Jesus, is the sacrifice bound with cords to the horns of the altar? Have we counted the cost, and are we solemnly ready to suffer all worldly loss for the Master's sake? The future gain will be an abundant reward, for Egypt's treasures are not to be compared with the glory to be revealed. Orpah is heard of no more; in glorious ease and idolatrous pleasure her life melts into the gloom of death; but Ruth lives in history and in heaven, for grace has placed her in the noble line from which sprung the King of kings. Blessed among women shall those be who for Christ's sake can renounce all; but forgotten and worse than forgotten shall those be who in the hour of temptation do violence to conscience and turn back to the world. Oh, that this morning we may not be content with the form of devotion, which may be no better than Orpah's kiss, but may the Holy Spirit work in us a cleaving of our whole heart to our Lord Jesus.

December 15 — Evening

And lay your foundations with sapphires. {Isaiah 54:11}

Not only what is seen by the church of God, but what is unseen, is fair and precious. Foundations are out of sight, and as long as they are firm it is not expected that they should be valuable; but in Jehovah's work everything is priceless, nothing is slurred, nothing is lowly. The deep foundations of the work of grace are as precious as sapphires, no human mind is able to measure their glory. We build upon the *covenant of grace*, which is firmer than adamant, and as enduring as jewels upon which age spends itself in vain. Sapphire foundations are eternal, and the covenant abides throughout the lifetime of the Almighty. Another foundation is *the person of the Lord Jesus*, who is clear and spotless, everlasting and beautiful as the sapphire; blending in one the deep blue of earth's ever rolling ocean and the azure of its all embracing sky. Once might our Lord have been likened to the ruby as he stood covered with his own blood, but now we see him radiant with the soft blue of love, love abounding, deep, and eternal. Our eternal hopes are built upon *the justice and the faithfulness of God*, which are as clear and cloudless as the sapphire. We are not saved by a compromise, by mercy defeating justice, or law suspending its operations; indeed, we defy the eagle's eye to detect a flaw in the groundwork of our confidence — our foundation is of sapphire, and will endure the fire.

The Lord himself has laid the foundation for his people's hopes. It is a matter for grave enquiry whether *our* hopes are built upon such a basis. Good works and ceremonies are not a foundation of sapphires, but of wood, hay, and stubble; neither are they laid by God, but by our own conceit. Foundations will all be tried before long: woe to him whose lofty tower shall come down with a crash, because it is based on quicksand. He who is built on sapphires may await storm or fire with equanimity, for he shall abide the test.

December 16 — Morning

{Daily Reading: James 1:1–5:20} {Quick Study: Hebrews 11:1–13:25}

Come to me. *{Matthew 11:28}*

The cry of the Christian religion is the gentle word, "Come." The Jewish law harshly said, "Go, take heed to your steps concerning the path in which you shall walk. Break the commandments, and you shall perish; keep them, and you shall live." The law was a dispensation of terror, which drove men before it as with a scourge; the gospel draws with bands of love. Jesus is the good Shepherd going before his sheep, bidding them to follow him, and always leading them onwards with the sweet word, "Come." The law repels, the gospel attracts. The law shows the distance which there is between God and man; the gospel bridges that awful chasm, and brings the sinner across it.

From the first moment of your spiritual life until you are ushered into glory, the language of Christ to you will be, "*Come, come to me.*" As a mother puts out her finger to her little child and woos him to walk by saying, "*Come,*" even so does Jesus. He will always be ahead of you, bidding you follow him as the soldier follows his captain. He will always go before you to pave your way, and clear your path, and you shall hear his animating voice calling you after him all through life; while in the solemn hour of death, his sweet words with which he will usher you into the heavenly world shall be — "Come, you blessed of my Father."

Indeed, further, this is not only Christ's cry to you, but, if you are a believer, this is your cry to Christ — "Come! Come!" You will be longing for his second advent; you will be saying, "Come quickly, even so come, Lord Jesus." You will be panting for nearer and closer communion with him. As his voice to you is, "Come," your response to him will be, "Come, Lord, and abide with me. Come, and occupy alone the throne of my heart; reign there without a rival, and consecrate me entirely to your service."

December 16 — Evening

*Indeed, you did not hear; indeed, you did
not know; indeed, from that time your
ear was not opened. {Isaiah 48:8}*

It is painful to remember that, in a certain degree, this accusation may be laid at the door of *believers*, who too often are, in a measure, *spiritually insensitive*. We may well bewail ourselves that we do not hear the voice of God as we ought, "Indeed, you did not hear." There are gentle motions of the Holy Spirit in the soul which are unheeded by us: there are whisperings of divine command and of heavenly love which are alike unobserved by our leaden intellects. Alas! We have been *carelessly ignorant* — "Indeed, you did not know." There are matters within which we ought to have seen, corruptions which have made headway unnoticed; sweet affections which are being blighted like flowers in the frost, untended by us; glimpses of the divine face which might be perceived if we did not wall up the windows of our soul. But we "have not known." As we think of it we are humbled in the deepest self-abasement. How must we adore the grace of God as we learn from the context that all this folly and ignorance on our part *was foreknown by God*, and, notwithstanding that foreknowledge, he still has been pleased to deal with us in a way of mercy! Admire the marvellous sovereign grace which could have chosen us in the sight of all this! Wonder at the price that was paid for us when Christ knew what we would be! He who hung upon the cross foresaw us as unbelieving, backsliding, cold of heart, indifferent, careless, lax in prayer, and yet he said, "I am the Lord your God, the Holy One of Israel, your Saviour. . . . Since you were precious in my sight, you have been honourable, and I have loved you: therefore I will give men for you, and people for your life!" Oh redemption, how wondrously resplendent you shine when we think how black we are! Oh, Holy Spirit, give us henceforth the hearing ear and the understanding heart!

December 17 — Morning

{Daily Reading: 1 Peter 1:1–2:25} {Quick Study: James 1:1–5:20}

I remember you. *{Jeremiah 2:2}*

Let us note that Christ delights to think upon his church, and to look upon her beauty. Just as the bird returns often to its nest, and as the wayfarer hurries to his home, so does the mind continually pursue the object of its choice. We cannot look too often upon that face which we love; we always desire to have our precious things in our sight. It is even so with our Lord Jesus. From all eternity "his delights were with the sons of men"; his thoughts rolled onward to the time when his elect should be born into the world; he viewed them in the mirror of his foreknowledge. "In your book," he says, "all my members were written, which in their days were fashioned, when as yet there were none of them." *{Psalms 139:16}* When the world was set upon its pillars, he was there, and he set the bounds of the people according to the number of the children of Israel. Many a time before his incarnation, he descended to this lower earth in the similitude of a man; on the plains of Mamre, *{Genesis 18:1}* by the brook of Jabbok, *{Genesis 32:24–30}* beneath the walls of Jericho, *{Joshua 5:13}* and in the fiery furnace of Babylon, *{Daniel 3:19–25}* the Son of Man visited his people. Because his soul delighted in them, he could not rest away from them, for his heart longed after them. They were never absent from his heart, for he had written their names upon his hands, and engraved them upon his side. Just as the breastplate containing the names of the tribes of Israel was the most brilliant ornament worn by the high priest, so the names of Christ's elect were his most precious jewels, and glittered on his heart. We may often forget to meditate upon the perfections of our Lord, but he never ceases to remember us. Let us chide ourselves for past forgetfulness, and pray for grace to always bear him in fondest remembrance. Lord, paint upon the eyes of my soul the image of your Son.

I am the door: by me if any man enters in, he shall be saved,
and shall go in and out, and find pasture. *{John 10:9}*

J esus, the great I AM, is the entrance into the true church, and the
way of access to God himself. He gives to the man who comes to
God by him four choice privileges.

1. *He shall be saved.* The fugitive manslayer passed the gate of the city
   of refuge, and was safe. Noah entered the door of the ark, and was
   secure. No one can be lost who takes Jesus as the door of faith to
   their souls. Entrance through Jesus into peace is the guarantee of
   entrance by the same door into heaven. Jesus is the only door, an
   open door, a wide door, a safe door; and blessed is he who rests all
   his hope of admission to glory upon the crucified Redeemer.

2. *He shall go in.* He shall be privileged to go in among the divine
   family, sharing the children's bread, and participating in all their
   honours and enjoyments. He shall go in to the chambers of
   communion, to the banquets of love, to the treasures of the covenant, to the storehouses of the promises. He shall go in to the
   King of kings in the power of the Holy Spirit, and the secret of
   the Lord shall be with him.

3. *He shall go out.* This blessing is much forgotten. We go out into
   the world to labour and suffer, but what a mercy to go in the
   name and power of Jesus! We are called to bear witness to the
   truth, to cheer the disconsolate, to warn the careless, to win
   souls, and to glorify God; and as the angel said to Gideon, "Go
   in this your might," even thus the Lord would have us proceed
   as his messengers in his name and strength.

4. *He shall find pasture.* He who knows Jesus shall never lack. Going
   in and out shall be equally helpful to him: in fellowship with
   God he shall grow, and in feeding others he shall be fed. Having
   made Jesus his all, he shall find all in Jesus. His soul shall be as a
   watered garden, and as a well of water whose waters do not fail.

December 18 — Morning

{Daily Reading: 1 Peter 3:1–5:14} {Quick Study: 1 Peter 1:1–5:14}

Rend your heart, and not your garments. *{Joel 2:13}*

GARMENT RENDING and other outward signs of religious emotion, are *easily seen* and are *frequently hypocritical*; but to feel true repentance is far more difficult, and consequently far less common. Men will attend to the most multiplied and minute ceremonial regulations — for such things are *pleasing to the flesh* — but true religion is too humbling, too heart-searching, too thorough for the tastes of carnal men; they prefer something more ostentatious, flimsy, and worldly. Outward observances are *temporarily comforting*; eye and ear are pleased; self-conceit is fed, and self-righteousness is puffed up: but they are *ultimately delusive*, for in the article of death, and at the day of judgment, the soul needs something more substantial than ceremonies and rituals to lean upon. Apart from vital godliness, all religion is *utterly vain*; offered without a sincere heart, every form of worship is a solemn sham and an impudent mockery of the Majesty of heaven.

HEART RENDING is *divinely wrought and solemnly felt.* It is a secret grief which is *personally experienced*, not in mere form, but as a deep, soul moving work of the Holy Spirit upon the innermost heart of each believer. It is not a matter to be merely talked about and believed in, but keenly and sensitively felt in every living child of the living God. It is *powerfully humiliating*, and *completely sin purging*; but then it is *sweetly preparative* for those gracious consolations which proud unhumbled spirits are unable to receive; and it is *distinctly discriminating*, for it belongs to the elect of God, and to them alone.

The text commands us to rend our hearts, but they are naturally hard as marble: how, then, can this be done? We must take them to Calvary: a dying Saviour's voice rent the rocks once, and it is as powerful now. Oh, blessed Spirit, let us hear the death cries of Jesus, and our hearts shall be rent even as men rend their vestures in the day of lamentation.

December 18 — Evening

Be diligent to know the state of your flocks, and
look well to your herds. *{Proverbs 27:23}*

Every wise merchant will occasionally hold a stock taking, when he will tally up his accounts, examine what he has on hand, and ascertain decisively whether his business is prosperous or declining. Every man who is wise in the kingdom of heaven, will cry, "Search me, oh God, and try me"; and he will frequently set apart special times for self-examination, to discover whether things are right between God and his soul. The God whom we worship is a great heart searcher; and of old his servants knew him as "the Lord who searches the heart and tries the reins of the children of men." Let me stir you up in his name to make diligent search and solemn trial of your state, lest you come short of the promised rest. What every wise man does, what God himself does with all of us, I exhort you to do with yourself this evening. Let the old saint look well to the fundamentals of his piety, for grey heads may cover black hearts: and do not let the young professor despise the word of warning, for the greenness of youth may be joined to the rottenness of hypocrisy. Every now and then a cedar falls into our midst. The enemy still continues to sow tares among the wheat. It is not my aim to introduce doubts and fears into your mind; indeed, truly, but I shall rather hope that the rough wind of self-examination may help to drive them away. It is not security, but carnal security, which we wish to kill; not confidence, but fleshly confidence, which we wish to overthrow; not peace, but false peace, which we wish to destroy. By the precious blood of Christ, which was not shed to make you a hypocrite, but that sincere souls might show forth his praise, I beseech you, search and look, lest at the last it is said of you, "Mene, Mene, Tekel: you are weighed in the balances, and are found wanting."

December 19 — Morning

{Daily Reading: 2 Peter 1:1–3:18} {Quick Study: 2 Peter 1:1–3:18}

The lot is cast into the lap, but the whole disposing of it is from the Lord. *{Proverbs 16:33}*

If the disposal of the lot is the Lord's, whose is the arrangement of our whole life? If the simple casting of a lot is guided by him, how much more the events of our entire life — especially when we are told by our blessed Saviour: "The very hairs of your head are all numbered: not a sparrow falls to the ground apart from your Father's will." It would bring a holy calm over your mind, dear friend, if you were always to remember this. It would so relieve your mind from anxiety, that you would be better able to walk in patience, quiet, and cheerfulness as a Christian should. When a man is anxious he cannot pray with faith; when he is troubled about the world, he cannot serve his Master, his thoughts are serving himself. If you would "seek first the kingdom of God and his righteousness," all things would then be added to you. You are meddling with Christ's business, and neglecting your own when you fret about your lot and circumstances. You have been trying "providing" work and forgetting that it is yours to obey. Be wise and attend to the obeying, and let Christ manage the providing. Come and survey your Father's storehouse, and ask whether he will let you starve while he has laid up so great an abundance in his garner. Look at his heart of mercy; see if that can ever prove unkind! Look at his inscrutable wisdom; see if that will ever be at fault. Above all, look up to Jesus Christ your Intercessor, and ask yourself, while he pleads, can your Father deal ungraciously with you. If he remembers even sparrows, will he forget one of the least of his poor children? "Cast your burden upon the Lord, and he will sustain you. He will never allow the righteous to be moved."

> My soul, rest happy in your low estate,
> Nor hope nor wish to be esteem'd or great;
> To take the impress of the Will Divine,
> Be that your glory, and those riches thine.

December 19 — Evening

And there was no more sea. *{Revelation 21:1}*

Scarcely could we rejoice at the thought of losing the glorious old ocean: the new heavens and the new earth are none the fairer to our imagination, if, indeed, literally there is to be no great and wide sea, with its gleaming waves and sandy shores. Is not the text to be read as a metaphor, tinged with the prejudice with which the Oriental mind universally regarded the sea in the olden times? It is mournful to imagine a real physical world without a sea; it would be an iron ring without the sapphire which made it precious. There must be a spiritual meaning here. In the new dispensation there will be no *division* — the sea separates nations and peoples from each other. To John in Patmos the deep waters were like prison walls, shutting him out from his brethren and his work: there shall be no such barriers in the world to come. Leagues of rolling billows lie between us and many a kinsman whom tonight we prayerfully remember, but in the bright world to which we go there shall be unbroken fellowship for all the redeemed family. In this sense there shall be no more sea. The sea is the emblem of change; with its ebbs and flows, its glassy smoothness and its mountainous billows, its gentle murmurs and its tumultuous roarings, it is never the same for long. Slave of the fickle winds and the changeful moon, its instability is proverbial. In this mortal state we have too much of this; earth is constant only in her inconstancy, but in the heavenly state all mournful change shall be unknown, and with it all fear of *storm* to wreck our hopes and drown our joys. The sea of glass glows with a glory unbroken by a wave. No tempest howls along the peaceful shores of paradise. Soon we shall reach that happy land where partings, and changes, and storms shall be ended! Jesus will waft us there. Are we in him or not? This is the grand question.

Indeed, I have loved you with an everlasting love. *{Jeremiah 31:3}*

Sometimes the Lord Jesus tells his church his love thoughts. "He does not think it is enough to say it behind her back, but in her very presence he says, 'You are all fair, my love.' It is true, this is not his ordinary method; he is a wise lover, and knows when to keep back the intimation of love and when to express it; but there are times when he will make no secret of it; times when he will put it beyond all dispute in the souls of his people." *{R. Erskine's Sermons}* The Holy Spirit is often pleased, in a most gracious manner, to witness with our spirits the love of Jesus. He takes the things of Christ and reveals them to us. No voice is heard from the clouds, and no vision is seen in the night, but we have a testimony more sure than either of these. If an angel should fly from heaven and inform the saint personally of the Saviour's love for him, the evidence would not be one whit more satisfactory than what is borne in the heart by the Holy Spirit. Ask those of the Lord's people who have lived the nearest to the gates of heaven, and they will tell you that they have had times when the love of Christ towards them has been a fact so clear and sure that they could no more doubt it than they could question their own existence. Yes, beloved believer, you and I have had times of refreshing from the presence of the Lord, and then our faith has mounted to the topmost heights of assurance. We have had confidence to lean our heads upon the bosom of our Lord, and we have no more questioned our Master's affection for us than John did when in that blessed posture; indeed, not so much: for the dark question, "Lord, is it I who shall betray you?" has been put far from us. He has kissed us with the kisses of his mouth, and killed our doubts by the closeness of his embrace. His love has been sweeter than wine to our souls.

December 20 — Evening

Call your labourers, and give them
their wages. *{Matthew 20:8}*

God is a good paymaster; he pays his servants while at work as
well as when they have done it; and one of his payments is
this: *an easy conscience.* If you have spoken faithfully about Jesus to
one person, when you go to bed at night you feel happy in thinking, "Today I have discharged my conscience of that man's blood."
There is a great *comfort in doing something for Jesus.* Oh, what a
happiness to place jewels in his crown, and give to him to see the
travail of his soul! There is also very great reward in *watching the
first buddings of conviction in a soul!* To say of that girl in the class,
"Her heart is tender, I do hope the Lord is working within her."
To go home and pray over that boy, who said something in the
afternoon which made you think he must know more about divine
truth than you had hoped! Oh, the joy of hope! But as for *the joy of
success!* It is unspeakable. This joy, overwhelming as it is, is a hungry
thing — you pine for more of it. To be a soul winner is the happiest
thing in the world. With every soul you bring to Christ, you get a
new heaven upon earth. But who can conceive of the bliss which
awaits us above! Oh, how sweet is that sentence, "Enter into *the joy
of your Lord!*" Do you know what the joy of Christ is over a saved
sinner? This is the very joy which we are to possess in heaven. Yes,
when he mounts the throne, you shall mount with him. When the
heavens ring with "Well done, well done," you shall partake in the
reward; you have toiled with him, you have suffered with him, you
shall now reign with him; you have sown with him, you shall reap
with him; your face was covered with sweat like his, and your soul
was grieved for the sins of men as his soul was, now your face shall
be bright with heaven's splendour as his countenance is, and now
your soul shall be filled with ecstatic joys even as his soul is.

December 21 — Morning

{Daily Reading: 1 John 4:1–5:21} {Quick Study: 2 John 1:1–13}

Yet he has made an everlasting covenant with me. *{2 Samuel 23:5}*

This covenant is *divine in its origin.* "HE has made an everlasting covenant with me." Oh that great word *HE!* Stop, my soul. God, the everlasting Father, has positively made a covenant with you; yes, that God who spoke the world into existence by a word; he, stooping from his majesty, takes hold of your hand and makes a covenant with you. Is it not a deed, the stupendous condescension of which might ravish our hearts for ever if we could really understand it? "HE has made a covenant with me." A king has not made a covenant with me — that would be something; but the Prince of the kings of the earth, Shaddai, the Lord all-sufficient, the Jehovah of ages, the everlasting Elohim, "He has made an everlasting covenant with me." But notice, it is *particular in its application.* "Yet he has made an everlasting covenant with ME." Here lies the sweetness of it to each believer. It is nothing for me that he made peace for the world; I want to know whether he made peace for me! It is little that he has made a covenant, I want to know whether he has made a covenant *with me.* Blessed is the assurance that he has made a covenant with me! If God the Holy Spirit gives me assurance of this, then his salvation is mine, his heart is mine, he himself is mine — *he is my God.*

This covenant is *everlasting in its duration.* An everlasting covenant means a covenant which had no beginning, and which shall never, never end. How sweet amidst all the uncertainties of life, to know that "the foundation of the Lord stands sure," and to have God's own promise, "I will not break my covenant, nor alter the thing that is gone out of my lips." Like dying David, I will sing of this, even though my house is not so with God as my heart desires.

December 21 — Evening

*Also I clothed you with embroidered cloth, and shod
you with badgers' skin, and I clothed you with
fine linen, and I covered you with silk.* {Ezekiel 16:10}

See the matchless generosity of the Lord as he provides for his people's apparel. They are so arrayed that the divine skill is seen producing an unrivalled *embroidered cloth*, in which every attribute takes its part and every divine beauty is revealed. There is no art like the art displayed in our salvation, no cunning workmanship like that seen in the righteousness of the saints. Justification has engrossed learned pens in all ages of the church, and will be the theme of admiration in eternity. God has indeed "intricately worked it." With all this elaboration there is mingled utility and durability, comparable to our being *shod with badgers' skins*. The animal here meant is unknown, but its skin covered the tabernacle, and formed one of the finest and strongest leathers known. The righteousness which is from God by faith endures for ever, and he who is shod with this divine preparation will tread the desert safely, and may even set his foot upon the lion and the adder. Purity and dignity of our holy vesture are brought out in *the fine linen*. When the Lord sanctifies his people, they are clad as priests in pure white; not even the snow itself excels them; they are in the eyes of men and angels fair to look upon, and even in the Lord's eyes they are without spot. Meanwhile, the royal apparel is as delicate and rich as *silk*. No expense is spared, no beauty withheld, no daintiness denied.

What, then? Is there no inference from this? Surely there is gratitude to be felt and joy to be expressed. Come, my heart, do not refuse your evening hallelujah! Tune your pipes! Touch your chords!

> Strangely, my soul, are you arrayed
> By the Great Sacred Three!
> In sweetest harmony of praise
> Let all your powers agree.

December 22 — Morning

{Daily Reading: 2 John 1:1–Jude 1:25} {Quick Study: 3 John 1–14}

I will strengthen you. *{Isaiah 41:10}*

God has a strong reserve with which to discharge this engagement; for he is able to do all things. Believer, until you can drain dry the ocean of omnipotence, until you can break into pieces the towering mountains of almighty strength, you never need to fear. Do not think that the strength of man shall ever be able to overcome the power of God. While the earth's huge pillars stand, you have enough reason to abide firm in your faith. The same God who directs the earth in its orbit, who feeds the burning furnace of the sun, and trims the lamps of heaven, has promised to supply you with daily strength. While he is able to uphold the universe, do not dream that he will prove to be unable to fulfil his own promises. Remember what he did in the days of old, in the former generations. Remember how he spoke and it was done; how he commanded, and it stood firm. Shall he who created the world grow weary? He hangs the world upon nothing; shall he who does this be unable to support his children? Shall he be unfaithful to his word for lack of power? Who is it that restrains the tempest? Does he not ride upon the wings of the wind, and make the clouds his chariots, and hold the ocean in the hollow of his hand? How can he fail you? When he has put such a faithful promise as this on record, will you for a moment indulge the thought that he has outpromised himself, and gone beyond his power to fulfil? Ah, no! You can doubt no longer.

Oh, you who are my God and my strength, I can believe that this promise shall be fulfilled, for the boundless reservoir of your grace can never be exhausted, and the overflowing storehouse of your strength can never be emptied by your friends or rifled by yours enemies.

Now let the feeble all be strong,
And make Jehovah's arm their song.

December 22 — Evening

The mark of his children. *{Deuteronomy 32:5}*

What is the secret mark which infallibly indicates the child of God? It would be vain presumption to decide this based on our own judgment; but God's Word reveals it to us, and we may tread with certainty where we have revelation to be our guide. Now, we are told concerning our Lord, "to as many as *received him*, he gave power to them to become the sons of God, even to as many as believed on his name." Then, if I have received Christ Jesus into my heart, I am a child of God. That reception is described in the same verse as *believing on the name of Jesus Christ*. If, then, I believe on Jesus Christ's name — that is, simply from my heart trust myself with the crucified but now exalted Redeemer, I am a member of the family of the Most High. Whatever else I may not have, if I have this, I have the privilege to become a child of God. Our Lord Jesus puts it in another way. "My sheep hear my voice, and I know them, and they follow me." Here is the matter in a nutshell. Christ appears as a shepherd to his own sheep, not to others. As soon as he appears, his own sheep recognise him — they trust him, they are prepared to follow him; he knows them, and they know him — there is a mutual knowledge — there is a constant connection between them. Thus, the one mark, the sure mark, the infallible mark of regeneration and adoption is a hearty faith in the appointed Redeemer. Reader, are you in doubt, are you uncertain whether you bear the secret mark of God's children? Then do not let an hour go by until you have said, "Search me, oh God, and know my heart." Do not trifle here, I admonish you! If you must trifle anywhere, let it be about some secondary matter: your health, if you will, or the title deeds of your estate; but about your soul, your never-dying soul and its eternal destinies, I beseech you to be in earnest. Make sure work for eternity.

December 23 — Morning

{Daily Reading: Revelation 1:1–2:29} {Quick Study: Jude 1–25}

Friend, go up higher. *{Luke 14:10}*

When first the life of grace begins in the soul, we do indeed draw near to God, but it is with great fear and trembling. The soul, conscious of guilt and humbled by it, is overawed with the solemnness of its position; it is prostrated to the earth by a sense of the grandeur of Jehovah, in whose presence it stands. With genuine bashfulness it takes the lowest room.

But in later life, as the Christian grows in grace, although he will never forget the solemnness of his position, and will never lose that holy awe which must encompass a gracious man when he is in the presence of the God who can create or can destroy; yet his fear has all its terror taken out of it; it becomes a holy reverence, and no more an overshadowing dread. He is called up higher, to greater access to God in Christ Jesus. Then the man of God, walking amid the splendours of Deity, and veiling his face like the glorious cherubim, with those twin wings, the blood and righteousness of Jesus Christ, will, reverent and bowed in spirit, approach the throne; and seeing there a God of love, of goodness, and of mercy, he will realise the covenant character of God rather than his absolute Deity. He will see in God his greatness rather than his goodness, and more of his love than of his majesty. Then the soul, bowing still as humbly as before, will enjoy a more sacred liberty of intercession; for while prostrate before the glory of the Infinite God, it will be sustained by the refreshing consciousness of being in the presence of boundless mercy and infinite love, and by the realisation of acceptance "in the Beloved." Thus, the believer is bidden to come up higher, and is enabled to exercise the privilege of rejoicing in God, and drawing near to him in holy confidence, saying, "Abba, Father."

So may we go from strength to strength, and daily grow in grace,
Until in your image raised at length, we see you face to face.

December 23 — Evening

The night also is yours. *{Psalms 74:16}*

Yes, Lord, you do not abdicate your throne when the sun goes down, nor do you leave the world all through these long wintry nights to be the prey of evil; your eyes watch us as the stars, and your arms surround us as the zodiac belts the sky. The dews of kindly sleep and all the influences of the moon are in your hand, and the alarms and solemnities of night are equally with you. This is very sweet to me when watching through the midnight hours, or tossing to and fro in anguish. There are precious fruits put forth by the moon as well as by the sun: may my Lord make me to be a favoured partaker in them.

The night of affliction is as much under the arrangement and control of the Lord of love as the bright summer days when all is bliss. Jesus is in the tempest. His love wraps the night around itself like a mantle, but to the eye of faith the sable robe is scarcely a disguise. From the first watch of the night even to the break of day the eternal Watcher observes his saints, and overrules the shadows and dews of midnight for his people's highest good. We believe in no rival deities of good and evil contending for the mastery, but we hear the voice of Jehovah saying, "I create light and I create darkness; I, the Lord, do all these things."

Gloomy seasons of religious indifference and social sin are not exempted from the divine purpose. When the altars of truth are defiled, and the ways of God forsaken, the Lord's servants weep with bitter sorrow, but they may not despair, for the darkest eras are governed by the Lord, and shall come to their end at his bidding. What may seem defeat to us may be victory to him.

> Though enwrapped in gloomy night,
> We perceive no ray of light;
> Since the Lord himself is here,
> 'Tis not fit that we should fear.

December 24 — Morning

{Daily Reading: Revelation 3:1–5:14} {Quick Study: Revelation 1:1–3:22}

For your sakes he became poor. *{2 Corinthians 8:9}*

The Lord Jesus Christ was eternally *rich*, glorious, and exalted; but "though *he was rich*, yet for your sakes he became poor." Just as the rich saint cannot be true in his communion with his poor brethren unless from his substance he ministers to their necessities, so (the same rule applies to the head as well as to the members), it is impossible that our divine Lord could have had fellowship with us unless he had shared with us from his own abounding wealth, and had become poor to make us rich. Had he remained upon his throne of glory, and had we continued in the ruins of the fall without receiving his salvation, communion would have been impossible on both sides. Our position by the fall, apart from the covenant of grace, made it as impossible for fallen man to communicate with God as it is for the devil to be in concord with Christ. In order, therefore, that communion might be accomplished, it was necessary that the rich kinsman should bestow his estate upon his poor relatives, that the righteous Saviour would give to his sinning brethren his own perfection, and that we, the poor and guilty, would receive his fulness grace for grace; that thus in giving and receiving, the One might descend from the heights, and the other ascend from the depths, and so be able to embrace each other in true and hearty fellowship. Poverty must be enriched by him in whom are infinite treasures before it can venture to commune; and guilt must lose itself in imputed and imparted righteousness before the soul can walk in fellowship with purity. Jesus must clothe his people in his own garments, or he cannot admit them into his palace of glory; and he must wash them in his own blood, or else they will be too defiled for the embrace of his fellowship.

Oh believer, herein is love! For *your sake* the Lord Jesus "became poor" so that he might lift you up into communion with himself.

December 24 — Evening

**The glory of the Lord shall be revealed,
and all flesh shall see it together.** *{Isaiah 40:5}*

We anticipate the happy day when the whole world shall be converted to Christ; when the gods of the heathen shall be cast to the moles and the bats; when Romanism shall be exploded, and the crescent of Mohammed shall wane, never again to cast its baleful rays upon the nations; when kings shall bow down before the Prince of Peace, and all nations shall call their Redeemer blessed. Some despair about this. They look upon the world as a vessel breaking up and going to pieces, never to float again. We know that the world and all that is in it will one day be burned up, and afterwards we look for new heavens and for a new earth; but we cannot read our Bibles without the conviction that —

> Jesus shall reign where'er the sun
> Does his successive journeys run.

We are not discouraged by the length of his delays; we are not disheartened by the long period which he allots to the church in which to struggle with little success and much defeat. We believe that God will never allow this world, which has once seen Christ's blood shed upon it, to be always the devil's stronghold. Christ came here to deliver this world from the detested sway of the powers of darkness. What a shout shall that be when men and angels shall unite to cry, "Hallelujah, hallelujah, for the Lord God omnipotent reigns!" What a satisfaction will it be in that day to have had a share in the fight, to have helped break the arrows of the bow, and to have aided in winning the victory for our Lord! Happy are those who trust themselves with this conquering Lord, and who fight side by side with him, doing their little in his name and by his strength! How unhappy are those on the side of evil! It is a losing side, and it is a great matter when to lose is to lose and to be lost for ever. On whose side are you?

December 25 — Morning

{Daily Reading: Revelation 6:1–8:13} {Quick Study: Revelation 4:1–5:14}

Behold, a virgin shall conceive, and bear a son,
and shall call his name Emmanuel. *{Isaiah 7:14}*

Today let us go down to Bethlehem, and in company with wondering shepherds and adoring Magi, let us see him who was born King of the Jews, for we by faith can claim an interest in him, and can sing, "*To us* a child is born, *to us* a son is given." Jesus is Jehovah incarnate, our Lord and our God, and yet our brother and friend; let us adore and admire. Let us notice at the very first glance *his miraculous conception.* It was a thing unheard of before, and unparalleled since, that a virgin should conceive and bear a son. The first promise ran thus, *"The seed of the woman,"* not the offspring of the man. Since venturous woman led the way in the sin which brought forth Paradise lost, she, and she alone, ushers in the Regainer of Paradise. Our Saviour, although truly man, was with respect to his human nature the Holy One of God. Let us reverently bow before the holy Child whose innocence restores to manhood its ancient glory; and let us pray that he may be formed in us, the hope of glory. Do not fail to notice *his humble parentage.* His mother has been described simply as "a virgin," not a princess, or prophetess, nor a matron of a large estate. It is true the blood of kings ran in her veins; nor was her mind a weak and untaught one, for she could sing most sweetly a song of praise; but yet how humble her position, how poor the man to whom she was engaged, and how miserable the accommodation afforded to the newborn King!

Emmanuel, God with us in our nature, in our sorrow, in our lifework, in our punishment, in our grave, and now with us, or rather we with him, in resurrection, ascension, triumph, and second advent splendour.

December 25 — Evening

*And it was so, when the days of their feasting had
run their course, that Job sent and sanctified them,
and rose up early in the morning, and offered burnt
offerings according to the number of them all: for Job
said, "It may be that my sons have sinned, and cursed
God in their hearts." Job did this continually.* {Job 1:5}

What the patriarch did early in the morning, after the family
festivities, it will be well for the believer to do for himself
before he rests tonight. Amid the cheerfulness of household gather-
ings it is easy to slide into sinful levities, and to forget our avowed
character as Christians. It ought not to be so, but so it is, that our
days of feasting are very seldom days of sanctified enjoyment, but
too frequently degenerate into unhallowed mirth. There is a way
of joy as pure and sanctifying as though one bathed in the rivers
of Eden: holy gratitude should be quite as purifying an element as
grief. Alas! for our poor hearts, that facts prove that the house of
mourning is better than the house of feasting. Come, believer, how
have you sinned today? Have you been forgetful of your high calling? Have you been even as others in idle words and loose speeches?
Then confess the sin, and flee to the sacrifice. The sacrifice sanctifies. The precious blood of the Lamb slain removes the guilt, and
purges away the defilement of our sins of ignorance and carelessness. This is the best ending for a Christmas day — to wash anew
in the cleansing fountain. Believer, come to this sacrifice continually; if it is so good tonight, it is good every night. To live at the
altar is the privilege of the royal priesthood; to them sin, great as
it is, is nevertheless no cause for despair, since they draw near yet
again to the sin atoning victim, and their conscience is purged from
dead works.

> Gladly I close this festive day,
> Grasping the altar's hallow'd horn;
> My slips and faults are washed away,
> The Lamb has all my trespass borne.

December 26 — Morning

{Daily Reading: Revelation 9:1–11:19} {Quick Study: Revelation 6:1–8:13}

The last Adam. *{1 Corinthians 15:45}*

Jesus is the federal head of his elect. As in Adam, every heir of flesh and blood has a personal interest, because he is the covenant head and representative of the race as considered under the law of works; so under the law of grace, every redeemed soul is one with the Lord from heaven, since he is the Second Adam, the Sponsor and Substitute of the elect in the new covenant of love. The apostle Paul declares that Levi was in the loins of Abraham when Melchizedek met him: it is a certain truth that the believer was in the loins of Jesus Christ, the Mediator, when in old eternity the covenant settlements of grace were decreed, ratified, and made sure for ever. Thus, whatever Christ has done, he has done for the whole body of his church. We were crucified in him and buried with him, *{Colossians 2:10–13}* and to make it still more wonderful, we are risen with him and even ascended with him to the seats on high. *{Ephesians 2:6}* It is thus that the church has fulfilled the law, and is "accepted in *the Beloved*." It is thus that she is regarded with complacency by the just Jehovah, for he views her in Jesus, and does not look upon her as separate from her covenant head. As the Anointed Redeemer of Israel, Christ Jesus has nothing distinct from his church, but all that he has he holds for her. Adam's righteousness was ours as long as he maintained it, and his sin was ours the moment that he committed it; and in the same manner, all that the Second Adam is or does, is ours as well as his, seeing that he is our representative. Here is the foundation of the covenant of grace. This is the gracious system of representation and substitution, which moved Justin Martyr to cry out, "Oh blessed change, oh sweet permutation!" This is the very groundwork of the gospel of our salvation, and is to be received with strong faith and rapturous joy.

December 26 — Evening

Lo, I am with you always. *{Matthew 28:20}*

The Lord Jesus is in the midst of his church; he walks among the golden lampstands; his promise is, "Lo, I am with you always." He is as surely with us now as he was with the disciples at the lake, when they saw coals of fire, and fish and bread laid on it. Not carnally, but still in real truth, Jesus is with us. And a blessed truth it is, for where Jesus is, *love becomes inflamed.* Of all the things in the world that can set the heart burning, there is nothing like the presence of Jesus! A glimpse of him so overcomes us, that we are ready to say, "Turn away your eyes from me, for they have overcome me." Even the smell of the aloes, and the myrrh, and the cassia, which drop from his perfumed garments, causes the sick and the faint to grow strong. Let there be only a moment's leaning of the head upon that gracious bosom, and a reception of his divine love into our poor cold hearts, and we are cold no longer, but glow like seraphs, equal to every labour, and capable of every suffering. If we know that Jesus is with us, *every power will be developed,* and every grace will be strengthened, and we shall throw ourselves into the Lord's service with heart, and soul, and strength; therefore, the presence of Christ is to be desired above all things. *His presence will be most realised by those who are most like him.* If you desire to see Christ, you must grow in conformity to him. Bring yourself, by the power of the Spirit, into union with Christ's desires, and motives, and plans of action, and you are likely to be favoured with his company. Remember, *his presence may be had.* His promise is as true as ever. He delights to be with us. If he does not come, it is because we hinder him by our indifference. He will reveal himself to our earnest prayers, and graciously allow himself to be detained by our entreaties, and by our tears, for these are the golden chains which bind Jesus to his people.

December 27 — Morning

{Daily Reading: Revelation 12:1–13:18} {Quick Study: Revelation 9:1–11:19}

Can the rush grow up without mire? *{Job 8:11}*

The rush is spongy and hollow, and even so is a hypocrite; there is no substance or stability in him. It is shaken to and fro in every wind just as formalists yield to every influence; for this reason the rush is not broken by the tempest, neither are hypocrites troubled with persecution. I would not willingly be a deceiver or be deceived; perhaps the text for today may help me to examine myself whether I am a hypocrite or not. The rush by nature lives in water, and owes its very existence to the mire and moisture where it has taken root; let the mire become dry, and the rush withers very quickly. Its greenness is absolutely dependent upon circumstances, a present abundance of water makes it flourish, and a drought destroys it at once. Is this my case? Do I only serve God when I am in good company, or when religion is profitable and respectable? Do I love the Lord only when temporal comforts are received from his hands? If so I am a base hypocrite and, like the withering rush, I shall perish when death deprives me of outward joys. But can I honestly assert that when bodily comforts have been few, and my surroundings have been rather adverse to grace than at all helpful to it, I have still held my integrity firmly? Then I have hope that there is genuine vital godliness in me. The rush cannot grow without mire, but plants of the Lord's right hand planting can and do flourish even in the year of drought. A godly man often grows best when his worldly circumstances decay. He who follows Christ for his bag is a Judas; they who follow for loaves and fishes are children of the devil; but those who attend him out of love for him are his own beloved ones. Lord, let me find my life in *you*, and not in the mire of this world's favour or gain.

December 27 — Evening

And the LORD shall guide you continually. *{Isaiah 58:11}*

"The *Lord* shall guide you." Not an angel, but JEHOVAH shall guide you. He said he would not go through the wilderness before his people, an angel should go before them to lead them in the way; but Moses said, "If *your* presence does not go with me, do not lead us there." Christian, God has not left you in your earthly pilgrimage to an angel's guidance: he himself leads the vanguard. You may not see the cloudy, fiery pillar, but Jehovah will never forsake you. Notice the word *shall* — "The Lord shall guide you." How certain this makes it! How sure it is that God will not forsake us! His precious "shalls" and "wills" are better than men's oaths. "I will never leave you, nor forsake you." Then observe the adverb *continually*. We are not merely to be guided sometimes, but we are to have a perpetual monitor; not occasionally to be left to our own understanding, and so to wander, but we are continually to hear the guiding voice of the Great Shepherd; and if we follow closely at his heels, we shall not err, but be led by a right way to a city to live in. If you have to change your position in life; if you have to emigrate to distant shores; if it should happen that you are cast into poverty, or uplifted suddenly into a more responsible position than the one you now occupy; if you are thrown among strangers, or cast among foes, yet do not tremble, for "the Lord shall guide you continually." There are no dilemmas out of which you shall not be delivered if you live near to God, and your heart is kept warm with holy love. He does not go amiss who goes in the company of God. Like Enoch, walk with God, and you cannot mistake your road. You have infallible wisdom to direct you, immutable love to comfort you, and eternal power to defend you. "Jehovah" — note the word — "Jehovah shall guide you continually."

December 28 — Morning

{Daily Reading: Revelation 14:1–16:21} {Quick Study: Revelation 12:1–14:20}

The life which I now live in the flesh,
I live by the faith of the Son of God. *{Galatians 2:20}*

When the Lord in mercy passed by and saw us in our blood, he first of all said, "Live"; and this he did *first*, because life is one of the absolutely essential things in spiritual matters, and until it is bestowed we are incapable of partaking in the things of the kingdom. Now the life which grace confers upon the saints at the moment of their conversion is none other than the life of Christ, which, like the sap from the stem, runs into us, the branches, and establishes a living connection between our souls and Jesus. Faith is the grace which perceives this union, having proceeded from it as its firstfruit. It is the neck which joins the body of the church to its all glorious Head.

> Oh Faith! You bond of union with the Lord,
> Is not this office yours? And your fit name,
> In the economy of Gospel types,
> And symbols fitting — the church's neck;
> Identifying her in will and work with him ascended?

Faith lays hold upon the Lord Jesus with a firm and determined grasp. She knows his excellence and worth, and no temptation can induce her to repose her trust elsewhere; and Christ Jesus is so delighted with this heavenly grace that he never ceases to strengthen and sustain her by the loving embrace and all-sufficient support of his eternal arms. Here, then, is established a living, sensible, and delightful union which casts forth streams of love, confidence, sympathy, complacency, and joy, from which both the bride and Bridegroom love to drink. When the soul can evidently perceive this oneness between itself and Christ, the pulse may be felt as beating for both, and the one blood as flowing through the veins of each. Then the heart is as near to heaven as it can be on earth, and is prepared for the enjoyment of the most sublime and spiritual kind of fellowship.

December 28 — Evening

**I did not come to send peace on
earth, but a sword.** *{Matthew 10:34}*

The Christian will be sure to make enemies. It will be one of his objects to make none; but if to do the right, and to believe the true, should cause him to lose every earthly friend, he will count it only a small loss, since his great Friend in heaven will be still more friendly, and reveal himself to him more graciously than ever. Oh, you who have taken up his cross, do you not know what your Master said? "I am come to set a man at variance against his father, and the daughter against her mother; and a man's foes shall be those of his own household." Christ is the great Peacemaker; but before peace, he brings war. Where the light comes, the darkness must retire. Where truth is, the lie must flee; or, if it remains, there must be a stern conflict, for the truth cannot and will not lower its standard, and the lie must be trodden under foot. If you follow Christ, you shall have all the dogs of the world yelping at your heels. If you wish to live to stand the test of the last tribunal, depend upon it, the world will not speak well of you. He who has the friendship of the world is an enemy to God; but if you are true and faithful to the Most High, men will resent your unflinching fidelity, since it is a testimony against their iniquities. Fearless of all consequences, you must do the right. You will need the courage of a lion unhesitatingly to pursue a course which shall turn your best friend into your fiercest foe; but for the love of Jesus you must thus be courageous. For the truth's sake to risk reputation and affection is such a deed that to do it constantly you will need a degree of moral principle which only the Spirit of God can work in you; yet do not turn your back like a coward, but play the man. Follow manfully in your Master's steps, for he has traversed this rough way before you. Better a brief warfare and eternal rest, than false peace and everlasting torment.

December 29 — Morning

{Daily Reading: Revelation 17:1–18:24} {Quick Study: Revelation 15:1–16:21}

So far the Lord has helped us. *{1 Samuel 7:12}*

The phrase "so far" seems like a hand pointing in the direction of the *past*. Twenty years or seventy, and yet, "so far the Lord has helped!" Through poverty, through wealth, through sickness, through health, at home, abroad, on the land, on the sea, in honour, in dishonour, in perplexity, in joy, in trial, in triumph, in prayer, in temptation, "so far the Lord has helped us!"

We delight to look down a long avenue of trees. It is delightful to gaze from end to end of the long vista, a sort of verdant temple, with its branching pillars and its arches of leaves; even so look down the long aisles of your years, at the green boughs of mercy overhead, and the strong pillars of lovingkindness and faithfulness which bear up your joys. Are there no birds singing in those branches? Surely there must be many, and they all sing of mercy received *"so far."*

But the word also points *forward*. For when a man gets up to a certain mark and writes "so far," he is not yet at the end, there is still a distance to be traversed. More trials, more joys; more temptations, more triumphs; more prayers, more answers; more toils, more strength; more battles, more victories; and then comes sickness, old age, disease, and death. Is it over now? No! There is more yet awakening in Jesus' likeness, thrones, harps, songs, psalms, white raiment, the face of Jesus, the companionship of saints, the glory of God, the fulness of eternity, and the infinity of bliss. Oh, be of good courage, believer, and with grateful confidence raise your "Ebenezer," for —

> He who has helped you hitherto
> Will help you all your journey through.

When read in heaven's light, how glorious and marvellous a prospect will your "so far" unfold to your grateful eye!

December 29 — Evening

What do you think of Christ? *{Matthew 22:42}*

The great test of your soul's health is, *What do you think of Christ?* Is he to you "fairer than the children of men" — "the chief among ten thousand" — the "altogether lovely?" Wherever Christ is thus esteemed, all the faculties of the spiritual man exercise themselves with energy. I will judge your piety by this barometer: does Christ stand high or low with you? If you have thought little of Christ, if you have been content to live without his presence, if you have cared little for his honour, if you have been neglectful of his laws, then I know that your soul is sick — God grant that it may not be sick even to death! But if the first thought of your spirit has been, how can I honour Jesus? If the daily desire of your soul has been, "Oh, that I knew where I might find him!" I tell you that you may have a thousand infirmities, and even scarcely know whether you are a child of God at all, and yet I am persuaded, beyond a doubt, that you are safe, since Jesus is great in your esteem. I do not care for your rags, what do you think of *his* royal apparel? I do not care for your wounds, though they bleed in torrents, what do you think of *his* wounds? Are they like glittering rubies in your esteem? I think none the less of you, though you lie like Lazarus on the dunghill, and the dogs lick you — I do not judge you by your poverty: what do you think of the King in his beauty? Has he a glorious high throne in your heart? Would you set him higher if you could? Would you be willing to die if you could only add another trumpet to the strain which proclaims his praise? Ah! Then it is well with you. Whatever you may think of yourself, if Christ is great to you, you shall be with him before long.

Though all the world my choice deride,
Yet Jesus shall my portion be;
For I am pleased with none beside,
The fairest of the fair is he.

December 30 — Morning

{Daily Reading: Revelation 19:1–20:15} {Quick Study: Revelation 17:1–19:21}

Better is the end of a thing than the beginning of it. *{Ecclesiastes 7:8}*

Look at David's Lord and Master; see his beginning. He was despised and rejected by men; a man of sorrows and acquainted with grief. Do you wish to see his end? He sits at his Father's right hand, waiting until his enemies are made his footstool. "Just as he is, so also we are in this world." You must bear the cross, or you shall never wear the crown; you must wade through the mire, or you shall never walk the golden pavement. Cheer up, then, poor Christian. "Better is the end of a thing than the beginning of it." See that creeping worm, how contemptible it appears! It is the beginning of a thing. See that insect with gorgeous wings, playing in the sunbeams, sipping at the flower bells, full of happiness and life; that is the end of it. That caterpillar is yourself, until you are wrapped up in the chrysalis of death; but when Christ shall appear you shall be like him, for you shall see him as he is. Be content to be like him, a worm and no man, so that like him you may be satisfied when you wake up in his likeness. That rough looking diamond is put upon the wheel of the lapidary. He cuts it on all sides. It loses much — much that seemed costly to itself. The king is crowned; the diadem is put upon the monarch's head with the trumpet's joyful sound. A glittering ray flashes from that coronet, and it beams from that very diamond which was just now so severely vexed by the lapidary. You may venture to compare yourself to such a diamond, for you are one of God's people; and this is the time of the cutting process. Let faith and patience have their perfect work, for in the day when the crown shall be set upon the head of the King, Eternal, Immortal, Invisible, one ray of glory shall stream from you. "They shall be mine," says the Lord, "in the day when I make up my jewels." "Better is the end of a thing than the beginning of it."

December 30 — Evening

**Do you not know that it will be bitterness
in the latter end?** *{2 Samuel 2:26}*

If, oh my reader! you are merely a professor, and not a possessor of the faith that is in Christ Jesus, the following lines are a true sketch of your end.

You are a respectable attendant at a place of worship; you go because others go, not because your heart is right with God. This is your beginning. I will suppose that for the next twenty or thirty years you will be spared to go on as you do now, professing religion by an outward attendance upon the means of grace, but having no heart in the matter. Tread softly, for I must show you the deathbed of such a one as yourself. Let us gaze upon him gently. A clammy sweat is on his brow, and he wakes up crying, "Oh, God, it is hard to die. Did you send for my minister?" "Yes, he is coming." The minister comes. "Sir, I fear that I am dying!" "Have you any hope?" "I cannot say that I have. I fear to stand before my God. Oh! Pray for me." The prayer is offered for him with sincere earnestness, and the way of salvation is for the ten thousandth time put before him, but before he has grasped the rope, I see him sink. I may put my finger upon those cold eyelids, for they will never see anything here again. But where is the man, and where are the man's true eyes? It is written, "In hell he lifted up his eyes, being in torment." Ah! Why did he not lift up his eyes before? Because he was so accustomed to hear the gospel that his soul slept under it. Alas! If you should lift up your eyes there, how bitter will be your wailings. Let the Saviour's own words reveal the woe: "Father Abraham, send Lazarus, so that he may dip the tip of his finger in water, and cool my tongue, for I am tormented in this flame." There is a frightful meaning in those words. May you never have to spell it out by the red light of Jehovah's wrath!

December 31 — Morning

{Daily Reading: Revelation 21:1–22:21} {Quick Study: Revelation 20:1–22:21}

In the last day, that great day of the feast, Jesus
stood and cried, saying, "If any man is thirsty,
let him come to me and drink." *{John 7:37}*

Patience had her perfect work in the Lord Jesus, and until the last day of the feast he pleaded with the Jews, even as on this last day of the year he pleads with us, and waits to be gracious to us. Admirable indeed is the longsuffering of the Saviour in bearing with some of us year after year, notwithstanding our provocations, rebellions, and resistance to his Holy Spirit. Wonder of wonders that we are still in the land of mercy!

Pity expressed herself most plainly, for Jesus *cried,* which implies not only the loudness of his voice, but the tenderness of his tones. He entreats us to be reconciled. "We *pray* you," says the apostle, "as though God *beseeched* you by us." What earnest, pathetic terms are these! How deep must be the love which makes the Lord weep over sinners, and like a mother woo his children to his bosom! Surely at the call of such a cry our willing hearts will come.

Provision is made most plenteously; all is provided that man can need to quench his soul's thirst. To his conscience the atonement brings peace; to his understanding the gospel brings the richest instruction; to his heart the person of Jesus is the noblest object of affection; to the whole man the truth as it is in Jesus supplies the purest nutriment. Thirst is terrible, but Jesus can remove it. Though the soul should be utterly famished, Jesus could restore it.

Proclamation is made most freely, that every thirsty one is welcome. No other distinction is made except that of thirst. Whether it is the thirst of avarice, ambition, pleasure, knowledge, or rest, he who suffers from it is invited. The thirst may be bad in itself, and be no sign of grace, but rather a mark of inordinate sin longing to be gratified with deeper draughts of lust; but it is not goodness in the creature which brings him the invitation, the Lord Jesus sends it freely, and without partiality.

Personality is declared most fully. The sinner must come to *Jesus*, not to works, ordinances, or doctrines, but to a personal Redeemer, who himself bare our sins in his own body on the tree. The bleeding, dying, rising Saviour, is the only star of hope to a sinner. Oh, for grace to come now and drink, before the sun sets upon the year's last day!

No waiting or preparation is so much as hinted at. Drinking represents a reception for which no fitness is required. A fool, a thief, a prostitute can drink; and so sinfulness of character is no bar to the invitation to believe in Jesus. We need no golden cup, no bejewelled chalice, in which to convey the water to the thirsty; the mouth of poverty is welcome to stoop down and quaff the flowing flood. Blistered, leprous, filthy lips may touch the stream of divine love; they cannot pollute it, but shall themselves be purified. Jesus is the fount of hope. Dear reader, hear the dear Redeemer's loving voice as he cries to each of us,

IF ANY MAN IS THIRSTY, LET HIM COME TO ME AND DRINK.

December 31 — Evening

**The harvest is past, the summer is ended,
and we are not saved.** *[Jeremiah 8:20]*

Not *saved!* Dear reader, is this your mournful plight? Warned of the judgment to come, bidden to escape for your life, and yet at this moment *not saved!* You know the way of salvation, you read it in the Bible, you hear it from the pulpit, it is explained to you by friends, and yet you neglect it, and therefore you are *not saved.* You will be without excuse when the Lord shall judge the quick and dead. The Holy Spirit has given more or less of blessing upon the Word which has been preached in your hearing, and times of refreshing have come from the divine presence, and yet you are without Christ. All these hopeful seasons have come and gone — your summer and your harvest have past — and yet you are *not saved.* Years have followed one another into eternity, and your last year will soon be here: youth has gone, manhood is going, and yet you are not saved. Let me ask you — *will you ever be saved?* Is there any likelihood of it? Already the most propitious seasons have left you unsaved; will other occasions alter your condition? Means have failed with you — the best of means, used perseveringly and with the utmost affection — what more can be done for you? Affliction and prosperity have alike failed to impress you; tears and prayers and sermons have been wasted on your barren heart. Are not the probabilities dead against your ever being saved? Is it not more than likely that you will remain as you are until death for ever bars the door of hope? Do you recoil from the supposition? Yet it is a most reasonable one; he who is not washed in so many waters will in all probability go filthy to his end. The convenient time never has come; why should it ever come? It is logical to fear that it never will arrive, and that Felix-like, you will find no convenient time until you are in hell. Oh, think of what that hell is, and of the dreadful probability that you will soon be cast into it!

Reader, suppose you should die unsaved, no words can picture your doom. Write out your dreadful estate in tears and blood, speak of it with groans and gnashing of teeth; you will be punished with everlasting destruction from the glory of the Lord, and from the glory of his power. A brother's voice would try to startle you into earnestness. Oh, be wise, be wise in time, and before another year begins, believe in Jesus, who is able to save to the uttermost. Consecrate these last hours to lonely thought, and if deep repentance is bred in you, it will be well; and if it leads to a humble faith in Jesus, it will be best of all. Oh, see to it that this year does not pass away, and you remain an unforgiven spirit. Do not let the New Year's midnight peals sound upon a joyless spirit! *Now*, NOW, NOW believe, and live.

> **ESCAPE FOR YOUR LIFE;**
> **DO NOT LOOK BEHIND YOU,**
> **NEITHER REMAIN**
> **IN ALL THE PLAIN;**
> **ESCAPE TO THE MOUNTAIN,**
> **LEST YOU ARE CONSUMED.**

Scripture Index

M = Morning

E = Evening

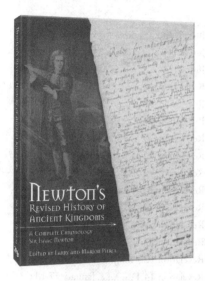

Newton's Revised History of Ancient Kingdoms

A Complete Chronology
by
Sir Isaac Newton

When you think of Sir Isaac Newton, you normally think of a great scientist and mathematician. His contributions to these areas of human knowledge are enormous. The same genius he applies to other disciplines, Newton also brings to bear on ancient history. Like a first-rate defense attorney, Newton cross-examines the ancient writers, using their own words against them to expose their logical inconsistencies. He then develops a more sound chronology using scientific method based on logic, observations, astronomy, and just plain common sense.

Newton worked on this project for over 40 years, but it was not published until 1728, a year after he died. Master Books is republishing this landmark book in a format and style suitable for today's readers, and most of secular ancient history before 700 B.C. will need drastic revision in the light of Newton's detailed findings.

- Contains diagrams of Solomon's Temple
- Critical analysis and investigation of historical sources
- Re-visits the chronologies of early and major civilizations
- Exposes the errors and exaggerations still commonly taken as fact today

8-1/2 x 11 • 208 pages • casebound
ISBN: 0-89051-556-3 • $19.99

Available at Christian bookstores nationwide